YEARS

THE THIRD THOUSAND YEARS

by

W. CLEON SKOUSEN

Bookcraft
Salt Lake City, Utah

Copyright
1964
BOOKCRAFT, INC.

27th Printing, 1994

ISBN: 0-88494-122-1

Lithographed in the United States of America
PUBLISHERS PRESS
Salt Lake City, Utah

To My Mother

RITA BENTLEY SKOUSEN

A mother of nine and a master teacher with
that rare ability to make the Biblical past
a vital part of the living present. I am only
one of the hundreds whose lives she touched,
influenced, molded, focussed, and inspired.

Preface

In the broad vista of human history few epics are more neglected by our generation than the thundering centuries of the third thousand years.

As the reader will recall, sacred literature divides the story of mankind into seven periods of a thousand years each. This book covers the third period which occurred between 2,000 and 1,000 B.C. These ten centuries included some of the most notable personalities of historical renown—Abraham, Isaac, Jacob, Joseph, Moses, Aaron, Joshua, Deborah, Gideon, Jephthah, Samson, Ruth, Samuel and Saul.

In this book we have attempted to capture the exciting historical reality of the life and times of those remarkable people. This is not a children's story of the Bible but a synthesis of the vast historical fabric of that entire period as seen through the eyes of the men and women who lived it and the prophets of God who wrote about it.

It was a brutal, harsh and violent time in which to live. Not only was it a desperate and challenging time for men to endure, but also for God to govern. It was a dark millennium of ferocity, fury and folly which could have been avoided. The Lord knew that through voluntary obedience to divine law the human race could have changed those heathenish dark ages into a renaissance of hope and happiness. It is for this reason that we have given special attention to the Lord's expressed point of view in offering the children of Israel a chance to build a society equal to that of the City of Enoch. And it is for the same reason that we have emphasized the tragic consequences which engulfed the whole civilized world of that era because Israel rejected that magnificent opportunity.

The format for this book closely follows that of the Bible. This was done so that the student could read the scriptures right along with *The Third Thousand Years*. Because of the antiquity of the Biblical text, occasional problems arise to challenge the modern reader. We have therefore dealt with these problems in this book. It is believed that when the

student has completed an examination of the gratifying answers which research and modern revelation have given us,
he will find the Old Testament making a lot more sense than
before.

This is particularly true with the Law of Moses. Many
students find it almost impossible to reconcile this law with
their conception of God since they know He is a personage
of justice and love. Special attention has been given to this
subject and we think the reader will be happily surprised
when he discovers how this famous code actually functioned.
In the appendix the reader will find the entire Law of Moses
broken down into topical sub-sections with explanatory notes
on each section. This is to supplement the general treatment
in the text itself.

In reading this book the student will of course appreciate
that it was the purpose of the author to try to share in the best
way he knew how the expansive reservoir of material which
relates to this stirring period. This necessarily implies a reservation to expand, clarify or improve upon any parts of this
book which future research might make possible. No writer
can approach a subject as profound and complicated as the
Old Testament without feeling its immensity. It is merely
the author's humble hope, therefore, that this material might
prove helpful. Any suggestions or observations which might
strengthen and further improve its contents will be heartily
welcomed.

The reader will also observe the rather heavy use of footnotes throughout this book. This is because the available
details are often scattered throughout many different scriptural sources and it is often tedious research to re-locate such
references once the material has become cold. Therefore, it
was to aid the author as much as the reader that these footnotes have been salted in rather heavily. This will also help
the student realize that these details came directly from the
scripture and not from the author's imagination.

In fact, wherever I have drawn a personal deduction, or
presented a suggested explanation which is not specifically
spelled out in the scriptures, I have deliberately tried to use
a signalling device so the reader can easily distinguish such
passages. These signals consist of phrases such as "it would

appear that," or "this would lead us to conclude," etc. Single words have also been used for this purpose such as "apparently," "probably," or "undoubtedly."

Because the King James translators sometimes used words which have now become obscure or obsolete, brackets have been used to enclose the author's suggested clarification.

ACKNOWLEDGMENTS

As this work comes to final fruition I find myself indebted to far more people than I could possibly acknowledge with genuine completeness. The following are therefore representative rather than all-inclusive.

My special appreciation must certainly go to Marvin Wallin, the publisher, who encouraged the writing of this book and patiently waited eight years for its completion.

I am also extremely grateful to the members of my family who diligently helped in every way possible—to my wife, Jewel, who spent many long weeks double checking all references and proof-reading the galleys; to my daughter, Julianne, who typed much of the final manuscript and made suggestions on art work and maps; to my son, David, who contributed several excellent suggestions as the result of his own research. I am also grateful to my other sons and daughters—to Sharon and Harold who helped in proof-reading the manuscript; and to Eric, Kathy, Paul and Brent who good naturedly sacrificed many pleasant projects we had planned as a family, but which the writing of this book necessarily postponed.

For the maps, art work and jacket design of this book I am indebted to the splendid talents of Paul Hasegawa. I am also most appreciative of the patient skill of Howard Gerber who worked 18-hour days on type setting and paging; and to Bill Sugden who did the makeup, I want to express my thanks. Paul R. Green had the task of pulling everything together and seeing that production and printing stayed on schedule. He and his team made a tremendous contribution.

For the striking motion picture stills of Biblical scenes I am extremely grateful to my good friend Henry Wilcoxon, associate producer of *The Ten Commandments,* to Y. Frank Freeman, Vice President of Paramount Pictures, and to

Florence Cole, secretary to the late Cecil B. deMille. I so appreciate the kindness of Paramount Pictures in granting me permission to use these photographs to illustrate the text.

To all of these and the many others who helped to make this book possible my abundant and heartfelt thanks!

W. Cleon Skousen

December 1, 1964
Salt Lake City, Utah

Contents

Gideon's Battle with the Midianites
Gideon Captures King Zebah and King Zalmunna
Gideon Refuses To Be the King of Israel

The Seizure of Power by Abimelech
The Parable of Jotham
The Days of Tola and Jair
The Rise of Jephthah
Jephthah Communicates with the King of the Ammonites
Jephthah Is Victorious Over the Ammonites
A Civil War Breaks Out in Israel
Thirty-Seven Years of Peace
A Few Notes on the Story of Samson
The Rise of Samson
Samson Makes a Fatal Mistake
The Marriage of Samson
The Philistines Send a Whole Army to Capture Samson
Samson and Delilah
The Death of Samson

Israel's Second Great Civil War
The Tribe of Benjamin Is Practically Wiped Out
The Book of Ruth
Ruth Meets Boaz
Naomi's Plan
Naomi's Plan is Threatened
How Ruth Became the Great Grandmother of David
The Life and Times of Eli
The Birth of Samuel
Eli Receives a Warning
Samuel Receives a Revelation
The Israelites Lose the Ark of the Covenant
God Intervenes to Restore the Ark to Israel
Samuel Launches a Reform and Conquers the Philistines

Samuel Discovers Apostasy in His Sons
What is the Nature of God's Government?
The Children of Israel Demand a Monarchy
The Calling of Saul
Saul Is Presented to the People
Saul's First Test—The Ammonite War
The Conference at Gilgal
The Beginning of the War with the Philistines
Jonathan Triggers a Surprising Victory
Saul Attempts to Kill Jonathan
The Campaign Against the Amalekites

APPENDIX:

Chronology
The Third Thousand Years

A complete chronology from Adam to Abraham will be found in the fly-leaf chart of *The First 2,000 Years.* The following chronology is a continuation from the birth of Abraham which is given as ....2,022 B.C.

Isaac born when Abraham 100 (Gen. 21:23) ....1,922 B.C.

Jacob born when Isaac is 60 (Gen. 25:26) ....1,862 B.C.

Abraham dies at the age of 175 (Gen. 25:7-8) ....1,847 B.C.

Joseph born when Jacob 91 (See note 96, chapter 3) ....1,771 B.C.

Joseph sold into Egypt at age of 17 (Gen. 37:2) ....1,754 B.C.

Isaac dies at age 180 (Gen. 35:28) ....1,742 B.C.

Joseph made prime minister of Egypt at 30 (Gen. 41:46) ......1,741 B.C.

Jacob moves to Egypt with his family at 130 (Gen. 47:9) ......1,732 B.C.

Jacob dies at age 147 (Gen. 47:28) ....1,715 B.C.

Joseph dies at age 110 (Gen. 50:22) ....1,661 B.C.

Moses is born 135 years after Jacob came to Egypt (See pages 186 to 188 of this book) ....1,597 B.C.

Moses leads Israel from Egypt at age 80 (Acts 7:23, 30)......1,517 B.C.

Moses dies at the age of 120 (Deut. 34:7) ....1,477 B.C.

Conquest of Canaan took 7 years (calculated from the words of Caleb in Joshua 14:7, 10) ....1,470 B.C.

The Judges lasted in excess of 400 years but the exact chronology is not given, therefore the following estimates are merely for the convenience of the reader:

Othniel ....1,434 B.C.

Ehud and Shamgar ....1,375 B.C.

Deborah ....1,333 B.C.

Gideon ....1,286 B.C.

Abimelech ....1,246 B.C.

Tola ....1,249 B.C.

Jair ....1,228 B.C.

Jephthah ....1,188 B.C.

Ibzan ....1,182 B.C.

Elon ....1,175 B.C.

Abdon ....1,167 B.C.

Samson ....1,139 B.C.

Eli ....1,119 B.C.

Samuel called as a prophet ....1,079 B.C.

Saul anointed king ....1,037 B.C.

THE TEN COMMANDMENTS — A Paramount Picture

"And it came to pass the selfsame day, that the Lord did bring the children of Israel out of the land of Egypt by their armies."

CHAPTER ONE

Who Are God's Chosen People?

Across the sweeping vista of human history there are whole chapters of blood-soaked pages which tell the torturous tales of brutal and passionate men who tried to set up a master race. With satanic zeal they set out to conquer the whole earth. Down through the ages, these sword-wielding conquerors emerged singly and in clusters from the major nations—the Babylonians, the Assyrians, the Medes, the Persians, the Egyptians, the Greeks, the Romans, the Mongols and the Moslems.

Today, the fallen, broken monuments of their fleeting glory lie crumbling in the dust.

But the tragic lessons they left for history seem wasted on many modern minds. The things which ancient greed and ferocious brutality failed to do, certain power-hungry men of modern times think they yet can do. They still seek to build by force and fear a master race which will become an "instrument of destiny." The Napoleons, Kaisers, Hitlers, Mussolinis, Tojos, and Stalins of modern centuries are merely the more recent counterparts of the caesars, pharaohs, emperors, kings and khans of the historic past.

GOD'S WAYS ARE NOT MAN'S WAYS

In contrast to all of this, God has proposed a completely different kind of leadership. God's plan does not call for a master race, but a society of "master servants," inspired men who lead with love, not lashes, and who excel in service, not suppression.

From earliest times the Lord has endeavored to promote this kind of leadership and this type of society. In the days of Enoch, God's revealed plan for happy living became the most dominant force on earth (Moses 7:17), but at other times it often dwindled to a mere shadow and was not allowed to have any significant influence among mankind whatever.

Nevertheless, whether accepted or rejected, God's society has always constituted the one and only way to achieve a lasting pattern of universal peace and universal prosperity.

Those who are willing to consecrate their total energies and resources to the building up of such a society are called God's "chosen people." He calls them "chosen," not because He would exclude the rest of mankind from the same blessings, but simply because these are they who *chose* to accept God's call to service. With the Lord, a call to leadership means a call to *service*, and therefore his chosen people are really his "master servants."

This whole concept was explained by a prophet of the Lord in these words:

"Behold, there are many called, but few are chosen. And why are they not chosen? Because their hearts are set so much upon the things of this world, and aspire to the honors of men, that they do not learn this one lesson—that the rights of the priesthood [God's service fraternity] are inseparably connected with the powers of heaven, and that the powers of heaven cannot be controlled nor handled only upon the principles of righteousness. That they may be conferred upon us, it is true; but when we undertake to cover our sins, or to gratify our pride, our vain ambition, or to exercise control or dominion or compulsion upon the souls of the children of men, in any degree of unrighteousness, behold, the heavens withdraw themselves; the Spirit of the Lord is grieved; and when it is withdrawn, Amen to the priesthood or the authority of that man. . . . We have learned by sad experience that it is the nature and disposition of almost all men, as soon as they get a little authority, as they suppose, they will immediately begin to exercise unrighteous dominion. Hence many are called but few are chosen." (Doctrine and Covenants 121:34-40)

A study of history will demonstrate that whenever the Lord has succeeded in developing a "chosen people," they have turned out to be a rare but tremendously impressive society. The individual members of that society are revealed to have been a singular and superior type of human being. In a moment we will discuss the personal attributes which characterized such people so that the student can measure his own qualities against the personality profiles of those who were acceptable to God in the past. Such a study makes it easy to see why, in the eyes of Heaven, these people were called, "the salt of the earth," "the elect," God's "peculiar people," and His "Royal Priesthood." In more modern terms we might almost be justified in calling them God's humble Supermen.

THE KEY TO BECOMING "CHOSEN" OF GOD

God has never had a chosen "race," only a chosen people.

The Prophet Nephi stated this precisely when he said, "Behold, the Lord esteemeth all flesh in one; he that is righteous is favored of God.[1] Paul was equally clear, "Tribulation and anguish, upon every soul of man that doeth evil . . . but glory, honour, and peace, to every man that worketh good . . . for there is no respect of persons with God."[2] The same doctrine was confirmed in modern times: "For I am no respecter of persons . . ." declared the Lord.[3] "I, the Lord, am bound when ye do what I say, but when ye do not what I say, ye have no promise."[4]

One of the most serious mistakes of mankind has been to assume that they were chosen and accepted of God just simply because of their illustrious ancestors. Now it is true that God does undertake to bless righteous parents with choice children. In fact, they are often referred to as "heirs according to the covenant,"[5] and "children of the prophets, and of the covenant."[6] Nevertheless, the righteousness of parents never can save their children. The children must be righteous on their own account or they will be treated like anyone else.

It is clear from the scriptures that some children or descendants of righteous ancestors have become proud and have assumed a sense of superiority just because of their blood line. This is an ethnical trap. The scriptures are bristling with warnings against those who think they are saved just because of their race or nationality. Jesus drove the point home when his tantalizers boasted that they were children of

---

1. 1 Nephi 17:35
2. Romans 2:9-11
3. Doctrine and Covenants 1:35
4. Doctrine and Covenants 82:10
5. Doctrine and Covenants 52:2
6. Acts 3:25

Abraham. Said the Master, "If ye were Abraham's children ye would do the works of Abraham. . . . Ye are of your father the devil, and the lusts of your father ye will do."[7]

These children of Abraham had been cut off from their righteous ancestors by their own wickedness. With God this is a very real principle. Paul pointed out specifically that it is not blood lines but *faith and obedience to God* which makes men and women the children of Abraham: "Know ye therefore that they which are of faith, the same are the children of Abraham. And the scripture, foreseeing that God would justify the heathen through faith, preached before the Gospel unto Abraham, saying, In thee shall all nations be blessed. So then they which be of faith are blessed with faithful Abraham."[8]

The lesson is clear. To be a descendant of Abraham is nothing unless a person qualifies for God's beneficence the same way Abraham did — by faith and obedience. This is the key to becoming "chosen" of God. Otherwise, a descendant of Abraham is rejected like anyone else. His blood line cannot save him.

God's Technique of Pruning and Grafting

Some people have wondered how a God of justice could have a "chosen" people and still be fair to the rest of the human family. The answer is simple. He does it on the two-pronged principle of *pruning* and *grafting*. One of God's favorite teaching devices is to compare his chosen people with a choice vine,[9] or a carefully cultivated olive tree.[10] As fast as the branches of the true vine or tame olive tree wither away and become dead wood, He *prunes* them off and casts them away.[11] In their place He *grafts* "wild" branches that have been observed to produce good fruit.[12] These are made a part of the tame tree so long as they produce good fruit.[13]

God's technique of grafting in the obedient and the righteous from among the gentiles or the heathens and there-after referring to them as the "Children of Israel" or "the

---

7. John 8:39-44
8. Galatians 3:7-9
9. Isaiah 5:1-7
10. Jacob Chapter 5

11. Jacob 5:7
12. Jacob 5:8-10
13. Jacob 5:18; 37

seed of Abraham," is called the principle of *adoption*. As the Lord said to Abraham, *"And I will bless them* (all nations) *through thy name; for as many as receive this Gospel shall be called after thy name,* AND SHALL BE ACCOUNTED THY SEED, *and shall rise up and bless thee,* AS THEIR FATHER."[14]

So from all nations the Lord seeks out those who will obey his voice and *adopts* them into his special group of chosen people. Paul propounds the same doctrine when he says: "For as many as are led by the Spirit of God, they are the sons of God . . . ye have received the Spirit of adoption. . . ."[15]

The "Spirit" referred to here is the Holy Ghost and Joseph Smith declared that, "The effect of the Holy Ghost upon a Gentile is to purge out the old blood, and make him actually of the seed of Abraham." Such a person has "a new creation by the Holy Ghost."[16] Obviously, from the Lord's standpoint, there is far more to the "Spirit of adoption" than the mere formality of joining his Kingdom.

To summarize, then, the call of God is to all people whether born of the covenant or not. If they are obedient they will be "chosen," and if they are chosen they will be grafted into the true vine or the seed of Abraham. On the other hand, those who belong to the true vine but turn toward wickedness and rebellion will be cut off. Salvation cannot be inherited. It has to be earned. *Obedience* is the one single, pulsating, throbbing source of virtue which permits God to call any of his children "chosen."[17]

CHARACTERISTICS OF GOD'S CHOSEN PEOPLE

A careful study of the lives and attitudes of those who were called "beloved of God" and designated "chosen" serv-ants will reveal a number of superior and exemplary cha-acteristics. These qualities are so universally typical of the Lord's leaders that they deserve to be itemized:

14. Abraham 2:9-10
15. Romans 8:14-15
16. *Teachings of Joseph Smith*, pp. 149-150
17. Hebrews 5:9; Matthew 7:21; Doc. & Cov. 41:5; 84:91

1—A spirit of personal sacrifice. A manifest zeal to serve God with heart, might, mind and strength. A willingness to live "sacrificially."

2—A personal code of stringent self discipline — morally, intellectually, physically, and spiritually.

3—Capacity to perform unbelievable quantities of hard, humble work.

4—Willingness to accept God's commandments without fear or reservation — even when a new commandment is in direct contradiction to a former commandment. An ability to recognize that God doesn't change, but circumstances do, and God's commandments will vary accordingly.

5—Possessing a world view of individuals as well as nations and recognizing the universal quality of God's program for human welfare. Appreciating that the Lord is neither provincial nor exclusive. His love and anxiety for mankind is all encompassing.

6—A willingness to engage in continuous study in order to catch the broad sweep of understanding necessary to appreciate heavenly principles from the Lord's point of view.

7—A willingness to tear up roots and help transplant civilizations from region to region and from continent to continent. (Notice how many prophets of God were raised up for the specific purpose of planting "islands of righteousness" in some new part of the earth — Enos, Enoch, Noah, Jared, Abraham, Jacob, Moses, Lehi, Nephi, and Alma are but a few examples.)

8—A willingness to strive valiantly to fill *all* of the purposes of earth life which the Lord calls the Second Estate:

   a. To raise up as large a family of well-trained and well-loved children as health and circumstances will permit.
   b. To prove worthy of continuous advancement in the Priesthood.
   c. To serve cheerfully in the Lord's Kingdom whatever the capacity.
   d. To serve willingly in public life when needed, including civil offices, elected posts and the military.

e. To teach, speak, travel, write, or otherwise serve in every possible way to promote righteousness in the earth whether spiritual or secular.

f. To be continually engaged in a good cause without having to be "commanded in all things" as is the case with "slothful servants."

g. To be a good provider and see that all of one's increase has been tithed unto the Lord.

h. To stand up and be counted when forces of evil sweep in to destroy God's Kingdom or the rights and liberties of his children.

Having itemized the qualities of exemplary character which God has ascribed to his "chosen" servants, we shall now turn our attention to the actual lives of those servants during ancient times. They were the men who headed up the dispensations of the Gospel in their day and who personified these very principles in action.

In *The First 2,000 Years*—the first book of this series— we discussed the lives of all the patriarchs from Adam to Abraham. Probably nowhere in the broad panorama of human history is the image of God's chosen servants more eloquently represented than in the hardships and achievements of the ancient patriarchs, particularly those who lived before the Great Flood. They were the pioneers of the race. They built whole civilizations and saw wickedness sometimes destroy them with forces as terrible and degenerate as any that will ever pollute humanity.[18] They built a golden age which survived for 365 years and was not only remembered after the Flood but became the illusive dream of Utopia which politicians and economists have tried to duplicate ever since.

As we proceed to examine the Old Testament, it should be kept in mind that this is the most ancient and the most neglected of all the scriptures. As a matter of fact, this is what makes it such a fascinating study. The student may expect to find new and exciting nuggets of history and doctrine hidden within its pages as we scrutinize the third thousand years — from 2,000 to 1,000 B.C.

---

18. Moses 7:36

THE HISTORICAL SETTING FOR THE THIRD THOUSAND YEARS

The face of the earth in the third thousand years of human history was different in many respects from its appearance today. No doubt the continental boundaries were very much the same, but the details of man's markings on the surface of those continents were different. Even the markings of nature were different. For example, where vast bodies of water once stretched across Middle Asia like the vestigial remnants of some great flood, there are only prairies and plains today. Where nature's fertile luxury once supported large city-states with populations in the tens of thousands there are today nothing but shifting seas of desolate sand dunes.

In the past century scientists have uncovered the ruins of cities from the third thousand years which were as large as Rome, but Rome knew nothing of them. Even then they were already too ancient to be remembered. By the third thousand years there were ganglia of highly organized humanity in Sumaria (the Shinar of the Bible) with metal works, textile manufacturing, monumental achitecture, and an efficient system of writing. By the third thousand years pockets of civilization were festering all up and down the great rivers — the Euphrates, Tigris, Indus and the Nile. Crash migrations by sturdy explorers and sometimes reckless adventurers were building comparable civilizations in Phoenicia, Crete, Syria and Jaredite-America. Everything scientists have been able to prove through archaeological and anthropological research has verified the accuracy of the broad outlines of history depicted in the scriptures by the prophet-historians.

Of course, the scriptures portray the past through the biographies of God's chosen servants and there is always the temptation to over-simplify the past when we study the lives of individuals. It is easy to miss the larger, swift-flowing flood of cross-currents which constitute the history of nations, empires and whole civilizations. Nevertheless, if we keep in mind the general cultural setting of a biography there is no more profitable research than the study of an individual who belonged to a particular age. With the philosopher we are compelled to conclude that in the final analysis, "there is no history, only biography." In fact, biography turns out to be the safer way to study history. As Will Durant comments in his story of civilization, "Most history is guessing, and the rest is prejudice."[19]

Students are turning more and more to the scriptural record and to archaeology to clarify their insights concerning the life and times of the ancient past. Today, in Israel, the favorite hobby is field studies in archaeology as students find it fascinating to correlate the account in the Bible with the artifacts to be found in the ruins and debris of the past. So important is this bilateral pursuit of knowledge through archaeology and the scriptures that when this author visited Palestine recently he was told that around 20% of every school day is devoted to a study of the Old Testament in the state schools of Israel. Christians, Mohammedans and Jews all study these scriptures together and then go out in the fields and mountains to locate the scientific evidence of the Biblical past. Once each year the nation of Israel sponsors a world-wide quiz on the Old Testament. The winner is then invited to match his knowledge with that of Israel's former prime minister, David Ben Gurion, who is one of the finest scholars of the Old Testament today.

CULTURAL SETTING FOR THE THIRD THOUSAND YEARS

It is clear from both scripture and archaeology that by the third thousand years the human epic was already an old story. The rhythmical pattern of growth and decay had already punctuated the course of human events. It had left its acccunt of some people so advanced that they (with Enoch) were able to experience inter-planetary transplantation,[20] while others were so depraved (such as those in the

---

19. Will Durant, *Our Oriental Heritage*, New York: Simon and Schuster, 1954, p. 12.

20. Doc. & Covenants 45:11-12; Inspired Version, Genesis 7:78; "By faith Enoch was translated that he should not see death; and was not found, because God had translated him. . . ." (Heb. 11:5)
"Many have supposed that the doctrine of translation was a doctrine whereby men were taken immediately into the presence of God, and into an eternal fullness, but this is a mistaken idea. Their place of habitation is that of the terrestrial order, and a place prepared for such characters He held in reserve to be ministering angels unto many planets, and who as yet have not entered into so great a fullness as those who are resurrected from the dead." (*Teachings of Joseph Smith,* p. 170)

days of Noah) that they had to be purged from the earth in a cataclysmic destruction by drowning.

In the year 2,000 B.C. at least two of those who had lived before the Great Flood were still alive. Noah was one of them, and the other was his second son, Shem. The Lord has verified that Noah did in fact live a total of 950 years, and that 350 of those years were after the Flood.[21] He has also verified that Shem lived 610 years and that 502 of those years were after the Flood.[22]

Noah had hoped that his descendants would remain righteous but by the time he died around 1,994 B.C., Noah had already seen the rise and fall of Babel, the confusion of tongues, the introduction of Nimrod's heathenism designed to compete with the Priesthood; also the introduction of vestal virgin prostitution and human sacrifices which were used as ritualistic embellishments in fertility worship and the diabolical mystery cults of devil worship.[23]

Ten generations down from Noah (and while Noah was still alive) Abraham was born into a cultural cesspool in the heathen-dominated city of Ur. In that city his own fathers had indulged in the most depraved heathen practices, even going so far as to sacrifice some of their own children, including Abraham.[24] Had not God intervened at the last moment, Abraham, who had been bound to the altar for sacrifice at the request of his own father, would have died in his youth under the knife of the priest of Elkenah.[25]

Fleeing from Ur, Abraham settled in Haran, but similar problems soon developed there,[26] and when he traveled on to Egypt, that opulent kingdom turned out to be tainted also.[27] Mankind had so corrupted their way upon the earth

---

21. "And Noah lived after the flood three hundred and fifty years. And all the days of Noah were nine hundred and fifty years: and he died." (Genesis 9:28-29)

22. Shem was born when Noah was 492 years old (Moses 8:12). This would make him 108 when the Great Flood occurred because Noah was then 600 (Genesis 7:11). We know Shem begat Arphaxad two years after the flood (Genesis 11:10), and lived 500 years thereafter (Genesis 11:11). This would mean that he lived 610 years and that 502 of those years were after the Flood.

23. See Clarke's *Bible Commentary*, Vol. 1, p. 565, 569; Lev. 17:7; Lev. 18:21-29.

24. Abraham 1:5-7

25. Abraham 1:7, 15

26. Abraham 2:5

27. Abraham 1:27

and established such a foothold of perverted debauchery that the Lord was compelled to undertake the reconstruction of a Gospel culture with one man. That man was Abraham.

Of course, there were islands of righteousness elsewhere, such as the people of Melchizedek at Salem, but they were soon to be removed from the earth to join the City of Enoch;[28] and there were the sporadic surges of righteousness in Jaredite-America, but the Lord knew those people would soon decline and eventually annihilate themselves in civil war.[29] Therefore, the hope of the Lord was in Abraham, and He blessed him accordingly. Abraham was told to return to Canaan. There he established himself at Hebron and Beer-sheba.

Isaac, First Patriarch in the Third Thousand Years

Just as the Lord was depending upon Abraham to establish a foothold of righteousness in the earth, so Abraham came to depend upon his son, Isaac, to carry on after him. Abraham had no other son worthy of being the one through whom the covenant could be projected and therefore Abraham nourished with the most jealous anxiety this slender thread of Priesthood perpetuity which Isaac represented.

In *The First* 2,000 *Years* we related the early life of Isaac, but at the risk of being slightly repetitious we will repeat the highlights of his younger days in order to pick up the threads of his story.

It will be recalled that Isaac was a miracle baby. He was born when his mother was 90 years of age and his father was 100![30]

His parents were told what his name should be a year before he was born.[31] Knowing what pleasure this child would bring to Abraham and Sarah, the Lord said to name him Isaac (laughter).[32]

The rite of circumcision was performed for Isaac when he was eight days old.[33] This was a relatively new ordinance

---

28. Inspired Version, Genesis 14:26-34
29. Ether 14:20-21
30. Genesis 17:17; 21:5
31. Genesis 17:19-21
32. Peloubet's *Bible Dictionary*, under *Isaac*.

which the Lord had initiated the year before. On that occasion Abraham, Ishmael and all of the male population in Abraham's household had been circumcised.[34] Now it was done
for Isaac.

It is important to keep in mind why the ordinance of
circumcision was introduced. A year earlier the Lord had
said to Abraham:

"My people have gone astray from my precepts, and
have not kept mine ordinances, which I gave unto their
fathers; and they have not observed mine anointing, and *the
burial, or baptism,* wherewith I commanded them. . . . And I
will establish a covenant of circumcision with thee . . . that
thou mayest know for ever that children are not accountable
before me until they are eight years old."[35]

From this we are able to see that circumcision was basic-
ally a reminder that just as a child was to be circumcised
when he was eight days old,[36] so also he was to be baptized
when eight *years* old.

This would therefore imply that when Isaac was eight
years of age he was baptized in accordance with the Lord's
commandment. The scripture does not mention this specific
event but we are certain it must have occurred since otherwise the ordinance of circumcision would have been meaningless.

THE OFFERING OF ISAAC AS A HUMAN SACRIFICE

As the aged Abraham carefully nurtured and guided
young Isaac toward maturity he knew he was molding a
choice child of God. Had not the Lord Himself declared that
he would be the channel through which the blessings of the
great covenant should pass? Had he not said to Abraham:
". . . thou shalt call his name Isaac: and I will establish my
covenant with him for an everlasting covenant, and with his
seed after him"?[37]

But even before young Isaac could have any posterity
and while he was still a "lad," the Lord gave a commandment

---

33. Genesis 21:4   36. Genesis 17:12
34. Genesis 17:11-14   37. Genesis 17:19
35. Inspired Version, Genesis 17:4-11

concerning him that was fantastic and incomprehensible to Abraham.

The Lord said, "Take now thy son, thine only son Isaac, whom thou lovest, and get thee into the land of Moriah; and offer him there for a burnt offering upon one of the mountains which I will tell thee of."[38]

This was impossible! To Abraham God just could not give a commandment like this. Had not Abraham's father, Terah, offered human sacrifices and thereby invoked the wrath of God?[39] Had not Abraham spent three quarters of a century following God's commandments in denouncing these abominable practices? How, then, could the Lord now ask Abraham to perform one of these sacrifices himself? And why young Isaac? Would not this terrible act wipe out every promise God had ever made to Abraham concerning the boy?

The desperate father received no answer to any of these questions. He was being tested as no other prophet had ever been tested.

Abraham arose early in the morning and prepared to make the journey from Beer-sheba to the area which today is called Jerusalem. He took two young men and Isaac with him. A pack animal was used to carry provisions and a quantity of chopped wood. Three days of continuous travel finally brought the party within sight of the place which was called Moriah. At this point Abraham told the two young men to wait while he and Isaac went ahead to worship. The two young men obeyed.

"And Abraham took the wood of the burnt offering, and laid it upon his back; and he took the fire in his hand, and a knife, and Isaac his son: and they went both of them together.

"And Isaac spoke unto Abraham his father, and said, My father! and he said, Here am I, my son. And he said, Behold the fire and the wood; but where is the lamb for a burnt offering?

---

38. Genesis 22:2   39. Abraham 1:5-7

"And Abraham said, My son, God will provide himself a lamb for a burnt offering."[40]

As Abraham led his son up the steep slopes to Mount Moriah he knew he was treading on sacred ground. Only a few years before this had been the site of Salem, the great city of Melchizedek. (In later centuries it would be called Jeru-salem.) Now Melchizedek and his people were gone. Modern revelation has disclosed that they "wrought right-eousness, and obtained heaven."[41] They had obtained the same blessing as that which had been given to the people of Enoch. To this sacred haven Abraham and Isaac now came. It was the same Mount Moriah where Solomon would later build his magnificent temple to God.[42] And two thous-and years later the Moslems would build their famous mosque over "the rock" where Isaac was believed to have been offer-ed as a sacrifice. No modern visitor to Old Jerusalem can help but feel the throbbing pulsation of its haunting history.

As for Abraham and Isaac, the scripture says, "And they came to the place which God told him of: and Abraham built an altar there, and laid the wood in order, and bound Isaac his son, and laid him on the altar upon the wood."[43]

There is no indication of any resistance by Isaac. Cer-tainly the anguish of Abraham's soul in this bitter hour would have wrung from him some explanation as he prepared his son for the shock of this terrible experience. Paul says Abra-ham approached the ordeal determined to offer up Isaac as commanded, but "accounting that God was able to raise him up, even from the dead."[44] Josephus attributes these words to Abraham as the moment of sacrifice drew near:

"Oh, son, I poured out a vast number of prayers that I might have thee for my son; when thou wast come into the world, there was nothing that could contribute to thy support for which I was not greatly solicitous, nor anything wherein I thought myself happier than to see thee grown up to man's

---

40. Inspired Version, Genesis 22:7-10. Note that Abraham carried the wood, not the "lad." This would indicate that Isaac was still quite young, perhaps only a child. The Inspired Version hereby corrects an error which had crept into our Standard Version of the Bible.

41. Inspired Version, Genesis 14:32-34   43. Genesis 22:9

42. 2 Chronicles 3:1   44. Hebrews 11:19

estate, and that I might leave thee at my death the successor to my dominion; but since it was by God's will that I became thy father, and it is now his will that I relinquish thee, bear this consecration to God with a generous mind; for I resign thee up to God who has thought fit now to require this testimony of honour to Himself, on account of the favours He hath conferred on me, in being to me a supporter and defender. Accordingly thou, my son, wilt now die, not in any common way of going out of the world, but sent to God, the Father of all men, beforehand, by thy own father, in the nature of a sacrifice. I suppose He thinks thee worthy to get clear of this world neither by disease, neither by war, nor by any other severe way, by which death usually comes upon men, but so that He will receive thy soul with prayers and holy offices of religion, and will place thee near to Himself, and thou wilt there be to me a successor and supporter in my old age; on which acount I principally brought thee up, and thou wilt thereby procure me God for my comforter instead of thyself."[45]

"And Abraham stretched forth his hand, and took the knife to slay his son."[46]

This was the final gesture of absolute obedience the Lord had been waiting for. Beyond the veil the angel of the Lord had watched the tense proceedings. At that very moment when Abraham raised the knife to slay his son, the angel cried out, "Abraham! Abraham!" The aged patriarch replied, "Here am I." And the angel said, "Lay not thine hand upon the lad, neither do thou anything unto him: for now I know that thou fearest God, seeing thou hast not withheld thy son, thine only son, from me."[47]

"And Abraham lifted up his eyes, and looked, and behold behind him a ram caught in a thicket by his horns: And Abraham went and took the ram, and offered him up for a burnt offering in the stead of his son."[48]

Abraham had met the crisis of his life. He had triumphed in it. From the murky swamp of total human despair he had

---

45. Josephus, *Antiquities of the Jews,* Book 1, Ch. 13:3
46. Genesis 22:10
47. Genesis 22:12
48. Genesis 22:13

been elevated suddenly to the exhilarating crest of ultimate achievement where the glory of God's approbation shown brightly upon him. From generation to generation, the events of this day would be proclaimed as possibly the most outstanding example of righteous faith ever exhibited by a member of the Priesthood. It would help others in later dispensations to trust in the Lord, particularly when His commandments seemed strange and incomprehensible.

To more fully appreciate the feelings of Abraham on this occasion, it is important to recall that many years before, in Ur of Chaldea, Abraham himself had been bound to an altar preparatory to being offered up as a human sacrifice. And a further irony was the fact that his own father had arranged it.[49] However, Abraham was to have been sacrificed to a heathen god. Abraham went through the terrifying experience of being bound to the heathen altar and seeing the fatal moment approach when the priest would plunge a dagger through his heart. Only at the last possible instant did the Lord intervene to save his life. In fact the impact of God's wrath was so powerful on that occasion that it not only miraculously released Abraham from the altar on which he was bound, but it killed the officiating priest and smashed the heathen altar to pieces.[50]

The relief which Abraham must have felt as he escaped from the brink of violent death in Ur, was similar, no doubt, to the sense of relief which swept over him in this later crisis as he cut the bonds and released his own son from the altar on Mount Moriah.

Surely there was no more grateful man on the face of the earth than Abraham as he joyfully led Isaac back down to the place where his two servants were waiting. Having packed their belongings, the four of them departed for home.

The Intervening Years and the Death of Isaac's Mother

As Isaac grew to maturity important events undoubtedly occurred but the canon of scripture is silent concerning them.

---

49. Abraham 1:5-7
50. Abraham 1:15, 20

It would be reasonable to expect, however, that during these impressionable years Abraham would have shared with this choice son the great secrets of heaven which had been revealed to him. Was Isaac instructed in the use of the Urim and Thummim? We know Abraham possessed these instruments[51] and that later they were used by Aaron.[52] Did Isaac get to study the ancient Priesthood records which Abraham had in his custody? These told the story of the creation and the history of mankind back to Father Adam.[53] And was he allowed to study the principles of astronomy, mathematics and perhaps other principles of science which had been revealed to Abraham by direct revelation.[54] Some day we will have all of the records of the ancient patriarchs and then we will know the answers to such questions.[55]

The next important event mentioned in the scripture was the death of Isaac's mother. By this time Isaac was 37 years of age and his mother was 127.[56]

The burial of Sarah presented a problem since Abraham owned no land. However, the affection and respect which the native princes held for Abraham was reflected in their willingness to have Abraham use their own personal tombs for Sarah's burial if he so desired. Although they wanted to have Abraham receive one of their tombs as a gift, he asked permission to buy a certain field which had a cave in its limestone cliffs. This transaction was succesfully negotiated and after paying 400 shekels of silver Abraham took permanent possession of this field. So Abraham and Isaac buried Sarah "in the cave of the field of Machpelah before Mamre: the same is Hebron in the land of Canaan."[57]

This sepulchre became more famous than almost any ancient burial place. It was not only the final resting place for the Shemite princess, Sarah, but also for Abraham,[58]

---

51. Abraham 3:1
52. Exodus 28:30; Leviticus; Deuteronomy 33:8
53. Abraham 1:31
54. Abraham Chapter 3; See discussion in *The First* 2,000 *Years,* pp. 285-295
55. Doctrine and Covenants 121:28; 101:32
56. Genesis 23:1; Genesis 17:17

Isaac,[59] Rebekah,[60] Leah,[61] and Jacob.[62] Today, the traditional site is covered by a large Mohammedan mosque.

<h2 align="center">ABRAHAM SEEKS A WIFE FOR ISAAC</h2>

Although Isaac was now 37, he had not married. This
was due to the fact that in Canaan there were none of his
own people to whom he could be married. After Sarah's
death, Abraham set about to remedy this situation.

Abraham called in his eldest servant "that ruled over
all that he had," and said: "Swear by the Lord, the God of
heaven, and the God of the earth, that thou shalt not take a
wife unto my son of the daughters of the Canaanites, among
whom I dwell."[63]

Since the Canaanites were of the Hamitic tribes who
could not enjoy the Priesthood, Abraham was greatly concerned about the marriage of Isaac to a young woman of the
proper lineage so that the promise of the Lord concerning
the Priesthood could be perpetuated through him. To marry
a Canaanite would cut the promise off because the children
of such a union could not receive the Priesthood. Abraham
therefore instructed his servant as follows: "But thou shalt go
unto my country, and to my kindred, and take a wife unto
my son Isaac."[64]

Abraham's servant hesitated to take an oath which he
might find difficult to fulfill. Said he: "Peradventure the
woman will not be willing to follow me unto this land . . .
from whence thou camest?" The servant thought that if
his own efforts to get a wife for Isaac failed it might help if
he took Isaac along with him so the young woman and her
family could approve of him for themselves. But Abraham
saw great danger in this.

Said he, "Beware thou, that thou bring not my son
thither again. The Lord God of heaven, which took me from
my father's house, and from the land of my kindred . . . sware

---

57. Genesis 23:17-19   61. Ibid.
58. Genesis 25:9   62. Genesis 50:13
59. Genesis 49:31   63. Genesis 24:3
60. Ibid.   64. Genesis 24:4

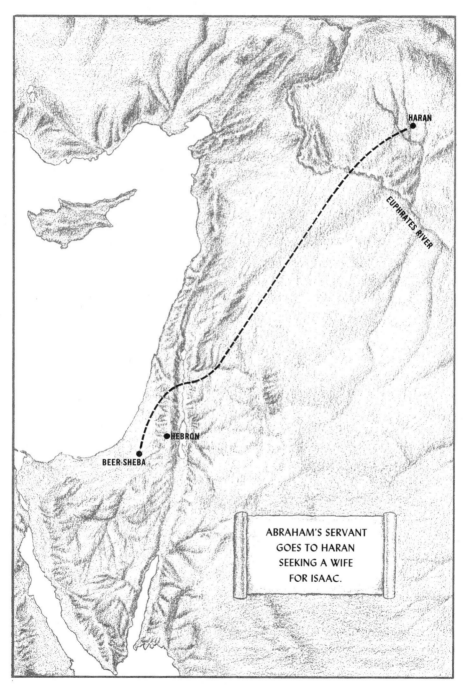

HARAN

EUPHRATES RIVER

HEBRON

BEER-SHEBA

ABRAHAM'S SERVANT
GOES TO HARAN
SEEKING A WIFE
FOR ISAAC.

unto me saying, Unto thy seed will I give this land."[65] Abraham believed his son must not be tempted by the prosperity of Mesopotamia, but must be determined to remain in Canaan where the Lord had promised an inheritance to Abraham and his descendants forever. Abraham therefore promised his servant that the Lord "shall send his angel before thee, and thou shalt take a wife unto my son from thence. And if the woman will not be willing to follow thee, then thou shalt be clear from this my oath: *only bring* not my son thither again."[66] Abraham was most emphatic that Isaac was not to go to Mesopotamia.

With this explanation the servant felt satisfied and took an oath to perform this service. He therefore set out with a large caravan of ten camels and a number of men and "went to Mesopotamia, unto the city of Nahor."[67]

The city of Nahor (named after Abraham's brother[68]) was located in the upper regions of the Euphrates River where Abraham had originally settled after leaving Ur.[69] The city where Nahor and his family lived was called Padan-aram, but it is clear that Padan-aram was either identical with Haran or in the district of Haran.[70] In sending his servant to the city of Nahor, Abraham could accurately describe it as "my country" and "my kindred".[71]

THE SERVANT OF ABRAHAM FINDS REBEKAH

When the servant of Abraham had arrived at the city of Nahor he made his camels kneel beside the well from which the people of the community obtained their water. Then he prayed to the Lord, saying:

"O Lord God of my master Abraham, I pray thee, send me good speed this day, and shew kindness unto my master Abraham.

"Behold, I stand here by the well of water; and the daughters of the men of the city come out to draw water:

65. Genesis 24:6-7
66. Genesis 24:7-8
67. Genesis 24:10, 32
68. Abraham 2:2. This name is spelled Nehor by Abraham.
69. Abraham 2:4, plus Genesis 29:4-5
70. Genesis 28:5, 10; 29:4-5
71. Genesis 24:4

And let it come to pass, that the damsel to whom I shall say, Let down thy pitcher, I pray thee, that I may drink; and she shall say, Drink, and I will give thy camels drink also: let the same be she that thou hast appointed for thy servant Isaac; and thereby shall I know that thou hast shewed kindness unto my master."[72]

Even before he had stopped speaking his prayer was answered: "Behold, Rebekah came out, who was born to Bethuel, son of Milcah, the wife of Nahor, Abraham's brother, with her pitcher upon her shoulder."[73]

The servant of Abraham noted that she was "very fair to look upon."[74] After Rebekah had filled her pitcher he asked her for a drink. The maiden was very gracious in complying. Though the man was a stranger she did not seem to fear him. When the servant of Abraham had finished drinking he heard the girl say: "I will draw water for thy camels also until they have done drinking." This was the sign which the servant had asked from the Lord. Nevertheless, he could not help wondering if it might not be a coincidence.[75] He therefore watched the girl as she "emptied her pitcher into the trough, and ran again unto the well to draw water." She did not stop until the camels had all been satisfied. To water ten camels was an arduous task. To perform this task without complaining or receiving assistance was a strong test. Still the servant of Abraham wondered, so he said to the girl: "Whose daughter art thou? tell me, I pray thee: is there room in thy father's house for us to lodge in?"

Her answer drove all doubt from the man's mind. Said she, "I am the daughter of Bethuel, the son of Milcah, which she bare unto Nahor." Then she added, "We have both straw and provender enough, and room to lodge in."[76]

As soon as the servant of Abraham heard this he reached forth and placed two gold bracelets on her arms and gave

---

72. Genesis 24:12-14
73. Genesis 24:15
74. Genesis 24:16. The Inspired Version gives even more concerning the beauty of this girl. It says: "And the damsel being a virgin, very fair to look upon, such as the servant of Abraham had not seen, neither had any man known the like unto her. . . ."
75. Genesis 24:21
76. Genesis 24:23-25

her jeweled earrings to wear. He was so gratified to have his mission such an unexpected success that the scripture says he "bowed his head" and publicly worshipped the Lord. He lifted his voice toward heaven saying, "Blessed be the Lord God of my master Abraham, who hath not left destitute my master of his mercy and his truth; I being in the way, the Lord led me to the house of my master's brethren!"[77]

These words told Rebekah for the first time who this stranger was. When she heard that he was the servant of none other than Abraham, her famous great-uncle, she ran immediately and told her people at home.

"And Rebekah had a brother, and his name was Laban . . . and it came to pass, when he saw the earring and bracelets upon his sister's hands, and when he heard the words of Rebekah his sister . . . he came unto the man; and, behold, he stood by the camels at the well.

"And he said, Come in, thou blessed of the Lord; wherefore standest thou without? for I have prepared the house, and the room for the camels.

"And the man came into the house: and he ungirded his camels, and gave straw and provender for the camels, and water to wash his feet, and the men's feet that were with him."[78]

REBEKAH'S GREAT DECISION

Laban wanted the servant of Abraham to eat but he said, "I will not eat, until I have told mine errand." Then he related the whole account of what had happened. He recited Abraham's instructions to him and the oath that Abraham had required of him. He told how he had asked the Lord for a sign and how astonished he was when Rebekah was the first girl who came to the well and had satisfied the sign in every particular. He said that his whole purpose in coming to Haran was to find a wife for Abraham's son, Isaac. Having delivered this forthright message he concluded by saying, "And now if ye will deal kindly and truly with my master, tell me: and if not, tell me; that I may turn to the right hand, or left."[79]

77. Genesis 24:27
78. Genesis 24:29-32

79. Genesis 24:49

No doubt this request came as a shock to the household of Rebekah. Rebekah's brother and father might have taken deep offense at this presumptuous request to have her suddenly leave home and travel with a stranger all the way to Canaan to marry a second cousin she had never seen. However, they were not offended: "Laban and Bethuel answered and said, The thing proceedeth from the Lord: we cannot speak unto thee bad or good."[80] In other words, the matter was not one for them to decide. The hand of the Lord had been so strongly manifested that the decision was already made. So they said, "Behold, Rebekah is before thee, take her, and go, and let her be thy master's son's wife, as the Lord hath spoken."[81] When the servant of Abraham heard this he was so overcome with gratitude that he once more fell to his knees and bowed himself to the earth and publicly thanked the Lord for this great blessing.

Then he took silver and gold and fine raiment and gave them to Rebekah. "He gave also to her brother and to her mother precious things.

"And they did eat and drink, he and the men that were with him, and tarried all night; and they rose up in the morning, and he said, Send me away unto my master.

"And her brother and her mother said, Let the damsel abide with us a few days, at the least ten; after that she shall go.

"And he said unto them, Hinder me not, seeing the Lord hath prospered my way; send me away that I may go to my master.

"And they said we will call the damsel, and enquire at her mouth.

"And they called Rebekah, and said unto her, Wilt thou go with this man? And she said, I will go."[82]

This entire series of incidents reflects a quality of character and spiritual strength in Rebekah which were becoming to a princess of Shem. She was a beautiful and noble girl

---

80. Genesis 24:50   82. Genesis 24:53-58
81. Genesis 24:51

—one of the choicest women on the face of the earth in her day and generation.

"And they blessed Rebekah and said unto her, Thou art our sister, be thou the mother of thousands of millions, and let thy seed possess the gate of those which hate them."[83]

These words seem to show that this family was entirely familiar with the great promise which had been made to Abraham and his descendants. In marrying Isaac, Rebekah was destined to become a "mother of nations."

"And Rebekah arose, and her damsels, and they rode upon the camels, and followed the man; and the servant took Rebekah, and went his way."[84]

Rebekah Meets Isaac

Few romances have had a more remarkable beginning than this one. There must have been anxious days for Rebekah as the caravan made its way slowly across Syria and down along the mountain ranges of Canaan.

But Rebekah was not the only one to feel anxiety. At least she had seen the power of God manifest in her selection and knew that her marriage with Isaac had the benediction of the Lord. But Isaac was in a completely different position. All he could do was wait and worry. He was under the necessity of patiently enduring until he could see what kind of judgment his father's servant would have in selecting a wife for him. More than once it must have occurred to Isaac that it was illogical to assume that the servant would bring any bride at all.

Isaac had gone out one evening into the field to meditate when he saw a caravan coming which he soon recognized as the one belonging to his father's steward. Isaac ran forward to meet it. As he drew near, Rebekah quickly inquired of Abraham's servant, "What man is this that walketh in the field to meet us?" and the servant replied, "It is my master!"[85]

---

83. Genesis 24:60
84. Genesis 24:61. Note that one of the "damsels" who accompanied Rebekah was Deborah, her nurse, whose death and burial are specifically mentioned later on. See Genesis 35:8.
85. Genesis 24:65

Immediately Rebekah alighted from the camel and covered her face with a veil to be prepared for the proper office of introduction after the manner of those times.

However, the servant of Abraham was not desirous of introducing Isaac to his prospective bride until Isaac had been told the whole exciting account of what had happened at Haran. He wanted Isaac to know how the Lord had led him to Rebekah and how she had accepted the many manifestations of divine approbation and was therefore prepared to become his wife even though she had never met him.

Then came the thrilling moment when these two important personalities met for the first time in earth life. There was a natural affinity between them. Their union was blessed of the Lord. Isaac took Rebekah to Abraham, and there must have been great joy in the heart of that aging patriarch as he joined them together in marriage after the pattern of the Holy Priesthood which is "for time and all eternity."

Finally the scripture says, "And Isaac brought her into his mother Sarah's tent, and took Rebekah, and she became his wife; and he loved her."[86] Isaac was now forty years of age.[87]

86. Genesis 24:67
87. Genesis 25:20

Scripture Reading and Questions on Chapter One

Scripture Reading Assignment: Genesis, chapters 21 to 24 inclusive.

1—On what principle does the Lord select his "chosen" people?

2—How can the Lord have a "chosen" people and still be fair and just?

3—Can a heathen or a gentile become the "seed of Abraham?"

4—What is the "Spirit of adoption?"

5—How does the Lord apply the principles of "pruning and grafting" to His Kingdom? What does it accomplish?

6—Name six outstanding characteristics of God's chosen people.

7—How long did Noah live after the Great Flood?

8—How long did Shem (Noah's heir) live after the Great Flood?

9—How old was Sarah when Isaac was born? How old was Abraham?

10—The Lord says the ordinance of circumcision was to remind parents of a more important ordinance. What was it?

11—Where did Abraham take Isaac to offer him up as a sacrifice? What made the place so famous? What is it called today?

12—Why did Abraham send to Haran to find a wife for his son?

13—Did the servant of Abraham go to Haran alone?

14—How did Abraham's servant happen to select Rebekah?

15—What relation was Rebekah to Isaac?

16—Why didn't her family object when Abraham's servant asked her to accompany him back to Canaan and marry a man she had never seen?

17—What were her physical attributes? Did she reflect qualities of spirituality?

18—What kind of blessing did Rebekah receive before she departed for Canaan? Did the family send her away alone?

19—When Rebekah saw Isaac walking out to meet them, what did she do?

20—What did Abraham's servant tell Isaac when he introduced Isaac to Rebekah?

CHAPTER TWO

Isaac Becomes the Father
of Two Nations

When Rebekah married Isaac, son and heir of the famous Abraham, she began a new chapter in her life which had all the ingredients for an existence of superlative happiness. But with the passing of time, Rebekah suffered a deep personal sorrow. She could have no children. For 19 years Rebekah was barren.[1]

This must have seemed especially strange since the Lord had given His benediction to this union,[2] and Rebekah had been brought all the way from Haran to be the wife of Isaac so that the blessings of Abraham (for a mighty posterity) might be perpetuated through her.[3] But after waiting nineteen years without having this blessing fulfilled, Isaac finally determined to ask for a special blessing from the Lord. And the Bible says, "Isaac entreated the Lord for his wife . . . and Rebekah his wife conceived."[4]

THE BIRTH OF THE TWINS—JACOB AND ESAU

By this time Issac is known to have been in his sixtieth year so we assume that Rebekah would necessarily have been around 40.[5]

Perhaps it was because of her age that Rebekah now found that her conception had brought upon her a season

---

1. Genesis 25:21 states Rebekah was "barren". The duration of this condition is determined by comparing Genesis 25:20 which says, "Isaac was forty years old when he took Rebekah" along with Genesis 25:26 which says Isaac was "three score years" before he had children. Rebekah was therefore barren for 19 of those years and gave birth to her twins in the twentieth year.
2. Genesis 24:50-51
3. Genesis 24:60
4. Genesis 25:21
5. Genesis 25:26. We know that Issac was 40 when he married Rebekah (Genesis 25:20) and therefore 20 years had transpired. Assuming Rebekah was approximately 20 years old when her marriage began, she would now be around 40.

of unexpected distress. Her illness was intense. The scriptures say she became so ill she felt she could not endure it.
Therefore, "she went to inquire of the Lord."[6]

"And the Lord said unto her, Two nations are in thy
womb . . . and the one people shall be stronger than the
other people; AND THE ELDER SHALL SERVE THE
YOUNGER."[7]

So Rebekah knew from this revelation that she was
going to have twins, and she knew that the younger of the
twins was going to prevail over the elder.

It was in or about the year 1862 B.C. that Rebekah's
twins were born.[8] Both were boys just as she had been
promised, but it was immediately apparent that they were
not identical twins. The firstborn was "red all over like an
hairy garment," and therefore he was given the name of
Esau which means, "hairy".[9] Later he was called Edom,
which means "red",[10] and the nation which grew out of him
became known as the Edomites.[11]

The second twin was smooth of skin and when he was
being born he reached forth his hand and grasped the heel
of the twin who came first. This incident, coupled with the
fact that the Lord had revealed that this second twin would
prevail over his elder brother, led Isaac and Rebekah to
name him Jacob, which means "supplanter".[12]

THE GREAT PATRIARCH ABRAHAM DIES AT THE AGE OF 175

When the twins had reached the age of fifteen[13] the most
notable event in their lives occurred. Their famous grandfather, Abraham, died. He had reached the age of 175.[14]

---

6. Genesis 25:22
7. Genesis 25:23
8. See "chronology" preceding chapter 1. This is four years earlier than the date
   given by Dr. Adam Clarke (Vol. 1, p. 158) but is believed to be more accurate as a result of data revealed in modern times.
9. Peloubet's Bible Dictionary under Esau.
10. Peloubet's Bible Dictionary under Edom
11. Ibid.
12. Peloubet's Bible Dictionary under Jacob.
13. Since Isaac was 60 when his twins were born (Genesis 25:26) and 75 when
    Abraham died (Genesis 21:5 plus 25:7) the intervening period would be 15
    years.
14. Genesis 25:7

Abraham had been a rare combination of excellence both as a servant of God and a man of affairs. He had been a prophet and seer,[15] a pioneer,[16] a soldier,[17] an astronomer and mathematician,[18] a man of great wealth [19] and a man of great influence in Ur,[20] Haran,[21] Egypt,[22] and Canaan.[23] He was the prophet whom the Lord called upon to initiate the ordinance of circumcision,[24] and he was the prophet to whom the Lord had made eight great promises.[25] The Lord had said:

"I will make of thee a great nation."

"I will bless thee above measure."

"I will . . . make thy name great among all nations."

"Thy seed . . . shall bear this ministry and Priesthood unto all nations."

"As many as receive the Gospel shall be . . . accounted thy seed."

"I will bless them that bless thee, and curse them that curse thee."

"I give unto thee a promise that this right [of the Priesthood] shall continue in thee."

"In thy seed after thee (that is to say, the literal seed or the seed of the body) shall all the families of the earth be blessed, even with the blessings of the Gospel."

---

15. Abraham 3:1-5
16. Abraham 2:3-4
17. Genesis 14:14-16
18. Abraham 1:31; Pearl of Great Price, p. 42 showing Abraham on the throne of Pharaoh "reasoning upon the principles of Astronomy." See also Josephus, *Antiquities of the Jews,* Book 1, Ch. 7:2: "He [Abraham] communicated to them arithmetic, and delivered to them the science of astronomy. . . ."
19. Genesis 13:2
20. Abraham 1:12-20
21. Abraham 2:4
22. Book of Abraham, p. 42, showing Abraham "sitting upon Pharaoh's throne, by the politeness of the king. . . ." See also Josephus, *Antiquities of the Jews,* Book 1, Ch. 7:1, "He [the Pharaoh] also made him [Abraham] a large present in money, and gave him leave to enter into conversation with the most learned among the Egyptians; from which conversation his virtue and his reputation became more conspicuous than they had been before."
23. Genesis 23:5-6
24. Genesis 17:11-12, 23-24
25. Abraham 2:10-11

Abraham had married three times. His first wife, Sarah, was his niece,[26] but she was unable to bear children and so she asked Abraham to marry her handmaid, Hagar. Hagar had a child when Abraham was 86[27] and he was named Ishmael. Later Sarah was able to bear Isaac when Abraham was 100.[28] Because Ishmael "mocked" Isaac, he and his mother were required to separate themselves from Abraham's household. Sarah then died at the age of 127[29] and Abraham married Keturah by whom he had six sons.[30]

Now the illustrious patriarch and prince of Shem was gone. His life span had covered 175 years, all filled with continuous achievement.

It was Isaac and Ishmael who buried Abraham.[31] Isaac was now 75 years old[32] and Ishmael was 89.[33] These two brothers joined forces to honor Abraham and place his remains beside those of Sarah in the cave of Machpelah, near Hebron.

THE EARLY YEARS OF JACOB AND ESAU

Except for the death of Abraham when Jacob and Esau were fifteen, we know of no other significant event during their early years. However, as they moved up toward young adulthood, an interesting development occurred. Young Esau became a "cunning hunter, a man of the field."[34] Young Jacob, on the other hand, seemed to love animals and instead of becoming a hunter he became a herder. He was a keeper of flocks, "a plain man, dwelling in tents."[35]

Then the Bible makes a cogent comment. It says, "Isaac loved Esau" while "Rebekah loved Jacob."[36]

---

26. Abraham 2:1-2
27. Genesis 16:16
28. Genesis 21:5
29. Genesis 23:1
30. Genesis 25:1-4
31. Genesis 25:9
32. Since Abraham was 100 when Isaac was born and 175 when he died this would make Isaac 75 when Abraham died.
33. By the same calculation, since Abraham was 86 when Ishmael was born, Ishmael would have to be 89 by the time Abraham was 175.
34. Genesis 25:27
35. Ibid.
36. Genesis 25:28

It is important to realize that by the time Jacob and Esau were 20 their father would be 80, for their father is described as being 60 when they were born.[37] Perhaps the age of Isaac may have had something to do with the way he felt toward Esau. He would have been impressed by favors bestowed upon him. The scripture specifically notes that one of the reasons the elderly Isaac loved Esau was because of the fine venison which Esau often brought his father.[38] Furthermore, we learn from a later scripture that Esau was not only a hunter but also a farmer, therefore it is understandable how both his venison and his bounties from the fruits of the field would tend to win the heart of the aging Isaac.[39]

Nevertheless, Rebekah kept her preference for Jacob. After all, the Lord had told her in a personal revelation that Jacob was to be the leader, and under the patriarchal Priesthood this meant that Jacob should be the one to receive the "birthright" of Isaac. In fact, this should not have been difficult for Father Isaac to accept, since he also was a second son who had been made heir in place of his older brother, Ishmael.[40] But in spite of this precedent, and in spite of God's declaration to Rebekah that Jacob should prevail over Esau, the elderly Isaac continued to shower his principal affections upon Esau.

JACOB DECIDES TO BARGAIN WITH ESAU FOR HIS BIRTHRIGHT

The unfolding of events we are now about to relate would indicate that Jacob began pressing for his brother's birthright at an early age. This could be attributed to avarice, but it is far more likely that Rebekah had shared with young Jacob the Lord's pronouncement that he was to prevail over Esau. Such knowledge would place Jacob in the complicated

---

37. Genesis 25:26
38. Genesis 25:28
39. Adam Clarke points out that "a man of the field" means that Esau earned part of his living by agriculture. Esau's cultivation of the fields is later referred to by Isaac when he thought he was giving Esau a blessing. He said: "See, the smell of my son is as the smell of the field which the Lord hath blessed; therefore, God give thee of the dew of heaven, and the fulness of the earth, and plenty of corn and wine." (Genesis 27:27-28) For such a blessing to be appropriate Esau would have to be a farmer, a tiller of the soil. See Clarke's Bible Commentary, Vol. 1, p. 158.
40. Genesis 21:9-12; 25:5

position of knowing that his claim to the birthright had the approval of Heaven, but it certainly did not seem to have the approval of his own father from whom the birthright blessing would have to come.

Jacob's problem was deciding how to proceed from here. How could he get Esau to give up the birthright and how could he get Father Isaac to bestow the blessing on his second son when he obviously favored the first?

As it turned out, circumstances permitted Jacob to solve the first problem rather easily, but he almost lost his birthright when he and his mother fell into a satanical trap trying to solve the second.

Getting Esau to sell his birthright was made easier by the fact that down through history prodigal heirs have often been willing to sell their future rights for some present advantage. One day the opportunity for such a transaction took place between Jacob and Esau.

Esau "came from the field" famished and faint from hunger. Instead of fixing himself some food, he demanded a meal from Jacob who had just cooked some "pottage". Jacob immediately saw a chance to exchange something he wanted for something Esau wanted. Therefore Jacob said unto Esau, "Sell me this day thy birthright."[41]

Ordinarily an heir to the Priesthood would have indignantly spurned such a proposition, particularly for a mere meal of pottage, but Esau let self-pity and his pangs of hunger combine to suppress any feelings of resistance. Said he, "Behold, I am at the point to die; and what profit shall this birthright do to me?" So he took an oath that Jacob should have his birthright and then sat down to eat.[42]

Now, if Esau had indeed been at the point of death this transaction would have been a great injustice, but we learn from the very next verse that Esau was not really starving but was simply a man of hearty appetite who thought he was going to die just because he felt a little faint after a long period of fasting. After a little pottage his recovery was

41. Genesis 25:31
42. Genesis 25:33

instantaneous. The scripture says, ". . . he did eat and drink, and rose up, and went his way."[43] Then, with a summary condemnation of Esau's impetuous conduct the scripture says, "Thus Esau despised his birthright."[44]

ANOTHER GREAT FAMINE STRIKES CANAAN

It was sometime after this event that the specter of starvation spread across Canaan.[45] It appeared to be a return of the terrible famine plague similar to the one which had engulfed the land during Abraham's day. Without seasonal rain the fields of Esau began to wither and burn and the

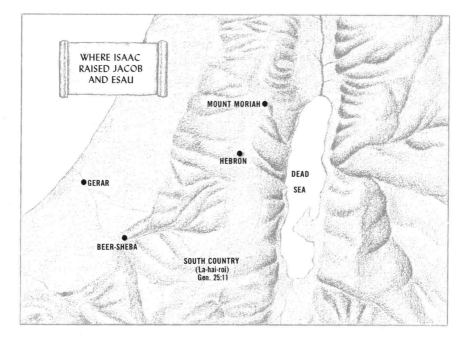

herds of Jacob began to die of starvation and thirst. Isaac therefore struck the tents of his nomadic village and headed toward Egypt, just as his father, Abraham, had done. He had barely started, however, when the Lord stopped him in the way and said:

43. Genesis 25:34
44. Ibid.
45. Genesis 26:1

"Go NOT down into Egypt; dwell in the land which I shall tell thee of: sojourn in this land, and I will be with thee, and will bless thee; for unto thee, and unto thy seed, I will give all these countries, and I will perform the oath which I sware unto Abraham thy father."[46]

The place in which Isaac had camped was the city of Gerar which was less than 30 miles southwest of Hebron. It was a place where Father Abraham had spent a little time nearly a century before.[47] This entire valley was filled with Philistines and Isaac found that the king was named "Abimelech" as was the king who had reigned in Abraham's day. It is believed that the people of Gerar may have called all of their kings "Abimelech" just as the Egyptians called all of their kings, "Pharaoh."

Because the Lord had commanded Isaac to settle in this place for the duration of the famine, Isaac attempted to carry out this order. However, he feared that he might have the same trouble with King Abimelech and the Philistines as his father, Abraham. It seems that these heathen kings and their princelings were in the habit of taking unto themselves any beautiful women in the realm who happened to catch their fancy, and the royal line of Shem was famous for its beautiful women. When Abraham had come to Gerar, the king had coveted Sarah even though she was nearly ninety years of age, and the Lord had been compelled to intervene to protect her from harm.[48] Now, nearly a century later, Isaac came into Gerar and feared that the beauty of Rebekah might cause a similar problem. The fact that a woman was already married was of no consequence to these heathen peoples since they could easily arrange to have a husband murdered. This is the explanation for the following passage of scripture:

"And the men of the place asked him of his wife; and he said, She is my sister: for he feared to say, She is my wife; lest, said he, the men of the place should kill me for Rebekah; because she was fair to look upon. And it came to pass, when he had been there a long time, that Abimelech

---

46. Genesis 26:2-3
47. Genesis 20:1
48. Genesis 20:3-17

king of the Philistines looked out at a window, and saw, and, behold, Isaac was sporting with Rebekah his wife. And Abimelech called Isaac, and said, Behold, of a surety she is thy wife: and how saidst thou, She is my sister? And Isaac said unto him, Because I said, Lest I die for her."[49]

The Hebrew custom of calling a near relative a "sister" or a "brother" as used here by Isaac was a technical device to escape being killed. This was exactly what the Lord had told Abraham to do in the case of Sarah.[50] However, as between Abraham and Sarah the term, "sister", was literally true because Abraham's father had adopted Sarah after her father, Haran, had died.[51]

This precedent may have led Isaac to justify himself in following a similar procedure even though he was not in as favorable a position to press the point as his father had been.

Nevertheless, when the king discovered the true relationship between Isaac and Rebekah, he issued a mandate saying, "He that toucheth this man or his wife shall surely be put to death."[52]

ISAAC BECOMES WEALTHY IN GERAR BUT IS FORCED TO LEAVE

Isaac now felt sufficiently secure to establish himself in the city of Gerar as a more or less permanent resident. He therefore "sowed in that land, and received in the same year a hundredfold: and the Lord blessed him."[53] Apparently in this region, at least, the famine was over.

Young Esau, the farmer and man of the field, undoubtedly had a lot to do with the success of this notable harvest, and apparently Jacob, the keeper of the flocks, also did his part, for the herds of Isaac prospered abundantly. The scripture says: "And the man [Isaac] waxed great, and

---

49. Genesis 26:7-9
50. Abraham 2:22-23
51. For a full consideration of this problem, see *The First 2,000 Years*, pp. 272-273; 292-294
52. Genesis 26:11
53. Genesis 26:12

went forward, and grew until he became very great: for he had possession of flocks, and possession of herds, and great store of servants: and the Philistines envied him."[54]

The Philistines not only envied him, but they developed an outright hostility toward Isaac and his family. The king became so concerned about Isaac that he finally said to him, "Go from us; for thou art much mightier than we."[55]

As a guest of the city, Isaac felt compelled to move. At first he just moved away from the city of Gerar and out into the valley which surrounded it. There he dug a well and started building an oasis, but as soon as the Philistines saw his success they moved their flocks in and said the water was theirs.[56] So Isaac and his sons tried again in a more distant place, but once more, as soon as they had dug and curbed a good well, the Philistines moved in on them and expropriated it. Isaac moved a third time.

It turned out that this third move took them sufficiently far so that it was no longer convenient for the Philistines of Gerar to molest them. Isaac was therefore able to keep this third well as his own. However, Isaac and his family were now so near the old homestead of Abraham at Beer-sheba that they decided to move again and see if they could find water there as Abraham had done.

It would appear that this whole area which Abraham's industry had once made so prosperous had become a desolation because all the wells which Abraham had dug "the Philistines had stopped them, and filled them with earth."[57] And without water the original community would have disappeared thereby allowing it to become a wilderness again.

As Isaac contemplated the possibility of rebuilding this city a wonderful revelation was given to him. The scripture says, "And the Lord appeared unto him the same night, and said, I am the God of Abraham thy father: fear not, for I am with thee, and will bless thee, and multiply thy seed for my servant Abraham's sake."[58]

---

54. Genesis 26:13-14
55. Genesis 26:16
56. Genesis 26:20

57. Genesis 26:15
58. Genesis 26:24

Isaac immediately put his servants to work in the arduous task of hand-digging a well sufficiently deep to reach water. While this was going on, Isaac and his sons were amazed to receive a surprise visit from King Abimelech and two of his personal advisors, including the chief captain of his army.

Isaac immediately challenged the king and said, "Wherefore come ye to me, seeing ye hate me, and have sent me away from you?"[59]

The king surprised Isaac by replying in the most conciliatory manner. Said he, "We saw certainly that the Lord was with thee: and we said, Let there be now an oath betwixt us . . . that thou wilt do us no hurt, as we have not touched thee, and as we have done unto thee nothing but good, and have sent thee away in peace: thou art now the blessed of the Lord."[60]

This was good news for Isaac and his sons. It meant that the king of Gerar was anxious for a truce. It meant there would be no more raids on their wells, no more forced moves. It also meant that the blessings of God had been showered upon Isaac and his family in such abundance that even the heathen King Abimelech could see that the Hebrew prophet was favored of God.

So Isaac prepared a feast and they had a time of rejoicing together. The next morning Isaac and King Abimelech went through the ceremonies of making a peace treaty sealed by an oath. It was exactly what Abraham had done a century earlier with another King Abimelech.[61] In fact, it was the reason Abraham had originally called this place Beer-sheba, meaning, "the well of the oath."[62]

Now Isaac had done the same thing in the same place with the King Abimelech of his day. And when the ceremony was over "Isaac sent them away, and they departed from him in peace."[63]

But barely was the king's party out of sight when great news came to Isaac. His servants had struck water! This

---

59. Genesis 26:27
60. Genesis 26:28-29
61. Genesis 21:29-31
62. Genesis 21:31 plus marginal note.
63. Genesis 26:31

meant that the old homestead of Abraham could be revived. Other wells could be dug and a thriving community built. What could be more appropriate than to name the new well in honor of the events of that day? Isaac therefore called it "Shebah" or "oath" so that once more the city became Beer-sheba — "the well of the oath" — just as Abraham had called it.[64]

ESAU MARRIES INTO A STRANGE TRIBE

As the years rolled on Isaac saw his two sons attain marriageable age. However, they were completely surrounded by members of the Hamitic tribes whom the descendants of Abraham had been forbidden to marry.[65] Therefore both Esau and Jacob remained single and passed over into a state of bachelorhood. Both of them remained bachelors until they reached forty, then Esau decided this was as long as he could endure. Consequently the scripture says:

"And Esau was forty years old when he took to wife Judith the daughter of Beeri the Hittite, and Bashemath the daughter of Elon the Hittite."[66]

Elsewhere the scripture makes it clear that these two girls were both descendants of the tribe of Ham and therefore any sons born to them could not receive the Priesthood.[67] It was for this reason that those bearing the Priesthood line had been forbidden to marry any Canaanites or other Hamitic tribes. Nevertheless, Esau had done it.

---

64. Genesis 26:33; compare Genesis 21:31
65. Abraham explains that a certain lineage of Ham "could not have the rights of the Priesthood." (Abraham 1:26-27) This would include all of those who had descended through Ham's son, Canaan, and who composed the principal inhabitants of this land which had been named after Canaan. This explains Abraham's action described in Genesis 24:3 where he has his servant take an oath that he will not allow Isaac to marry from among "the daughters of the Canaanites," since this would introduce the Canaanite blood into Abraham's covenant lineage and cut them off from the Priesthood. In Genesis 28:1, Isaac calls Jacob to him and says: "Thou shalt not take a wife of the daughters of Canaan." Esau had already married into this lineage and it was "a grief of mind unto Isaac and to Rebekah." (Genesis 26:35) Rebekah was continually worried lest the same thing might happen to Jacob. She said, "I am weary of my life because of the daughters of Heth: if Jacob take a wife of the daughters of Heth, (who were Canaanites, see Genesis 28:8) such as these which are of the daughters of the land, what good shall my life do me?" (Genesis 27:46) All her descendants would be cut off of the Priesthood and thereby lose the promises of the covenant.
66. Genesis 26:34
67. Genesis 26:34 plus 28:8 plus 9:22 plus Abraham 1:26-27

Father Isaac was 100 years of age[68] by this time and when he learned that his son, Esau, had married these two Canaanite girls the scripture says it was "a grief of mind unto Isaac and to Rebekah."[69] Esau had married outside the covenant.

A CRISIS DEVELOPS AS TO WHO SHALL BE ISAAC'S HEIR

This incident should have demonstrated to Isaac why the Lord had proclaimed from the beginning that Jacob was to be preferred over his brother, Esau, nevertheless, Isaac had grown old preferring Esau. Not only had he grown old, he also had become blind.[70] Isaac felt that death might not be too far away and so he said, "Behold now, I am old, I know not the day of my death."[71] As it turned out, he still had around 63 years to live,[72] but his state of mind was such that he felt he should delay no longer in conferring upon his favorite son the birthright blessing.

To commemorate the occasion, Isaac called Esau to him and said, ". . . take, I pray thee, thy weapons, thy quiver and thy bow, and go out to the field, and take me some venison; and make me savoury meat, such as I love, and bring it to me, that I may eat; that my soul may bless thee before I die."[73]

So Esau went joyously forth. What cared he if his birthright had been sold to Jacob? Or what did it matter if he had sworn by an oath to disclaim it forever? Was not all of that long ago when both of them were much younger? Anyway, who could blame Esau if their father were determined to give the blessing to his eldest son? Could Jacob complain? Was not this their father's decision? Esau went forth with jubilance to fulfill his father's wish.

But the scripture says that Rebekah's sharp ears had overheard this whole conversation between Isaac and Esau.

---

68. Since he was 60 when Esau and Jacob were born (Genesis 25:26) an additional 40 years would make him 100.
69. Genesis 26:35
70. Genesis 27:1
71. Genesis 27:2
72. He did not die until he was 180 (Genesis 35:28).
73. Genesis 27:3-4

She was frantically disturbed by this sudden turn of events. What was her husband thinking about to give the birthright blessing to a son who had already married outside the covenant? And what about Esau's oath? What about the revelation from the Lord concerning Jacob prevailing over Esau? With anguish in her soul, Rebekah resolved to halt this threatening tragedy.

REBEKAH MAKES A SERIOUS MISTAKE

Under the anxiety and pressure of these difficult circumstances, Rebekah allowed herself to be drawn into a satanical trap. Without counseling with Isaac or waiting for the Lord to reveal to her husband that he was following the wrong course, Rebekah decided to take matters into her own hands. No sooner was Esau out of sight than Rebekah launched on a desperate stratagem to get the birthright blessing placed on the head of Jacob.

First of all, Rebekah used her maternal rank to "command" Jacob to obey her in carrying out the scheme.[74] She told him to kill two young goats from which she would make a "savoury meat for thy father such as he loveth."[75] She instructed Jacob to present the savoury meat as though he were Esau and thereby get the blessing from his aged and blind father.

Jacob protested. He didn't like the scheme. He began to make excuses to try to get out of it. Said he, "Behold, Esau my brother is a hairy man, and I am a smooth man. My father peradventure will feel me, and I shall seem to him as a deceiver; and I shall bring a curse upon me, and not a blessing."[76]

But his mother was not to be diverted from her objective. Rebekah exclaimed, "Upon me be thy curse, my son: only obey my choice. . . ."[77]

So the savoury meat was prepared and Rebekah took the skins of the two young goats and somehow attached portions of the hair to Jacob's hands and the smooth part of

---

74. Genesis 27:8   76. Genesis 27:11-12
75. Genesis 27:9   77. Genesis 27:13

his neck. She dressed Jacob in his brother's finest clothing and then sent him with the delicious delicacy of savoury meat to greet his father.

"And he [Jacob] came unto his father, and said, My father: And he [Isaac] said: Here am I; who art thou, my son?

"And Jacob said unto his father, I am Esau thy firstborn. I have done according as thou badest me: arise, I pray thee, sit and eat of my venison, that thy soul may bless me.

"And Isaac said unto his son, How is it that thou hast found it so quickly, my son? And he said, because the Lord thy God brought it to me.

"And Isaac said unto Jacob, Come near, I pray thee, that I may feel thee, my son, whether thou be my very son Esau or not.

"And Jacob went near unto Isaac his father; and he felt him, and said, The voice is Jacob's voice, but the hands are the hands of Esau."[78]

Then, just to reassure himself for the last time, Isaac asked for one final confirmation. Said he, "Art thou my very son Esau?" And with complete finality Jacob replied, "I am."[79]

So Isaac ate heartily of the savoury meat which Jacob had presented to him. When the meal was finished the elderly Isaac prepared to give his son the coveted blessing.

"And his father Isaac said unto him, Come near now, and kiss me, my son. And he came near, and kissed him."[80]

During this embrace Isaac immediately caught the perfumed fragrance of the "goodly raiment" Jacob was wearing, clothes which belonged to Esau's rich wardrobe.[81] It apparently reminded the aged Isaac of the blossoms of the field which his blind eyes would never see again, therefore he began his blessing in these words:

"See, the smell of my son is as the smell of a field which the Lord hath blessed: Therefore God give thee of the dew

---

78. Genesis 27:18-22
79. Genesis 27:24
80. Genesis 27:26-27
81. Genesis 27:15 plus 27:27

of Heaven, and the fatness of the earth, and plenty of corn and wine:

"Let people serve thee, and nations bow down to thee: be Lord over thy brethren, and let thy mother's sons bow down to thee: cursed be every one that curseth thee, and blessed be he that blesseth thee."[82]

Here indeed was a birthright blessing, but would it take effect? If Jacob and his mother had been more experienced in Priesthood procedure they would have known that no blessing of the Priesthood can be obtained by deception or fraud. A blessing, to be effective, must be ratified both by the person giving it and by the Holy Spirit of Promise. Otherwise it is null and void.[83] In this case Isaac had intended to bless Esau, not Jacob, therefore the blessing would have given nothing to Jacob had it not been for one thing: Isaac subsequently *ratified* this blessing for Jacob after he learned what had happened!

Here is the way the Bible describes it:

"And it came to pass, as soon as Isaac had made an end of blessing Jacob, and Jacob was yet scarce gone out from the presence of Isaac his father, that Esau his brother came in from his hunting.

"And he also made savoury meat, and brought it unto his father, and said unto his father, Let my father arise, and eat of his son's venison, that thy soul may bless me.

"And Isaac his father said unto him, Who art thou? And he said, I am thy son, thy firstborn Esau.

"And Isaac trembled very exceedingly, and said, Who? where is he that hath taken venison, and brought it me, and I have eaten of all before thou camest, and have blessed him? YEA, AND HE SHALL BE BLESSED."[84]

By these last six words Father Isaac elected to ratify the blessing he had given Jacob rather than declare it void as he might have done. When Esau heard it, he was practically beside himself with grief.

---

82. Genesis 27:27-29
83. Doctrine and Covenants 132:7
84. Genesis 27:30-33

". . . he cried with a great and exceeding bitter cry, and said unto his father, Bless me, even me also, O my father.

"And he [Isaac] said, Thy brother came with subtility, and hath taken away thy blessing.

"And he [Esau] said, Is not he rightly named Jacob? for he hath supplanted me these two times: he took away my birthright; and, behold, now he hath taken away my blessing. And he said, Hast thou not reserved a blessing for me?

"And Isaac answered and said unto Esau, Behold, I have made him thy Lord, and all his brethren have I given to him for servants; and with corn and wine have I sustained him: and what shall I do now unto thee, my son?

"And Esau said unto his father, Hast thou but one blessing, my father? bless me, even me also, O my father. And Esau lifted up his voice, and wept.

"And Isaac his father answered and said unto him, Behold, thy dwelling shall be the fatness of the earth, and of the dew of heaven from above; and by the sword shalt thou live, and shalt serve thy brother; and it shall come to pass when thou shalt have the dominion, that thou shalt break his yoke from off thy neck."[85]

Then, the scripture says, "Esau hated Jacob because of the blessing wherewith his father blessed him. . . ."[86]

Of course, legally speaking, Esau's lamentation did not have the merit he pretended. In the first place, Esau could not say Jacob had "taken" his birthright from him, for Esau had deliberately sold it to him for a mess of pottage, and had even taken a sacred oath that Jacob should have it. Secondly, the giving of the blessing was merely the formal ritual of conferring the birthright, therefore Esau could not complain on that account either.

If anyone had a right to complain it was Isaac who had been deceived, but since Isaac was flying in the face of the Lord's expressed will concerning the selection of an heir, perhaps he considered the circumstances a timely opportunity

---

85. Genesis 27:34-40
86. Genesis 27:41

to rectify his own blunder. At least we know he made no attempt to transfer the blessing from Jacob to Esau which he could have done. He simply ratified the blessing which he had conferred upon Jacob, and this allowed the Holy Spirit of Promise to seal it up in accordance with the Lord's original declaration before Jacob was born.

As for Jacob, he did not escape God's judgment. The passing years saw him repaid in kind for this deception of his father. Jacob's own children did in time deceive him to a point where it left him prostrate with grief.

Thus God has dealt with the weaknesses of his servants in every age. It is amazing how consistently the biographies of great Bible leaders commence in weakness and then grow to strength. This is true in both the Old and New Testaments. For example, Peter commenced his mission impetuous and vacillating but became the President of the early Christian Church. Paul commenced his life's labors prejudiced and over zealous for the wrong side, but he ended up the greatest missionary the Christian Church ever produced. Jeremiah and Enoch both trembled with timidity because of their youth-fulness and inability to speak, yet both became trumpets of thunder in the cause of God's righteousness.

God knew each of these servants to be diamonds in the rough, and while their polishing often involved the shock and heartbreak of many bitter experiences, nevertheless they each finally came forth as polished gems of brilliant integrity.

Jacob was one of these who went through the polishing mill. The offense in his earlier life of trying to deceive his father finally faded into the shadows as God taught him a complete purity of purpose and helped him rise to the pinnacle of his best potential self. As it was said of another, so it might be said of Jacob, ". . . yet learned he obedience by the things which he suffered."[87]

---

87 .Hebrews 5:8

Scripture Reading and Questions on Chapter Two

Scripture Reading Assignment: Genesis, chapters 25 to 27 inclusive.

1—How old was Isaac when Rebekah had her twins?

2—What did the Lord tell Rebekah about her twins before they were born? What is the meaning of the name, *Esau?* What is the meaning of *Jacob?*

3—What significant event happened when the twins were 15 years old?

4—Why did Isaac favor Esau? Who favored Jacob?

5—How did Isaac happen to take his family to Gerar?

6—Why did Isaac and his sons have to rebuild Beer-sheba?

7—Why did Esau's marriage at the age of forty offend his parents?

8—Why was Rebekah so distressed when she learned that Isaac was about to give the birthright blessing to Esau?

9—What was Jacob's reaction when Rebekah told him to obtain the the birthright blessing by deception?

10—What did she say to Jacob to persuade him to go ahead?

11—What made Isaac suspicious that Jacob was deceiving him?

12—What was unusual about the clothing Jacob wore when he went in to get his blessing?

13—Name three important elements in the blessing which Isaac gave Jacob.

14—What did Isaac say which clearly identified this blessing as the "birthright" blessing?

15—What two things are essential before any blessing or ordinance of the Priesthood becomes binding?

16—Could Isaac have repudiated the blessing which he gave Jacob by mistake? What made it binding?

17—Did Esau have a legitimate reason to feel cheated?

18—What blessing did Esau finally receive? Was he satisfied?

19—Did Jacob escape God's judgment for having deceived his father?

20—Name two other famous Biblical personalities who started their careers in weakness but who eventually became pillars of spiritual strength,

Jacob Flees From Canaan to Escape Being Murdered

Esau was so enraged when he found that he had really lost his birthright to his younger twin, that he resolved to kill him. But knowing that his father was old and blind, he decided to wait until the aged Isaac had passed on. Said Esau, "The days of mourning for my father are at hand; then will I slay my brother Jacob."[1]

But the scripture says, "these words of Esau . . . were told to Rebekah."[2] Immediately the agile mind of this frightened mother went to work. She called in Jacob and said, ". . . flee thou to Laban my brother to Haran; and tarry with him a few days, until thy brother's fury turn away."[3] She promised to send for him as soon as she considered it safe. Neither of them realized that Jacob would not be gone for "a few days" but for nearly half a century and certainly Rebekah would never have guessed that this would be the last time she would ever see her son. All she was concerned with at this moment was getting Jacob away from his older twin who was bent on murdering him.

Rebekah also had the problem of getting the aged Isaac to consent to have one of his sons leave at this critical time when the old man thought the end of his days was near. However, there was one thing which she felt fairly certain would persuade him. In deepest anguish she declared to Isaac: "I am weary of my life because of the daughters of Heth: if Jacob take a wife of the daughters of Heth, such as these which are of the daughters of the land, what good shall my life do me?"[4]

---

1. Genesis 27:41
2. Genesis 27:42
3. Genesis 27:43-44
4. Genesis 27:46

Here was a barb that went like a shaft straight to the center of Isaac's soul. If Jacob should marry a Canaanite girl his posterity would be deprived of both the Priesthood and Abraham's covenant. Esau had already cut himself off by marrying into a Canaanite tribe so Jacob was the only hope of perpetuating the Patriarchal Priesthood.

Father Isaac immediately called Jacob to him and straightway commanded him, "Thou shalt not take a wife of the daughters of Canaan. Arise, go to Padan-aram, to the house of Bethuel thy mother's father; and take thee a wife from thence of the daughters of Laban thy mother's brother."[5]

Before Jacob left, however, his father gave him a blessing. Without restraint or rancor for the deception which had previously been perpetrated upon him, the aged Isaac bestowed this benediction upon Jacob, "And God Almighty bless thee, and make thee fruitful, and multiply thee, that thou mayest be a multitude of people: and give thee the blessing of Abraham, to thee, and to thy seed with thee: that thou mayest inherit the land wherein thou art a stranger, which God gave unto Abraham."[6]

So Jacob departed. His destination was a country up toward the headwaters of the Euphrates River where Laban, his uncle, resided. Jacob did not travel with the comfort of a caravan or with servants or even a guide. With staff in hand he strode out on the long trek which would take him to upper Mesopotamia.

Esau Makes an Unexpected Move

As soon as Esau learned what had happened to his brother it seemed to give him a whole new perspective of life. He was particularly impressed with the fact that "Isaac had blessed Jacob . . . and that as he blessed him, he gave him a charge, saying, Thou shalt not take a wife of the daughters of Canaan."[7] For the first time Esau appears to have realized how much a marriage "within the covenant"

---

5. Genesis 28:1-2
6. Genesis 28:3-4
7. Genesis 28:6

meant to his father and mother. Esau could now see why his marriage into the Canaanite tribe had been "a grief of mind unto Isaac and to Rebekah."[8] So the scripture says, "And Esau seeing that the daughters of Canaan pleased not Isaac his father; then went Esau unto Ishmael. . . ."[9]

Notice that Esau did not go where Jacob had been sent. Instead of going to the land of his mother's brother, Esau went to the land of his father's brother, to Ishmael, who lived in the region south of the Dead Sea. There he arranged to marry Mahalath, his first cousin,[10] and there he apparently remained. From this union came the mighty Edomites,[11] the rich and powerful desert tribes who later challenged Moses and the children of Israel as they attempted to pass up toward Jordan and enter the promised land. It is important to remember the origin of the Edomites. They have an important place in Bible history.

JACOB RECEIVES HIS FIRST REVELATION

Shortly after Jacob left home he reached a point which was about 48 miles from Beer-sheba. There he camped not far from the ancient settlement or city called Luz.[12] During the night he received a magnificent revelation which, so far as we know, is the first time the heavens had been opened to him. Jacob saw a gigantic ladder with the messengers of God going and coming between Heaven and earth. He saw the personage of the Lord standing at the portals of glory who spoke to him and said:

"I am the Lord God of Abraham thy father, and the God of Isaac: the land whereon thou liest, to thee will I give it, and to thy seed; and thy seed shall be as the dust of the earth, and thou shalt spread abroad to the west, and to the east, and to the north, and to the south: and in thee and in thy seed shall all the families of the earth be blessed."[13]

Here was the identical covenant which God had made with Abraham and now it was being conferred in its entirety upon Jacob, Abraham's grandson. But that was not all. The

8. Genesis 26:34-35
9. Genesis 28:8-9
10. Ibid.

11. Peloubet's *Bible Dictionary* under "Edom".
12. Genesis 28:19
13. Genesis 28:13-14

Lord comforted Jacob and assured him of protection on his journey:

"And, behold, I am with thee, and will keep thee in all places whither thou goest, and will bring thee again into this land; for I will not leave thee, until I have done that which I have spoken to thee of."[14]

Then Jacob awoke. He was deeply moved by this vivid experience. Therefore he took the stone on which he had been leaning for a pillow and hefted it into an erect position so that it made sort of a pillar. Then he poured oil upon it and made a promise to the Lord that as God blessed him with the bounties of the earth he would faithfully return one tenth to the Lord.[15] Jacob's covenant on this occasion was his affirmation of the ancient law of tithing which Abraham had also honored.[16] In fact, we have reason to believe that "tithing" had been the law of the Lord ever since the City of Enoch had been taken away with its higher law of Consecration or United Order.[17] Now that tithing was the law, Jacob resolved to fulfill it faithfully.

Jacob named that place Beth-el, meaning "God's house."[18] It was to become a most important place in the history of Israel.

The revelation which Jacob had received must have been a great comfort to him. It meant that in spite of his mistakes and weaknesses of the past, he was now acceptable to God and would receive his continuous blessings if he could remain valiant. At this early state, Jacob could never have guessed the treasures which Heaven held in store for him if he could just remain faithful.

JACOB ARRIVES IN HARAN

From his earliest childhood, Jacob's mother must have told him about the riches and wonders of her home in Mesopotamia. So far as we know she had never returned since

---

14. Genesis 28:15
15. Genesis 28:22
16. Genesis 14:18-20
17. For a discussion of the law of consecration or United Order see *The First 2,000 Years*, pp. 173-177.
18. Genesis 28:19 plus marginal note.

leaving it as a young woman, but now her son was returning to the place where Rebekah was born — Haran.

Haran, in the land of Padan-aram, had been originally settled by Abraham on his flight from Ur.[19] It had been named after Abraham's brother who had starved to death during the terrible famine in Ur.[20] But Abraham had been blessed in Haran and had stayed there long enough to rebuild his depleted flocks before proceeding to Canaan.[21] Abraham's other brother, Nehor (spelled Nahor in Genesis) had decided to make Haran his permanent residence.[22] Abraham's wicked and idolatrous father, Terah, had also elected to remain in this place.[23]

Down through the years Abraham and his family had always maintained some contact with his relatives in Haran. It was to this place that he had sent his servant to get a wife for his son, Isaac, and now Isaac had sent his own son to this place to obtain a wife.

It will be recalled that Jacob had been told by Isaac to look for Rebekah's brother, Laban, a leading citizen of Haran. As Jacob came near the settlement of Haran the road passed by a well where flocks of sheep were waiting to be watered. Jacob asked the local herdsmen if they by any chance might know Laban. They did indeed. In fact, they pointed out that one of his daughters, named Rachel, was at that moment approaching with a flock of Laban's sheep to water them.

Jacob had never lived or been closely associated with any kinsmen other than his own immediate family, so when he found that Rachel was his very own flesh and blood he "kissed Rachel, and lifted up his voice, and wept."[24] Rachel was just as excited as Jacob. As soon as she found out who he was "she ran and told her father."[25]

When Laban received the news he was excited too. Laban "ran to meet him, and embraced him, and kissed him, and brought him to his house."[26] It was a glorious reunion.

---

19. Abraham 2:4
20. Abraham 2:1, 4
21. Abraham 2:4-5
22. Genesis 24:15

23. Abraham 2:5
24. Genesis 29:11
25. Genesis 29:12
26. Genesis 29:13

Jacob Enters Into a Marriage Contract for Rachel

Laban's family apparently did everything possible to welcome Jacob into their home. Jacob reciprocated by helping Laban run the affairs of his estate and manage his flocks. This congenial relationship continued for a month, whereupon Laban decided he may be imposing on his nephew. He therefore said to Jacob, "Because thou art my brother [meaning a relative], shouldest thou therefore serve me for naught? Tell me, what shall thy wages be?"[27]

Of course, Jacob had not come to Haran to get a job. He was the heir apparent to a fortune in Beer-sheba. Nevertheless, here was an opportunity to help Laban and at the same time gain his permission to secure that which he had come to Haran to obtain — a wife. His father Isaac had even given him specific instructions that he was to seek a wife from among "the daughters of Laban."[28] Already Jacob knew which daughter he would like to have as his wife because he had fallen in love with Rachel who is described as "beautiful and well favoured."[29]

Jacob therefore said to Laban, "I will serve thee seven years for Rachel thy younger daughter."[30] Laban replied that he did not know of anyone he would rather have for a son-in-law. He accordingly accepted Jacob's offer and said, "Abide with me."[31]

Altogether, this was an unusual arrangement. It was, of course, customary in arranging marriages to have the side seeking the favor offer a gift or dowry. But this gift of seven years of free labor was unique. It was not as though Jacob were poor and unable to afford a dowry. His father Isaac in Beer-sheba could have provided a handsome dowry and then Jacob could have taken his bride and returned home. But here was precisely the problem. Jacob could not return home. His brother would kill him.

What, therefore, could have been more ideal than to strike up an agreement which would permit him to provide a dowry gift to Laban and at the same time remain away from

27. Genesis 29:15
28. Genesis 28:2
29. Genesis 29:17
30. Genesis 29:18
31. Genesis 29:19

home until it was safe to return? Nevertheless, seven long years seems an unreasonable length of time for Jacob to postpone his marriage. Some authorities have suggested that perhaps Rachel was still quite young and that Jacob had specified seven years because by that time she would be fully mature. We do know that it was not unusual for young girls to be betrothed long before the time of their actual marriage. Perhaps this was the case with Rachel. In any event, Jacob commenced his seven years of work for Laban which was literally a "labor of love."

LABAN BETRAYS JACOB

It was amazing to Jacob how fast the time began to fly. Actually there are three different kinds of time. There is *mechanical* time which is measured by the ticking of a watch or by a tiny stream of sand pouring through the neck of an hour glass. There is *solar* time which reflects the rotation of the earth in relation to the sun. Last of all there is *psychological* time. Psychological time is merely the awareness that time is passing. It depends neither on seconds, sand nor sun, but operates according to the dynamic law of personal interest. When circumstances are exciting, psychological time flies quickly. There is scarcely any awareness of time at all. However, when a person is bored, the awareness of time is like an anchor around the neck.

The Bible is very specific in describing Jacob's feelings during the seven years he was working out a dowry for the beautiful Rachel:

"And Jacob served seven years for Rachel; and they seemed unto him but a few days, for the love he had to her."[32]

And when the seven years were finished Jacob anxiously awaited the marriage ceremony. For him this was not just a routine romantic excursion. It was a beautiful and sacred conclusion to a lifetime of patient preparation. The casual reader of the scripture may miss the rather dramatic fact that by the most conservative calculation, Jacob was now at least 64 years of age![33]

---

32. Genesis 29:20
33. See the discussion of this problem at the close of this chapter.

Of course, human longevity being what it was in those days when most men lived far longer than they do today, the age of 64 would be comparable to perhaps 35 or 40 in modern man, but the fact remains that for 64 long years Jacob had patiently waited for the right person and the right circumstances to marry. It was a great personal triumph of human integrity as he approached the conclusion of this long vigil.

Jacob's future father-in-law also seemed excited about the coming wedding and was rushing about making the necessary preparations. The scripture says, "Laban gathered together all the men of the place, and made a feast."[34] This was no casual affair. It was a big event for the most notable family in Haran.

The scripture says "in the evening" when the wedding feast was over, Laban brought the veiled and beautifully gowned bride to Jacob. Laban also brought along a handmaid for the bride, a young servant girl from Laban's household named Zilpah. We shall become better acquainted with Zilpah as this history unfolds. Thus Jacob entered the sacred state of matrimony.

But when the wedding night was past, the bridegroom had the shock of his life. He looked at his bride and could scarcely believe his eyes. She was not the beautiful Rachel at all. It was the "tender-eyed" Leah, Rachel's older sister! After seven long years of working and waiting, Jacob had been tricked.

It was certainly no tender-eyed Jacob who went storming in to Laban. "What is this thou hast done unto me?" he cried. "Did I not serve with thee for Rachel? Wherefore then hast thou beguiled me?"[35]

But the shrewd old sheik of Haran was ready with an answer. Said he, "It must not be so done in our country, to give the younger before the firstborn."[36]

Then he made a proposition to the wrath-filled bridegroom. Laban said that if Jacob would go ahead and fulfill

34. Genesis 29:22   36. Genesis 29:26
35. Genesis 29:25

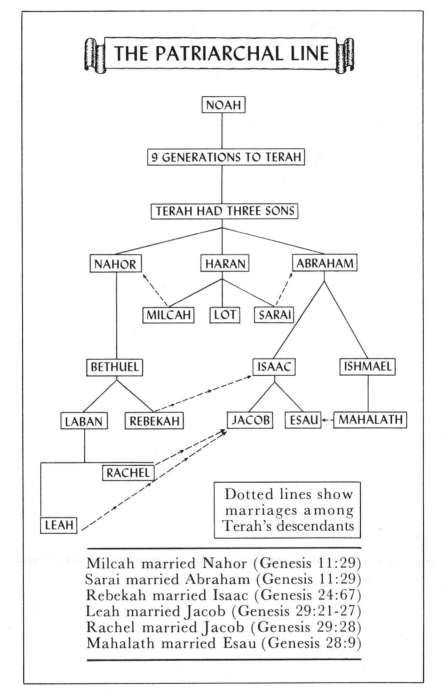

THE PATRIARCHAL LINE

NOAH

9 GENERATIONS TO TERAH

TERAH HAD THREE SONS

NAHOR   HARAN   ABRAHAM

MILCAH   LOT   SARAI

BETHUEL   ISAAC   ISHMAEL

LABAN   REBEKAH   JACOB   ESAU ← MAHALATH

RACHEL

Dotted lines show
marriages among
Terah's descendants

LEAH

Milcah married Nahor (Genesis 11:29)
Sarai married Abraham (Genesis 11:29)
Rebekah married Isaac (Genesis 24:67)
Leah married Jacob (Genesis 29:21-27)
Rachel married Jacob (Genesis 29:28)
Mahalath married Esau (Genesis 28:9)

the customary honeymoon or "marriage week" with Leah, he would then give Jacob the bride he had been expecting. Of course, the wily Laban added, if Jacob now took Rachel as a wife it would cost Jacob "yet seven other years."[37] But Laban said he was willing to make a concession. He would trust Jacob. He would let him have Rachel at the end of Leah's marriage week and then depend upon Jacob to fulfill his obligation of working out the additional seven years of dowry. Jacob consented.

Jacob Commences a Period of Travail

When this incident was finally closed, Jacob knew a lot more about the cunning character of Laban than he had realized before. This was not by any means to be the last act of treachery which Jacob would suffer at the hands of his father-in-law. Once the old man had Jacob in his power he began to exploit and abuse him. Jacob was a man of good will who would go the "second mile," or even the third mile, but Laban began to demand ten.

As Jacob set about to give Laban another seven years of labor, he was apparently paid some kind of wages for his subsistence. After all, he now had a household to maintain. But his wages from Laban were most uncertain. Laban changed the amount ten different times.[38] Furthermore, if any of the animals in Jacob's care were killed by wild animals or stolen by thieves, Jacob was required to make it up to his father-in-law from his wages.[39] The scripture leaves little doubt as to the craft and greed of Laban.

The Challenge of Jacob's Marital Life

While Jacob was working out the dowry for Rachel, children began to be born to him. But only by Leah. Rachel was barren.

In the beginning the scripture says "Leah was hated,"[40] because she had been foisted upon Jacob by fraud, but this strong antagonism began to disappear as Jacob's resentment

---

37. Genesis 29:27
38. Genesis 31:41

39. Genesis 31:38-40
40. Genesis 29:31

subsided. It helped when Leah was able to present Jacob with his first-born son. Leah named him Reuben which means, "See, a son!"[41]

She then conceived again and brought forth a son whom she named Simeon. This name means "hearing" and was adopted by Leah because she felt the Lord had heard her prayers.[42]

Soon Leah noticed that she definitely was progressing in gaining the confidence and affection of Jacob, so when her third son was born she named him Levi which means "joined".[43] Finally, when her fourth son was born she felt she had been completely victorious in solving this problem with her husband and so she called his name Judah, which means "praise".[44]

The scripture says that Jacob loved Rachel "more than Leah,"[45] but by this time Rachel was in despair. Her older sister had borne Jacob four fine sons while she remained barren. The record says Rachel "envied her sister" and complained to Jacob, "Give me children, or else I die."[46] This shows how strongly the women of Shem looked upon the blessing of motherhood. Unless they could bare children they felt they were a total failure and life held no meaning for them.

Jacob was angry with Rachel because of her sudden demand and accusation against him. Said he, "Am I in God's stead, who hath withheld from thee the fruit of the womb?"[47]

Jacob's First Wives Ask Him to Take Two More Wives

Rachel finally decided to take a step which was permissible in those days. Rachel urged Jacob to take her handmaid as his wife which would allow Rachel to have children vicariously. In fact, this was one of the purposes of giving a maid to a bride at the time of her marriage. If a wife found she was unable to bare children she was able to give her maid to her husband as a wife and thereby provide the children

41. Genesis 29:32 plus marginal note
42. Genesis 29:33 plus marginal note
43. Genesis 29:34 plus marginal note
44. Genesis 29:35 plus marginal note

45. Genesis 29:30
46. Genesis 30:1
47. Genesis 30:2

which the original marriage was expected to produce. So Rachel proposed to Jacob that he accept Bilhah, her maid, as his wife.[48] It was exactly the same action Jacob's grandmother, Sarah, had taken when she asked Abraham to take her maid, Hagar, as his wife so that Abraham might have children.

When Bilhah became the wife of Jacob, she conceived and gave birth to a son who was given the name of Dan. The meaning of the name is "judging" which refers to the fact that Rachel felt that God had judged her worthy of having a son vicariously through Bilhah.[49] Then Bilhah conceived again and this son was named Naphtali which means "wrestling". This refers to the struggle which Rachel felt she was having with her sister in order to merit the confidence of Jacob.[50]

Now all of this was too much for Leah. It was true that she had already given Jacob four sons, but she was apparently unable to bare any more.[51] She knew if this continued Rachel would soon catch up with her through Bilhah's babies. Leah decided to accept the challenge. She went to Jacob and asked him to take to wife her own maid, Zilpah. Jacob consented and Leah was delighted when Zilpah had a son. She was sure this was only the beginning. She cried out, "A troop cometh!" so the baby was named Gad or "troop" because he was considered the first of a multitude.[52]

Then much to Leah's delight Zilpah had another son. Leah was so overjoyed that she named this one Asher, which means "my happiness."[53]

And so the contest went on. Finally, Leah determined to have more children herself. Apparently Jacob had become discouraged with Leah and was therefore making his residence exclusively with Rachel. Leah therefore decided to make a bargain with her more favored sister. She waited until she had something very special which Rachel would desire. It turned out to be a harvest of mandrakes (something modern scholars are no longer able to identify). Rachel wanted some.

48. Genesis 30:3-4
49. Genesis 30:6 plus marginal note
50. Genesis 30:8 plus marginal note

51. Genesis 30:9
52. Genesis 30:11 plus marginal note
53. Genesis 30:13 plus marginal note

Leah agreed on condition that Rachel would consent to have Jacob stay with her for a season. Rachel consented and Leah therefore went forth to meet Jacob as he came from the field. After she had explained what had happened Jacob consented to go with her.[54]

The Twelve Sons of Jacob in the Order of Their Birth

Name	Mother	Meaning of Name
Reuben	Leah	See, a Son!
Simeon	Leah	Hearing
Levi	Leah	Joined
Judah	Leah	Praise
Dan	Bilhah	Judging
Naphtali	Bilhah	Wrestling
Gad	Zilpah	Troop
Asher	Zilpah	My Happiness
Issachar	Leah	A Reward
Zebulun	Leah	Dwelling
Joseph	Rachel	Adding
Benjamin	Rachel	My right hand

Now Leah's greatest hopes were realized as she once more delivered a son. This one she called Issachar which means "there is a reward."[55] Shortly afterwards she conceived and had another son which was her sixth. This son was named Zebulun which means "dwelling". This apparently referred to her feeling that Jacob would no longer lose confidence in her but would be willing to make his dwelling with her from this time on.[56]

Later, Leah had one more child, a little girl whom she named Dinah.[57] Among all of Jacob's children, this was the only daughter born to him.

---

54. Genesis 30:16
55. Genesis 30:18 plus Peloubet's *Bible Dictionary* under "Issachar".
56. Genesis 30:20 plus marginal note
57. Genesis 30:21

But Leah was not the only one to have cause for rejoicing. Suddenly Rachel was able to announce that she, too, had finally conceived. Jacob rejoiced also, and when the little boy was born Rachel named him Joseph. This means "adding" and clearly reflected her hope that someday God would bless her with additional children.[58] However, she was only able to have one more son and that was many years later. As we shall see, he was the last of Jacob's 13 children and his name was Benjamin. For the time being Rachel had to be satisfied with Joseph.

AN INTERESTING INTERVIEW BETWEEN JACOB AND LABAN

The scripture says that shortly after Joseph was born, Jacob decided to take his family and return to Beer-sheba. Just what the motivation was we are not told. The record simply says, "Jacob said unto Laban, Send me away, that I may go unto mine own place and to my country. Give me my wives and my children, for whom I have served thee, and let me go, for thou knowest my service which I have done thee."[59]

This came as a great shock to Laban. What would he do without Jacob who had been so successful in building up Laban's possessions? Laban immediately became very humble and ingratiating. He begged Jacob to stay. Said he, "I have learned by experience that the Lord hath blessed me for thy sake."[60] He asked Jacob to name his price and he would get it.[61]

Jacob was fully aware of the contribution he had made through the years to Laban's wealth and he was not unmindful of Laban's selfish greed which had made him an unfair master. So Jacob decided to set the record straight and then make Laban a proposition.

"Thou knowest," Jacob began, "how I have served thee, and how thy cattle was with me. For it was little which thou hadst before I came, and it is now increased unto a multitude; and the Lord hath blessed thee since my coming: and now when shall I provide for mine own house also?"[62]

---

58. Genesis 30:24 plus marginal note
59. Genesis 30:25-26
60. Genesis 30:27
61. Genesis 30:28
62. Genesis 30:29-30

Laban was in complete agreement. All of these facts could be fully admitted. Now if Jacob would just name his price and agree to stay, all would be well. "What shall I give thee?" asked Laban.

Jacob repied, "Thou shalt not give me anything; if thou wilt do this thing for me, I will again feed and keep thy flock. I will pass through all thy flock today, removing from thence all the speckled and spotted cattle, and all the brown cattle among the sheep, and the spotted and speckled among the goats: and of such shall be my hire."[63]

Laban was delighted. This was a great bargain. The speckled and spotted goats and the brown sheep were so few in number! Laban seized upon the offer immediately and made it binding.

Jacob and His Family Become Wealthy in Haran

So Jacob separated the few speckled goats and brown sheep and gave them to his sons to herd while he continued tending the flocks of Laban. He told his sons to keep the flocks separated by a three days journey so there would be no possibility of their becoming mixed again.[64] Then Jacob tried an experiment.

There was an ancient belief that has continued down to relatively modern times that what a female parent sees during pregnancy marks her offspring. Apparently Jacob gave some credence to this belief so he went to work cutting rods of green poplar, hazel and chestnut, and then stripped away the bark here and there so as to make them spotted. If the sheep and goats which were carrying young could be influenced to transfer these peculiar markings to their lambs and kids then they would bear the markings which would make them belong to Jacob.

To make certain the experiment would be a success, Jacob set the limbs and rods in the watering troughs so the female animals could not help but look at them.[65] Jacob was even particular to see that the most virile of the flock received this treatment.[66]

---

63. Genesis 30:31-32   65. Genesis 30:37-38
64. Genesis 30:35-36   66. Genesis 30:41-42

And sure enough, when the lambing season came, there were a great many brown sheep and ring-streaked and spotted goats. It seemed to be proof beyond question that this technique worked.

But Jacob received a revelation from the Lord explaining what had really happened. He was shown the mating process and he saw that the sires were all "ring-streaked, speckled and grisled."[67] Of course, Jacob knew that he had removed all of the rams of this description from Laban's flocks so the revelation had a deeper meaning. What the Lord was trying to tell him was the fact that even though the rams in Laban's flocks were not ring-streaked, speckled or grisled, nevertheless they were passing these characteristics on to their offspring. Ordinarily these characteristics would be recessive, but it was an easy thing for the Lord to make them dominant so that the majority of the flocks would bear marked offspring even though neither of the parents bore these marks. Modern scientific genetics has given us an understanding of the way inherited characteristics are passed along from parents to offspring. The Lord wanted Jacob to know that it was divine intervention working through the natural breeding processes and not Jacob's speckled tree limbs that had made Jacob suddenly rich.

The Lord explained why he had done this for Jacob. Said He, "I have seen all that Laban doeth unto thee."[68] This miraculous harvest of brown sheep and speckled goats was to balance the scales of equity between Jacob and his avaricious father-in-law.

For six years the wealth of Jacob and his family multiplied.[69] The scriptures declare that his possessions "increased exceedingly" so that he had "much cattle, and maid-servants, and men servants."[70] Jacob had come to Haran with virtually nothing and now he possessed both posterity and prosperity. He was ready to return home.

JACOB DEPARTS FROM HARAN IN HASTE

As it turned out, Jacob found it propitious to leave Haran in a hurry. He discovered that a belligerent spirit of jealousy

---

67. Genesis 31:10
68. Genesis 31:12
69. Genesis 31:41
70. Genesis 30:43

and anger was fomenting in Laban's sons. They complained bitterly, saying, "Jacob hath taken away all that was our father's; and of that which was our father's hath he gotten all this glory."[71] Jacob noticed that the bitterness of the sons was beginning to show in Laban, their father. The Lord said unto Jacob, "Return unto the land of thy fathers, and to thy kindred; and I will be with thee."[72]

Jacob was apparently in the fields when this last message came to him. He immediately called Rachel and Leah to meet him in the field where they could counsel together. Said he: "I see your father's countenance, that it is not toward me as before . . . and ye know that with all my power I have served your father. And your father hath deceived me, and changed my wages ten times; but God suffered him not to hurt me. . . . God hath taken away the cattle of your father, and given them to me."[73] Then he told Rachel and Leah of the vision in which the Lord had explained to him how so many of the sheep and goats happened to be marked so that Jacob could claim them. It had been a judgment against Laban.

Both Rachel and Leah expressed earnest sympathy for Jacob. They pointed out that their father, Laban, had even treated them as strangers rather than as his daughters and had deprived them of their rightful inheritance.[74] They told Jacob they felt that God had dealt justly with their greedy father in giving these riches to Jacob. They said, "Whatsoever God hath said unto thee, do."[75] Jacob did.

He gathered all of his family, his flocks, and his servants together and hurried away while Laban was off a considerable distance shearing his sheep.[76] Rachel felt so indignant toward her father that prior to leaving Haran she went to Laban's house and secretly took something which we later learn was of tremendous value to Laban. Rachel took her father's made-man gods or "images".[77]

From this we learn that the idolatry which Laban's great grandfather, Terah, had brought from Ur, had tainted the community of Haran including the household of Laban.[78]

71. Genesis 31:1
72. Genesis 31:3
73. Genesis 31:5-9
74. Genesis 31:14-16

75. Genesis 31:16
76. Genesis 31:17-20
77. Genesis 31:19
78. Abraham 2:15

LABAN PURSUES JACOB

Laban did not hear of Jacob's departure for three days, but as soon as word came to him he immediately set off in hot pursuit.[79] It took him seven days to catch up with Jacob. By this time Jacob had crossed the Euphrates river and was headed toward Canaan as fast as his flocks could be driven.[80]

It is of interest to note that just before Laban caught up with Jacob the Lord spoke to Laban in a dream and said, "Take heed that thou speak not to Jacob either good or bad."[81] This last phrase is better understood in the original Hebrew which says, "from good to evil."[82] In other words, do not begin with "Peace be unto thee," and then proceed to do violence to him.

When Laban caught up with Jacob, he could not resist rebuking him at least to some extent. Said he, "What hast thou done, that thou hast stolen away unawares to me, and carried away my daughters, as captives taken with a sword?"[83] With cunning insinuation he added, "I might have sent thee away with mirth, and with songs, with tabret, and with harp."[84] He even threatened Jacob by saying, "It is in the power of my hand to do you hurt. . . ." but then he explained that God had warned him not to do evil to Jacob.[85] Finally he told Jacob the reason for the deepest offense of all. In a spirit of ominous accusation he said, "Wherefore hast thou stolen my gods?"[86]

Jacob was amazed by this accusation, but he decided first of all to explain why he had left Haran secretly and then deal with this charge of theft. Said Jacob, "I was afraid; for I said, Peradventure thou wouldest take by force thy daughters from me."[87] Now as for the accusation that he had stolen Laban's gods, Jacob challenged Laban directly, saying, "With whomsoever thou findest thy gods, let him

---

79. Genesis 31:22-23
80. Genesis 31:21-23
81. Genesis 31:24
82. See Clarke's *Bible Commentary* Vol. 1, p. 191.
83. Genesis 31:26
84. Genesis 31:27
85. Genesis 31:29
86. Genesis 31:30
87. Genesis 31:31

not live!" Then the scripture adds, "Jacob knew not that Rachel had stolen them."[88]

Laban thought Jacob was bluffing and so he took up Jacob's challenge and began an immediate search. First, he started with Jacob's tent, then Leah's, and finally he ransacked the tents of the maid-servants. The gods were nowhere to be found. Last of all he strode into the tent of Rachel. Here is what the record says happened:

"Now Rachel had taken the images and put them in the camel's furniture, and sat upon them. And Laban searched all the tent, but found them not. And she said to her father, Let it not displease my Lord that I cannot rise up before thee: for the custom of women is upon me. And he searched, but found not the images."[89]

When the search was over, Jacob was triumphant. At the same time he was indignant with rage. He rebuked Laban: "What," he demanded, "is my trespass? What is my sin, that thou hast so hotly pursued after me? . . . This twenty years have I been with thee, thy ewes and thy she-goats have not cast their young, and the rams of thy flock have I not eaten. That which was torn of beasts I brought not unto thee; I bare the loss of it; of my hand didst thou require it, whether stolen by day, or stolen by night. Thus I was; in the day the drought consumed me, and the frost by night; and my sleep departed from mine eyes. Thus have I been twenty years in thy house; I served thee fourteen years for thy two daughters, and six years for thy cattle: and thou hast changed my wages ten times. Except the God of my father, the God of Abraham, and the fear of Isaac, had been with me, surely thou hadst sent me away now empty. God hath seen mine affliction and the labour of my hands, and rebuked thee yesternight."[90]

In reply, Laban spluttered something about "These daughters are my daughters, and these children are my children, and these cattle are my cattle, and all that thou seest is mine. . . ."[91] but then his blustering bravado collapsed. Laban capitulated completely and offered to enter into a peace pact with Jacob. Jacob agreed.

88. Genesis 31:32
89. Genesis 31:34-35
90. Genesis 31:36-42
91. Genesis 31:43

They set up a pillar and a heap of stones and Laban said: "This heap be witness, and this pillar be witness, that I will not pass over this heap to thee, and that thou shalt not pass over this heap and this pillar unto me, for harm."[92] Jacob made the same covenant and then offered a sacrifice after which he invited all of the company to eat and stay together for the night.

Thus were the two families reconciled. "And early in the morning Laban rose up, and kissed his sons and his daughters, and blessed them; and Laban departed, and returned unto his place."[93]

Jacob also was now free to proceed in peace toward his own homeland.

How Long Was Jacob in Haran?

In closing this epic in the life of Jacob we have just one final problem to dispose of. How long was Jacob in Haran?

At first the problem appears to have a simple answer, for Jacob, himself, told Laban, "Thus have I been twenty years *in thy house;* I served thee fourteen years for thy two daughters, and six years for thy cattle. . . ."[94]

It soon becomes apparent, however, that "in thy house" does not mean the same as "in Haran," for it would have been literally impossible for Jacob to achieve what he did "in Haran" during a mere 20 years. For example, he worked seven years for Laban before he even married. Then he had 12 children, all of whom appear to have been born in separate years. The youngest child born in Haran was Joseph and Jacob then stayed an additional six years before returning to Canaan.[95] Obviously, we are dealing with a much longer period "in Haran" than just 20 years.

It is clearly established that Jacob spent the first 14 years in Laban's house working off his dowry contracts for Leah and Rachel, and we also know he spent the last six years in Laban's house acquiring a flock of his own. It is

---

92. Genesis 31:52   94. Genesis 31:41
93. Genesis 31:55   95. Genesis 30:24-31; plus Genesis 31:41

nevertheless apparent that in between these two periods Jacob must have spent as much as 20 additional years raising his family and functioning more or less independent of Laban. Therefore this would make the stay in Haran more like 40 years than 20.

We know that Jacob was 91 when Joseph was born[96] and therefore he was 97 when he left Haran.[97] It is certainly illogical to assume that he came to Haran only 20 years before this, seeking a wife at the age of 77. A man of that age would be most unlikely to offer to work seven years before receiving his wife.

On the other hand, if the stay in Haran was approximately 40 years it would mean that Jacob was around 57 when he arrived at Laban's house and 64 when he married. These age factors would fit the known circumstances far more logically than age 77. A period of 40 years would also allow time for the sequence of events which are known to have transpired. This is easily demonstrated in the following table:

```
 1. ⎫
 2. ⎪
 3. ⎪
 4. ⎬  Jacob worked 7 years for Laban prior to his marriage
 5. ⎪
 6. ⎪
 7. ⎭
 8. Jacob marries Leah and Rachel
 9. Reuben is born to Leah
10. Simeon is born to Leah
11. Levi is born to Leah
12. Judah is born to Leah
13. Jacob marries Bilhah
```

---

96. This is easily calculated from the following scriptures: Jacob says he was 130 when he went to Egypt (Genesis 47:9). By adding the dates given in Genesis 41:46, 48 and 45:11 we know that Joseph was 39 when his father came into Egypt. Therefore, if Joseph was 39 when his father was 130, he would have been born when his father, Jacob was 91 years of age.

97. Genesis 30:24-31 states that Jacob agreed to work for Laban right after Joseph was born, i.e., when Jacob was 91. Genesis 31:41 states that his labor lasted six years, so Jacob would have been 97 by the time he left Haran.

14. Dan is born to Bilhah
15. Naphtali is born to Bilhah
16. Jacob marries Zilpah
17. Gad is born to Zilpah
18. Asher is born to Zilpah
19. Leah again seeks to have more children
20. Issachar is born to Leah
21. Zebulun is born to Leah
22. Dinah is born to Leah
23.
24.
25.   NOTE: Dinah would require around 18 years to
26.   mature sufficiently so that she would be of marriage-
27.   able age by the time Jacob left Haran. That such was
28.   the case is clear from the circumstances set forth in
29.   Genesis 34:1-4
30.
31.
32.
33.
34. Joseph is born to Rachel when Jacob is 91 (see note 96)
35.
36.
37.   Jacob works for Laban 6 more years in order to ac-
38.   quire flocks of his own
39.
40.
41. Having completed his agreement, Jacob leaves Haran

A careful study of these events will demonstrate that it would be difficult if not impossible to condense them into any period of time much less than 40 years. This is why leading Bible scholars have set the period of Jacob's stay in Haran at approximately 40 years rather than 20.[98]

So far as we know, Jacob never returned to Haran again. As Jacob proceeded with his flocks and family toward Canaan he had only one worry. What would happen when he met Esau? After all these years would his twin brother still want to kill him?

---

98. See various authorities cited on this problem in Clarke's *Bible Commentary*, Vol. 1, pp. 194-197.

Scripture Reading and Questions on Chapter Three

Scripture Reading Assignment: Genesis, chapters 28 to 31 inclusive.

1—After Esau lost his birthright to Jacob, what action did he intend to take against his younger brother? Why did he postpone it?

2—What excuse did Rebekah use to get Jacob out of the country?

3—Where did Esau go after Jacob left? Did he stay there?

4—What did the Lord promise Jacob at Bethel? What did Jacob promise the Lord?

5—About how old is Jacob believed to have been when he married?

6—After being tricked into marrying Leah, how long did Jacob have to wait until he married Rachel?

7—How many sons were born to Leah? Can you name them?

8—Who were the sons of Zilpah?

9—Who were the sons of Bilhah?

10—Who were the sons of Rachel?

11—Jacob worked six years for Laban to get flocks of his own. What did he do to get "speckled and spotted" cattle and brown sheep? Did it seem to work?

12—What did the Lord reveal to be the real explanation for Jacob's good fortune?

13—Why did Jacob leave Haran in such a hurry? Did the Lord approve?

14—What did Rachel take from her father's house prior to their departure. What was the significance of these objects being in her father's house?

15—How many days passed before Laban heard that Jacob had departed? How long did it take him to catch up with Jacob? Had Jacob crossed the great Euphrates river yet?

16—What revelation did the Lord give to Laban just before he caught up with Jacob?

17—When Laban searched for his missing property, did he ever find it?

18—What were the feelings between Jacob and Laban when they finally parted?

19—Why do Bible scholars believe Jacob was in Haran nearly 40 years?

20—How old was Jacob when Joseph was born?

CHAPTER FOUR

Jacob Returns to Canaan

When Jacob finally separated from his avaricious father-in-law, it must have given him a feeling of satisfaction and relief. But it was not to be for long.

As Jacob returned to the land of his birthright he knew there was one man who would count him a mortal enemy. That would be Esau, his red-haired brother. Perhaps, after being gone so long, there was a remote chance that Esau's wrath may have softened, but on the other hand, their aged father, Isaac, was nearing the end of his life, and had not Esau sworn he would kill Jacob as soon as their father was dead?[1]

In any event, Jacob determined to try to make some kind of peace pact with his brother, and so, to this end, Jacob dispatched a servant to tell Esau he was coming. In his message of greeting Jacob emphasized that he was now a prosperous man. He did not want Esau to think he was returning home as a prodigal begger. He said his purpose in contacting Esau was simply to "find grace in thy sight."[2]

AN UNEXPECTED TURN OF EVENTS

When the servant returned he had an alarming message for Jacob. "He cometh to meet thee," said the servant, "and four hundred men with him!"[3]

Jacob could have panicked and fled back across the Euphrates, but here was a test of his faith. Had not God commanded him to return to the land of his birthright and had not He said, "I will be with thee?"[4] Jacob determined to stay. Nevertheless, both Jacob and his family knew there was a terrible risk involved in this decision. How would

1. Genesis 27:41-43
2. Genesis 32:5
3. Genesis 32:6
4. Genesis 31:3

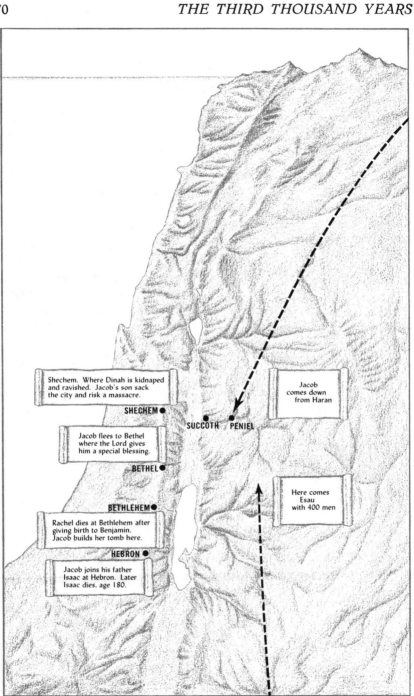

Shechem. Where Dinah is kidnaped
and ravished. Jacob's son sack
the city and risk a massacre.

SHECHEM

Jacob
comes down
from Haran

SUCCOTH   PENIEL

Jacob flees to Bethel
where the Lord gives
him a special blessing.

BETHEL

BETHLEHEM

Here comes
Esau
with 400 men

Rachel dies at Bethlehem after
giving birth to Benjamin.
Jacob builds her tomb here.

HEBRON

Jacob joins his father
Isaac at Hebron. Later
Isaac dies, age 180.

Jacob and his servants stand off 400 men? It was impossible. And what about the women and children? There might be a massacre.

Frantically, Jacob divided his followers and his herds into two groups. He thought if Esau attacked the first group it would perhaps allow his family in the second group to escape.[5] Having taken this preliminary precaution, Jacob threw himself upon the mercy of the Lord. In prayerful pleading he said, "Deliver me, I pray thee, from the hand of my brother, from the hand of Esau; for I fear him, lest he will come and smite me, and the mother with the children."[6]

Jacob then undertook to provide a series of rich gifts to placate Esau. He sent one servant out to meet Esau with a flock of 220 goats. Another servant followed some distance behind him with a flock of 220 sheep. Behind these he sent a servant with 30 milk camels and their young. Then came a servant with 50 head of cattle. And finally, a servant brought up the rear with a gift of 20 female pack animals (donkeys) with their colts.[7]

Each servant was to present his flock or herd to Esau and say, "Behold, thy servant Jacob is behind us. For he said, I will appease him with the present that goeth before me, and afterward I will see his face; peradventure he will accept of me."[8]

Having made all these preparations, Jacob determined to make one final plea with the Lord. The scripture makes it plain that by this time Jacob was already well into the land of Canaan. He had remained on the east side of Jordan, however, and was about half way between the Sea of Galilee and the Dead Sea. He had camped on the banks of the river, Jabbok, which runs directly into the Jordan. In order to be assured of privacy, Jacob sent his flocks and his family across the river and then remained behind to meditate and pray throughout the night.

5. Genesis 32:7-8
6. Genesis 32:11
7. Genesis 32:13-19
8. Genesis 32:20

In a Time of Crisis Jacob Gets a New Name and a Blessing

While Jacob was pleading with the Lord, a messenger suddenly appeared to him. The scripture calls him a "man," but it also makes it clear that he was a divine messenger with a physical tabernacle and not just a spirit. He may have been a member of the Priesthood from the City of Enoch which was specifically set up to provide ministering angels to God's creations.[9] In fact, divine messengers similar to the one which now appeared before Jacob had previously ministered to Father Abraham.[10]

Jacob knew the messenger which had come to him was not a disembodied spirit because Jacob had a physical encounter with him. Jacob wanted the heavenly messenger to give him a special blessing and a promise of protection against his impetuous brother, Esau. The messenger attempted to depart without doing so. Jacob seized him and they struggled together. During the struggle, Jacob's thigh was thrown out of joint.[11] Nevertheless, Jacob desperately persisted. Finally, the messenger said, "Let me go, for the day breaketh." Jacob replied, "I will not let thee go except thou bless me."[12]

The messenger actually could have had no purpose in coming to Jacob except for the purpose of giving him comfort and a blessing and therefore it appears that his reluctance in giving the blessing was by design and for a purpose. He seemed to be pushing Jacob's faith to the highest possible pinnacle. When this had been achieved the messenger challenged Jacob.

---

9. "Now the doctrine of translation is a power which belongs to this Priesthood. There are many things which belong to the powers of the Priesthood and the keys thereof, that have been kept hid from before the foundation of the world; they are hid from the wise and prudent to be revealed in the last times. Many have supposed that the doctrine of translation was a doctrine whereby men were taken immediately into the presence of God, and into an eternal fullness, but this is a mistaken idea. Their place of habitation is that of the terrestrial order, and a place for such characters He held in reserve to be ministering angels unto many planets, and who as yet have not entered into so great a fullness as those who are resurrected from the dead." (*Teachings of Joseph Smith*, p. 170)

10. Genesis 18:1-22. Note the description of these men as it appears in the Inspired Version: "And the angels which were holy men, and were sent forth after the order of God. . . ." (Insp. Version, Genesis 18:23)

11. Genesis 32:25

12. Genesis 32:26

"What is thy name?" The exhausted Jacob told him. Obviously, the messenger already knew his name but apparently this was his way of making a point of emphasis. He said, "Thy name shall be called no more Jacob, but Israel: for as a prince hast thou power with God and with men, and hast prevailed."[13]

This was a glorious victory for Jacob. The struggle had not been in vain. In a spirit of intimate appreciation he said to the messenger, "Tell me, I pray thee, thy name." But the messenger brushed it aside saying, "Wherefore is it that thou dost ask after my name?" Then the messenger blessed Jacob and departed.[14]

Jacob was so thrilled with this powerful testimonial of God's interest in his affairs that he called the place Peniel and said, "I have seen God face to face, and my life is preserved."[15] Actually, the messenger had withheld his identity but Jacob apparently felt that such a glorious being must have been the Lord in person. A similar error in mistaking an angel for the Lord was made by John on the Isle of Patmos.[16]

After the messenger had left, Jacob found the sinew of his thigh had shrunk and it had left him lame. "Therefore the children of Israel eat not of the sinew which shrank, which is upon the hollow of the thigh, unto this day."[17]

Esau Comes With 400 Men

As the new day broke, "Jacob lifted up his eyes and looked, and, behold, Esau came, and with him four hundred men."[18]

Jacob frantically arranged his family so that if there were trouble, his beloved Rachel and her son, Joseph, would be the least likely to get hurt.[19] This constant manifestation of a strong preference for one part of his family was something Jacob was never successful in hiding. Evidence of it spilled over continually and later created bitter feelings in

---

13. Genesis 32:28
14. Genesis 32:29
15. Genesis 32:30
16. Revelations 22:8-9
17. Genesis 32:32
18. Genesis 33:1
19. Genesis 33:2

his family which he might have avoided with more careful or prudent management.

In any event, Jacob was now ready to confront Esau.

Jacob went out to meet Esau and "bowed himself to the ground seven times, until he came near to his brother."[20] What would Esau do? With 400 men he could spread havoc, and Jacob knew it. Imagine his amazement, therefore, when the mighty Esau ran eagerly toward Jacob and welcomed him with open arms like the long lost brother that he was. The scripture says, "And Esau ran to meet him, and embraced him, and fell on his neck, and kissed him. . . ." Both men wept.[21]

No blessing could have been more welcomed to Jacob than this one. His fears and his tears evaporated together. Joyfully he brought forth each member of his family and introduced them to Esau. It was a proud reunion.[22]

Then Esau, in a warm and hearty spirit, said, "What meanest thou by all this drove which I met?" This had reference to all the sheep, goats, cattle, camels and donkeys Jacob had sent ahead as gifts.

Jacob replied, "These are to find grace in the sight of my Lord."

Esau protested, "I have enough, my brother; keep that thou hast unto thyself."

But Jacob would not hear of it. He pleaded with Esau to accept this token of his esteem that henceforth only trust and affection might exist between them. Finally Esau consented.[23]

Esau was so delighted to have his brother back that he wanted Jacob to immediately accompany him to his desert kingdom at Mount Seir.[24] But Jacob deferred that pleasure until some future time. Esau then offered to leave behind some of his desert warriors to provide Jacob with safe passage, but Jacob also declined this additional offer of kindness.[25] Little did he know that within a short time he could have used the whole band of 400.

---

20. Genesis 33:3
21. Genesis 33:4
22. Genesis 33:5-7

23. Genesis 33:8-11
24. Genesis 33:12-14
25. Genesis 33:15

So this historic meeting was terminated, and "Esau returned that day on his way unto Seir."[26]

DINAH, JACOB'S ONLY DAUGTER, IS KIDNAPPED AND RAVISHED

In studying the life of Jacob, it soon becomes apparent that the biography of this distinguished servant of God was a continuous series of critical situations, some of which ended in the profoundest tragedy. One such incident occurred at this time.

After Esau had departed for Seir, Jacob established a temporary settlement half-way between Peniel and the Jordan River. He called it Succoth (booths) because there he "made booths for his cattle."[27] Later, Jacob succeeded in fording the Jordan with his herds and flocks and proceeded toward a group of Canaanite settlements which were federated together around Shechem.[28] This spot was sacred to the memory of Jacob and his family for it was here that Abraham had first stopped when he came into Canaan.[29] Perhaps this accounts for Jacob's decision to build an estate there. He bought a tract of land from Hamor, the ruling prince of Shechem, spread his tent upon it, established his flocks there and then set up a place of worship with an altar of sacrifice. Jacob called this new home El-Elohe-Israel, meaning, "God, the God of Israel."[30]

All was going well for Jacob until one day his daughter, Dinah, found the attraction of the nearby settlement of Shechem too fascinating to resist. Without any companions or protection whatever, she "went out to see the daughters of the land" who dwelt in the city.[31] Because she was the only girl in Jacob's family it is understandable why she felt attracted to the young women her own age in this nearby com-

---

26. Genesis 33:16
27. Genesis 33:17 Succoth is identified today as Dayr Alla
28. Genesis 33:18 Shechem is identified today as Balatah
29. Genesis 12:6 But not difference in spelling. All authorities agree that Sichem (or Sychem) and Seechem are identical and they are so rendered in the Revised Version. See Dummelow's *Bible Commentary* under Genesis 12:6.
30. Genesis 33:20 plus marginal note
31. Genesis 34:1

munity. Nevertheless, she soon had occasion to regret deeply what she had done.

In this city was a young man named Shechem. Perhaps he was a namesake for the person after whom the city had been named. Shechem was the son of Hamor, the ruling prince of the city who had sold the tract of land to Jacob. Apparently young Shechem was impulsive and accustomed to taking anything he wanted, therefore, when he saw Dinah, the beautiful daughter of Jacob, walking about the streets unprotected "he took her, and lay with her and defiled her."[32]

For Dinah and her people this was a revolting act of violence, but for Shechem it was a routine episode, a romantic conquest after the manner of the heathen Canaanites. The scripture says, "he loved the damsel, and spake kindly unto the damsel."[33] However, instead of liberating Dinah, Shechem continued to hold her prisoner with the intent of making her his wife.

Under the circumstances the arrangements for a marriage would require the most delicate handling, therefore Shechem went to Hamor, his father, and asked him to beg permission of Jacob so that he could marry the beautiful Hebrew girl. Hamor agreed to try.

Jacob Hears a Strange Proposal

So from Hamor, the father of the reckless youth who had kidnapped and ravished his daughter, Jacob heard the shocking confession of what had happened and thereafter listened to the proposal that Shechem and Dinah be allowed to get married.[34] Had Hamor known the abhorrence which Jacob held toward intermarriage with the Canaanites, he might never have ventured on this mission, nevertheless, Jacob kept his feelings under control and sent for his sons. When the sons of Jacob came in from the fields and heard what had happened, they were outraged.[35] Hamor pleaded with them:

"Make ye marriages with us, and give your daughters unto us, and take our daughters unto you. And ye shall dwell

---

32. Genesis 34:2   34. Genesis 34:4-5
33. Genesis 34:3   35. Genesis 34:7

with us: and the land shall be before you; dwell and trade ye therein, and get you possessions therein."[36]

Even Shechem dared to come out to plead with them, saying, "Let me find grace in your eyes, and what ye shall say unto me I will give. Ask me never so much dowry and gift, and I will give according as ye shall say unto me: but give me the damsel to wife."[37]

But to the sons of Jacob this was all treachery. Their sister had been kidnapped and ravished and even now, while she was being held a prisoner, her abductor dared to come out and brazenly bargain for permanent possession of her.

Very well, the sons of Jacob could be clever, too. Without telling Jacob, they concocted a scheme to recapture their sister and avenge her debauchery. In furtherance of their scheme this is what they said to Hamor and Shechem, "We cannot do this thing, to give our sister to one that is uncircumcised; for that were a reproach unto us: but in this will we consent unto you: If ye will be as we be, that every male of you be circumcised, then will we give our daughters unto you, and we will take your daughters to us, and we will dwell with you, and we will become one people."[38]

The scripture says these "words pleased Hamor, and Shechem. . . ."[39] Therefore they went hurriedly back to their city to confer with the men of the town. Would they submit to circumcision? To persuade them, Hamor and Shechem pointed out the tremendous economic advantage of having the wealth and influence of the Hebrews in the community. Said they, "Shall not their cattle and their substance and every beast of theirs be ours? only let us consent unto them, and they will dwell with us."[40] The idea of keeping Jacob and his wealth in their community appealed to the men of Shechem, therefore they consented to submit themselves and their male children and servants to circumcision.

---

36. Genesis 34:9-10
37. Genesis 34:11-12
38. Genesis 34:14-16

39. Genesis 34:18
40. Genesis 34:23

JACOB'S SONS DECLARE WAR ON SHECHEM

Now the older sons of Jacob were almost ready to act.

They waited until the third day when the men of this community were virtually helpless because of their operations, then "Simeon and Levi, Dinah's brethren [being sons of Leah, they were full brothers], took each man his sword and came upon the city boldly, and slew all the males. And they slew Hamor and Shechem his son with the edge of the sword, and took Dinah out of Shechem's house, and went out."[41]

They then apparently returned with some of the other "sons of Jacob" and "spoiled the city, because they had defiled their sister."[42] With no men left to defend it the sacking of the city resulted in the seizure of all the women and children, the cattle, oxen, sheep, and "all their wealth."[43]

For such a small band to be able to completely conquer Shechem would indicate that the city was of a limited population even though it was the tribal capital of that region. There is the additional likelihood that the older sons of Jacob who conducted this war recruited their servants, herders, and workers to assist them, particularly in gathering up the spoils.

However, as soon as Jacob found out what was happening he was outraged. This attack amounted to reckless stupidity and created the very real possibility of a retaliatory attack by nearby Canaanites which could wipe out the whole Hebrew camp. Jacob therefore denounced and berated the two leaders, Simeon and Levi. Said he, "Ye have troubled me to make me to stink among the inhabitants of the land, among the Canaanites and Perizzites; and being few in number, they shall gather themselves together against me, and slay me; and I shall be destroyed, I and my house."[44]

The brothers of Dinah could only mutter back wrathfully. "Should he deal with our sister as with an harlot?"[45]

---

41. Genesis 34:25-26
42. Genesis 34:27
43. Genesis 34:28-29

44. Genesis 34:30
45. Genesis 34:31

JACOB FLEES TO BETHEL

At this point the Lord intervened and commanded Jacob to leave immediately and go to Bethel. Jacob was told that when he arrived there he should build an altar.[46] This meant that Jacob and his family must offer sacrifice and cleanse themselves. Jacob therefore commanded his wives and children and all his followers to submit themselves to the deepest humility and repentance. He ordered his followers from Haran to get rid of their heathen images or gods, and "be clean." He ordered them to change their garments which often were embroidered with the symbols of heathen cult worship as well as their jewelry.

The scripture says, "And they gave unto Jacob all the strange gods which were in their hand, and all their earrings which were in their ears; and Jacob hid them under the oak which was by Shechem."[47]

As the caravan made its way toward Bethel Jacob must have watched anxiously for the possibility of ambush or counter-attack by the Canaanites and Perizzites. However, nothing happened. As Jacob came in site of Bethel, he was once more back in familiar territory. At Bethel God had given him his first revelation nearly a half-century before.[48] Here was the tomb of his mother's handmaid, Deborah.[49] This was also the second stopping place of Abraham when he first came to Canaan,[50] and the place to which he returned after coming up out of Egypt.[51]

As soon after reaching Bethel as possible, Jacob built the altar which God had commanded. He was rewarded with an open revelation which started out by confirming the new name which Jacob had previously received from the divine messenger with whom he had wrestled. The Lord declared:

". . . thy name shall not be called any more Jacob, but Israel shall be thy name; and he called his name Israel."[52]

---

46. Genesis 35:1
47. Genesis 35:4
48. Genesis 28:11-16
49. Genesis 35:8
50. Genesis 12:8
51. Genesis 13:3-4
52. Genesis 35:10

Then the Lord conferred upon Jacob his final blessing. It was the assurance that he was acceptable to God as the legitimate heir of both Abraham and Isaac.

"And God said unto him, I am God Almighty; be fruitful and multiply; a nation and a company of nations shall be of thee, and kings shall come out of thy loins. And the land which I gave Abraham and Isaac, to thee I will give it, and to thy seed after thee will I give the land.

"And God went up from him in the place where he talked with him."[53]

Jacob straightway built a pillar to memorialize this great event. On the pillar he poured a drink offering and holy oil to sanctify it.[54]

Jacob Loses His Beloved Rachel

Now Jacob was ready to move quickly toward Hebron where his aged father, Isaac, awaited him. But before that was accomplished the specter of another tragedy suddenly loomed across the pathway of Jacob's life. It was to have been a moment of rejoicing, for Jacob's beloved Rachel who had been so anxious to give him at least one more son was about ready to be delivered of another child. No doubt Jacob expected that the caravan would reach Hebron in time for the wonderful event but this was not to be.

As the company reached the outskirts of Ephrath (Bethlehem)[55] Rachel announced that she could proceed no further. The caravan was abruptly stopped and there, some 1,738 years before the birth of Jesus Christ, Rachel undertook to be delivered of her son. However, Rachel was no longer a young woman. By the most careful calculations it would appear that Rachel was now considerably past 50 years of age.[56] No doubt this contributed to the difficulty of

---

53. Genesis 35:10-13
54. Genesis 35:14
55. Genesis 35:16, 19
56. Jacob fell in love with Rachel when he first met her (Genesis 29:18) so she must have been at least 14 at that time. He then worked 7 years before he married her which would make her at least 21. We have seen from Jacob's chronology that around 27 years passed before Joseph was born which would make Rachel 48. Then 6 more years passed before Jacob and his family left Haran. (Genesis 30:25 plus 31:41) bringing Rachel's age to 54. It appears that Benjamin was born the year after they came out of Haran, so this would make her at least 55.

her delivery. The hours of painful labor wore on and finally became so intense that Rachel almost despaired, but "the midwife said unto her, Fear not; thou shalt have this son also."[57]

Finally the baby came but the travail had been more than the aging mother could endure. As Rachel felt her life ebbing away she whispered the boy's name. "Ben-oni," she called him, which means "the son of my sorrow."[58] But the grief-stricken Jacob did not want such a mark to be carried by this choice child whose life had been gained by the sacrifice of his mother. Therefore Jacob called him "Benjamin," which means "the son of the right hand."[59]

In deepest mourning Jacob buried his beloved Rachel near the shepherd town of Bethlehem. Several hundred years later either Moses or a subsequent scribe made this note in Genesis, "And Jacob set a pillar upon her grave; that is the pillar of Rachel's grave unto this day."[60]

THE DISGRACE OF REUBEN

But this was not the terminal point of tragedy for this part of Jacob's life. Another deep sorrow came to Jacob soon after the death of Rachel. The scripture says, "And Israel journeyed, and spread his tent beyond the tower of Edar."[61] One more move and his company would reach Hebron! But while they were camped near the tower of Edar, Jacob's eldest son, Reuben, became morally involved with Bilhah, the handmaid of Rachel.[62] This was the handmaid which Rachel had asked Jacob to take as his third wife.[63] Jacob had consented and Bilhah had borne Jacob two sons, namely, Dan and Naphtali. Now this sacred family relationship had been violated by Reuben's act of incest.

Because of this crime against himself, his father, and his God, Reuben was later deprived of his entire birthright. Just before his death, Jacob gave a pronouncement upon each of his sons. For most of them he had a blessing, but not for

57. Genesis 35:17
58. Genesis 35:18 plus marginal note
59. Ibid.
60. Genesis 35:20

61. Genesis 35:21
62. Genesis 35:22
63. Genesis 30:3-4

Reuben. Future events would disclose that in the wisdom of God the birthright of Abraham, Isaac and Jacob was going to by-pass Reuben and go to a younger brother, Joseph, whose son, Ephraim, would become the birthright holder for all Israel. But that was something for the future.

Jacob Arrives in Hebron

Meanwhile, Jacob hastened on to Hebron to join his aged father, Isaac. For some reason Isaac did not remain in Beer-sheba. He had moved up to Hebron where Father Abraham lived for so many years and where both Abraham and Sarah were buried.

It must have been a touching reunion when Jacob and Isaac were finally re-united. Both of them were now old men. Isaac was nearing the termination of his life which would come at age 180. Jacob was now well past 100 but still had many years of vitality left.

There is no mention of Rebekah so we assume that she must have died some years before. The date of her death is not stated, but we do know she was buried here at Hebron in the Cave of Machpelah along with others of this notable family.[64]

Isaac Dies

As nearly as we can tell Isaac became blind sometime prior to the age of 117 and had been expecting death to take its toll ever since.[65] Nevertheless, he had continued on until he became 180.[66] There is no indication that he ever regained his eyesight so these must have been quiet, reflective years. It is difficult to comprehend the sorrow he must have felt when Rebekah finally died and left him alone. It would be equally difficult to appreciate the joy which came to him when he learned that Jacob had arrived with abundant wealth, many flocks, and a large family, after having been absent for almost half a century.

---

64. Genesis 49:30-31
65. Genesis 27:1-2
66. Genesis 35:28

It would appear that Jacob and Isaac enjoyed several years together in Hebron before the ravages of time finally brought the life of the aged Isaac to a close. When the end came his two sons, Jacob and Esau joined together to honor their illustrious father and lay him to rest in the Cave of Machpelah along with his parents and his wife.[67]

Thus came to a conclusion one of the notable personalities of Biblical history. Let us review the highlights of his remarkable career. His birth was predicted a year before it occurred,[68] and his name was given by direct revelation on the same occasion.[69] He was born when his mother was 90,[70] and his father 100.[71] As a "lad" he thought he was going to be offered up as a human sacrifice but was saved after he had been bound and laid on the altar.[72] His mother, Sarah, died when he was 37[73] and when he was 40 he married Rebekah, his cousin, of Haran in Mesopotamia, who was selected for him by a servant of the household acting under divine guidance.[74]

Twenty years passed away before any children were born to Isaac and Rebekah and then they had twins. As we have already seen, Isaac fixed his affection on the oldest twin even though revelation had given preference to the younger and it was some time before Isaac became reconciled. During a severe famine he moved down among the Canaanites at Gerar and became very prosperous there even though he was finally compelled to move out and rebuild the old homestead of Abraham at Beer-sheba. By the time he was approximately 117 Isaac had become blind and thought he was soon going to die.[75] Through the stratagem of Rebekah he gave the birthright blessing to Jacob even though he intended to give it to Esau. He subsequently ratified the bless-

---

67. Genesis 49:31
68. Genesis 17:21
69. Genesis 17:19
70. Genesis 17:17
71. Genesis 21:5
72. Genesis 22:9-12
73. Genesis 23:1. Since Sarah was 90 (Genesis 17:17) when Isaac was born, he would be 37 when she died at age 127.
74. Genesis 24:42-48
75. Genesis 27:1-2

ing given to Jacob and had to send Jacob to Mesopotamia to keep Esau from murdering him. Jacob did not return for nearly half a century but when he did the two twins were completely reconciled and Isaac had the comfort of spending his last few years of life with Jacob in Hebron. Isaac died at the good old age of 180[76] after apparently spending approximately 63 years without his sight. Both Jacob and Esau joined forces in honoring Isaac and burying him in the Cave of Machpelah alongside his parents and his wife.

With the passing of Isaac, Jacob assumed full responsibility for the perpetuation of God's covenant people. Even before Isaac's death this assignment had assumed monumental proportions. Jacob found that he had only one son who seemed completely dedicated to the preservation of the Patriarchal Priesthood. That was Joseph.

Once Jacob had made up his mind that Joseph was the hope of all Israel, he poured his unlimited affection and confidence upon him. From that point on, the life of Jacob gravitated almost exclusively around this favored son. It is toward Joseph, therefore, that our history now turns.

---

76. Genesis 35:28

Scripture Reading and Questions on Chapter Four

Scripture Reading Assignment: Genesis, chapters 32 to 35 inclusive.

1—Why did Jacob send word to Esau that he was coming back to Canaan? What startling news did the messenger bring back?

2—What did Jacob do to placate Esau's feelings?

3—What happened when Jacob pleaded with the Lord for help?

4—Did the Lord appear in person or was it a translated being?

5—Why did Jacob wrestle with the angelic messenger?

6—What did the heavenly messenger tell Jacob? What is meaning of the name, *Israel*?

7—What was Jacob's mistake when he named this place Peniel? Who else made a similar mistake?

8—What happened when Jacob met Esau? Was Jacob surprised?

9—What happened to the gifts Jacob had sent to Esau? Did Esau want them? Did he finally take them?

10—After crossing the Jordan river, where did Jacob settle and buy land?

11—What were the circumstances leading up to the kidnapping and ravishing of Jacob's only daughter?

12—Who told Jacob about the tragedy? What was his purpose in doing so? Did Shechem ever come out to plead his case?

13—How did the older sons of Jacob avenge their sister?

14—What happened to Hamor, to Shechem, and to Dinah?

15—What was Jacob's reaction to his sons' rash behavior? What did he fear might happen as a result?

16—What did the Lord tell Jacob to do? What did Jacob tell his followers to do in order to cleanse themselves?

17—What did the Lord tell Jacob at Bethel? What was the full significance of this revelation?

18—Where did Rachel die? What were the circumstances? Where was she buried?

19—What did Reuben do to disgrace himself and become disinherited?

20—How old was Isaac when he died? About how many years had he been blind? Where was he buried?

CHAPTER FIVE

Young Joseph—a Shepherd, a Seer, and Then a Slave

Of all the Old Testament prophets, the life of Joseph who was sold into Egypt is undoubtedly one of the most fascinating. He started his career as a prophet while still a teen-ager. He ended his career as the virtual ruler of one of the great nations of the earth. As with Enoch, the Lord shared some of his most intimate secrets of the future with Joseph. This eleventh son of Jacob knew that eventually the tribes of Israel would become slaves in Egypt. He also knew both Moses and Aaron by name[1] even though they would not be born until two generations after Joseph. He knew the work they would do, and the power God would give them to perform miracles and divide the Red Sea.[2] He knew about the great work which God would do in America, particularly in the latter days, when one of Joseph's namesakes[3] would be raised up to prepare the world for the Second Coming of the Messiah. This Joseph was one of the great prophets of all time.

Joseph was born in Haran when his father was 91[4] and his mother was approximately 48.[5] A little over six years later his father brought him out of Haran along with the rest of his family.[6] Joseph was too young to have been involved in the sacking of Shechem and was probably only 7 or 8

---

1. Inspired Version, Genesis 50:34-35; 2 Nephi 3:17
2. Ibid.
3. Inspired Version, Genesis 50:33; 2 Nephi 3:6, 14-15
4. As we shall see later, Jacob says he was 130 when he went down into Egypt (Genesis 47:9). By adding the dates given in Genesis 41:46,48 and 45:11, we know that Joseph was 39 when his father came into Egypt. Therefore, if Joseph was 39 when his father was 130, he would have had to be born when his father, Jacob, was 91 years of age.
5. See note 56, previous chapter.
6. Genesis 30:25 plus 31:41

when his mother died near Bethlehem after giving birth to Joseph's only full brother who was named Benjamin.[7]

JACOB'S LOVE FOR JOSEPH

Because of the intense and abiding love which Jacob had always felt for Rachel, it was almost to be expected that he would transfer a major portion of that affection to her oldest son after she died. The scripture specifically says that "Israel loved Joseph more than all his children, because he was the son of his old age. . . ."[8]

When Joseph was 17 he happened to be herding sheep with his half-brothers, the "sons of Bilhah" and "the Sons of Zilpah." Joseph saw these men doing things which were evil. We are not told just what these offenses were but Joseph felt they were sufficiently serious to warn Jacob, so "he brought unto his father their evil report."[9] This incident proved to Jacob that his best beloved son was both discerning and loyal, but it created only hatred in the hearts of these brothers for Joseph.

Apparently they were even further offended when they saw that their father had made for young Joseph a "coat of many colours." The scripture says "they hated him and could not speak peaceably unto him."[10]

YOUNG JOSEPH RECEIVES THE GIFT OF SEERSHIP

However, the most offensive thorn which began pricking the hearts of these brothers was a series of dreams which Joseph received. They were such unusual and startling dreams that Joseph could not keep them to himself. After the first dream he said, "Hear, I pray you, this dream which I have dreamed: for, behold, we were binding sheaves in the field, and, lo, my sheaf arose, and also stood upright; and, behold, your sheaves stood round about, and made obeisance to my sheaf."[11]

This was disgusting. "And his brethren said to him, Shalt thou indeed reign over us? or shalt thou indeed have

---

7. Genesis 35:16-20
8. Genesis 37:3
9. Genesis 37:2

10. Genesis 37:4
11. Genesis 37:6-7

dominion over us? and they hated him yet the more for his dreams, and for his words."[12]

But Joseph was not taken aback in the least. He came to them with another dream. "Behold," he said, "I have dreamed a dream more; and, behold, the sun and the moon and the eleven stars made obeisance to me."[13]

As a rule, leadership does not rest easily on young or inexperienced shoulders and human nature being what it is, young Joseph was manifesting the typical bravado of a boy his age who knows he is just coming into his own. Therefore, the telling of these dreams was not so much an exhibition of boasting as it was a manifestation of the rich and exultant feelings which come to a youth when he suddenly realizes that he has a mission in life and a role to fill. He probably thought his family would be pleased to know of these prophecies of his future leadership. But his brothers were bitter at what appeared to be a most preposterous presumption. This last dream even shocked Jacob. The scripture says, ". . . his father rebuked him, and said unto him, What is this dream that thou hast dreamed? Shall I and thy mother and thy brethren indeed come to bow down ourselves to thee to the earth?"[14]

No doubt this rebuke sent Joseph away crestfallen and hurt, but as Jacob reflected on this dream and its possible implications he decided it might have more significance than he and his family were willing to admit. The record says the brothers remained angry and envious but "his father observed the saying."[15]

JOSEPH IS NEARLY MURDERED

It was right after this that Jacob decided to send his flocks from Hebron to Shechem. We know that Jacob owned land at Shechem,[16] but it is surprising that he felt safe in sending his herds back to the exact area from which he had fled some ten years earlier when his older sons had sacked the principal Canaanite settlement there.[17] Nevertheless this

---

12. Genesis 37:8
13. Genesis 37:9
14. Genesis 37:10
15. Genesis 37:11
16. Genesis 33:18-19
17. Genesis 34:27-29

is what was done. Apparently all ten of the older brothers went on this trek while Joseph and his young brother, Benjamin, remained behind.

After a period of time Jacob said to Joseph, "Go, I pray thee, see whether it be well with thy brethren, and well with the flocks; and bring me word again."[18] But Joseph could not find his father's flocks at Shechem. "And a certain man found him, and, behold, he was wandering in the field: and the man asked him, saying, What seekest thou? And he said, I seek my brethren: tell me, I pray thee, where they feed their flocks. And the man said, They are departed hence; for I heard them say, Let us go to Dothan."[19]

So Joseph went to Dothan and finally located the flocks of his father. But his brothers saw him coming, "And they said one to another, Behold, this dreamer cometh. Come now therefore, and let us slay him, and cast him into some pit, and we will say, Some evil beast hath devoured him: and we shall see what will become of his dreams."[20]

This murderous conspiracy was headed off, however, by none other than Reuben, the oldest of the brothers. He agreed to have Joseph thrown into a pit but he said, "Let us not kill him."[21] The scripture says Reuben went along with the plot to throw him into the pit only because he thought this would save Joseph's life and that afterwards Reuben could "rid him out of their hands, to deliver him to his father again."[22]

As soon as Joseph had come into their midst the brothers leaped upon him, stripped off his beautiful "coat of many colours," and lowered him into a deep pit or well. However, the record says "the pit was empty, there was no water in it."[23]

After their exertions were over, the ten brothers went back to their camp and "sat down to eat bread: and they lifted up their eyes and looked, and, behold, a company of Ishmaelites came from Gilead with their camels bearing

---

18. Genesis 37:14
19. Genesis 37:15-17
20. Genesis 37:19-20

21. Genesis 37:21
22. Genesis 37:22
23. Genesis 37:24

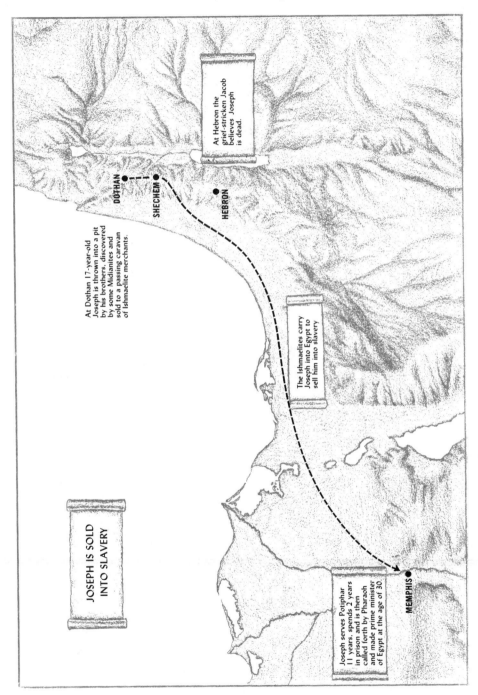

At Hebron the grief-stricken Jacob believes Joseph is dead.

At Dothan 17-year-old Joseph is thrown into a pit by his brothers, discovered by some Midianites and sold to a passing caravan of Ishmaelite merchants.

The Ishmaelites carry Joseph into Egypt to sell him into slavery.

JOSEPH IS SOLD INTO SLAVERY

Joseph serves Potiphar 11 years, spends 2 years in prison and is then called forth by Pharaoh and made prime minister of Egypt at the age of 30.

DOTHAN

SHECHEM

HEBRON

MEMPHIS

spicery and balm and myrrh, going to carry it down to Egypt."[24]

These Ishmaelites were distant relatives and the sight of them gave Judah an idea. Said he, "What profit is it if we slay our brother, and conceal his blood? Come, and let us sell him to the Ishmaelites, and let not our hand be upon him; for he is our brother and our flesh."[25] This idea of making a good business deal and getting rid of Joseph at the same time appealed to the brothers as a splendid idea. They would do it.

A Surprise Development

But before any of these brothers could get back to the well a group of merchantmen who were Midianites came along and accidentally found Joseph. They immediately dragged him to the surface and then did exactly what Joseph's brothers were going to do. They sold him to the Ishmaelites for 20 pieces of silver. It is very likely that by the time the Ishmaelites came in sight of the camp where the ten brothers were eating, they already had Joseph in their possession.

It was Reuben who first discovered that Joseph was gone. He had raced back to the pit ahead of the others with the apparent intention of rescuing Joseph and delivering him to his father, but "behold, Joseph was not in the pit; and he rent his clothes. And he returned unto his brethren, and said, The child is not; and I, whither shall I go?"[26] Whether Joseph had escaped from the pit or been killed he did not know.

As far as Joseph was concerned he thought the whole thing had been engineered by his brothers. He had heard his brothers plotting to throw him into the pit and when he was unexpectedly pulled out by the Midianites and sold to the Ishmaelites he thought it was all part of the plot. Years later he would accuse his brothers of selling him into bondage.[27]

Meanwhile, the brothers were frantic with consternation. What would they tell their father? The ten brothers knew their father would hold them accountable for Joseph and

24. Genesis 37:25   26. Genesis 37:29-30
25. Genesis 37:26-27   27. Genesis 45:4-5

since they did not know for certain exactly what had happened to him, they hatched up a new conspiracy. "And they took Joseph's coat, and killed a kid of the goats, and dipped the coat in the blood; and they sent the coat of many colours, and they brought it to their father; and said, This have we found: know now whether it be thy son's coat or no. And he knew it, and said, It is my son's coat, an evil beast hath devoured him; Joseph is without doubt rent in pieces."[28]

The reaction of the aged Jacob to this calamity was vehement. "And Jacob rent his clothes, and put sackcloth upon his loins, and mourned for his son many days. And all his sons and all his daughters rose up to comfort him; but he refused to be comforted; and he said, For I will go down into the grave unto my son mourning. Thus his father wept for him."[29]

HAVING LOST HIS SON, JACOB ALSO
LOSES ISAAC, HIS FATHER

Jacob was 108 years old when he lost Joseph.[30] The years that followed were bitter and empty. Twelve years after the disappearance of Joseph, Jacob was further bereaved by the loss of his patriarchal parent, Isaac.[31] We have already discussed the death of Isaac but it should be mentioned here to keep the sequence of events in their proper order.

Isaac had lived to the venerable age of 180,[32] and so far as we know he had spent approximately the last 63 of those years afflicted with total blindness.[33] In fact, he had been expecting to die during all that period, and apparently his family had thought so, too.[34]

Now, at last, however, the spirit of Isaac was finally called home. The scripture closes with this note, "And Isaac gave up the ghost and died, and was gathered unto his people, being old and full of days. . . ."[35]

---

28. Genesis 37:31-33
29. Genesis 37:34-35
30. Joseph was 17 when he was sold into Egypt (Genesis 37:2) and since Jacob was 91 when Joseph was born (see note 4, this chapter) he would now be 108.
31. Genesis 35:28-29
32. Genesis 35:28   34. Genesis 27:1 plus 27:41
33. Genesis 27:1   35. Genesis 35:29

From the rugged mountain oasis of his wilderness domain came Esau, Jacob's red haired twin brother, who now, as a man of 120, flourished with his posterity in wealth and influence at Mount Seir.[36] Together, Jacob and Esau buried their father alongside of Abraham, Sarah, and Rebekah, in the cave of Machpelah, near Hebron.[37]

THE POLITICAL CLIMATE WHEN JOSEPH
ARRIVED IN EGYPT

As we now turn to the history of Joseph in Egypt, it is important to remember that the amazing experiences of Joseph in that land would have been practically impossible if the traditicnal rulers of Egypt had still been in power there. The original Egyptian Pharaohs were descendants of Ham[38] and many of them possessed a passionate hatred for strangers and people of other nationalities and races.[39]

It just so happened, however, that some time before Joseph was brought into Egypt, the country had been conquered by the famous Hyksos invaders. The Hyksos were the "shepherd kings" from the Shemites of Arabia, Canaan and Syria. They were therefore distant relatives of Abraham and his descendants which would, of course, include Joseph.

A well known writer, Dr. Werner Keller, makes reference to this most fortunate political climate which developed in Egypt just prior to the time Joseph arrived there.

"Suddenly as a bolt from the blue, warriors in chariots drove into the country like arrows shot from a bow, hooves thundered past the frontier posts, rang through city streets, temple squares and the majestic court of Pharaoh's palaces. Even before the Egyptians realized it, it had happened; their country was taken by surprise, overrun and vanquished. The giant of the Nile, who never before in his history had seen foreign conquerors, lay bound and prostrate.

---

36. Esau had indicated his affluence even earlier, see Genesis 33:1,9

37. Genesis 49:31

38. Abraham 1:23-25

39. Werner Keller, *The Bible As History*, p. ·93, declares, "under the (native) Pharaohs a sand-dweller could never have become viceroy." The term "sand-dweller" was a favorite Egyptian epithet for surrounding foreigners.

"The rule of the victors began with a bloodbath. The Hyksos, Semitic tribes from Canaan and Syria, knew no pity. With the fateful year 1730 B.C. [Dr. Keller says this is only approximate] the thirteen-hundred-year rule of the dynasties came to an abrupt end. The Middle Kingdom of the Pharaohs was shattered under the onslaught of these Asian peoples, the 'rulers of foreign lands.' That is the meaning of the name Hyksos."[40]

Manetho, best known of the ancient Egyptian historians, describes these same events as follows:

"We had a king called Tutimaeus. In his reign, it happened. I do not know why God was displeased with us. Unexpectedly from the regions of the East, came men of unknown race. Confident of victory they marched against our land. By force they took it, easily, without a single battle. Having overpowered our rulers, they burned our cities without compassion, and destroyed the temples of the gods. All the natives were treated with great cruelty, for they slew some and carried off the wives and children of others into slavery. Finally they appointed one of themselves as king. His name was Salitis and he lived in Memphis and made Upper and Lower Egypt pay tribute to him . . . and when he found a city in the province of Sais which suited his purposes (it lay east of the Bubasite branch of the Nile and was called Avaris) he rebuilt it and made it very strong by erecting walls and installing a force of 240,000 men to hold it. Salitis went there every summer partly to collect his corn and pay his men their wages, and partly to train his armed troops and terrify foreigners."[41]

Dr. Werner Keller points out that this Avaris mentioned by Manetho is the same city which was eventually named Pi-Ramses. As we shall see later, it was one of the treasure cities where the children of Israel were required to labor in bondage.[42]

The Hyksos are said to have remained in control of Egypt for some 200 years.[43] When they were finally driven out the Egyptians could be expected to smash their monu-

---

40. Ibid., pp. 86-87   42. Exodus 1:11
41. Ibid. pp. 87-88   43. Will Durant, *Our Oriental Heritage*, p. 152

ments, burn their records, efface their stone-carved histories and vengefully wipe out every possible trace of these hated foreigners. Historians, archaeologists, and students of Egyptology verify that this is precisely what was done.[44] There is no doubt but that somewhere in the havoc and shambles of that deliberate, methodical destruction was the remarkable story of the Hebrew viceroy of Egypt named Joseph. Today the only suggestion of the influence of this Biblical personality is to be found in the name of the ancient canal at Medinet-el-Faiyum lying 80 miles south of Cairo. This artificial canal is over 200 miles long and carried the water of the Nile into a district which became extolled as the "Venice of Egypt." Dr. Keller states that, "In the lush gardens of this flourishing oasis grew oranges, mandarins, peaches, olives, pomegranates, and grapes."[45] To this day the ancient waterway which made all of this possible is known as "Bahr Yusuf"—"Joseph's Canal."[46]

However, the details of the life of Joseph cannot be found in Egypt. The monuments which once upon a time undoubtedly told his story have probably been lost forever. Only in the sacred writings of the Hebrews is there any original source material concerning him.

JOSEPH'S CAREER COMMENCES IN EGYPT

When Joseph was carried down into Egypt by the Ishmaelites, they sold him to one of the king's officials named Potiphar.[47] The English Bible describes Potiphar as "captain of the guard,"[48] but the original Hebrew text calls him "Chief of the butchers," meaning that he was the head of the Pharaoh's elite guard which summarily took life or spared it according to the whims of the despotic ruler of this rich land.[49]

---

44. Werner Keller, *The Bible As History*, p. 86, ". . . they discovered neither documents nor monuments out of this whole period. The records which showed hardly a break for centuries suddenly stopped 1730 BC. From then on for a long time an impenetrable darkness lay over Egypt. Not before 1580 B.C. did contemporray evidence appear once again."
45. Ibid., p. 90
46. Ibid.
47. Genesis 39:1
48. Ibid.
49. Clarke's *Bible Commentary*, Vol. 1, p. 221

At first Joseph was just a house-boy, but as time went on "his master saw that the Lord was with him, and that the Lord made all that he did to prosper in his hand."[50]

Potiphar had extensive possessions, not only a wealthy home with slaves and servants, but fields requiring supervision and cultivation. Gradually young Joseph's responsibilities were increased until he became superintendent of Potiphar's entire estate:

"And Joseph found grace in his sight, and he served him: and he made him overseer over his house, and all that he had he put into his hand . . . and the blessing of the Lord was upon all that he had in the house, and in the field."[51]

Not only did Potiphar make Joseph his general superintendent and overseer, but he came to trust him so implicitly that he did not even keep accounts and inventories any more but "left all that he had in Joseph's hand; and he knew not ought he had, save the bread which he did eat."[52]

POTIPHAR'S WIFE SEEKS TO SEDUCE JOSEPH

As Joseph gained full maturity the Hebrew text says he became "beautiful in his person, and beautiful in his countenance."[53] This attractive personal appearance of Joseph became traditional so that down through the centuries the writers of the Middle East created some of their most eloquent literature on this one subject.[54] In fact, the entire twelfth chapter of the *Koran* is devoted to the beauty, piety, and admirable personality traits of Joseph.

It is no wonder, therefore, that in a culture where morals were preached but brazenly violated, Joseph would become the amorous target of some voluptuous and infatuated Egyptian woman. It turned out to be about the most dangerous woman Joseph could have encountered—the wife of Potiphar, "chief of the butchers."

50. Genesis 39:3
51. Genesis 39:4-5
52. Genesis 39:6
53. Clarke's *Bible Commentary*, Vol. 1, p. 226
54. Ibid. pp. 226-227

"And it came to pass . . . that his master's wife cast her eyes upon Joseph; and she said, Lie with me. But he refused, and said unto his master's wife, Behold, my master wotteth not what is with me in the house, and he hath committed all that he hath to my hand; There is none greater in this house than I; neither hath he kept back any thing from me but thee, because thou art his wife: how then can I do this great wickedness, and sin against God?"[55]

But the wife of Potiphar was persistent. Joseph's virtue and integrity made him all the more alluring to her. Day after day she made romantic advances toward him, but without success.[56]

Finally one day she saw an opportunity to compromise Joseph. "And it came to pass about this time, that Joseph went into the house to do his business; and there was none of the men of the house there within. And she caught him by his garment, saying, Lie with me: and he left his garment in her hand, and fled, and got him out."[57]

The poets have said there is no anger so hot as that of a woman repulsed. Joseph found it so with this woman. Having tried to impose her attentions on Joseph by physical force and being left empty handed with nothing but his cloak, her rage knew no bounds. So she resolved to make believe the situation had been reversed and that it was Joseph who had tried to force his attentions on her. Since she could not trap him romantically, she would destroy him.

"And it came to pass, when she saw that he had left his garment in her hand, and was fled forth, that she called unto the men of her house, and spake unto them, saying, See, he hath brought in an Hebrew unto us to mock us; he came in unto me to lie with me, and I cried with a loud voice: And it came to pass, when he heard that I lifted up my voice and cried, that he left his garment with me, and fled, and got him out."[58]

Having established this alleged outrage with the house servants, this seditious woman waited the return of her

---

55. Genesis 39:7-9
56. Genesis 39:10

57. Genesis 39:11-12
58. Genesis 39:13-15

husband. "And she laid up his garment by her, until his lord came home. And she spake unto him according to these words, saying, The Hebrew servant, which thou hast brought unto us, came in unto me to mock me: and it came to pass as I lifted up my voice and cried, that he left his garment with me and fled out."[59]

To all of this Potiphar reacted about the way his wife had expected. After all the trust and authority Potiphar had showered upon this slave, such treachery was monstrous. The scripture says Potiphar's "wrath was kindled," and no doubt he would have killed Joseph had not this most uncommon slave established such an affection and confidence in Potiphar's heart. Therefore Potiphar had Joseph seized and thrown "into the prison, a place where the king's prisoners were bound. . . ."[60]

JOSEPH IN PRISON

The word used for "prison" in the original Hebrew text actually means "round house."[61] We learn later that it was built with administrative quarters above ground for those in charge while prisoners were confined below the ground in a dungeon. Joseph specifically refers to the fact that his quarters were in the dungeon.[62]

But even here Joseph soon gained the confidence of the warden or officer in charge and this improved his circumstances considerably. All his life, Joseph seems to have had a superior sense of service and accommodation. He was always surprising his superiors with greater capacity and efficiency than they expected. As a result he gained special blessings and advantages which would have otherwise been denied him.

Before long the scripture says, "And the keeper of the prison committed to Joseph's hand all the prisoners that were in the prison: and whatsoever they did there, he was the doer of it. The keeper of the prison looked not to any thing that was under his hand; because the Lord was with him, and that which he did, the Lord made it to prosper."[63]

---

59. Genesis 39:16-18
60. Genesis 39:20
61. Clarke's *Bible Commentary*, Vol. 1, p. 227
62. Genesis 40:15
63. Genesis 39:22-23

It seems that this particular prison was used primarily for the Pharaoh's servants or workmen who had offended him. The Pharaoh had authority to exercise the power of life or death over anyone in his realm, and more especially those who personally served him. As a result, two of the people in prison with Joseph were servants of the king who had offended him and were waiting for the decision of the Pharaoh as to what should become of them. One of these was Pharaoh's chief butler who served the king's table, and the other was the Pharaoh's chief baker.

It was customary for the Pharaoh to require his personal servants to be selected from among the most illustrious families of the land.[64] It is likely, therefore, that the chief butler and chief baker were no ordinary slaves or servants. This is borne out by the fact that when Joseph was cast into the dungeon, he was assigned by Potiphar to serve these two prisoners.[65]

JOSEPH GAINS A REPUTATION FOR INTERPRETING DREAMS

One day Joseph came to the quarters of the butler and baker and found them both perplexed and sad. They had each experienced a strange kind of dream. Each said his dream was so vivid and left such a profound impression that he felt it might be some kind of omen of the future. However, each dream was so obscure that neither the butler nor baker had any idea what the meaning of his dream might be, hence their perplexity.

When they related this problem to Joseph he said, "Do not interpretations belong to God? tell me them [the dreams] I pray you."[66]

So they began to relate their dreams. The chief butler said he saw a vine with three branches and upon the branches grapes grew. The Butler said that in the dream he took the grapes and used them to make juice for the Pharaoh's cup and that he gave the cup to Pharaoh to drink.[67]

"And Joseph said unto him, This is the interpretation of it: the three branches are three days: yet within three days

---

64. Clarke's *Bible Commentary*, Vol. 1, p. 228
65. Genesis 40:4
66. Genesis 40:8
67. Genesis 40:9-11

shall Pharaoh lift up thine head, and restore thee unto thy place: and thou shalt deliver Pharaoh's cup into his hand, after the former manner when thou wast his butler."[68]

Joseph could not have known the meaning of this dream any better than the butler had not the Lord revealed it to him, but once Joseph knew what was going to happen to the butler he saw an opportunity to take advantage of the situation. Joseph said to the butler, "But think on me when it shall be well with thee, and shew kindness, I pray thee, unto me, and make mention of me unto Pharaoh, and bring me out of this house: for indeed I was stolen away out of the land of the Hebrews: and here also have I done nothing that they should put me into the dungeon."[69]

Now the chief baker demanded to have his dream interpreted. The baker said he had seen himself with 3 white baskets on his head. The top basket was filled with a variety of delicious baked goods for the Pharaoh, but before the baker could deliver them they were devoured by a flock of birds.

"And Joseph answered and said, This is the interpretation thereof: the three baskets are three days: yet within three days shall Pharaoh lift up thy head from off thee, and shall hang thee on a tree; and the birds shall eat thy flesh from off thee."[70]

It was significant that both the butler and the baker had but three days to wait in order to discover whether Joseph was an inspired seer or merely a self-appointed phoney soothsayer. No doubt the hapless baker hoped he would turn out to be the latter.

It was further significant that the "third day" was the Pharaoh's birthday on which he planned to have a great feast for all his household.[71] Incidental thereto the Pharaoh intended to dispose of the case of the chief butler and the chief baker. Therefore he "lifted up" these men from their prison cells and had them brought before him. No doubt all the household of the king waited anxiously to see what would become of their former associates. And just as Joseph had

---

68. Genesis 40:12-13
69. Genesis 40:14-15

70. Genesis 40:18-19
71. Genesis 40:20

predicted so it came to pass. The chief baker was found guilty and sentenced to death. If the customary procedure were followed it would mean that the baker was beheaded by Potiphar, the "chief of the butchers," and then hung from a tree by his hands or by hooks.[72] As for the chief butler, he was either found innocent or was forgiven. Just as Joseph had predicted, he was allowed to return to the side of the Pharaoh and serve once more as the king's proud cup-bearer.[73]

All of this should have meant good news for Joseph, but nothing changed. The butler was supposed to have brought Joseph's predicament to the attention of Pharaoh and to have told him how Joseph had been kidnapped "out of the land of the Hebrews," and sold into slavery. He was also supposed to have pleaded Joseph's innocence and pointed out that the young Hebrew had done nothing to warrant confinement in the miserable dungeon of the round house. Obviously, a word from the powerful Pharaoh and Joseph could be free, but the scripture says:

"Yet did not the chief butler remember Joseph, but forgat him."[74]

Joseph Finally Comes to the Attention of Pharaoh

Joseph was forgotten for two whole years![75] The wretched months must have dragged slowly. He must have been thoroughly aware of what could happen. Under the despotic rule of those days an innocent person could be left to rot in one of Pharaoh's filthy prisons. Under such circumstances only the ravages of time and the debilitating tentacles of disease could release a prisoner from the misery of his dungeon life through the liberation of a merciful death. Was this to be the fate of Joseph?

One night Pharaoh had two dreams. Both dreams were so ominous and irrational that they deeply disturbed him. He therefore called in his magicians and professional holy men to see if they could detect any special significance in these strange night visions. The magicians were masters in the

---

72. Clarke, *Bible Commentary*, Vol. 1, p. 230   74. Genesis 40:23
73. Genesis 40:21   75. Genesis 41:1

secret cult of wonder workers who not only entertained with their tricks but used these mysterious and fascinating talents to gain influence over the people, including the king. On the other hand, the "wise men" or professional holy men were the classical scholars of the day. "Contemplation of the stars, self purification, arithmetic and geometry, and singing hymns in honour of their gods, was their continual employment."[76]

But after listening to the king's dreams neither the magicians nor the professional wise men dared risk a guess as to their meaning.

It was then that the Pharaoh's chief butler suddenly thought of the young Hebrew in the king's prison. *He* could interpret dreams! A guilty feeling swept over him as he painfully recalled that this young man had been depending on the butler to plead his case with the Pharaoh.

"Then spake the chief butler unto Pharaoh, saying, I do remember my faults this day."[77] He immediately told the Pharaoh all about the remarkable talent which Joseph possessed to interpret dreams. He related the events which he and the king's baker had witnessed two years earlier when Joseph had told them both what would happen in three days. "And it came to pass, as he interpreted to us, so it was. . . ." concluded the butler.[78]

That was enough for the Pharaoh. He sent for the Hebrew in the dungeon.

It must have been like sighting a welcomed port in the storm of life when Joseph finally heard the tremendous news that Pharaoh wanted to see him. At last he would be able to plead his case. Of course, the filthy dungeon had made Joseph unfit to appear before the king so the Pharaoh's servants "brought him hastily out of the dungeon: and he shaved himself and changed his raiment, and came in unto the Pharaoh."[79]

It is difficult to imagine the feelings of this future heir to the house of Jacob as he came out from the stench and darkness of his prison and gazed about at the flowers, shrubs and

76. Clarke, *Bible Commentary*, Vol. 1, p. 231   78. Genesis 41:13
77. Genesis 41:9   79. Genesis 41:14

trees, the radiant sunshine, and the bustling activity of the Pharaoh's palace as he was ushered along its corridors. After two miserable years what a relief it must have been to be once more above ground, to be clean again, and to be dressed in decent clothes.

JOSEPH IN THE PRESENCE OF PHARAOH

As Joseph was ushered into the king's presence it must have created curious feelings in the heart of this Pharaoh. Could this young Hebrew actually decipher dreams? Though Pharaoh did not know it, he was looking into the face of the most important person he would ever meet in his entire life.

"And Pharaoh said unto Joseph, I have dreamed a dream, and there is none that can interpret it: and I have heard say of thee, that thou canst understand a dream to interpret it."[80]

Unless Joseph had been advised of this in advance, the Pharaoh's request must have come as a great surprise. It meant that Joseph had not been brought out to plead his case at all. He had been released from the dungeon merely to interpret a dream. And Joseph knew that this would be impossible unless the Lord would give him a direct revelation. So he said to the Pharaoh, "It [i.e., the power to interpret dreams] is not in me." Then, before Pharaoh could register anger or disappointment, Joseph quickly added, "God shall give Pharaoh an answer of peace."[81]

Very well, so be it. Pharaoh began to recite his dream.

"In my dream," he said, "behold, I stood upon the bank of the river: and, behold, there came up out of the river seven kine, fatfleshed and well favoured; and they fed in a meadow: and, behold, seven other kine came up after them, poor and very ill favoured and leanfleshed, such as I never saw in all the land of Egypt for badness: and the lean and the ill favoured kine did eat up the first seven fat kine."[82]

Then Pharaoh said he had another dream but this time he saw ears of corn instead of cows. Nevertheless, as in the

---

80. Genesis 41:15   82. Genesis 41:17-20
81. Genesis 41:16

previous dream, seven lean, wind-withered ears devoured seven fat, fully developed ears.

As Joseph listened intently to Pharaoh's recitation, the word of the Lord came to him. This revelation disclosed that Pharaoh's troublesome night visions were not merely the casual consequences of indigestion or restless slumber. Both dreams were planted in the king's mind by the Lord and were intended to reveal to Pharaoh an important message. Therefore, as Pharaoh completed his speech, Joseph was ready to tell him with the utmost confidence, "God hath shewed Pharaoh what he is about to do."[83]

Joseph explained that both dreams were intended to convey the same warning. Then he gave the interpretation. "Behold, there come seven years of great plenty throughout all the land of Egypt: and there shall arise after them seven years of famine; and all the plenty shall be forgotten in the land of Egypt; and the famine shall consume the land; and the plenty shall not be known in the land by reason of that famine following; for it shall be very grievous. And for that the dream was doubled unto Pharaoh twice; it is because the thing is established by God, and God will shortly bring it to pass."[84]

Joseph Makes a Proposal Which Produces Astonishing Consequences

With the revelations of God permeating his whole being, Joseph was no longer speaking as a prisoner or slave but as a prophet of God. He exhibited no hesitation whatever as he interpreted the king's dream and he was equally confident as he stepped forward to suggest to Pharaoh the steps he should take to avert the great calamity which was sweeping down on Egypt. Said he:

"Now therefore let Pharaoh look out a man discreet and wise, and set him over the land of Egypt. Let Pharaoh do this, and let him appoint officers over the land, and take up the fifth part [of the harvest] of the land of Egypt in the seven plenteous years. And let them gather all the food of

---

83. Genesis 41:25   84. Genesis 41:29-32

those good years that come, and lay up corn under the hand of Pharaoh, and let them keep food in the cities. And that food shall be for store to the land against the seven years of famine, which shall be in the land of Egypt; that the land perish not through the famine."[85]

Pharaoh was inspired and fascinated as he listened to this magnificent young Hebrew who had sweltered so long in the cavernous labyrinths of the king's own dungeon. Here was a man, barely 30 years old,[86] who had brilliant revelations direct from God, who could interpret incomprehensible dreams, who had offered the Pharaoh administrative remedies as great as the calamities he predicted. As the Pharaoh looked around he could see that his servants were equally impressed.[87]

Very well, so Joseph had recommended that the Pharaoh appoint a man "discreet and wise" to put in charge "over all the land of Egypt." Pharaoh knew exactly what he would do. Turning to all his servants and assistants he challenged them with this question: "Can we find such a one as this is, a man in whom the Spirit of God is?"[88]

Turning to the young Hebrew bond servant, Pharaoh made this royal proclamation:

"Joseph, Forasmuch as God hath shewed thee all this, there is none so discreet and wise as thou art: thou shalt be over my house, and according unto thy word shall all my people be ruled: only in the throne will I be greater than thou. . . . See, I have set thee over all the land of Egypt."[89]

It was a miracle. In a single day, Joseph, the eleventh son of Jacob, had gone from a woe-begotten dungeon slave to the prime minister of all Egypt!

85. Genesis 41:33-36
86. Genesis 41:46
87. Genesis 41:37

88. Genesis 41:38
89. Genesis 41:39-41

Scripture Reading and Questions on Chapter Five

Scripture Reading Assignment: Genesis, chapters 36 to 37 and 39 to 41.

1—Where was Joseph born? About how old was he when his mother died? How old was he when he began receiving the gift of seership?

2—What was Joseph's first inspired dream? What was the second? Why did the second dream offend his father?

3—Where was Joseph when his brothers seized him with intent to kill him?

4—Who pleaded that his life be spared? Did he consent to have Joseph thrown into the pit? Then what did he intend to do?

5—Who suggested selling Joseph to a caravan of Ishmaelites? But who actually discovered Joseph in the pit and did the selling?

6—Who did Joseph think sold him into slavery?

7—What was Reuben's reaction when he found Joseph gone?

8—What did the brothers decide to tell their father? What was Jacob's reaction when they did tell him?

9—What fortunate political upheaval took place in Egypt just before Joseph arrived there?

10—How do archaeologists account for the lack of any reference to Joseph in Egyptian histories or on Egyptian monuments?

11—How completely did Potiphar trust Joseph?

12—What caused him to throw Joseph in the king's prison house? What assignment did Joseph get? Was he above ground or in the dungeon?

13—What was the dream of the chief butler? What was the dream of the chief baker?

14—What did Joseph say each dream meant? Did it come to pass?

15—How did Joseph expect that his interpretation of the butler's dream might help get him released from the prison? How much longer did he have to stay in prison?

16—How did he come to the attention of the Pharaoh? How old was he by this time?

17—What were the Pharaoh's two dreams? What did Joseph say they meant?

18—What did Joseph tell the Pharaoh to do?

19—What did the Pharaoh say to his officers? Did they object?

20—What did the Pharaoh say to Joseph? Did he object?

CHAPTER SIX

Joseph -- Prime Minister of All Egypt

Had there been fast communications or newspapers around 1,741 B.C., the news would have been flashed to every corner of the civilized world that a sensational political upheaval had taken place in Egypt. The Pharaoh had turned over the entire government of Egypt to a newly liberated bond servant. A Hebrew!

Such news would have flown through the commercial centers of the big cities and eventually filtered out into the sheep camps and villages of the Great Crescent. Eventually, it would have reached Hebron. There it would have found the aging Jacob in continuous mourning, not only for Joseph whom he believed to be dead, but also for Isaac who had died just the year before.[1] What a tidal wave of joy it would have brought to the sorrowing father of Joseph if he had known that his son was not only alive but had just been promoted to vice-regent or prime minister of one of the world's most powerful potentates.

As it was, however, the blind misery of death and despair hung heavy over Hebron. There was no hope, no thrilling challenge, no prospect of joy. Only the awesome reality of growing old in the shadows of Machpelah, cave of the family tombs. From one source alone did the saddened Jacob find comfort. That was from Benjamin, his youngest son, now around 23 years of age, who had been motherless from the time of his birth. Events were shaping up, however, which would threaten to take even Benjamin away from him.

---

1. This calculation is determined by the following facts. Isaac was 60 when Jacob was born. (Gen. 25:26) Jacob was 91 when Joseph was born. (See note 96, chapter 3) Joseph was 30 when he was made prime minister (Gen. 41:46) These total 181 years. Since Isaac died at age 180 (Gen. 35:28) he would have died the year before Joseph became prime minister.

JOSEPH GETS A NEW NAME AND A NEW BRIDE

When Pharaoh made Joseph his prime minister, there was no doubt about the impression Pharaoh intended to make upon his own people. "And Pharaoh took off his ring from his hand, and put it upon Joseph's hand, and arrayed him in vestures of fine linen, and put a gold chain about his neck; And he made him to ride in the second chariot which he had; and they cried before him, Bow the knee: and he made him ruler over all the land of Egypt."[2]

The totalitarian power of the Pharaoh was also shared with Joseph. He told Joseph that henceforth "shall no man lift up his hand or his foot in all the land of Egypt," if Joseph objected.[3]

Pharaoh also gave Joseph a new name with profound mystical meaning which was a popular device among the Egyptians. Joseph was called Zaphnath-paaneah, which is believed to have meant "The Revealer of Secrets."[4]

At the time these marvelous developments occurred, Joseph was 30 years of age.[5] It was time he got married. For this purpose, Pharaoh chose for Joseph the beautiful daughter of the priest of On. The priest's name was Poti-pherah (no relation to Potiphar, chief of the butchers,) and his beautiful daughter was named Asenath.[6] The city of On where Asenath had been living, is better known by its Greek name, Heliopolis, or "City of the Sun." It was located just below the point of the Delta, and about 20 miles northeast of Memphis. This city was famous for its priestly scholars who worshipped the sun. No doubt Poti-pherah was one of these. Some 1,400 years later Plato went to On and studied under the scholars of that day.

In front of the city of On were erected two majestic monoliths of marble called obelisks. Augustus Ceasar took them to Alexandria about 23 A.D. and from there they were taken away to embellish the modern world. One of these now stands on the Thames embankment in London and the other is in Central Park, New York City.

2. Genesis 41:42-43
3. Genesis 41:44
4. Clarke's *Bible Commentary*, Vol. 1, p. 235
5. Genesis 41:46
6. Genesis 41:45

There is reason to believe that Joseph's new bride had an exciting biography in her own right, but the Bible does not provide it. As we have already mentioned, the ruling class of Egypt at this time were Semitic peoples from the Penninsula of Arabia who had swept in from the desert and conquered the native Hamitic Egyptians. The wife of Joseph was probably of this Semitic nation which at this time made up the aristocratic class of Egypt. Joseph therefore had the double task of not only gaining the love and confidence of his new bride, but also teaching her the fulness of the gospel.

THE SEVEN YEARS OF PLENTY

With his honeymoon over, Joseph set to work. It says, "And Joseph went out from the presence of Pharaoh, and went throughout all the land of Egypt."[7] We later learn that he constructed vast storage depots or granaries in every city. He then filled them with the double-tithe (described as "one-fifth"—Gen. 41:34) of the harvest which the Pharaoh had authorized him to store each year. Joseph's prophecy of seven abundant years followed by seven years of famine may have been known among the people, but if it did the people took no heed of it. Among themselves they made no preparations for the famine but lived it up to the hilt as long as the years of plenty lasted. Had not Joseph followed out the inspired "welfare plan" of that day, hundreds of thousands of people undoubtedly would have died from starvation.

The flow of "corn" into the granaries built by Joseph reached such a flood tide that it was "as the sand of the sea, very much, until he left numbering; for it was without number."[8]

TWO SONS ARE BORN TO JOSEPH

During the period of prosperity and plenty, Joseph had two sons born to him. The firstborn was named Manasseh (forgetfulness) because Joseph said, "God . . . hath made me forget all my toil, and all my father's house."[9] This is a highly significant comment.

---

7. Genesis 41:46
8. Genesis 41:49
9. Genesis 41:51

It meant that the thirteen years of slavery which Joseph had endured plus the vivid recollection of the plot of his brothers to murder him, had all left a dark and ugly memory in the mind of Joseph. That is why the arrival of a new son was such a pleasant distraction. It made him forget all the hate, envy and malice of those elder brothers. Later we see that he had not forgotten his father nor his younger brother, Benjamin, both of whom he continued to hold in the deepest affection.

Joseph's second son was named Ephraim (fruitful) because Joseph said, "God had caused me to be fruitful in the land of my affliction."[10]

These are the only children ever born to Joseph insofar as we know. It was out of these two that God would raise up some of the choicest leadership for His entire kingdom and create one of the largest tribal populations in all Israel.[11]

Ephraim appears to have been born just before the famine struck. Immediately following a description of his birth, the scripture says: "And the seven years of plenteousness, that was in the land of Egypt, were ended. And the seven years of dearth began."[12]

THE FAMINE COMMENCES

All that is necessary to create a famine in Egypt is to have the rains fail up around the headwaters of the Nile. This prevents the annual inundation of the farm lands on each side of the Nile where the river ordinarily deposits its rich silt collections. It also forces the water level of the Nile down to a point where even the irrigation canals cease to function. In the deserts of Egypt the absence of rain is of little significance, but when there is a failure of the rains at the headwaters of the Nile, the river itself seems to lose its life.

But it seemed deeply significant that the famine on this occasion was not confined to Egypt. The scripture says the whole Mediterranean basin was devastated "because that the famine was so sore in all lands." Therefore, "all countries came into Egypt to Joseph to buy corn."[13]

---

10. Genesis 41:52
11. Numbers, Chapter 1

12. Genesis 41:53
13. Genesis 41:57

A seven-year famine is a desperate contest for survival; therefore Joseph did not give away the grain lest it be wasted. He sold it in carefully supervised amounts. In all of these arrangements, the Pharaoh required the people to submit completely to Joseph's judgment. At the beginning they had gone to the Pharaoh pleading for foodstuffs, but he had said, "Go unto Joseph; what he saith to you, do."[14]

Not only Egyptians but even foreigners were required to go to Joseph or his officers in order to buy grain. It was by this means that the Lord now brought to pass his own beneficent designs.

Truth is Stranger than Fiction

The scripture gives us no explanation as to why Joseph had made no attempt to contact his family during the seven years of plenty, especially since he was serving as the governor of all Egypt. It is plain, however, that he did not do so. Neither he nor they had any idea what had happened during the twenty years which had intervened since that dark day of doom when Joseph had disappeared from the pit in the wilderness.

But after the famine had been in progress for approximately a year and Joseph's people at Hebron had practically consumed all of their food, Jacob learned that there was grain to be had in Egypt He immediately dispatched all ten of his older sons to Egypt for the purpose of exchanging some of the family gold and silver for grain. Only Benjamin was required to stay behind "lest peradventure mischief befall him."[15]

It would appear that Joseph personally supervised purchase by foreigners; at least he supervised the sale of grain to the men from Hebron. And as they came forward, he suddenly recognized them as his brethren. It must have been a shock to see them actually standing before him after all those years. However, instead of throwing his arms around them and revealing that he was still alive, he chose a different tactic. Obviously they did not recognize their former 17-year-old brother who had now reached the age of 38. Joseph

---

14. Genesis 41:55   15. Genesis 42:4

did two strange things. First, he spoke to them through a translator[16] even though he knew perfectly well every single word they said. Secondly he accused them of being spies![17]

They pleaded with Joseph. They were not spies, they said, but hungry men from Canaan. To further persuade him, they began reciting all about themselves, that they were ten brothers and that there were two other brothers, but one was home with their father and the other "is not."[18]

Very well, the governor of Egypt would prove them. He said one of them could go back and get their younger brother to prove they were not lying. Meanwhile they would be held hostages in prison. Joseph thereupon had all of his ten brothers taken into custody for three days. At the end of the three days he went to them with a proposition. He declared through a translator that nine of the brothers could return but one must stay behind as a hostage. He also said they could take grain for their families to last them for the time being.[19]

As these hardened nomads from Canaan contemplated their critical predicament they began to wonder why God would deal with them in such a manner. They knew their father was a prophet of God and a patriarch of the covenant. Now that they had fulfilled his commandment to come into Egypt to buy grain they were in all kinds of trouble. They began to wonder if perhaps this was the retribution of God for what they had done to their younger brother, Joseph, many years ago. As their conversation centered around their past offense, Reuben chastised them by reminding them that it was he who had pled for Joseph's life: "And Reuben answered them, saying, Spake I not unto you, saying, Do not sin against the child; and ye would not hear? therefore, behold, also his blood is required."[20]

Then the scripture says:

"And they knew not that Joseph understood them; for he spake unto them by an interpreter. And he turned himself about from them, and wept; and returned to them again and

---

16. Genesis 42:23
17. Genesis 42:9
18. Genesis 42:13

19. Genesis 42:15-20
20. Genesis 42:22

communed with them, and took from them Simeon, and bound him before their eyes."[21]

Then Joseph told his officers to fill the grain sacks of the men from Hebron and to put their money in with the grain. This was done and the nine brothers departed. Enroute home, they discovered the money in their grain sacks. They couldn't figure it out. What was happening?

When Jacob's nine sons finally reached home they told their father everything that had happened. Jacob was outraged. He appreciated the grain, but obviously they had made fools of themselves. What kind of bargaining was this? "And Jacob their father said unto them, Me have ye bereaved of my children: Joseph is not, and Simeon is not, and ye will take Benjamin away: all these things are against me."[22]

Reuben tried to reassure his father saying, "Slay my two sons, if I bring him [Benjamin] not to thee: deliver him unto my hand, and I will bring him to thee again." But Jacob said, "My son shall not go down with you; for his brother is dead, and he is left alone: if mischief befall him by the way in the which ye go, then shall ye bring down my gray hairs with sorrow to the grave."[23]

THE RETURN OF JOSEPH'S BROTHERS TO EGYPT

It was only when "they had eaten up the corn which they had brought out of Egypt" and starvation faced the settlement once more that Father Jacob finally capitulated and agreed to let Benjamin go with his brothers to get additional supplies and secure the freedom of Simeon. It was a weary and broken Jacob who sent them away saying, "If I be bereaved of my children, I am bereaved."[24]

When the caravan of ten brothers (which now included Benjamin) reached the capital city of Egypt they once more sought out Joseph. But he did not deal with them personally. Instead, Joseph's steward took them to Joseph's home.[25] This frightened the brothers. They interpreted this to mean they were going to become bonded servants for not paying for the grain on their first trip.[26]

---

21. Genesis 42:23-24   24. Genesis 43:14
22. Genesis 42:36   25. Genesis 43:17
23. Genesis 42:38   26. Genesis 43:18

They took the steward into their confidence and pleaded with him not to condemn them for failing to pay for the first grain because they did not know how the money got back into their sacks. The steward reassured them: "Peace be to you, fear not: your God, and the God of your father, hath given you treasure in your sacks: I had your money."[27] The brothers were perplexed. What did this mean? Shortly thereafter Simeon was brought out to them.

Now the eleven brothers prepared to meet Joseph. Their father had sent a gift for the Egyptian governor and when Joseph came in they "bowed themselves" clear to the ground and presented it to him.[28]

JOSEPH AND YOUNG BENJAMIN MEET

Joseph no longer "spoke roughly" to them. Instead, this is what the scripture says: "And he asked them of their welfare, and said, is your father well, the old man of whom ye spake? Is he yet alive? And they answered, Thy servant our father is in good health, he is yet alive. And they bowed down their heads, and made obeisance. And he lifted up his eyes, and saw his brother Benjamin, his mother's son, and said, Is this your younger brother, of whom ye spake unto me? And he said, God be gracious unto thee, my son. And Joseph made haste; for his bowels did yearn upon his brother: and he sought where to weep; and he entered into his chamber, and wept there. And he washed his face and went out, and refrained himself, and said, Set on bread."[29]

Not only were the brothers astonished to be invited to eat with Joseph but something else puzzled them. When he sat them down around the table Joseph put each man in his own position according to his age or birthright."[30] How did he know their ages? ". . . the men marvelled one at another."[31]

During the meal the brothers noticed that when the Egyptian governor dished up the food, Benjamin received far bigger helpings than they. However, it didn't spoil their appetites. They ate and drank and "were merry" with the

---

27. Genesis 43:23
28. Genesis 43:26
29. Genesis 43:27-31

30. Genesis 43:33
31. Ibid.

governor.[32] They must have felt exuberant with joy as they saw how well everything was working out for them.

JOSEPH'S BRETHREN DEPART AND ARE ENSNARED

So once again the caravan of the men from Canaan was loaded with grain, and once again Joseph's steward put the money in the mouth of each man's sack. In addition, Joseph told his steward to put Joseph's silver cup in Benjamin's sack.[33]

Early next morning the caravan departed but it had barely gotten beyond the city limits when Joseph's steward overtook them. He said one of them had stolen the Egyptian governor's silver cup. The eleven brothers, who but a moment ago could scarcely believe their good fortune, could now scarcely contain their dismay. They assured the steward they had not stolen the cup. Said they, "With whomsoever of thy servants it be found, both let him die, and we also will be my lord's bondmen [slaves]."[34] So the sacks were searched and to the utter disbelief of the ten brothers, young Benjamin was found to be guilty of having the cup. The brothers tore their clothes in anguish and all went back to Joseph's house with the steward. When they came before Joseph "they fell before him on the ground."[35]

"And Judah said, What shall we say unto my lord? what shall we speak? or how shall we clear ourselves? God hath found out the iniquity of thy servants: behold, we are my lord's servants, both we, and he also with whom the cup is found."[36]

Joseph said it would be sufficient for Benjamin to remain behind. The rest could go. The brothers did not move. The prospect of facing Father Jacob without Benjamin was impossible. In the greatest humility, Judah stepped forward and said: "O my lord, let thy servant, I pray thee, speak a word in my lord's ears, and let not thine anger burn against thy servant: for thou art even as Pharaoh."[37]

---

32. Genesis 43:34
33. Genesis 44:1-2
34. Genesis 44:9
35. Genesis 44:14
36. Genesis 44:16
37. Genesis 44:18

Judah then said that Benjamin was the child of his father's old age and the best beloved of all his children who yet remained alive.

"Now therefore when I come to thy servant my father, and the lad be not with us; seeing that his life is bound up in the lad's life; It shall come to pass, when he seeth that the lad is not with us, that he will die: and thy servants shall bring down the gray hairs of thy servant our father with sorrow to the grave."[38]

As a final supplication Judah said: "Now therefore, I pray thee, let thy servant abide instead of the lad a bondman to my lord; and let the lad go up with his brethren. For how shall I go up to my father, and the lad be not with me? lest peradventure I see the evil that shall come on my father."[39]

JOSEPH "RETURNS FROM THE DEAD"

Judah's overwhelming grief and supplication induced Joseph to change his plan.

He was apparently intending to keep his identity hidden for some time yet. Perhaps he hoped that by keeping Benjamin in Egypt, his beloved father would come down to get him. But whatever the strategy, Joseph now abandoned it.

Suddenly he ordered all of the Egyptians from the room. When they were gone and he was alone with his brothers, he looked into their faces and prepared to tell them who he was. But the flood dikes of emotion broke within him. All the pent up loneliness of being separated from his family for a quarter of a century flooded to the surface and broke his composure. In an instant he ceased to be the all-powerful governor of Egypt and was once again just Joseph, their younger brother. There is something strange and profound when a strong man weeps. The scripture says, "he wept aloud: and the Egyptians and the house of Pharaoh heard."[40]

But Joseph was unashamed. Before him stood his own flesh and blood, more important to him than the whole kingdom of Egypt. He said, "I am Joseph."[41]

---

38. Genesis 44:30-31
39. Genesis 44:33-34

40. Genesis 45:2
41. Genesis 45:3

The eleven brothers stood petrified. They had been surprised when he started to weep but what he now said to them defied all rational comprehension. He was out of his senses!

"And Joseph said unto his brethren, Come near to me, I pray you . . . I am Joseph your brother, whom ye sold into Egypt. Now therefore be not grieved, nor angry with yourselves, that ye sold me hither, for God did send me before you to preserve life.

"For these two years hath the famine been in the land: and yet there are five years, in the which there shall neither be earing nor harvest.

"And God sent me before you to preserve you a posterity in the earth, and to save your lives by a great deliverance.

"So now it was not you that sent me hither, but God: and he hath made me a father to Pharaoh, and lord of all his house, and a ruler throughout all the land of Egypt.

"Haste ye, and go up to my father, and say unto him, Thus saith thy son Joseph, God hath made me Lord of all Egypt: come down unto me, tarry not:

"And thou shalt dwell in the land of Goshen, and thou shalt be near unto me, thou, and thy children, and thy children's children, and thy flocks, and thy herds, and all that thou hast:

"And there will I nourish thee; for yet there are five years of famine; lest thou, and thy household, and all that thou hast, come to poverty.

"And, behold, your eyes see, and the eyes of my brother Benjamin, that it is my mouth that speaketh unto you.

"And ye shall tell my father of all my glory in Egypt, and of all that ye have seen; and ye shall haste and bring down my father hither."[42]

Having now revealed himself, Joseph embraced each of his brothers, starting with Benjamin. As the reality of this reunion touched the heart of this youngest brother he could not keep back the flood of tears himself. Both he and Joseph

---

42. Genesis 45:5-13

wept together as they held each other briefly and a rapture of unspeakable love seemed to cry out within them. It seemed to weld these two sons of Rachel into a sacred bond of spiritual oneness.

Then the record says:

'Moreover he kissed all his brethren, and wept upon them: and after that his brethren talked with him.''[43]

And what a lifetime of information there was to exchange; about Jacob and all the family's affairs at Hebron; the death of Grandfather Isaac, Joseph's 13 years of slavery, the dreams of the baker, the butler, and the Pharaoh; Joseph's nine years as governor of Egypt, his marriage to Asenath, the birth of Manasseh and Ephraim.

REACTION OF THE PHARAOH

All this excitement was magnificent news to be chanted from mouth to mouth, through every hall and chamber of the Pharaoh's palace. "Joseph's brethren are come!"[44]

The respect and admiration of the Pharaoh for Joseph is never more apparent than is found in his reaction to this news about Joseph's brethren. Not only was the Pharaoh pleased, but here is what he told Joseph to tell his brothers:

"Say unto thy brethren, this do ye, lade your beasts, and go, get you unto the land of Canaan; And take your father and your households, and come unto me: and I will give you the good of the land of Egypt, and ye shall eat the fat of the land. Now thou art commanded, this do ye; take you wagons out of the land of Egypt for your little ones, and for your wives, and bring your father, and come. Also regard not your stuff; for the good of all the land of Egypt is yours.''[45]

No ruler could better express the affection which he felt for Joseph than to make this overwhelmingly generous offer to a people who were foreigners in the land.

---

43. Genesis 45:15
44. Genesis 45:16
45. Genesis 45:17-20

The Aged Jacob Gets the News

Joseph "gave them wagons, according to the commandment of Pharaoh, and gave them provisions for the way."[46] This meant provisions for the trip to Canaan and back to Egypt.

The provisions included "change of raiment" for each of the brothers, but "to Benjamin he gave three hundred pieces of silver, and five changes of raiment."[47] And Joseph sent his father ten donkeys "laden with the good things of Egypt," and ten other donkeys "laden with corn and bread and meat for his father by the way."[48] This refers to prepared materials which could be readily used on the return trip.

As the wagons and donkeys and eleven brothers came trooping into Hebron it must have been a sight to behold. And the exuberance of the eleven brothers who were in possession of the most exciting information Jacob would ever hear, must have been close to impossible to contain. One can imagine the scene when they finally reached their father and excitedly blurted out the news: Joseph is alive, Joseph is alive, and he is governor over all the land of Egypt![49]

Their father's reaction was immediate and decisive: "Jacob's heart fainted, for he believed them not."[50]

His eleven sons hastened to explain that it was true. They pointed to the loaded wagons and burdened donkeys as proof that Joseph was not only alive but that he wanted his father and family to hasten to Egypt: "and when he [Jacob] saw the wagons which Joseph had sent to carry him, the spirit of Jacob their father revived: And Israel said, It is enough; Joseph my son is yet alive: I will go and see him before I die."[51]

---

46. Genesis 45:21
47. Genesis 45:22
48. Genesis 45:23

49. Genesis 45:26
50. Ibid.
51. Genesis 45:27-28

Scripture Reading and Questions on Chapter Six

Scripture Reading Assignment: Genesis, chapter 41:42 to chapter 45.

1—What was the name of Joseph's new bride? What was her nationality? What was her religion? How old was Joseph when he married her?

2—How much of the grain harvest did Joseph store up during each of the years of plenty?

3—What was the name of Joseph's oldest son? What did his name signify?

4—What was the name of Joseph's second son? What did his name signify?

5—How extensive was the famine when it struck?

6—When Jacob sent ten of his sons to Egypt for grain, why did he keep Benjamin home?

7—How long had the famine been in progress when Jacob sent his sons to Egypt for grain?

8—When Joseph recognized his brothers what accusation did he make against them?

9—What did he say they had to do? Which brother was held as hostage until they fulfilled their promise?

10—What did Jacob say when his sons returned? What made him change his mind?

11—When Jacob's sons returned to Egypt, where did Joseph meet them?

12—What was unusual about the way Joseph seated them at his table? What was Joseph's treatment of Benjamin?

13—When Benjamin was found with Joseph's silver cup in his grain sack, who offered to be Joseph's servant in Benjamin's place?

14—What were the circumstances when Joseph revealed his true identity to his brothers?

15—What was the reaction of the brothers? What did Benjamin do as Joseph embraced him? What did Joseph do?

16—What was the reaction of Pharaoh when he heard the news?

17—What did the Pharaoh invite Joseph to do?

18—What kind of vehicles did the Pharaoh tell Joseph to send back with his brothers? For what purpose were they to be used?

19—What happened to Jacob when his sons brought back the news that Joseph was still alive?

20—What finally convinced him that the report was true? What did he say?

CHAPTER SEVEN

Joseph Settles His Family in Egypt

In the literature of fiction it is customary to begin with vast quantities of conflict and threatening disaster but nevertheless have the story conclude with a happy ending. In real life, it is seldom so. Human history reveals that more often than not the villains have won. The most brutal and vicious specimens of humanity have dominated history, plundering the innocent and violating the weak.

It is for this very reason that the Lord has emphasized to his servants that the final judgment of mankind must wait until the very end of the Second Estate. Only after the winding up scene will rewards and punishments be meted out to every man "according to his works."[1]

Occasionally, however, there is a true life story of a great national leader which actually does have a happy ending right here on earth. Joseph's biography is one of them. It moves from darkness to light.

Briefly, it will be recalled that his life began in Haran where a continuing feud existed between his father and his maternal grandfather. While the family was moving back to Canaan they stopped near Shechem and there his sister, Dinah, was kidnaped and ravished. Immediately afterwards his older brothers declared war on Shechem, killed the ruler and his son, wiped out the entire male population and sacked the city. When Joseph was near age seven his mother died. When he was 17 his older brothers plotted to kill him and while they had him imprisoned in a pit, he was discovered by some Midianites who sold him to a caravan of Ishmaelite merchants and these, in turn, sold him into slavery in Egypt.

---

1. Revelations 20:12; Doc. and Covenants 19:1-20

Even though a slave, Joseph worked diligently and became the chief servant of his master. But after eleven years of service he was arrested on false charges and thrown into a dungeon for two years. Finally, because of God's revelations to him concerning the dreams of Pharaoh, he was released from slavery and made the prime minister with no superior over him save the Pharaoh himself.

From that day forward, his happiness increased. He was given a beautiful girl for a wife and they had two sons. All Joseph then needed to make his happiness complete was the joy of seeing his father's face again and being united with his family. Through the intervention of heaven, even this was achieved.

WHY WAS JACOB AFRAID TO GO INTO EGYPT?

When Joseph invited Father Jacob to join him in Egypt, he did not mean as a visitor but as a permanent resident. This left Father Jacob with a deeply perplexing decision.

Abraham and Isaac had both risked their lives in order to maintain a residence in Canaan. The Lord had told them specifically it was their promised land. But now this promised land was dying. The perpetual heat of the blistering sun and the wilting blast of the desert winds had left this rainless land completely desolate. The flocks were dying, the people were dying, the gaunt specter of famine was everywhere. Even wealthy tribal chieftains like Jacob barely had the means to survive. And without help from Egypt, perhaps even he would have died.

So, reluctantly, Jacob prepared to leave the family home in Hebron and take "all that he had down to Egypt."[2] Enroute, he put in at Beer-sheba which was his southern headquarters, and there Jacob "offered sacrifices unto the God of his father Isaac."

It was at Beer-sheba while Jacob was in the midst of a deep sleep that the vision of the Almighty quietly descended upon him. The Lord called him saying, "Jacob, Jacob," and the aged patriarch replied, "Here am I."[3]

2. Genesis 46:1
3. Genesis 46:2

And the Lord declared unto him, "I am God, the God of thy father: fear not to go down into Egypt; for I will there make of thee a great nation: I will go down with thee into Egypt, and I will also surely bring thee up again: and Joseph shall put his hand upon thine eyes."[4]

So, the hand of the Lord was in it!

The depth of Jacob's apprehension and the need for this divine manifestation is better appreciated when it is realized that there was a prophetic warning handed down from Abraham that had quoted the Lord as saying: ". . . Abram, Know of a surety that thy seed shall be a stranger in a land that is not theirs, and shall serve them; and they shall afflict them . . . . And also that nation, whom they shall serve, will I judge: and afterward shall they come out with great substance."[5]

Since that time, each of the patriarchs — Abraham, Isaac and Jacob — must have wondered when this prophecy would be fulfilled, and where. Surely Jacob must have felt a particularly profound sense of anxiety in moving to Egypt when he knew this might turn out to be the period of slavery and affliction which the Lord had been talking about.

But no matter, the Lord had now spoken. The move southward had His blessing. Without compunction or fear Jacob could go joyfully into Egypt to meet Joseph.

The Family of Jacob Joins Joseph in Egypt

"And they took their cattle, and their goods, which they had gotten in the land of Canaan, and came into Egypt, Jacob, and all his seed with him."[6]

The number who belonged to Jacob's immediate family — sons and grandsons — are given as 70 in the Old Testament[7] and 75 in the New Testament.[8] However, the Septuagint version of the Old Testament also gives the number as 75 and includes five descendants of Manasseh and Ephraim which are not listed in the King James version of the Old Testament.[9] We therefore conclude that this is the

---

4. Genesis 46:3-4
5. Genesis 15:13
6. Genesis 46:6

7. Genesis 46:27
8. Acts 7:14
9. Clarke, *Bible Commentary*, Vol. 1, p. 252

correct figure. In addition to the immediate family of Jacob there must have been many times more than these who were servants and maid-servants, together with their families. Apparently Jacob still had considerable cattle which had survived the famine[10] and no doubt he would bring along all of his herders and house servants who had been with him since he left Haran.[11]

On this trek to Egypt Jacob was leaving behind the mothers of eight of his children. Rachel had died when Benjamin was born[12] and some time afterwards Leah had died. Jacob had buried Rachel in her own tomb near Bethlehem[13] but Leah apparently died in Hebron and was buried in the cave of Machpelah along with Abraham, Sarah, Isaac and Rebekah.[14]

Jacob now sent Judah ahead to have Joseph direct them to the place where they should settle.[15] Joseph had previously told them to go to Goshen because "thou shalt be near unto me."[16] Apparently Joseph maintained his headquarters in the capital city of Memphis where Pharaoh is believed to have had his seat of government. Goshen was not far distant, and we know that is where Joseph directed Judah to settle Jacob and his family.

Joseph must have felt the deepest anxiety as he contemplated the joy of seeing his father again. It had been 22 years since they parted (13 years of slavery plus seven good years plus two years of famine). Joseph therefore mounted his royal chariot and hastened to Goshen.[17] To the Egyptians Joseph was a calculating and efficient administrator, a man of affairs, a man of business, but to his family he was tender-hearted as a woman. When Joseph saw his father he rushed forward, embraced him and "wept . . . a good while."[18] The aged patriarch looked at his son and said: "Now let me die, since I have seen thy face, . . . thou art yet alive."[19] The twenty-two years of mourning had left their mark. Jacob could not have been more overjoyed if Joseph had literally returned from the dead.

10. Genesis 46:6
11. Genesis 30:43
12. Genesis 35:16-19
13. Genesis 35:19-20
14. Genesis 49:31
15. Genesis 46:28
16. Genesis 45:10
17. Genesis 46:29
18. Ibid.
19. Genesis 46:30

JOSEPH PRESENTS HIS FATHER AND FIVE OF HIS BROTHERS TO PHARAOH

In a sense it was a delicate thing for Joseph to bring his father's colony from Canaan and settle them in Egypt, particularly during one of the severest famines in the history of the country. Joseph therefore desired to keep his people separate from the Egyptians and still have them fairly close to the place where Joseph lived. Goshen was a rich and fertile part of Egypt and an ideal area for their flocks of cattle. This is why Joseph had selected it. He now had the task of getting it approved by the Pharaoh. Therefore, he instructed his father and brothers as follows:

"And it shall come to pass, when Pharaoh shall call you, and shall say, What is your occupation? That ye shall say, Thy servants' trade hath been about cattle from our youth even until now, both we, and also our fathers: that ye may dwell in the land of Goshen; for every shepherd is an abomination unto the Egyptians."[20]

Accordingly, Joseph took his father and five of his brothers to the palace of Pharaoh.[21] We do not know why only five were taken nor do we know which five they were. Joseph presented his brothers to the Pharaoh, and just as Joseph had predicted, the Pharaoh asked them their occupation.[22] They answered precisely the way Joseph had suggested.[23] Pharaoh then turned to Joseph and said: "The land of Egypt is before thee; in the best of the land make thy father and brethren to dwell."[24]

This was excellent. Things were going exactly as Joseph had hoped they would.

---

20. The Egyptians despised shepherds for at least two reasons. First, the Hyksos who conquered them and at this time ruled over them, were shepherds and are called the "shepherd kings." Second, the Bedouin raiders which continually preyed upon the outposts of Egypt were professional shepherds. The native Egyptians felt a natural hostility towards them. Of course, the Egyptians kept flocks of their own, but even the Egyptian shepherds were often quarrelsome outlaws who were deeply mistrusted and belonged to the lowest, meanest class. All of these factors led Joseph to conclude that it was wisdom to get Pharaoh's permission to have the people of Israel live apart from the Egyptians and dwell in nearby Goshen. (For additional discussion, see Clarke's *Bible Commentary*, Vol. 1, p. 254.)

21. Genesis 47:2
22. Genesis 47:3
23. Genesis 47:4
24. Genesis 47:6

Then Pharaoh added: "In the land of Goshen let them dwell: and if thou knowest any men of activity among them, then make them rulers over my cattle."[25] Pharaoh knew competent people when he saw them. Since Joseph had been such a splendid steward he hoped other members of the family might be available.

Now Joseph brought his aged father before Pharaoh. As Jacob came into the presence of Pharaoh, he saluted the Egyptian monarch with a greeting and a blessing.[26] The Pharaoh said: "How old art thou?"[27] and Jacob gave an interesting reply. Said he: "The days of the years of my pilgrimage are a hundred and thirty years; few and evil have the days of the years of my life been, and have not attained unto the days of the years of the life of my fathers in the days of their pilgrimage."[28]

It is obvious that Jacob felt his life was drawing to a close much faster than Abraham who had lived to be 175[29] or Isaac who had lived to be 180.[30] Actually, Jacob would live in Egypt for another 17 years before he passed away at the age of 147.[31] As people grow older they often feel ready to go before their time. Abraham was called "old and well stricken in age" when he was 140,[32] but he remarried and had six sons after that. Isaac thought he was through at the age of around 110,[33] but he lived for almost another three quarters of a century. Each generation has had to learn that the secret formula for a happy old age is to keep going right down to the last flicker of physical vitality.

The record concludes this episode by saying: "And Joseph placed his father and his brethren, and gave them a possession in the land of Egypt, in the best of the land, in the land of Rameses, as Pharaoh had commanded."[34]

How Pharaoh Acquired the Wealth of Egypt

Now Joseph turned his attention back to the chore of nurturing the starving multitudes of Egypt and the surround-

25. Ibid.
26. Genesis 47:7
27. Genesis 47:8
28. Genesis 47:9
29. Genesis 25:7-8
30. Genesis 35:28
31. Genesis 47:28
32. Genesis 24:1
33. Genesis 27:2
34. Genesis 47:11

ing countries so they could survive the famine which was not even half over. Because of the prudent storage of grain during the years of plenty there was enough to get them by, but only if it were distributed with the most careful kind of rationing. Perhaps it was to avoid hoarding or waste that Joseph continued to sell the grain rather than give it away. This worked all right as long as the people had money but when that was gone he suggested they bring in their personal property. "And they brought their cattle unto Joseph."[35]

The next year they were once more depleted of resources, so Joseph suggested that they market their land to the Pharaoh in exchange for the grain they needed. "And Joseph bought all the land of Egypt for Pharaoh; for the Egyptians sold every man his field, because the famine prevailed over them, so the land became Pharaoh's."[36] Then apparently to conserve the supplies available and maintain a closer supervision of its rationing. Joseph brought the people into the cities where they could remain until the famine was over.[37]

As soon as the seven years had run their course, Joseph knew from the Lord's revelation concerning Pharaoh's dream that the people could now return to the land and reap a good harvest, so he said unto them:

"Lo, here is seed for you, and ye shall sow the land. And it shall come to pass, in the increase, that ye shall give the fifth part unto Pharaoh, and four parts shall be your own, for seed of the field, and for your food, and for them of your households, and for food for your little ones."[38]

At first it might have appeared to the people that Joseph was exploiting them for the sake of the Pharaoh, but now, as he placed them back on the land, gave them seed, and levied a tax of only 20% of their increase for the benefit of the central government, they knew they were dealing with a man of both prudence and justice. So the people said, "Thou hast saved our lives: let us find grace in the sight of my Lord, and we will be Pharaoh's servants. And Joseph

---

35. Genesis 47:17
36. Genesis 47:20
37. Genesis 47:21
38. Genesis 47:23-24

made it a law over the land of Egypt unto this day, that
Pharaoh should have the fifth part. . . ."[39]

How different from many other kingdoms where the
taxes often ran as high as 50 per cent, and how different
from the way the stewards of future Pharaohs would treat
the children of Israel — taking from them their full labor and
abusing them as abject slaves.

THE PEOPLE OF ISRAEL BECOME ESTABLISHED IN EGYPT

When the ravages of the famine had passed, it must
have taken Joseph several years to rehabilitate the vast domain
of Pharaoh. Since all the Egyptians had been brought into the
major cities during the last part of the famine,[40] they now had
to be encouraged to take the seed which Joseph had given
them and once more develop the agricultural resources of the
Delta and the Nile Valley. The sprawling network of canals
would have to be cleaned out and repaired. The towns and
villages which had been abandoned during the famine would
have to be rebuilt and re-occupied. The normal patterns of
commerce and trade in Egypt's ports and commercial centers
would have to be restored and regulated. We are certain
that the years which followed the famine were busy, challenging years for Joseph, prime minister of Egypt.

As for the people of Israel, the scripture leaves no doubt
as to the blessings of heaven which now showered their
abundance upon Jacob and his family in their new homeland.
It says, "And Israel dwelt in the land of Egypt, in the country
of Goshen; and they had possessions therein, and grew, and
multiplied exceedingly."[41]

From here on the Israelites became engrossed in the
task of multiplying their numbers and building up their possessions. As we shall see later, they apparently averaged
around ten or more children per family during the next
several generations, and eventually achieved a size which
caused a later Pharaoh of Egypt to cry out in alarm, "Behold,
the people of the children of Israel are more and mightier
than we!"[42] But that was to be in a future day.

---

39. Genesis 47:25-26   41. Genesis 47:27
40. Genesis 47:21   42. Exodus 1:9

During Joseph's time, the personal popularity and prestige of Joseph gave the people of Israel the enviable role of a prosperous and favored minority. This was the case as long as he lived and for many years afterwards.

The Aged Jacob Approaches the End of His Life

The scripture says, "And Jacob lived in the land of Egypt seventeen years . . . and the time drew nigh that Israel must die. . . ."[43]

As Jacob thought he saw the end of his life approaching he became increasingly disturbed over the possibility that he and his family might still be in Egypt at the time of his death. If this were the case he undoubtedly would be buried in Egypt and this he did not want. Therefore the scripture says, ". . . he called his son Joseph, and said unto him, If now I have found grace in thy sight, put I pray thee, put thy hand under my thigh,[44] and deal kindly and truly with me; bury me not, I pray thee, in Egypt: But I will lie with my fathers, and thou shalt carry me out of Egypt, and bury me in their burying place."[45]

Under the circumstances, this was almost an impossible request, and, as we shall see later, it constituted a most challenging promise to fulfill; nevertheless, Joseph comforted his father and said, "I will do as thou hast said."[46]

But Jacob was not satisfied. He said to Joseph, "Swear unto me." So Joseph took the customary oath in the name of God that he would do as his father requested. Only then was Jacob reconciled. The depth of his anxiety over this matter is reflected by the fact that as soon as his mind was relieved by the knowledge that Joseph would do this for him, Jacob felt exhaustion overcome him so that "Israel bowed himself upon the bed's head."[47]

---

43. Genesis 47:28-29
44. Joseph Smith gave this phrase, "under my thigh" as "under my hand." (See Inspired Version, Genesis 24:2) However, since the Inspired Version was never completed, this phrase was left uncorrected in Genesis 47:29.
45. Genesis 47:29-30
46. Genesis 47:30
47. Genesis 47:31

JACOB ADOPTS EPHRAIM AND MANASSEH

It was only a short time after this that a messenger came once more to Joseph and said, "Behold, thy father is sick .... "[48] Joseph hurriedly left the capital for Goshen and took with him his two sons, Ephraim and Manasseh. Before his aged father passed away Joseph wanted him to confer a blessing upon these two young men who were now reaching their maturity. Little did he know that Jacob also had been thinking about giving a blessing to Ephraim and Manasseh but it was to be a far greater blessing than even Joseph would have guessed.

Jacob's problem was that his two oldest sons, Reuben and Simeon, had both disgraced themselves. Reuben had been guilty of incest many years before at Edar[49] and Simeon was guilty of being the leader in the murderous attack on the settlement of Shechem which had wiped out the entire male population of that community and nearly precipitated the massacre of Jacob and his family.[50] Levi and the older sons of Jacob had been allied with Simeon in this terrible affair,[51] but apparently Jacob held Simeon primarily responsible for instigating it.

Now, as Jacob approached the end of his life, he felt he must take formal action against these two eldest sons. He felt that as far as the covenant was concerned, he must formally disinherit them. Jacob had made up his mind to replace them with his two grandsons, Ephraim and Manasseh.

Although Jacob was very ill, the opportunity to take care of this matter presented itself when Jacob heard that Joseph was coming to see him with his two sons. The scripture says that as soon as Joseph had decided to visit his sick father, a messenger ran ahead and said to Jacob, "Behold, thy son Joseph cometh unto thee."[52] Because of his illness, this was a difficult time for the old patriarch, but he endeavored to rise to the occasion. The scripture says he "strengthened himself, and sat upon the bed."[53]

---

48. Genesis 48:1
49. Genesis 35:21-22
50. Genesis 34:25-30
51. Genesis 34:25-27
52. Genesis 48:2
53. Ibid.

As Joseph entered the room to greet his father, Jacob immediately unfolded to him his plan for adopting Ephraim and Manasseh in place of Reuben and Simeon. He started out by saying:

"God Almighty appeared unto me at Luz in the land of Canaan, and blessed me, and said unto me 'Behold, I will make thee fruitful, and multiply thee, and I will make of thee a multitude of people; and will give this land to thy seed after thee for an everlasting possession."[54]

No doubt it was obvious to Joseph what was troubling Jacob. The elderly patriarch had been given this marvelous blessing by the Lord but he had certain sons who were not worthy to have this blessing passed on to them. Jacob therefore disclosed what he wanted to do:

"And now thy two sons, Ephraim and Manasseh, which were born unto thee in the land of Egypt before I came unto thee into Egypt, are mine: as Reuben and Simeon, they shall be mine."[55]

So that was it. Joseph must have caught the full implication of this plan immediately. It meant that his sons would be moved up as direct heirs of Jacob, each of them receiving one twelfth of Jacob's estate. It also meant that in the pattern of the Priesthood these two sons would be adopted by Jacob to replace Reuben and Simeon, as his first and second sons. This meant that Joseph's house would be the major beneficiary, both materially and spiritually, of Jacob's priceless legacy.

The Blessing of Ephraim and Manasseh

The scripture says that "the eyes of Israel were dim for age so that he could not see."[56] Apparently he was not totally blind but was unable to see distinctly, therefore it was not until he had finished the above conversation with Joseph that he "beheld Joseph's sons."[57] His eyesight was too poor to identify them and so he said, "Who are these?"[58] Joseph replied, "They are my sons, whom God hath given me in this place."[59]

---

54. Genesis 48:3-4
55. Genesis 48:5
56. Genesis 48:10
57. Genesis 48:8
58. Ibid.
59. Genesis 48:9

This was splendid. Jacob said, "Bring them, I pray thee, unto me, and I will bless them."[60] Joseph brought them forward and the scripture says Jacob "kissed them, and embraced them."[61]

In presenting his sons for this blessing, Joseph was careful to arrange them so that the right hand of Jacob would rest on the head of Manasseh, the elder of the two, and his left hand on Ephraim, the younger. But as the aged Jacob prepared to bless these two young heirs, he crossed his hands and placed the right hand "upon Ephraim's head, who was the younger, and his left hand upon Manasseh's head, guiding his hands wittingly: for Manasseh was the first-born."[62]

The blessing which he gave them was as follows, "God, before whom my fathers Abraham and Isaac did walk, the God which fed me all my life long unto this day, the Angel which redeemed me from all evil, bless the lads; and let my name be named on them, and the name of my father Abraham and Isaac; and let them grow into a multitude in the midst of the earth."[63]

It was obvious to Joseph that his sons were receiving Jacob's principal blessing, putting them in line to be his direct heirs in the Priesthood. In view of this, the crossing of Jacob's hands suddenly became very significant. It placed Ephraim, the younger son, in a preferred position over Manasseh, the elder. This was very disturbing to Joseph because he thought his father was too weak and sick to realize that he had made a mistake. Therefore he deliberately lifted Jacob's hand up from Ephraim's head and said, "Not so, my father: for this is the firstborn; put thy right hand upon his head."[64]

To Joseph's surprise Jacob replied, "I know it, my son, I know it: he [Manasseh, the elder] also shall become a people, and he also shall be great: but truly his younger brother shall be greater than he, and his seed shall become a multitude of nations."[65]

---

60. Ibid.
61. Genesis 48:10
62. Genesis 48:14

63. Genesis 48:15-16
64. Genesis 48:18
65. Genesis 48:19

So Joseph held his peace and Jacob completed the bless-ing. In it he included a prophecy that the blessings upon these two young men would be so great that all Israel would use them as an example and say to each other, "God make thee as Ephraim and as Manasseh."[66]

Jacob Makes His Final Pronouncement on His Twelve Sons

After Jacob had completed blessing Ephraim and Man-asseh he determined to make his last pronouncement on each of his sons. Although extremely weak and afflicted with the advanced stages of his final illness, Jacob roused himself to fulfill this important obligation. He called all of his sons and said, "Gather yourselves together, that I may tell you that which shall befall you in the last days."[67]

First, Jacob called forth the six sons of Leah for his prediction concerning them:

REUBEN: ". . . thou art my firstborn," said Jacob, "my might, and the beginning of my strength, the excellency of dignity, and the excellency of power."[68] But Reuben had lost all of these because of immorality. Therefore his father had no blessing for him but simply said, "Unstable as water, thou shalt not excel; because thou wentest up to thy father's bed: then defiledst thou it. . . ."[69]

SIMEON AND LEVI: Here were two more sons who had been a great trial to Jacob. They had combined together to avenge the kidnapping and ravishing of their sister at Shechem by killing not only her abductor but the whole male population of that community. Therefore Jacob said of them: "Simeon and Levi are brethren; instruments of cruelty are in their habitations. O my soul, come not thou into their secret; unto their assembly, mine honour, be not thou united: for in their anger they slew a man, and in their selfwill they digged down a wall. Cursed be their anger, for it was fierce; and their wrath, for it was cruel: I will divide them in Jacob, and scatter them in Israel."[70]

---

66. Genesis 48:20
67. Genesis 49:1
68. Genesis 49:3

69. Genesis 49:3-4
70. Genesis 45:5-7

It is interesting to note that Levi received the same judgment as Simeon because he was a party to the crime against Shechem. However, in the days of Moses, the men of this tribe vindicated themselves by showing forth greater faithfulness than any of the others[71] and therefore received the exclusive rights to the Aaronic Priesthood from then until the dispensation of Jesus Christ. Nevertheless, the tribe of Levi did not receive an inheritance in the promised land but was "scattered" among all the other tribes of Israel. Even this turned out for the best, however, since it facilitated the administration of religious services among the various tribes.

JUDAH: This fourth son of Leah had also committed serious offenses in his lifetime,[72] but apparently he was forgiven and restored to the full confidence of his father as of this time. Said Jacob: "Judah, thou art he whom thy brethren shall praise: thy hand shall be in the neck of thine enemies; thy father's children shall bow down before thee. Judah is a lion's whelp. . . ."[73] Jacob then promised Judah three specific things:

1. Judah would be a tribe of courageous warriors.[74]

2. The Kingdom of Judah would remain intact as a political entity until the coming of the Messiah.[75]

3. The Messiah would be of the tribe of Judah and would come riding on a donkey's colt.[76]

ZEBULUN: This son's descendants were blessed to receive an inheritance on the Mediterranean Sea which would extend inland to the Sea of Galilee and as far north as Sidon.[77] Unfortunately this tribe, like several of the others, was dilatory and never achieved the full extent of its inheritance.

ISSACHAR: His descendants are described as bearing two burdens — interpreted to mean patient in great labor but

---

71. Exodus 32:26-28
72. Genesis Ch. 38
73. Genesis 49:8-9
74. Genesis 49:9
75. Genesis 49:10
76. Genesis 49:10-11. Although the modern text is very obscure, this is the interpretation of Genesis 49:11 given by Jewish authorities (Clarke's *Bible Commentary*, Vol. 1, p. 266) and also by Matthew in the New Testament (Matthew 21:2-5). The basic idea is more clearly presented in Zachariah 9:9.
77. Genesis 49:13 plus Joshua 19:10

invincible in war.[78] Concerning this tribe, Jacob said, "And he saw that rest was good, and the land that it was pleasant; and bowed his shoulder to bear, and became a servant unto tribute."[79] So for this tribe there would be blessings from the earth but tribulation from man.

Having given a prophecy to each of Leah's six sons, Jacob now called forth the two sons of Zilpah who was Leah's maid, and the two sons of Bilha, Rachel's maid.

DAN: This son of Bilhah was told, "Dan shall judge his people, as one of the tribes of Israel. Dan shall be a serpent by the way, an adder in the path, that biteth the horse heels, so that his rider shall fall backward."[80] Dr. Adam Clarke suggests the following interpretation: "Dan, whose name signifies judgment, was the oldest of Jacob's sons by Bilhah, Rachel's maid, and he is here promised an equal rule with those tribes that sprang from either Leah or Rachel. . . . It is intimated that this tribe should gain the principal part of its conquests more by cunning and stratagem, than by valour; and this is seen particularly in their conquest of Laish (Judges 18) and even in some of the transactions of Samson (who belonged to this tribe), such as burning the corn of the Philistines, and at last pulling down their temple, and destroying three thousand at one time."[81]

GAD: This son of Zilpah was told, "a troop shall overcome him: but he shall overcome at the last."[82] This prophecy undoubtedly refers to the frequent disturbances to which this tribe would be exposed as one of the three occupants of Trans-Jordan.

ASHER: To this son of Zilpah, Jacob said: "Out of Asher his bread shall be fat, and he shall yield royal dainties."[83] This simply refers to the great fertility of the region which the tribe of Asher would inherit. Moses makes reference to the blessings and prosperity which would be the lot of this tribe.[84]

NAPHTALI: To this son of Bilhah, Jacob declared: "Naphtali is a hind let loose; he giveth goodly words."[85]

78. Clarke's *Bible Commentary*, Vol. 1, p. 268
79. Genesis 49:14-15
80. Genesis 49:17
81. Clarke's *Bible Commentary*, Vol. 1, p. 268
82. Genesis 49:19
83. Genesis 49:20
84. Deut. 33:24
85. Genesis 49:2 1

There are too few references to this tribe in the Bible to indicate the exact meaning of this prophecy. Perhaps in the original text it was more meaningful.

Last of all Jacob called forth the two sons of his beloved Rachel:

JOSEPH: To his eleventh son Jacob gave the coveted birthright blessing. It contained six specific promises.

1. Joseph's posterity would not be confined to the land of Canaan but would be like a "fruitful bough by a well; whose branches run over the wall."[86] Eventually his descendants would be extended "unto the utmost bound of the everlasting hills.[87]

2. Joseph's descendants would be subject to the ferocious violence of war but would be known as valiant men who would abide in their places and would be blessed of God so they would come off victorious in the end.[88]

3. The tribe of Joseph would enjoy the blessings of heaven with its life-giving moisture necessary to make their inheritance productive.[89]

4. They would have the blessing of the great deep, reminding one of the successful Lehi migration, halfway round the world, mostly by water.[90]

5. They would be blessed with a great posterity possessing fertility and strength. These were called the "blessings of the breast and of the womb."[91] Today the descendants of Joseph are found in every corner of the earth. They are mixed in with many other nationalities but their blessings still boldly manifest themselves wherever the seed of Joseph is found.

6. Finally, Joseph received the birthright blessing. Jacob said, "The blessings of thy father have prevailed above the blessings of my progenitors unto the utmost bound of the everlasting hills; they shall be on the head of Joseph, and on the crown of the head of

86. Genesis 49:22
87. Genesis 49:26
88. Genesis 49:23-24

89. Genesis 49:25
90. Ibid.
91. Ibid.

him that was separate from his brethren."[92] This was the greatly coveted blessing which each patriarch held in reserve for the choicest of his children. From Joseph it would go to Ephraim.

BENJAMIN: Apparently the second son of Rachel was not nearly the caliber of the first. As with most of the others, the pronouncement on his head was not so much a blessing as a prophcey: "Benjamin shall ravin as a wolf; in the morning he shall devour the prey, and at night he shall divide the spoil."[93] This prophecy was literally fulfilled in the history of Benjamin's descendants. They invariably displayed a rude courage and a war-like ferocity, particularly in their conflicts with the other tribes. On one occasion they had two great victories and then were nearly exterminated.[94] Finally, they mixed with the tribe of Judah until they were no longer mentioned as a separate people.

It is not difficult to read these various blessings and prophecies pronounced by Jacob without being able to immediately pick out the two sons who had the historic roles of important leadership. One was Joseph, the other was Judah. Through one would pass the birthright blessing and through the other would come the Messiah.

The Death of Jacob

Having pronounced these blessings and prophecies on the heads of his sons, Jacob had only one more instruction before he died. It is obvious that the importance of it preyed upon his mind. Said he,

"I am to be gathered unto my people: bury me with my fathers in the cave that is in the field of Ephron the Hittite. . . . There they buried Abraham and Sarah his wife; there they buried Isaac and Rebekah his wife; and there I buried Leah."[95] Already Joseph had made a solemn oath that he would comply with this desire, but apparently the dying patriarch wanted all of his sons to assume some of the responsibility in carrying out this death-bed wish. Having made this final plea, the scripture says Father Jacob "gathered up his feet into the bed, and yielded up the ghost and was

---

92. Genesis 49:26
93. Genesis 49:27

94. Judges 20:12-48
95. Genesis 49:29-31

gathered unto his people."[96] This specific reference to the immortality of the soul and the uniting of Jacob with his loved ones in the spirit world is significant. As the writer of Ecclesiastes would later say, "Then shall the dust return to the earth as it was; and the spirit shall return unto God who gave it."[97]

The death of Jacob marked the closing of a great human adventure lasting 147 years.[98] As Joseph realized the great loss that all of them had suffered through the death of this great prophet, he could not contain his feelings. The scripture says "Joseph fell upon his father's face and wept upon him and kissed him."[99] There is no question as to the depth of affection which existed between this father and son.

JACOB'S FUNERAL BECOMES A STATE AFFAIR

Now Joseph had the task of fulfilling his sacred oath to bury the body of Jacob with his people in Hebron. By this time Joseph was thoroughly familiar with the embalming procedure practiced by the Egyptians and so he determined to have the body of his father embalmed so as to permit it to be transported up into Canaan.[100] Joseph therefore placed the body in the hands of the "physicians" and "the physicians embalmed Israel."[101] This required forty days[102] and after that there was a season of mourning both among Israelites and Egyptians for 70 days.[103]

When the days of mourning were over, Joseph went to Pharaoh saying, "My father made me swear, saying, Lo, I die; in my grave which I have digged for me in the land of Canaan, there shalt thou bury me. Now therefore let me go up, I pray thee, and bury my father, and I will come again."[104]

Once more Pharaoh exhibited the admiration and respect which he felt for his Hebrew prime minister. Said he, "Go up, and bury thy father, according as he made thee

---

96. Genesis 49:33
97. Ecclesiastes 12:7
98. Genesis 47:28
99. Genesis 50:1
100. See Appendix article, "Herodotus Describes the Egyptian Embalming Process."
101. Genesis 50:2   103. Ibid.
102. Genesis 50:3   104. Genesis 50:5

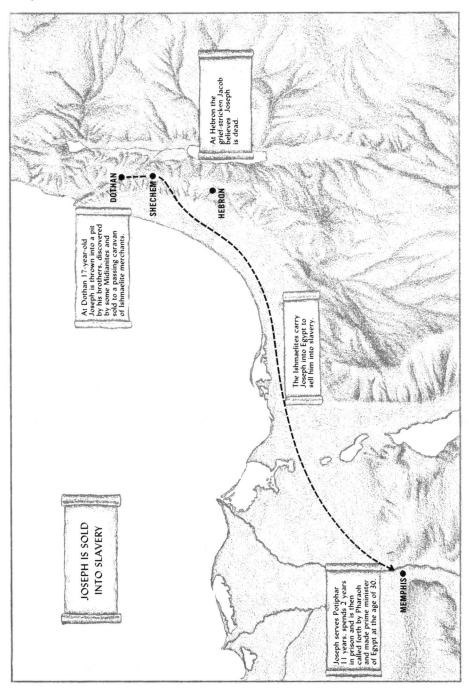

At Hebron the grief-stricken Jacob believes Joseph is dead.

At Dothan 17-year-old Joseph is thrown into a pit by his brothers, discovered by some Midianites and sold to a passing caravan of Ishmaelite merchants.

DOTHAN

SHECHEM

HEBRON

The Ishmaelites carry Joseph into Egypt to sell him into slavery.

JOSEPH IS SOLD INTO SLAVERY

Joseph serves Potiphar 11 years, spends 2 years in prison and is then called forth by Pharaoh and made prime minister of Egypt at the age of 30.

MEMPHIS

swear."[105] Then Pharaoh did a remarkable thing. He made the funeral procession to Canaan an official affair. Rarely in history are there instances where a powerful government has honored a foreigner who happened to die within its borders, but in the case of Jacob the Pharaoh sent all of the officials of his own palace and all of the top dignitaries of the entire government of Egypt.[106] In addition, Pharaoh ordered up a splendid military guard of honor, "both chariots and horsemen,"[107] and they together with the large retinue of Egyptian officials constituted "a very great company."[108] Up from Memphis, over through Goshen, and finally onto the king's highway, the royal retinue wound its way carrying the body of Jacob toward Canaan.

During this journey Joseph must have marveled at the wonders God had wrought. It had been just 39 years before that he had been dragged across these desert roads by Ishmaelite merchants to be sold into Egyptian slavery. And only 17 years before his father and family had traveled down to Egypt along these roads to escape starvation. Now the whole family was returning to Canaan as part of a royal Egyptian cortege specifically designed by the Pharaoh to honor Jacob and show respect to Joseph.

The whole family of Jacob participated in this pilgrimage. ". . . only their little ones, and their flocks, and their herds, they left in the land of Goshen."[109]

When the great retinue came into the borders of Canaan and camped for seven days of mourning at Atad the people of Canaan were astonished and said, "This is a grievous mourning to the Egyptians!"[110] The Canaanites were so impressed that they ever afterwards called the place of that camp "the mourning place of the Egyptians."[111]

And so it was done unto Jacob as he had pleaded before he died. "For his sons carried him into the land of Canaan, and buried him in the cave of the field of Machpelah."[112] There he was laid to rest beside his wife, Leah, and in com-

---

105. Genesis 50:6
106. Genesis 50:7
107. Genesis 50:9
108. Ibid.

109. Genesis 50:8
110. Genesis 50:11
111. Ibid. plus marginal note
112. Genesis 50:13

pany with his parents, Isaac and Rebekah, as well as his grandparents, Abraham and Sarah.[113] A large tower, some ten miles distant, marked the final resting place of his beloved Rachel.[114]

Thus another generation in the great patriarchal line of God's chosen servants passed into history.

---

113. Genesis 49:31
114. Genesis 35:20

Scripture Reading and Questions on Chapter Seven

Scripture Reading Assignment: Genesis, chapters 46 to 50:13.

1—When Joseph invited his father to move to Egypt, why did Jacob hesitate? What did the Lord say?

2—How many Israelites of the same contemporary period established their homes in Egypt under Joseph's direction? Which appears to be the correct figure, the one in the New Testament or the one in the Old Testament?

3—In what district of Egypt did the Israelites settle?

4—What was the professional reputation of shepherds in Egypt? Could this have caused the Israelites trouble?

5—Why did Joseph want his family to emphasize to Pharaoh that they were shepherds?

6—Why were the Hyksos rulers likely to have a different attitude toward shepherds than the native Egyptians?

7—What did Jacob say to Pharaoh about his age? How much longer did Jacob actually live?

8—Is there any indication that the Egyptians had stored supplies in their homes preparatory to the famine?

9—Do you see any advantage in gathering the people in the cities for the duration of the famine?

10—Do you see any advantage in requiring the people to give something in exchange for the wheat instead of just rationing it out on a per capita basis?

11—After the land was sold to the Pharaoh for food, how long was it before Joseph gave the land back to the people? What else did he give them?

12—How much "income" or "harvest tax" did Joseph require the people to pay each year? Was this reasonable or excessive?

13—As Jacob approached the end of his life what worried him? What did Joseph do to reassure him?

14—What did Jacob do with his oldest sons? Why? Who replaced them?

15—Why did Jacob cross his hands when he blessed Ephraim and Manasseh?

16—What three promises did Jacob make to Judah?

17—To whom did Jacob give his birthright blessing?

18—Then to whom did it pass? What relation is he to you?

19—How do these blessings explain the Lord's declaration that the Twelve Tribes will get their endowments from Ephraim in the last days? (See the Doctrine and Covenants 133:30-32)

20—What other tribe is practically co-equal with Ephraim? Does this explain the need for two Jerusalems during the Millennium?

CHAPTER EIGHT

The Last Days of Joseph and His Remarkable Prophecies Concerning the Future

When Joseph and his brothers returned from Canaan they had probably seen their "promised land" for the last time in this life. Although they had been told it was to be the place of their inheritance, Joseph learned from the Lord that it would be their posterity who would possess it, not they, and this would not happen until many years in the future.[1] Meanwhile, the children of Israel had a mission to perform in Egypt.

JOSEPH'S BRETHREN SUFFER FROM A GUILT COMPLEX

Once Joseph and his eleven brothers had returned to Egypt a strange psychological reaction set in. Ten of them (all except Benjamin) manifested new symptoms of an old guilt complex. Knowing their own treacherous natures and realizing that Father Jacob was no longer around to intercede for them, they began to fear that Joseph might now have a change of heart toward them. ". . . they said, Joseph will peradventure hate us, and will certainly requite us all the evil which we did unto him."[2] They knew, of course, that Joseph had totalitarian authority in Egypt, which meant that he had power over life and death among the subjects of Pharaoh. If he had a change of heart towards his brothers because of their betrayal of him, they might very soon be dead men.

The more the guilty brothers thought about it the deeper became their mental torment. Finally all ten of them decided to hasten to Joseph and throw themselves at his feet in

---

1. Inspired Version, Genesis 50:24, 34-35
2. Genesis 50:15

humble supplication. The scripture discloses that Jacob, prior to his death, had anticipated this very development. He had told them to go to Joseph as a group and petition him for his complete forgiveness.[3] Therefore, in a spirit of deepest humiliation they now prepared to make this plea.

First, they sent a messenger to the capitol to tell Joseph they were coming. They also indicated that they were coming to do something their father had told them to do. This was their message to Joseph: "Thy father did command before he died, saying, So shall ye say unto Joseph, Forgive, I pray thee now, the trespass of thy brethren, and their sin; for they did unto thee evil: and now, we pray thee, forgive the trespass of the servants of the God of thy father."[4]

Of course, Joseph had long since demonstrated both verbally and by his whole behavior that he had forgiven them.[5] Therefore this new plea for mercy apparently came as a great surprise. He was especially amazed when they came into his presence and "fell down before his face," and pleaded that they be allowed to be his "servants."[6]

"And Joseph wept when they spake unto him."[7]

This was not the kind of relationship he wanted with his brothers. He did not want them cowering before him. He told them not to be afraid and then he spoke to them in a spirit of moderate rebuke saying, ". . . am I in the place of God?"[8]

He wanted them to get up off the ground and stand before him as brethren and equals, not servants. He did not condone their sin but neither did he hold it against them. Said he, ". . . ye thought evil against me, but God meant it unto good, to bring to pass, as it is this day, to save much people alive.. Now therefore fear ye not: I will nourish you, and your little ones."[9]

Then the scriptures conclude, ". . . and he comforted them, and spake kindly unto them."[10]

---

3. Genesis 50:16-17
4. Ibid.
5. Genesis 45:4-15
6. Genesis 50:18

7. Genesis 50:17
8. Genesis 50:19
9. Genesis 50:20-21
10. Ibid.

The End of the Life and Reign of Joseph in Egypt

Joseph was around 17 when he came into Egypt,[11] and we know he was 30 when he became governor of Egypt.[12] Seven additional years were used in preparing the storage of grain and seven more were absorbed in administering its distribution during the famine. So far as we know, he continued to serve as the prime minister of Egypt until his death at the age of 110.[13] This would mean that Joseph governed Egypt for a total of 80 years! Joseph was 56 when his father died[14] so he still had 54 years to govern Egypt following the events we have just described.

We are not told how many Pharaohs Joseph served under, but in all likelihood he served under more than one. Joseph lived to see "Ephraim's children of the third generation: the children also of Machir, son of Manasseh."[15]

As the thrilling story of Joseph's life began to draw toward a conclusion, he exhibited the same anxiety his father had felt. He wanted to be buried in Canaan with his progenitors. As we shall see shortly, Joseph had been given many remarkable revelations concerning the future of Israel and he already knew about the coming of Moses and Aaron to liberate the children of Israel following their cruel period of bondage. With this in mind, he said to his children, ". . . God will surely visit you, and ye shall carry up my bones from hence."[16] Of course, he knew this event would not transpire until many years in the future. It is interesting to note that when it did come time to leave Egypt, the leaders of Israel did not forget the promise which their fathers had made to Joseph. They took his body with them.

It was around the year 1,661 B.C., as nearly as we can tell, that the great Hebrew administrator and prime minister of Egypt passed to his reward. Because Joseph reached the age of only 110 he died younger than any of his paternal

---

11. Genesis 37:2, 36
12. Genesis 41:46
13. Genesis 50:22
14. Jacob was 91 when Joseph was born (see note 96, Ch. 3) and since he died at the age of 147 (Genesis 47:28) this would make Joseph 56 when his father passed away.
15. Genesis 50:23
16. Genesis 50:25

ancestors. The Lord, in his wisdom, undoubtedly had a special purpose in taking him this soon. Perhaps one of the factors was the pending overthrow of the Hyksos kings which would change the whole political climate of Egypt.

The scripture says that after Joseph had died, steps were taken to preserve his body so it could be carried out of Egypt and buried in accordance with Joseph's desires. Therefore, ". . . they embalmed him, and he was put in a coffin in Egypt."[17] The sarcophagus of Joseph was laid in some honored place to await the day when Israel would carry it triumphantly back to Canaan and bury it at Shechem.

THE LOST PROPHECIES OF JOSEPH

Sometime prior to Joseph's death he recorded some rather amazing prophecies. Until these were restored in modern times it was assumed that Joseph had only a vague idea of what would happen after his death. It now turns out that he knew all about the period of Israel's bondage. He knew the name of Moses and the name of Aaron. He knew that the daughter of Pharaoh would adopt Moses as her own son. He also knew that Moses would have power over the Red Sea and would perform many other marvelous miracles.

It was more than a century later, when Moses was living upon the earth and writing the book of Genesis, that he got hold of these prophecies by Joseph and included them in what became the fiftieth chapter of Genesis. It must have been astonishing to Moses to learn how much the Lord had disclosed about his life — even before he was born.

Today, unfortunately, all of this marvelous information is missing from Genesis. Some warped or apostate scribe of the distant past stripped it out. The Lord warned Moses that this would happen. Said He: "And in a day when the children of men shall esteem my words as naught and take many of them from the book which thou shalt write, behold, I will raise up another like unto thee; and they shall be had again among the children of men — among as many as shall believe." (Moses 1:41)

---

17. Genesis 50:26

Today, those who are familiar with the phenomenal mission of Joseph Smith, know that a part of this material has been restored. It is contained in the so-called "Inspired Version." In fact, Joseph Smith found that the prophecies of Joseph had not only been written up by Moses for the Book of Genesis but they also had been written up by Joseph for the Book of Remembrance in his own family.

Joseph's Descendants Produce a Family Canon of Scripture

We now know that a rare and precious scriptural treasure was put together by Joseph's descendants and passed down from father to son, each of whom recorded the writings of the particular prophet who lived in his day. Naturally, Joseph's prophecies occupied a conspicuous place in this family heirloom.

In order to preserve this priceless record from fire or other destructive elements, the entire contents were laboriously transcribed onto metal plates made of brass.[18] We now have a rather detailed description of the contents of these famous brass plates. We are told that ". . . they did contain the five books of Moses, which gave an account of the creation of the world, and also of Adam and Eve, who were our first parents; and also a record of the Jews from the beginning even dowr to the commencement of the reign of Zedekiah, king of Jdah, and also the prophecies of the holy prophets, from the beginning, even down to the commencement of the reign of Zedekiah; and also many prophecies which have been spoken by the mouth of Jeremiah."[19]

Jeremiah was the presiding prophet at the very time this statement was made. The fact that Jeremiah's writings were already inscribed on the brass plates demonstrates that these historical records were kept right up-to-date.

We are also told that as of that time, which was 600 B.C., the plates were in the custody of "Laban [who] also was a descendant of Joseph, wherefore he and his fathers had kept the records."[20]

---

18. 1 Nephi 3:3
19. 1 Nephi 5:11-13
20. 1 Nephi 5:16

However, this same year these records were taken from Laban by another of Joseph's descendants named Nephi.[21] Shortly thereafter they were brought to the western hemisphere.[22]

Nephi's father, Lehi, studied these brass plates diligently and discovered the remarkable prophecies which Joseph had written. Lehi therefore abstracted them into his own writings. Lehi's writings then came into our possession as soon as the Book of Mormon was translated in 1829 and this gave us our second version of Joseph's prophecies — the first one from the restored or inspired version of Genesis and the second through Lehi's account in the Book of Mormon.

As might be expected, these two presentations differ slightly. The version from the restored text of Genesis is more detailed in certain places; however, the Book of Mormon version has some quotations which the Genesis account does not mention at all.

Joseph Smith's integrity as a translator is demonstrated by the fact that he did not try to make these two separate renditions agree with each other just to be consistent. He translated each of them just as it was written.

The following presentation of these two versions in parallel columns will make it easier for the reader to appreciate the valuable contribution represented by these two accounts of Joseph's "lost" prophecies.

COMPARING THE TWO MODERN SOURCES OF JOSEPH'S LOST PROPHECIES

GENESIS 50 (Inspired Version)	2 NEPHI Chapter 3 (Book of Mormon)
24. And Joseph said unto his brethren, I die, and go unto my fathers; and I go down to my grave with joy. The God of my father Jacob be with you, to deliver you out of affliction in the days of your bondage: for the Lord hath visited me, and I have obtained a promise of the Lord, that out of the fruit of my loins, the Lord God will raise up a righteous branch out of my loins;	5. Wherefore Joseph truly saw our day. And he obtained a promise of the Lord, that out of the fruit of his loins the Lord God would raise up a righteous branch unto the house of Israel;

21. 1 Nephi Ch. 3 and 4
22. Omni, verse 14; Alma 37:3-4

GENESIS 50 (Inspired Version)

2 NEPHI Chapter 3 (Book of Mormon)

and unto thee, whom my father Jacob hath named Israel, a prophet; (not the Messiah who is called Shilo;) and this prophet shall deliver my people out of Egypt in the days of thy bondage.

not the Messiah,

25. And it shall come to pass that they shall be scattered again; and a branch shall be broken off, and shall be carried into a far country; nevertheless they shall be remembered in the covenants of the Lord, when the Messiah cometh; for he shall be made manifest unto them in the latter days, in the Spirit of power; and shall bring them out of darkness into light; out of hidden darkness, and out of captivity unto freedom.

but a branch which was to be broken off, nevertheless, to be remembered in the covenants of the Lord that the Messiah should be made manifest unto them in the latter days, in the spirit of power, unto the bringing of them out of darkness unto light—yea, out of hidden darkness and out of captivity unto freedom.

26. A seer shall the Lord my God raise up, who shall be a choice seer unto the fruit of my loins.

6. For Joseph truly testified, saying: A seer shall the Lord my God raise up, who shall be a choice seer unto the fruit of my loins.

27. Thus saith the Lord God of my fathers unto me, A choice seer will I raise up, out of the fruit of thy loins, and he shall be esteemed highly among the fruit of his loins, his brethren; and unto him will I give commandments that he shall do a work for the fruit of thy loins.

7. Yea, Joseph truly said: Thus saith the Lord unto me: A choice seer will I raise up out of the fruit of thy loins and he shall be esteemed highly among the fruit of thy loins. And unto him will I give commandment that he shall do a work for the fruit of thy loins, his brethren, which shall be of great worth unto them, even to the bringing of them to the knowledge of the covenants which I have made with thy fathers.

28. And he shall bring them to a knowledge of the covenants which I have made with thy fathers;

and he shall do whatsoever work I shall command him.

8. And I will give unto him a commandment that he shall do none other work, save the work which I shall command him.

29. And I will make him great in mine eyes, for he shall do my work;

And I will make him great in mine eyes for he shall do my work.

and he shall be great like unto him whom I have said I would raise up unto you, to deliver my people, O house of Israel,

9. And he shall be great like unto Moses, whom I have said I would raise up unto you, to deliver my people, O house of Israel.

out of the land of Egypt; for a seer will I raise up to deliver my people out of the land of Egypt; and he shall be called Moses. And by this name he shall know that he is of thy house; for he shall be nursed by the king's daughter, and shall be called her son.

10. And Moses will I raise up, to deliver thy people out of the land of Egypt.

GENESIS 50 (Inspired Version)

30. And again, a seer will I raise up out of the fruit of thy loins, and unto him will I give power to bring forth my word unto the seed of thy loins; and not to the bringing forth of my word only, saith the Lord, but to the convincing them of my word, which shall have already gone forth among them in the last days;

31. Wherefore the fruit of thy loins shall write, and the fruit of the loins of Judah shall write; and that which shall be written by the fruit of thy loins, and also that which shall be written by the fruit of the loins of Judah, shall grow together unto the confounding of false doctrines, and laying down of contentions, and establishing peace among the fruit of thy loins, and bringing them to a knowledge of their fathers in the latter days; and also to the knowledge of my covenants, saith the Lord.

32. And out of weakness shall he be made strong, in that day when my work shall go forth among all my people, which shall restore them, who are of the house of Israel, in the last days.

33. And that seer will I bless, and they that seek to destroy him shall be confounded; for this promise I give unto you; for I will remember you from generation to generation;

and his name shall be called Joseph, and it shall be after the name of his father; and he shall be like unto you; for the thing which the Lord shall bring forth by his hand shall bring my people unto salvation.

34. And the Lord sware unto Joseph, that he would preserve his seed for ever,

saying, I will raise up Moses, and a rod shall be in his hand, and he shall gather together my people, and he shall lead them as a flock, and he shall smite the waters of the Red Sea with his rod.

2 NEPHI Chapter 3 (Book of Mormon)

11. But a seer will I raise up out of the fruit of thy loins; and unto him will I give power to bring forth my word unto the seed of thy loins — and not to the bringing forth my word only saith the Lord, but to the convincing them of my word, which shall have already gone forth among them.

12. Wherefore, the fruit of thy loins shall write; and the fruit of the loins of Judah shall write; and that which shall be written by the fruit of thy loins, and also that which shall be written by the fruit of the loins of Judah, shall grow together, unto the confounding of false doctrines and laying down of contentions, and establishing peace among the fruit of thy loins, and bringing them to the knowledge of their fathers in the latter days, and also to the knowledge of my covenants, saith the Lord.

13. And out of weakness he shall be made strong, in that day when my work shall commence among all my people, unto the restoring thee, O house of Israel, saith the Lord.

14. And thus prophesied Joseph, saying: Behold, that seer will the Lord bless; and they that seek to destroy him shall be confounded; for this promise, which I have obtained of the Lord, of the fruit of my loins, shall be fulfilled. Behold, I am sure of the fulfilling of this promise.

15. And his name shall be called after me; and it shall be after the name of his father. And he shall be like unto me; for the thing, which the Lord shall bring forth by his hand, by the power of the Lord shall bring my people unto salvation.

16. Yea, thus prophesied Joseph: I am sure of this thing, even as I am sure of the promise of Moses; for the Lord hath said unto me, I will preserve thy seed forever.

17. And the Lord hath said: I will raise up a Moses; and I will give power unto him in a rod;

GENESIS 50 (Inspired Version)

2 NEPHI Chapter 3 (Book of Mormon)

35, And he shall have judgment and shall write the word of the Lord. And he shall not speak many words, for I will write unto him my law by the finger of mine own hand. And I will make a spokesman for him, and his name shall be called Aaron.

and I will give judgment unto him in writing. Yet I will not loose his tongue, that he shall speak much, for I will not make him mighty in speaking. But I will write unto him my law, by the finger of mine own hand; and I will make a spokesman for him.

36. And it shall be done unto thee in the last days also, even as I have sworn. Therefore, Joseph said unto his brethren, God will surely visit you, and bring you out of this land, unto the land which he swear unto Abraham, and unto Isaac, and to Jacob.

37. And Joseph confirmed many other things unto his brethren, and took an oath of the children of Israel, saying unto them, God will surely visit you, and ye shall carry up my bones from hence.

18. And the Lord said unto me also; I will raise up unto the fruit of thy loins; and I will make for him a spokesman. And I, behold, I will give unto him that he shall write the writing of the fruit of thy loins, unto the fruit of thy loins; and the spokesman of thy loins shall declare it.

19. And the words which he shall write shall be the words which are expedient in my wisdom should go forth unto the fruit of thy loins. And it shall be as if the fruit of thy loins had cried unto them from the dust; for I know their faith.

20. And they shall cry from the dust; yea, even repentance unto their brethren, even after many generations have gone by them. And it shall come to pass that their cry shall go, even according to the simpleness of their words.

21. Because of their faith their words shall proceed forth out of my mouth unto their brethren who are the fruit of thy loins; and the weakness of their words will I make strong in their faith, unto the remembering of my covenant which I made unto thy fathers.

The Two Sources For Joseph's Prophecies

Joseph's descendants kept a family scripture called the Brass Plates. This included the Prophecies of Joseph.

The Prophecies of Joseph were copied onto the plates of Nephi.

The Plates of Nephi were incorporated into the plates of Mormon.

Moses originally wrote the prophecies of Joseph in the concluding portion of Genesis.

Holy Bible

The modern Bible is based on an ancient collection of texts from which the prophecies of Joseph had been deleted.

Book of Mormon

The Plates of Mormon were translated into English and published in 1830.

Inspired Version of the Holy Bible

A portion of the original text was restored by direct revelation. This included the prophecies of Joseph as recorded by Moses.

A SUMMARY OF JOSEPH'S KNOWLEDGE CONCERNING MOSES

Supposing a famous man died in 1900 and just prior to his death he told all about a baby who would be born in 1964. This would be comparable to Joseph's prophecies concerning Moses. The death of Joseph and the birth of Moses were about 64 years apart.

From what we have already seen in the material quoted above, it is obvious that Joseph knew his people would go into bondage after his death but in due time they would be liberated. This is why Joseph was able to say from his death bed, "I go down to my grave with joy. The God of my father Jacob be with you, to deliver you out of affliction in the days of your bondage; for the *Lord hath visited me,* and I have obtained a promise of the Lord, that . . . the Lord God will raise up . . . a prophet (not the Messiah who is called Shilo;) and this prophet shall deliver my people out of Egypt in the days of thy bondage."[23]

In connection with this great liberation, Joseph knew nine specific things:

1. He knew that the name of the great emancipator would be "Moses". (Insp. Version, Genesis 50:29, 34; 2 Nephi 3:10)

2. He knew Moses would be raised by the king's daughter and would be called her son. (Insp. Version, Genesis 50:29)

3. He knew Moses would have a rod with which he could perform stupendous miracles. (Insp. Version, Genesis 50:34; 2 Nephi 3:17)

4. He knew Moses would have the power to "smite the waters of the Red Sea." (Insp. Version, Genesis 50:34)

5. He knew that Moses would be slow of speech because the Lord would not loosen his tongue. (2 Nephi 3:17)

6. He knew Moses would have a spokesman appointed to speak for him. (Insp. Version, Genesis 50:35; 2 Nephi 3:17)

---

23. Insp. Version, Genesis 50:24

7. He knew that the name of Moses' spokesman would be "Aaron." (Ibid.)

8. He knew that while Moses would be slow of speech he would have great skill in writing. (Insp. Version, Genesis 50:35; 2 Nephi 3:17)

9. He knew that the Lord would personally inscribe the law for Moses "by the finger of mine own hand." (Insp. Version, Genesis 50:35; 2 Nephi 3:17)

A Summary of Joseph's Knowledge Concerning His Own Descendants

We have also seen from a review of the "lost" prophecies of Joseph that he had a remarkably detailed understanding concerning the future destiny of his own descendants. He knew that their mission would be more or less separate from that of the rest of Israel and that it would be in a "far country." A careful analysis of Joseph's prophecies reveals that he knew at least 22 specific things concerning the future mission and destiny of his posterity.

1. He knew that God would raise up a righteous branch from among his descendants and that these would be "broken off and shall be carried into a far country." (Insp. Version, Genesis 50:25; 2 Nephi 3:5)

2. He knew this branch of his posterity would be remembered "when the Messiah cometh." (Insp. Version, Genesis 50:25; 2 Nephi 3:5)

3. He knew the Messiah would appear to his descendants "in the latter days," and would bring his posterity "out of the darkness into light," and "out of captivity unto freedom." (Insp. Version, Genesis 50:25; 2 Nephi 3:5)

4. He knew among his descendants in that "far country" a great prophet or seer would be raised up who would be "esteemed highly" by Joseph's posterity. (Insp. Vers. Gen. 50:25-26, 30; 2 Nephi 3:6-7)

5. He knew that the seer of the latter days would do a great work for Joseph's posterity and that he would be "great" in the eyes of God because he would

occupy himself exclusively in the work which God would assign to him. (Insp. Vers., Gen. 50:27-29; 2 Nephi 3:7-8)

6. He knew this latter-day seer would be given revelations and have the "power to bring forth my word" unto the descendants of Joseph. (Insp. Vers., Gen. 50:30; 2 Nephi 3:11)

7. He knew this seer would have the ability to rebuild their faith in the scriptures which had already come into their possession "in the last days." (Ibid.)

8. He knew his descendants would write a testament of God's revelations to them. (Insp. Vers., Gen. 50:31; 2 Nephi 3:12)

9. He knew the Jews would write a testament of God's revealed word to them. (Ibid.)

10. He knew these two testaments would grow together and become a single canon of scripture. (Ibid.)

11. He knew that these two testaments would combine to put down false doctrines, eliminate contentions, and establish peace among Joseph's descendants of the latter days. (Ibid.)

12. He knew that those who undertook to destroy the Lord's seer in the latter days would be confounded. (Insp. Vers., Gen. 50:33; 2 Nephi 3:14)

13. He knew the Lord's seer who would be raised up in the latter days would be named "Joseph". (Insp. Vers., Gen. 50:33; 2 Nephi 3:15)

14. He knew the father of this seer would also be named Joseph. (Ibid.)

15. He knew the seer of the latter days would be like unto Joseph who was sold into Egypt. (Ibid.)

16. He knew this seer would also have those qualities which would make him comparable to Moses. (Insp. Vers., Gen. 50:20; 2 Nephi 3:13)

17. He knew that this seer would begin his calling in abject weakness but would "be made strong." (Insp. Vers., Gen. 50:32; 2 Nephi 3:13)

18. He knew that Joseph of the latter days would in-augurate a program of gathering and restoring Israel. (Insp. Vers., Gen. 50:32; 2 Nephi 3:13)

19. He knew this Joseph would have a spokesman even as Moses. (2 Nephi 3:18)

20. He knew that this seer would have the power to restore that which Joseph's posterity had written "many generations" earlier. (2 Nephi 3:18-20)

21. He knew that these writings would come from some secret burial place in the earth so that their words would, as it were, "cry from the dust . . . after many generations have gone by." (2 Nephi 3:20)

22. He knew these writings would not be spectacular and eloquent but would be noted for their "simple-ness" and though they would be called "weak" by many, still God would make them strong in convert-ing Israel and establishing his covenant with them. (2 Nephi 3:21)

Anyone familiar with the work and mission of Joseph Smith will immediately recognize the literal fulfillment of these prophecies. In fact, his life was so remarkable that even many who have heard of it find it difficult to believe. Nevertheless, the work which he started is rolling forward with such speed that this generation may live to see the final fruition of everything Joseph in Egypt predicted concerning the work of the latter-day Joseph.

Modern Jews Expecting a "Joseph" to Prepare the Way for the Coming of Their Messiah

Now that we know the Hebrew scriptures originally contained all of these prophecies concerning a latter-day seer named "Joseph," we are able to account for a persistent tradition among the Jews which has previously puzzled schol-ars. From the most ancient times, Jewish tradition has pro-claimed that a great servant of God from the House of Joseph would come in the latter days to prepare the way for the coming of Shilo, the Great Messiah.[24]

---

24. See Joseph Klausner, *The Messianic Idea in Israel*, New York: the Macmillan Co., 1955, chapter 9 is devoted exclusively to this subject.

In fact, so profound was the respect of the rabbis for this "Joseph" that they began calling him," Messiah ben Joseph," and called their Shilo, "Messiah ben David." Literally translated, these appellations mean, "The anointed One, son of Joseph," and "The anointed One, son of David."

A comprehensive study of this mysterious "Messiah ben Joseph" was made by Dr. Joseph Klausner, Professor Emeritus of Hebrew literature and Jewish history at the Hebrew University in Jerusalem. Dr. Klausner did everything possible to explain away this "Joseph" but, being an honest scholar, he was compelled to put down the basic attributes which Jewish tradition variously ascribed to him. These include the following:

1. He will rise up shortly before the coming of Shilo, the great Messiah ben David. (p. 486)
2. He will be a descendant of Joseph through Ephraim. (p. 487)
3. His mission will commence about the time the prophet Elijah comes as promised in Malachi 4:5-6. (p. 498)
4. In preparing mankind for the coming of Shilo, Messiah ben Joseph will enter into a great contest with the anti-Christ forces. (p. 496)
5. In the heat of this contest with the anti-Christ, Messiah ben Joseph will be killed. (p. 496)

Dr. Klausner points out that the Samaritans were particularly zealous in proclaiming the coming of Messiah ben Joseph since they claimed to be remnants of Joseph who had survived the Assyrian conquest. They took great pride in the fact that the prophet who would come to prepare the way for Shilo would be from the House of Joseph. The Samaritan version of this latter-day Joseph is extremely interesting.

1. They said he would be a descendant of Joseph through Ephraim and they sometimes referred to him as "son of Ephraim." (p. 484)
2. They called him Teal, meaning "a restorer," "he who returns," or, according to others, "he who causes to return." (p. 484)

3. They believed he would call the people to repentance and bring back better days for Israel.

4. They said this Joseph of the latter day "will restore everywhere the true Law to its former validity and convert all peoples, *especially the Jews,* to the Samaritan [Ephraimite] religion." (p. 484)

The Samaritans did not like the idea of having their prophet Joseph killed by the anti-Christ so they said he would overcome Gog and Magog and "die a natural death after fulfilling his mission in the world." (p. 484)

As might be expected, there are a number of contradictions in the traditions concerning Messiah ben Joseph, but considering the vast number of centuries through which these stories have been handed down it is almost a miracle that they remained so much like the original prophecy as they did.

When Were Joseph's Prophecies Lost?

Dr. Klausner admits that it is historically repugnant to the Jewish scholars to think that anything good could come out of Ephraim. As Joseph's heir, Ephraim took its place at the head of the twelve tribes. When Judah rebelled around 937 B.C. and set up a separate capital it was almost inevitable that the most bitter kind of hostility would persist between Judah and Ephraim. Even after the Northern Kingdom (under Ephraim) had been conquered by the Assyrians around 722 B.C., and carried off to an unknown destination, the hostility of Judah continued to be vented on the Samaritans who were said to have a remnant of Ephraimite blood in them.

Since we now know that Joseph's prophecies were once a part of the authentic text of Genesis as recorded by Moses, it is likely that the hostility of some ancient scribe resulted in the deliberate purging of this material from the official canon of scripture which was kept in the temple at Jerusalem. During the bitter days of strife between Judah and the Northern Kingdom it would have been easy for a leading scribe to speculate that perhaps these prophecies about a latter-day Joseph were apocryphal and then persuade himself that they had been inserted by some zealous Josephite who wanted to rob Judah of her honored position in being the tribe through whom the great Messiah would come.

It must also be remembered that this was a period of flagrant apostasy. The sanctity and prestige of holy writ was at its lowest ebb. Possibly a scribe of that period would have had little compunction in slashing from the Jewish scriptures any prediction that said a great leader would rise up out of the tribe of Joseph. Such a prophecy might have been counted an intolerable political liability, particularly when the leaders at Jerusalem were struggling so desperately to build up an undying hostility toward the Josephites and the Northern Kingdom.

Nevertheless, the removal of these great prophecies from the scriptural canon in Jerusalem did not remove them from the minds of the people. As Dr. Klausner points out, down through the centuries persistent references to a coming "Messiah ben Joseph" crept into the writings of the most respected rabbis. Modern Jewish scholars are still trying to explain it.

MESSIAH BEN JOSEPH HAS COME!

If these fine scholars only knew it, the most exciting message of the modern age is now sweeping across the earth: "Messiah ben Joseph has come!" A few devout and believing Jews have already stopped to hear the message. They have accepted it knowing that it portends the nearness of the coming in glory of the great Messiah ben David for whom they have waited so long.

Even those who have not heard of the modern Joseph but who have read the prophecies of the Old Testament, recognize that great days are coming for Israel. Things are happening which were given as the signs by which the nearness of the Messianic reign could be recognized. The most significant of these is the massive migration of the Jews back to Palestine and the creation of the nation of Israel. Jewish scholars count this of great messianic significance. They accept the fact that the hand of God is in it. As Dr. Klausner says in the chapter of his book called, "The Ingathering of the Exiles:"

"According to *Shemoneh Esreh* it is God Himself who will 'sound the great horn for freedom' and 'lift up the ensign to gather our exiles, and gather us quickly from the four corners of the earth' just before Messiah's coming." (p. 470)

However, Dr. Klausner is deeply disappointed about one thing. He says the people of Judah who are returning to Palestine have not yet adopted the correct principles which are necessary in order for them to enjoy God's richest blessings and become "a light of the Gentiles" as predicted by Isaiah."[25] Instead, Dr. Klausner says the Jewish leaders are experimenting in Israel with certain cultural and social principles which he believes they must someday abandon. Here are his words from the preface to his book:

". . . the idea of redemption in Israel (Palestine) has spread and overflowed into many hearts like a flood of mighty waters. And to this idea there has become attached another idea, which has organic connexion with it: viz., the idea of social equality and righteousness. For the idea of redemption is impossible without the positive element of the eternal vision of the prophets of truth and righteousness — the Messianic idea, the idea of the knowledge of God as revealed in the prophetic ethic, the idea of the brotherhood of man and the rule of righteousness in the world.

"But alas! it is not the Hebraic, the prophetic, the Messianic-Israelitic social conception which has become a basis for bringing about redemption in the land of vision and promise, but a foreign social conception, linked up with economic and historical materialism,[26] to which the prophetic idealism is a mockery. All this is not Jewish, not Palestinian, and therefore is not truly humanitarian either. Zionist social policy cannot be based on an authoritarian materialism, which brings about equality by deeds of violence; it must be prophetic, saturated with the Jewish Messianic idea, or else not be at

---

25. Isaiah 42:6
26. "Economic and historic materialism" are ideas created and promoted by Karl Marx to justify the use of violence and revolution to establish a communist state. When his Communist Party was outlawed in 1851, Marx turned around and used these same ideas but proposed a plan for the acquisition of dictatorial control by what he called "peaceful means." He proposed to work through the regular legislative bodies to gradually gain control of farms, industries, and other productive property. Marx called this second method *Socialism*. It is sometimes called *Marxist-Socialism* to distinguish it from the utopian variety which tried unsuccessfully to make these principles work on a voluntary basis. Marx said they would work under compulsion of government control. These are the principles of "economic and historic materialism" Dr. Klausner is castigating.

all. If this book can succeed in giving an idea of the close connexion between the political redemption of Israel in its own land and the ideal of righteousness, peace, and brotherhood among all peoples; and if a prophetic social outlook can be gained from this idea, and can be laid as a foundation stone in the building of our politico-spiritual National Home, I shall know that my labors of many years have not been in vain."[27]

JOSEPH'S PROPHECIES BEING FULFILLED

At the time Dr. Klausner wrote this he had no idea that God had already launched His program to make the Messianic dream an eventual reality. To facilitate the day of redemption for Israel, Messiah ben Joseph had been sent. God had already revealed Himself just as he promised he would. A prophet had been raised up who was indeed a direct descendant of Joseph. His name was Joseph. His father's name was Joseph. He had already brought forth the sacred records of Joseph's posterity who were a branch "broken off" and carried to America, that "far country" seen by Joseph in Egypt.

In fact, this modern Joseph had originally begun his work under divine guidance clear back in 1820. By 1829 he had finished translating the metal plates which contained the history of Joseph's descendants in the western hemisphere and which had been buried in the earth for nearly 1400 years. By 1830 he had followed revealed instructions and set up the organization of the restored Church and Kingdom of God. In 1841 he had one of his associates carry out the Lord's instruction to have the land of Jerusalem dedicated for the return of the Jews. From 1820 until 1844 this modern Joseph was engaged in a deadly conflict with the forces of the anti-Christ which combined against him. On June 27, 1844, he was slain by a mob at Carthage, Illinois, even though he was in protective custody of the Governor of that state at the time.

Since then the work he started has continued to roll forth without diminution. Today, God's modern kingdom is in the process of putting 25,000 unpaid, full-time mission-

---

27. See preface to Dr. Klausner's book, *The Messianic Idea in Israel*, pp. IX-X. The parenthesis in this quote are mine.

aries into the field to tell the world that God has spoken again, that the fulness of His Gospel has been restored, and that the Second Advent of the great Messiah is near.

This is a message to Christians, Jews, and all the rest of humanity alike. No longer need Judah look upon Ephraim with envy, nor Ephraim look upon Judah with hostility. The prophets predicted that these two great branches of Israel would join hands in the last days to usher in the long awaited Messianic reign. Concerning this period the prophet proclaimed:

"And he shall set up an ensign for the nations, and shall assemble the outcasts of Israel, and gather together the dispersed of Judah from the four corners of the earth.

"The envy also of Ephraim shall depart, and the adversaries of Judah shall be cut off: Ephraim shall not envy Judah, and Judah shall not vex Ephraim."[28]

---

28. Isaiah 11:12-13

Scripture Reading and Questions on Chapter Eight

Scripture Reading Assignment: Genesis 50:14-26; 2 Nephi, chapter 3.

1—Why did Joseph's brothers ask to be made his servants?

2—What was Joseph's reaction? What did he say to them?

3—How long did Joseph govern Egypt following his father's death? How old was Joseph when he died?

4—What did Joseph ask his descendants to do with his body? Where was it finally buried?

5—In what two records were the prophecies of Joseph originally written? In what two records can they be found today?

6—List five things which Joseph knew about the liberation of Israel from Egyptian bondage.

7—What did Joseph say about his people being "broken off" from the rest of Israel?

8—What did Joseph say would happen to his descendants when the Savior came?

9—What did he say the Savior would do for his descendants in the latter days?

10—List four things Joseph knew about the great prophet who would be raised up by the Lord in the latter days.

11—What did Joseph say about the Bible? Did he know about the Book of Mormon?

12—What have the Jews known about a "Joseph" who would be raised up to prepare the way for the Messiah? What do the Jews call him?

13—How would the Jews have a tradition about this Joseph when their scriptures no longer contain this prophecy?

14—Why would the Samaritans be especially anxious to keep alive the prophecy about the coming of a "Joseph" in the latter days?

15—What great modern movement has signalled to the Jews that the appearance of their Messiah must be drawing near?

16—Do Jewish scholars see the hand of God in the gathering of the Jews to Palestine?

17—What does Dr. Klausner say is disappointing to him in the Jewish gathering thus far? Is it significant that since Dr. Klausner's book was written, the Jewish leaders have been turning away from "authoritarian materialism" and creating a more open society similar to the kind envisioned by the American founding fathers?

18—List five predictions concerning "Messiah Ben Joseph" which were literally fulfilled in the life of Joseph Smith.

19—What is the basic message which the modern servants of God are taking to the world?

20—What feelings are supposed to exist between Ephraim and Judah in the last days?

CHAPTER NINE

The Writings of Joseph Discovered in Egypt

We cannot conclude the epic of Joseph without mentioning one more extremely important development which is still in the process of unfolding. This was the discovery of a whole volume of Joseph's writings in the catacombs of Egypt.

As we have already mentioned, archaeologists had searched in vain for the slightest fragment of evidence relating to the administration of Joseph in Egypt. So far as they were able to determine his entire ministry was during the period of the Hyksos shepherd kings. Therefore, it was assumed that when those hated Shemite foreigners were finally driven out by the native Egyptians, they systematically demolished every sign of the Hyksos occupation, including all possible references to the great Hebrew prime minister, Joseph.

So thorough was this destruction that it created a chasm-like gap in the history of Egypt extending across a bleak and unmarked period of more than 150 years. At first this was baffling to Egyptologists because they knew the native Egyptians were immaculate record keepers. Dr. Werner Keller comments on this phenomenon:

"No country in the ancient East has handed down its history so faithfully as Egypt. . . . No other people have recorded so meticulously their important events, the activities of their rulers, their campaigns, the erection of temples and palaces, as well as their literature and poetry.

"But this time Egypt gave the scholars no answer. As if it were not enough that they found nothing about Joseph, they discovered neither documents nor monuments out of this whole period. The records which showed hardly a break for centuries suddenly stopped about 1730 B.C. From then on for a long time an impenetrable darkness lay over Egypt. Not before 1580 B.C. did contemporary evidence appear once again. How could this absence of any information whatever over so long a period be explained, especially from such a highly developed people and civilization?"[1]

Dr. Keller answers his own question by pointing out that this turned out to be the time when the "Hyksos, Semitic tribes from Canaan and Syria," were ruling over Egypt.[2]

The dates of "about" 1730 to 1580 B.C. which Dr. Keller cites as the duration of the Hyksos occupation are not fixed by historians with absolute exactness but they are believed to be very close, give or take a decade or two. Certainly it turned out to be a remarkable coincidence that this period was the identical time dimension for three significant events:

1. The time when Joseph was living in Egypt.
2. The time when the Hyksos shepherd kings were ruling over Egypt.
3. The time which later Egyptians tried to totally obliterate from their history.

If this reconstruction is correct — and current findings seem to strongly support it — then it explains why the Egyptians would wish to wipe out this despised period of their history and it also explains why the archaeologists were unable to find any monuments, obelisks, pillars or historical records referring to the Hebrew prime minister, Joseph.

But even if it were the intention of the vengeful Egyptians to erase every vestige of Joseph's history along with that of the Hyksos, we now know that they providentially missed a most priceless volume of Joseph's writings which was buried with a royal mummy in one of Egypt's sacred pit-tombs. Under the circumstances, it is almost miraculous that this lengthy papyrus of Joseph's writings should have survived.

Sometime between 1818 and 1823 A.D. a free-lance

---

1. Dr. Werner Keller, *The Bible as History*, New York: William Morrow and Company, 1956, p. 86.
2. Ibid. p. 87

treasure seeker named Antonio Lebolo[3] opened up a section
of the Egyptian catacombs near the ancient city of Thebes
and accidentally stumbled into this royal sanctuary where the
writings of Joseph were hidden. Lebolo never lived long
enough to learn the value of what he had discovered, but no
modern student of the Bible should be ignorant of it.

THE AMAZING STORY OF ANTONIO LEBOLO

The correct dates and many significant details concerning the Lebolo exploration were not documented until fairly
recently. Dr. Sidney B. Sperry of Brigham Young University
started digging into the Lebolo story a number of years ago.
Then Dr. James R. Clark, also of Brigham Young University,
decided to make this area of research an important part of
his life's work. It turned out to be an exciting adventure.

All of the far-flung facts which have been unearthed so
far have been compiled in a book written by Dr. Clark,
entitled, *The Story of the Pearl of Great Price.*[4] This book
is presently used as a text at Brigham Young University and
in it will be found a summary of the Lebolo exploration and
the subsequent events related to it. The highlights are as
follows:

Antonio Lebolo did his exploring in Egypt under the
sponsorship of Chevalier Drovetti, the French Consul, who
had obtained a special license from Mehemmet Ali, the Viceroy of Egypt. Lebolo was only one of a great many adventurers and explorers who dug into the catacombs during the
early part of the nineteenth century. However, in spite of
all the digging, this was not by any means the "golden age"
of archaeology in Egypt. It would more appropriately fall in
the classification of a wild and reckless age when ruffians
were raiding the royal tombs of Egypt in an effort to find
mummies and artifacts which could be legally shipped out of

---

3. This name may be more familiar to the reader as Antonio Sebolo since that is
   the way it originally appeared in *Documentary Church History*, Vol. 2, p. 348.
   However, the correct spelling has now been conclusively established as "Lebolo."
   In fact, this is precisely the way Parley P. Pratt spelled the name in 1842 when
   he published the Book of Abraham in the *Millennial Star* in England. The error
   in the *Documentary History of the Church* may have resulted from the mistaking
   of a cursive "L" for a cursive "S" in the longhand manuscript.
4. See James R. Clark, *The Story of the Pearl of Great Price*, Salt Lake City:
   Bookcraft, Inc., 1955, 253 pages.

Egypt and sold for a handsome profit to the museums and collectors of Europe.[5]

Because many of these tombs had remained sacred, unde-filed, and unmolested for over 3,000 years, they represented a virtually priceless repository of archaeological treasure. How-ever, since the professional tomb robbers of this period were not scientists but looters, it was inevitable that only the most valuable and the best preserved objects would be saved.

A man named Giovanni Belzoni who was working in the same area as Lebolo, describes what it was like to break into one of these ancient royal tombs. Each vault or pit-tomb often contained hundreds of mummified bodies. Belzoni says, "every step I took I crushed a mummy in some part or other. . . . When my weight bore on the body of an Egyptian it crushed like a band-box. I sank altogether among the broken mummies with a crash of bones, rags and wooden cases. . . . I could not avoid being covered with bones, legs, arms and heads rolling from above. . . ."[6]

It was down into just such a dark and musty royal tomb located near Thebes and containing hundreds of mum-mies that Antonio Lebolo made entry sometime prior to 1823.[7]

Antonio Lebolo's nephew, Michael Chandler, is reported to have furnished the following details concerning this explor-ation:[8]

A work force involving 433 men consisting of Egyptian or Turkish soldiers, were employed at a wage of six cents per day and worked four months and two days before they discovered the entrance to this particular tomb. After forcing an entry into the catacomb, Lebolo discovered that it con-tained around 100 mummies which were of "the first order" of embalming, and from 200 to 300 mummies which were

---

5. Dr. Clark treats this problem and cites Glyn E. Daniel, lecturer in Archaeology at Cambridge University. See *The Story of the Pearl of Great Price*, pp. 81-83.
6. Ibid., p. 81.
7. The nephew of Lebolo, Michael Chandler, allegedly gave the date of his uncle's penetration into the tomb as June 7, 1831 (See *Documentary History of the Church*, Vol. 2, p. 348). However, since there is now rather compelling evidence that Lebolo died in 1823, we conclude that his exploration would have necessarily occurred prior to the 1823 date, perhaps June 7, 1821, instead of 1831.
8. Except as otherwise noted, all of these details are set forth in the report of Chand-ler's account which is contained in the *Documentary History of the Church*, Vol. 2, pp. 348-350. I have condensed the information and included a few additional matters with their sources cited.

of the second and third order. All of these were located in the "grand cavity" or vaulted catacomb.

The first order of mummies were in coffins which were standing erect in niches carved in the catacomb walls. The remainder were laid out upon the floor. The antiquity of these mummies was such that none of those on the floor could be removed. They fell apart with the slightest handling. However, among the 100 mummies of the first order, 11 were found to be in a good state of preservation. Lebolo promptly boxed these up for shipment to Paris.

It is stated that none of the Egyptian coffins or sarco- phagi were opened by Lebolo[9] so he did not know that within these coffins would be found original documents older than the writings of Moses.

Unfortunately, Lebolo never reached his destination with these mummies so we do not have his personal account of this exploration except through his nephew, Michael Chandler, to whom he presumably communicated the above information by letter. Lebolo was stricken by a severe illness while en- route to Paris and had to have the ship put in at Trieste, Italy, where he died ten days later. Prior to his death, how- ever, Lebolo made out a will to his nephew, Michael Chand- ler, and bequeathed to him the 11 mummies. Perhaps it was at this same time that he wrote out for the benefit of his nephew the manner in which the mummies had been dis- covered. We know that Chandler claimed to have a know- ledge of a great many details concerning these mummies from some source.

It was a long time, however, before Chandler received the bulky crates containing these 11 Egyptian coffins. In fact, according to his own account, they did not reach him until the spring of 1833. Since we now have documentation from contemporary sources indicating that Lebolo died in 1823,[10] it is obvious that there was a delay of approximately 10 years before the mummies came into the possession of Michael Chandler.

9. "Up to this time they (the mummies) had not been taken out of the coffins, nor the coffins opened." Ibid. p. 349.
10. See the British compilation quoted by Dr. Clark in *The Story of the Pearl of Great Price*, pp. 77-78.

Part of the delay was due to the fact that Michael Chandler had originally been living in Dublin, Ireland, and it was to this destination that the mummies were initially shipped. However, when these Egyptian antiquities arrived at the Thames port in England,[11] it was somehow learned that Chandler had moved to America so his friends arranged to have the shipment sent directly to New York.

Michael Chandler Receives the 11 Mummies

Having paid the assessed custom charges, Chandler took possession of the mummies in April, 1833, and prepared to take them to his home in Philadelphia. However, either because it was required by the custom officials, or because he could not wait to discover what kind of Egyptian treasures his uncle had sent him, Michael Chandler opened the coffins right there at the New York custom house. Not finding anything inside the coffins but linen-bound mummies, he decided to unwrap the bodies and view them for himself. In the process it was discovered that two of the bodies each had a cylinder shaped object lying on the breast beneath the folded hands which crossed each other in a fashion customary to many of the Egyptian dead.[12]

These objects had been carefully wrapped in linen and sealed tightly with bitumen. When they were opened Chandler discovered that they were papyrus scrolls covered with Egyptian writing and hieroglyphics in black and red.[13]

When Chandler opened some of the other coffins he also found a number of smaller papyrus scrolls containing

---

11. For this detail we are indebted to Parley P. Pratt who mentions it in the *Millennial Star* for July 1, 1842. Dr.Clark quotes it in *The Story of the Pearl of Great Price*, p. 84.
12. The words, "lying upon the breast" are also the words of Parley P. Pratt in the same source just cited. Dr. J. R. Riggs, a contemporary of Parley P. Pratt, described it a little differently though it could be his version of the same thing. Professor N. L. Nelson attributes the following description to Dr. Riggs: "Lying transversely on the stomach, beneath the folded hands of one of the mummies, was found the relic in question." (See *The Story of the Pearl of Great Price*, p. 87, where Dr. Clark furnishes a photostatic copy of all this material.)
13. Seven medical doctors who saw the papyrus scrolls in Philadelphia at a later date signed a certificate which said among other things, "The papyrus covered with black or red ink, or paint, in excellent preservation, are very interesting." This entire certificate is in *Documentary History of the Church*, Vol. 2, p. 350. When Joseph Smith saw these scrolls in 1835 he described them very similarly as " . . . beautifully written on papyrus with black and a small part red, ink or paint, in perfect preservation." Ibid. p. 348.

mathematical and astronomical data. However, since he had hoped to find jewelry or gold ornaments in these cylinder-shaped objects,[14] he was bitterly disappointed to find nothing but ancient, unreadable documents. Had he been told what he held in his hands he might never have believed it. These documents were worth more than the Hope diamond!

Apparently the coffin opening had attracted quite a crowd at the New York custom house and when the rolls of papyrus were being displayed someone told Chandler that no one could translate them in New York City but that undoubtedly Joseph Smith could do it since he had already translated some Egyptian writings.[15] Chandler had never heard of Joseph Smith but he made a mental note of his name.[16]

CHANDLER ATTEMPTS TO GET THE SCROLLS TRANSLATED

During the next two years or so, Chandler traveled up and down the Atlantic seaboard with his mummies and scrolls. He visited cities such as Baltimore, Philadelphia, New York City, and Harrisburg, Pennsylvania. He was constantly look-ing for experts on ancient languages who might translate the Egyptian scrolls. However, the science of Egyptology was still so primitive that only the meaning of a minor fragment or two could be interpreted successfully. It is reported that on several occasions people brought up the name of Joseph Smith again and urged Chandler to test Joseph Smith's trans-lating ability by taking these documents to him.[17]

Finally through circumstances not yet entirely known, Chandler did make a trip to the frontier community of Kirt-land, Ohio, for the specific purpose of showing the Egyptian writings to Joseph Smith.

By then it was July, 1835. Chandler had sold seven of the mummies and one or more of the shorter papyrus scrolls containing astronomical calculations.[18] Four mummies re-

---

14. "When Mr. Chandler discovered that there was something with the mummies, he supposed or hoped it might be some diamonds or valuable metal, and was no little chagrined when he saw his disappointment." Ibid., p. 349.
15. Ibid.
16. Ibid. pp. 349-350.
17. See statement by Parley P. Pratt quoted in *The Story of the Pearl of Great Price,* p. 84, and the statement of Dr. J. R. Riggs, a contemporary, quoted in the same source, p. 87.
18. Ibid. p. 97

mained, together with the two larger papyrus scrolls and two or three of the smaller ones. When Chandler met Joseph Smith he attempted to test his ability by asking Joseph Smith to translate the same small fragments as those which had been deciphered by linguists in the East. Chandler was delighted when Joseph Smith promptly came up with the meaning of the hieroglyphics and verified to a remarkable extent what the so-called experts had previously told him. Chandler was so impressed that he immediately sat down and wrote a personal testimonial concerning Joseph Smith's ability to translate these Egyptian characters. Here is the statement:[19]

Kirtland, July 6, 1835

This is to make known to all who may be desirous, concerning the knowledge of Mr. Joseph Smith, Jun., in deciphering the ancient hieroglyphic characters in my possession, which I have, in many eminent cities, showed to the most learned; and, from the information that I could ever learn, or meet with, I find that of Mr. Joseph Smith, Jun., to correspond in the most minute matters.

Michael H. Chandler

Traveling with, and proprietor of, Egyptian Mummies

News of this incident rapidly spread through the village of Kirtland and created considerable excitement. Several citizens were so impressed that they thought Joseph Smith should have an opportunity to study these scrolls further. It appears that they discussed this with Joseph Smith and he urged them to secure these antiquities if at all possible.[20] These citizens therefore raised $2,000[21] which seemed to satisfy Mr. Chandler and after making an outright purchase of the mummies and papyrus scrolls they presented them to Joseph Smith as a gift.

---

19. *Documentary History of the Church*, Vol. 2, p. 235
20. A reporter for the Quincy Whig interviewed Joseph Smith and reported that Joseph Smith indicated that the mummies were purchased "at his suggestion." (Quincy Whig, Quincy, Ill., October 17, 1840, p. 1, and quoted by Dr. Clark in *The Story of the Pearl of Great Price*, p. 70) Dr. J. R. Riggs who was associated with Joseph Smith is reported to have said that Joseph Smith was "eager to purchase the manuscripts. . . ." See *The Academic Review*, Brigham Young Academy, Provo, Utah, Vol. 1, No. 6, March, 1885. Also quoted by Dr. Clark in *The Story of the Pearl of Great Price*, p. 87.
21. The figure of $2,000 is attributed to Dr. J. R. Riggs, Ibid., p. 87

Joseph Smith 1805-1844

Joseph Smith Makes a Thrilling Discovery

Why did Joseph Smith urge his friends to try to purchase these particular antiquities?

It is worthy of note that since he was completely dependent upon the Lord for the gift of translation, it must have struck him as extremely singular that the Lord would give him the gift of translation in connection with these particular records. He must have sensed that there was undoubtedly something unusual and significant about them. How significant, he soon discovered.

As Joseph Smith received the gift of translation for the first of the two scrolls, he found it commenced as follows: "In the land of the Chaldeans, at the residence of my father, I, Abraham. . . ."[22]

ABRAHAM! What in the providence of God had suddenly fallen into his hands? For days Joseph Smith poured over this ancient text. It was literally overflowing with lost history, lost revelation, and lost principles of astronomy. What was this sacred document doing clasped to the breast of a mummified Egyptian?[23]

As Joseph Smith continued the translation he was told that there were some matters mentioned by Abraham which should not be disclosed for the present; matters both sacred and profound, which in the wisdom of God were best kept within the cloistered knowledge of those in the charge of the new dispensation.[24] But even so, the material which Joseph Smith was authorized to publish was cause for abundant satisfaction since it constituted a whole storehouse of new, original source material.

---

22. Abraham 1:1
23. With which mummies the scrolls were found is not clear. We are definitely told that one of the papyrus scrolls was found on the body of a "female" mummy (see statement of Parley P. Pratt quoted in *The Story of the Pearl of Great Price*, p. 84), however, Joseph Smith quotes Chandler as stating that he found the two main scrolls on two different bodies and the smaller scrolls on yet other bodies. See *Documentary History of the Church*, Vol. 2, p. 349. The four mummies which finally came into the possession of Joseph Smith are reported to have been identified as "a king, a queen, a princess, and a slave." See statement of Dr. J. R. Riggs quoted in *The Story of the Pearl of Great Price*, p. 87.
24. When Joseph Smith later published portions of the Egyptian hieroglyphics along with his translation of it, he clearly identified those items which he had not been permitted to disclose. See, for example, facsimile No. 2 in the *Pearl of Great Price*, p. 34, where 13 items are identified as matters which "ought not be revealed at the present time."

Joseph Smith finally went on to the next scroll. When the gift of translation was obtained for this second papyrus, its contents turned out to be as great a surprise as the first. It was Egyptian writing containing the words of Joseph who was sold into Egypt! In fact, the information contained in this scroll was a continuation of the scriptural history commenced in the previous papyrus written by Abraham.[25] It is interesting that Joseph Smith was given to understand that the papyrus of Abraham was "written by his own hand,"[26] and that both the papyrus of Abraham and that of Joseph are referred to as though they were original works personally written by their respective authors and not a copy. Joseph Smith specifically calls them "the writings of the Fathers, Abraham, and Joseph,"[27] and Parley P. Pratt speaks of these combined scrolls as "a record written partly by the father of the faithful, Abraham, and finished by Joseph when in Egypt."[28]

Apparently, the two scrolls together constituted a history of the world from the creation down to the time of the patriarchs, and a prophetic history of the world from then until the final judgment.[29]

THE SCROLL OF JOSEPH CREATES TREMENDOUS INTEREST

Joseph Smith obtained the papyrus scrolls and mummies in July, 1835. During December, 1835, his secretary and scribe, Oliver Cowdery, wrote a lengthy letter which

---

25. "The record is now in course of translation . . . and proves to be a record written partly by the father of the faithful, Abraham, and finished by Joseph when in Egypt." Statement of Parley P. Pratt quoted in *The Story of the Pearl of Great Price*, p. 84.
26. Joseph Smith introduced the first published portion of the Book of Abraham by saying it was "written by his own hand. . . ." *Times and Seasons*, March 1, 1842, Vol. 3, p. 704. This was the understanding conveyed to Wilford Woodruff who wrote in his Manuscript Diary under date of February 19, 1842: "Joseph the Seer has presented us some of the Book of Abraham which was written by his own hand. . . ."
27. *Documentary History of the Church*, Vol. 2, pp. 350-351.
28. Statement of Parley P. Pratt in the *Millennial Star*, July 1, 1842, and quoted in *The Story of the Pearl of Great Price*, p. 84.
29. Dr. James R. Clark is of the opinion — and I am strongly inclined to agree — that Joseph's scroll very likely contained a prophetic history of the world similar to the information given to the brother of Jared. The revelation to the brother of Jared was so sacred that it has remained hidden until now. It constitutes the sealed portion of Mormon's gold plates which cannot be revealed until a later time. (Ether 4:4-7) Was it for this same reason that the papyrus of Joseph was not published along with the Book of Abraham?

dealt almost exclusively with the scroll of Joseph.[30] He was greatly animated, he said by the fact that this record discussed the creation, the fall, the nature of the Godhead, the history recorded on the pillars of Enoch (not mentioned in the modern Bible, but referred to by Josephus), and so forth. Oliver Cowdery also gives a description of "the inner end" of the scroll of Joseph which presents a prophetic description of the final judgment.

Sometime after this a man named William S. West visited Kirtland and interviewed Joseph Smith concerning the mummies and scrolls. At this time there appears to have been little discussion about the writings of Abraham. Once again the whole conversation centered around the papyrus of Joseph. Mr. West afterwards published a pamphlet describing the contents of the record of Joseph. He says he was given to understand that it contained ". . . important information respecting the creation, the fall of man, the deluge, the patriarchs, the Book of Mormon, the lost tribes, the gathering, the end of the world, the judgment, etc. etc."[31] He also said he was told that when the contents of these papyrus scrolls are finally translated, "a larger volume than the Bible will be required to contain them."[32] This is the only known reference to the estimated amount of scriptural material contained in these ancient texts.

For reasons best known to the Lord, this sacred treasury of scriptures written up by Joseph was never published. Just as Joseph Smith was getting well along with the translation of these documents, a flood of persecution suddenly descended upon both him and his followers which drove them from Kirtland, Ohio, to Missouri, and from Missouri to Illinois.

It was not until December, 1841, that Joseph Smith once again found the peace and opportunity to continue this im-

---

30. *LDS Messenger and Advocate,* Kirtland, Ohio, December, 1835, Vol. 2, pp. 235-238. Quoted in *The Story of the Pearl of Great Price,* pp. 95-97.

31. This quotation from a pamphlet by William S. West was discovered by Dr. James R. Clark in the Coe Collection of the Yale University Library. Dr. Clark brought this important pamphlet to my attention and kindly approved my use of the quotations which he had abstracted from the original. The reference for this pamphlet is given as follows: William S. West, *A Few Interesting Facts Respecting the Rise, Progress and Pretentions of the Mormons,* Warren, Ohio, 1837, 16 pp.

32. Ibid.

A FACSIMILE FROM THE BOOK OF ABRAHAM

No. 3

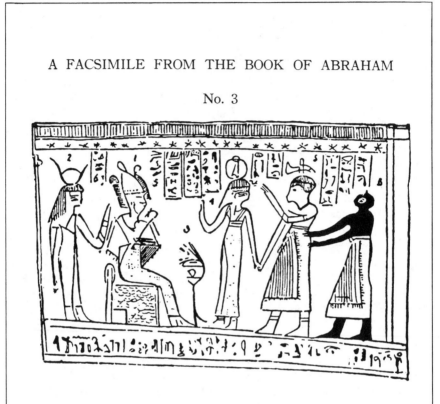

EXPLANATION OF THE ABOVE CUT

1. Abraham sitting upon Pharaoh's throne, by the politeness of the king, with a crown upon his head, representing the Priesthood, as emblematical of the grand Presidency in Heaven; with the scepter of justice and judgment in his hand.

2. King Pharaoh, whose name is given in the characters above his head.

3. Signifies Abraham in Egypt—referring to Abraham, as given in the ninth number of the *Times and Seasons*. (Also as given in the first facsimile of this book.)

4. Prince of Pharaoh, King of Egypt, as written above the hand.

5. Shulem, one of the king's principal waiters, as represented by the characters above his hand.

6. Olimlah, a slave belonging to the prince.

Abraham is reasoning upon the principles of Astronomy, in the king's court.

portant project. He started in with the first scroll, the writings of Abraham, and as soon as a substantial portion had been translated, he published it. This occurred early in 1842. Not only did he publish his English version of the Egyptian text, but in order to share with the public a deeper appreciation of the miraculous break-through which God had permitted his modern servants to achieve, Joseph Smith printed several illustrations of the Egyptian text with the inspired translation beside it. Here indeed was a challenge to the skeptic and the scholar!

JOSEPH SMITH'S TRANSLATION OF THE EGYPTIAN SCROLLS RECEIVES NATIONAL PUBLICITY

The challenge was immediately seized upon by several major newspapers in the East. They printed the Egyptian hieroglyphic facsimile which Joseph Smith had published and also his accompanying translation.

James Gordon Bennett, editor of the powerful New York Herald devoted a prominent portion of the editorial page to Joseph Smith and the translation of the Egyptian scrolls in the issue of Sunday, April 3, 1842. Wrote Bennett:

"We give in this day's paper, a very curious chapter from the 'Book of Abraham,' which we find published in the last number of a weekly journal, called the 'Times and Seasons,' conducted by Joe Smith the great Mormon Prophet, in the city of Nauvoo, Hancock county, Illinois. . .

"This Joe Smith is undoubtedly, one of the greatest characters of the age. He indicates as much talent, originality, and moral courage as Mahomet, Odin, or any of the other great spirits that have hitherto produced the revolutions of past ages. In the present infidel, irreligious, material, ideal, geological, animal-magnetic age of the world, some such singular prophet as Joe Smith is required to preserve the principle of faith, and to plant some new germs of civilization that may come to maturity in a thousand years. While modern philosophy, which believes in nothing but what you can touch, is overspreading the Atlantic States, Joe Smith is creating a spiritual system, combined also with morals, industry, that may change the destiny of the race."[33]

Three days later the Boston Ledger published the same material as the New York Herald. The editor, William Bartlett, was also impressed by Joseph Smith, not only as a translator but also as an exceptionally competent leader. His editorial included such comments as the following:

"Joe Smith is decidedly the greatest original of the present day. He carries all before him when he undertakes an enterprise — knows no impediment — and never halts in his course till he has accomplished his object. His post, at the head of the Mormons, is a conspicuous one, and in a few years with such advancement as he has met with for the past year, will give him a numberless host of followers. . . .

"The chapter from the recently recovered Book of Abraham, and the unique cut which illustrates it, on our outside, has occasioned us some expense; but we care not for that, so long as we please our patrons, which we mean to do at all hazards; trusting to the good sense of the most enlightened public in this, or any other universe, for suitable remuneration.

"The Mormons hold meetings in Boston regularly on the sabbath, somewhere in Commercial Street, and are equally successful in saving souls, healing the sick, and restoring sight to the blind. . . ."[34]

Joseph Smith published three segments from the Book of Abraham in the *Times and Seasons* while he was serving as editor. These appeared in the issues dated March 1, 1842, March 14, 1842, and May 16, 1842. Months later, in the *Times and Seasons* for February, 1843, we find the announcement: "We would further state that we have the promise of Br. Joseph, to furnish us with further extracts from the Book of Abraham."[35] This promise was never fulfilled. The translating of the papyrus scrolls from Egypt was only one of a dozen tremendously important projects in which Joseph Smith was engaged when his whole monumental career was suddenly stopped by the bullets of a mob.

33. *New York Herald*, April 3, 1842, page 2, col. 1.
34. *Boston Daily Ledger*, April 7, 1842.
35. Quoted by Clark in his *Story of the Pearl of Great Price*, p. 98.

Had Joseph Smith lived a few more years who knows what additional scriptural treasures might have been extracted from the Egyptian scrolls. As it turned out, the tornadoes of persecution, harrassment and threatened destruction, began to pour down their fury upon him shortly after the above announcement was made, and after a tempestuous sixteen months of false charges, false law suits, and false arrests, he was finally murdered by a mob at Carthage, Illinois, June 27, 1844, while in the protective custody of the Governor.

WHAT HAPPENED TO THE EGYPTIAN SCROLLS?

Immediately afterwards, the storm broke on his followers. They eventually were driven from their homes and were forced to flee to the wilderness of the West. They left behind them their temple, which was soon burned, their homes, and many of their most precious possessions.

Among the precious possessions left behind were the mummies and the priceless papyrus scrolls of Abraham and Joseph, which were left in the custody of a trustee.[36] Tragically, this trustee allowed these invaluable treasures of antiquity to get out of his hands and when an attempt was made to recover them it was found impossible.[37] Unsympathetic members of Joseph Smith's family are believed to be the ones who sold the Egyptian relics to one or more museums.[38]

---

36. "Notable is the fact that it was Almon W. Babbitt, the trustee in Trust of Church Property in Nauvoo, appointed by Brigham Young, that took care of Mother Smith (Joseph Smith's mother) and evidently turned over to her the mummies and the papyrus scrolls for her to place on exhibit and thus be in a measure self-asupporting . . ." J. R. Clark, *ibid.,* p. 152.

37. In the *Journal History of the Church* under date of January 31, 1847, there is a letter from Almon W. Babbitt, Trustee in Trust of Church Property at Nauvoo, which states, "William Smith has got the mummies from Mother Smith and refuses to give them up . . ." See *Ibid.*, p. 148.

38. Most researchers have been inclined to believe that it was Joseph Smith's mother who sold the mummies and scrolls prior to her death in 1855. However, Dr. J. R. Riggs who came west with the Church and settled in Provo, is reported to have stated that it was Lucy Smith (the sister of Joseph, rather than his mother) who, together with her husband, a Mr. Milliken, negotiated the sale of at least part of the Egyptian collection. *Ibid.* p. 87. One source says that for a period of time Mother Smith lived with her youngest daughter, Lucy, who had married Arthur Milliken. *Ibid.*, p. 151. George B. Arbaugh, in a doctor's dissertation at the Univ. of Chicago (*Revelation in Mormonism*) in 1945, suggests that the mummies which went to the St. Louis Museum were sold through Isaac Sheen and William Smith, Joseph's younger brother, *Ibid.*, p. 162.

Two mummies and "part of the records" were traced by Dr.
James R. Clark to the St. Louis Museum which is believed
to have acquired them between 1851 and 1856.[39] The two
mummies are described in the St. Louis Museum Catalogue
of 1859 (page 45) as "a female, about forty — the other,
that of a boy, about fourteen."[40] However, it seems that the
entire contents of the St. Louis Museum were moved to Chicago in 1863 and the Egyptian exhibit became part of the
Wood Museum in that city. The mummies are listed on
page 42 of the 1863 catalogue of the Chicago Museum —
usually referred to as the Wood Museum — with exactly
the same description as that given for them in St. Louis.[41]
There is documented evidence that these two mummies were
at the Wood Museum as late as 1869,[42] and it has therefore
been assumed that they were destroyed in 1871 when this
museum was consumed in the Great Chicago Fire of that
year. If they were not destroyed, no one has been able to
locate them since.

The major question therefore remains, what happened
to the other two mummies and the rest of the papyrus records?
Charles Haggerty, an associate researcher with Dr. James
R. Clark and the Librarian of the public library at Danville,
Illinois, wrote August 29, 1950: "I have traced the other two
mummies and at least one or two bits of papyrus to the
Philadelphia Museum. This was in the same building known
as the Philadelphia Arcade in which Michael Chandler exhibited the mummies in 1834 or 35."[43] Ever since this exciting
news reached Brigham Young University the search has
been intensified. Someone, somewhere, probably without even
knowing the value of these antiquities, is in possession of
these two mummies and what is undoubtedly the oldest scriptural record to be discovered thus far. The current attempt

39. "The St. Louis Museum acquired these mummies sometime between 1844 and 1856.
    The Curator of the Museum, J. P. Bates, states in the catalog that he spent the
    years from 1851 to 1856 making additions 'from our own territory.' This
    statement argues strong that he acquired the mummies between 1851 and 1856."
    Ibid., p. 162.
40. Ibid., p. 159.
41. Ibid., p. 159.
42. This reference is the 1869 Salt Lake City Directory and Business Guide, quoted in
    Clark's Story of the Pearl of Great Price, p. 151.
43. Ibid., p. 163

to locate this material is probably the most important single project in historical research being carried on today.

The painful disappointment of not having the writings of Joseph to study today is ameliorated by the fact that we know he left a comprehensive record of his experiences in Egypt and also a scriptural history of all the patriarchs who had preceded him. Someday, in the wisdom of God, we shall have these writings again.

Reading Assignment and Questions on Chapter Nine

Reading Assignment: Documentary History of the Church, Vol. 2, pp. 235 and 348-351.

1—How do archaeologists explain the fact that no reference to Joseph can be found among the histories or monuments of Egypt?

2—Who was Antonio Lebolo? Why is he sometimes called Antonio Sebolo?

3—Were the writings of Joseph discovered near Memphis or Thebes?

4—What happened to Antonio Lebolo?

5—How did he dispose of his eleven mummies?

6—How long was it before they reached Michael Chandler in New York?

7—Where were the Egyptian coffins first opened?

8—What did Michael Chandler hope to find in these coffins besides mummies?

9—Where did Michael Chandler first hear of Joseph Smith and his ability to translate Egyptian?

10—To what extent were the experts able to translate the papyrus scrolls for Chandler?

11—Was Chandler pleased or disappointed with Joseph Smith's ability to translate Egyptian? What did he do to show it?

12—What astonishing discovery was made by Joseph Smith when he began translating the first papyrus scroll?

13—Whose writings did he find in the second scroll?

14—When the mummies and scrolls were first exhibited which scrolls seemed to have aroused the most interest and discussion?

15—What specific subject matter did William S. West say the writings of Joseph contained?

16—Do we have any recorded estimate of the amount of material contained in the two scrolls and how big a book would be required to publish the English translation of their contents?

17—Which part of the two scrolls was published in 1842? Is there evidence that Joseph Smith had expected to publish more? What prevented it?

18—What happened to the Egyptian scrolls following Joseph Smith's death?

19—Were they destroyed in the great Chicago fire or is there evidence that they are still in existence?

20—What was in the scroll of Joseph's writings which the Lord may not have wished published until a later time?

CHAPTER TEN

The Rise of Moses

It is a rare moment in the upward struggle of the race when a single life flashes across the horizon of human history with so much brilliance that its power for good remains un-dimmed 3,400 years later. Such was the life of Moses.

Except for Jesus Christ, there is more information concerning the prophet Moses and the works of his hands than any other personality in the Bible. His interests and capacities were almost encyclopedic. His career involved sixteen different functions, any one of which would have been a notable accomplishment. Moses was all of the following things:

A *scholar*, "learned in all the wisdom of the Egyptians."

A *military leader*, with victories which Josephus says made him Egypt's national hero.

A *writer* who recorded more full-length books in the Bible than any other one man.

A *historian*, who put together 2,500 years of the great human saga.

A *crown prince*, whose adoption by the king's daughter could have made him the next Pharaoh of Egypt.

A *shepherd*, who patiently followed his flocks by day and by night for forty years.

An *emancipator*, whose liberation of between two and three million Israelites from Egyptian slavery is a classic event in history.

A *prophet*, raised up by God at the age of eighty to perform a labor which could have overwhelmed a younger man.

A *seer*, who saw God face to face, and spoke to him, as one man speaketh to another.

A *revelator*, who recorded the Creation Story and other scriptures as they were given to him by the Lord.

A *High Priest*, who functioned in that holy office from his ordination by Jethro to the time of his death.

A *miracle-worker*, the greatest of which was the dividing of the Red Sea.

A *legislator*, who enunciated the divine laws which still serve as the sinews of entire civilizations.

A *judge*, who presided as chief justice over Israel for forty years.

A *pioneer*, who set up 40 different city-camps in the desert wilderness of Egypt and Arabia during four strenuous nomadic decades.

A *temple-builder*, who built by divine blueprint a portable house of holiness and established God's approved pattern of worship from then until the coming of Christ.

In addition to all these, Moses was a faithful husband, a loving father, a good neighbor, a wise counsellor, and a staunch friend.

But with all his achievements, Moses had the usual frailties of the race. Although a great writer, he was slow of speech and had extreme difficulty expressing himself. His inferiority complex resulting from this impediment was so great that God had to appoint an official spokesman for him.

When called by God to liberate the Israelites he became so frightened the Lord had to sustain him with an endowment of miraculous power in order to build up his confidence.

Even after receiving his prophetic calling he neglected to perform a sacred ordinance and almost lost the life of his son as a penalty.

He was extremely soft-hearted where relatives were concerned and pleaded for Aaron and the leaders of Israel when the Lord said it would be better if they were returned to the spirit world.

He was slow to delegate authority to others and had to be reprimanded by Jethro, his father-in-law, so he would not kill himself off from overwork.

An occasional streak of egotism and pride shot through his personality and one unfortunate display of boasting cost him the privilege of leading Israel into the promised land. Such was the man, Moses.

Nevertheless, these human weaknesses all turned out to be a blessing to Moses when viewed through the long telescope of history. He was so fantastically brilliant and successful in so many different fields that without a few such weaknesses he would seem too good to be true. His weaknesses make him less formidable and more inspirational to his fellow men who cannot help but view his life sympathetically as they likewise seek to manifest strength in achievement despite personal weaknesses.

Moses in Prophecy

As we have already seen, Joseph was told many details concerning the life of Moses.[1] As to his identity, the Lord had said to Joseph:

". . . for a seer will I raise up to deliver my people out of the land of Egypt; and he shall be called Moses. And by this name he shall know that he is of thy house [in other words, an Israelite]; for he shall be nursed by the king's daughter, and shall be called her son."[2]

Joseph was also told many details concerning the mission and miraculous powers which would be given to Moses:

"I will raise up Moses, and a rod shall be in his hand, and he shall gather together my people, and he shall lead them as a flock, and he shall smite the waters of the Red Sea with his rod. And he shall have judgment and shall write the word of the Lord. And he shall NOT speak many words,

---

1. See Inspired Version, Genesis 50:29-35; 2 Nephi 3:10-17
2. Inspired Version, Genesis 50:29

for I will write unto him my law by the finger of mine own hand. And I will make a spokesman for him, and his name shall be called Aaron."[3]

Probably not since Noah had there been so much information revealed about a prophet before he was born.

How Many Years Separated Joseph from Moses?

The Book of Exodus opens with the death of Joseph and then implies that within a relatively short period of time — a generation or two — Moses was born. Great confusion has prevailed among students as to the length of time Israel was in Egypt, and the answer to this problem has a direct bearing on the number of years between Joseph and Moses.

There are four passages of scripture which refer directly to this question. The first passage is Genesis Chapter 15, verse 13, which says: "And he said unto Abram, Know of a surety that thy seed shall be a stranger in a land that is not theirs, and shall serve them; and they shall afflict them; four hundred years."

The second passage is a New Testament reference to this same scripture which says: "And God spake on this wise, That his seed should sojourn in a strange land; and that they should bring them into bondage, and entreat them evil four hundred years."[4]

The third passage deals with an entirely different figure and seems to contradict the two passages above. Exodus 12:40 says: "Now the sojourning of the children of Israel, who dwelt in Egypt, was four hundred and thirty years."

Authorities point out that this passage is emasculated in our modern Bible. In all of the Samaritan copies of Exodus this passage is rendered differently and the Alexandrian copy of the Septuagint which is reputed to be one of the most reliable agrees with it exactly. In these books, the passage is given as follows:

---

3. Ibid., 50:34-35
4. Acts 7:6-7

"Now the sojourning of the children of Israel, and of *their fathers*, which they sojourned in the *land of Canaan* and in the land of Egypt, was 430 years."[5]

Paul also cites the figure 430 years from the time Abraham received the covenant until the giving of the law: "And this I say, that the covenant, that was confirmed before of God in Christ, the law, which was four hundred and thirty years after, cannot disannull, that it should make the promise of none effect."[6] In other words, the covenant which was made with Abraham was not annulled by the giving of the law which came 430 years after.

So our problem boils down to this, what period of 400 years would satisfy the first pair of passages and what period of 430 years would satisfy the second pair of passages?

The first passages (based on Genesis 15:13) would appear to be dealing with four generations of 100 years each. Three verses later the Lord calls these 400 years "four generations."[7] This would imply that this passage is therefore talking in broad general terms, namely, that shortly after 400 years or four generations the children of Israel would come out of bondage.

The second pair of passages, however, appear to be speaking in terms of a specific number of years, namely, 430 years. If this is correct then our only concern is with this second figure, which is the only one pretending to be an exact period of time.

It is clear from the Samaritan text of Exodus 12:40 which we quoted above, that these 430 years are supposed to represent the time that the children of Israel were in Egypt plus the time their fathers, Abraham, Isaac and Jacob, lived in Canaan prior to the captivity. Taking this as a lead we come up with the following information:

From Abraham's entry into Canaan to the birth of Isaac was 25 years,[8] Isaac was 60 years old when Jacob was born,[9] and Jacob was 130 when he brought his family down into

---

5. Clarke's *Bible Commentary*, Vol. 1, p. 356
6. Galatians 3:17   8. Genesis 12:4 plus 17:1-21
7. Genesis 15:16   9. Genesis 25:26

Egypt.[10] This adds up to 215 years or half of the 430 years. What happened in the remaining 215 years?

Since Moses was 80 when Israel went out of Egypt,[11] we subtract this from 215[12] to determine when Moses was born. This would mean his birth occurred 135 years after Jacob came down into Egypt. Does this fit the other known facts relating to this period? In Exodus 6:14-20 we are told that there were only two generations between Jacob and the father of Moses. In fact, it says there was only one generation between Jacob and the mother of Moses. This would definitely fit into the framework of 135 years very satisfactorily, certainly better than a period of more than four centuries.

Then how many years separated Joseph and Moses?

Having established the approximate lapse of 135 years between the arrival of Jacob in Egypt and the birth of Moses we can now determine with relative exactness the answer to this question. We know that Joseph lived 71 years after Jacob came down to Egypt.[13] Subtract 71 from 135 and we come up with 64 years as the number of years between Joseph's death and the birth of Moses.

As we shall see in a moment this fits both historically and logically into all of the other known facts related to this period.

However, one important problem remains.

WHAT ABOUT ISRAEL'S POPULATION EXPLOSION?

If, between the arrival of Jacob and the birth of Moses, there was an elapsed time of only 135 years, how could the Israelites have multiplied sufficiently to give reason for the Pharaoh to accuse the Israelites of being "more and mightier than we"?[14]

---

10. Genesis 47:9
11. Acts 7:23, 30
12. As previously indicated, 215 would be the number of years between the arrival of Jacob in Egypt and the Exodus.
13. By adding the dates given in Genesis 41:46, 48 plus 45:11 we know Joesph was 39 when his father came into Egypt. Since Joseph died when he was 110 (Genesis 50:22) it therefore follows that he lived 71 years after his father's arrival (110-39=71).
14. Exodus 1:9

For this to be true, several factors would have to be present. Was it possible that the kingdom of Egypt had been torn and decimated by some recent conflict — such as the overthrow of the Hyksos shepherd kings, for example? There is no doubt the Pharaoh was worried about powerful enemies of some sort. Said he: "Come on, let us deal wisely with them [the Israelites]; lest they multiply, and it come to pass, that, when there falleth out any war, they join also unto our enemies, and fight against us. . . ."[15] In such a war the Pharaoh appears to have felt that the Israelites would definitely hold the balance of power.

It would further appear from all the circumstances that the Pharaoh at this time had dominion over merely the Delta area, called the Lower Kingdom.[16] We know he was building treasure cities in the vicinity of the Delta and he appears to have had his capital at Memphis. No reference is made to any circumstances which would imply his control of the Upper Kingdom (meaning the upper region of the Nile) with its capital at Thebes. In fact, Josephus tell us that by the time Moses was grown, the Ethiopians came down and practically conquered the whole of Egypt with little difficulty.[17] All of this seems to imply political weakness and perhaps the availability of only a limited population to provide military forces.

But even so, how could the Israelites start out with 75 people and be "more and mightier" than the Egyptians within 135 years? Accepting the fact that the Israelites practiced plural marriage and often had large families, it is still astonishing to think that this could have been achieved in so short a time. We do not have any actual population figures to go by at the end of 135 years, but we do have the basis for a population count some 80 years later when the Israelites had begun their Exodus. In other words, we do have some basis for an estimate of Israel's size at the end of 215 years in Egypt. A little over a year after the Exodus began a census was taken of all males over twenty years old who were capable of bearing arms. The number of men fit to bear arms

---

15. Exodus 1:10
16. Memphis appears to have been the capital, not Thebes. During the plagues Moses was never very far away from the Pharaoh nor his own people. All of this argues for a limited kingdom centered at the vortex of the Delta.
17. Josephus, *Atiquities of the Jews,* Book 2. Chapter 10.

was in excess of 600,000![18] This number of men together with their wives and families would undoubtedly constitute a total population of between two and three million.

Israel's Population Explosion

The Bible indicates that during 215 years Israel grew from 75 souls to a vast host of between two and three million. Specifically, it states that in the second year following the Exodus, Israel could number over 600,000 men who were beyond 20 and able to bear arms. This number of men, plus wives and children, would undoubtedly total close to 3,000,000. In the following tabulation we discover that if, during these 215 years, each family had averaged 10 children — and this means children who grew up, married, and had children of their own — the population of between 2 and 3,000,000 could be readily reached. To illustrate:

32 years:	If the 75 Israelites who came down to Egypt combined to make 37 couples and they had 10 children per couple, it would increase the population by 370 (185 new couples).
64 years:	If these 185 couples had 10 children per couple it would increase the population 1,850 (925 new couples.)
96 years:	If these 925 couples had 10 children per couple it would increase the population 9,250 (4,625 new couples).
128 years:	If these 4,625 couples had 10 children per couple it would increase the population 46,250 (23,125 new couples).
160 years:	If these 23,125 couples had 10 children per couple it would increase the population 231,250 (115,625 new couples).
192 years:	If these 115,625 couples had 10 children per couple it would increase the population 1,156,250 (578,125 new couples).
215 years:	578,125 couples in a half generation could easily push this census to the population of 2 to 3,000,000 and by this time 600,000 of the men certainly would be over 20 and able to bear arms as indicated in Numbers, Chapter 1.

---

18. Numbers 1:46. This census was conducted during the second year after the Exodus. (See Numbers 1:1-2)

Is it reasonable to believe that 75 people could multiply to such a multitude in 215 years? The population table on the preceding page tells the story. If the Israelites averaged ten children per generation for 6½ generations of 32 years each, the last generation would bring the population to a figure which would correlate closely with the one the Bible reflects. The scripture specifically says the Israelites became notable for their prolific population explosion. It says they "were fruitful, and increased abundantly, and multiplied, and waxed exceeding mighty; and the land was filled with them."[19] Plural marriage was being practiced at this time and we know that Hebrew families of a later date reached as high as 70 children.[20] It would seem reasonable, therefore, that using the average figure of 10 children per family — and that means children who matured, married and had children of their own — would be a conservative estimate.

Was Moses Jewish?

Contrary to widespread popular belief, Moses was not Jewish. He was a pure Levite. The highly interesting genealogy of Moses is portrayed in the accompanying chart. Note that his mother was Jochebed, "a daughter of Levi,"[21] while his father was Amram, the grandson of Levi.[22] Moses was therefore the grandson of Levi through Jochebed, his mother, and the great-grandson of Levi through Amram, his father!

Just to make certain that the reader would not misunderstand, the Bible specifically states that "Amram took him Jochebed his father's sister to wife; and she bare him Aaron and Moses."[23] In other words, Amram married his own aunt.

In Exodus 2:1 it calls Jochebed "a daughter of Levi." Some students have felt that this is meant in a general sense. They suggest that she was "a descendant" of Levi rather than

---

19. Exodus 1:7
20. Gideon had 70 sons but no mention is made of the number of daughters (Judges 8:30); Ibzan had 30 sons and 30 daughters making a total of 60 children (Judges 12:8-9); Abdon had 40 sons but the number of daughters is not mentioned (Judges 12:13-14).
21. Exodus 2:1
22. Exodus 6:16-20
23. Exodus 6:20

his own personal daughter. However, Exodus 6:16-20 completely explodes this possibility as it traces the genealogy of Moses through both his parents and identifies Jochebed as Levi's personal daughter. Levi lived until he was 137 years of age and apparently had children long after he was a hundred just as Abraham did.[24] If Jochebed were born in Levi's later years she could have easily been the same age as her nephew, Amram, and could have married him precisely as the Bible says she did.

A reconstruction of the time element based on the data given in the Bible would indicate that Jochebed was probably around 55 when Moses was born and this may account for the fact that he was the last of her children.[25]

MOSES WAS CONDEMNED TO DEATH BEFORE HE WAS BORN

Evil and cruel days had fallen on Israel prior to the birth of Moses. A lot of things can happen in 65 years. The Bible says ". . . there arose up a new king over Egypt, which knew not Joseph."[26] He not only did not know Joseph, but he had no respect for his ministry, his memory, his people nor the principles for which he stood. He looked upon all Israel as potential subversives who might take advantage of the very next war to betray Egypt and join her foes.

Egypt always had two permanent enemies at her very borders — the Shemite nomads pushing west from Arabia and south from Canaan; and the Ethiopian tribes who could overflow Egypt like a flood from their retreat in the highland country of the upper Nile.

---

24. Exodus 6:16; Genesis 25:1-2
25. The time element can be reconstructed rather accurately from the following facts: Levi was born when Father Jacob was around 75 years of age (see data at the end of chapter 4 indicating that Levi was born about 11 years after Jacob married Leah). Jacob was 130 when he went down into Egypt (Genesis 47:9) which means Levi was around 55 (130-75=55). Now, since we know Levi was 137 when he died (Ex. 6:16) this would mean he resided in Egypt 82 years (137-55=82.) We have already seen in this present chapter that the period from the arrival of Jacob's family in Egypt (which included Levi) to the birth of Moses was 135 years. This means that Levi died 53 years before the birth of Moses (135—82=53). If Levi's daughter, Jochebed, were born in his last days, say two years before his death, she would be 55 when Moses was born (53+2= 55). As we have already seen in the case of Rachel (Ch. 4, note 56) childbearing at this age was not uncommon in those early days.
26. Exodus 1:8

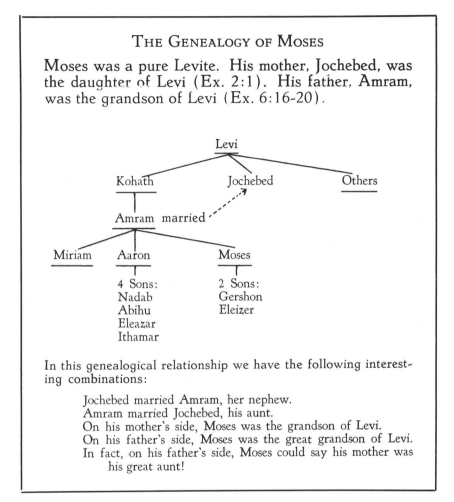

THE GENEALOGY OF MOSES

Moses was a pure Levite. His mother, Jochebed, was the daughter of Levi (Ex. 2:1). His father, Amram, was the grandson of Levi (Ex. 6:16-20).

In this genealogical relationship we have the following interesting combinations:

Jochebed married Amram, her nephew.
Amram married Jochebed, his aunt.
On his mother's side, Moses was the grandson of Levi.
On his father's side, Moses was the great grandson of Levi.
In fact, on his father's side, Moses could say his mother was his great aunt!

As we have already seen, it was the Shemite nomads who had conquered Egypt just prior to Joseph's coming into the land. They had ruled for nearly two centuries as the hated Hyksos shepherd kings, but after Joseph's death the Hyksos were driven out and the native Egyptians once more assumed control of their land. It would seem that the new Pharaoh who "knew not Joseph" was part of that victorious regime which had ousted the shepherd kings and therefore hated all Shemites whether called Hyksos or Israelites. Dr. Keller and others suggest that this is one reason the new Pharaoh became so alarmed by the prolific increase among the Israelites and said:

"Behold, the people of the children of Israel are more and mightier than we: Come on, let us deal wisely with them; lest they multiply, and it come to pass, that, when there falleth out any war, they join also unto our enemies, and fight against us, and so get them up out of our land."[27]

Like the Pharaohs before him, this Egyptian king had ambitions to build vast public works, new capitals, new shrines, monuments, obelisks and roads. The Israelites were the principal source of manpower for these gigantic undertakings and so he was most anxious that they not "get them up out of the land." To prevent it, the king literally enslaved the whole populace of Israel by setting "over them taskmasters to afflict them with their burdens."[28] According to Exodus 1:16 the immediate object of the Pharaoh was to build two treasure cities called Pithom and Raamses.

The scripture says: "And the Egyptians made the children of Israel to serve with rigour; And they made their lives bitter with bondage, in morter, and in brick, and in all manner of service in the field: all their service, wherein they made them serve, was with rigour."[29] Notice that they did not just work in the clay pits making bricks but they did "all manner of service in the field," as well.

To prevent a complete imbalance in population ratios between Egyptians and Israelites, the Pharaoh decided to have the Israelites *kill their own male children* as soon as they were born. The king called upon two women of Israel, Shiphrah and Puah, who apparently had charge of the Hebrew midwives. He commanded them to kill all male Hebrew children as soon as they were born. The midwives secretly defied the king because they "feared God," and they "saved the men children alive."[30] When the Pharaoh accused these women of treachery, they said that the Hebrew women had their children so fast no midwife could get there in time. In bitter anger, the king called upon "his people," the Egyptians, to spy upon the Hebrews. Said he: "Every son that is born ye shall cast into the river, and every daughter ye shall save alive."[31]

27. Exodus 1:9-10
28. Exodus 1:11
29. Exodus 1:13-15

30. Exodus 1:17
31. Exodus 1:22

So these were the circumstances when Jochebed, daughter of Levi, found she was with child. Her baby was condemned to death before he was born.

An Unnamed Slave Child Becomes Moses, the Adopted Son of the Pharaoh's Daughter

It is difficult to comprehend the terror of a mother who must await the birth of her child knowing that if it is a boy he will be assassinated on sight by the agents of the government. Such was the fear which gripped the heart of the aging Jochebed as she looked forward to the birth of her third and last child. She already had a daughter, Miriam, who was now a young girl, and Aaron, a boy, age three.[32] When the new baby arrived it was a son and the scripture says the mother saw that he was a "goodly child." But, goodly or not, the harsh realities of life were obvious. This baby was a capital fugitive carrying the Pharaoh's death warrant. Frightened and distraught, she attempted to hide him away.

Jochebed was only able to hide him in her home for about three months. In such crowded quarters as the slaves occupied she must have known that the cries of the child would eventually attract the attention of the night watchmen, the king's taskmasters, or the paid informers of Pharaoh. In desperation she took the chance of hiding him in a tiny waterproof casket made of bulrushes and coated with tar.[33] This little ark was placed among the reeds on the bosom of the great River Nile — the very river in which the king had ordered all newborn male Hebrews to be drowned.

The baby's older sister, Miriam, watched the precious cargo from "afar off" on the river bank.[34] What happened very shortly is a well-known story. "And the daughter of Pharaoh came down to wash herself at the river; and her maidens walked along by the river's side; and when she saw the ark among the flags, she sent her maid to fetch it."[35]

---

32. Exodus 7:7
33. The word *slime* in the Old Testament is translated from a Hebrew word which means asphalt or tar, sometimes called *bitumen*. (Clarke's *Bible Commentary* Vol. 1, p. 87—note on Genesis 11:3)
34. Exodus 2:4
35. Exodus 2:5

"And when she could not longer hide him, she took for him an ark of bulrushes . . . and put the child therein and she laid it in the flags by the river's brink."

THE TEN COMMANDMENTS — A Paramount Picture

Apparently the little casket was completely covered over and had to be opened. The scripture says:

"And when she [the daughter of Pharaoh] had opened it she saw the child: and, behold, the babe wept. And she had compassion on him, and said, This is one of the Hebrew's children."[36]

The next thing this Egyptian princess knew, a young Hebrew girl was standing beside her. It was Miriam.

"Shall I go and call to thee a nurse of the Hebrew women, that she may nurse the child for thee?"[37]

"Go," said the daughter of Pharaoh.

It must have been an excited Miriam who ran breathlessly to the slave encampment to fetch Jochebed, her mother. When Jochebed came down to the river and met the princess, the daughter of Pharaoh said to her, "Take this child away, and nurse it for me, and I will give thee thy wages."[38]

Jochebed knew her baby had been saved. But who will count the anguish of this mother sometime later as she finally made that fateful pilgrimage to the Pharaoh's palace and turned her child over to the waiting arms of the Egyptian woman. Jochebed had saved her son from drowning in the river, but for what?

It was the Egyptian princess who gave the child his name. "And she called his name Moses: and she said, Because I drew him out of the water."[39]

MOSES BECOMES THE CROWN PRINCE OF EGYPT

The whole story of the birth and youth of Moses as it appears in the modern Bible occupies only 10 verses. However, the Jewish historian, Josephus, states that when Jerusalem was conquered during 70 A.D., he was allowed to secure the whole sacred library before the temple was torn down.[40] From these records he was able to glean consider-

---

36. Exodus 2:6
37. Exodus 2:7
38. Exodus 2:9
39. Exodus 2:10
40. Josephus says: "Titus Caesar, when the city of Jerusalem was taken by force, persuaded me frequently to take whatever I pleased out of the ruins of my country; for he told me that he gave me leave so to do . . . I also had the holy books by his concession." (Quoted by William Whiston in his Dissertation IV on the *Antiquities of the Jews* by Josephus).

ably more about the youth of Moses and this information is incorporated in his *Antiquities of the Jews*.

Josephus says the infant Moses was remarkable for his beauty and form. The handsome qualities of Moses from the time of his childhood are emphasized on several occasions. Stephen, in his final sermon, specifically mentioned that the child, Moses, "was exceeding fair,"[41] and Josephus says:

". . . they (the people who saw the infant Moses) left what they were about, and stood still a great while to look on him; for the beauty of the child was so remarkable and natural to him on many accounts, that it detained the spectators, and made them stay longer to look upon him."[42]

Not only was the daughter of Pharaoh taken up with the little Hebrew boy because of his beauty, but Josephus says the fact that she could have no children of her own made her determined to offer this adopted son to her father as the heir to the throne of Egypt. Josephus continues:

"And when one time she had carried Moses to her father, she showed him to him, and said she thought to make him her father's successor, if it should please God she should have no legitimate child of her own; and said to him, 'I have brought up a child who is of divine form, and of a generous mind; and as I have received him from the .bounty of the river, in a wonderful manner, I thought proper to adopt him for my son, and the heir of thy kingdom.' And when she had said this, she put the infant into her father's hands; so he took him, and hugged him close to his breast; and on his daughter's account, in a pleasant way, put his diadem upon his head. . . ."[43]

Josephus says the shrewd and powerful priests of Egypt watched this new development in jealous anger. They promptly acquired such a hatred for Moses that they finally had the reckless audacity to suggest to the Pharaoh that he ignore his daughter's request concerning Moses. They even went further. In their desperation they tried to get the Pharaoh to kill Moses. They argued that the elevation of a

---

41. Acts 7:20
42. Josephus, *Antiquities of the Jews*, Vol. 2, Ch. 9:6
43. Ibid., 9:7

Hebrew child to such eminence might give hope and encouragement to the Hebrew slaves and thereby lead to an uprising.

However, the Pharaoh's love for his daughter prevailed and in spite of the priests' protest, Moses was accepted as the heir-apparent to the Pharaoh's throne.

When news of this amazing development reached the slave camps of Israel, there was rejoicing indeed, and hope did rise in the hearts of the people just as the priests of Egypt had feared. Josephus says, "So the Hebrews depended on him and were of good hopes that great things would be done by him."[44]

As a young prince of Egypt, Moses is said to have received the finest education and training the land could provide. This would necessarily include horsemanship, handling a chariot, training with weapons, becoming learned in the history and culture of the Egyptians, and knowing courtly procedures and protocol. The New Testament speaks of the education of Moses: ". . . Moses was learned in all the wisdom of the Egyptians, and was mighty in words and in deeds."[45]

How Moses Became a National Hero

What were some of the mighty deeds of young Moses? The Bible is silent except to assure us that there were some. However, Josephus draws on the supplementary documents which he possessed and shares with us the details of one notable achievement which made Prince Moses a national hero.

It was sometime after Moses reached maturity that one of the fiercest attacks on Egypt occurred, something the Pharaoh had been fearfully expecting ever since he first put the Israelites in bondage. However, the attack was not by the Shemites or nomads from the Arabian desert, but from the Ethiopian armies which came pouring down out of the highlands surrounding the headwaters of the Nile. Here is the way Josephus describes it:

---

44. Ibid.
45. Acts 7:22

"The Ethiopians, who are next neighbours to the Egyptians, made an inroad into their country, which they seized upon and carried off the effects of the Egyptians, who, in their rage, fought against them, and revenged the affronts they had received from them; but being overcome in battle, some of them were slain, and the rest ran away in a shameful manner, and by that means saved themselves; whereupon the Ethiopians followed after them in the pursuit, and thinking that it would be a mark of cowardice if they did not subdue all Egypt, they went on to subdue the rest with greater vehemence; and when they had tasted the sweets of the country, they never left off the prosecution of the war; and as the nearest parts had not courage enough at first to fight with them, they proceeded as far as Memphis, and the sea itself, while not one of the cities was able to oppose them."[46]

So serious was the crisis and so frightened were the Egyptian leaders that they asked their priests to use their oracles to hurriedly obtain divine guidance in this hour of peril. Josephus says the priests saw an opportunity to save the country and get rid of Moses all in one plan of action. They therefore told the king to prevail upon his daughter to let Moses lead the troops. Apparently they felt confident Moses could rally the forces of Egypt and thereby drive out the Ethiopians, but it was their hope that during the great conflict Moses would be killed. The plan was adopted.

However, once Moses had rallied the Egyptian troops he struck out into the wilderness and traveled overland rather than engage in heavy fighting by going up the river as the Ethiopians were expecting. It was the objective of Moses to cut off the enemy from behind and then launch an attack. However, he knew that there was one stretch of country which was thickly infested with snakes and his soldiers would be afraid to pass over it. Therefore Moses brought with him from the Nile large cages containing sacred Egyptian birds, the ibises. These long-legged creatures with their curved bills were notorious for their ability to destroy serpents.

Josephus writes, "As soon, therefore, as Moses was come to the land which was the breeder of these serpents, he

---

46. Josephus, *Antiquities of the Jews*, Vol. 2, Ch. 10:1

let loose the ibes, and by their means repelled the serpentine kind, and used them for his assistants before the army came upon that ground. When he had therefore proceeded thus on his journey, he came upon the Ethiopians before they expected him; and, joining battle with them, he beat them, and deprived them of the hopes they had of success against the Egyptians, and went on in overthrowing their cities, and indeed made a great slaughter of these Ethiopians. Now when the Egyptian army had once tasted of this prosperous success, by the means of Moses, they did not slacken their diligence, insomuch that the Ethiopians were in danger of being reduced to slavery, and all sorts of destruction; and at length they retired to Saba, which was a royal city of Ethiopia, which Cambyses afterwards named Meroë, after the name of his own sister."[47]

Here, at their national capital, the Ethiopians intended to make their stand. Moses therefore made complete preparations for a long siege. Josephus describes the difficulties involved:

"The place was to be besieged with very great difficulty, since it was both encompassed by the Nile quite round, and the other rivers, Astapus and Astaboras, made it a very difficult thing for such as attempted to pass over them; for the city was situated in a retired place, and was inhabited after the manner of an island, being encompassed with a strong wall, and having the rivers to guard them from their enemies, and having great ramparts between the wall and the rivers, insomuch that when the waters come with the greatest violence, it can never be drowned [or submerged so as to get over them]; which ramparts make it next to impossible for even such as are gotten over the rivers to take the city."[48]

With such a combination of monumental difficulties, how could the Ethiopian capital be taken? No one — not even Moses — would have guessed what was about to happen. Josephus says:

". . . while Moses was uneasy at the army's lying idle, (for the enemies durst not come to a battle,) this accident happened: Tharbis was the daughter of the king of the Ethi-

---

47. Ibid. 10:2   48. Ibid.

opians: she happened to see Moses as he led the army near the walls, and fought with great courage; and admiring the subtility of his undertakings, and believing him to be the author of the Egyptians' success, when they had before despaired of recovering their liberty, and to be the occasion of the great danger the Ethiopians were in, when they had before boasted of their great achievements, she fell deeply in love with him; and upon the prevalency of that passion, sent to him the most faithful of all her servants to discourse with him about their marriage."[49]

This was an almost unbelievable stroke of good fortune. Moses saw an immediate opportunity to end the war and avoid the destruction of many thousands of lives on both sides. Josephus says Moses "thereupon accepted the offer, on condition she would procure the delivering up of the city; and gave her the assurance of an oath to take her to his wife and that when he had once taken possession of the city, he would not break his oath to her."[50]

"Duty" marriages of this type were a common practice from the most ancient times. A marriage between members of two royal families was considered one of the best guarantees by both nations that peace would be preserved between them; therefore Josephus concludes:

"No sooner was the agreement made, but it took effect immediately; and when Moses had cut off the Ethiopians, he gave thanks to God, and consummated his marriage, and led the Egyptians back to their own land."[51]

What a glorious and heroic return this victory march to Memphis must have been. The Egyptian nation which so recently had trembled on the very brink of total conquest had suddenly emerged as the complete victor and massive bloodshed had been avoided through the marriage of Prince Moses to Princess Tharbis.

As for this marriage, we have no further knowledge of it. We have no hint that Moses took the Ethiopian princess back to Egypt with him, nor is there any indication that he ever had any occasion to be associated with her again.

---

49. Ibid.   51. Ibid.
50. Ibid.

All we know is that more than forty years later when Moses was in the process of commanding the great Exodus of Israel, Miriam and Aaron ridiculed Moses and "spake against Moses because of the Ethiopian woman whom he had married; for he had married an Ethiopian woman."[52] They even implied that because of this they might be more worthy than Moses to receive revelations.

This passage not only supports the account given by Josephus concerning the Ethiopian marriage but it vividly reflects the strong opposition which Israelites maintained toward marriage with any person of the Hamitic tribes.

However, in this case the Lord ruled against Miriam and Aaron. Whatever the circumstances of that marriage might have been, it is clear that the Lord had no complaint against Moses concerning it. He punished both Miriam and Aaron for their sedition against Moses. Miriam was struck with leprosy for a time and Aaron received a personal reprimand from the Lord.[53]

Thus closes a highly significant but little known segment of history which occurred while Moses was a young man. The victory over the Ethiopians made Prince Moses a national hero in Egypt.

---

52. Numbers 12:1
53. Numbers 12:4-15

Scripture Reading and Questions on Chapter Ten

Scripture Reading Assignment: Exodus, chapt. 1 to chapt. 2, verse 10.

1—Can you name eight of the sixteen functions which Moses fulfilled successfully?

2—What earlier prophet was told about the coming of Moses? Can you name five of the specific things he knew about Moses?

3—As nearly as we can tell, how many years after the death of Joseph was Moses born?

4—If the Israelites were in Egypt 215 years, how many children would each family have to average in order to create a population of two to three million? Under the circumstances then existing does this seem possible?

5—Why did Pharaoh say he was afraid of the increased population of the Israelites?

6—What was the first method Pharaoh tried to use in an effort to cut down the growth of Israel? Why did it fail?

7—What was the second order given by Pharaoh to destroy the male children of Israel? To whom was the order specifically given?

8—Since women slaves worked right along with the men, what was Pharaoh's logic in killing the male children but saving the females?

9—Was Moses Jewish? What relation was the mother of Moses to Levi? What did this make Moses on his mother's side?

10—Were the duties of all the Israelites confined to making bricks? What was Pharaoh using the slave labor of the Israelites to build?

11—How much older than Moses was Aaron? What was the name of of their sister who was older than both of them?

12—Who gave Moses his name? Why did she select this particular name?

13—What skills would Moses have to acquire in order to be "learned in all the wisdom of the Egyptians?"

14—How did Josephus happen to get hold of the collected historical records of the Jews around 70 A.D.?

15—According to Josephus, who induced the Pharaoh to make Moses the heir to his throne?

16—When the Pharaoh's daughter adopted Moses, what effect did this have on the aspirations of the Israelites?

17—According to Josephus, how did Moses become a national hero in Egypt?

18—What does he say Moses achieved by marrying Princes Tharbis of Ethiopia? What was the strategic design of political marriages between the members of royal families?

19—Under what circumstances does the Bible make mention of the marriage of Moses to an "Ethiopian"?

20—Since this marriage took place long before Moses came under the influence of Israel's law, did the Lord condemn him for it?

Chapter Eleven

Moses, the Mighty Prince, Becomes Moses, the Humble Shepherd

So far as we can determine, Moses more or less accepted his role as a prince of Egypt until he neared the age of forty. In fact, the scripture says it was ". . . when he was full forty years old, it came into his heart to visit his brethren the children of Israel."[1]

This was no casual visit. With it came an overwhelming compulsion to give up his adopted status in the palace of the Pharaoh and somehow identify himself with his own people even though it might mean becoming a slave with them. Paul describes the situation as follows:

"By faith, Moses, when he was come to years, refused to be called the son of Pharaoh's daughter, choosing rather to suffer affliction with the people of God, than to enjoy the pleasures of sin for a season; esteeming the reproach of Christ greater riches than the treasures in Egypt. . . ."[2]

Moses Becomes a Fugitive

But Moses was scarcely prepared for what he was about to see. No doubt he had a general idea of the sufferings of his people and may have seen some of it in his earlier years. But now he identified himself with Israel's suffering in a very personal way. These were "his brethren."[3]

His sudden indignation against the whole slavery system was triggered by the sight of an Egyptian taskmaster "smiting an Hebrew, one of his brethren."[4] Being a man of

---

1. Acts 7:23
2. Hebrews 11:24-26
3. Exodus 2:11
4. Ibid.

authority and power himself, Moses could not hold back. A feeling of righteous wrath surged through him as he prepared to charge into the Egyptian. This was a dangerous thing to do and Moses knew it. To challenge the authority of an Egyptian taskmaster could cost a Hebrew his life, but Moses "looked this way and that way, and when he saw that there was no man," he took on the Egyptian in physical combat. After the struggle was over the Egyptian was dead. Moses hastily buried his body in the sand and immediately hurried away.[5]

We do not know what happened to the Hebrew whom Moses had rescued from the lash of the Egyptian, but it is apparent from the record that Moses felt confident that the killing of the Egyptian would certainly be kept a secret by the person he tried to protect. However, the very next day Moses learned differently when he went out among the Hebrews again. This time he found two of his fellow Israelites beating on each other. Apparently Moses came up in time to see who started it and so "he said to him that did the wrong, Wherefore smitest thou thy fellow?"[6]

Moses was soon to learn that slavery had brutalized many of the Hebrews, and this man was one of them. He turned on Moses with a snarling challenge, saying, "Who made thee a prince and a judge over us? Intendest thou to kill me, as thou didst the Egyptian?"[7]

This stopped Moses in his tracks. His secret was out! The scripture says, "Moses feared, and said, Surely this think is known."[8] It was indeed, and not just in the slave camps.

Among slaves there are always informers who seek special favors from their masters by passing along information of misconduct or insurrection among the ranks. Consequently, it was not long before Pharaoh had heard this whole story. It is easy to imagine the scandal it created in the court of Egypt's omnipotent ruler. Not only had the adopted son of the Pharaoh's daughter turned renegade and gone

5. Exodus 2:12   7. Exodus 2:14
6. Exodus 2:13   8. Ibid.

back to his people, but he had dared to kill an Egyptian officer. This could almost be counted an act of treason. It even might have started an insurrection and a strike for freedom by the Egyptian slaves. In the mind of Pharaoh this act of Moses was unforgivable. He caught the full political implication of this whole situation. The priests had been right. The Pharaoh's royal wrath reached such heights that he forgot all about the mighty deeds of the past which Moses had wrought for Egypt. The Pharaoh angrily ordered his soldiers to hunt Moses down and kill him on sight.[9]

What would the former crown prince do? Moses was far too well acquainted with the cruel and cunning mind of the Egyptian ruler to take a chance on pleading for mercy or justice. He quickly determined to flee from Egypt and abandon the land of his birth forever.

Moses Flees to Midian

The desert east of Egypt's delta region is a virtual desolation of burning sand and barren rock. This is the desert Moses crossed to escape the terrors of the Pharaoh's vengeance. Josephus provides the following details concerning the flight from Egypt:

". . . when he had learned beforehand what plots there were against him, he went away privately; and because the public roads were watched, he took his flight through the deserts, and where his enemies could not suspect he would travel; and, though he was destitute of food, he went on, and despised that difficulty courageously; and when he came to the city Midian, which lay upon the Red Sea, and was so denominated from one of Abraham's sons by Keturah, he sat upon a certain well, and rested himself there after the laborious journey, and the affliction he had been in."[10]

Not only the Midianites, but many of the desert tribes were distant relatives of the Israelites and direct descendants of Abraham. As indicated by Josephus, the Midianites had descended from Abraham's fourth son, through Keturah,

---

9. Exodus 2:15
10. Josephus, *Antiquities of the Jews,* Book 2, Ch. 11:1

the wife of his last days.[11] These people had settled along the east fork of the Red Sea which today is called the Gulf of the Akaba. Some of the Midianites followed the occupation of shepherds while others were merchants who roamed the fertile crescent buying, bargaining, selling and trading. Years ago, it had been just such a group of Midianite merchants who had discovered Joseph in the well and had sold him to their cousins, the Ismaelites, who in turn had sold him into Egypt.[12] But more than 250 years had passed since then and evil days had befallen the people of Joseph during the intervening years. Now Moses had come from the Israelites to seek refuge at the hands of the people whose merchants originally had helped to sell Joseph into slavery. The freakish course of history had run its full cycle.

What was to become of him, Moses did not know, but as he sat by the well of the Midianites he could at least be thankful for water to drink and the companionship of fellow Shemites. But of course the Midianites did not look upon Moses as a Shemite. As we shall see in a moment he was dressed and spoke as an Egyptian, and was therefore mistaken for one.

MOSES MEETS JETHRO

While Moses was resting by the well he saw seven girls come with their flocks of sheep which they intended to water. Although Moses did not know it, these were the daughters of Jethro, the Priest of Midian.[13] The girls carefully and laboriously hauled up the water from the well to fill the drinking troughs, but just as they were finished and about to bring up their sheep to drink, a band of ruffian shepherds tried to drive the girls away and stampede their flocks[14]

Moses was outraged. In spite of his fatigue, he rose up and drove off the shepherds, and then helped the girls water their sheep. Little did Moses know that this single act of kindness would open the door for a whole new life in Midian.

---

11. Genesis 25:1-2
12. Genesis 37:28
13. Exodus 2:16; 3:1
14. Exodus 2:16-17

After watering their sheep, the girls went to their home. Their father was surprised; "How is it," he said, "that you are come so soon today?"[15] The girls had an exciting tale to tell: "An Egyptian delivered us out of the hand of the shepherds, and also drew water enough for us and watered the flock."[16]

"And where is he?" asked the father. "Why is it that ye have left the man? Call him that he may eat bread."[17]

So the girls ran to find Moses and invite him to their home. It was probably a most grateful and famished Moses who came forth weary but welcomed to the house of Jethro.

But Moses turned out to be a most singular guest. He was the original "man who came to dinner" but who stayed for forty years! No doubt with the warm encouragement of Jethro's seven daughters, the handsome man from Egypt was asked to visit awhile. The visit became a stay, and the stay became a permanent residence. Jethro took to this Moses. In due time Jethro not only invited Moses to make his home with the family, but he offered him the job of managing his flocks. Eventually he offered Moses one of his daughters to marry. Moses chose Zipporah. Jethro also ordained Moses to the Melchizedek Priesthood (Doc. & Cov. 84:6).

To Moses and Zipporah were born two sons. The first one was named Gershom which means "a stranger here."[18] Sometime later he had a second son whom Moses named Eliezer, meaning "My God is my help."[19]

So from the rank of a proud prince in Egypt, Moses had come to the role of a humble shepherd in Midian. It was a new life but a good life. The Bible says Moses was "content."[20] For forty years Moses served in this quiet, nomadic occupation of his great patriarchal ancestors.

MOSES RECEIVES HIS FIRST REVELATION FROM GOD

Moses had lived out two-thirds of his life before he received his first communication from heaven.

---

15. Exodus 2:18
16. Exodus 2:19
17. Exodus 2:20

18. Exodus 2:22 plus marginal note
19. Exodus 18:4 plus marginal note
20. Exodus 2:21

The scripture says it was about the time when Moses was eighty[21] that he happened to be feeding his flock "on the backside of the desert, and came to the mountain of God, even to Horeb."[22]

This mountain range had never before been named in scripture as "the mountain of God," but events were about to transpire there which would make it so. This vast pile of jagged peaks at the lower end of the Sinai peninsula juts its rugged cliffs of solid granite directly out of the floor of the wilderness around it. It is a bleak, barren and forbidding mountain range which in ancient times was known in its entirety as Horeb.[23]

As Moses foraged his flock on the desert plain at the base of this range, he was attracted by a strange phenomenon on the slopes of one of its peaks. It was a burning bush. What amazed him was the fact that it seemed to burn brightly but was not consumed. Moses said, "I will now turn aside, and see this great sight, why the bush is not burnt."[24]

Since Moses later named one whole peak of the Horeb range "Mount Sinai," (taken from the Hebrew word, *seneh*, meaning a bush) it is suggested by various authorities that the bush actually may have been high up along the side of this peak or even among its crags and crevices. We know that when Moses came to commune with the Lord in later years he always went into the very summit of Sinai to receive his revelations.[25]

But wherever the bush was, Moses now approached it. "And when the Lord saw that he turned aside to see, God called unto him out of the midst of the bush and said, Moses, Moses."[26] In astonishment Moses replied, "Here am I."[27]

The Lord said, "Draw not nigh hither: put off thy shoes from off thy feet, for the place whereon thou standest is holy ground."[28]

---

21. Exodus 7:7; Acts 7:23,30
22. Exodus 3:1
23. Clarke, *Bible Commentary*, Vol. 1, p. 30
24. Exodus 3:3
25. See for example, Exodus 19:20; 34:2
26. Exodus 3:4
27. Ibid.
28. Exodus 3:5

THE TEN COMMANDMENTS — A Paramount Picture

"... and he looked, and, and, behold, the bush burned with fire, and the bush was not consumed. And Moses said, I will now turn aside to see this great sight, why the bush is not burnt."

As Moses hastened to obey, the Lord continued:

"I am the God of thy father, the God of Abraham, the God of Isaac, and the God of Jacob."[29]

Moses was so frightened by this unexpected announcement that he turned his face away lest he look upon the glory of God and die.

But the Lord knew his fear would diminish as the interview progressed, therefore the Lord wasted no time on preliminaries but went directly to the purpose of this visitation. Said He:

"I have surely seen the affliction of my people which are in Egypt, and have heard their cry by reason of their taskmasters; for I know their sorrows; and I am come down to deliver them out of the hand of the Egyptians, and to bring them up out of that land unto a good land and a large, unto a land flowing with milk and honey; unto thy place of the Canaanites, and the Hittites, and the Amorites, and the Perizzites, and the Hivites, and the Jebusites."[30]

Up to this point Moses must have been thrilled with all the Lord was saying. Forty years earlier it had been maddening to Moses to see the suffering of Israel and not be able to do anything about it. Now at last God was going to intervene. But then the Lord shocked Moses. He announced that He was not going to do this marvelous work of liberation by Himself. To Moses he unexpectedly declared:

"I will send thee unto Pharaoh, that thou mayest bring forth my people the children of Israel out of Egypt."[31]

What was this? Impossible! It was virtual suicide! Did not the Lord know he was a fugitive from Egypt with a death sentence hanging over his head? If he returned to Egypt he would be killed the moment they identified him. Furthermore, he was not a person of any consequence in Egypt any more. His pleas to the Pharaoh to liberate Israel would be ridiculed and he would be arrested and slain. All of these fears, frustrations, and the firm determination of Moses to reject this calling were reflected in the conversation

29. Exodus 3:6   31. Exodus 3:10
30. Exodus 3:7, 8

which followed. Moses started out by pleading with the Lord,

"Who am I, that I should go unto Pharaoh, and that I should bring forth the children of Israel out of Egypt?" And the Lord replied, "Certainly I will be with thee."[32]

But who would believe him? Would the Israelites? Moses said: "Behold, when I come unto the children of Israel, and shall say unto them, the God of your fathers hath sent me unto you; and they shall say to me, what is his name? what shall I say unto them?

"And God said unto Moses, I AM THAT I AM: . . . Thus shalt thou say unto the children of Israel, I AM hath sent me unto you."[33] Then the Lord outlined the detailed manner in which Moses should approach the children of Israel as well as the Pharaoh to liberate them from bondage.[34]

But Moses was not convinced. He said:

". . . they will not believe me, nor hearken unto my voice: for they will say, The Lord hath not appeared unto thee."[35]

At this point Moses did not have the faith to believe that God literally meant it when He said, "I will be with thee."[36] Therefore the Lord undertook to remove the timidity of this new prophet by giving his faith something tangible to feed upon. Moses did not know it, but he was about to go through a series of frightening experiences. The Lord said to Moses:

"What is that in thine hand? Moses replied, "A rod." The Lord commanded him saying, "Cast it on the ground." Moses did. But barely had it touched the ground when it changed its very nature. Instead of a rod it passed through some kind of metamorphosis and began wriggling about. It had become a serpent.[37]

That was enough for Moses. He ran away, or as the scripture says, he "fled from before it."[38]

---

32. Exodus 3:11-12
33. Exodus 3:13-14
34. Exodus 3:15-22
35. Exodus 4:1

36. Exodus 3:12
37. Exodus 4:3
38. Ibid.

But the Lord called him back and said, "Put forth thine hand, and take it by the tail."[39]

When Moses finally worked up the courage to do so, the snake promptly became a rod again in his hand. It was unbelievable.

The Lord now told Moses that he was authorized to show this same miracle to the Israelites so that they would know he came to them with the power of God as a witness to his calling.

However, the Lord was not through with Moses. Said He:

"Put now thine hand into thy bosom." Moses did so and "when he took it out, behold, his hand was leprous as snow."[40]

This was the most hated and frightening disease in the whole Middle East. What was the Lord doing to him? With perfect reassurance the Lord said to him:

"Put thine hand into thy bosom again. And he put his hand into his bosom again; and plucked it out of his bosom, and, behold, it was turned again as his other flesh."[41]

The Lord then declared that if the turning of the rod into a serpent did not persuade them then "they will believe the voice of the latter sign"—the sign of the leprous hand. And just in case Moses felt he needed yet another proof of his authority, the Lord said:

". . . if they will not believe also these two signs, neither hearken unto thy voice, that thou shalt take of the water of the river, and pour it upon the dry land: and the water which thou takest out of the river shall become blood upon the dry land."[42]

One might presume that at the conclusion of such a miraculous demonstration of God's power, this 80-year-old servant of the Lord would have hastened toward Egypt with the most complete and enthusiastic confidence. But not Moses. Great leaders often contain a strong, stubborn streak in

39. Exodus 4:4   41. Exodus 4:7
40. Exodus 4:6   42. Exodus 4:9

their natures which makes them seem to hold out to the bitter end. What Moses had seen so far was good enough, but he had some other important excuses he wanted to try out on the Lord. Said he:

"O my Lord, I am not eloquent, neither heretofore, nor since thou hast spoken unto thy servant: but I am slow of speech, and of a slow tongue."[43]

The Lord replied: "What hath made man's mouth? or who maketh the dumb, or deaf, or the seeing, or the blind? have not I the Lord? Now therefore go, and I will be with thy mouth, and teach thee what thou shalt say."[44] When Enoch had made a similar complaint and received a similar answer he had been content. As a result the Lord had healed him of his affliction and made a great orator out of him.[45]

But Moses was not Enoch. Instead of humbly responding Moses exhibited one final thrust of stubbornness. However, he did not argue with the Lord, in fact, his offense was that he stopped arguing. Without any justification whatever, he just simply said he thought the Lord had better send somebody else. Authorities agree that this is the meaning of the statement, "O my Lord, send I pray thee, by the hand of him whom thou wilt send."[46]

This was a reckless step Moses should never have taken. "And the anger of the Lord was kindled against Moses, and he said, Is not Aaron the Levite thy brother? I know that he can speak well. And also, behold, he cometh forth to meet thee: and when he seeth thee, he will be glad in his heart. And thou shalt speak unto him, and put words in his mouth: and I will be with thy mouth, and with his mouth, and will teach you what ye shall do."[47]

So his older brother, Aaron, was coming! At least they could share this tremendous new calling together. Moses was finally reconciled. He accepted his calling.

---

43. Exodus 4:10
44. Exodus 4:11-12
45. Moses 6:31-39
46. Exodus 4:13
47. Exodus 4:14-15

THE RELIGIOUS EDUCATION OF MOSES BEGINS

Even though Moses was 80 years old by this time,[48] his spiritual development was that of a timid adolescent. This was awkwardly evident during his first conversation with the Lord which we have just discussed. But no one knew this problem better than the Lord, so he prepared to give Moses the necessary background of celestial knowledge which would build this new prophet into a pillar of spiritual granite. The Lord, Himself, was the instructor in the religious education of Moses.

We know this series of revelations occurred after the incident of the burning bush because Moses refers to the burning bush as a past event,[49] and we know it was before he had liberated Israel from Egypt, because during this revelation the Lord said, "thou shalt be made stronger than many waters" and "thou shalt deliver my people from bondage."[50] Obviously, rescuing Israel was still a future event.

To receive his spiritual education Moses was brought to "an exceedingly high mountain . . . the name of which shall not be known among the children of men."[51] Then the record continues:

"And he saw God face to face, and he talked with him, and the glory of God was upon Moses; therefore Moses could endure his presence. And God spake unto Moses, saying: Behold, I am the Lord God Almighty . . . And, behold, thou art my son; wherefore look, and I will show thee the workmanship of mine hands; but not all, for my works are without end, and also my words, for they never cease. Wherefore, no man can behold all my works, except he behold all my glory; and no man can behold all my glory, and afterwards remain in the flesh on the earth."[52]

Here was a heavenly vision of the most extraordinary kind. In his quickened condition Moses was first permitted to gaze upon the personage of God " face to face." Then he was told he would see a broad vista of God's creative handiwork. The Lord warned Moses, however, that what

---

48. Exodus 7:7; Acts 7:23,30   51. Moses 1:1, 42
49. Moses 1:17   52. Moses 1:2-5
50. Moses 1:25-26

he was about to see was only a token of His workmanship, since a complete disclosure of His glory and dominion is impossible if a man is to remain in the flesh. Nevertheless, what he was about to see would give him at least some appreciation of the divine personality who now stood before him.

Almost immediately this revelation made reference to Jesus Christ:

"And I have a work for thee, Moses, my son; and thou art in the similitude of mine Only Begotten; and mine Only Begotten is and shall be the Savior, for he is full of grace and truth; but there is no God beside me, and all things are present with me for I know them all."[53]

Although Moses did not know it, he was going to receive a series of revelations.

For this first lesson, the Lord merely wished to give Moses a broad historical perspective. Therefore he said,

"And now, behold, this one thing I show unto thee, Moses, my son; for thou art in the world, and now I show it [the world] unto thee. And it came to pass that Moses looked, and beheld the world upon which he was created; and Moses beheld the world and the ends thereof, and all the children of men which are, and which *were* created...."[54]

Apparently Moses was given a sweeping view of the entire human race in all parts of the earth. He not only saw those who existed in his own day, but those who had existed before. When this comprehensive vista of history had been presented to Moses the scripture says "he greatly marveled and wondered,"[55] The Lord knew that this was the man who would later write Genesis, therefore He gave him this panoramic vision which provided a broad appreciation of what happened to mankind during the previous 2,500 years. This made Moses a far better informed historian than most modern scholars have been willing to admit.

But suddenly the vision ended. "The presence of God withdrew from Moses, that his glory was not upon Moses;

53. Moses 1:6   55. Moses 1:8
54. Moses 1:7-8

and Moses was left unto himself. And as he was left unto himself, he fell unto the earth.[56]"

Moses now learned what other prophets had learned; namely, that the departure of the quickening power of God following a celestial manifestation to one who is not used to it, leaves the recipient as weak as water. "And it came to pass that it was for the space of many hours before Moses did again receive his natural strength like unto man; and he said unto himself: Now for this cause I know that man is nothing, which thing I never had supposed. But now mine own eyes have beheld God; but not my natural, but my spiritual eyes, for my natural eyes could not have beheld; for I should have withered and died in his presence; but his glory was upon me; and I beheld his face, for I was transfigured before him."[57]

This is the finest passage in all scripture describing the quickening process through which men must pass in order to come into the presence of God. Elsewhere we learn that the more often a person goes through this experience the less impact it has on his physical nature.[58]

Moses Suddenly Realizes He Has Just Missed a Great Opportunity

The once proud prince of Egypt had been so humbled by this revelation that he erroneously concluded that "man is nothing." Like all new students, the light of knowledge had temporarily blinded him. Later he would learn that while man should remain humble, he neverthless is God's most precious and most deeply beloved possession. Future lessons would teach him this.

However, something else occurred to Moses which was more realistic. He suddenly realized he had just missed a

---

56. Moses 1:9
57. Moses 1:10-11
58. Philo Dibble was present while Joseph Smith and Sidney Rigdon were recording the 76th Section of the Doctrine and Covenants. They had received an open revelation lasting several hours. He says, "Joseph appeared as strong as a lion but Sidney seemed as weak as water. Joseph, noticing his condition smiled and said: 'Brother Sidney is not as used to it as I am." (Quoted by N. B. Lundwall in *The Vision*, Salt Lake City: Bookcraft, 1948, p. 11, original source given as the *Eighth Book of Faith Promoting Series*, pp. 80-81.)

magnificent opportunity. He had been so excited he had forgotten to ask any questions!

Like all men, Moses must have puzzled over the mysteries of the universe. Over the years a thousand questions had probably tumbled through his mind. Why hadn't he taken advantage of this wonderful opportunity to ventilate these problems while he stood in the presence of God? The very fact that he had been granted such an interview made him bold in hoping for another one. Said he, "I will not cease to call upon God: *I have other things to inquire of him.* . . ."[59]

But before Moses could receive another revelation from the Lord he was to be subjected to a severe trial. He was to be exposed to a satanical exhibition of power administered by the prince of darkness in person. Apparently God wished to impress upon His newly commissioned servant that there are two great forces in the universe — one constructive, the other destructive. He wanted Moses to be able to distinguish between them. Lucifer, therefore, was permitted to appear before Moses and bring his whole influence to bear upon him. First he tempted Moses just as he later tempted the Savior, and when this failed to ensnare him, Satan struck out in a violent rage and tried to intimidate him with a terrorizing demonstration which caused Moses to "fear exceedingly; and as he began to fear, he saw the bitterness of hell. Nevertheless, calling upon God, he received strength, and he commanded saying: Depart from me, Satan, for this one God only will I worship, which is the God of glory."[60]

The vital lesson which the Lord wanted Moses to gain had been learned. When Satan saw that he had failed to deceive Moses he cried out against him in a wild denunciation. The record states that in the bitterness of his frustration he "cried with a loud voice, with weeping, and wailing, and gnashing of teeth."[61] Finally he departed.

Moses was now prepared to receive one of the greatest revelations ever given to man.

59. Moses 1:18   61. Moses 1:22
60. Moses 1:18-22

Moses Has a New Opportunity to Inquire of the Lord

"And it came to pass that when Satan had departed from the presence of Moses, that Moses lifted up his eyes unto heaven, being filled with the Holy Ghost . . . and calling upon the name of God, he beheld his glory again, for it was upon him; and he heard a voice, saying: Blessed art thou, Moses, for I, the Almighty, have chosen thee, and thou shalt be made stronger than many waters; for they shall obey thy command as if thou wert God. And lo, I am with thee, even unto the end of thy days; for thou shalt deliver my people from bondage, even Israel my chosen."[62]

With this, the vision of eternity suddenly opened again before Moses. He saw exactly what he had seen in the first vision—the earth and all of its inhabitants. Moses gazed intently at the scene. He "beheld the earth, yea, even all of it; and there was not a particle of it which he did not behold, discerning it by the spirit of God. And he beheld also the inhabitants thereof, and there was not a soul which he beheld not . . . and their numbers were great, even numberless as the sand upon the sea shore."[63]

This was the opportunity Moses had hoped for. This was his chance to ask directly concerning the questions which had been troubling him. Just as any modern scholar would have done, Moses longed to know the origin and purpose of all the things he had beheld. "Tell me, I pray thee, why these things are so, and by what thou madest them?"[64]

This was a decisive moment in the spiritual education of the man whose writings would later become part of the most widely read book in the world. In order that men of all ages and dispensations might afterwards appreciate the authoritative source of this revelation, Moses was endowed with additional glory so that he once again stood in the presence of God. "And the Lord God said unto Moses: For mine own purpose have I made these things. Here is wisdom and it remaineth in me."[65]

---

62. Moses 1:24-26
63. Moses 1:27-28
64. Moses 1:30
65. Moses 1:31

Moses Learns That There Are Many Inhabited Planets

Then the Lord gave Moses cause for more wonderment. Since he had been so impressed by the vision of this planet, the Lord shared with him another secret of the heavens. He told Moses that there are millions of other inhabited planets in the universe. "Worlds without number have I created," said the Lord. "For behold, . . . there are many that now stand, and innumerable are they unto man; but all things are numbered unto me, for they are mine and I know them."[66]

Moses had been a shepherd for forty years and on moonless nights he had gazed into the blue-black heights of the vaulted sky and watched the pinpoints of twinkling light coming through from the vast region of outer space where great star-giants wheel their way through the orbits of our galaxy. Now he was told by this omnipotent and holy personage — this divine personality who stood before him — that many of these great solar dynamos are no different than our own sun and they are circumscribed by whirling planets which — like our own earth — sustain life upon them.

Here was cause for real wonderment as Moses contemplated the vastness of the Lord's creations!

God Places Limitations on the Revelation to Moses

But the Lord quickly added that He did not intend to emphasize distant things in this particular revelation. "Only an account of *this* earth and the inhabitants thereof give I unto you," said the Lord.[67]

This was a most significant restriction placed upon the revelation which Moses was about to receive. It meant that nothing would be revealed at this time concerning possible relationships existing between this earth and other earths. It meant that if other, older, planets were used as a source of plant and animal life for this earth, such facts would not be revealed because it would involve a discussion of planets

---

66. Moses 1:33, 35
67. Moses 1:35

other than our own. It meant that Moses would be required to accept some things without explanation for the time being.

History confirms the wisdom of God in refusing to excite the human imagination concerning matters which have no immediate bearing on life here, and would only distract the human race from the business of making life more profitable on our own planet. It is only a temporary restriction, however, for the Lord has promised that when the time is ripe all this information concerning faraway things and places will be fully revealed. "A time to come in the which nothing shall be withheld, whether there be one God or many gods, they shall be manifest. All thrones and dominions, principalities and powers, shall be revealed and set forth upon all who have endured valiantly for the gospel of Jesus Christ. And also, if there be bounds set to the heavens or to the seas, or to the dry land, or to the sun, moon, or stars — all the times of their revolutions, all the appointed days, months, and years, and all the days of their days, months, and years, and all their glories, laws and set times, shall be revealed in the days of the dispensation of the fulness of times."[68]

It is understandable, nevertheless, why Moses was disappointed when he first learned of this restriction. The human mind is inherently desirous of knowing all truth whether it is ready for that truth or not. However, once Moses realized there was going to be this restriction he exhibited the genuine faith of an obedient son; if he could not receive the whole answer, he would still appreciate all the Lord would share with him. Said he, "Be merciful unto thy servant, O God, and tell me concerning *this* earth, and the inhabitants thereof . . . then thy servant will be content."[69]

MOSES LEARNS THE IMPORTANCE OF THE HUMAN RACE

But the Lord had one more seed to plant in the mind of Moses before He began the revelation on the "history of the race." The words which came next from the Lord constitute one of the most precious diadems of truth ever vouchsafed to man from the heavens:

---

68. Doctrine & Covenants 121:28-31
69. Moses 1:36

"Behold," said the Lord, *"this is my work and my glory —to bring to pass the immortality and eternal life of man."*[70]

Here is the answer to the inquiry of King David when he said, "What is man that thou takest knowledge of him?"[71]

Man is the pride and pleasure of God and the object of his infinite devotion. He is no whimsical fantasy of God's creative power. He is no mere creature of chance cast upon the horizon of existing things by fickle circumstances. In fact, God was soon to reveal to Moses the thrilling fact that the spirit which is embodied in each and every human being is a *literal offspring of God*—a fact which Paul would later confirm, as does modern revelation.[72]

Man is so important to the "work and glory" of God that earths are created for the express purpose of being inhabited by him.[73] The plant and animal kingdom which are placed upon these planets are for men to cultivate, subdue and make a part of his pleasant dominion.[74]

Since God is man's literal Father and Creator He looks upon His children like any other father. Their proper rearing is His "work," and their individual attainment is His "glory."

Moses Is Finally Ready to Receive "Genesis"

"And now, Moses, my son," said the Lord, "I will speak unto thee concerning this earth upon which thou standest; and thou shalt *write* the things which *I shall speak*. And in a day when the children of men shall esteem my words as naught and take many of them from the book which thou shalt write, behold, I will raise up another like unto thee; and they shall be had again among the children of men — among as many as shall believe."[75]

The above passage reveals a glaring error on the part of many modern Bible scholars who have been teaching for many years that Genesis is not of divine origin but merely

---

70. Moses 1:39
71. Psalms 144:3
72. Acts 17:29; Hebrews 12:9; Doc. & Cov. 76:24

73. Isaiah 45:18
74. Moses 2:26
75. Moses 1:40-41

a compilation of the *oral traditions* of the Hebrews which Moses collected and wrote down for the first time. The teaching of these scholars has had the effect of reducing the major portion of Genesis to the level of superstitious hearsay. Almost cheerfully, they have gone about the business of discrediting and destroying confidence in the historicity and authenticity of Genesis.[76]

But here we have the truth of the matter. Genesis is based upon a direct revelation from the Creator of this planet. It does not pretend to furnish all of the details. The Lord says he has reserved that until his Second Coming: "Yea, verily I say unto you, in that day when the Lord shall come, he shall reveal all things — things which have passed, and hidden *things which no man knew,* things of the earth, by which it was made, and the purpose and the end thereof . . . things that are in the earth, and upon the earth and in heaven."[77]

Nevertheless, what we do have in Genesis is from the Lord, not from the imaginations of man.

It must have been a thrilling experience for Moses as he began to record under divine instruction the material which constitutes the first several chapters of the book of Genesis in the Bible. Of course the Lord had warned Moses that many important parts of what he was writing would be stripped away and lost but he was comforted by the fact that in the last days, God would restore it again.[78]

---

76. Volume 1 of *The Interpreter's Bible* goes to great length to explain Genesis as myth and oral tradition. This 12-volume set which is one of the most popular commentaries is typical of the reckless handling of these ancient texts. In this source Dr. Arthur Jeffery writes: "The story of the growth of Hebrew Literature is in no fundamental way different from that of the growth of literature among other peoples. Everywhere the beginnings of national literature is oral." (Vol. 1, p. 33) Notice that the inspired origin of the Bible is completely discounted. With such men serving as their teachers it is no wonder that so many young ministers come from their seminaries possessing an attitude of deepest cynicism and suspicion toward the Bible.

77. Doctrine and Covenants 101:32-34

78. In 1830 Joseph Smith received the "restored" text of Genesis. This text gives us the opening chapters of Genesis the way Moses originally recorded them. In this restored text we find answers to many questions which have puzzled scholars for centuries. To appreciate the serious emasculation which had taken place in Genesis down through the years, it is significant that our modern version of Genesis contains only 151 verses of scripture whereas the restored version given to Joseph Smith contains 314 verses—more than twice as much. An actual calculation shows that 52% of the original Genesis up to verse 13 of chapter 6 had been lost.

So Moses concluded this great revelation. He now had a far better understanding of what had happened in the earth prior to his own arrival.

MOSES PREPARES TO LEAVE FOR EGYPT

Now Moses prepared to leave for Egypt. The respect which he held for his aged father-in-law, Jethro, is reflected in the following passage:

"And Moses went and returned to Jethro his father-in-law, and said unto him, Let me go, I pray thee, and return unto my brethren which are in Egypt, and see whether they be yet alive. And Jethro said to Moses, Go in peace."[79]

In spite of the warm relation between Moses and Jethro there is no indication that Moses felt authorized to share with Jethro these sacred experiences which had been coming from the Lord. To be able to keep a secret is one of the first prerequisites of a prophet.[80]

The Lord now told Moses something which He had been apparently holding back: "Go, return into Egypt," the Lord said, *"for all the men are dead which sought thy life."*[81] Pharaoh dead? Who had replaced him? Undoubtedly Moses reflected on the strange circumstances which had taken him away from Egypt 40 years earlier. Had he remained in Egypt, perhaps he would now be the Pharaoh.

No matter, Moses now had a calling more precious than all the thrones of the whole world.

Once more the Lord assured Moses that he would be successful on this new mission. Moses was even given advance notice that if the Pharaoh proved completely stubborn and immovable the Lord was prepared to go as far as taking the life of Pharaoh's eldest son.[82]

A short time later, the Lord was threatening to take away the life of Moses' eldest son!

---

79. Exodus 4:18
80. As Brigham Young stated, "The Lord has no confidence in those who reveal secrets, for he cannnot safely reveal himself to such persons. (Discourses of Brigham Young, pp. 62-63.)
81. Exodus 4:19
82. Exodus 4:23

Moses Learns a Lesson in Obedience

Moses was about to learn that heavenly visions and angelic revelations never saved any man. Only *obedience* to God's commandments can earn His blessings. As Moses, Zipporah, and their two sons were proceeding on their way, the Lord suddenly confronted Moses with the possibility of losing Gershom, his firstborn. Moses had not placed his sons under the covenant of Abraham through the rite of circumcision. This was something new for Moses. He must have hesitated. The scripture says that when Zipporah saw that she might lose one of her sons through her husband's neglect she did not wait for Moses to perform the circumcision. She did it herself.

"Cutting the flesh" in those days was usually accomplished by means of a flint knife because it could be chipped and honed to an extremely fine cutting edge.[83] So the scripture says Zipporah circumcised her son with a "sharp stone."[84] Then she made a statement which is said to mean, "a spouse by blood art thou unto me because of the circumcision."[85]

It should be kept in mind that all of these weaknesses and criticisms of Moses were put into the record by Moses himself. This book is his own writing. It demonstrates his honesty as a historian and his humility as a prophet. When it came time to write this history he could look back on his life and see how patient God had been with him down through the years.

After the incident of the neglected circumcision, Moses for some reason decided that he had better send Zipporah and her sons back to Jethro while he proceeded to Egypt alone.[86] However, he did not go to Egypt directly. We find that he first returned to the "mount of God."

Moses Receives a Pleasant Surprise

Now the Lord took steps to fulfill a promise He had made to Moses when He spoke to him from the burning

---

83. Clarke. *Bible Commentary*, Vol. 1, p. 311
84. Exodus 4:25
85. Ibid., plus Clarke, *Bible Commentry*, Vol. 1, p. 311
86. This fact is not revealed until later in the narrative, see Exodus 18:2-3.

bush. He had assured Moses that Aaron, his older brother, was coming up from Egypt to meet him. So far as we know Aaron and Moses had been out of touch with each other for nearly forty years. Perhaps the long and powerful arm of Pharaoh's vengeance had made it too dangerous for Moses to make contact. Surely, if the family of Moses had known where he was they would have told him that the old Pharaoh had died, and it was safe to return. From all the circumstances it would appear that they had no idea what had happened to him. Now, however, the Lord revealed the whereabouts of Moses to Aaron. He must have told Aaron exactly where to find Moses, for the scripture says, "And the Lord said to Aaron, Go into the wilderness to meet Moses. And he went, and met him in the mount of God, and kissed him."[87]

This was a glorious day for these two brothers. "And Moses told Aaron all the words of the Lord who had sent him, and all the signs which he had commanded him."[88]

So these two grandsons of Levi were ready for their call.[89] Together they headed back across the desert wilderness toward the precincts of mighty Egypt.

---

87. Exodus 4:27
88. Exodus 4:28
89. They were grandsons of Levi through their mother, great-grandsons through their father. See Exodus 6:16-20.

Scripture Reading and Questions on Chapter Eleven

Scripture Reading Assignment: Exodus 2:11 through chapter 3; also Moses, chapter 1.

1—How old was Moses when he returned to his people? Did he renounce his adoption at this time?

2—Did Moses therefore slay the Egyptian taskmaster in his role as the adopted son of Pharaoh's daughter or after he had assumed the role of a Hebrew?

3—Did the slaying of the taskmaster remain a secret? How did Moses discover that his act was known?

4—When Pharaoh heard of it what did he do? What did Moses do?

5—Where is Midian? Did Moses have difficulty reaching it?

6—How did Moses happend to meet Jethro? Did they know he was a Hebrew?

7—What three things did Moses receive through the generosity of Jethro?

8—How long did Moses serve Jethro as a shepherd? Then how old was Moses when he received his call?

9—What is the meaning of Sinai? Who named it? Why?

10—When Moses learned of his new calling what was his reaction?

11—What three signs was Moses authorized to show the Israelites in order to convince them that he had the approval of God?

12—What did Moses say that angered the Lord?

13—Approximately when did Moses receive the revelation which is recorded in the first chapter of the Book of Moses?

14—After the revelation closed, what was the physical impact on Moses? Why did Moses suddenly realize he had just missed a great opportunity?

15—What was Moses told about Jesus Christ?

16—What was Satan's purpose in appearing before Moses?

17—When Moses received his next revelation what restriction did the Lord put on it? If you had been Moses, would this have been a disappointment to you?

18—Where did Moses get the information for Genesis? What did the Lord say would happen to the writings of Moses in the coming centuries? Was this prophecy fulfilled?

19—How did Moses come close to losing the life of his eldest son?

20—Did Moses take his wife and sons with him into Egypt? Who did go with him?

CHAPTER TWELVE

Moses Returns to Egypt

Forty long years had passed since Moses had seen the land of his birth.

In Goshen there were kinsmen to welcome him—Miriam, his sister, the four sons of Aaron, Aaron's wife, no doubt many others. But equally important was the welcome of the thousands of Israelites to whom Moses was a figure of heroic tradition. By this time two whole generations had heard the story countless times of the Hebrew baby who was adopted by the Pharaoh's daughter and grew up in the palace of the king. And then there were the feats of courage in the Ethiopian War. Finally, there was the tragic ending, the killing of the Egyptian slave master, the death edict of the Pharaoh and the mysterious disappearance of the great Moses.

But somewhere in those slave camps of Goshen were Ephraimites with the record of Joseph. Whoever had that record knew this Moses was a child of prophecy and a man of destiny. They knew that somehow, sometime, Israel would hear from Moses again.

What a charge of excitement must have electrified the slave quarters of Israel as the word spread throughout all Goshen: "Moses is back! Moses is back!"

MOSES PRESENTS GOD'S PLAN OF LIBERATION TO THE ELDERS OF ISRAEL

When greetings and social amenities were over, Moses and Aaron prepared to deliver their volatile message. However, they called no mass meetings of the people to announce the purpose of their mission. Instead, they called together the responsible leaders of Israel.[1]

---

1. Exodus 4:29

This was an occasion of the utmost solemnity. Aaron served as spokesman and unfolded the sacred plan of the Lord to liberate Israel.[2] At the appropriate moment Moses stepped forward and called upon these elders of Israel to witness the fact that he did not come to them as a self-appointed liberator but as a servant of God with power to perform the wonders of God.

As Moses threw his staff to the ground it immediately became transformed, coiling and writhing as a living serpent. When he grasped it by the tail it once more became a simple shepherd's staff. It was fantastic. Then, standing before them he thrust his hand beneath his robe and brought it forth white and ulcerated with the panic-provoking plague of leprosy. Thrusting his hand back again within his robe he brought it forth cleansed and healed, glowing with the robust radiance of healthy flesh.

Thus Moses and Aaron "did the signs in the sight of the people," and the flame of hope was kindled in the hearts of all the Israelites. They could see that the hand of God was with these two new leaders.

"And the people believed; and when they heard that the Lord had visited the Children of Israel, and that he had looked upon their affliction, then they bowed their heads and worshipped."[3]

Moses and Aaron Face the New Pharaoh

Next came the real challenge, convincing the Pharaoh. Moses and Aaron left Goshen and made the short journey to the world-famous Egyptian capital which, during this period, was Memphis. There they requested an audience with the new Pharaoh. Strong, conflicting emotions must have swept through the heart and mind of Moses as he walked the streets and palace corridors where once he had the honor of being the crown prince of Egypt. Where was his foster mother, daughter of the old Pharaoh, the woman who had loved him so deeply? What had happened to his old friends and associates of those earlier days? On

2. Exodus 4:30
3. Exodus 4:31

all such details the scriptures are silent, but without doubt Moses must have pondered such questions.

When Moses and Aaron had been ushered into the presence of the new Pharaoh they delivered their message. The scripture says, "And afterward Moses and Aaron went in, and told Pharaoh, Thus saith the Lord God of Israel, Let my people go, that they may hold a feast unto me in the wilderness."[4]

Certainly no crowned head of any country ever heard a petition quite like this, especially from slaves. What did they mean invoking the "Lord God of Israel" to promote their paper-thin scheme to escape from Egypt? This petition was a plot. It was contemptible. Sneeringly, the Pharaoh replied, "Who is the Lord, that I should obey his voice to let Israel go? I know not the Lord, neither will I let Israel go."[5]

But Moses and Aaron persisted. They said: "The God of the Hebrews hath met with us: let us go, we pray thee, three days' journey into the desert, and sacrifice unto the Lord our God; lest he fall upon us with pestilence, or with the sword."[6]

The logic of this request is explained by Dr. Adam Clarke as follows:

"The Israelites could not sacrifice in the land of Egypt, because the animals they were to offer to God were held sacred by the Egyptians; and they could not omit this duty, because it was essential to religion even before the giving of the law." (*Bible Commentary*, Vol. 1, p. 313).

But there was no logic in all of this for Pharaoh. He determined to put down this sudden display of independence with finality and firmness. He would teach these slaves to waste time dreaming about some ridiculous religious festival in the desert.

"And the king of Egypt said unto them, Wherefore do ye, Moses and Aaron, let the people from their works? Get you unto your burdens."[7]

---

4. Exodus 5:1   6. Exodus 5:3
5. Exodus 5:2   7. Exodus 5:4

Then calling to him the officers and taskmasters who had charge of the Israelites he proclaimed:

"Ye shall no more give the people straw to make brick, as heretofore: let them go and gather straw for themselves.

"And the tale [tally] of the bricks, which they did make heretofore, ye shall lay upon them; ye shall not diminish ought thereof: for they be idle; therefore they cry, saying, Let us go and sacrifice to our God.

"Let there more work be laid upon the men, that they may labour therein; and let them not regard vain words."[8]

So this became the Pharaoh's order and his officers were prompt and harsh in executing it. The people frantically spread abroad, trying to find straw, but when they failed to find enough, they began pulling up the "stubble instead of straw."[9] This took so much time that the tally of bricks diminished and after two days the taskmasters took the officers of the Israelites and beat them, saying, "Wherefore have ye not fulfilled your task in making brick both yesterday and to day, as heretofore?"[10]

The answer to this ridiculous question seemed obvious.

Moses and Aaron Lose the Support of the Elders of Israel

The order of the Pharaoh was so unreasonable and senseless that the elders of Israel knew they would never meet its requirements regardless of their effort. They therefore decided to go directly to the Pharaoh and plead for a more tolerable arrangement.

"Then the officers of the children of Israel came and cried unto Pharaoh, saying, Wherefore dealest thou thus with thy servants?

"There is no straw given unto thy servants, and they say to us, Make brick: and, behold, thy servants are beaten; but the fault is in thine own people.

---

8. Exodus 5:7-9   10. Exodus 5:14
9. Exodus 5:12

"But he [the Pharaoh] said, Ye are idle, ye are idle: therefore ye say, Let us go and do sacrifice to the Lord.

"Go, therefore now, and work; for there shall no straw be given you, yet shall ye deliver the tale of bricks.

"And the officers of the children of Israel did see that they were in evil. . . ."[11]

Having been dismissed by the Pharaoh, the elders of Israel came out of the palace and found Moses and Aaron anxiously waiting to hear what had happened. The elders of Israel were boiling with wrath. Said they, "The Lord look upon you, and judge; because ye have made our savour to be abhorred in the eyes of Pharaoh, and in the eyes of his servants, to put a sword in their hand to slay us."[12]

Neither Moses nor Aaron could answer this rebuke. They also wondered why the Lord was not fulfilling His promise, smoothing the path, and opening the way? What was the sign of the rod turning into a serpent or the sign of the leprous hand if the Lord now failed to keep His promises? Apparently Moses had missed the full implication of the Lord's previous warning concerning the hardness of Pharaoh's heart.[13] In puzzled wonderment and deepest disappointment Moses attempted to make contact with the Lord. His prayer was a mixture of supplication and anger. He still had much to learn. Said he:

"Lord, wherefore hast thou so evil entreated this people? Why is it that thou hast sent me, For since I came to Pharaoh to speak in thy name, he hath done evil to this people; neither hast thou delivered thy people at all."[14]

Like a patient father dealing with a child, the Lord replied: "Now shalt thou see what I will do to Pharaoh: for with a strong hand shall he let them go. . . ."[15]

On five previous occasions the Lord had specifically promised Moses that he would ultimately liberate Israel from bondage.[16] Now he repeated the promise twice more.[17]

11. Exodus 5:15-19
12. Exodus 5:21
13. Exodus 3:19-20
14. Exodus 5:22-23
15. Exodus 6:1
16. Exodus 3:8; 3:10; 3:12; 3:17; 3:20
17. Exodus 6:1, 7

With this new assurance Moses returned to the Children of Israel to gird up their courage and deliver the latest promise of God's deliverance. But he found Goshen in chaos. The whip lashes across the backs of the people were deeper and more convincing than the words of Moses. Therefore the scripture says: ". . . they hearkened not unto Moses for anguish of spirit, and for cruel bondage."[18]

MOSES AND AARON GO IN BEFORE PHARAOH THE SECOND TIME

"And the Lord spake unto Moses, saying, Go in, speak unto Pharaoh king of Egypt, that he let the children of Israel go out of his land."[19]

But Moses had not achieved pure faith as yet. He had to be persuaded. Said he, "Behold, the children of Israel have not hearkened unto me; how then shall Pharaoh hear me . . . ?"[20]

Now the Lord took a new approach. It was no longer a question of merely letting the Children of Israel go. The Lord now issued a command or a "charge" unto the Children of Israel, and unto Pharaoh, king of Egypt, to bring the Children of Israel out of the land of Egypt.[21]

The Lord then warned Moses and Aaron not to expect Pharaoh to respond,[22] but to proceed exactly the way the Lord instructed them and they would eventually triumph. In fact, from here on the Lord told them just how Pharaoh would behave on each occasion and how they should deal with him.

As Moses and Aaron appeared before Pharaoh the second time they delivered God's commandment that the Pharaoh should "bring the Children of Israel out of Egypt." The Pharaoh challenged them to prove they were servants of God by displaying the power of God. Aaron, who was serving as spokesman, cast down the rod of Moses and it became a serpent. Instead of accepting this amazing phenomenon as a sign of divine power the Pharaoh called in his

---

18. Exodus 6:9   21. Exodus 6:13
19. Exodus 6:10-11   22. Exodus 7:4
20. Exodus 6:12

"magicians". Lo and behold, they had developed a cunning magician's trick by which they also seemed to be able to turn rods into serpents. Paul, the apostle, knew the identity of the two leaders of the magicians. They were called Jannes and Jambres.[23]

The difference between a prophet and a magician is that one uses the power of God to perform a miracle, while the other uses the power of deception and trickery to make it *seem* that he has performed a miracle. But from the Pharaoh's point of view he considered one equal to the other. However, an interesting thing happened as all these "miracle" serpents slithered on the floor before Pharaoh. The serpent that belonged to Aaron suddenly began devouring all the magician's serpents. This should have been an omen to Pharaoh, but Pharaoh's heart was hardened and he believed it not.[24] Aaron and Moses departed.

THE TEN TERRIBLE PLAGUES

The Lord now commanded Moses to launch the contest of miracles known as the ten plagues. This contest between Moses and Aaron on the one hand and the Pharaoh's magicians on the other, became world famous. Dr. Adam Clarke points out that the Greek historian, Pliny, specifically refers to Moses by name and identifies contemporary "magicians" as Jamnes and Jotapes which are undoubtedly the same as those referred to by Paul even though their names are spelled differently.[25]

The summary of the plagues which were inflicted on Egypt at this time was as follows:

1. The water is turned into blood.

2. The plague of the frogs.

---

23. 2 Timothy 3:8
24. Several times in Exodus it says the Lord hardened Pharaoh's heart, but the correct translation is "and Pharaoh's heart was hardened." Dr. Adam Clarke points out Exodus 7:22 among others where the correct translation is given. However, these same words are incorrectly translated in many other places. (Clark, *Bible Commentary*, Vol. 1, p. 322) Joseph Smith made the same correction in the Inspired Version.
25. Pliny stated: "There is also another faction of magicians which took its origin from the Jews, Moses Jamnes, and Jotapes, many thousands of years after Zoroaster." (Clarke, Ibid., p. 324)

3. The plague of the lice.

4. The plague of the flies (insects).

5. The plague of murrain among the cattle.

6. The plague of boils and blains.

7. The plague of fire mingled with hail.

8. The plague of locusts.

9. The plague of thick darkness.

10. The slaying of the first-born.

Now let us deal with each plague in more detail.

First—Turning Water Into Blood

"And the Lord said unto Moses, Pharaoh's heart is hardened, he refuseth to let the people go.

"Get thee unto Pharaoh in the morning; lo he goeth out unto the water; and thou shalt stand by the river's brink against he come. . . . Say unto Aaron, take thy rod, and stretch out thine hand upon the waters of Egypt, upon their streams, upon their rivers, and upon their ponds, and upon all their pools of water, that they may become blood; and that there may be blood throughout all the land of Egypt, both in vessels of wood, and in vessels of stone."[26]

The next day Moses and Aaron did exactly as the Lord had commanded them. Aaron, "lifted up the rod, and smote the waters that were in the river, in the sight of Pharaoh and in the sight of his servants; and all the waters that were in the river were turned to blood.

"And the fish that was in the river died; and the river stank, and the Egyptians could not drink of the water of the river; and there was blood throughout all the land of Egypt."[27]

This was an amazing display of power but Pharaoh determined to attribute it to trickery or sorcery rather than God so long as his magicians could match it. And they did! Obviously, the magicians were unable to do it on the

---

26. Exodus 7:14-15, 19   27. Exodus 7:20-21

scale that Moses and Aaron had achieved since all surface water had been previously turned into blood but they did know a way to turn water into something which looked like blood that that was enough for Pharaoh. The scripture says, "And Pharaoh's heart was hardened, neither did he hearken unto them; as the Lord had said."[28]

However, his contemptuous disdain did not alter the stubborn fact that all of this area of Egypt was without any kind of drinking water. The plague of blood lasted seven days and during that time the people had to scramble about digging wells to secure subterranean water for themselves and their cattle. As the scripture says, "And all the Egyptians digged round about the river for water to drink; for they could not drink of the water of the river. And seven days were fulfilled after that the Lord had smitten the river."[29]

SECOND—THE PLAGUE OF FROGS

Now came a plague which turned out to be more loathsome than the blood. The Lord said to Moses:

"Go unto Pharaoh, and say unto him, Thus saith the Lord, let my people go, that they may serve me. And if thou refuse to let them go, behold, I will smite all thy borders with frogs: And the river shall bring forth frogs abundantly, which shall go up and come into thine house, and into thy bedchamber, and upon thy bed, and into the house of thy servants, and upon thy people, and into thine ovens, and into thy kneading troughs."[30]

When Pharaoh failed to respond to this latest plea, the second plague descended upon Egypt. Millions of frogs came up from the river. Their slippery, cold, half-reptile bodies were everywhere, indoors and out. The whole conglomoration of croaking, hopping, squatting swamp creatures brought a cry of despair throughout the land. The magicians rushed forward to produce even more frogs from the river, but this was little comfort to the Pharaoh. The problem was to get rid of the frogs, not produce more. Since the magicians could neither stop the plague nor reduce its intensity, the

28. Exodus 7:22
29. Exodus 7:24-25
30. Exodus 8:1-4

Pharaoh finally called for Moses and Aaron. To them he said, "Intreat the Lord that he may take away the frogs from me, and from my people; and I will let the people go, that they may do sacrifice unto the Lord."[31]

This sudden display of humility on the part of Pharaoh was the first glimmer of encouragement Moses and Aaron had received. Moses immediately offered the Pharaoh the privilege of naming the very hour when the plague would cease so that he would have his own personal testimony that the hand of God was in it. Pharaoh accepted the challenge, naming the exact time. Moses replied, "Be it according to thy word: that thou mayest know that there is none like unto the Lord our God. And the frogs shall depart from thee, and from thy houses, and from thy servants, and from thy people; they shall remain in the river only."[32]

Moses then went forth to seek the Lord in prayer and ask him to ratify his servant's promise that the plague of frogs would cease at the precise time the Pharaoh had picked.

"And the Lord did according to the word of Moses; and the frogs died out of the houses, out of the villages, and out of the fields. And they gathered them together upon heaps; and the land stank."[33]

At last the Pharaoh had a personal witness that there was indeed a supernatural power behind Moses and Aaron which could not be explained away as mere coincidence, sorcery, or a magician's trick. He had given his royal oath that if they would perform, he would fulfill. Moses and Aaron had performed, the plague was stayed, now what of the Pharaoh?

The scripture says, "But when Pharaoh saw that there was respite, he hardened his heart, and hearkened not unto them; as the Lord had said."[34] Up to this time there may have been some excuse for the heathen Pharaoh to rationalize away each manifestation of God's power because the magicians seemed to be able to do something similar. However, the magicians could not stop a plague while Moses and Aaron had done so, and they had allowed the Pharaoh to fix

---

31. Exodus 8:8   33. Exodus 8:13-14
32. Exodus 8:10-11   34. Exodus 8:15

the time. For the Pharaoh his royal oath was, in the light of this evidence, a clear sign that he was choosing a course of action similar to Cain when he said, "Who is the Lord that I should know him."[35] In other words, what does it matter if it is the work of God? He would defy God.

THIRD—THE PLAGUE OF LICE

This is all the Lord needed to establish. The first two plagues had been unpleasant and inconvenient, now the Lord resorted to a pestilence of torment. Without any further warning to Pharaoh the following command was given to Moses: "Say unto Aaron, Stretch out thy rod, and smite the dust of the land, that it may become lice throughout all the land of Egypt. And they did so; for Aaron stretched out his hand with his rod, and smote the dust of the earth, and it became lice in man, and in beast; all the dust of the land became lice throughout all the land of Egypt."[36]

Once more the magicians hastened to prove to Pharaoh that this was just another trick which they, themselves, could do. *But this time they failed.* Whether they had expected to do it by deceptive manipulation or by sorcery we do not know. The scripture simply says that when they found they could not duplicate this amazing phenomenon they were beaten. There is an old saying that "if you can't beat them, join them." This is what the Pharaoh's magicians did: "Then the magicians said unto Pharaoh, This is the finger of God!"[37]

One would have thought this would have most certainly impressed Pharaoh, but it did not. The scripture says, "and Pharaoh's heart was hardened, and he hearkened not unto them." Now the Pharaoh was resisting both the prophets of God and his own magicians.

FOURTH—THE SWARM OF INSECTS AND FLIES

As a result, another plague of torment was unleashed on the Egyptians. This time it came in the form of great swarms of insects. The English bible says "flies" but author-ities point out that the original Hebrew term includes "dif-

---

35. Moses 5:16   37. Exodus 8:19
36. Exodus 8:16-17

ferent kinds of insects, such as flies, wasps, hornets, etc."[38] There is no doubt that this plague was a torture to the people.

To prove to Pharaoh that this plague was a sign from God and not a mere happenstance, the Lord told Moses to intercept Pharaoh as he came down to the river the following day and declare unto him: "Thus saith the Lord, Let my people go, that they may serve me. Else, if thou wilt not let my people go, behold, I will send swarms of flies [insects] upon thee. . . . And I will sever in that day the land of Goshen, in which my people dwell, that no swarms of flies [insects] shall be there; to the end thou mayest know that I am the Lord in the midst of the earth."[39]

This would imply that prior to this time the plagues had been universal, meaning that during the plagues of the blood, the frogs and the lice, the Israelites had suffered right along with the Egyptians. Now, however, it would be different. The Lord said, "And I will put a division between my people and thy people: to morrow shall this sign be."[40]

This is precisely what happened: ". . . there came a grievous swarm of flies [insects] into the house of Pharaoh, and into his servant's houses, and into all the land of Egypt: the land was corrupted by reason of the swarm of flies [insects]."[41]

Finally Pharaoh begged for mercy. It would seem that his magicians were no longer available to support him, and the cry of protest from the people became unbearable. However, he did not intend to capitulate completely, he just offered to compromise. He told Moses to go ahead and sacrifice, but do it "in the land."[42] This meant that they were to offer their sacrifices in Goshen without leaving Egypt.

Moses replied that this was impossible: "It is not meet so to do," said he, "for we shall sacrifice the abomination of the Egyptians to the Lord our God: lo, shall we sacrifice the abomination of the Egyptians before their eyes, and will they not stone us?"[43]

---

38. Clarke, *Bible Commentary*, Vol. 1, p. 328
39. Exodus 8:20-22
40. Exodus 8:23
41. Exodus 8:24
42. Exodus 8:25
43. Exodus 8:26

The Egyptians would sacrifice a human being to their gods but they believed animals were too sacred to sacrifice. In fact, the very animals which God had commanded the Hebrews to sacrifice were the ones held the *most* sacred by the Egyptians. These included the ram (sheep), the goat, the heifer or the bullock. According to Eusebius, the Egyptians believed that during a war between supernatural beings their gods were forced to flee to the earth and had hidden in the bodies of various animals. Jupiter, for example, was believed to have taken the body of a ram, Apollo a crow, Bacchus a goat, Diane a cat, Juno a heifer, Venus a fish, Mercury a bird (the ibis).[44] All of these animals were given protective sanctuary in Egypt. This is why the Egyptians would form into a mob and stone the Israelites if they were so reckless as to kill any of these sacred animals and offer them up as sacrifices.

Pharaoh caught the point and he had to agree. Nevertheless, he stubbornly refused to capitulate entirely. He was determined not to lose the slave power of the Israelites if he could help it, therefore he said, "I will let you go, that ye may sacrifice to the Lord your God in the wilderness; *only ye shall not go very far away*: intreat for me."[45]

So Moses agreed to ask the Lord to remove the plague of insects, but he warned Pharaoh, ". . . let not Pharaoh deal deceitfully any more in not letting the people go to sacrifice to the Lord."[46]

However, it was a repeat performance. No sooner had the plague been terminated than the fickle mind of Pharaoh went into reverse and repudiated his promise.

FIFTH—THE MURRAIN OF THE CATTLE

From here on the Lord began to send a series of plagues which attacked the possessions of the people. The fifth plague was aimed directly at the Egyptian cattle. As they began to die off in great numbers, Pharaoh sent messengers to Goshen to see if this were just a routine epidemic which

44. Quoted in Clarke's *Bible Commentary*, Vol. 1, p. 329
45. Exodus 8:28   47. Exodus 9:7
46. Exodus 8:29   48. Exodus 9:3

occasionally struck Egypt or whether, on this particular occasion, it was being inflicted exclusively upon the cattle of the Egyptians.

When the report came back it confirmed Pharaoh's worst fears: ". . . and behold there was not one of the Israelite cattle dead."[47] Among the domestic flocks of the Egyptians, however, there was death everywhere. This included sheep, goats, oxen, camels, donkeys and horses.[48]

Dr. Clarke states, "The murrain is a very contagious disease among cattle, the symptoms of which are hanging down and swelling of the head, abundance of gum in the eyes, rattling in the throat, difficulty of breathing, palpitation of the heart, staggering, a hot breath, and a shining tongue; which symptoms prove that a general inflammation has taken place."[49]

In spite of the plague among the Egyptian cattle, however, the king would not concede. ". . . the heart of Pharaoh was hardened, and he did not let the people go."[50]

SIXTH—THE PLAGUE OF BOILS AND BLAINS

The sixth plague struck both man and beast. "And the Lord said unto Moses and unto Aaron, Take to you handfuls of ashes of the furnace, and let Moses sprinkle it toward the heaven in the sight of Pharaoh. And it shall become small dust in all the land of Egypt, and shall be a boil breaking forth with blains upon man, and upon beast, throughout all the land of Egypt."[51]

Moses and Aaron did as they were told and immediately boils and blains began breaking out on all the people and their cattle which had survived the murrain. For the Egyptians, it was the terrible plague of Job. One boil will torment the body, but a plague of boils will torture it. The master magicians who had formerly taunted Moses and Aaron found this plague striking them just as it did the ordinary people. "And the magicians could not stand before Moses because

---

49. Clarke, *Bible Commentary*, Vol. 1, p. 331   51. Exodus 9:8-9
50. Exodus 9:7

of the boils; for the boil was upon the magicians, and upon all the Egyptians."[52] This is the last reference to the magicians.

But, even as before, the Pharaoh continued to resist.

SEVENTH—THE PLAGUE OF FIRE MINGLED WITH HAIL

The seventh plague was aimed at the precious Egyptian crops and the remainder of the Egyptian cattle. The Lord had Moses and Aaron warn the Egyptians: "Send therefore now, and gather thy cattle, and all that thou hast in the field; for upon every man and beast which shall be found in the field, and shall not be brought home, the hail shall come down upon them, and they shall die."[53]

Some of the Pharaoh's attendants had seen enough of Moses and Aaron to fear their words. It says, "He that feared the word of the Lord . . . made his servants and his cattle flee into the houses; And he [like Pharaoh] that regarded not the word of the Lord left his servants and his cattle in the field."[54]

When the storm struck, it was much more than a hail storm. It was a frightening electrical storm which thundered and roared across the land. The record says, "and the Lord sent thunder and hail, and the fire ran along upon the ground. . . . So there was hail, and fire mingled with the hail, very grievous, such as there was none like it in all the land of Egypt since it became a nation. . . . Only in the land of Goshen, where the Children of Israel were, was there no hail." (Exodus 9:23-26)

Once again, the resistance of Pharaoh finally collapsed and he "called for Moses and Aaron and said unto them, I have sinned this time: the Lord is righteous, and I and my people are wicked. Intreat the Lord (for it is enough) that there be no more mighty thunderings and hail; and I will let you go, and ye shall stay no longer."[55]

Ordinarily, such a confession of humility and repentance by the Pharaoh would have been most persuasive, but not to Moses. The Lord had already warned Moses over and over again that this was a man whose hypocrisy was chronic,

---

52. Exodus 9:11
53. Exodus 9:19

54. Exodus 9:20-21
55. Exodus 9:27-28

his royal oath meant nothing, his repentance was a sham. "And Moses said unto him, As soon as I am gone out of the city, I will spread abroad my hands unto the Lord; and the thunder shall cease, neither shall there be any more hail; that thou mayest know how that the earth is the Lord's. But as for thee and thy servants I know that ye will not yet fear the Lord God."[56]

The Bible says the two crops most severely damaged by the hail and fire were the flax and barley because "the barley was in the ear, and the flax was bolled." Two other major crops, "The wheat and the rie were not smitten: for they were not grown up."[57]

As soon as the plague had ceased, Pharaoh conducted himself in his customary fashion by completely repudiating his promise. The scripture says, "he sinned yet more, and hardened his heart, he and his servants."[58]

EIGHTH—THE PLAGUE OF LOCUSTS

Now the Lord prepared to scorch the earth with a plague which would destroy the crops left over from the fire and hail. As before, Pharaoh was warned in advance: "And Moses and Aaron came in unto Pharaoh, and said unto him, Thus saith the Lord God of the Hebrews, How long wilt thou refuse to humble thyself before me? let my people go, that they may serve me. Else, if thou refuse to let my people go, behold, to morrow will I bring the locusts into thy coast: and they shall cover the face of the earth, that one cannot be able to see the earth: and they shall eat the residue of that which is escaped which remaineth unto you from the hail, and shall eat every tree [plant] which groweth for you out of the field: and they shall fill thy houses, and the houses of all they servants, and the houses of all the Egyptians; which neither thy fathers, nor thy fathers' fathers have seen, since the day that they were upon the earth unto this day."[59]

---

56. Exodus 9:29-30
57. Exodus 9:32. The marginal note for "not grown up" says the original Hebrew means "hidden" or still in the "dark." This would imply that the wheat and rye had been planted but they had not yet sprouted.
58. Exodus 9:34
59. Exodus 10:3-6

Once again Pharaoh pleaded for mercy and once again Moses went before the Lord to intercede in his behalf. As before, the miracle which brought the plague was no greater than the miracle which suddenly ended it. "And the Lord turned a mighty strong west wind, which took away the locusts, and cast them into the Red Sea; there remained not one locust in all the coasts of Egypt."[63]

However, the locust plague was not the only thing which was gone with the wind. So was Pharaoh's humility. Once more his heart became as stone and his countenance like flint.

NINTH—THE PLAGUE OF THICK DARKNESS

The long enduring patience of the Lord was now worn to near exhaustion. As a final exertion to persuade the Pharaoh that he was rapidly approaching the point of no return, the Lord imposed the ninth plague. This was a plague of terror. It was a shroud of enveloping darkness so thick that *it could be felt.*[64]

When this ghostly vapor of evil descended upon Egypt it caught the people completely unawares and immobilized them wherever it found them. "They saw not one another, neither rose any from his place for three days: but all the children of Israel had light in their dwellings."[65]

The significance of this last statement may arise from the fact that this particular kind of darkness which is so thick it can be felt prevents any fire being kindled or any light being provided. Here is the description of this kind of darkness given by a Nephite prophet who experienced it some 1600 years later. Said he: "And it came to pass that there was thick darkness upon all the face of the land, insomuch that the inhabitants thereof who had not fallen could feel the vapor of darkness; and there could be no light, because of the darkness, neither candles, neither torches, neither could there be fire kindled with their fine and exceedingly dry wood, so that there could not be any light at all."[66]

Assuming that the Egyptians had the same kind of darkness to deal with as the Nephites, it would be highly

---

63. Exodus 10:19
64. Exodus 10:21

65. Exodus 10:23
66. 3 Nephi 8:20-21

significant that during the three days of darkness "all the children of Israel had light in their dwellings."

When the darkness had finally lifted, Pharaoh sent for Moses and offered one more concession. Said he, "Go ye, serve the Lord; only let your flocks and your herds be stayed: let your little ones also go with you."[67] Pharaoh was now saying that the Israelites could take their families with them but they must leave their flocks behind. The Pharaoh correctly surmised that if they had no flocks they would starve in the wilderness and be forced to return to the slave camps of Goshen.

Moses told the Pharaoh his proposal was completely unacceptable. He declared that when the people left they intended to take all their possessions with them.

Suddenly the light of reason went out of Pharaoh's mind, leaving his whole being dark with rage and hatred. Up to this time Pharaoh had always left the way open for future negotiations, but after the ninth plague he intended to close off all possibilities of any future communication. He turned to Moses with an ultimatum and a death sentence:

"And Pharaoh said unto him, Get thee from me, take heed to thyself, see my face no more; for in that day thou seest my face thou shalt die. And Moses said, Thou hast spoken well, I will see thy face again no more."[68]

This was it. The stage was now set for the great last act of this terrible drama. The tenth and final plague was about to be invoked.

THE FEAST OF THE PASSOVER

Before imposing the final devastating punishment on Egypt, Moses was instructed to get the people of Israel fully prepared for flight because, as the Lord told Moses, after the tenth plague the Pharaoh "shall surely thrust you out hence altogether."[69]

Here is the way the Lord described the tenth plague:

---

67. Exodus 10:24   69. Exodus 11:1
68. Exodus 10:28-29

"About midnight will I go out into the midst of Egypt: and all the firstborn in the land of Egypt shall die, from the firstborn of Pharaoh that sitteth upon his throne, even unto the firstborn of the maidservant that is behind the mill; and all the firstborn of beasts. And there shall be a great cry throughout all the land of Egypt, such as there was none like it, nor shall be like it any more.

"But against any of the children of Israel shall not a dog move his tongue, against man or beast: that ye may know how that the Lord doth put a difference between the Egyptians and Israel."[70]

In commemoration of this great event the Lord instructed Moses to memorialize the month by making it the first month of the year,[71] to memorialize the day by celebrating it with a " feast of passover,"[72] to memorialize their flight with a "feast of unleavened bread,"[73] and to memorialize their bondage in Egypt by collecting from the Egyptians vast quantities of gold, silver and raiment.[74]

The immediate task was to initiate the great Feast of the Passover. The Lord said each family or group of persons comparable to an average family should select a lamb or goat on the tenth day of the month of Nisen and keep it until the eve of the Exodus which the Lord predicted would be the fourteenth of Nisen. Said he:

"Your lamb shall be without blemish, a male of the first year: ye shall take it out from the sheep, or from the goats: and ye shall keep it up until the fourteenth day of the same month: and the whole assembly of the congregation of Israel shall kill it in the evening. . . . And they shall eat the flesh in that night, roast with fire, and unleavened bread; and with bitter herbs they shall eat it. Eat not of it raw, nor sodden |boiled| at all with water, but roast with fire: his head with his legs, and with the purtenance thereof. . . . And that which remaineth of it until the morning ye shall burn with fire. And thus ye shall eat it; with your loins girded, your shoes on your feet, and your staff in your hand; and ye shall eat it in haste: it is the Lord's passover."[75]

---

70. Exodus 11:4-7
71. Exodus 12:1-2
72. Exodus 12:3-14

73. Exodus 12:15-20
74. Exodus 11:2, 12:35-36
75. Exodus 12:5-11

In connection with the slaying of the lamb the Lord said the people were to mark their doors with its blood as a sign and a token:

"And they shall take of the blood, and strike it on the two side posts and on the upper door post of the houses, wherein they shall eat it. . . . And the blood shall be to you for a token upon the houses where ye are: and when I see the blood, I will pass over you, and the plague shall not be upon you to destroy you, when I smite the land of Egypt."[76]

The slaying of the paschal[77] lamb was to be a permanent memorial and celebrated "throughout your generations."[78]

It is interesting to note that when the Jews were driven from the land of their inheritance in 70 A.D., they suspended all blood sacrifices including that of the paschal lamb. However, they continued to memorialize the Feast of the Passover as best they could. Dr. Adam Clarke makes this comment:

"It is remarkable that though the Jews have ceased from the whole of their sacrificial system, so that sacrifices are no longer offered by them in any part of the world, yet they all, in all their generations and in all countries, keep up the remembrance of the passover, and observe the feast of un-leavened bread. But no lamb is sacrificed. Their sacrifices have all totally ceased, ever since the destruction of Jerusalem by the Romans. Even the flesh that is used on this occasion [of the Passover Service] is partly roasted and partly boiled, that it may not even resemble the primitive sacrifice; for they deem it *unlawful* to sacrifice out of Jerusalem."[80]

All authorities agree that the paschal lamb was symbolic of the coming Messiah.[81] It memorialized the future advent of the Son of God who would be slain, but no bone broken, and whose blood would save all who came under its atoning efficacy. After the death and resurrection of Jesus, the Feast of the Passover was no longer celebrated by the followers

76. Exodus 12:7, 13
77. Taken from the word *pasch*, meaning to pass over.
78. Exodus 12:14
79. Exodus 12:25
80. Clarke, *Bible Commentary*, Vol. 1, p. 351
81. Ibid., p. 353

as ye have said. Also take your flocks and your herds, as ye have said, and be gone; AND BLESS ME ALSO."[87]

Had Pharaoh really meant it, these last four words could have saved his soul and brought a whole new life to the king and his country. But unfortunately, it was only a passing sentiment growing out of this hour of grief and despair. Within a few weeks this same Pharaoh who had so humbly asked for a blessing from Moses would launch a military campaign designed to reconquer or massacre the whole population of Israel.

Nevertheless, at this moment, the sweeping tide of public opinion centered on one single, compelling objective: get the Israelites out of Egypt! Not only Pharaoh wanted them gone, but the rest of the people as well: "And the Egyptians were urgent upon the people [of Israel], that they might send them out of the land in haste; for they said, We be all dead men."[88]

THE ISRAELITES COLLECT THE WEALTH OF EGYPT AS THE WAGES FOR THEIR BONDAGE

The last act of the Israelites prior to their departure from Egypt was to follow the commandment of the Lord by asking the Egyptians for gold, silver, and raiment. The miracle of the plagues had suddenly put these harshly treated Hebrew slaves in a powerful bargaining position. The Egyptians were literally pleading with them to depart quickly out of the land. Very well, it was time for a reckoning. After so many hard years of cruel, compulsory labor the Israelites should not be sent away empty handed. The Egyptians agreed. They willingly, almost enthusiastically, poured out their wealth, their gold, their silver and their raiment.

For such a thing to happen was almost as great a miracle as one of the ten plagues, nevertheless, the scriptures leave no doubt as to its literal reality: "And the children of Israel did according to the word of Moses; and they borrowed of the Egyptians jewels of silver, and jewels of gold, and raiment: And the Lord gave the people favour in the sight of

87. Exodus 12:31-32
88. Exodus 12:33

the Egyptians, so that they lent unto them such things as they required. And they spoiled the Egyptians."[89]

One word in this passage is misleading. It is the word "borrowed." This word implies that something is taken with the understanding it will be returned. The original Hebrew word, *shaal* means "to ask, request, demand, require." It does not imply that the thing received shall be returned. Dr. Adam Clarke says, "This is certainly not a very correct translation. . . ." He then points out that the English version is the only one which uses the idea of "borrow." He says this ". . . is a gross mistake into which scarcely any of the versions ancient or modern have fallen except our own."[90] The word "lent" in this passage is also misleading and should be translated "allowed" or "gave them" what they required.

Certainly there is no other occasion in history where a whole nation of slaves marched out of captivity with the riches of their slavemasters voluntarily showered upon them.

No doubt the rustic Israelites could scarcely believe their good fortune. Overnight they had gone from the slave-operated slime pits of the brickyards to a life of personal freedom embellished with an abundance of gold, silver and fine raiment. Little did they know that much of their gold would end up in the idolatrous image of a golden calf, the worship of which would cost 3,000 of them their lives; but that was in the future. At the moment there was only the sweet wine of unmitigated triumph. They were free! They were rich! They were leaving Egypt!

---

89. Exodus 12:35-36
90. Clarke, *Bible Commentary*, Vol. 1, p. 305

Scripture Reading and Questions on Chapter Twelve

Scripture Reading Assignment: Exodus, chapters 4 to 12 inclusive.

1—To whom did Moses and Aaron reveal the Lord's plan for the liberation of Israel? Did Moses show them the miraculous signs?

2—What did Moses and Aaron ask the Pharaoh? Why couldn't they offer their sacrifices in Egypt?

3—What penalty did Pharaoh put on the Israelites for making this request? What happened to the elders of Israel as a result?

4—When did Moses and Aaron find they had lost the confidence of the Israelites?

5—What was the attitude of Moses when he prayed to the Lord for help? How does the recording of these facts reveal the integrity of Moses as a historian?

6—When Moses saw Pharaoh the second time was it to plead or command?

7—What did Pharaoh challenge them to do? What happened?

8—When the water was turned to blood for seven days, what did the people have to do to get water?

9—Which was the first miracle the magicians could not duplicate? What did they say to the Pharaoh? Did Pharaoh heed them?

10—Name the first five plagues.

11—Name the last five plagues.

12—Did Pharaoh admit during any of these plagues that he was sinning against God in refusing to let the Israelites go?

13—What is the Feast of the Passover designed to commemorate? What does *paschal* mean? What then is the *paschal lamb*? What is it supposed to represent?

14—After the plague of thick darkness what did Pharaoh threaten to do to Moses if he ever saw him again?

15—What was the worst plague of all? When he called for Moses again what did he say to him? Did he fulfill his threat against Moses?

16—What significant request did Pharaoh make as he ordered Moses to take the Israelites and leave?

17—Did the Lord allow the Israelites to leave Egypt in poverty? What did he have them do?

18—How do you account for the liberality of the Egyptians?

19—Did the Egyptians "lend" them this wealth? Where did this idea come from?

20—Over what three things could the Israelites now rejoice?

CHAPTER THIRTEEN

The Great Exodus Begins

When the Israelites were suddenly granted their freedom, it was a glorious day for Jacob's children. But it is
one thing to glory in freedom and quite another thing to move
a mass of some three million human beings across a bleak
and barren wilderness in order to keep that freedom.

Moses knew that wilderness. The Israelites did not.
It was ugly and violently desolate; windswept during the
deadly monsoon season, and sun-drenched to the point of
creating a boiling, blistering sterility during six months of
the year. Its 120 degree heat could suck the breath of life
from every man, woman and child.

What would they eat? What would they drink? How
would their flocks and herds survive? At the moment, these
matters may not have worried the hosts of Israel. They
were just grateful to be free. But Moses had reason to be
worried. He knew that without these necessities this people
might learn through bitter suffering in the wilderness to hate
their precious freedom and actually long to return to the flesh
pots and slavery of Egypt. The problem for Moses was not
merely to get free, but to *stay* free.

THE DEPARTURE OF ISRAEL FROM EGYPT

Apparently the central gathering place for Israel was
Rameses.[1] This was one of the treasure cities which was being built for the Pharaoh with Hebrew slave labor.[2] Rameses
was also the capital of Goshen, the district where the Israelites had resided for some 215 years.[3]

---

1. Exodus 12:37. The correct spelling of this city is Rameses as shown here and
   in Genesis 47:11. Somehow the translators took the same Hebrew word and
   spelled it *Raamses* in Exodus 1:11.
2. Exodus 1:11
3. See Peloubet's *Bible Dictionary,* under "Exodus," and previous discussion of
   this problem in Chapter 10 of this present writing.

From Rameses the great throng of excited, newly rich, newly dressed, newly liberated Israelites marched forth with their geese and goats, sheep and cattle, household goods and private possessions. It was the beginning of one of the strangest migrations in all human history.

The scriptures declare that this was no small conglomerate of nomadic tribesmen, but a monstrous concourse of humanity which included "600,000 on foot that were men," not counting women and children, the Levites, or the "mixed multitude" which went with them.[4] As we learn elsewhere, this 600,000 constituted the male Israelites over 20 years of age who were fit and able to fight in defense of the others.[5] This host of over half a million men is accurately referred to in Exodus as the "armies" of Israel.[6]

They, together with their wives and children (not counting the "mixed multitude") are believed to have constituted a total population of between two and three million people.[7] As we pointed out in Chapter Eleven, in order for the Israelites to have attained such a population in 215 years it would have been necessary for each family in each generation to have averaged around ten children. We also pointed out that when all of the circumstances are taken into consideration, this unexpected expansion in population is entirely plausible.

It is interesting, however, that the Israelites did not go out of Egypt alone. There were some, at least, who threw in their lot with them. As the record states, "And a mixed multitude went up also with them; and flocks, and herds, even very much cattle."[8]

In connection with these "strangers" in their midst, the Lord laid down the principle that everyone be treated alike. They were to be treated alike both as to obligations and privileges. It was to be one law for all people. The Lord declared, "One law shall be to him that is homeborn, and

---

4. Exodus 12:37-38
5. Numbers, chapter 1, note especially verse 3.
6. Exodus 12:51
7. See the discussion of this problem in chapter 10 of this book. Dr. Adam Clarke comes to the same conclusion in his *Bible Commentary*, Vol. 1, pp. 355-356.
8. Exodus 12:38

unto the stranger that sojourneth among you."⁹ Modern
societies could learn much from this divine injunction.

Among the bulky paraphernalia which the Israelites
carted out of Egypt, there was one object among the cargo
which received the most careful attention from Moses. It
was the sarcophagus containing the body of Joseph. The
scripture says, "And Moses took the bones of Joseph with
him: for he [Joseph] had straitly sworn the children of Israel,
saying, God will surely visit you; and ye shall carry up my
bones away hence with you."¹⁰

Succoth—The First Major Camp Site

It was the 15th day of the month Abib (sometimes called
Nisan) and around the year 1,517 B.C.,¹¹ that Israel departed
out of Rameses, Egypt. "And the people took their dough
before it was leavened, their kneadingtroughs being bound up
in their clothes upon their shoulders."¹²

They had begun eating unleavened bread the night
before in connection with the Feast of the Passover and the
Lord said they were to eat it for seven days more or from
the 15th to the 21st day of the month inclusive. This was
to be known as the Feast of Unleavened Bread to commemorate their hasty departure from Egypt.¹³

The first major step was Succoth, which means "booths"
or "tents" and was probably a great camping ground—the
first of more than forty gigantic camp cities which these
Israelites would build between here and Canaan.¹⁴

While the people rested at Succoth, the Lord gave this
commandment to Moses: "Sanctify unto me all the firstborn, whatsoever openeth the womb among the children of
Israel, both of man and of beast: it is mine."¹⁵

The Lord knew this new commandment would create
questions in the minds of future generations, and so he said:
"And it shall be when thy son asketh thee in time to come,
saying, What is this? that thou shalt say unto him, By

---

9. Exodus 12:49
10. Exodus 13:19
11. Exodus 13:4, plus Numbers 33:3 which fixes the day of the month.
12. Exodus 12:34   14. Exodus 12:37
13. Exodus 12:14-20   15. Exodus 13:2

strength of hand the Lord brought us out from Egypt, from the house of bondage: and it came to pass, when Pharaoh would hardly let us go, that the Lord slew all the firstborn in the land of Egypt, both the firstborn of man, and the firstborn of beasts: therefore I sacrifice to the Lord all that openeth the matrix, being males; but all the firstborn of my children I redeem."[16]

The "sanctification" of the first-born among the sheep, goats, and cattle consisted of making a sacrifice of it. Among other domestic animals, however, such as the donkey, the first-born was to be redeemed by sacrificing a lamb, and giving to the Lord's servants five shekels which weighed a stipulated amount.[17] The sanctification of the first-born of their own children required a similar redemption.[18] In addition to this, the Lord later demanded the dedication of all the male Levites to Priesthood service in lieu of this requirement for the first-born among all the tribes.[19] This we will discuss further on.

THE ORIGIN OF PHYLACTERIES

At this point the Lord also said something which became the basis for the custom of wearing phylacteries. After explaining the sanctification of the first-born, the Lord said: "And it [the process of sanctifying the first-born] shall be for a token upon thine hand, and for frontlets between thine eyes: for by strength of hand the Lord brought us forth out of Egypt."[20]

The Israelites took this and similar passages literally and began wearing a copy of these passages of scripture on their persons. These were called phylacteries, which were of two kinds. One was worn on the head, the other on the arm or in the hand.

The one on the head (called the frontlets) consisted of four passages of scripture, written on parchment or vellum and encased in four separate, tiny compartments, which were attached to a band or thong. These were worn on the

---

16. Exodus 13:14-15
17. Exodus 13:13; Numbers 18:15-16
18. Numbers 18:15-16

19. Numbers 8:14-17
20. Exodus 13:16

center of the forehead "for frontlets between thine eyes."
The passages of scriptures contained in the phylacteries were
Exodus 13:2-10; Exodus 13:11-16; Deuteronomy 6:4-9; and
Deuteronomy 11:13-21.

The one for the arm or hand had the scriptures written
on a single piece of parchment or vellum and was placed
in a single container which was worn just above the elbow
on the inside of the left arm (nearest the heart), or attached
to the wrist and carried in the hand.

The phylacteries were worn while praying or reading
the scriptures and were frequently called "prayer ornaments."[21]

In addition to the above, Moses later instructed the
people to wear a blue ribbon with a fringe at the hem of their
garments. The multitude of individual threads comprising the
fringe were to remind them to live each and every part of
the law so that, like the tiny, individual threads, their lives
would gradually be woven into a beautiful fabric of faith and
good works.[22]

THE AMAZING ROUTE OF THE EXODUS

After leaving Succoth, the children of Israel "encamped
in Etham, in the edge of the wilderness."[23] From here they
could reach Canaan by any one of three routes. They could
go up north along the wall of Egyptian fortifications until
they reached the Mediterranean and then take the Philistine
route which was only 150 miles to Canaan. Or they could
have taken the Beersheba route which Jacob probably followed when he came down to Egypt some 215 years earlier.
With a small company this route was satisfactory, but since
it cut straight across the wilderness it was no place to take
two or three million people. The third route was called the
Red Sea route. From Etham this route went around the
Suez gulf of the Red Sea to the Horeb range (where mount
Sinai was located), across to the Aqaba gulf of the Red Sea
and then up the Arabah valley to Canaan.

---

21. Clarke, *Bible Commentary*, Vol. 1, p. 362
22. Numbers 15:38-39
23. Exodus 13:20

The Lord ruled out the first two routes because the Israelites would thereby find themselves involved in a desert war. The scripture says: "And it came to pass that God led them not through the way of the land of the Philistines, although that was near; for God said, Lest peradventure the people repent [literally, 'turn back'] when they see war, and they return to Egypt."[24]

In view of this divine declaration, the Israelites undoubtedly expected they would follow the Red Sea route. There wasn't really any alternative. But if the Lord did this he would have had to take the Israelites around the northern tip of what was then the Gulf of Suez. Oddly enough, he did not. Even though this was the only known way to get to the eastern side of the Suez gulf, the Lord routed the Israelites down the *western* side of the Red Sea.

It should be kept in mind that the Egyptian tongue of the Red Sea (the Gulf of Suez) formerly extended much further north than it does today. Authorities believe the lower region of the modern Suez Canal is actually built on the remnants of the old Gulf of Suez which once comprised a solid body of water extending up to what is now called Lake Timsah.

Professor J. R. Dummelow of Cambridge states, "There is little doubt that at the time of the Exodus the Gulf of Suez extended much further north than it does now, and that the modern Lake Timsah and the Bitter Lakes were connected with each other. . . . It is pretty certain that the Israelites crossed at some point north of the modern Suez." (Dummelow's Bible Commentary, p. 60)

This meant that the logical route for the Israelites would have been to go around this northern tip of the Gulf of Suez in order to reach the Sinai peninsula. But this they did not do.

Since the Philistines occupied the desert area east cf what is now the Suez Canal, there is no doubt but what the sight of between two and three million Israelites coming around the point of the Gulf (now Lake Timsah) would have caused them to mobilize their whole people and sweep down

---

24. Exodus 13:17

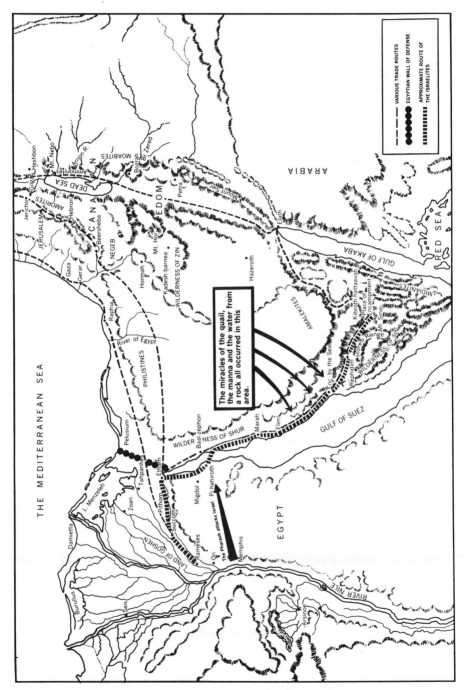

on Israel in a whirlwind of spears and flashing sabers. This, the Lord avoided by leading the people of Israel down the *west* side of the Gulf of Suez. However, this complicated matters. It trapped the Israelites between Egypt and the Red Sea. How would they cross?

Ordinarily the Israelites might have accused Moses of making a serious tactical error, but in this case they could not. All Israel knew it was God who had led them, not Moses. The visible evidence of God's leadership was constantly before them. "And the Lord went before them by day in a pillar of a cloud, to lead them the way; and by night in a pillar of fire, to give them light; to go by day and night: He took not away the pillar of the cloud by day, nor the pillar of fire by night, from before the people."[25]

By this means the Lord led the people from Etham southward until they came to the western shores of the Red Sea "over against Baal-zephon."[26] There the Lord told them to make camp, "by the sea."[27]

Moses Receives Word of a Threatening Disaster

The Lord now revealed to Moses the news of a sensational development back in Egypt. The mighty Pharaoh who had so recently asked Moses to bless him and had urged the whole nation of Israel to leave Egypt, had undergone a complete change of heart. Apparently he had sent his spies to see where the Israelites had gone and learned the exciting news that they were trapped between Egypt and the Red Sea.[28]

Pharaoh discussed this whole situation with his royal advisors and they said among themselves, "Why have we done this, that we have let Israel go from serving us?"[29]

As they tantalized their minds with this unbelievably good fortune which had placed the Israelites where they could be easily recaptured, these slavemasters of the Nile found it impossible to resist the temptation:

---

25. Exodus 13:21-22
26. Exodus 14:2
27. Ibid.

28. Exodus 14:5
29. Ibid.

"And he [the Pharaoh] made ready his chariot, and took his people with him: and he took six hundred chosen chariots, and all the chariots of Egypt, and captains over every one of them."[30] In addition, Pharaoh took "his horsemen, and his army. . . ."[31] It was no small matter to head off between two and three million people and drive them back to the slime pits of the Goshen brickyards. Pharaoh was taking no chances. He had mobilized the total available military strength at his command. He would teach those woe-begotten rebellious Hebrew brickmakers!

THE PHARAOH'S HOSTS SPEED EAST

Apparently Moses did not feel it wise to share with Israel the advance notice that he had received from the Lord concerning developments in Egypt, therefore the realization that Pharaoh's hosts were sweeping down upon them came to the Israelites as a complete surprise. The word did not reach Israel until the royal charioteers, cavalry and marching Egyptian battalion had pushed up over the horizon and stood in clear view of the whole people. Israel's reaction was one of absolute terror.

The scripture says they were "sore afraid,"[32] and therefore a great cry went up from the camps of Israel. They felt completely helpless before Pharaoh and his hosts. They were unarmed, untrained, and in every other respect totally unprepared for any kind of battle. What was God doing to them? In a state of near panic, the people rushed in upon Moses. They cried out, "Because there were no graves in Egypt, hast thou taken us away to die in the wilderness? wherefore hast thou dealt thus with us, to carry us forth out of Egypt? Is not this the word that we did tell thee in Egypt, saying, Let us alone, that we may serve the Egyptians? For it had been better for us to serve the Egyptians, than that we should die in the wilderness."[33]

These harsh words indicate the difficulty Moses had endured trying to get the Israelites to support him in the first place. Now they were saying, "We told you so!"

---

30. Exodus 14:6-7
31. Exodus 14:9. The Egyptians who "marched after them" are mentioned in Exodus 14:10
32. Exodus 14:10   33. Exodus 14:11-12

THE TEN COMMANDMENTS — A Paramount Picture

"But the Egyptians pursued after them, all the horses and chariots of Pharaoh, and his horsemen, and his army . . . ."

If the people ever needed reassurance, this was the moment. Moses said, "Fear ye not, stand still, and see the salvation of the Lord, which he will shew to you to day: for the Egyptians whom ye have seen to day, ye shall see them again no more for ever. The Lord shall fight for you, and ye shall hold your peace."[34]

But of course these brave words meant nothing unless the Lord would back them up. Apparently Moses pleaded with the Lord to respect him in this hour of threatened disaster for in the very next verse the Lord says, "Moses, wherefore criest thou unto me? speak unto the children of Israel, that they go forward."[35]

Yes, but "forward" would take them directly into the Red Sea! To the Lord this was no obstacle. He said to Moses: "But lift up thy rod, and stretch out thine hand over the sea, and divide it: and the children of Israel shall go on dry ground through the midst of the sea."[36]

Israel Marches into the Sea

In obedience to the commandment of the Lord, Moses instructed the hosts of Israel to hastily break camp and march toward the sea. But could they reach it before being overrun by Pharaoh's hosts? Suddenly a strange thing happened. The great pillar which had led them as a cloud by day and a pillar of fire by night, rapidly began to shift its position. It circled the camps of the Israelites until it "stood behind them."[37]

It was like an ominous curtain thrust in between Pharaoh's speeding hosts and the lumbering masses of Israel. There it remained to hold Pharaoh back. To the Egyptians this pillar became "a cloud and darkness to them."[38] They dared not penetrate it. They were cut off. However, as night came on, the eastern side of the cloud became luminous for Israel so that it cast a powerful radiance over them and lighted their path toward the sea.[39]

---

34. Exodus 14:13-14
35. Exodus 14:15
36. Exodus 14:16

37. Exodus 14:19
38. Exodus 14:20
39. Ibid.

there finally opened to the view of Pharaoh the escape route of the Israelites. By this time it was "the morning watch" (around sunrise)[45] "and the Egyptians pursued, and went in after them to the midst of the sea, even all Pharaoh's horses, his chariots, and his horsemen."[46] It is apparent that the whole vast entourage got well within the canyon of water before they began to have serious trouble. Then the chariots began to mire down, they lost their wheels and drove "heavily."[47]

Finally, the Egyptians became panicky. What if these towering walls of water came tumbling down upon them? For the moment they were held up by a kind of power they did not understand, and that power was terribly real, but so were their troubles. Finally, they said to one another, "Let us flee from the face of Israel; for the Lord fighteth for them against the Egyptians."[48]

But even as the Egyptians tried to wheel around and race back to the western shore, they suddenly found it was too late. By this time the last of the Israelites had struggled safely up onto the beaches of the eastern shore, "And the Lord said unto Moses, Stretch out thine hand over the sea, that the waters may come again unto the Egyptians, upon their chariots, and upon their horsemen. And Moses stretched forth his hand over the sea, and the sea returned to his strength when the morning appeared; and the Egyptians fled against it. . . . And the waters returned, and covered the chariots and the horsemen, and all the host of Pharaoh that came into the sea after them; there remained not so much as one of them."[49]

What sensations must have coursed through the brains of those thousands of vengeance-ridden Egyptians as they saw those giant walls of water suddenly begin to collapse and come thundering down upon them in a colossal debacle of total chaotic destruction. It was over in an instant. The smothering billows churned them about like driftwood and shortly left them just as lifeless. No nation's army was ever

---

45. See Peloubet's *Bible Dictionary* under "Watches of Night."
46. Exodus 14:23
47. Exodus 14:24-25
48. Exodus 14:25
49. Exodus 14:26-28

destroyed so completely or so quickly. Pharaoh and all his hosts were drowned.[50]

It must have been almost unbelievable to the Israelites to see this dreaded array of military might which so shortly before had threatened to annihilate or enslave them, suddenly disappear in the froth and brine of the pounding waves of the Red Sea. Before long there came up from the depths the mute evidence of the Pharaoh's disaster: "And Israel saw the Egyptians dead upon the seashore."[51]

So Pharaoh and all his multitude were dead![52] To the Israelites there was first the horror of it and then the relief. The latter was so great that the Israelites could not contain their feelings. Moses led the people in a song of thanksgiving and triumph.[53] Then the aged Miriam, sister of Moses, took a timbrel and led the women of Israel in dancing and singing. She cried out: "Sing ye to the Lord, for he hath triumphed gloriously; the horse and his rider hath he thrown into the sea."[54]

ISRAEL HEARS THE GOSPEL OF JESUS CHRIST

There is no doubt that the Israelites were vividly impressed by the miraculous manifestation of God's power in their behalf at the Red Sea. The scripture says, "And Israel saw that great work which the Lord did upon the Egyptians: and the people feared the Lord, and believed the Lord, and his servant Moses."[55] Obviously, this would have been an ideal time to preach the Gospel to them.

These bedraggled and brutalized Hebrews who had been exposed to the licentious idolatry of Egypt for approximately 215 years and who had been in bondage for at least a full generation, were covered with the physical and spiritual scars of their experiences. How deeply they had been scarred became all too evident as Moses became better acquainted with them.

Nevertheless, the Apostle Paul makes it very clear that Moses did everything possible to share the Gospel of Jesus

---

50. Exodus 14:28
51. Exodus 14:30
52. Exodus 14:28
53. Exodus 15:1-19
54. Exodus 15:21
55. Exodus 14:31

Christ with these people and promote the spiritual regeneration which they so badly needed. In writing to the Corinthians, Paul declared, "Moreover, brethren, I would not that ye should be ignorant, how that all our fathers were under the cloud, and all passed through the sea; and were all baptized unto Moses in the cloud and in the sea; and did all eat of that same spiritual meat; and did all drink the same spiritual drink: for they drank of that spiritual Rock that followed them: and that Rock was Christ."[56]

Paul emphasized the same point in writing to the Hebrews. He speaks of those "that came out of Egypt by Moses," and says, "For unto us was the gospel preached as well as unto them: but the word preached did not profit them, not being mixed with faith in them that heard it."[57]

It should be kept in mind the Israelites had the Melchizedek Priesthood in their midst even though it may have become tarnished and neglected. The Lord refers to their "priests"[58] long before the lower, or Levitical, Priesthood was set up, so we know from this that the Melchizedek Priesthood was functioning at least to some extent and that it was recognized by the Lord. It was the purpose of Moses to sanctify this people and make them a whole "kingdom of priests" after the order of Melchizedek and the Lord encouraged Moses in this ambition as long as the lives of the Israelites would permit it.[59] Only when they had completely collapsed did the Lord withdraw the Melchizedek Priesthood from their midst and require them to live under the Levitical Priesthood which administers only the temporal ordinances — animal sacrifices, daily incense burning, circumcision, baptism, administering to the physical needs of the people, and serving as housekeepers and custodians of the Tabernacle and places of worship.[60]

ISRAEL MOVES FROM THE RED SEA TO THE WILDERNESS

In due time the camps of Israel moved toward Sinai. They left the shores of the Red Sea and pushed into the barren, treeless wastes of the "wilderness of Shur."[61] For

---

56. 1 Corinthians 10:1-4
57. Hebrews 3:16; 4:2
58. Exodus 19:22
59. Exodus 19:6
60. *Doctrine and Covenants* 84:25-27
61. Exodus 15:22

three days they wandered in this area but found no water.[62] Finally, when the whole multitude was becoming desperate, they discovered a body of water, but it was bitter and brack- ish so that neither they nor their flocks could drink it. There- fore they called the place Marah, meaning "bitterness." How- ever, the people's complaints were as bitter as the water. They said to Moses, "What shall we drink?"[63]

Moses took the problem to the Lord and was told to look for a certain kind of tree nearby which could be cast into the water to sweeten it. Moses did so and the people soon found that the water had lost its bitterness just as the Lord had promised.

The Lord used this incident of sweetening the water to emphasize the importance of physical health: "If thou [the people of Israel] wilt diligently hearken to the voice of the Lord thy God, and wilt do that which is right in his sight, and wilt give ear to his commandments, and keep all his statutes, I will put none of these diseases upon thee, which I have brought upon the Egyptians: for I am the Lord that healeth thee."[64]

As we shall see later, God was preparing them to re- ceive a "Word of Wisdom" which would help them protect themselves against the kind of diseases which were prevalent in those days. In that future statute the Lord would lay down the famous dietary laws and put religious support behind the fundamental rules of sanitation and good health.

In modern times, God has given a different "Word of Wisdom" which lays stress on the dangers of alcohol, tobac- co, and certain harmful "hot drinks" which the Lord said would be promoted by "conspiring men in the last days."[65] All of this simply demonstrates God's concern for the physi- cal well-being of mankind regardless of the age in which they live.

When the children of Israel had replenished their water supply, they pressed forward to Elim where they found twelve wells of water and an oasis of palm trees. This gave them a pleasant respite after which they migrated further

62. Ibid.
63. Exodus 15:24
64. Exodus 15:26
65. *Doctrine and Covenants* 89:4

down the Sinai Peninsula and entered the wilderness of Sin. The scripture says the Israelites had now been absent from Egypt exactly one month.[66]

THE MIRACLE OF THE MEAT AND THE MANNA

It will be recalled that the Israelites had left Egypt with their unleavened dough and whatever food supplies they could haul with them. However, one month in the wildernness had depleted their meal and flour so that, except for their flocks, they had no source of food whatever. Like little children, the Israelites were soon sending up their voluble complaints to Moses. Said they, "Would to God we had died by the hand of the Lord in the land of Egypt, when we sat by the flesh pots, and we did eat bread to the full; for ye have brought us forth unto this wilderness, to kill this whole assembly with hunger."[67]

Moses petitioned the Lord for relief and was no doubt astonished by the Lord's prompt response. The Lord said to him, "Behold, I will rain bread from heaven for you. . . ."[68] With this assurance Moses took Aaron and went back to the people and said, ". . . your murmurings are not against us, but against the Lord."[69] Aaron was then instructed to call all of the people into a huge conference while Moses went out to the cloudy pillar which stood before the camp. He wanted the people to witness for themselves that God was with them and that what was about to happen was through His divine intervention. "And it came to pass, as Aaron spake unto the whole congregation of the children of Israel, that they looked toward the wilderness, and behold, the glory of the Lord appeared in the cloud.

"And the Lord spake unto Moses, saying, I have heard the murmurings of the children of Israel: speak unto them, saying, At even ye shall eat flesh, and in the morning ye shall be filled with bread; and ye shall know that I am the Lord your God."[70]

---

66. Exodus 16:1. Since they left the 15th day of the first month (Numbers 33:3) and since it was now the 15th day of the second month, the journey thus far had consumed one full month.
67. Exodus 16:3
68. Exodus 16:4
69. Exodus 16:8
70. Exodus 16:10-12

That evening a great quantity of quail moved in upon the hungry Israelites until these low-flying birds literally "covered the camp."[71] Here indeed was the meat the Lord had promised. And during the night a heavy dew fell upon the rocks and bushes and the ground which left a residue of substance. It was so new and strange to the Israelites that they called it "manna," meaning "What is this?"[72]

We have several descriptive references to this manna. One says that each particle of the manna was "a small round thing, as small as the hoar frost on the ground."[73] Another scripture says, ". . . and it was like coriander seed, white; and the taste of it was like wafers made with honey."[74] Still another says, "And the people went about, and gathered it, and ground it in mills, or beat it in a mortar, and baked it in pans, and made cakes of it: and the taste of it was as the taste of fresh oil."[75]

PECULIAR QUALITIES OF MANNA

There were certain amazing characteristics about this manna which deserve mentioning.

First, it had to be gathered early in the morning or it would melt "when the sun waxed hot."[76]

Second, in spite of the fact that manna would melt in the sun, the people could bake it into bread like a cereal.[77]

Third, the supply gathered during the first five days of the week was subject to almost immediate spoilage. Moses told the people to gather only enough for their individual needs and not to save any of it over from one day to the next. "And Moses said, Let no man leave [any] of it till the morning. Notwithstanding they hearkened not unto Moses; but some of them left of it until the morning, and it bred worms, and stank: and Moses was wroth with them."[78]

Fourth, manna which fell on the morning of the *sixth* day was not subject to immediate spoilage. Therefore, every

---

71. Exodus 16:13
72. Exodus 16:15 and marginal note
73. Exodus 16:14
74. Exodus 15:31
75. Numbers 11:8
76. Exodus 16:21
77. Exodus 16:23
78. Exodus 16:19-20

family collected enough on the sixth day to fill their needs over the Sabbath.

Fifth, when some of the people tried to secretly gather extra manna on the Sabbath, "they found none."[79] This was the only day it did not fall.

Sixth, except for the days of the Sabbath the "miracle of the manna" occurred every single day for forty years.[80] In other words, this miracle was performed on more than 12,400 separate occasions.

Seventh, under certain circumstances dictated by the Lord, it was possible to keep manna permanently. Hence the Lord told Moses to "Fill an omer of it to be kept for your generations; that they may see the bread wherewith I have fed you in the wilderness, when I brought you forth from the land of Egypt."[81]

THE MIRACLE OF WATER SPRINGING FROM A ROCK

According to the Book of Numbers, the camps of Israel left the wilderness of Sin and moved as rapidly as possible toward Sinai, stopping first at Dophkah, then at Alush, and finally at Rephidim near Mount Horeb. The Book of Exodus does not mention the first two places because apparently nothing of historical importance occurred there.

It was at Rephidim, however, that the first miracle occurred involving the bringing forth of water from a rock. The circumstances were ugly. With their liberty merely a few weeks old, the Israelites only stayed as close to the Lord as the satisfying of their physical comforts seemed to require. At the slightest provocation or inconvenience they turned on the Lord and His prophet with a snarl and a tongue lashing. This happened at Rephidim. The people were just one stop away from Sinai but they had run out of water.

"And the people thirsted there for water; and the people murmured against Moses, and said, Wherefore is this that thou hast brought us up out of Egypt, to kill us and our children and our cattle with thirst?"[82]

---

79. Exodus 16:27
80. Exodus 16:35
81. Exodus 16:32
82. Exodus 17:3

They claimed Moses was trying to kill them but they were so filled with hatred they were thinking of killing him!

"And Moses cried unto the Lord, saying, What shall I do unto this people? they be almost ready to stone me."[83]

The Lord told Moses what to do. He was to take his staff and go with the elders of Israel to a certain place nearby where the Lord's power would be manifest "upon the rock in Horeb."[84] There Moses was to smite the rock and bring forth water for the multitudes of Israel and their flocks. So Moses did as the Lord commanded him and the miracle occurred just as the Lord had promised.

"And he [Moses] called the name of the place Massah [temptation], and Meribah [chiding], because of the chiding of the children of Israel, and because they tempted the Lord, saying, Is the Lord among us, or not?"[85]

Anyone who has visited the mountains of Horeb will realize what a miracle this divine dispensation of power turned out to be. The harsh, desolate, barren granite cliffs of this mountain range are piled high above the surrounding desert floor. In this vicinity the children of Israel were to remain a whole year. Without the miraculous "bringing forth of water" and the daily rations of manna, it would have been impossible.

THE DESCENDANTS OF ESAU SWEEP DOWN ON ISRAEL

Moses had barely started settling the people in this new camp sight near Horeb when the warlike tribes from among the descendants of Esau came charging down from their mountain headquarters and began despoiling the hapless Israelites. The attack was not against the main body of Israel but against the stragglers who were weary and faint and had fallen behind.[86] The attackers turned out to be Amalekites who were descendants of Amalek, grandson of Esau. Since Esau was Jacob's twin brother, the people of Israel were kinsmen of the Amalekites, but after so many generations who cared about relatives? The Amalekites attacked with great ferocity.

---

83. Exodus 17:4
84. Exodus 17:6
85. Exodus 17:7
86. Deuteronomy 25:17-18

In this moment of crisis, Moses called forth a trusted young Ephraimite who was destined to become a famous personage in Hebrew history. His name was originally Hoshea, son of Nun, but Moses changed his name to Joshua (meaning savior)[87] the very name which the Son of Mary would be given some 1500 years later.[88]

Moses ordered Joshua to choose a body of men and go to battle against the Amalekites the following day. To insure their victory, Moses took Aaron and Hur,[89] who seem to have served as counsellors, and went to a high hill overlooking the battlefield where they could petition God's blessings.[90]

When the battle began, Moses held up his staff or rod and the Israelites prevailed, but when he became tired and lowered his arm, the Amalekites prevailed. Aaron and Hur saw what was happening and so they prepared a stone on which Moses could sit, and "Aaron and Hur stayed up his hands, the one on the one side, and the other on the other side; and his hands were steady until the going down of the sun."[91]

Thus the Israelites vanquished the Amalekites completely and forced the survivors to flee for their lives.

Then the Lord told Moses to take a book and write in it concerning this great victory. The Lord also gave Moses a prophecy that one day the Amalekites would be "utterly put out of remembrance . . . from under heaven."[92] This prophecy was fulfilled 400 years later.[93]

Note that Exodus 17:14 talks about writing a book. This is the first reference to "writing" in the Bible, and some authorities had assumed that alphabetical writing must have

---

87. Numbers 13:16
88. The Hebrew name of the Messiah was Joshua and that was the only name he ever knew. We call him Jesus but that is simply the English transliteration for Joshua. Notice that the New Testament references to "Joshua, son of Nun," are also translated "Jesus." See Acts 7:45 and Hebrews 4:8, plus marginal notes.
89. This is our first acquaintance with Hur. Josephus, who is supported by the oldest Jewish scholars, say Hur was Miriam's husband and therefore the brother-in-law of Moses. (Josephus, *Antiquity of the Jews*, Book 3, 2:4)
90. Exodus 17:9-10   92. Exodus 17:14
91. Exodus 17:12   93. I Samuel 15:3

been invented about this time.[94] However, modern revelation discloses the fact that this assumption is a serious error. Writing existed among men from the days of Adam. In fact, the Lord states that Adam taught his children to write a language which was pure and undefiled.[95] Zephaniah predicts that this pure language will be restored in the last days.[96] We have already discussed the writings of both Abraham and Joseph which were found in the catacombs of Egypt. Certainly these were prepared long before Moses. We are assured from these and other sources of evidence that writing had been a fine art centuries before Moses was born.

THE ARRIVAL OF JETHRO WITH THE WIFE AND SONS OF MOSES

It would appear that almost immediately after the defeat of the Amalekites, the heart of Moses was cheered by the arrival of his father-in-law, Jethro, Priest of Midian. And better still, he brought with him the wife of Moses and their two sons, Gershom and Eliezer. Originally Zipporah and her sons had started to Egypt with Moses, but for some reason had turned back.[97] Now they joined Moses in his hour of triumph.

"And Moses went out to meet his father-in-law, and did obeisance, and kissed him; and they asked each other of their welfare; and they came into the tent.

"And Moses told his father-in-law all that the Lord had done unto Pharaoh and to the Egyptians for Israel's sake, and all the travail that had come upon them by the way, and how the Lord had delivered them.

"And Jethro rejoiced for all the goodness which the Lord had done to Israel, whom he had delivered out of the hand of the Egyptians."[98]

Moses was anxious to have the princes of Israel meet the Priest of Midian who was not only his father-in-law, but the man from whom he had received the Priesthood.[99] Moses

---

94. See Clarke, *Bible Commentary*, Vol. 1, p. 388.
95. Moses 6:4-6
96. Zephaniah 3:9
97. Exodus 18:2-3
98. Exodus 18:7-9
99. *Doctrine and Covenants* 84:6

therefore invited Aaron and all the leaders of Israel to a great feast where they honored Jethro.

JETHRO TEACHES MOSES HOW TO GOVERN THE PEOPLE

The very next day an interesting thing happened. The scripture says;

"And it came to pass on the morrow, that Moses sat to judge the people: and the people stood by Moses from the morning unto the evening.

"And when Moses' father-in-law saw all that he did to the people, he said, What is this thing that thou doest to the people? why sittest thou thyself alone, and all the people stand by thee, from morning unto even?

"And Moses said unto his father in law, Because the people come unto me to inquire of God:

"When they have a matter, they come unto me; and I judge between one and another; and I do make them know the statutes of God, and his laws."[100]

Of course all of this had the highest motivations and the best possible intentions, but it did not please Jethro at all. The High Priest of Midian had several generations of Priesthood training and experiences behind him, extending clear back to Father Abraham.[101] He therefore said to Moses:

"The thing that thou doest is not good.

"Thou wilt surely wear away, both thou, and this people that is with thee: for this thing is too heavy for thee; thou art not able to perform it thyself alone.

"Hearken now unto my voice, I will give thee counsel, and God shall be with thee: Be thou for the people to God-ward, that thou mayest bring the causes unto God:

"And thou shalt teach them ordinances and laws, and shalt shew them the way wherein they must walk, and the work that they must do.

---

100. Exodus 18:13-16
101. *Doctrine and Covenants* 84:6-13

"Moreover thou shalt provide out of all the people able men, such as fear God, men of truth, hating covetousness; and place such over them, to be rulers of thousands, and rulers of hundreds, rulers of fifties, and rulers of tens:

"And let them judge the people at all seasons: and it shall be, that every great matter they shall bring unto thee, but every small matter they shall judge: so shall it be easier for thyself, and they shall bear the burden with thee.

"If thou shalt do this thing, and GOD COMMAND THEE SO, then thou shalt be able to endure and all this people shall also go to their place in peace."[102]

The remarkable quality of this powerful declaration is enhanced by the humility of this master teacher who gave it. So far as the scriptures show, Jethro had never divided the Red Sea. Jethro had never changed a staff into a serpent, nor performed the miracle of the leprous hand. Jethro had never been called upon to liberate between two and three million people from slavery nor command ten terrible plagues to ravage the highhanded dictatorial authority of the Egyptian aristocracy. Jethro had never produced honey-dew bread from heaven nor made water gush forth in a flood from a rock. Jethro had not done any of these things for the simple reason that God had never commanded him to do them. Nevertheless, he knew that the Priesthood which he, Jethro, had conferred upon Moses, was the channel of power through which these mighty deeds were done. And now, when he saw Moses, this same mighty miracle-worker, this beloved son-in-law and husband of Zipporah, foolishly failing to delegate Priesthood responsibility to others, the wise old patriarch knew it was time to speak out.

But when he was all through, when he had given the best advice which the principles of Priesthood procedure would seem to require, he humbly concluded by asking Moses to verify this advice with the Lord. "If thou shalt do this thing, AND GOD COMMAND THEE SO, then thou shalt be able to endure and all this people shall also go to their place in peace." These were the last words recorded in scripture from this wise and humble man. Jethro there-

---

102. Exodus 18:17-23

upon bade his loved ones farewell and departed once again into his own country.[103]

Moses never forgot these inspired instructions from Jethro. At the very first opportunity he carried them out. But that opportunity did not come for nearly a year.[104]

Moses did not know it but he was about to pass through the most tempestuous and frustrating experiences of his entire career as a prophet.

The next stop was Sinai. There he would become engulfed in a rapid-fire sequence of events which would toss him alternately from the celestial heights of glorious heavenly visions down to the fathomless depths of darkness where he would have direct personal contact with the forces emanating from the satanic labyrinths of Lucifer's subversive, conspiratorial kingdom. During this series of experiences Moses would find himself caught in the furious vortex of a titanic struggle between eternal beings — a combat which began as "the War in Heaven" but which continues on the earth as Lucifer seeks to dethrone God and wipe out the human family with his "abomination of desolation."

Moses was about to feel the fury of that violent and very real war between the hosts of heaven and the hosts of hell.

---

103. Exodus 18:27
104. Deuteronomy 1:6-18

Scripture Reading and Questions On Chapter Thirteen

Scripture Reading Assignment: Exodus, chapters 13 to 18 inclusive.

1—How many years does it appear that the Israelites were in Egypt? Who went with the Israelites when they left? How did the Lord say they should be treated?

2—What is a phylactery? Do you think the Lord intended these to be worn in a literal sense or was he speaking symbolically?

3—Was the route the Israelites took out of Egypt a logical one? Who was responsible for leading the Israelites down the west side of the Red Sea?

4—Did Moses have advance notice that Pharaoh was coming with his army? Did he tell the people? What was their reaction when the Egyptians came in sight?

5—What kept the Egyptians from attacking the Israelites? How long did it take the Israelites to cross the Red Sea?

6—Was the dividing of the Red Sea merely the result of the wind blowing it back? What did the Israelites observe which no amount of wind could have achieved?

7—What were the Egyptians trying to do just as the banks of water broke and came pouring down upon them?

8—Did any of the Egyptians escape? What happened to the Pharaoh?

9—Did the Israelites ever hear of Jesus Christ? Were they taught Christianity? Were they baptized and confirmed?

10—After crossing the Red Sea what was the first miracle the Lord performed for the Israelites? What was the second? The third?

11—Describe three unusual qualities of "manna." Why was it called by this name? How long did the miracle of the manna last?

12—From whom had the Amalekites descended? Did they attack the main body of Israel? Who led the Israelites in defeating them?

13—When does the Lord say the art of writing first began? Why do you think the more primitive types of writing have been so prevalent among archaeological findings? Is it possible that more advanced writing was done on less durable material?

14—What was the reaction of Moses when Jethro arrived? What did he do to honor him? Who did Jethro bring with him?

15—The day after his arrival, what did Jethro watch Moses do? What was Jethro's reaction? Was Jethro right?

16—What kind of men was Moses told to select as judges?

17—What were the numerical divisions into which the Israelites were to be divided?

18—In what way would such divisions be helpful to Moses?

19—How would this new procedure be helpful to the people?

20—Did Jethro stay with Moses? How long before Moses was able to carry out Jethro's instructions?

CHAPTER FOURTEEN

The Revelations of God Pour Down from Mt. Sinai

For Moses, the towering peak of Mount Sinai was like a sanctuary of the Almighty. This was the mountain where he had first seen the burning bush and had named the peak "Sinai" or "bush" to commemorate it. This was where the Lord had spoken to Moses the very first time and said, "put off thy shoes . . . for the place whereon thou standest is holy ground."[1]

It was here that he had first encountered the glory of God and received his commission to liberate Israel. It was here that he had first received the witness of the rod turning into a serpent and had beheld the miracle of the leprous hand. This is where he had met Aaron just before going into Egypt. This was the mountain to which he had been told to return with the hosts of Israel.

To fulfill this commandment Moses and Aaron had gone through the plagues of blood, frogs, lice, flies, murrain, boils, fire, hail, locusts, and the death of the first-born. To survive their journey they had been given power to divide the Red Sea, produce great quantities of quail for meat, gather honey-dew manna for bread, and command water to come gushing forth from solid rock. Not at any time in all the history of the whole human race had there been such an avalanche of miraculous power manifested through divine intervention and exercised on behalf of the same group of people over such an extended period of time.

With God, the stakes were high and the effort necessary. With Moses, it was just one continuous series of supernatural surprises that made the incredible believable and the impossible an accomplished fact.

---

1. Exodus 3:5

Moses Meets the Lord at Mount Sinai

It appears to have been but a short journey from Rephidim to Mount Sinai. This was the move the children of Israel now made.

The open terrain at the base of this monolithic granite mountain is called the wilderness of Sinai or the desert of Sinai.[2] The scripture says that "there Israel camped before the mount."[3]

It had now been exactly two months since the Israelites had begun their flight to freedom. They had left Rameses on the fifteenth day of the first month and they arrived at Sinai the "same day" or the fifteenth day of the third month.[4]

As soon as the camp had been settled, Moses climbed the steep and difficult heights of Sinai to present himself to the Lord. Once again he was allowed to penetrate that higher dimension of cosmic reality and become "quickened" so he could speak directly to the Lord.

The Lord said he was now prepared to enter into a covenant with Israel and give them a great blessing if they were obedient. He told Moses to return to the people and ask them if they were willing to enter into such a contract. If so, the Lord said He was willing to make the children of Israel his "chosen people" through whom God would do his great work among the children of men in that day. Moses was to tell the people:

"Now therefore, if ye will obey my voice indeed, and keep my covenant, then ye shall be a peculiar treasure unto me above all people: for all the earth is mine: and ye shall be unto me a kingdom of priests, and an holy nation."[5]

The True Significance of God's Covenant with Moses

This was the same covenant and blessing given in the days of Enoch when that prophet was allowed to raise up a people who became so powerful and righteous that "The fear of the Lord was upon ALL NATIONS, so great was the glory of the Lord, which was upon his people. And the Lord

---

2. Exodus 19:1-2   4. Exodus 19:1
3. Exodus 19:2   5. Exodus 19:5-6

blessed the land, and they were blessed upon the mountains, and upon the high places, and did flourish. And the Lord called his people ZION, because they were of one heart and one mind, and dwelt in righteousness; and there was no poor among them."[6]

This same covenant and blessing was offered to the Brother of Jared and his people around 2,200 B.C. when they were brought to the western hemisphere and told by the Lord, "I will bless thee and thy seed, and raise up unto me of thy seed, and of the seed of thy brother, and they who shall go with thee, a great nation. *And there shall be NONE GREATER than the nation which I will raise up unto me of thy seed, upon all the face of the earth.*"[7]

This is the same covenant and blessing received by Melchizedek, Prince of Salem, who avoided the abomination of desolating war in his day by getting the people to repent, live under this covenant, and eventually refine themselves through righteous living until they were able to be translated like the people of Enoch. The scripture says: "And now, Melchizedek was a priest of this order [the higher order of the Priesthood]; therefore he obtained peace in Salem, and was called the Prince of peace. And his people wrought righteousness and obtained heaven, and sought for the city of Enoch which God had before taken. . . ."[8]

This same covenant and blessing was offered to the Saints in the days of Christ which led Peter to exclaim: "But ye are a chosen generation, a royal priesthood, an holy nation, a peculiar people: that ye should shew forth the praises of him who hath called you out of darkness into his marvelous light; which in the time past were not a people, but are now the people of God. . . ."[9] Unfortunately, apostasy overtook the early Christians so they never did enjoy the complete fulfillment of this blessing.

In the latter days the Lord has promised to build a great civilization with this same covenant and blessing. As He ushered in the last dispensation of the fullness of times the Lord declared: "For Zion must increase in beauty, and in holiness;

6. Moses 7:17-18
7. Ether 1:43
8. Inspired Version, Genesis 14:33-34
9. I Peter 2:9-10

her borders must be enlarged; her stakes must be strengthened; yea, verily I say unto you, Zion must arise and put on her beautiful garments. Therefore, I give unto you this commandment, that ye bind yourselves by this covenant, and it shall be done according to the laws of the Lord."[10]

These passages help us catch the point of view of the Lord when he was talking to Moses on Sinai. These Hebrews were being offered the kingdom of God on earth, a restoration of the golden age of Enoch, a duplication of the orderly society achieved by Melchizedek, a taste of government and glory such as the whole earth will enjoy during the millennium. All this was being offered to Israel. The fact that they bungled this opportunity is one of the greatest tragedies in human history.

THE THREE THINGS MOSES WANTED TO DO FOR ISRAEL

But Moses never intended that Israel should bungle it. As we shall see in a moment, Moses had a passionate zeal to achieve for Israel in his day everything which Enoch and Melchizedek had achieved for ancient peoples in their day.

To bring this about, Moses had to do three things: *First,* he had to regenerate the lives of the people of Israel to a level of righteousness where God could walk and talk with them as He did with the people of Enoch. *Second,* he had to confer upon all who were worthy, the higher, or Melchizedek Priesthood which holds the keys to a true knowledge of God and the power whereby men and women may come into His very presence.[11] *Third,* he had to build a temple in which the holy ordinances could be administered to the people which are specifically designed to prepare people for the great privilege of communicating personally with God. This is called the Endowment.[12] Concerning this the Lord has said in modern times:

"For, for this cause I commanded Moses that he should build a tabernacle, that they should bear it with them in the wilderness, and to build a house [the temple of Solomon] in

10. Doctrine and Covenants 82:14-15
11. Doctrine and Covenants 84:20-22
12. Doctrine and Covenants 105:11-12, 33; 110:9

the land of promise, that those ordinances [of the higher priesthood] might be revealed which had been hid from before the world was."[13]

Concerning these ordinances of the higher Priesthood the Lord said, "And this greater priesthood administereth the gospel and holdeth the key of the mysteries of the kingdom, even the KEY OF THE KNOWLEDGE OF GOD. Therefore, in the ordinances thereof, and the authority of the priesthood, the power of godliness is manifest. And without the ordinances thereof, and the authority of the priesthood, the power of godliness is not manifest unto men in the flesh; for WITHOUT THIS NO MAN CAN SEE THE FACE OF GOD, EVEN THE FATHER, AND LIVE."[14]

So Moses knew exactly what he had to do to achieve this for his people.

Moses went down from the presence of the Lord to the people. He explained the covenant which God was willing to make with them and then asked them if they were willing to commit themselves to a divine pattern for happy living which the Lord was about to reveal.

"And all the people answered together, and said, All that the Lord hath spoken we will do."[15] So be it. "Moses returned the words of the people unto the Lord."[16]

Moses Attempts to Get Israel a Scientific Witness of God's Reality

It was apparently at about this point that Moses made his special request of the Lord. He wanted all Israel to come into the very presence of God and see him face to face as Moses had seen Him. He wanted them to hear His voice and see His glory.

This exciting disclosure concerning the motivations of Moses in wanting to bring the people into the immediate presence of God is specifically mentioned in a modern revelation. The Lord says:

---

13. Doctrine and Covenants 124:38   15. Exodus 19:8
14. Doctrine and Covenants 84:19-22   16. Ibid.

"Now this Moses plainly taught to the children of Israel in the wilderness [between Egypt and Sinai[17]], and sought diligently TO SANCTIFY HIS PEOPLE THAT THEY MIGHT BEHOLD THE FACE OF GOD.

"But they hardened their hearts and could not endure his presence: therefore the Lord in his wrath, for his anger was kindled against them, swore that they should not enter into his rest while in the wilderness, WHICH REST IS THE FULNESS OF HIS GLORY.

"Therefore, he took Moses out of their midst, and the holy [or higher] priesthood also: and the lesser priesthood continued, which priesthood holdeth the key of the ministering of angels and the preparatory gospel: which gospel is the gospel of repentance and of baptism, and the remission of sins, and the law of carnal commandments, which the Lord in his wrath caused to continue with the house of Aaron among the children of Israel until John. . . ."[18]

This golden nugget of revelation casts a completely new light on the nineteenth chapter of the Book of Exodus and the events immediately following. It means that ever since Moses had left Egypt he had taken every opportunity during these two months in the wilderness to elevate the vision of this people toward the days when they would become "a kingdom of priests and an holy nation."[19] He wanted them to have a holy temple in which the people could walk and talk with God as had the people of Enoch. As the Lord later said, "And let them make me a sanctuary that I MAY DWELL AMONG THEM."[20] Moses wanted every person in Israel to become worthy to enjoy a personal, scientific, witness that God lives, that men are made in his image, and that the Lord is prepared to bless them beyond their most vivid expectations if they will but remain obedient.

As we shall see later Moses achieved this partially with Aaron, Nadab, Abihu, and 70 others (including Joshua), but none else. It was the most bitter disappointment of his life.

---

17. At Sinai the calamity occurred which cut Israel off from any possibility of coming into the presence of God. Therefore, this time element referred to in the phrase, "Now this Moses plainly taught to the children of Israel in the wilderness" would have to be during the wilderness trek between Egypt and Sinai. (D. & C. 84·23)
18. Doctrine and Covenants 84:23-27
19. Exodus 19:6   20. Exodus 25:8

THE INITIAL ATTEMPT TO SANCTIFY THE PEOPLE OF ISRAEL

But that is getting ahead of our story. The nineteenth chapter of Exodus opens with Moses exhibiting the joyous anticipation that he would be successful. The Lord said He was willing to show great signs to the children of Israel, and personally communicate with them, but they must not attempt to come into the presence of his glory at this initial stage of their spiritual development or they would be consumed in an instant. Here is the way the Lord stated it to Moses:

"Lo, I come unto thee in a thick cloud, that the people may hear when I speak with thee, and believe thee for ever. . .

"Go unto the people, and sanctify them today and to morrow, and let them wash their clothes, and be ready against the third day: for the third day the Lord will come down in the sight of all the people, upon Mount Sinai. And thou shalt set bounds unto the people round about, saying, Take heed to yourselves, that ye go not up into the mount, or touch the border of it; whosoever toucheth the mount shall be surely put to death."[21]

Moses did as the Lord commanded. The people washed their clothes, bathed, resolutely set their minds on the things of God, and did everything else they could to sanctify themselves. This continued for three days. Then they waited expectantly for the manifestation of God's power which he had promised.

What happened exceeded their wildest expectations.

First, of all, a luminous storm cloud descended upon the mount. The thunders roared out across the wilderness and crashing bolts of lightning set the earth to shaking.[22] Then the people heard the sounding of a trumpet which blew louder and louder until the people found themselves trembling for fear.[23]

At this point Moses brought the hosts of Israel out of their camps and had them converge around the boundaries which had been set at the base of the mountain. A fearful display of sight and sound then took place before them:

---

21. Exodus 10:9-12   22. Exodus 19:16-18   23. Exodus 19:16

"And Mount Sinai was altogether on a smoke, because the Lord descended upon it in fire: and the smoke thereof ascended as the smoke of a furnace, and the whole mount quaked greatly."[24]

A NEAR CATASTROPHE OCCURS

The Lord then directed Moses to come up "to the top of the Mount" to meet Him. For an eighty-year-old man this required tremendous exertion but it was such a thrilling reward at the end of the climb that Moses went up with enthusiastic eagerness. But barely had he struggled to the summit when the Lord commanded him to go quickly back down again. A monumental catastrophe was about to occur. The impetuous Israelites were so fascinated by the fact that God's very presence was on this mountain that they were on the verge of defying the boundaries which Moses had established and follow him up into the mountain.

Said the Lord: "Go down, charge the people, lest they break through unto the Lord to gaze, and many of them perish."[25]

Moses just could not believe the Isaelites would be so brazen and rash, so he said to the Lord, "The people cannot come up to Mount Sinai: for thou chargedst us, saying, Set bounds about the mount, and sanctify it."[26]

But this was no time to argue. There is a science to the heavens as well as the earth, and the Lord knew immediate destruction awaited the Israelites if they ventured into the precincts of this mountain while the glory of God was upon it. So the Lord spoke sharply to Moses and said:

"Away get thee down, and thou shalt come up, thou, and Aaron with thee; but let not the priests and the people break through, to come up unto the Lord, lest he break forth upon them."[27]

So Moses hurried down the mountain far faster than he had come up. After all the careful preparations, what kind of stupidity possessed these reckless renegades?

---

24. Exodus 19:18   26. Exodus 19:23
25. Exodus 19:21   27. Exodus 19:24

The Israelites Hear Moses Receive the Ten Commandments

The scripture says "Moses went down unto the people and spake unto them."[28] The text of his words is not given but they probably constituted a blistering declamation. Then the people heard another voice. From the fiery heights of Sinai came the powerful and penetrating voice of the Lord. They actually heard the Lord speaking to Moses. This is exactly what the Lord had previously promised when he said, "Lo, I come unto thee in a thick cloud, that the people may hear when I speak with thee, and believe thee forever."[29]

The pronouncement which the Lord made on this occasion was the famous Ten Commandments.[30] Later God would write these commandments on tablets of stone with his own finger, but at this point He declared them through the spoken word in the presence of all the people.

One would have thought that the sign-seeking Israelites who only a short time before were willing to risk annihilation to see God, would have rejoiced at this condescension of God to speak to Moses in their presence where all could hear. But their reaction was not joy but terror. They panicked and fled in a body "afar off."

Moses could not stop them. They said, "Speak thou with us, and we will hear: but let not God speak with us, lest we die."[31]

Moses replied, "Fear not: for God is come to prove you, and that his fear may be before your faces, that ye sin not."[32]

They feared all right, but they were not willing to stand forth and be proved. They wanted Moses to go back and get the word of the Lord. Meanwhile, they would stay at a safe distance.

So Moses went back to receive the rest of the law from the Lord. He confidently moved up "near unto the thick darkness, where God was."[33]

---

28. Exodus 20:25
29. Exodus 19:9
30. Exodus 20:1-17
31. Exodus 20:19
32. Exodus 20:20
33. Exodus 20:21

"And the Lord said unto Moses, Thus thou shalt say unto the children of Israel, YE HAVE SEEN THAT I HAVE TALKED WITH YOU FROM HEAVEN."[34] But since they did not dare return to hear the rest of the law, the Lord began dictating it to Moses.

MOSES RECEIVES GOD'S LAW OF EQUITY AND JUSTICE

The laws which the Lord now gave to Moses were the laws for the governing of a nation. They do not represent the broad constitutional basis for a nation, but rather the day-to-day rules of justice, equity, and righteousness by which a community, a state, a country, or the whole world can best govern itself.

These laws were the rules for a theocracy — a government in which the Lord is at the helm with instructions, counsel, and nominations for leadership, but where the people are given the right to accept or reject the principles and the leadership offered them.

Many of these laws were civil in nature, and appear very similar to those adopted by later civilizations such as Greece and Rome. However to the Israelites they were religious laws because they came directly from God; they were administered by the servants of the Lord and violations considered an offense against God as well as the community. As we shall see later, all of these laws were written down by Moses and the people voluntarily accepted them as part of a sacred, solemn covenant between them and the Lord. In other words they voted to be bound by them as the religious laws under which they would live.

It is very probable that these rules were the same as those which God had revealed for the governing of Enoch's people as well as other great kingdoms which the Lord had raised up in the past. Not at any time has the Lord repudiated them. These do not constitute "the law of Moses" which was "added because of transgression"[35] and then taken away at the time of Christ. Paul makes it clear that the laws which were "added" after Israel's apostasy were the dietary laws and the strict religious rituals. He says these

---

34. Exodus 20:22   35. Galatians 3:19

were the laws "Which stood only in meats and drinks, and divers washings, and carnal ordinances, imposed on them [the Israelites] until the time of reformation [the coming of Christ].[36]

However, the Ten Commandments plus the laws which Moses received before the apostasy of Israel, were permanent principles of the Gospel, many of which the Lord repeated as the governing rules of His Church in modern times.[37]

As previously mentioned, it is interesting that both Greece and Rome adopted many of these same basic principles to govern their empires. These principles also constitute the warp and woof of the Common Law of England which formed the foundation for American law. These laws therefore deserve more than passing interest. They should be studied today. The student may find the original law from the Lord to be far superior to the "patch on patch" statutes which in so many cases have been adopted to replace them.

CRIMES, TORTS AND GENERAL POLICIES

Moses had already been told by his father-in-law, Jethro, how best to organize the people after the Priesthood pattern with judges over tens, fifties, hundreds, thousands, etc., and with himself as chief judge. Jethro had told Moses to "provide out of all the people able men, such as fear God, men of truth, hating covetousness;"[38] and he said, "Thou shalt teach them ordinances and laws, and shalt shew them the way wherein they must walk, and the work that they must do."[39]

What Moses now received directly from the Lord was an important part of the code of the law Jethro was talking about. We will summarize all of these laws, using the modern legal terms to describe them so that the student can appreciate how comprehensive the Lord's "Law of the Covenant" actually was.

---

36. Hebrews 9:10
37. See, for example, almost all of Section 42 of the Doctrine and Covenants, especially verses 18-29; 54-57; 79-93
38. Exodus 18:21
39. Exodus 18:20

1. Laws governing bond servants.[40]
2. Laws governing deliberate murder specifically distinguished from accidental homicide.[41]
3. Law against the abuse of parents.[42]
4. Law against kidnapping.[43]
5. Law against battery.[44]
6. Law against the abuse of servants.[45]
7. Law against injury of expectant mothers.[46]
8. Law governing punishment for mayhem.[47]
9. Law against animals destroying human life.[48]
10. Law against animals injuring other animals.[49]
11. Law against wells or pits left uncovered.[50]
12. Law against cattle-stealing.[51]
13. Law governing the killing of a nighttime burglar.[52]
14. Law governing the killing of a daytime burglar.[53]
15. Law against animals being deliberately placed on the property of another to feed.[54]
16. Law against arson—fire setting.[55]
17. Law against embezzlement—breach of trust.[56]
18. Law against seduction.[57]
19. Law against sodomy.[58]
20. Law against heathen sacrifices.[59]
21. Policy concerning the treatment of strangers.[60]
22. Policy governing the treatment of widows and orphans.[61]
23. Policies and regulations relating to usury and loans.[62]
24. The people expected to honor and sustain their judges and rulers.[63]
25. Religious obligations of the people whether in sacrifices or oblations to be submitted promptly.[64]

---

40. Exodus 21:2-11
41. Exodus 21:12-14
42. Exodus 21:15, 17
43. Exodus 21:16
44. Exodus 21:18-19
45. Exodus 21:20, 26-27
46. Exodus 21:22
47. Exodus 21:23-25
48. Exodus 21:28-32
49. Exodus 21:35-36
50. Exodus 21:33-34
51. Exodus 22:1, 4
52. Exodus 22:2
53. Exodus 22:3
54. Exodus 22:5
55. Exodus 22:6
56. Exodus 22:7-15
57. Exodus 22:16-17
58. Exodus 22:19
59. Exodus 22:20
60. Exodus 22:21; 23:9
61. Exodus 22:22-24
63. Exodus 22:28
62. Exodus 22:25-27
64. Exodus 22:29-30

26. Animals killed or torn in combat not to be eaten.[65]
27. Law against bearing false witness.[66]
28. Law against raising or joining a mob.[67]
29. Law against the abuse of the poor in the courts.[68]
30. Law against bribery.[69]
31. Regulations governing the use of the land.[70]
32. Regulations governing the celebration of the three feasts or religious festivals of the Israelites.[71]
33. Law against the heathen practice of "seething a kid in his mother's milk."[72]
34. Law against idolatry.[73]

There were many unique features about the Lord's law which we will discuss further on as we deal with later passages where Moses gives a more complete treatment of these and related laws. It is sufficient here to simply state that the principles and practices of the "Mosaic Code" have been seriously misunderstood and a better understanding of these laws reveals them to be a far more advanced system of jurisprudence than any which exists on the earth today.

The Lord Makes Five Promises to Israel if They Will Swear to Obey These Laws

The laws we have just listed were followed by several promises from the Lord. He said that if the people respected these laws and tried to live under them to the very best of their ability, five blessings would come to Israel:

First, an angel of the Lord would lead them into the promised land.[74]

Second, the Israelites would be blessed with good health.[75]

Third, they and their flocks would multiply greatly.[76]

Fourth, they would succeed in their war against the heathen nations, so as to gradually take over the promised land.[77]

---

65. Exodus 22:31
66. Exodus 23:1
67. Exodus 23:2
68. Exodus 23:3,6
69. Exodus 23:8
70. Exodus 23:10-11
71. Exodus 23:14-17
72. Exodus 23:19
73. Exodus 23:24
74. Exodus 23:20-23
75. Exodus 23:25
76. Exodus 23:26
77. Exodus 23:27-31

Fifth, Israel would ultimately inherit everything from the Red Sea to the Euphrates River.[78]

Thus the revelation on the Lord's covenant with Israel concluded.

"And Moses wrote all the words of the Lord, and rose up early in the morning and builded an altar under the hill, and twelve pillars according to the twelve tribes of Israel. And he sent young men of the children of Israel, which offered burnt offerings, and sacrificed peace offerings of oxen unto the Lord. And Moses took half of the blood, and put it in basons; and half of the blood he sprinkled on the altar. And he took the book of the covenant, and read in the audience of the people: and they said, ALL THAT THE LORD HATH SAID WILL WE DO, AND BE OBEDIENT.

"And Moses took the blood, and sprinkled it on the people, and said, Behold the blood of the covenant, which the Lord hath made with you concerning all these words."[79]

Moses Is Finally Permitted to Bring 73 Israelites into God's Presence

One of the most thrilling moments in the life of Moses now occurred. The Lord gave him permission to provide a scientific witness to 73 of the Israelites concerning God's reality, His personal appearance, and His glory.

The Lord said to Moses: "Come up unto the Lord, thou, and Aaron, Nadab, and Abihu [the two eldest sons of Aaron], and seventy of the elders of Israel; and worship ye afar off. And Moses alone shall come near the Lord: but they shall not come nigh; neither shall the people go up with him."[80]

We learn later that two of those fortunate enough to be included among the seventy elders of Israel were Hur and Joshua. We also learn from later events that this pilgrimage was only part way up Mount Sinai. Moses alone was allowed to go to the summit.

Here is the way the scripture describes what happened:

---

78. Exodus 23:31   79. Exodus 24:4-8   80. Exodus 24:1-2

"Then went up Moses, and Aaron, Nadab and Abihu, and seventy of the elders of Israel. And they saw the God of Israel: and there was under his feet as it were a paved work of a sapphire stone, and as it were the body of heaven in his clearness.. And upon the nobles of the children of Israel he laid not his hand: also they saw God, and did eat and drink."[81]

Apparently they were relieved that the Lord did not lay his hand on them to destroy them for having come into his presence, and when the glorious experience had passed they apparently sat down to enjoy a repast of food and drink which they had brought along. But Moses did not stay with them. "And the Lord said unto Moses, Come up to me into the mount, and be there: and I will give thee tables of stone, and a law, and commandments which I have written; that thou mayest teach them."[82]

Moses and Joshua Ascend Higher into Mount Sinai

"And Moses rose up, and his minister Joshua: and Moses went up [higher] into the mount of God. And he said unto the elders, Tarry ye here for us, until we come again unto you: and, behold, Aaron and Hur are with you: if any man have any matters to do, let him come unto them. And Moses [and Joshua] went up into the mount, and a cloud covered the mount."[83]

During the absence of Moses, Aaron and Hur were to be in charge, but apparently Moses, himself, did not realize he would be gone forty days and forty nights! In fact, six days passed before Moses even got to see the Lord.

"And the Glory of the Lord abode upon Mount Sinai, and the cloud covered it six days: and the seventh day he called unto Moses, out of the midst of the cloud. And the sight of the glory of the Lord was like devouring fire on the top of the mount in the eyes of the children of Israel. And Moses went into the midst of the cloud, and gat him up [higher] into the mount. . . ."[84]

Apparently Joshua stayed at the level where he and Moses had been waiting during the previous six days. The

---

81. Exodus 24:9-11
82. Exodus 24:12

83. Exodus 24:13-15
84. Exodus 24:16-18

MOSES CONFERS
WITH THE LORD
34 DAYS

MOSES AND JOSHUA
WAIT SIX DAYS

AARON, NADAB, ABIHU
AND 70 OF THE ELDERS OF
ISRAEL ARE ALLOWED TO
ASCEND THE MOUNT PART
WAY AND SEE GOD

amazing integrity of Joshua was demonstrated by the fact that when Moses came down some five weeks later, Joshua was still there, patiently waiting. We know that during all that time Moses was spiritually quickened so that he "neither ate bread nor drank water."[85] but what Joshua did we have no idea. All we know is that he faithfully waited, and somehow survived.

Further down the mountain, Aaron, his two sons, and the seventy elders of Israel were also waiting — but not for long. Apparently, they soon ran out of food and patience and made their way back down the mountain to the comforts of the camp. The day would come when Aaron would realize that this weakness in disobeying Moses and returning to camp was the beginning of the biggest blunder in his life.

Meanwhile Moses was transfigured in the exquisite sublimation of spiritual "quickening" which permitted him to survive without food or drink while enjoying a series of magnificent revelations extending over a period of 34 days.[86]

---

85. Exodus 34:28; Deuteronomy 9:9
86. This figure is derived from the fact that we know he was in the mount forty days and forty nights (Exodus 24:18) but did not begin his conversation with the Lord until after the sixth day.

MOSES RECEIVES THE SPECIFICATIONS FOR A
PORTABLE TEMPLE

Moses had come into the mountain to receive the promised tablets on which were written the law by the finger of God. As we shall see later, these tablets also contained the sacred temple ordinances of the higher Priesthood which were so necessary to prepare the people for the privilege of coming into the presence of God. However, temple ordinances are not usually given until there is the prospect of a temple in which to administer them. Therefore the Lord began this series of revelations with a detailed blueprint for a portable temple. To distinguish it from permanent temples, (such as Solomon's,) this portable model was referred to as the Tabernacle.

The amazing thing about this revelation is the minute detail of every aspect of the structure. The doors, veils, walls, decorations, coverings, utensils, altar, and Ark of the Covenant are all described down to the most precise measurement and architectural detail.

Altogether, there are three revelations in the Bible giving the architectural specification for temples. Each of them is remarkably detailed. The first is the present revelation on the Tabernacle,[87] the second is the revelation on the Temple of Solomon which was given to David,[88] and the third is Ezekiel's detailed revelation for the temple to be built in Jerusalem by the Jews just prior to the coming of the Messiah.[89]

In all three cases the person receiving the revelation was not only given the measurements, but he seems to have been shown a vision of the complete structure. The Lord said to Moses, "And thou shalt rear up the tabernacle according to the fashion thereof which was shewed thee in the mount."[90] Concerning Solomon's temple, the pattern was given by revelation to David who turned it over to his son for execution. The scripture says the pattern was given to David "by the spirit. . . . All this, said David, the Lord made me under-

87. Exodus, Chapters 25 and 27 inclusive
88. I Chronicles 28:11-19; II Chronicles Chapters 3-4.
89. Ezekiel, Chapters 41 and 42   90. Exodus 26:30

stand in writing by his hand upon me, even all the works of this pattern."[91] Ezekiel likewise had a vision portraying the magnificent temple which would be built in Jerusalem preparatory to the coming of the Messiah, and the angel of the Lord took Ezekiel through the entire structure in vision, measuring it as he went.[92] This description is so carefully chronicled that the Jews could make up their architectural plans for this temple and start building it just as soon as they gain access to Old Jerusalem.

WHAT IS THE ENDOWMENT?

We now know that the Tabernacle was originally designed for the Endowment or the higher ordinances pertaining to the Melchizedek Priesthood. As we have already mentioned, this is specifically referred to in a modern revelation. The Lord said:

"For, for this cause I commanded Moses that he should build a tabernacle, that they should bear it with them in the wilderness . . . THAT THOSE ORDINANCES MIGHT BE REVEALED WHICH HAD BEEN HID FROM BEFORE THE WORLD WAS."[93]

These ordinances "which had been hid from before the world was" constitute the higher Priesthood ordinances or Endowment which have never been performed in public as were the animal sacrifices and other ordinances belonging to the lower Priesthood. The higher ordinances were always kept "hid" or private because of their sacred character.

In 1912 the Church published *The House of the Lord,* in which Dr. James Talmage gave this authorized description of the Endowment ordinances. These ordinances have been essentially the same since the days of Adam. Concerning them Dr. Talmage wrote:

"The temple endowment, as administered in modern temples, comprises instruction relating to the significance and sequence of past dispensations. . . . This course of instruction

---

91. I Chronicles 28:12,19   93. Doctrine and Covenants 124:38
92. Ezekiel, Chapters 41 and 42

includes a recital of the most prominent events of the creative period, the condition of our first parents in the Garden of Eden, their disobedience and consequent expulsion from that blissful abode, their condition in the lone and dreary world when doomed to live by labor and sweat, the plan of redemption by which the great transgression may be atoned, the period of the great apostasy, the restoration of the gospel with all the ancient powers and privileges, the absolute and indispensable conditions of personal purity and devotion to the right in present life, and a strict compliance with gospel requirements. . . .

"The ordinances of the endowment embody certain obligations on the part of the individual, such as a covenant and promise to observe the law of strict virtue and chastity, to be charitable, benevolent, tolerant and pure; to devote both talent and material means to the spread of truth and the uplifting of the race; to maintain devotion to the cause of truth; and to seek in every way to contribute to the great preparation that the earth may be made ready to receive her King, the Lord Jesus. With the taking of each covenant and the assuming of each obligation a promised blessing is pronounced, contingent upon the faithful observance of the conditions.

"No jot, iota, or tittle of the temple rites is otherwise than uplifting and sanctifying. In every detail the endowment ceremony contributes to covenants of morality of life, consecration of person to high ideals, devotion to truth, patriotism to nation, allegiance to God."[94]

In the days of Moses the temple or Tabernacle was only designed for those getting their own endowments. Vicarious work for the dead referred to by Paul[95] was only permitted after Jesus had preached to the spirits in prison[96] and had been resurrected. The structure of the ancient temples was therefore much more simple than the layout for modern temples. Today, each temple must have many rooms for the large companies doing ordinance work for the dead. In the Tabernacle this was not the case.

---

94. James E. Talmage, *The House of the Lord*, pp. 99-101
95. I Corinthians 15:29   96. I Peter 4:6

The Approximate Procedure for the Ministering of the Ordinances in the Tabernacle

Because the ordinances revealed on the mount to Moses have been restored in modern times, we are able to reconstruct with approximate accuracy what it would have been like to participate in the temple service which the Lord originally designed for the Tabernacle. Because of apostasy, this procedure had to be altered, but we gain a better appreciation of the Tabernacle by examining the ritual as the Lord originally designed it.

From the accompanying illustration it will be seen that the Israelite would approach the Tabernacle through the eastern gate of the courtyard which surrounded the Tabernacle. This courtyard was called the "court of the congregation" and consisted of a rectangular wall of linen curtains five cubits high (7½ feet).[97] These curtains were strung

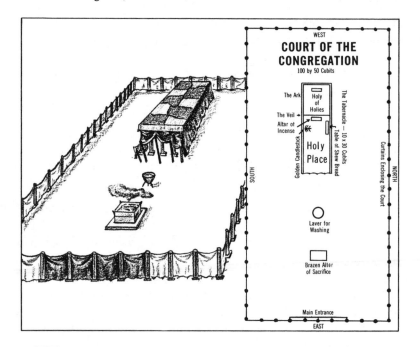

97. See Exodus 27:9-18; Concerning the length of the cubit Peloubet's *Bible Dictionary* treats it under "Weights and Measures". He says, ". . . the cubit, originally the length of the human arm from the tip of the middle finger to the elbow. The ordinary equivalent for this is 18 inches. . . ."

on bronze poles and extended around the enclosure which measured 100 by 50 cubits (150 by 75 feet).[98]

Inside the enclosure the Israelite would first come to the altar of sacrifice, sometimes called the brazen altar.[99] This was a hollow, bronze-lined and bronze-covered box of the finest wood, measuring 7½ feet square and 5 feet high. It was partially filled with earth and in the center a fire was kindled beneath a grate. There the sacrifices or burnt offerings were made. The Israelites would offer to the priest a lamb, goat or two doves (if he were poor) which would be killed and offered as a sacrifice according to a procedure which we will describe later.[100]

Proceeding toward the Tabernacle the Israelite would come to a large laver or basin filled with water. Here the washing with water and anointing with oil took place. When pronounced ceremonially clean, he would be escorted into the Tabernacle.[101]

DESCRIPTION OF THE TABERNACLE

The Tabernacle was surprisingly small — about 45 feet

---

98. Exodus 27:18
99. Exodus 27:1-8
100. Those familiar with modern temple ceremonies will recognize that this part of the ceremony is not presently practiced. However, Joseph Smith said someday it will be reinstituted after the temple is built in Jerusalem: ". . . it is generally supposed," he said, "that sacrifice was entirely done away when the Great Sacrifice (i.e.,) the sacrifice of the Lord Jesus was offered up, and that there will be no necessity for the ordinance of sacrifice in the future; but those who assert this are certainly not acquainted with the duties, privileges and authority of the Priesthood, or with the Prophets . . .
   "These sacrifices, as well as every ordinance belonging to the Priesthood, will, when the Temple of the Lord shall be built, and the sons of Levi be purified, be fully restored and attended to in all their powers, ramifications, and blessings. This ever did and ever will exist when the powers of the Melchizedek Priesthood are sufficiently manifest; else how can the restitution of all things spoken of by the Holy Prophets be brought to pass. It is not to be understood that the law of Moses will be established again with all of its rites and variety of ceremonies; this has never been spoken of by the prophets; but those things which existed prior to Moses' day, namely, sacrifice, will be continued.
   "It may be asked by some, what necessity for sacrifice, since the Great Sacrifice was offered? In answer to which, if repentance, baptism, and faith existed, prior to the days of Christ, what necessity for them since that time?" (Documentary History of the Church, Vol. 4, pp. 211-212.)
101. This part of the Priesthood ritual is practiced in modern times. All washings, anointings and being dressed in the garment of the Prisethood occur prior to the time the candidate enters the temple proper. Being dressed in the robes of the Priesthood takes place after entering the temple.

(or 30 cubits) long by 15 feet (10 cubits) wide.[102] This rectangular room was divided by a veil which cloistered the last one third of the Tabernacle.[103] This cloistered area was called the Holy of Holies, whereas the larger room was called the Holy Place.[104] As the candidate entered the outside he would see, straight in front of him against the veil at the far end of the room, the golden altar of incense.[105] To the right of it was the golden table of shew bread.[106] To the left was the golden candlestick which had seven tapers and provided the only light.[107]

The sides of the tabernacle were hung with curtains of fine linen, dyed blue, purple and scarlet, and embroidered or woven with figures of cherubim.[108] The ceiling was also of linen[109] and above it were three protective coverings — one of goats' hair, one of rams' skins dyed red,[110] and one of badgers' skins or seal skins from the Red Sea.[111]

It is important to distinguish the two separate apartments of the Tabernacle, namely, the Holy Place and the Holy of Holies. It was in the first of these — the Holy Place—that the candidate would receive all of the higher ordinances, be clothed in the robes of the Priesthood, and make his sacred vows. He would then be presented at the veil and introduced into the Holy of Holies.

The Holy of Holies

The Holy of Holies was the place where the High Priest came to receive revelations from the Lord. It was the most sacred place on earth to which a son or daughter of God might come. Here was located the famous Ark of the Covenant.[112] It was made of the finest wood and covered inside and out with plates of pure gold. The Ark was designed to contain the two tablets of stone on which the Law had been inscribed

---

102. Exodus 26:1-30
103. Exodus 26:31-33
104. Exodus 26:33
105. Exodus 30:1-9
106. Exodus 25:23-30
107. Exodus 25:31-40
108. Exodus 26:7-13

109. Exodus 26:1-6
110. Exodus 26:14
111. Exodus 26:15; The English translation says "badgers' skins," and the Revised Version says, "sealskins."
112. Exodus 25:10-22; 26:34

by the finger of God.[113] It also contained a vessel of manna.[114] Later, the miraculous rod of Aaron was placed with the Ark.[115]

The lid of the Ark of the Covenant was called the Mercy Seat.[116] It was elaborately decorated, having a cherubim at each end with their extended wings covering the Mercy Seat. Here the presence of God was to be made manifest. The Lord said, "I will commune with thee from above the mercy seat, from between the two cherubims which are upon the ark of the testimony. . . ."[117]

The Ark of the Covenant (sometimes called the Ark of Testimony, as above) was not large. It measured 2½ cubits in length, 1½ cubits wide and 1½ cubits high.[118] This would make it approximately 45 inches long, 27 inches wide and 27 inches high.

For the ordinary Israelite, the privilege of coming into the Holy of Holies at the conclusion of the Endowment ceremony would be a once-in-a-lifetime experience. To have the further privilege of seeing the objects of "testimony" in the Ark of the Covenant would be a thrilling climax to a sacred occasion.

Unfortunately, however, since the Endowment or higher Priesthood ordinances were later withheld from the Israelites because of their rebellion, the use of the Tabernacle by the people as a whole was never inaugurated. As the scripture says, the Israelites "hardened their hearts and could not endure his presence; therefore, the Lord in his wrath . . . took Moses out of their midst, and the Holy Priesthood also; and the lesser priesthood continued, which priesthood holdeth the key of the ministering of angels and the preparatory gospel."[119]

The "lesser Priesthood" ordinances had to do with repentance, baptism, animal sacrifices and the various carnal commandments which were nearly all performed outside the Tabernacle.[120] Therefore the ceremonies in the Tabernacle

---

113. Exodus 31:18; 34:28: Deuteronomy 10:5; Hebrews 9:4
114. Exodus 16:33-34; Hebrews 9:4   118. Exodus 25:10
115. Numbers 17:10; Hebrews 9:4   119. Doctrine and Covenants 84:24-26
116. Exodus 25:17-22   120. Doctrine and Covenants 84:27
117. Exodus 25:22

were limited almost exclusively to the lighting of the incense each day and the annual visit of the high priest to the Holy of Holies on the Day of Atonement.[121]

WERE GOD'S LEADERS ALLOWED TO RECEIVE THE ENDOWMENT?

We have reason to believe that even though the Lord withheld the Endowment and related Melchizedek Priesthood ordinances from the main body of Israel, He nevertheless permitted this sacred ordinance to be received by his chosen leaders. This is strongly inferred from two sources.

First of all, we know that Moses had the Melchizedek Priesthood,[122] and several generations later we find the heirs of that Priesthood building a temple in the promised land (Solomon's Temple) and ministering the Endowment. In a modern revelation the Lord makes specific reference to this fact. The Lord says He commanded his servants "to build a house in the land of promise [Solomon's Temple], that those ordinances might be revealed which had been hid from before the world was."[123] As we have already pointed out, this particular phraseology has reference to the higher ordinances in the temple. The very next verse in the Doctrine and Covenants so identifies it.[124]

This would therefore indicate that those who traced their Priesthood from Moses were ministering in these higher ordinances in the Temple of Solomon.

As a further evidence that the Lord allowed His chosen leaders to receive the Endowment from generation to generation, we have the statement that these blessings stopped with Elijah. Joseph Smith learned that "Elijah was the last Prophet that held the keys of the [higher] Priesthood,"[125] He said these "keys" consist of "the revelations, ordinances, oracles, powers and endowments of the fulness of the Melchizedek Priesthood and of the Kingdom of God on earth. . . ."[126] These were restored during the ministry of Christ,[127] and had to be

121. Leviticus Chapter 16, especially 11-17
122. Doctrine and Covenants 84:6
123. Doctrine and Covenants 124:38
124. Doctrine and Covenants 124:39
125. Documentary History of the Church, Vol. 4, p. 211
126. Documentary History of the Church, Vol. 6, p. 251
127. Ibid.

restored again in the latter days.[128] Joseph Smith said that without the keys which Elijah held the higher temple ordinances "could not be administered in righteousness."[129]

We therefore find considerable evidence to support the belief that between Moses and Elijah — a period of some 600 years — the higher temple ordinances which were taken away from the main body of Israel were administered to the righteous leaders as God raised them up during that period.

THE VESTMENTS OF THE HIGH PRIEST AND HIS ASSISTANTS

While Moses was in the mount the Lord showed him how the High Priest and his assistants should be dressed when they came to minister in the sanctuary. These vestments were to be "holy garments" and were to be "for glory and beauty."[130]

However, they were described as "holy" because they were for sacred rather than public use. And they were for the glory and beauty of God's sanctuary, not for the pompous parading of God's servants before the envious eyes of a multitude. The Lord has specifically identified the ostentatious public display of rich vestments as being a sign of apostasy.[131]

These vestments were symbols of a calling, therefore they were *in addition* to the shirt, trousers and underclothing. The High Priest had six items, each of which is described minutely:

1. First, he would put on an EMBROIDERED COAT.[132] This was a short frock worn over the upper part of the body.

2. Then he put on the BLUE ROBE.[133] This was a solid piece of blue linen with a hole in the middle area to be slipped over the head. At the hem of the robe were embroidered blue, purple and scarlet pomegranates and in between each one was a golden bell which tinkled softly as the priest performed the service.

128. Doctrine and Covenants 110:13-16
129. Documentary History of the Church, Volume 4, p. 211
130. Exodus 28:2
131. I Nephi 13:6-8
132. Exodus 28:4, 39
133. Exodus 28:4; 39:22-26

3. Next came the EPHOD.[134] This was a waistcoat of "fine twined linen" and decorated with "cunning work." It was gold, blue, purple, and scarlet. On each of the shoulders was a large onyx stone set in a gold rosette. Each stone had engraved upon it six of the tribes of Israel. From these two onyx stones hung woven gold chains which held up the "breastplate."

4. About the waist the priest wore a linen GIRDLE[135] which matched the ephod.

5. Then came the BREASTPLATE.[136] This was not metal but made of embroidered, jewel-covered linen. It was about nine inches square and woven of gold, blue, purple and scarlet like the ephod. On it were twelve stones, each representing one of the tribes of Israel. The breastplate was "double"[137] meaning that it formed a pocket. In this pocket the High Priest placed the Urim and Thummim which facilitated the receiving of revelations.[138] The breastplate had gold rings at the top and on the sides. The top rings were fastened by a woven chain to each of the onyx stones on the shoulders of the ephod. The side rings also had woven gold chains attached which connected to the ephod around the waist in order to hold it firm.

6. The High Priest wore a MITRE[139] or linen cap which had a shield in the front bearing the inscription: HOLINESS TO THE LORD.[140]

It would appear that those who served with the High Priest (which in the case of Aaron were his sons) wore linen breeches[141] and an embroidered linen coat with a girdle.[142] On their heads they wore "bonnets."[143] They did not wear a blue robe, an ephod, breast-plate or mitre, since these belonged exclusively to the office of the High Priest.

THE FINAL HOURS ON THE MOUNT

As the visions and instructions concerning the laws, the Tabernacle, the implements, vestments and ordinances finally came to a close, Moses received several important commandments and comments from the Lord.

---

134. Exodus 28:6-14
135. Exodus 28:4, 8
136. Exodus 28:15-30; 39:8-21
137. Exodus 39:9
138. See article in the appendix, "The History and Significance of the Urim and Thummim."   141. Exodus 28:42
139. Exodus 28:4; 39:28   142. Exodus 29:8-9
140. Exdous 39:30-31   143. Exodus 28-40

First of all, he was told that when the Tabernacle was completed he should consecrate Aaron to be the High Priest and his sons were to be ordained as assistants. This ceremony was to last a week. The Lord wanted it set before the people as a great religious event. He even outlined the ritual which was to be followed.

The Lord also wanted Moses to understand that there was nothing which any generation of Saints in ancient times had enjoyed but what the Lord would gladly provide for Israel. He even assured Moses that when the Tabernacle had been completed and sanctified, He would show Himself to the people as He did in the days of Enoch. The Lord said, "And I will dwell among the children of Israel, and will be their God. And they shall know that I am the Lord their God, that brought them forth out of the land of Egypt, that I may dwell among them. . . ."[144] One of the greatest blessings received by the people of Enoch was the fact that "the Lord came and dwelt with his people, and they dwelt in righteousness."[145] The Lord was now saying that with the same righteousness, Israel could have the same blessing.

The Lord also said that keeping the Sabbath day holy would be the way the people of Israel could show whether or not they intended to continue honoring their covenant with God: "Wherefore the children of Israel shall keep the Sabbath, to observe the Sabbath throughout their generations, for a perpetual covenant. It is a sign between me and the children of Israel for ever. . . ."[146]

MOSES RECEIVES THE SACRED TABLETS OF STONE INSCRIBED BY THE FINGER OF GOD

When Moses went into the mount he already knew he was to receive the tablets of stone on which the Lord would write the Law.[147] So far as we know, the Lord prepared these first two tables of stone Himself. He said, "I will give thee tables of stones, and a law, and commandments which I have written: that thou mayest teach them."[148]

---

144. Exodus 29:45-46
145. Moses 7:16
146. Exodus 31:16-17

147. Exodus 24:12
148. Exodus 24:12

The very last thing the Lord did before sending Moses back down from the mount was to give him these two tables of stone. The scripture says, "And he gave unto Moses, when he had made an end of communing with him upon mount Sinai, two tables of testimony, tables of stone, written with the finger of God."[149]

Another passage tells us that they were written on both sides. ". . . the tables were written on both their sides; on the one side and on the other were they written."[150]

Moses also made clear in the original text of Exodus that this first set of tables contained material pertaining to the "priesthood" and "my holy order, and the ordinances thereof."[151]

With the receipt of the precious tables of stone written by the Lord with his own finger, Moses was prepared to descend to the plain below where the vast tent-city of Israel spread away toward the horizon. Moses must have felt jubilant. In his two hands he held one of the greatest treasures any prophet had received since the days of Adam.

Moses was 80 years old and he had gone without food or water during the entire time he had been in the mountain. This amounted to 40 days and 40 nights. Moses later bore personal testimony of this fact when he said to Israel, "When I was gone up into the mount to receive the tables of stone, even the tables of the covenant which the Lord made with you, then I abode in the mount forty days and forty nights, I neither did eat bread nor drink water."[152]

Only two other persons are known to have duplicated this feat. One was the Prophet Elijah,[153] and the other was the Savior.[154] But, as we shall see shortly, Moses appears to have done something which no other person ever duplicated. He went on a second forty-day fast within two or three days after this first one was completed! How this came about will be the subject of the next chapter.

---

149. Exodus 32:18
150. Exodus 32:15
151. Inspired Version, Exodus 34:1
152. Deuteronomy 9:9
153. I Kings 19:8
154. Matthew 4:2

Scripture Reading and Questions On Chapter Fourteen

Scripture Reading Assignment: Exodus, chapters 19 to 29 inclusive.

1—How long had Israel been in the wilderness before they reached Sinai? Why was Sinai so significant to Moses?

2—What was so significant about the covenant God immediately made with Israel? Had other people ever received such a covenant?

3—What were the three things Moses wanted to do for Israel?

4—While Moses was up conversing with the Lord, what did the people try to do? Was this dangerous? Why?

5—Where was Moses when the Lord enunciated the Ten Commandments the first time? Where were the people? When they heard the voice of God what did they do? What did they ask Moses to do?

6—Could the Israelites have heard the Lord dictate the laws of the covenant to Moses? What prevented it?

7—Name three of the five promises which the Lord made to Israel if they would keep the law of the covenant. Did the people vote to abide by the covenant or did they vote to reject it?

8—What scientific witness did Aaron, Nadab, Abihu and seventy of the elders of Israel receive in the mount?

9—Were these seventy-three men allowed to see God at close range? Who had that privilege?

10—What did Moses tell these men to do while he went higher up into the mount? Did they do it?

11—Who went with Moses into the mount? Did he go all the way? How long was it before the Lord spoke to them? What did he tell Moses to do?

12—How much detail did the Lord reveal concerning the architecture of the Tabernacle? What two temples are described in the Bible with equal detail?

13—Has the Church ever published a statement on the nature of the endowment? Was this ever revealed during Old Testament times?

14—What procedure permits members of the Church in modern times to go through the endowment ceremony more than once? Was this done before the resurrection?

15—Was Aaron's breastplate made of metal? What was it made of?

16—Were the vestments of the Priesthood to be worn in public? Why not?

17—What did the Israelites have to do before God could "dwell among them?" What does this mean?

18—Did the stone tablets have anything on them besides the Ten Commandments? What else?

19—Did Moses carve the words of God on the tablets of stone? Who did?

20—Who else is known to have fasted 40 days and 40 nights besides Moses?

CHAPTER FIFTEEN

How the Israelites Lost Their Chance to Become Another City of Enoch

When Moses had completed his spiritual pilgrimage of 40 days and 40 nights on Mount Sinai he was prepared to return triumphantly to his people.

What a treasure of knowledge he now possessed to share with all Israel. How thrilled they would be to see the two tablets of stone inscribed on both sides by the very finger of God. Moses now had the necessary knowledge to build a temple, to establish the temple service, to set up all of the ordinances, ceremonies, sacraments and laws of conduct necessary to organize the true Church of God on earth.[1] With this knowledge he could build a nation as Enoch had done, a nation that had produced a golden age of peace, prosperity and righteousness never surpassed in human history. The Lord had even told Moses he would come and "dwell" with Israel just as he had done with the people of Enoch.

But Moses was missing something. He lacked a people worthy of these blessings.

MOSES HEARS AN ASTONISHING ANNOUNCEMENT FROM THE LORD

Of course, Moses had no idea what had happened during his absence from Israel, but the Lord did. Even while the Lord had been conversing with Moses, His omniscient mind had been observing the outrageous apostasy which was rising like a tide in Israel and was fomenting itself into a

---

1. Acts 7:38

seething rebellion both against God and against Moses. The Lord therefore interrupted the sublime spiritual mood which Moses had so richly enjoyed and brought him suddenly to the bitter realities of the hour.

"Go, get thee down," commanded the Lord, "for thy people, which thou broughtest out of the land of Egypt, have corrupted themselves."[2]

Moses could not believe it. In six weeks? What could they have done? The Lord gave Moses a hint.

"They have turned aside quickly out of the way which I commanded them: they have made them a molten calf, and have worshipped it. . . ."[3]

But, as Moses was soon to discover, the situation was far worse than simply worshipping a golden calf. The people really had corrupted themselves. Without furnishing all of the morbid details, the Lord shocked Moses by abruptly announcing that He was about to usher that vast multitude of Israelites back into the spirit world in one mighty avalanche of vengeance and destruction.

The Lord warned Moses not to try to stop Him: ". . . let me alone that my wrath may wax hot against them, and that I may consume them . . ." Then, to comfort Moses and assure him that God's prophecies and promises would not be cut off by such action, he told Moses: "I will make of THEE a nation mightier and greater than they."[4]

In other words, from this point forward, God's purposes would be fulfilled exclusively in Moses and those who were valiant and obedient; those who were vigorously willing to keep pace with him spiritually. The Lord's intent was to divide the wheat from the tares as He had done in the days of Enoch. He would cleanse the ranks of Israel and build a nation exclusively from those who would live by their covenants.

But such a cataclysmic destruction of Israel — even though they were rebellious — seemed horrifying to Moses. He could not conceive of anything they might have done

---

2. Exodus 32:7   4. Deuteronomy 9:14; Exodus 32:10
3. Exodus 32:8

THE TEN COMMANDMENTS — A Paramount Picture

"And the Lord said Unto Moses, Go, get thee down; for thy people . . . have corrupted themselves . . . they have made them a molten calf, and have worshipped it."

which would justify such a terrible judgment. Said he, "Why doth thy wrath wax hot against thy people, which thou hast brought forth out of the land of Egypt with great power and with a mighty hand?"[5] Little did he realize that within a few hours he would be so disgusted and shocked by what he would see the Israelites doing that he would order the execution of several thousand of them himself!

At this moment, however, he plead for the Israelites. He said that if the Lord destroyed such a multitude of Israelites the Egyptians would be jubilant. They would say, "For mischief did he bring them out, to slay them in the mountains, and to consume them from the face of the earth."[6] In deepest anguish Moses cried out to the Lord:

"Turn from thy fierce wrath. Thy people will repent of this evil; therefore come thou not out against them. [This is taken from the Inspired Version. Note that it is 'thy people' or Israel who must repent, not God. In the King James Version Moses calls on God to repent!]

"Remember Abraham, Isaac, and Israel, thy servants, to whom thou swarest by thine own self, and saidst unto them, I will multiply your seed as the stars of heaven, and all this land that I have spoken of will I give unto your seed, and they shall inherit it for ever.

"And the Lord said unto Moses, If they will repent of the evil which they done, I will spare them, and turn away my fierce wrath; but behold, thou shalt execute my judgment upon all that will not repent of this evil this day. Therefore, see thou do this thing that I have commanded thee, or I will execute all that which I had thought to do unto my people."[7]

Moses was quick to agree with this proposal. He would gladly punish the unrepentant if the Lord would just spare the remainder of the people. Little did he realize that before he was through this commitment would require him to execute over three thousand Israelites!

MOSES DESCENDS FROM THE MOUNT

As Moses came down from the heights of Mount Sinai he was joined at a lower level by Israel's commander in chief,

---

5. Exodus 32:11   7. Inspired Version, Exodus 34:12-14
6. Exodus 32:12

Joshua. This valiant Ephraimite had faithfully waited for the Lord's prophet 34 days.[8] What Joshua had done to sustain himself during this lonely vigil we do not know, but it is obvious that there is a wonderful and heroic story of supreme loyalty in this incident which is missing from the scripture.

Joshua had no knowledge of what the Lord had told Moses concerning events in the camps of Israel, and therefore he was somewhat alarmed as they came down out of the Mount to hear the noise of a great tumult ascending up from the plain below. Joshua immediately concluded that the hosts of Israel must be under attack. He exclaimed to Moses, "There is a noise of war in the camp."[9] But a moment later he knew this could not be true for he heard singing with the shouting and tumult.[10] To Israel's great soldier it was a mystifying thing. Moses and Joshua hurried downward.

When they finally came into full view of the great city of tents which Israel called its home, the two men were better able to appreciate what was actually happening.

A great multitude of the Israelites were right in the midst of celebrating the degenerate and abominable rites of the ancient heathen cult of fertility worship. It was the excuse which heathen nations used for a season of wild, drunken, immoral debauchery. Such practices were often built around the worship of a young bullock.[11] It was the custom in Egypt and wherever fertility rites of this type were practiced, to have the people dance naked before the idol. They would provoke themselves into a frenzy of tempestuous emotion and then abandon every vestige of decency and morality as they flung themselves into one continuous indulgence of profligate and degrading dissipation. Therefore, "when Moses saw that the people were naked,"[12] and when Moses "saw the calf and the dancing,"[13] he knew exactly what was taking place. His fury was almost without bounds. Here was a multitude of the Israelites who had aspired to become

---

8. Joshua and Moses spent the first six days out of the 40 waiting for God to tell them what to do (Exodus 24:16-18). Moses was then ordered to come to the summit which left Joshua alone 34 days.
9. Exodus 32:17
10. Exodus 32:18
11. See Peloubet's *Bible Dictionary* under "Aaron"
12. Exodus 32:25
13. Exodus 32:19

man that brought us up out of the land of Egypt, we wot not what is become of him."[20] They had demanded that Aaron make them a golden calf or bullock so that they might have festivities and pass the time away more pleasantly. Aaron admitted that he had tried to pacify them by melting down their gold ornaments and then fashioning it into the image of a calf.[21] Aaron even did the tooling and engraving of the idol.[22]

In fairness to Aaron it should be noted that he did try to divert the people from their tumultuous "mischief" by ordering a "feast to the Lord."[23] However, having made a golden calf to tempt them, the feast was no diversion at all. That very morning the people started out with "burnt offerings" and "peace offerings" to the Lord.[24] However, just as soon as they were through with these formalities they then "sat down to eat and drink" and the next thing Aaron knew they "rose up to play."[25]

As we have already seen, this frolic or "play" was no innocent display of youthful exuberance, but an evil and calculated conspiracy to involve the weaker moral characters of the camp in an obscene Egyptian esoteric orgy. The record blames Aaron for allowing them to become naked and thereby disgrace themselves and become an object of ridicule before their enemies who were no doubt spying in the vicinity.[26]

For all of this the Lord was so angry with Aaron that He was ready to destroy him. Moses later risked his own salvation in an effort to save his stumbling brother as well as the weak, corrupted Israelites.[27]

Moses Invokes "Direct Action" Against Israel

Taking up a position at the gate of the camp, Moses now challenged the whole multitude of Israel. He cried out, "Who is on the Lord's side? Let him come unto me."[28]

Not all of the people had participated in these licentious heathen rites, but even those who had stood on the sidelines seemed to feel deeply guilty for having permitted this evil to

---

20. Exodus 32:23   23. Exodus 32:5   26. Exodus 32:25
21. Exodus 32:24   24. Exodus 32:6   27. Exodus 32:32
22. Exodus 32:4   25. Ibid.   28. Exodus 32:26

occur. Therefore they held back when Moses called the men of the camps to come unto him. Of all the hundreds of thousands from the various tribes who heard the message, only the men from the tribe of Levi responded. For this act of courage they would later receive a great reward.

But Moses wanted more than mere lip service from these sons of Levi. He ordered them to take their swords and go down among the revelers and slay every person who was guilty of participating in the sensual corruption of these heathen rites. Moses said it was the commandment of God that they were to spare none, even if the guilty person turned out to be a brother, a companion, or a neighbor. All who were guilty must die.[29]

The terrible consequences of all this mixed up maze of heathen immorality is described in this single, tragic passage:

"And the children of Levi did according to the words of Moses: and there fell of the people that day, about three thousand men."[30]

Moses Once More Ascends Mount Sinai to Plead with the Lord

All of the events we have just described appear to have occupied one full day. "On the morrow," the Bible says, Moses told the people he was going back up into the Mount to seek out the Lord and plead for mercy on behalf of Israel.[31] Moses had no illusion about the responsibility he was undertaking. This people had sinned against light and knowledge.

They had rebelled against the Almighty when He had showered upon them more manifestations of miraculous power than any generation since the days of Enoch. They had been saved by divine intervention from slavery in Egypt, from drowning in the Red Sea, from conquest by the Midianites, from starvation in the wilderness, and from dying of thirst in the desert. They had been allowed to hear the voice of God. They had been given a pillar of cloud to guide

---

29. Exodus 32:27   31. Exodus 32:30
30. Exodus 32:28

them by day and a pillar of fire to guide them by night. This wicked and rebellious people were so corrupted by their selfish, ungrateful conduct that Moses was risking his own salvation by even asking God to allow them to continue as His servants.

Knowing all of this, Moses decided to throw the weight of his own good offices on the scales and try to save these apostate Israelites one more time. On this occasion Moses actually bargained with his own soul. As he came into the presence of the Lord on the summit of Sinai, he cried out:

"Oh, this people have sinned a great sin, and have made them gods of gold; yet now, if thou wilt, forgive their sin; and IF NOT, BLOT ME, I PRAY THEE, OUT OF THY BOOK, WHICH THOU HAST WRITTEN."[32]

Moses was talking about the sacred Book of Life later referred to by John the Beloved when he saw a vision of God's great last judgment.[33] A modern revelation describes it as the "book of the names of the sanctified, even them of the celestial world."[34]

But the Lord brushed aside this monumental offer of Moses. The Lord does not allow one man to bargain with his soul for the sins of another. The Lord declared, "Whosoever hath sinned against me, HIM will I blot out of my book."[35]

Then the Lord declared that Moses should get on with the business of preparing to go up to Canaan where God would yet allow this people to possess the land. However, the Lord said the children of Israel would no longer have the glory of His presence to guide them, for they were so weak and rebellious that if He were to be among them in person it would be a temptation to "consume them in the way."[36] Nevertheless, the Lord said He would not leave them without guidance. "I will send an angel before thee."[37]

So Moses hastened down to the people and told them what had happened. He told them they would still receive the promised land "flowing with milk and honey," but that

---

32. Exodus 32:31-32
33. Revelations 20:12
34. Doctrine and Covenants 88:2

35. Exodus 32:34
36. Exodus 33:3
37. Exodus 33:2

from here on God's personal guidance would not be available. They would have to be satisfied with ministering angels.[38]

"And when the people heard these evil tidings, they mourned: and no man did put on him his ornaments."[39]

MOSES ERECTS A TEMPORARY TABERNACLE

To further propitiate the Lord, Moses hastily erected a temporary tabernacle of worship outside the camp.[40] When Moses and Joshua entered the tabernacle the people were relieved to see the Lord's miraculous "cloudy pillar" descend to the door of the tabernacle. The people knew Moses was at that very moment communicating directly with the Lord and pleading their cause, therefore, "all the people rose up and worshipped, every man in his tent door."[41]

However, Moses was so discouraged at this point that the Lord's "cloudy pillar" was not enough to restore his hope for the apostate Israelites. Therefore he asked for an assurance from God that He would not forsake Israel and leave them wandering helpless and alone in the wilderness. He pleaded with the Lord, saying, "Now therefore, I pray thee, if I have found grace in thy sight, shew me now thy way, that I may know thee, that I may find grace in thy sight: and consider that this nation is thy people."[42]

God's mercy and capacity to forgive are among the most prominent qualities of His personality. He is quickly moved with any sincere manifestation of true humility. As He beheld this 80-year-old Moses kneeling in humble supplication, He reversed His former proclamation to the effect that He would not personally go with Israel into Canaan. Unexpectedly He said, "My presence SHALL go with thee, and I will give thee rest."[43]

But Moses was not prepared for such a sudden change on the part of the Lord. He feared something else might happen to again lose the Lord's favor. Consequently, he said, "If thy presence go not with me, carry us not up hence [into the promised land]."[44] Moses knew the only way they

---

38. Exodus 33:2-3
39. Exodus 33:4
40. Exodus 33:7
41. Exodus 33:8-10

42. Exodus 33:13
43. Exodus 33:14
44. Exodus 33:15

could successfully take over the promised land would be by the power of God's presence going before them. The Lord again assured Moses that He would indeed accompany Israel on its pilgrimage to Canaan. Still Moses felt insecure. As a final proof that the Lord was not just being pleasant but really did intend to stand by them through all adversity, Moses attempted to test the relationship between himself and the Lord by saying: "I beseech thee, shew me thy glory."[45]

In reply, the Lord revealed that there were still some strong vestiges of wrath left in Him from the provocation of the day before. The Lord replied, "Thou canst not see my face at this time, lest mine anger is kindled against thee also, and I destroy thee, and thy people; for there shall no man among them see me at this time, and live, for they are exceeding sinful. And no sinful man hath at any time, neither shall there be any sinful man at any time, that shall see my face and live."[46] But the Lord comforted Moses by telling him that there was a place in the Mount where Moses could go and "stand upon a rock," and there he would see God's glory pass before him. Nevertheless, the Lord said, "I will . . . cover thee with my hand while I pass by. And I will take away mine hand, and thou shalt see my back parts, but my face shall not be seen, as at other times; for I am angry with my people Israel."[47]

The English version of this passage is emasculated and has greatly puzzled scholars. In the restored version, which we have just quoted, it is perfectly clear. As we have previously pointed out, God lives in an environment of science and law, just as we do. He conducts Himself accordingly. The power emanating from the face of the Lord during this period of great emotional distress had a very real and dangerous effect on any being of a lower dimension who might come into His presence. Therefore, He wanted Moses to understand that in the Lord's present disturbed condition, the radiating wrath of His countenance would destroy any man, even Moses. Hence the warning.

---

45. Exodus 33:18
46. Inspired Version, Exodus 33:20
47. Inspired Version, Exodus 33:23

THE SECOND SET OF TABLETS

Now the Lord started Moses out all over again. He told him to go once more and "Hew thee two tables of stone like unto the first. . . ."[48] But for the rest of this passage we turn to the Inspired Version because the English Version is incomplete. In fact, the English Version says the very opposite of what Moses originally wrote. Apparently some ancient scribe wanted the oncoming generations to believe that the second set of tablets was as great as the first, so he altered the text. Actually, the second set of stone tablets lacked some of the most precious items from the first set. The Lord said this was intentional. Here is the full text:

"And the Lord said unto Moses, Hew thee two other tables of stone, like unto the first, and I will write upon them also, the words of the law, according as they were written at the first on the tablets which thou brakest; BUT IT SHALL NOT BE ACCORDING TO THE FIRST, FOR I WILL TAKE AWAY THE PRIESTHOOD OUT OF THEIR MIDST: THEREFORE MY HOLY ORDER, AND THE ORDINANCES THEREOF, SHALL NOT GO BEFORE THEM: FOR MY PRESENCE SHALL NOT GO UP IN THEIR MIDST, LEST I DESTROY THEM."[49]

So the second set of plates did not have "my holy order, and the ordinances thereof" which prepare men and women to come into the presence of God in the Holy of Holies. The Lord was not going to "dwell" with Israel as He had with the people of Enoch. Israel had lost the privilege.

Nowhere in the scripture is Moses condemned for breaking the first set of stone tablets. The Lord was so angry Himself that He seems to have fully appreciated why Moses had broken the first tablets after seeing what the Israelites had done. However, in connection with the second set of tablets, the Lord made it clear that He did not want them broken. He commanded Moses to protect them as a permanent testimony of God's covenant with Israel by placing them in the Ark.[50]

---

48. Exodus 34:1
49. Inspired Version, Exodus 34:1

50. Deuteronomy 10:5

Now the Lord told Moses to come up into the Mount for a second session of instruction and revelation. Said the Lord, "And be ready in the morning, and come up in the morning unto Mount Sinai, and present thyself there to me in the top of the mount. And no man shall come up with thee, neither let any man be seen throughout all the mount; neither let the flocks nor herds feed before that mount."[51]

So Moses "hewed two tables of stone like unto the first, and Moses rose up early in the morning, and went up unto Mount Sinai, as the Lord had commanded him, and took in his hand the two tables of stone."[52]

MOSES BEGINS A SECOND PERIOD OF 40 DAYS AND NIGHTS ON MOUNT SINAI

Now commenced a second period of 40 days and 40 nights in which "he did neither eat bread, nor drink water."[53] After what appears to have been a respite of only two or three days, Moses went from one 40-day fast into another one, thereby making a total of 80 days of fasting with only a brief interval between.

In a previous account Moses described what it was like to move across the veil into the dimension of the spirit. He said "I could not look upon God, except his glory should come upon me, and I were strengthened before him."[54] It is obvious that this quickening process permits the body to remain in suspended animation without the debilitating effects which usually accompany long periods of fasting. In fact, the absence of water alone can destroy life in a matter of ten days.

A friend of the author, John Noble, spent 9½ years in a Russian slave camp, and on one occasion his guards tried to starve him to death. In his well-known book, *I Found God in Soviet Russia,* John Noble describes the rapid deterioration of brain and body under compulsory fasting over a period of a few days:

"Each day my strength diminished. After an entire week without a morsel of food to eat, I found myself too

---

51. Exodus 34:2-3
52. Exodus 34:4

53. Exodus 34:28
54. Moses 1:14

weak to walk. . . . By this time my weakness was so great that I could no longer sleep at night. I did not feel any pain but felt dizzy and giddy, as if I were intoxicated. It was difficult to keep my thoughts collected. At times, I became delirious . . .

"On the ninth day of the fast, both my bodily strength and my mental processes had sunk to such a level that, in one of the few lucid moments I had in my delirium, I realized death could not be far away. . . .

"The starvation regime continued four or five days longer. During the time, more and more prisoners died, until over half our number had gone. The rest were at death's door . . .

"The period of systematic starvation did finally come to an end after twelve hideous days. On Tuesday morning, August 14, without explanation, the 'liquid diet' order [consisting of a daily cup of warm water which the guards called 'coffee'] was suddenly lifted and we received bread with our coffee. It was not a full slice but some stale crumbs on a piece of paper, amounting in all to perhaps two ounces. However, it was our first nourishment of any kind and when I received these crumbs in my hand, I must have sat transfixed for at least a quarter of an hour, trying to comprehend that it was real and that the Lord had seen fit to save my life. Tears ran from my eyes and I offered a prayer of gratitude to God. Then I ate each crumb slowly, as though I were partaking of the communion wafer."[55]

These few paragraphs help us to better appreciate the significance of a fast lasting 80 days with only two or three days respite after the first half of the fast. Unless Moses had been quickened by the Lord and "strengthened before him" such a fast would have been impossible.

Moses Converses with the Lord

When Moses had ascended the summit of Mount Sinai, the Lord had Moses stand in the "cleft of a rock" as he had previously promised, and the eyes of Moses were covered

---

55. John Noble, *I Found God in Soviet Russia*, pp. 41-47.

until the personage of the Lord had passed by, then he was able to look upon Him from the back without seeing His face.[56] The scripture says, "And Moses made haste, and bowed his head toward the earth, and worshipped."[57]

The Lord then told Moses that He is a forgiving and long-suffering Being, but He nevertheless cannot ignore the wicked acts of the guilty when they do not reform or repent.[58]

Moses responded by pleading with the Lord to forgive Israel. Moses said, "If now I have found grace in thy sight, O Lord, let my Lord, I pray thee, go among us; for it is a stiff-necked people; and pardon our iniquity and our sin, and take us for thine inheritance."[59]

Finally, the Lord agreed to make a new covenant with Israel and bless them in securing the "land of milk and honey." However, He warned Moses that the Lord was going to use the rebellious Israelites to execute judgment on a vile and degenerate people who were corrupting themselves, their children, and all who came in contact with them. Later, He would disclose to Moses that it was not because of Israel's righteousness that they would capture the promised land but only because of the totally vicious, violent lives of their enemies that they would be allowed to conquer them.[60]

The harsh reality of the terrible destruction which would accompany the cleansing of the promised land, now received the Lord's attention. He said to Moses, ". . . it is a terrible thing that I will do with thee. Observe thou that which I command thee this day; behold, I drive out before thee the Amorite, and the Canaanite, and the Hittite, and the Perizzite and the Hivite, and the Jebusite. Take heed to thyself lest thou make a covenant with the inhabitants of the land whither thou goest, lest it be for a snare in the midst of thee. But ye shall destroy their altars, break their images, and cut down their groves: for thou shalt worship no other god: for the Lord, whose name is Jealous, is a jealous God: Lest thou make a covenant with the inhabitants of the land, and they go a whoring after their gods, and do sacrifice unto their

56. Exodus 33:21-33
57. Exodus 34:8
58. Exodus 34:6-7

59. Exodus 34:9
60. Deuteronomy 9:5

gods, and one call thee, and thou eat of his sacrifice; And thou take of their daughters unto thy sons, and their daughters go a whoring after their gods, and make thy sons go a whoring after their gods."[61]

As it turned out, this was exactly what eventually happened. By failing to completely cleanse the land as the Lord here commanded, Israel became ensnared by the corruption of the heathens. The student of the Old Testament should realize that Israel was not like the obedient people of Enoch or Melchizedek. They were more like the Jaredites. Never at any time did the Israelites rise to their full potential as a people of God. Nevertheless, the Lord did everything in His power to undergird them so as to prevent, or at least postpone, their tendency to collapse.

At this point it is easier to see why Israel's fatal folly in consorting with the heathen cult rites at Sinai brought down the whirlwind of God's wrath upon them.

Moses Receives the Law of Carnal Commandments

During this period of 40 days and 40 nights the Lord instructed Moses in the new order. As the Lord declared, "I will give unto them the law as at the first, but it shall be after the law of carnal commandment for I have sworn in my wrath, that they shall not enter into my presence, into my rest, in the days of their pilgrimage."[62]

As we examine the law in Leviticus, Numbers and Deuteronomy and compare it with Exodus, we note two basic differences: *First*, the original statement of the law is rather simple. It is then expanded into a far more complex, detailed code. It is as though God were dealing with little children who needed every tiny minutia spelled out in the most finite detail.

Second, the Lord added the dietary laws, a health code, and a singular array of ordinances, rules, regulations and new requirements. It appears as though the Lord intended to keep the Israelites so completely involved in "busyness" that they would not have time for wickedness. It was

---

61. Exodus 34:10-16   62. Inspired Version, Exodus 34:2

preventive medicine, a "schoolmaster," as Paul calls it, to keep them from exploding to the four winds until after they had brought forth the Christ.[63]

Paul had a particularly keen insight into the purpose of the "law of carnal commandments." The word, *carnal* means worldly, materialistic, and pertaining to things of the flesh. Paul says that because the Israelites would not elevate their loyalty to a pattern for happy living based on spiritual laws, (i.e., the Gospel), the law of carnal commandments "was added because of transgressions, till the seed should come to whom the promise was made. . . ."[64] Paul identifies "thy seed as Christ."[65] He says the carnal commandments added to the original simple Gospel a whole volume of statutes dealing with "meats and drinks, and divers washings, and carnal ordinances, imposed on them until the time of reformation."[66]

As we have pointed out previously, these "additions" must not be confused with the basic principles of good government which have always been part of the Gospel. In the next chapter we shall cover the entire system of laws under which Israel lived, and distinguish the basic Gospel principles from the carnal commandments which were added.

Moses Comes Down Among the People While Partially Transfigured

At last Moses was ready to go back down to the people. Once again he had a set of stone tablets on which the covenant of God had been inscribed with His own finger. Of course, it was a lesser law, a schoolmaster, but it was a tangible witness that God had not rejected Israel completely and was willing to struggle along with them in spite of their weaknesses. Nevertheless, Moses knew the Israelites were paying a terrible penalty for their wickedness and rebellion. This was a heartbreak he would have to live with the rest of his life.

---

63. Galatians 3:24
64. Galatians 3:19

65. Ibid. 3:16
66. Hebrews 9:10

Moses also knew the people would be anxiously awaiting him, but he was astonished as he came down among them to find them fleeing from him rather than welcoming him. The scripture says:

"And it came to pass, when Moses came down from Mount Sinai with the two tables of testimony in Moses' hand . . . that Moses wist not that the skin of his face shone while he [the Lord] talked with him. And when Aaron and all the children of Israel saw Moses, behold, the skin of his face shone; and they were afraid to come nigh him. And Moses called unto them . . ."[67]

Apparently Aaron and the leaders of the people were able to get the message to Moses that they did not dare approach him because of the luminous glory which still emanated from his face. As soon as Moses realized they were afraid of him he obtained a veil and placed it over his face. ". . . and Aaron and all the rulers of the congregation returned unto him: and Moses talked with them. And afterward ALL the children of Israel came nigh: and he gave them in commandment all that the Lord hath spoken with him in mount Sinai. And till Moses had done speaking with them, he put a vail [Bible spelling] on his face."[68]

As soon as he had communicated this message, Moses apparently went into the temporary tabernacle to report to the Lord. "But when Moses went in before the Lord to speak with him, he took the vail off, until he came out. And he came out and spake unto the children of Israel that which he was commanded. And the children of Israel saw the face of Moses that the skin of Moses' face shone: and Moses put the vail upon his face again until he went in to speak with him."[69]

It must have given the Israelites an uncanny feeling as they stood solemnly listening to their great prophet who was compelled to talk to them from behind a veil because they were afraid to look upon the glory of his countenance. Apparently it was some time before the visible influence of the transfiguration finally disappeared.

---

67. Exodus 34:29-31   69. Exodus 34:34-35
68. Exodus 34:31-33

MATERIALS GATHERED FOR THE BUILDING OF
THE TABERNACLE

Because of their disastrous experience in allowing their weaker members to worship the golden calf, the Israelites were truly humble for a season. They even seemed anxious to have the Lord command them to do something just so they could exhibit their willingness to obey. Such a commandment now came to them. They were told to build a beautiful portable temple to be called the "Tabernacle of the Congregation."[70]

As we have previously seen, the architectural specifications of this structure had been given to Moses in the most comprehensive detail while he was in the Mount. Apparently Moses had even seen a vision of the completed structure so the Lord now told him to construct it with all its appointments just as he had seen these things. Said the Lord: "And look that thou make them after their pattern which was showed thee in the mount."[71] It was to be similar in all of its basic features to the permanent temple which the Lord would later command His servants to build in Jerusalem.[72]

However, the Lord did not want the newly repentant Israelites to build the Tabernacle under any sense of compulsion. He gave the most strict commandment to Moses that nothing should go into the Tabernacle except that which was given as a free will offering. The Lord said, "Speak unto the children of Israel, that they bring me an offering: of every man that giveth it willingly with his heart ye shall take my offering."[73] This was to be the procedure no matter what was needed, whether it was gold, silver, onyx, fine linen, dyed skins, expensive and rare woods, spices, anointing oil, incense, or any other contribution. Nothing was to be taken from the people by force for this structure.

Moses called all the people together and itemized the articles which were needed. Many of them, particularly the precious metals, jewels, and fine linen were brought from

---

70. Exodus 31:7
71. Exodus 25:40
72. See Clarke, *Bible Commentary, Volume* 1, p. 628
73. Exodus 25:2; Exodus 35:5

Egypt by the Israelites.[74] But other things they would have to manufacture themselves.

The response of the people to this challenge was amazing. The scripture says, "And they came, every one whose heart stirred him up, and every one whom his spirit made willing, and they brought the Lord's offering to the work of the tabernacle of the congregation, and for all his service, and for the holy garments. And they . . . brought bracelets, and earrings and rings, and tablets, all jewels of gold . . . [and fine spun cloth of] blue, and purple, and scarlet, and fine linen, and goats' hair, and red [dyed] skins of rams, and badgers' skins . . . and spice, and oil for the light and for the anointing oil, and for the sweet incense."[75]

The next thing Moses knew the people had piled up such treasures of cloth, jewels and precious metal that it was far in excess of what was needed. He therefore had the satisfaction of sending out the word that contributions could now cease and the Tabernacle would be speedily built.[76]

THE TABERNACLE IS BUILT IN SIX MONTHS

By direct revelation the Lord had selected the two master builders to be responsible for the actual mechanics of building the Tabernacle. One of these was Bezaleel of the tribe of Judah,[77] and the other was Aholiab of the tribe of Dan.[78]

These two craftsmen were men of remarkable skills so that between them they could construct, manufacture and artistically create practically every device for the building and embellishment of a holy structure such as the Tabernacle. It is obvious that they could not have learned these skills during their year of flight in the wilderness so undoubtedly these two men were artisans of renown who had been trained in the luxurious and intricate arts which were so highly developed in Egypt.

The scripture says these two men were filled with the Spirit of God and had great wisdom in all manner of workmanship "to devise curious works, to work in gold, and in

---

74. Exodus 11:2-3
75. Exodus 35:21-28
76. Exodus 36:5-7

77. Exodus 35:30
78. Exodus 35:34

silver, and in brass, and in the cutting of stones, to set them, and in carving of wood . . . of the engraver, and of the cunning workman, and of the embroiderer, in blue, and in purple, in scarlet, and in fine linen, and of the weaver, even of them that do any work, and of those that devise cunning work."[79]

Moses found others with special skills who could help in this great project. The scripture says, "Then wrought Bezaleel and Aholiab, and every wise hearted man, in whom the Lord put wisdom and understanding to know how to work all manner of work for the service of the sanctuary, according to all that the Lord had commanded."[80]

It apparently took around six months of extremely arduous effort to complete the Tabernacle.[81] When all of the materials were finished and ready, Moses personally managed the actual erection of the sacred structure.

The Israelites had been gone from Egypt just 15 days short of one year.[82] The scripture says that it was New Year's Day when the Tabernacle was completed and raised up.[83]

"And Moses reared up the tabernacle, and fastened his sockets, and set up the boards thereof, and put in the bars thereof, and reared up his pillars."[84] Then he covered the walls and ceiling of this framework with the beautiful linen curtains which had been dyed blue, purple, and scarlet and embroidered with cherubim.[85] Above these came the covering of goats' hair, then the covering of rams' skins dyed red, and finally the protective covering of badgers' skins or seal skins.[86]

Inside the Tabernacle he divided the Holy Place from the Holy of Holies by hanging the "veil of the temple."[87] A veil was also hung over the doorway to the Tabernacle[88]

---

79. Exodus 35:32-35
80. Exodus 36:1
81. See Clarke, *Bible Commentary*, Volume 1, p .490
82. They had left on the fifteenth day of the first month (Exodus 13:4 plus Numbers 33:3 which fixes the day of the month).
83. Exodus 40:17
84. Exodus 40:18
85. Exodus 26:7-13
86. Exodus 26:1-14
87. Exodus 26:31 II Chronicles 3:14; Matthew 27:51
88. Exodus 40:28

so the sacred veil which covered the Holy of Holies is sometimes called the *second* veil.[89] Once the Holy of Holies was cloistered, Moses took the beautiful gold-plated Ark of the Covenant, placed the sacred tablets of the law within it, and then placed the Ark in the Holy of Holies. The lid of the Ark or the Mercy Seat with its elaborately carved cherubim spreading their wings above it, was also put into place.[90]

On the other side of the veil, in the Holy Place, Moses arranged the furnishings exactly as the Lord commanded. In front of the veil he placed the golden altar of incense.[91] To the right of it (on the north side) he placed the golden table of shew bread.[92] On the left (the south side) he placed the golden candlestick with its seven tapers.[93] Since the Tabernacle had no windows, Moses immediately lighted the golden candlesticks[94] and then hung the veil over the doorway through which the only light had been coming.[95]

Outside the Tabernacle he set up the "altar of burnt offering"[96] which was a huge hollow box of the finest wood, which measured 7½ feet square and 5 feet high. This appears to have been partially filled with earth and then a fire lighted beneath a grate which burned perpetually. There the sacrifices or burnt offerings were made.[97]

Then, the scripture says, Moses "set the laver between the tent [tabernacle] of the congregation and the altar, and put water there, to wash withal. And Moses, and Aaron, and his sons, washed their hands and their feet thereat: when they went into the tent of the congregation, and when they came near unto the altar, they washed, as the Lord commanded Moses."[98]

Last of all, Moses erected the protective curtain or wall which surrounded all of the items described above and formed the "court of the congregation." This wall formed a "court round about the tabernacle and the altar. . . ."[99] It consisted of a rectangular wall of linen curtains five cubits high (7½

---

89. Hebrews 9:3
90. Exodus 40:20
91. Exodus 40:26-27
92. Exodus 40:22
93. Exodus 40:24
94. Exodus 40:25

95. Exodus 40:28
96. Exodus 40:29
97. Exodus 27:1-8
98. Exodus 40:30-32
99. Exodus 40:33

feet) which were strung on bronze poles and extended around an enclosure measuring 100 cubits by 50 cubits (150 feet by 75 feet.)[100]

This was the final touch and the scripture says, "So Moses finished the work."[101]

It was a great achievement, and the magnificent burst of energy and sacrifice which had made it possible, received the full approbation of the Lord. Immediately after Moses had completed this work on New Year's Day "a cloud covered the tent [tabernacle] of the congregation, and the glory of the Lord filled the tabernacle. And Moses was not able to enter into the tent of the congregation, because the cloud abode thereon; and the glory of the Lord filled the tabernacle."[102]

Thus we come to the conclusion of that monumental historical record called the Book of Exodus. It begins with the birth of Moses and ends with the building of the Tabernacle. In between were 81 years of triumph and tragedy highlighted by a spectacular display of God's miraculous power which have been a source of amazement and wonderment during all of the 3,500 years since.

---

100. Exodus 27:18
101. Exodus 40:33
102. Exodus 40:34-35

Scripture Reading and Questions On Chapter Fifteen

Scripture Reading Assignment: Exodus, chapters 30 to 40 inclusive.

1—What did the Lord propose to do when the Israelites started worshipping the golden calf? Did Moses agree?

2—Did Moses come down from the mount alone? Who was with him? Did he know about Israel's apostasy?

3—What was it about idolatry that made it such an abomination before the Lord? Were the Israelites guilty of this?

4—What did Moses do with the stone tablets? What did he do with the golden calf?

5—When Moses asked who was on the Lord's side, which of the tribes responded? What did Moses require them to do? How many were slain?

6—In asking the Lord to forgive the Israelites, how much of a risk did Moses take? For whose sake did the Lord agree to give the rest of the Israelites another chance?

7—When Moses asked to see the Lord again "face to face" what was the Lord's reason for refusing him? What was done instead?

8—Was the second set of stone tablets the same as the first? What was the difference?

9—What frightened the people when Moses descended from the mount with the new set of tablets in his hand? What did he do so they would not be frightened?

10—Did Moses tax the Israelites in order to get the expensive materials for the Tabernacle? What did he do? What was the response?

11—How long did it take to build the Tabernacle? Was Moses the actual builder or did the Lord appoint someone else?

12—What was in the Holy of Holies? What three items were in the Holy Place?

13—As a person entered the Court of the Congregation did he first come to the altar of sacrifice or the laver for washing?

14—How long had the Israelites been gone from Egypt when the Tabernacle was completed?

15—On what day was the Tabernacle erected the first time? Who did it?

16—Did the Tabernacle have any windows? How was light provided?

17—Was the Tabernacle a large structure? What were its approximate measurements?

18—What was the approximate size of the Court of the Congregation?

19—What happened immediately after Moses had erected the Tabernacle?

20—How old was Moses by this time? Does his age appear to have affected his strength or vigor?

CHAPTER SIXTEEN

The Impact of the Carnal Commandments on Israel

As soon as the Tabernacle was erected the children of Israel had their first taste of the law of carnal commandments. It began with the anointing and consecrating of Aaron and his sons to the service of the Tabernacle. This ceremony occupied seven days and was followed by a convocation of the people in a general conference on the eighth day. In connection with this general conference the people were introduced to the elaborate ceremonies and offerings which had been "added" to the basic Gospel law.

The entire book of Leviticus is devoted to the events of these eight days and the recitation of the new law of carnal commandments. There is also an extensive recitation of the Law of the Covenant (erroneously called the Law of Moses) to which the carnal commandments had been added. In this chapter we shall try to get better acquainted with all of these.

THE ANOINTING OF AARON AND HIS SONS

Moses personally supervised the anointing and consecrating of Aaron and his sons. All the congregation was called together to witness these important events.

First, there were the washings,[1] then Moses took Aaron and dressed him in his robes as the High Priest. This consisted of six vestments. He first put on the embroidered coat which was like a frock that covered the upper part of the body.[2] Then came the blue robe which was a solid piece of blue linen with a hole in the middle which slipped over the head. At the hem of this robe were embroidered blue, purple and scarlet pomegranates and in between each one was a golden bell which tinkled softly as Aaron performed

---

1. Leviticus 8:6   2. Exodus 28:4, 39

the various rites.[3] Over the robe was worn the ephod which was a multi-colored waistcoat with onyx stones on the shoulders from which hung woven gold chains to fasten to the breastplate.[4] A multi-colored girdle which matched the ephod was worn around the waist.[5] The breastplate was a colorful linen container about nine inches square.[6] On it were twelve stones which represented each one of the twelve tribes. Inside the pocket of the breastplate, Moses placed the famous transparent stones, the Urim and Thummim, which were used for revelation,[7] for the ascertaining of God's judgment in difficult cases,[8] and for the interpreting of ancient records.[9] Last of all, Moses placed upon Aaron's head the mitre or head covering which bore a shield declaring "Holiness to the Lord."[10]

Following this, Moses took the holy oil of consecration and anointed each sacred item that the Lord had designated as a part of the worship service — the Tabernacle and all of its fixtures within, then the laver and altar without.[11] Next, he anointed Aaron's head and sanctified him to the service of God.[12]

When this was completed, Moses took Aaron's four sons and dressed them in embroidered linen coats, linen breeches and bonnets.[13]

At this point the children of Israel saw for the first time a series of complicated rituals in the form of special animal sacrifices which were part of the carnal commandments. Each sacrifice was executed in the most exacting manner and required the greatest physical exertion on the part of Moses, Aaron, Nadab, Abihu, Eleazar and Ithamar.

The first ritual was called a Sin Offering. This consisted of slaying a young bullock, skinning it, burning certain parts

3. Exodus 28:33-35; 39:22-26
4. Exodus 28:6-14
5. Exodus 28:4,8 39:5
6. Exodus 28:15-30; 39:8-21
7. Numbers 27:21
8. Exodus 28:30
9. Doctrine and Covenants 10:1; Ether 3:23-24
10. Exodus 28:4; 39:27-31
11. Leviticus 8:10-11
12. Leviticus 8:12
13. Leviticus 8:13

on the brazen altar and disposing of the rest of it as the Lord commanded.[14]

The second ritual was a Burnt Offering which consisted of the slaying of a ram and disposing of its carcass by burning it in a prescribed manner.[15]

14. THE SIN OFFERING. This had reference to a specialized type of Burnt Offering made for sins which had been committed in ignorance but subsequently discovered. The Sin Offering was for offenses that could not be undone or repaired. If the offense could be repaired, a Trespass Offering was made which differed slightly in its ritual requirements. The ritual for a Sin Offering varied according to the rank of the offender. If the High Priest found he had committed a sin ignorantly his sacrifice had to be a young bullock (Leviticus 4:3); if the sin was ignorantly committed by the whole congregation then the sacrifice had to be a young bullock (Leviticus 4:14) or a male goat (Numbers 15:24); if a ruler was involved, his sacrifice had to be a male goat (Leviticus 4:23); and if an ordinary person had committed the sin in ignorance his sacrifice could be a she-goat (Leviticus 4:28), a ewe-lamb (Leviticus 4:32), a pigeon (Leviticus 5:7) or a meal offering (Leviticus 5:11). One distinction of the Sin Offering over the regular Burnt Offering was the disposition of the blood. The priest smeared the blood of the victim on the horns of the altar of incense inside the Tabernacle and then poured out the rest at the base of the brazen altar of sacrifice outside. When a high priest or the whole congregation was making a Sin Offering a small portion of blood was carried into the Tabernacle and sprinkled seven times before the veil of the sanctuary (Leviticus 4:5-6, 16-17). On the annual Day of Atonement the distinctive aspect of the Sin Offering was the fact that the priest took some of the blood clear into the Holy of Holies and sprinkled it before the Mercy Seat (Leviticus 16:14). The ritual in sacrificing a Sin Offering was to burn the internal fat and kidneys on the altar of sacrifice and then the carcass was saved and later eaten by the priests (Leviticus 6:26). However, when a Sin Offering was being made for a High Priest, none of it was eaten, it was all burned (Leviticus 4:11-12; 6:30). The scripture suggests the type of offenses for which the Sin Offering would be appropriate; withholding needed testimony (Leviticus 5:1), touching a carcass, or unclean person or thing (Leviticus 5:2-3), making rash oaths (Leviticus 5:4). Provisions were made so that if a poor person needed to make a Sin Offering and could not afford the lamb or goat he was to bring two turtle doves or two young pigeons. One was to be offered as a Sin Offering and the other as a regular Burnt Offering, (Leviticus 5:7). And if he were so poor he could not afford these he was to bring a Meat (meal) Offering consisting of one tenth of an ephah (bushel) of fine flour (Leviticus 5:11).

15. THE BURNT OFFERING: Sometimes called the *Whole* Burnt Offering because the entire animal was consumed (Leviticus 1:9). The sacrificial victim had to be a male without blemish from among cattle, sheep, goats, turtle-doves or pigeons (Leviticus 1:3-17). Procedure: 1—Animal presented at door of Tabernacle and dedicated by the owner laying his hands upon the animal's head (Leviticus 1:4); 2—Animal slain by person offering it (Leviticus 1:5); 3—Blood caught in a bowl by the priest and spread around the altar (Leviticus 1:5); 4—Animal skinned (the priest kept the skin—Leviticus 7:8), and the animal was then divided or opened up. The entrails and legs were washed with water and then the entire carcass was placed on the altar and completely burned. When the Burnt Offering was made by the poor and turtle doves or pigeons were used, the procedure was somewhat different (Leviticus 1:14-17). The Burnt Offering, completely consumed by the fire, represented a complete surrender of the individual to the will and purposes of God. This is the sacrifice inaugurated in the days of Adam (Moses 5:4-8), and which was always a part of the Priesthood ritual. Under the law of Moses there was a Burnt Offering of lamb each morning and each night on behalf of all Israel (Exodus 29:38-42). The morning sacrifice was to burn all day, and the evening sacrifice was to burn all night (Leviticus 6:9). The priests were to see that the fire of the altar was kept burning perpetually (Leviticus 6:13).

This was followed by a Peace Offering[16] which involved the slaying of another ram. Moses dipped his finger into the blood of this ram and touched the right ear, the thumb of the right hand and the large toe of the right foot of Aaron and each of his sons. *Leviticus* calls the ram in this particular Peace Offering "the ram of consecration."[17]

In connection with the above ritual, Moses also made a Wave Offering.[18]

By this time the children of Israel must have begun to feel the tedious burden of the law of carnal commandments. Certainly the student of the Old Testament will have begun to feel its wearisome weight! But there were three other offerings which we shall mention here so that all of the offerings can be treated together in our footnotes. These consisted of the Trespass Offering,[19] the Meat (meal) Offering,[20] and the Drink Offering.[21]

---

16. THE PEACE OFFERING: This was an offering which was shared by the altar of God, the priest, and the family of the person making the offering. It was a feast of concilation, a feast of communion, a feast of thanksgiving. The sacrificial victim could be chosen from among the cattle, the sheep or the goats. As the animal was brought to the door of the Tabernacle, the owner laid his hands upon its head and offered a prayer of thanksgiving. Therefore this offering is sometimes called a "Thank Offering." After the animal was killed at the altar, the kidneys and internal fat (and in the case of Syrian sheep, the fat tail) were burned on the altar. The breast and the right thigh were given to the priest after they had been waved in the direction of the Tabernacle, thereby signifying that it had been given to God and was now conferred upon the servants (Leviticus 7:28-34). The rest of the meat was eaten by the offerer and his family at a so-called "sacrificial" meal, or meal of "Thanksgiving." (Leviticus 7:15-16)

17. Leviticus 8:22

18. THE WAVE OFFERING: Sometimes called the "Heave Offering." This ceremony was performed in connection with a peace offering (Leviticus 8:29), the first fruits of the harvest (Leviticus 23:11-12), and of the two loaves at the Feast of Weeks (Leviticus 23:20). It was also used in connection with the cleansing of a leper (Leviticus 14:12, 24). The "waving" or "heaving" consisted of taking the breast and the right shoulder of a sacrificial animal or the first fruits of the harvest and moving them horizontally in the direction of the sanctuary. It was to signify that these choice parts of the sacrifice were first presented to God and then returned by Him to the officiating priests for their use.

19. THE TRESPASS OFFERING: Often callled the GUILT Offering. This offering was appropriate in those cases where a person discovered that he had sinned or trespassed against the Lord or his neighbor, but was able to remedy or repair the damage (Leviticus 5:16; 6:4-5). The scripture suggests two types of offenses where the Trespass Offering would be appropriate: where a person found that he had held back or consumed something which belonged to the Lord—tithes, firstborn of his flocks, etc. (Leviticus 5:15). The penalty was to not only restore to the sanctuary of the Lord that which had been withheld, but to add one fifth thereto as a penalty (Leviticus 5:16). The Trespass Offering consisted of the sacrificing of a ram (Leviticus 5:16) or sometimes a

From here on the priests of Israel would be required to make a burnt offering, a meat (meal) offering and a drink offering every morning and every night.[22] Members of the congregation would also be required to make various offerings for almost every type of offense imaginable. There was no doubt about it, the law of carnal commandments was going to be a strict schoolmaster.

THE BURDEN OF ISRAEL BECOMES GOD'S GREAT SORROW

But way out and beyond all of this complex and tedious business of continuous sacrifices and offerings there was the muffled sound of heaven weeping. In the days of the patriarchs, animal sacrifices had been very simple. They were made with only one purpose in mind and that was to point toward the great sacrifice of the Son of God in the meridian of time.[23] Now, however, the carnal commandments made these sacrifices a rigid teaching device, an attention-holder, a gargantuan burden of ritualistic mechanics designed to form habits of obedience.

---

male lamb (Numbers 15:24). A second example was where something had been withheld or disallowed to a neighbor by deceit (Leviticus 6:2-3). Here again he had to restore that which had been lost by his neighbor plus one fifth of its value for a penalty. Value had to be estimated in silver shekels, as used in the sanctuary (Leviticus 5:15-16). The Trespass Offering was a ram or a male lamb (Leviticus 6:4-7).

20. THE MEAT OFFERING: More properly called the MEAL Offering because today "meat" implies flesh whereas this offering was of the fruits of the field. This offering took several forms. Usually it consisted of fine flour which could be presented raw (Leviticus 2:1-3), or baked into cakes in an oven (v. 14) and/or in a pan (v. 5). The meal was mixed with oil (v. 4) and salt (v. 13). However, it was not to contain any leaven or honey (v. 11). A "memorial" or portion of the meal was burned on the altar of sacrifice (v. 9), but the remainder of the offering was eaten by the High Priest and those officiating with him . . . (in the beginning, Aaron and his sons—v. 10). Concerning the first-fruits from the field such as grain, it was to be "dried by the fire" and "beaten out of full ears" (v. 14). A "memorial" or small portion of it was then mixed with oil and frankincense and burned on the altar. The remainder (with oil but no frankincense) was presented to the priest (v. 16). The priest was required to make a Meat (Meal) Offering for the whole congregation each morning and each night right along with the Burnt Offering (Exodus 29:41-42). Since this offering was by a priest, it was fully burned and none of it was eaten (Leviticus 6:23).

21. THE DRINK OFFERING: This was often used to express thanksgiving to the Lord. It consisted of "the fourth part of a hin" of wine (Leviticus 23:13) which would be about three pints. This offering was simply a libation which was poured out before the Lord. This offering occurred every morning and every night along with the Burnt Offering and the Meat (Meal) Offering (Exodus 29:39-40).

22. Exodus 29:39-42

23. Moses 5:6-8

It is clear from a number of scriptures that the Lord yearned for the day when His children would grow up spiritually so that all of these ritualistic crutches could be thrown away. Nowhere is this more eloquently portrayed than in the following passage. It might be called, "God's Lamentation:"

"To what purpose is the multitude of your sacrifices unto me? saith the Lord: I am full of the burnt offerings of rams, and the fat of fed beasts; and I delight not in the blood of bullocks, or of lambs, or of he goats . . . Bring no more vain oblations: insense is an abomination unto me; the new moons and sabbaths, the calling of assemblies, I cannot away with [them]; it is iniquity, even the solemn meeting . . . And when ye spread forth your hands, I will hide mine eyes from you: yea, when ye make many prayers, I will not hear: your hands are full of blood."[24]

Then the Lord follows this lamenation with a plea which radiates the spirit of both the Beatitudes and the Sermon on the Mount. Said He, "Wash you, make you clean; put away the evil of your doings from before mine eyes; cease to do evil; learn to do well; seek judgment, relieve the oppressed, judge the fatherless, plead for the widow. Come now and let us reason together, saith the Lord: though your sins be as scarlet, they shall be as white as snow: though they be red like crimson, they shall be as wool. IF YE ARE WILLING AND OBEDIENT YE SHALL EAT THE GOOD OF THE LAND."[25]

All through the Old Testament this message resounds.[26] It is the pathetic plea of a Heavenly Parent who has been betrayed.

Fire from Heaven

The Lord commanded Aaron and his sons to remain within the Tabernacle courtyard for a total of seven days. Each day they were to repeat the various ordinances and sacrifices to impress them firmly in their minds. The penalty

---

24. Isaiah 1:11-15
25. Isaiah 1:16-19
26. Hoseah 6:6; Micah 6:6-8; Amos 5:21

for abandoning their calling during this period of consecration was death.[27]

It is a simple thing for the Lord to transfer a human spirit from earth life to the spirit world. As we shall see shortly, the most narrow and confining aspect of the law of carnal commandments was that it carried the death penalty for many types of serious violations. However, we are also going to discover that this ominous aspect of the law was not nearly so harsh nor unreasonable as it may at first seem. Nevertheless, in the very beginning, the Lord did administer the carnal commandments very strictly and the death penalty was invoked a number of times during the period of wandering in the wilderness.

It was on the morning of the eighth day that Moses was told to convene the congregation once more that they might see the power of God manifest.[28]

The conference began with Aaron sacrificing a young bullock for himself and his sons as a Sin Offering,[29] and then sacrificing a ram for himself and his sons as a Burnt Offering.[30]

The congregation was then called upon to make offerings in their own behalf. They were required to bring Aaron and his sons a young goat for a Sin Offering, then a calf and a lamb for Burnt Offerings. This was followed by a bullock and a ram for a Peace Offering. Last of all came the Meat (meal) Offering.[31]

By the time all of these offerings had been completed, Aaron and his sons must have been exhausted for this ordinance work required strenuous physical exertion. Furthermore, by this time the brazen altar was piled high with the animals and the parts of animals which had been slain as offerings and laid upon it. In the case of Burnt Offerings the whole carcass was placed on the altar, whereas the other offerings involved only the fat and certain parts of the animal. The fire on the altar was not particularly large so this quantity of sacrifices would have been consumed very slowly.

---

27. Leviticus 8:33-36
28. Leviticus 9:5-6
29. Leviticus 9:2
30. Ibid.
31. Leviticus 9:3-4

Nevertheless, the work was done, "And Aaron lifted up his hand toward the people, and blessed them, and came down from offering of the sin offering, and the burnt offering, and peace offerings."[32]

Then Moses and Aaron reported to the Lord in the Tabernacle. When they came out they again blessed the people. And immediately the pillar of cloud over the Tabernacle illuminated so that "the glory of the Lord appeared unto all the people."[33] This was a glorious satisfaction since it meant that God had accepted the anointing and consecrating of Aaron and his sons, and it also meant that the offerings of the people were accepted.

But suddenly something happened which was both frightening and glorious. "And there came a fire out from before the Lord," which struck the altar on which the Burnt Offerings were stacked. The fire consumed the entire offering and caused such a reaction among the people that the scripture says, "they shouted, and fell on their faces."[34]

A Tragedy Strikes the Family of Aaron

Barely had Aaron received the joy of being accepted by the Lord in his new calling before a shaft of tragedy struck his family.

It will be recalled that Aaron's two oldest sons, Nadab and Abihu, had been closely associated with Aaron in his spiritual calling. These two sons had gone into the Mount with Aaron and the 70 elders of Israel to behold the glorious personage of the Lord.[35] They had been selected by direct revelation from among the hundreds of thousands of Israelites to minister with Aaron in the Tabernacle.[36] Together with their two younger brothers, Nadab and Abihu they had been washed, anointed, clothed and consecrated to serve as priests in the great Levitical order. But then something happened.

When Nadab and Abihu undertook to go into the Tabernacle "before the Lord" they experimented with an incense

32. Leviticus 9:22   35. Exodus 24:1, 9-10
33. Leviticus 9:23   36. Exodus 28:1
34. Leviticus 9:24

offering which was different from the one the Lord had prescribed. The scripture describes their offering as "strange
fire" and the consequences of this reckless act would indicate
that they must have imitated some heathen ritual. The Israelites who had danced naked before the golden calf had demonstrated that they were thoroughly familiar with the Egyptian
rites and had no doubt participated in them before. Was
this the explanation for the conduct of Nadab and Abihu?
Had they also been tainted by the influence of the heathen
rites in Egypt?

Based on the record in the Bible their conduct is incomprehensible. Nevertheless, we are assured it did happen;
"And Nadab and Abihu, the sons of Aaron, took either of
them his censer, and put fire therein, and put incense thereon,
and offered strange fire before the Lord, which he commanded them not."[37]

The results were immediate and devastating. "And there
went out fire from the Lord, and devoured them, and they
died before the Lord."[38]

Aaron was so shocked and overwhelmed with grief that
he no doubt would have sent up a cry of protest against
the gates of heaven, but before he could do so, Moses stopped
him short. Moses reminded his older brother that this was
exactly the thing concerning which the Lord had been warning them. The Lord was not going to permit the sacraments
of the Tabernacle to be corrupted or desecrated. This apparently brought Aaron to his senses because the scripture says
"Aaron held his peace."[39]

Moses called Mishael and Elzaphan, second cousins of
Nadab and Abihu, and told them to carry the bodies of the
two dead Levites away from the Lord's altar and dispose
of them outside the camp. "So they went near, and carried
them in their coats out of the camp; as Moses had said."[40]
We learn from this that the fire of the Lord had taken the
lives of Nadab and Abihu but had not destroyed their bodies.

Moses then turned to Aaron and his two remaining
sons, Eleazar and Ithamar, and commanded them not to in-

37. Leviticus 10:1
38. Leviticus 10:2
39. Leviticus 10:3
40. Leviticus 10:5

dulge in the customary mourning by uncovering their heads or rending their clothes. This judgment of God should be accepted for what it was — a well-deserved application of justice. Moses warned these relatives that any further complaint against the Lord might bring death to Aaron and his sons and wrath upon "all the people."[41]

Then the word of the Lord came to Aaron saying, "Do not drink wine nor strong drink, thou, nor thy sons with thee, when ye go into the tabernacle of the congregation, lest ye die."[42] Some authorities have wondered if this problem of "strong drink" did not have something to do with the reckless acts of Nadab and Abihu when they brought "strange fire" before the Lord. It was immediately after their deaths that this commandment was given and the *reason* the Lord gave for the commandment seemed to point to Nadab and Abihu. The Lord said it was essential for the priests to be sober and in possession of their faculties so that "ye may put difference between holy and unholy, and between unclean and clean; and that ye may teach the children of Israel all the statutes which the Lord hath spoken unto them, by the hand of Moses."[43]

As this difficult day wore on, Moses noticed that Aaron and his two remaining sons had not eaten the food which was set aside from the sacrifices as the priests' portion. Moses reprimanded them for not eating this food which had been sanctified to their use, but Aaron said that after "such things have befallen me," he wondered if he were even worthy to eat of these priestly rations.[44] Moses could see that his brother was completely broken in spirit and so "when Moses heard that, he was content."[45]

Moses and Aaron Receive the Dietary Laws

Authorities point out that the greatest single device used by the Lord to keep the Israelites separate from the heathen or gentile nations, was their strict dietary laws.[46]

41. Leviticus 10:6
42. Leviticus 10:9
43. Leviticus 10:10-11
44. Leviticus 10:19
45. Leviticus 10:20
46. See Leviticus Chapter 11 plus Clarke, *Bible Commentary*, Vol. 1, Page 538.

It meant that while these Hebrews might mingle with other nations for business or civic reasons, they would nevertheless tend to refrain from fraternizing or socializing with them at the table or festive board because to the Israelites many of their foods would be *taboo.* Separate diets tend to preserve separate cultures — not completely, of course — but sufficiently to keep them distinct and independent.

These laws also had a second purpose, and that was to keep the people from becoming victims of diseases which are known to be prevalent in certain types of animals, particularly the swine. the hare, and many creatures of the scavenger variety. To this extent, these laws were like an ancient Word of Wisdom.[47] The Lord has always been interested in the physical welfare of His people.

A third purpose for these dietary laws may have been the desire of the Lord to put religious influence behind the domestication of flocks and the building of civilization. Chapter 11 of *Leviticus* which sets forth the dietary laws, clearly demonstrates that the Lord was prohibiting the use of many of the animals, birds and forms of sea life which were the common fare of the wild, nomadic tribes which inhabited this part of the world. The dietary laws would therefore tend to make this wild, bare-subsistence type of life repugnant to them. At the same time — as we pointed out above — these dietary laws would also tend to keep them separate and socially isolated from the heathen or gentile populations which inhabited the towns and cities.

We know that these laws were more or less temporary and of arbitrary nature, since they were declared "fulfilled" and made obsolete as soon as the Messiah had come. Paul makes this clear. He points out that the carnal commandments which were "added because of transgression"[48] included these laws which "stood only in meats and drinks, and divers washings and carnal ordinances, imposed on them until the time of reformation."[49]

---

47. The modern Word of Wisdom is contained in the Doctrine and Covenants, Section 89. It warns against harmful substances and encourages the use of others which will promote good health.
48. Galatians 3:19
49. Hebrews 9:10

With the coming of Christ the law of the Gospel took over again. This law provides that "all things" are to be consumed or rejected in terms of "wisdom" and "good judgment" rather than *taboo*. As the Lord said in modern times:

"The fulness of the earth is yours, the beasts of the field and the fowls of the air, and that which climbeth upon the trees and walketh upon the earth; yea, and the herb, and the good things which come of the earth, whether for food or for raiment, or for houses, or for barns, or for orchards, or for gardens, or for vineyards; yea, all things which come of the earth, in the season thereof, are made for the benefit and the use of man, both to please the eye and to gladden the heart; yea, for food and for raiment, for taste and for smell, to strengthen the body and to enliven the soul. And it pleaseth God that He hath given all these things unto man; for unto this end were they made to be used, with JUDGMENT, not to excess, neither by extortion."[50]

After the restrictions of the dietary laws were lifted for the early Christians, Paul wrote to the Saints, "Let no man therefore judge you in meat, or in drink, or in respect of an holyday, or of the new moon, or of the sabbath days: which are a shadow of things to come. . . ."[51] Nevertheless, Paul declared that in his missionary work he would respect the customs of others if it might otherwise hinder them from joining the Kingdom. In other words, the whole spirit of the new law was to be one of "good judgment."[52]

PURIFICATION AND HEALTH LAWS

The Lord now revealed a series of commandments dealing with purification and health laws. The twelfth chapter of Leviticus deals with the ordinances and procedures following the birth of a child. The child was to be circumcised eight days after birth[53] and then the mother was to remain in an isolated state of purification for 33 days (a different period was designated for girl babies) following which she would take a lamb to the priest for a Burnt Offering, and a young pigeon or turtle-dove for a Sin Offering (for sins

50. Doctrine and Covenants 59:16-20   52. I Corinthians 8:13; Romans 14:15, 21
51. Colossians 2:16-17   53. Leviticus 12:3

committed in ignorance).[54] If she were too poor to afford a lamb, she could bring a dove or young pigeon instead of a lamb for the Burnt Offering.[55] It is significant that when Mary and Joseph fulfilled this requirement following the birth of Jesus, they brought two doves or young pigeons, one of which was used for the Burnt Offering in place of a lamb, and one for the Sin Offering.[56]

In connection with the health laws for Israel, Moses and Aaron were told how to detect infectious diseases such as leprosy and those involving running sores. The procedures for the protection of the community and the ceremonial cleansing of the victim were then set forth.[57]

ISRAEL'S ANNUAL DAY OF ATONEMENT

The tenth day of the seventh month (Tishri) was set aside by the Lord as the annual day of atonement. Modern Jews celebrate this day as "Yom Kippur" which comes each year early in the fall.

There are two significant things connected with the original Day of Atonement. The first was the fact that on this one day alone, Aaron and his successors were allowed to go into the Holy of Holies to perform ordinances in connection with the sacrifices being conducted at the brazen altar in the courtyard. The second significant thing was the oral confession of all the sins of the whole people during the previous year. This confessional was pronounced while Aaron laid his hands on the head of a goat — called the scape goat.[58] The recital of the weaknesses of the people during the previous year was primarily to remind them of their failings since the last general conference. This goat on whose head these sins were laid, was then taken by a "fit man" and carried or driven to a distant land which was "not inhabited."[59] This was to remind the people that their offenses were now carried away and that if they would repent and avoid such errors in the future the Lord would no longer remember them.

---

54. Leviticus Chapter 4; 12:4,6
55. Leviticus 5:7; 12:8
56. Luke 2:24

57. Leviticus Chapters 13, 14, and 15
58. Leviticus 16:21
59. Leviticus 16:21-22

GETTING ACQUAINTED WITH "THE LAW OF MOSES"

We have now reached a point in our account where we need to pause and examine one of the great mysteries of the Old Testament.

There is probably no subject which is more baffling to the beginning student of the Old Testament than the so-called "Law of Moses." The confusion grows out of the fact that the Mosaic Law is really a combination of two systems—the higher law of the Gospel covenant (much of which Israel was commanded to retain even after the golden calf incident), and the law of carnal commandments which was added as a "schoolmaster," to bring them to Christ.[60]

In this discussion we will treat these two systems of law separately. The Law of Carnal Commandments has already been introduced, and we noted that the maze of ordinances, sacrifices and offerings were a most elaborate complex of procedural repetition designed to teach the people the rhythm of obedience. All of these were symbolic and pointed to the coming of Christ. This is why we are told they were fulfilled or made obsolete when the Messiah finally came.

As Jesus stated in the Sermon on the Mount, Matt. 5:17: "Think not that I am come to destroy the law, or the prophets: I am not come to destroy, but to fulfill." And, as Paul points out, it was the Law of Carnal Commandments which were fulfilled in Christ. After the coming of Christ the "schoolmaster" part of the law was taken away.[61]

Concerning the remainder of the law (the law of the Gospel covenant), Jesus specifically stated that it was still in force: "Whosoever therefore shall break one of these least commandments, and shall teach men so, he shall be called the least in the kingdom of heaven: but whosoever shall do and teach them, the same shall be called great in the kingdom of heaven."[62]

In His Sermon on the Mount Jesus stated that the Gospel laws against killing, adultery, etc., were not only to continue, but that He wanted His disciples to push the refinement of

---

60. Galatians 3:19,24
61. Galatians 3:24-26
62. Matthew 5:19

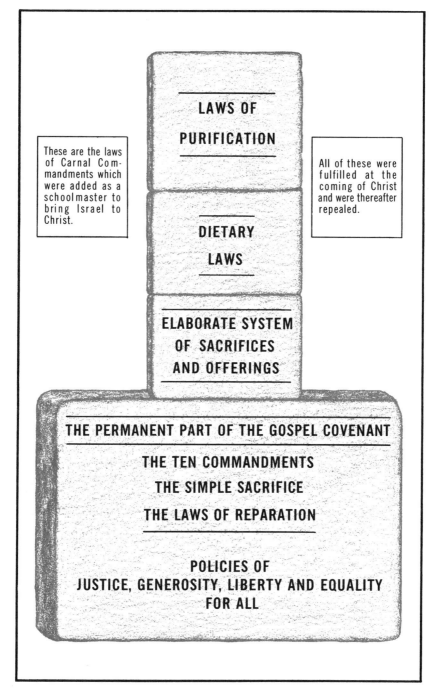

LAWS OF

PURIFICATION

These are the laws of Carnal Commandments which were added as a schoolmaster to bring Israel to Christ.

All of these were fulfilled at the coming of Christ and were thereafter repealed.

DIETARY

LAWS

ELABORATE SYSTEM
OF SACRIFICES
AND OFFERINGS

THE PERMANENT PART OF THE GOSPEL COVENANT

THE TEN COMMANDMENTS

THE SIMPLE SACRIFICE

THE LAWS OF REPARATION

POLICIES OF
JUSTICE, GENEROSITY, LIBERTY AND EQUALITY
FOR ALL

their lives even higher. The basic Law of the Covenant which said "Thou shalt not commit adultery" was to be refined to the point where even lustful thoughts were overcome.[63] The Law of the Covenant which said "Thou shalt not kill" was to be refined to the point where hatred was eliminated and disputes were conciliated.[64] The law of an eye for an eye and a tooth for a tooth which is based on the principle of equity or reparation was to be refined to the point where the Saints would not be looking continually for some cause of offense, but would "turn the other cheek" and go the second mile.[65]

In other words, the Law of the Covenant which existed from the most ancient times is a permanent part of the Gospel, but it is the floor of the Gospel, not the ceiling. Therefore, Jesus wanted His disciples to use it as a minimum performance and then refine their lives to higher dimensions. When the Gospel was restored in modern times, the Ten Command- ments and related principles of the Gospel Covenant were laid down once again.[66] The Lord pointed out that if the Saints could rise above these minimal requirements it would be accounted unto them for righteousness. Said He: ". . . if men will smite you, or your families, once, and ye bear it patiently and revile not against them, neither seek revenge, ye shall be rewarded."[67] Then He pointed out that if there is additional abuse and it can still be absorbed without striking back, it is counted as an even greater achievement.[68] How- ever, even from the first, a person is justified on the basis of equity and justice in protecting himself.[69] He is not con- demned by the Lord for standing up for his rights because this is the Law of the Covenant, i.e., equal justice. So, even while encouraging the Saints to hold back as long as possible, the Lord says, "Nevertheless, thine enemy is in thine hands; and if thou rewardest him according to his works thou art justified; if he has sought thy life, and thy life is endangered by him, thine enemy is in thine hands and thou art justified."[70] This gives us a deeper insight into the effort of the Lord to use the Law of the Covenant as a guide line for justice,

---

63. Matthew 5:27-28
64. Matthew 5:21-24
65. Matthew 5:38-39
66. Doctrine and Covenants Section 42

67. Doctrine and Covenants 98:23
68. Ibid., verses 25-30
69. Ibid., v. 24
70. Ibid., v. 31

but nevertheless maintain an upward pressure to have his disciples rise to the highest possible capacity for tolerance, love and forgiveness.

Just knowing that the Law of the Covenant is a permanent part of the Gospel makes it more interesting to study. In examining this remarkable system of laws, however, it should be pointed out that while basic concepts such as "charity for the poor," loving one's neighbor, being honest in business dealings, etc., will apply in our day as much as in ancient times, nevertheless the method of carrying out such principles will vary with circumstances. Therefore, some of the mechanics of the Law of the Covenant in the days of Moses are not used today, but the underlying principles are in full force. This will become evident as we proceed.

THE GENIUS OF THE MOSAIC LAW

Authorities point out that the part of the Law of Moses which we call the Law of the Covenant had a genius for the achieving of justice and equity which no other ancient code comes anywhere close to matching. Most ancient codes such as that of Hammurabi, incorporated special privileges for certain classes and the application of the law depended upon the class to which a person belonged. Other codes such as that of Confucius, Menu and Zoroaster contained substantive weaknesses which are summarized by Dr. Adam Clarke.[71]

Most modern students have the impression that the Law of the Covenant was extremely harsh, but that is because these laws and the procedure under which they were administered are not generally understood.

Take, for example, the idea of "an eye for an eye and a tooth for a tooth." Many people visualize a wretched prisoner having his eye put out with a hot iron or his tooth extracted with a pair of pincers. But this is not what happened.

If a person deliberately attacked another person and during the struggle the victim lost an eye, then it was necessary for the assailant to provide "satisfaction" to the victim or lose his own eye. In other words, the threat of losing his

---

71. *Clarke, Bible Commentary*, Vol. I, pages 840-841

own eye, or tooth, was the reason why the offender would desperately extend himself to make it right with his victim.

As one might expect, in most cases this "satisfaction" was in the form of a money payment.[72] If a man did not have money he could sell his personal services for any period of time up to six years for the purpose of raising the money.[73] Today, for a similar crime, a man may be sentenced to many years in prison where his time is virtually wasted and where he is completely separated from his family and the community. Under the Law of Moses the offender could continue his normal life while working out the necessary "satisfaction" for the person he had injured.

Notice also that the purpose of the Mosaic Law was to balance the scales of justice *with the victim,* not the state. Under modern law, fines are almost invariably paid to the city, county or federal government. If the victim wants any remedy he must sue for damages in a civil court. However, as everyone knows, by the time a criminal has paid his fines to the court, he is usually depleted of funds or consigned to prison where he is earning nothing and therefore could not pay damages even if his victim went to the expense of filing a suit and getting a judgment. As a result, modern justice penalizes the offender, but does virtually nothing for the victim. To this extent, justice is robbed, and one is led to conclude that the Mosaic Law was far more fair to the victim of a crime or a tort[74] than modern law.

England has recently recognized this defect in modern justice and has therefore passed a law that people who are victims of crimes shall be compensated by the government. But this compensation must come from the taxpayers which means that non-criminals are paying for the violence and damages perpetrated by criminals. This whole procedure has been challenged. Two wrongs do not make a right. Admitting that the acts of the criminal are wrong, it does not satisfy justice for the government to use its authority to extract money (in taxes) from people who are not criminals to pay for the misdeeds of those who are.

---

72. See for example Exodus 21:22,30
73. Exodus 22:3; Exodus 21:2
74. "A wrongful act for which damages can be obtained."

The Law of Moses avoided this whole problem by making the criminal "give satisfaction" to his victim or suffer the consequences.

How Capital Crimes Were Handled Under the Law of Moses

A great many offenses under the Law of Moses carried a maximum penalty of death. Yet the student finds this was very seldom used and he cannot avoid wondering why. The answer is simple. Only *one* type of crime carried a *compulsory* death sentence and that was the crime of first degree murder.[75] In other words, capital punishment was absolutely inevitable only where human life had been destroyed deliberately, with premeditation and full criminal intent.[76]

In the case of all other offenses—where the maximum penalty was death — the offender had two alternatives. One was to "be cut off from among his people" and the other was to "make satisfaction." To be cut off from among one's people could be accomplished by self-exile. The use of this term "cut off," in the scripture invariably refers to an offender being cut off from among "his" people; not ALL People.[77] This would be accomplished if a person or group of persons fled to another country or society outside of Israel.

Since the original assignment of Israel was the same as the one given to the City of Enoch, namely, to build up a whole community of people willing to obey God's law, it was a logical procedure to give serious offenders the alternative of voluntarily leaving the society where God's laws prevailed and go to one of a lower order. Therefore, a person guilty of a serious offense which corrupted the culture of Israel was under the necessity of either reforming and making satisfaction or fleeing to another society. To insure this, serious offenses were made a capital crime which meant that if the offender would not make satisfaction but nevertheless attempted to remain in Israel, he did so at the peril of his life.

However, if he were repentant and wanted to become accepted so he could remain among "his" people, he had to

---

75. Numbers 35:31
76. Exodus 21:12-14
77. Exodus 30.33; Exodus 30:38; Leviticus 7:20-21, 25 17:4; 19:8; 20:6; 23:29; Numbers 9:13

"make satisfaction." Concerning this matter of making monetary satisfaction the scripture makes it clear that this not only
applied to damages for an eye or a tooth but even in capital
crimes. Moses gives an example of one of these capital offenses and says: "If there be laid on him a sum of money,
then he shall give for the ransom of his life whatsoever is
laid upon him."[78] However, as already stated under no circumstances could a person make satisfaction or a ransom for
his life if he were guilty of murder: "Moreover ye shall take
no satisfaction for the life of a murderer, which is guilty of
death: but he shall be surely put to death."[79]

In later centuries a great dispute arose between the
Jewish intellectuals as to the meaning of "satisfaction." The
Pharisees, consisting of the rabbis and principal leaders of
the people, held to the traditional position laid down by
Moses that in all cases except murder a monetary or similar
"satisfaction" could be made to remedy a wrong. However,
the Sadducees, a small aristocratic party which thought
salvation came through the sacrifice and carnal commandments, wanted a literal interpretation of an eye for an eye and
a tooth for a tooth. This was the cause of a great contention
between Sadducees and Pharisees.[80] A careful perusal of
the scriptures will leave no doubt as to what the Lord had
intended.

This clearly demonstrates that the Law of Moses was
not a *Lex Talionis* (law of retaliation) as so many have
claimed. Rather, it was a law of *reparation*. The object was
not vengeance, but equity and justice. Its purpose was not
to destroy the offender but compel him to restore his victim
to a state of well-being comparable to that which existed
before the crime was committed. Modern law makers might
learn much from a study of the law of the covenant!

How Was the Law of Moses Enforced?

One further question remains to be discussed and that
was the method of enforcing the Mosaic Law. One of the
unique features about the Mosaic code was the fact that it

---

78. Exodus 21:30
79. Numbers 35:31
80. See James E. Talmage, *Jesus the Christ*, pp. 66-67

was not administered by a body of "enforcement officers" but by the people themselves.

It did not have any army of semi-military civilians constantly policing the people to see if there were any violators of God's law. Instead, the judges waited until the people brought a complaint. Then the judges had the sacred responsibility to "inquire diligently" to see if the charge were true.[81] This implies an investigation as well as a hearing. The judges then came to a decision, and passed judgment.

But even the execution of the judgment depended to a large extent upon the people. This was particularly true in a case involving the death sentence.

As we have already pointed out, the only time the judges were duty-bound to invoke a death sentence was in the case of murder.[82] However, the death sentence could be invoked for a great variety of offenses if the offender refused to leave the land or make "satisfaction." But even in these cases the original accusers or witnesses to the offense had to be the ones to cast the first stone.[83] It is one thing to accuse a person of a capital crime and have the Government officers do the investigation and the executing. It is quite another thing for private citizens who brought the original charges or who served as the principal witnesses to be required to initiate the execution. This is exactly what was required under the Mosaic Law. It states: "At the mouth of two witnesses, or three witnesses, shall he that is worthy of death be put to death; but at the mouth of one witness he shall not be put to death. *The hands of the witnesses shall be first upon him to put him to death, and afterward the hands of all the people.*"[84]

Note that no matter how inflamed a community might be against the accused, they could not execute him until *after* the citizens who had brought the charges (and thereby inflamed the community's wrath) had cast the first stone. If these witnesses failed to act then it was presumed that there was something wrong with their testimony. That is why the elders of a community were legally prohibited from carrying out the death sentences unless the accusing witnesses would strike the first blow.

---

81. Deuteronomy 17:4; 19:18
82. Numbers 35:31

83. Deuteronomy 13:9; 17:7
84. Deuteronomy 17:6-7

A good example of the way the Mosaic Law was administered can be found in the provisions for dealing with a
dissolute, disobedient and obstreperous son. Here, certainly,
it would seem harsh to impose the death penalty, and so it
was. Yet, every son of Israel knew that it was a most serious
offense to rebel against parents because it was a capital
offense.

At the same time, the law required parents to exhibit the
utmost patience with a rebellious son and try to work with him
in order to overcome his evil ways. This is evident from the
fact that before parents could declare their son *anathema*
the following was required of them:

"If a man have a stubborn and rebellious son, which
will not obey the voice of his father, or the voice of his mother,
and that, when they have chastened him, will not hearken unto them; then shall his father and his mother lay hold on him,
and bring him out unto the elders of his city, and unto the
gate of his place; and they shall say unto the elders of his
city, This our son is stubborn and rebellious, he will not obey
our voice; he is a glutton, and a drunkard."[85]

At this point the parents had to pick up a stone and
be the first to strike their son down. No wonder we have
no record of this procedure ever being used! Parents, no
matter how provoked, would be extremely unlikely to resort
to such desperate measures. Nevertheless, the provision in
the law had an important psychological value. It impressed
upon the youth of Israel that their parents did have the legal
power over their very lives if they became violently rebellious.

What About Offenses for Which "Satisfaction" Was Not Possible?

As we have already seen, most offenses under the Mosaic Law could be remedied by having the offender provide
"satisfaction" to his victim. Not only did he have to restore
anything he had taken but he had to give back more to make
up for the inconvenience or fear to which he had subjected
his victim. The penalty for the ordinary theft was to return

---

85. Deuteronomy 21:18-20

twice as much as had been taken.[86] In certain cases, such as the theft of cattle and sheep, the thief had to return even more.[87]

But what about those offenses which were not against a person but against the good order of the whole community? This would include offenses such as breach of the peace, drunkenness, public prostitution, instigating a riot, and so forth. What would be the punishment for offenses of this nature? The Mosaic Law provided that all such evils which did violence to the whole community were to be punished by whippings:

"And it shall be, if the wicked man be worthy to be beaten, that the judge shall cause him to lie down, and to be beaten before his [the judge's] face, according to his fault, by a certain number. Forty stripes he may give him, and not exceed: lest, if he should exceed and beat him above these with many stripes, then thy brother should seem vile unto thee."[88]

Notice that in order to safeguard a prisoner against possible abuse by his guards and, at the same time, to prevent the assigned number of stripes from being diminished, the judge who gave the sentence was required to personally witness the whipping. The number of "stripes" depended upon the seriousness of the offense, but the absolute maximum was forty. To make sure this commandment was not exceeded, it became customary to limit the maximum number of stripes to thirty-nine.

After the prisoner had been whipped he was released. Under the Law of Moses the authorities could not throw an offender in some dark dungeon to starve or die, nor could they mutilate him, torture him, or subject him to any of the brutal and inhuman cruelty which was customary in those days.

But what kind of instrument was the whip? The one used by Jesus to cleanse the temple is specifically described as being made "with small cords."[89] These cords or thongs were usually of rope or leather and were attached to a wooden

86. Exodus 22:4
87. Exodus 22:1
88. Deuteronomy 25:2-3
89. John 2:15

handle. The thongs were designed to sting and welt the skin but not to break it.

When herders and caravan drivers found this type of whip to be ineffective in dealing with tough-skinned animals such as oxen, donkeys or camels, they tied pieces of bone or metal along the thongs which cut deeply into the flesh. The use of sharp metal or bone at the end of the thongs is what characterized the infamous "cat o' nine tails." The employment of this type of whip on human beings was so destructive and cruel that it gave the whole idea of "punishing by whipping" a repulsive and uncivilized reputation. In fact in most modern nations whipping has been outlawed as a means of punishment because it was so often abused. However, Canada and the State of Delaware have continued to authorize its use in certain cases where the prisoner elects to be whipped in preference to spending many tedious years in useless prison life.

For several years, psychologists who have to work with seriously delinquent youth have noted the therapeutic value of physical punishment when it has been used judiciously. Some have wondered if there might not be equal merit in dealing with adults who would elect to receive corporal punishment in preference to spending long years wasting away in the cell of a prison. The reason the Canadian government has kept this provision on the books is because this procedure was preferred by some prisoners. It appeared that prisoners who were whipped and released had a lower rate of recidivism (return to criminality) than ordinary prisoners. Here, as under the Mosaic code, the whip employed for the punishment leaves a "stripe" on the back of the offender but not a lacerated wound.

CONCLUSION

With this background on the Mosaic Law, the student can better appreciate the pattern of legal provisions in this code which were far more reasonable and compatible with modern thinking than many have supposed. Because the Law of Moses is scattered throughout four different books of the Bible, it is rather difficult to study. We have therefore gathered together all of these statutes and arranged them in logical categories for the convenience of the student. This compilation will be found in the appendix.

Scripture Reading and Questions on Chapter Sixteen

Scripture Reading Assignment: the entire Book of Leviticus.

1—How many days does the Book of Leviticus cover? What happened the first seven days? What happened on the eighth day?

2—What was an ephod? Describe the breastplate worn by Aaron. Was it similar to the breastplate found with the plates of Mormon?

3—What did a Burnt Offering signify? When was a Sin Offering appropriate?

4—Who shared in a Peace Offering? What gave the "Wave Offering" its name? Did the Meat Offering involve flesh of any animal?

5—When was a Trespass Offering appropriate? What was a Drink Offering?

6—What three offerings were the Priests required to make every morning and every evening?

7—What was the purpose of the Carnal Commandments which were added to the law of the covenant?

8—Name three purposes of the dietary laws in the Old Testament. When were these laws "fulfilled"? What law replaced them?

9—What lesson do we draw from the death of Nadab and Abihu? What appears to have been their offense?

10—Did Jesus say his Gospel did away with the law of the covenant as given to Moses? What did he say? Do the Ten Commandments apply today?

11—Under the law of "an eye for an eye and a tooth for a tooth," did an offender automatically lose his eye or his tooth? What was the actual application of this principle? Why do we call this the "law of reparation?"

12—If a person committed first degree murder (with premeditation, malice and criminal intent) what did the Lord say the punishment should be? Was it mandatory? Has the Lord ever replaced this instruction?

13—Was the law of reparation which Moses received more just and equitable than modern law? Why?

14—Was the death penalty mandatory for any offense other than deliberate murder?

15—What could a person do to avoid the death penalty in those offenses not involving the shedding of innocent blood?

16—When the death penalty was carried out, who had to strike the first blow? What was the purpose of this rule?

17—How many witnesses were required to convict a person? Why is this a good rule?

18—Under the Law of Moses, who had the responsibility of seeing that the law was enforced? Should we have more of this today?

19—Was there any provision for sentencing a guilty person to long terms in prison?

20—If a person were whipped what was the maximum number of stripes? Who had to witness the whipping? Were they allowed to use a whip which was designed to cut or tear the skin? Do any governments allow prisoners to choose a whipping in preference to prison today?

CHAPTER SEVENTEEN

Organizing Israel for the March on Canaan

By this time, Moses was well over the threshold of his second year in the wilderness. However, if he had anticipated that this second year was going to be smoother than the first one, he must have been deeply disappointed. On New Year's Day Moses had erected the Tabernacle and then eight days later he had anointed Aaron and his sons to their new calling. Barely was this over when two of those sons, Nadab and Abihu, brought a calamity down upon themselves by offering "strange fire" before the Lord. They had lost their lives instantaneously. Moses also had the frustrating disappointment of seeing the people lose the higher ordinances, the endowment, the Melchizedek Priesthood, and receiving in their place the complicated, intricate ritual of strict obedience called the carnal commandments.

But the Lord did not allow Moses time to fret about his disappointments. This second year was going to be a big one and Moses was required to be immediately up and doing.

THE FIRST CENSUS OF ISRAEL

Moses was instructed to count his soldiers. As Israel marched up toward Canaan to reconquer it, Moses needed to know his military resources. Furthermore, the hosts of Israel needed to be organized the way Jethro had suggested over a year earlier.[1]

So on the first day of the second month Moses was instructed to number every man of military age who was "twenty years old and upward" and who was "able to go forth to war in Israel."[2]

---

1. Exodus 18:13-23   2. Numbers 1:3

This brings us to the Book of Numbers which takes its name from this census. However, the Book of Numbers is known in the Hebrew version by a more appropriate title. It is called "In the Wilderness."[3] This is a more fitting title since the Book of Numbers covers the entire historical trek from Sinai to the borders of the Promised Land. Taking a census and organizing the camp along military lines was part of the preparation for this journey.

The outcome of the census was as follows:

The tribe of Reuben 46,500
The tribe of Simeon 59,300
The tribe of Gad 45,650
The tribe of Judah 74,600
The tribe of Issachar 54,400
The tribe of Zebulun 57,400
The tribe of Ephraim (Joseph) 40,500
The tribe of Manasseh (Joseph) 32,200
The tribe of Benjamin 35,400
The tribe of Dan 62,700
The tribe of Asher 41,500
The tribe of Naphtali 53,400

Grand Total .... 603,550[4]

It will be observed that the Lord did not permit Moses to take a census for the tribe of Levi at this time because the Lord did not intend to use them in war. He was about to give a special calling to the entire tribe of Levi.[5] We shall discuss this in just a moment.

ORGANIZING THE CAMP AROUND THE TABERNACLE

Having completed the census, Moses was now told to reorganize the camp of Israel so that the various tribes surrounded and protected the Tabernacle on all four sides. Nevertheless, they were to pitch their tents far out from the Tabernacle and only approach it for the purpose of worship. As we shall see later, the tribe of Levi was to be settled immediately around the Tabernacle so this left eleven tribes to

3. Clarke, *Bible Commentary,* Vol. 1, p. 604
4. Numbers 1:46   5. Numbers 1:49-50

guard the four outer flanks. Because this was an uneven number, the tribe of Joseph was split into Ephraim and Manasseh to make a total of twelve. The camp of Israel was then set up as follows:[6]

On the East—Judah, Issachar and Zebulun

On the South—Reuben, Simeon and Gad

On the West—Ephraim, Manasseh and Benjamin

On the North—Dan, Asher and Naphtali

THE LORD ADOPTS THE TRIBE OF LEVI IN PLACE OF THE FIRSTBORN

It will be recalled that a little over a year earlier (while Israel was still in Egypt), the Pharaoh and all the families of the Egyptians had lost their firstborn as the terrible climax to the ten plagues. The Israelites, of course, had not lost their firstborn children, and therefore the Lord claimed them as His own. Since then, all of the firstborn had been consecrated to the Lord. Now, however, the Lord told Moses that He was going to adopt the entire tribe of Levi and use them for His Tabernacle service in lieu of the firstborn from the other tribes.[7]

Moses was told to get a count of the males in the tribe of Levi who were one month old or more.[8] It was found that there were 22,000.[9] He was then told to find out the number of the firstborn among the other tribes of Israel. This turned out to be 22,273.

The Lord said that since there were 273 more firstborn among the various tribes than the total for the tribe of Levi, He would require the various tribes to redeem this difference of 273 by paying a monetary contribution into the sanctuary of the Tabernacle.[10] This was done.

Now the tribe of Levi was set apart as the consecrated servants of the Lord to function in the Levitical Priesthood and perform the various spiritual services for the entire camp of Israel. Of course, not all 22,000 were available for this purpose since the population tally included all male Levites

---

6. Numbers, chapter 2
7. Numbers 3:5-12
8. Numbers 3:40

9. Numbers 3:39
10. Numbers 3:51

who were one month old or more. Moses said the qualifications for service in the Tabernacle of the Congregation required that a Levite be "without blemish" and between the ages of 30 and 50.[11] Out of the 22,000 male Levites, a total of 8,580 were able to qualify.[12]

Moses then divided all of the Levites into three groups. Each group represented the descendants of one of Levi's

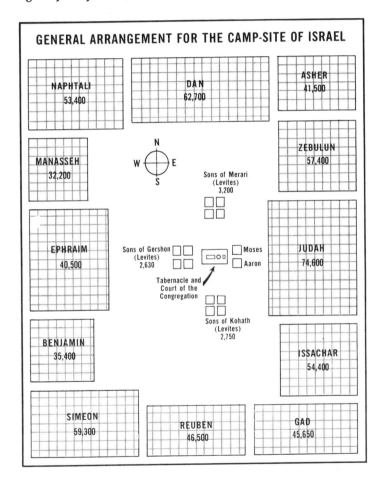

GENERAL ARRANGEMENT FOR THE CAMP-SITE OF ISRAEL

---

11. See Numbers 4:30, 35, 39. The age requirements changed occasionally as the need for more Levites increased. For example, in Numbers 8:24 the Levites are ordered to enter the service at age 25. In I Chronicles 23:24 the Levites are ordered to enter the service at 20. It is obvious that the age re-requirement was flexible and depended upon circumstances.
12. Numbers 4:47-48

sons[13] and was assigned a separate camp immediately around the Tabernacle. The descendants of Gershon pitched their tents on the west side of the Tabernacle,[14] those who had descended from Kohath pitched their tents south of the Tabernacle,[15] and those who descended from Merari pitched their tents on the north side.[16] This left only the front of the Tabernacle to the east unprotected. The Lord ordered Moses and Aaron and their families to occupy the east side.[17]

DIVISION OF LABOR AMONG THE LEVITES

The three branches of Levites were also given separate duties in connection with the transporting and setting up of the Tabernacle each time the camp moved. The Kohathites were to transport on their shoulders all of the artifacts within the Tabernacle — the Ark of the Covenant, the golden altar of incense, the golden candlestick, and the golden table of shew bread.[18] However, the Lord said they were not to enter the Tabernacle to obtain those things until each item had been carefully covered by Aaron and his sons.[19] The Gershonites were to transport the curtains of the Tabernacle[20] and the sons of Merari were to handle the boards, bars, sockets and pillars.[21] The Tabernacle and all of its facilities represented a tremendous amount of weight. (Dr. Clarke estimates the metal alone weighed almost ten tons.)[22] Therefore the princes or tribal leaders of Israel came forward with a gift of six covered wagons and twelve oxen to facilitate the transportation of the Tabernacle.[23] These wagons were given to the sons of Gershon who carried the curtains,[24] and the sons of Merari who carried the heavy framework.[25] No wagons were given to the sons of Kohath because this body of

---

13. Numbers 3:17
14. Numbers 3:23
15. Numbers 3:29
16. Numbers 3:35
17. Numbers 3:38
18. Numbers 4:15-20
19. See Numbers 4:5-15.
20. Numbers 4:22-26
21. Numbers 4:29-33
22. Clarke, *Bible Commentary*, Vol. 1, p. 627
23. Numbers 7:3
24. Numbers 7:7
25. Numbers 7:8

Levites were required to carry the Ark of the Covenant, the altar of incense, the table of shew bread and the golden candlestick on their shoulders.[26]

When the whole program of the Levitical service had been presented to the Levites, Moses prepared them for a solemn consecration service to induct them into their new calling. The men of the tribe washed, shaved and dressed themselves in clean clothing, whereupon they were presented to the Lord "for an offering."[27] All the congregation were asked to "put their hands upon the Levites"[28] which probably means that they sustained them with their uplifted hands in a vote of confidence just as officers of the Priesthood are sustained in modern times.[29]

Of course, the setting aside of one whole tribe to institutionalize the spiritual aspects of the Mosaic program (including *both* the carnal commandments and the Law of the Covenant) was a temporary crutch. From the Lord's standpoint it was an act of desperation. It was to keep this people from destroying themselves. The Lord's preferred way is to have a *"kingdom* of priests" not a tribe of priests. The Lord would like to have *every* worthy person enjoy priesthood privileges, but when a whole nation rejects the responsibilities of Priesthood service as Israel had done, the Lord's only alternative was to build a firm core of responsible leadership in whatever group seemed most likely to carry the load. *In a time of crisis it had been the Levites who had met the test.* This occurred when Moses had stood at the gates of the camp right after the ugly incident of worshipping the golden calf and had cried out, "Who is on the Lord's side? let him come unto me."[30] The scripture says: "And all the sons of Levi gathered themselves together unto him."[31] Not another single tribe had stepped forward. Now the Levites received their reward for that act of courageous commitment.

THE NAZARITE

Nevertheless, the Lord made provision for anyone in Israel to participate in a period of service, study, and prayer,

---

26. Numbers 7:9
27. Numbers 8:11
28. Numbers 8:10
29. Doctrine and Covenants 20:63, 65

30. Exodus 32:26
31. Exodus 32:26
32. Numbers 6:1-21

by taking the vow of "separation."[32] In other words, while
the Tribe of Levi had the exclusive responsibility of perpetuating the Levitical Priesthood functions, any person could
volunteer for a mission of dedicated service and study. Such a
person could be either a man or a woman.[33] During the period
of service they were individually referred to as "one separated." This is the Hebrew meaning of the term, "Nazarite".
Therefore any person who had assumed a vow of being separated from his usual occupation and activities for a season
in order to participate in spiritual development was called a
Nazarite.

However, the Nazarite vow is always referred to in
scripture as a vow of limited duration, never for life unless
commanded by the Lord as with Samson and Samuel. It is
obvious that the Lord never intended that groups of people
in a state of "separation" or as Nazarites should band together and become a monastic order. Yet this is what happened during the period of Israel's apostasy. As Dr. Adam
Clarke points out, "From the Nazarites sprang the Rechabites, from the Rechabites the Essenes, from the Essenes, the
Anchorites or Hermits, and in imitation of these, the different
[Christian] monastic orders."[34] It was the order of the
Essenes (meaning "the pious ones") which produced the
"Dead Sea Scrolls."

THE GREAT LEVITICAL PRAYER

It was shortly after the consecrating of the tribe of Levi
to the Lord that a prayer was given by direct revelation
which Aaron was instructed to use in blessing the people and
giving them encouragement during the difficult days ahead.
This inspired supplication and benediction is brief just as
the Lord's Prayer in the New Testament, nevertheless it is
filled with a profound essence of spirituality which has made
it one of the most popular and most frequently repeated
passages in the Bible:

"The Lord bless thee, and keep thee;
"The Lord make his face shine upon thee,
"And be gracious unto thee:

33. Numbers 6:2
34. Clarke, *Bible Commentary*, Vol. 1, p. 634

"The Lord lift up his countenance upon thee,
"And give thee peace."[35]

MOSES RECEIVES THE COMMAND TO MARCH TOWARD THE PROMISED LAND

The hosts of Israel had been camped at the foot of Mount Sinai for ten months.[36] Now the Lord said to Moses: "Ye have dwelt long enough in this mount . . . Behold, I have set the land before you: go in and possess the land which the Lord sware unto your fathers, Abraham, Isaac, and Jacob, to give unto them and to their seed after them."[37]

This new command undoubtedly gave Moses a surge of enthusiastic hope. It implied that Israel could occupy the "land of milk and honey" before the next season! Subsequent events disclosed that this was exactly what the Lord had in mind. The conquest of Canaan could commence in this, the second year out of Egypt.

Once again Israel was going to be presented with a choice, and once again, in spite of the thrilling prospect, Israel was going to go braying off into the wilderness. In fact, it would result in 38 years in the wilderness. Out there in those desolate wastes there would be massive apostasy, cowardice, rebellion, a plot to overthrow Moses, and plagues that would decimate the ranks of Israel. Except for Joshua and Caleb, not a single adult Israelite was going to survive this trek and enter into the Promised Land. They would be consumed in the wilderness and die off at the rate of more than 16,000 per year. This terrible destruction could have been avoided, of course, but Israel made the wrong choice.

MOSES ORGANIZES THE HOSTS OF ISRAEL

A year earlier the father-in-law of Moses (Jethro), had told Moses how to organize the hosts of Israel. Moses had been told to delegate and disperse the responsibilities of leadership.[38] There were to be captains of tens, captains

---

35. Numbers 6:24-25
36. Exodus 19:1; Numbers 10:11
37. Deuteronomy 1:6, 8. The first verse refers to "Horeb" rather than Sinai. It is believed that Horeb was the general range of mountains in this area, Sinai being one of its major peaks.
38. Exodus 18:21-23

of fifties, captains of hundreds and captains of thousands. These captains were to be judges as well as administrative leaders. Apparently Moses had never presented this proposed organization to the people of Israel before this time, but now the camp must start its trek, so he could postpone it no longer. To all the people he declared:

"I am not able to bear you myself alone: the Lord your God hath multiplied you, and behold, ye are this day as the stars of heaven for multitude . . . How can I myself alone bear your cumbrance, and your burden, and your strife?"[39]

Then Moses presented to them the suggestion which had come from Jethro, his father-in-law: "Take you wise men, and understanding, and known among your tribes, and I will make them rulers over you."[40] The leaders of the various tribes responded with enthusiasm: "The thing which thou has spoken is good for us to do."[41]

So the tribes of Israel were organized with captains of tens, fifties, hundreds, and thousands. Notice that Moses gave the tribes the privilege of selecting the candidates, then Moses said he would make the formal appointment. This meant that Moses had reserved the right to exclude any whom he considered unworthy to serve in this sacred calling. The scripture states that as soon as these captains were nominated by the tribes and were officially appointed by Moses, he promptly brought them together in a school of instruction. Moses charged them as follows:

"Hear the causes between your brethren, and judge righteously between every man and his brother, and the stranger that is with him. Ye shall not respect [favor] persons in judgment: but ye shall hear the small as well as the great; ye shall not be afraid of the face of man; for the judgment is God's: and the cause that is too hard for you, bring it unto me, and I will hear it."[42]

THE MARCH ACROSS THE WILDERNESS BEGINS

With between two and three million people to lead across the desert wilderness, Moses was commanded by the

39. Deuteronomy 1:9-12
40. Deuteronomy 1:13
41. Deuteronomy 1:14
42. Deuteonomy 1:16-17

Lord to provide a signalling system. This consisted of two sacred silver trumpets, the blowing of which would provide a piercing clarion call. These were to be used to call an assembly of the congregation, to indicate the order of march, to sound an alarm in time of war, and to celebrate holidays or feast days.[43]

These silver trumpets were sacred instruments to be blown only by the sons of Aaron.[44] No doubt this was to fix responsibility for the initial signal. Other trumpets could then pass the signal throughout the camp. Note that in the beginning there were only two signalling trumpets because only two of Aaron's sons were alive. In the days of Joshua the number of trumpets would be increased to seven. They would also be made of rams' horns rather than silver because they were needed mostly for battle.[45] In the days of Solomon the priests would use 120 trumpets which undoubtedly provided a magnificent concert of instrumentation in connection with feast day celebrations.[46]

THE LINE OF MARCH

The scripture says, "And it came to pass, on the twentieth day of the second month, in the second year, that the cloud was taken up from off the tabernacle of the testimony. And the children of Israel took their journeys out of the wilderness of Sinai. . . ."[47]

It must have been a majestic spectacle to see this vast encampment take up its orderly line of march. When the silver trumpets blew the first time, the vanguard moved out in front.[48] This consisted of three tribes with Judah in the lead. The other two tribes were Issachar and Zebulun.[49]

Immediately behind the vanguard came two sections of the Levites (the sons of Gershon and the sons of Merari) transporting the dismantled Tabernacle with all its curtains, framework, fixtures and sacred utensils.[50] The Tabernacle was sent ahead early so it could be set up and in complete

---

43. Numbers 10:1-10
44. Numbers 10:8
45. Joshua 6:4
46. 2 Chronicles 5:12

47. Numbers 10:11-12
48. Numbers 10:5
49. Numbers 10:14-16
50. Numbers 10:17

readiness when the Ark of the Covenant and other sacred furnishings arrived.[51]

The second sounding of the trumpets[52] brought up the tribe of Reuben accompanied by the hosts of Simeon and Gad.[53]

These were followed by the group of Levites called the sons of Kohath who carried on their shoulders the Ark of the Covenant; the golden altar of incense, the table of shew bread and the golden candlestick.

The third bugling of the trumpets[54] brought up the tribe of Ephraim accompanied by the hosts of Manasseh and Benjamin.[55]

The fourth brought up Dan accompanied by the tribes of Asher and Naphtali.[56] These constituted the rear guard.

THE BROTHER-IN-LAW OF MOSES REFUSES TO GO

As the multitudes of Israel moved out on their great migration northward, an incident occurred which Moses felt was worth recording. A man named Hobab refused to go along. This man turns out to be the son of Jethro, and therefore the brother-in-law of Moses.[57] Moses strenuously urged Hobab to accompany them, saying, "We are journeying into the place of which the Lord said, I will give it you: come thou with us, and we will do thee good: for the Lord hath spoken good concerning Israel."[58] But Hobab felt duty-bound to stay with his own people. Said he, "I will not go, but I will depart to mine own land, and to my kindred."[59]

---

51. Numbers 10:21
52. Numbers 10:6
53. Numbers 10:18-20
54. The third and fourth alarms are not mentioned in the King James version, but appear in the *Septuagint* as follows: "And when ye blow a third alarm or signal, the camps on the west shall march: and when ye blow a fourth alarm or signal, the camps on the north shall march." (Clarke, *Bible Commentary*, Vol. 1, p. 648.)
55. Numbers 10:22-24
56. Numbers 10:25-27
57. Hobab is described as the son of Roquel, a Midianite. But this same Hebrew name is spelled Reuel in Exodus 2:18 and it is explained that this "Reuel" is the same as Jethro, the father-in-law of Moses (Exodus 4:18; 18:5).
58. Numbers 10:29
59. Numbers 10:30

So Hobab, like his father, Jethro,[60] felt compelled to stay with the Midianites, most of whom had apparently apostatized and turned to idolatry along with the rest of the seed of Abraham in this region. Jethro and Hobab obviously felt a deep sense of responsibility toward these wayward relatives. However, we discover later that some of these people did go along with the Israelites and settled in Judah.

THE TRIALS OF A PROPHET

When the camps of Israel marched into the desert there was the expectant excitement of adventure, new scenes and new settlements. But after a three days' journey[61] from the Horeb range, the blazing sun and blistering sand had sapped the enthusiasm of these tenderfooted nomads and left the people weary, worried and contentious.

It was not long before an outburst of complaints and lamentations sent a poisonous taint throughout the ranks of Israel and produced an ugly mood everywhere. As their howl of sorrow and self-pity ascended to heaven it brought down a reply of consuming fire. It was obvious that the hosts of Israel were pressing the patience of the Lord beyond endurance. The scripture says this spectacular fire of consumption struck "the uttermost parts of the camp" and commenced to destroy them.[62] In childlike terror the people pleaded with Moses to intercede for them. The scripture says, "When Moses prayed unto the Lord, the fire was quenched."[63]

But people who live with miracles often come to take them for granted. Immediately after this volatile display of inflammatory destruction, those who were not directly affected by it went right ahead seeking additional excuses for their complaints. The scripture says this second wave of contentious rebellion began among "the mixed multitude" of non-Israelites who had come out of Egypt with them.[64] Then it spread to the Israelites themselves. The basic complaint was concerning food. The miracle of the manna was ungratefully denounced. The people cried out: "Who shall give

---

60. Exodus 18:27
61. Numbers 10:33
62. Numbers 11.1

63. Numbers 11:2
64. Numbers 11:4; Exodus 12:38

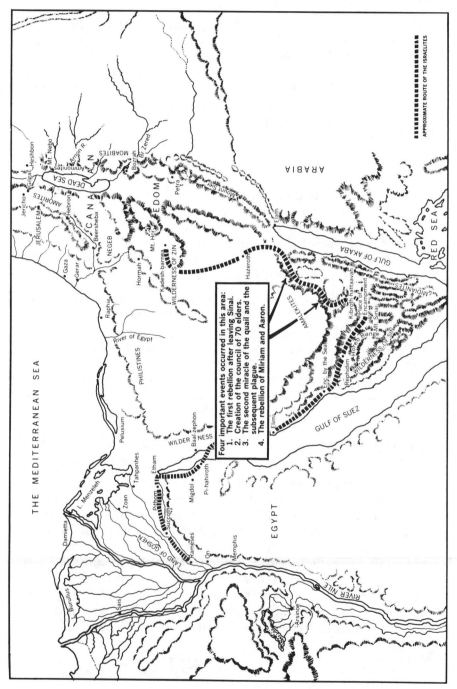

Four important events occurred in this area:
1. The first rebellion after leaving Sinai.
2. Creation of the council of 70 elders.
3. The second miracle of the quail and the subsequent plague.
4. The rebellion of Miriam and Aaron.

us flesh to eat? We remember the fish, which we did eat in Egypt freely; the cucumbers, and the melons, and the leeks, and the onions and the garlick: But now our soul is dried away: there is nothing at all, beside this manna, before our eyes."[65]

Now this thankless, woe-begotten people were pressing their leader beyond the point of tolerant endurance. The scriptures say that not only "the anger of the Lord was kindled greatly," but "Moses also was displeased."[66] In the past Moses had offered to forfeit the salvation of his own soul in an effort to get the Lord to spare these wretched people, but now Moses was wondering if he had taken upon himself an impossible task. He cried out:

"Lord, wherefore hast thou afflicted thy servant? and wherefore have I not found favour in thy sight, that thou layest the burden of all this people upon me? Have I conceived all this people? have I begotten them, that thou shouldest say unto me, Carry them in thy bosom, as a nursing father beareth the sucking child, unto the land which thou swarest unto their fathers? Whence should I have flesh to give unto all this people?"[67] In a final burst of anguish he declared: "I am not able to bear all this people alone, because it is too heavy for me. And if thou deal thus with me, kill me, I pray thee, out of hand, if I have found favour in thy sight; and let me not see my wretchedness."[68]

To this fervent plea the Lord gave an answer.

THE CREATION OF THE COUNCIL OF SEVENTY ELDERS

About a year earlier, the Lord had given a special spiritual testimony to seventy "elders" who had been chosen from the various tribes. He had allowed them to come up part way into Mount Sinai to see the personage of the Lord from a distance.[69] Now, a year later, the Lord tells Moses to "Gather unto me seventy men of the elders of Israel whom thou knowest to be the elders of the people, and officers over them; and bring them unto the tabernacle of the congregation that they may stand there with thee."[70]

---

65. Numbers 11:4-6
66. Numbers 11:10
67. Numbers 11:11-13
68. Numbers 11:14-15
69. Exodus 24:9-11
70. Numbers 11:16

The writings of Moses do not indicate whether this group was identical with the one taken in the mount the year before, but since this new Council of Seventy was to be given another great spiritual endowment, it is likely that Moses would have selected as many as possible from those who had already ascended the higher dimensions of spiritual realization the year before. The Lord told Moses to gather together this group of seventy, "And I will come down and talk with thee there: and I will take of the spirit which is upon thee, and will put it upon them; and they shall bear the burden of the people with thee, that thou bear it not thyself alone."[71]

When these men were assembled together Moses "set them round about the tabernacle."[72] They did not know it but they were about to hear the voice of the Lord and enjoy a great endowment of spiritual power which would give them a scientific knowledge of God's capacity to sublimate the human mind to a point of refinement far beyond their previous comprehension. Moses later wrote: "And the Lord came down in a cloud and spake unto him, and took of the spirit that was upon him, and gave it unto the seventy elders: and it came to pass, that, when the spirit rested upon them, they prophesied, and did not cease."[73] Here was the forerunner to a similar thrilling occasion which would occur on the Day of Pentecost, fifty days after the crucifixion of Christ.[74]

Moses had written down the names of the seventy men who were appointed as members of the council, but two of them had not shown up for the conference. He had therefore gone ahead with the other sixty-eight. We are not told what had detained these two absent members but there must have been compelling reasons for the Holy Ghost sought them out "in the camp" and gave them the same spirit of prophecy as that which was being enjoyed at the Tabernacle.[75]

A young man ran to the Tabernacle and obtained an audience with Moses to tell him that "Eldad and Medad do prophesy in the camp."[76] Joshua was standing nearby

---

71. Numbers 11:17   74. Acts 2:1-4
72. Numbers 11:24   75. Numbers 11:26
73. Numbers 11:25   76. Numbers 11:27

and apparently assumed that Eldad and Meldad were presumptuously prophesying to the people when this was the specific calling of their great leader, Moses. Joshua therefore said, "My Lord Moses, forbid them."[77]

But Moses replied, "Enviest thou for my sake? Would God that all the Lord's people were prophets and that the Lord would put his Spirit upon them."[78] Any person who enjoys the true spirit of Priesthood service will never envy the manifestations of God's approval in another. He will rejoice in his neighbor's acceptance by the Lord because he knows that the power of God manifested in one is a benefit and a blessing to all.

The great council of seventy set up by Moses is believed by authorities to be the origin of the body which became known in later centuries as the Sanhedrin. Although it eventually fell into evil days and evil ways, the purpose of the Sanhedrin was to bring together the men of greatest wisdom and ability. It was the supreme court of Israel and also had a variety of administrative duties. Until the destruction of Jerusalem (70 A.D.) the Sanhedrin convened in a hall called Gazith, or the Chamber of Hewn Stone situated on the southern edge of the inner court of the temple. Its place of meeting was moved from Jerusalem to Tiberias after the fall of the capital, and remained there until it became extinct in 425 A.D.[79] It has never met since.

THE COMING OF THE QUAIL CARRYING A DEADLY CURSE

It will be recalled that the Lord set up the Council of Seventy in direct response to the plea of Moses that "I am not able to bear all this people alone." Obviously, this was a legitimate complaint and the Lord dealt with it accordingly. But then there came the whining and whimperings of the people about wanting "flesh" and mocking the daily ration of manna as though it were repugnant to them. This was counted by the Lord as an epidemic of "lusting" rather than a legitimate complaint. He rewarded this complaint as follows: A great migration of quail "from the sea" came rid-

---

77. Numbers 11:28
78. Numbers 11:29
79. See Peloubet's *Bible Dictionary* under "Sanhedrin."

ing in on a high wind.[80] No doubt those Israelites who believed in the philosophy that the "squeaky wheel gets the grease," must have disdainfully smirked at their more patient brethren who had refused to join in their noisy demand for "flesh." Was it not evident that even God responds to those who cry out the most? Little did they guess that this bounteous quantity of quail carried with it a deadly curse. The scripture says, "And the people stood up all that day, and all that night, and all the next day, and they gathered the quails: he that gathered least gathered ten homers: and they spread them all abroad for themselves round about the camp [to cure the meat by drying it]."[81] Ten homers would fill two bushel baskets.

In describing the quantity of the quail, the English Bible says they "were two cubits high upon the face of the earth."[82] Many students took this to mean that the birds were stacked to a depth of two cubits throughout the area. Such a situation would have been a calamity indeed! The correct meaning of this passage appears in the *Vulgate* which says, "And they [the quail] flew in the air, two cubits high above the ground."[83] In other words, it was easy to gather large numbers of the quail because they flew low where they could be quickly caught.

Apparently some of the people who had "lusted" for flesh did not waste time preserving the birds for future use but went ahead stuffing themselves like gluttons. "And while the flesh was yet between their teeth, ere it was chewed, the wrath of the Lord was kindled against the people, and the Lord smote the people with a very great plague. And he [Moses] called the name of that place Kibroth-hataavah [the graves of lust]: because there they buried the people that lusted."[84]

As soon as they had buried their dead, the Israelites struck camp and headed for their next stop which was called Hazeroth.[85]

---

80. Numbers 11:31
81. Numbers 11:32
82. Numbers 11:31
83. See Clarke, *Bible Commentary*, Vol. 1, p. 654
84. Numbers 11:33-34
85. Numbers 11:35

AARON AND MIRIAM TURN AGAINST MOSES

The biography of Moses vividly demonstrates that the calling of a prophet does not remove in the slightest degree the daily frustrations and travails of ordinary earth-life. After all the mutinous complaints Moses had endured from the rebellious ranks of the Israelites, one might have supposed that he certainly would have been supported by the unflinching loyalty of his immediate family. But human nature being what it is, this bastion of support also collapsed occasionally and left Moses struggling alone. One of these unfortunate incidents occurred at Hazeroth.

It will be recalled that Miriam and Aaron were both older than Moses. Perhaps this was one of the factors which led them to begin looking down upon Moses in a self-righteous and critical manner. Because Miriam is mentioned first and because she later received the greater penalty, it appears that she was the originator of the plot. The complaint they conjured up was a fragile one. In attempting to magnify the faults of Moses and justify their own self-righteousness, Miriam and Aaron had to go back some 60 years to find a basis for accusing Moses. They mocked him because they said that in his early life he had married an "Ethiopian woman."[86]

It will be recalled that Josephus, the Jewish historian, relates the details of this marriage, and states that while Moses was the crown prince of Egypt he was called upon to save Egypt from the conquest of the Ethiopians. In doing so, he drove the armies of that nation back up into the headwater country of the Nile and besieged the Ethiopian capital of Saba. As he was rendezvousing his troops near the city wall, the Ethiopian princess, Tharbis, saw Moses and fell in love with him, whereupon she sent her most trusted servant to propose marriage to Moses. He agreed on condition that the city be surrendered without bloodshed. The princess induced her father to agree and the war ended. The subsequent marriage between Moses, the "prince of Egypt," and Tharbis, the "princess of Ethiopia" served as a guarantee that peace would prevail between the two countries in the future. As we pointed out earlier, such "duty" marriages were commonplace down through history. There is no indication that

---

86. Numbers 12:1

the Ethiopian princess ever accompanied Moses to Egypt or that they had any further association with each other after political peace had been restored between the two countries.

For an Israelite, a marriage to an Ethiopian was forbidden, and it was for this offense that Miriam and Aaron now condemned their younger brother. The scripture says: "And Miriam and Aaron spake against Moses because of the Ethiopian woman whom he had married: for he had married an Ethiopian woman."[87]

The injustice of their accusation is obvious when it is realized that Moses is described in the scripture as being "full forty years old" before "it came into his heart to visit his brethren the children of Israel."[88] Since Moses had led their conquest of Ethiopia many years earlier, it is doubtful that he was even aware of any prohibition against such a marriage. Certainly the Lord had no condemnation against Moses for what had happened, and Aaron and Miriam were about to find it out. In fact, we discover that their complaint against Moses for his marriage to the Ethiopian princess was not the honest reason for their grumbling. They actually were looking for an excuse to express their envy toward him. Said they, "Hath the Lord indeed spoken only by Moses? hath he not spoken also by us?[89] Here was the real bone in their throats. They were boiling over with jealousy!

The scripture says, "And the Lord heard it."[90] Not only did He hear it, but He promptly took action. "And the Lord spake suddenly unto Moses, and unto Aaron, and unto Miriam, Come out ye three unto the tabernacle of the congregation."[91] In dread of the consequences, Moses, Miriam, and Aaron obeyed. At the Tabernacle, the glory of God was manifest in the brilliance of the cloud. Then the Lord called to Aaron and Miriam and told them to draw near.

"Hear now my words," said the Lord. "If there be a prophet among you, I the Lord will make myself known unto him in a vision and will speak unto him in a dream. My servant Moses is not so, who is faithful in all mine house. With him will I speak mouth to mouth, even apparently,

---

87. Ibid.
88. Acts 7:23
89. Numbers 12:2

90. Ibid.
91. Numbers 12:4

and not in dark speeches; and the similitude of the Lord shall he behold: WHEREFORE THEN WERE YE NOT AFRAID TO SPEAK AGAINST MY SERVANT MOSES?"[92]

With this, the cloud of the Lord's glory abruptly departed from off the Tabernacle, and when it did so, Miriam suddenly discovered to her horror that she was covered with leprosy. It is not difficult to understand the panic which seized her. Aaron turned frantically to Moses and pleaded from the depths of his heart:

"Alas, my lord, I beseech thee, lay not the sin upon us, wherein we have done foolishly, and wherein we have sinned. Let her not be as one dead, of whom the flesh is half consumed when he cometh out of his mother's womb."[93]

Of course, Moses loved Miriam as much as Aaron, and he was also touched by Aaron's humility. Therefore he turned to the Lord and cried out, "Heal her now, O God, I beseech thee."[94]

To this the Lord consented, but He said Miriam was to be treated as an unclean person and stay outside of the camp for seven days. So the scripture closes the incident with this statement: "And Miriam was shut out from the camp seven days: and the people journeyed not till Miriam was brought in again."[95] This was a critical delay since Israel was almost in sight of the promised land; nevertheless, out of consideration for Miriam who was greatly respected in Israel, the tribes remained another full week at Hazeroth. Then went up the cry, "On to Canaan!"

---

92. Numbers 12:6-8
93. Numbers 12:11-12
94. Numbers 12:13
95. Exodus 12:15

Scripture Reading and Questions on Chapter Seventeen

Scripture Reading Assignment: Numbers, chapters 1 to 12 inclusive.

1—What period of Israel's history does the Book of Numbers cover?

2—When the census of Israel was taken who was eligible to be numbered? How many were there (in round figures)? What do authorities estimate the total population of Israel to have been at this time?

3—How did the Lord happen to claim the firstborn of the Israelites? Did he also claim the firstborn of their domestic animals?

4—What was the purpose of the Lord in adopting the tribe of Levi?

5—What was a Nazarite? Was it intended to be a monastic order?

6—Repeat the Levitical prayer revealed by the Lord.

7—If the Israelites had remained righteous, when could they have entered the Promised Land?

8—What signalling device were the Israelites told to use? Who was given the responsibility of sounding the first signal?

9—After the Israelites had marched into the wilderness three days what did they do? What did the Lord do?

10—How was the plague stopped?

11—Who started the next wave of rebellion? Did Moses complain about it?

12—What was the purpose of the council of seventy elders? What kind of spiritual experience did they have?

13—How does the scripture prove that Moses wanted to share the manifestations of the Spirit rather than restrict them to himself?

14—What was the attitude of the Israelites toward the daily ration of manna?

15—How did the Lord provide "flesh?" In what quantity? Were the quail actually piled up "two cubits high" throughout the camp?

16—What happened to those who had "lusted" after flesh? Did Moses try to stop it or did he let it run its course?

17—What did Miriam and Aaron say Moses had done to offend the Lord? What was the real reason for their rebellion against Moses?

18—What happened to Miriam as a result of her role in leading this rebellion?

19—What was the reaction of Aaron? What did he ask Moses to do?

20—Did Moses apparently forgive Miriam? What did the Lord say would be required of her? Did the Israelites respect Miriam?

Chapter Eighteen

Israel Wanders 38 Years in the Wilderness

When the Israelites prepared to break camp at Hazeroth they knew their next stop would be on the borders of Canaan. In fact, the next camp would be their base for the invasion and conquest of the "promised land." Among the hosts of Israel there was undoubtedly a mounting surge of excitement and expectation as "the people removed from Hazeroth, and pitched in the wilderness of Paran."[1]

This "wilderness of Paran" must not be confused with an earlier "Paran" mentioned in Deuteronomy 1:1, which was located very near the Horeb range of mountains which included Sinai. The wilderness of Paran or the wilderness of Zin into which the Israelites had now come consisted of combined stretches of rugged terrain located about 90 miles south of Jerusalem. This is the famous Negeb or "south country" of Abraham's day,[2] and its principal settlement was Kadesh-Barnea.[3]

A good geographical description of Kadesh-Barnea is found in Geikie's Bible series:

"Out from the barren and desolate stretch of the burning desert, we had come with magical suddenness, into an oasis of verdure and beauty, unlooked for and hardly conceivable in such a region. A carpet of grass covered the ground. Fig trees, laden with fruit nearly ripe, dotted the sheltered southern hillside. Shrubs and flowers were in profusion. Running water gurgled in the waving grass. Bees hummed and birds flitted from tree to tree. Huge ant-hills of green grass seed, instead of sand, were numerous. The water which

---

1. Numbers 12:16
2. Genesis 20:1
3. Numbers 13:26

made this beauty rose from springs under the limestone rock and was gathered into two great wells, with large pools beyond them, down the slope, to retain the overflow, but still beyond these, it flowed away down the wady under the grass. This was the place where Moses fixed his headquarters [off and on] for nearly forty years."[4]

But Moses had no idea he would be in this general vicinity for nearly 40 years — 38½ to be exact. The slow and tedious journey to the borders of Canaan was for the express purpose of taking possession of this land as the Lord had commanded them when they left Sinai only a few weeks earlier. Moses felt that the sooner they took it the better.

The First Signs of Timidity Appear Among the Israelites

As the Israelites contemplated the approaching zero hour when they would send their hosts from Paran to Canaan, Moses encouraged them by saying, "Ye are come unto the mountain of the Amorites, which the Lord our God doth give unto us. Behold the Lord thy God hath set the land before thee; go up and possess it, as the Lord God of thy fathers hath said unto thee: fear not, neither be discouraged."[5]

The leaders of Israel hesitated. They said, "We will send men before us, and they shall search us out the land, and bring us word again by what way we must go up, and into what cities we shall come."[6]

This seemed to make sense to Moses and so he consented.[7] The Lord also consented.[8] But it is one thing to spy out a land to see how it shall be taken; it is quite another thing to spy out a land looking for evidence that it *cannot* be taken. The Lord said to send one man from each tribe.[9]

---

4. Cunningham Geikie, *Hours with the Bible,* Vol. 2, p. 364
5. Deuteronomy 1:20-21
6. Deuteronomy 1:22
7. Numbers 13:2
8. Deuteronomy 1:23
9. Since the tribe of Levi was not involved in the military conquest of Canaan, this tribe was not represented. However, both Ephraim and Manasseh were represented so the total number of spies was 12.

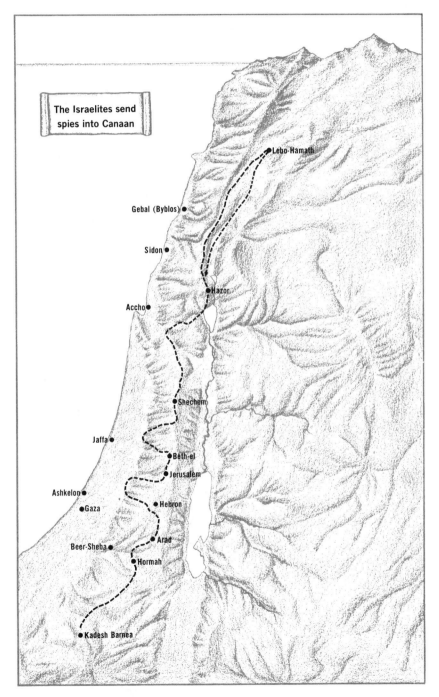

The Israelites send
spies into Canaan

Caleb represented Judah[10] and Joshua represented Ephraim.[11] The names of the other ten are also listed in scripture,[12] but they are not individuals about whom further background is known. To these twelve men Moses gave the following instructions:

"Get you up this way southward, and go up into the mountain; And see the land, what it is; and the people that dwelleth therein, whether they be strong or weak, few or many; and what the land is that they dwell in, whether it be good or bad; and what cities they be that they dwell in, whether in tents, or in strong holds; and what the land is, whether it be fat or lean, whether there be wood therein or not. And be ye of good courage, and bring of the fruit of the land."[13]

The length of Canaan is about 180 miles and the average width between the Mediterranean Sea and the River Jordan is about 40 miles. The twelve spies of Israel spent about six weeks covering it. The scripture says "they went up, and searched the land from the wildernness of Zin unto Rehob, as men come to Hamath."[14]

On the return journey they concentrated their surveillance in the south because that was where the first attack would have to occur. Two things impressed them. First, they were amazed at the fertility of some of these valleys and they carried back various kinds of fruit to show to Moses as he had requested. At the brook of Eshcol they cut down one huge cluster of grapes which required two men to carry it on a staff.[15] The second thing which impressed these spies was the exceptionally large-statured men at Anak.[16] These giant-like specimens of humanity were among the last of a whole nation of over-sized people who had developed among the Canaanites and occupied parts of this territory. We shall hear of the Anaks later in our account.

After forty days, the spies returned to report.[17]

As Moses listened to them it was easy to see that there was unanimous and enthusiastic agreement that this was

10. Numbers 13:6
11. Numbers 13:8,16
12. Numbers 13:4-15
13. Numbers 13:17-20

14. Numbers 13:21
15. Numbers 13:23
16. Numbers 13:22, 33
17. Numbers 13:25

undoubtedly the most fertile, prosperous and productive country they had ever seen. They showed Moses the pomegranates, figs and grapes they had brought with them.[18] But when it came to a report on the military aspects of Canaan these spies were heatedly divided.

The maritime plain along the coast of the Mediterranean was occupied primarily by the Canaanites who had built fleets of merchantmen and warships which made calls at all of the ports of the known world. These Canaanites had also migrated east from the maritime plain to cross the mountainous backbone of Judea and Samaria, and had spilled over into the Jordan Valley. The mountains themselves were occupied by the Hittites and Jebusites in what came to be called Judea, while the area which came to be known as Samaria was occupied by the Hivites. The northern mountains on the west of Galilee were occupied by the Perizzites.[19]

THE MILITARY REPORT OF THE SPIES

As the spies made their reports on the possibility of conquering this territory, ten of them vehemently declared it was impossible. Said they:

"We came unto the land whither thou sentest us, and surely it floweth with milk and honey; and this is the fruit of it. Nevertheless the people be strong that dwell in the land, and the cities are walled, and very great; and moreover we saw the children of Anak there. The Amalekites dwell in the land of the south: and the Hittites, and the Jebusites, and the Amorites, dwell in the mountains; and the Canaanites dwell by the sea, and by the coast of Jordan."[20]

Apparently the leaders of the tribes and many of the Israelites had gathered to hear the report. As soon as they heard these words they were deeply disturbed and began to murmer. Caleb, who had represented the tribe of Judah, objected to this report. He "stilled the people before Moses" and then declared boldly: "Let us go up at once, and possess it; for we are well able to overcome it."[21] Joshua, who represented the tribe of Ephraim, agreed with Caleb.[22]

18. Numbers 13:23
19. Dummelow's *Bible Commentary*, p. 107
20. Numbers 13:27-29
21. Numbers 13:30
22. Numbers 14:6-9

But the other ten continued to rebel against the Lord's announced program of occupation. Said they: "We be not able to go up against the people; for they are stronger than we. . . . The land through which we have gone to search it, is a land that eateth up the inhabitants thereof:[23] and all the people that we saw in it are men of a great stature. And there we saw the giants, the sons of Anak, which come of the giants: and we were in our own sight as grasshoppers, and so we were in their sight."[24]

THE MILITARY REPORT RESULTS IN MUTINY

When the people had heard the spies' full report — particularly the part about the ferocious giants of Anak — they spent the whole night howling and weeping in bitter protest against Moses and Aaron. By morning they had worked themselves into a hysterical uproar. The scripture says:

"And the whole congregation said unto them [Moses and Aaron]: Would God that we had died in the land of Egypt! or would God we had died in this wilderness! And wherefore hath the Lord brought us unto this land, to fall by the sword, that our wives and our children should be a prey? were it not better for us to return into Egypt?"[25]

This fantastic and cowardly compulsion to flee "when no man pursueth" clearly reflected the psychological scars of the years of slavery in Egypt. Here they were safely encamped at Kadesh without the slightest danger of attack, yet they behaved as though the giants of Anak were already pouncing down upon them. Not only did their emotional intoxication drive them to plot an insurrection against Moses and Aaron, but they proposed to abandon the purpose of their long journey from Egypt, select a new leader, and march back to the slime-pits of the brickyards on the Nile. Said they:

"Let us make a captain, and let us return into Egypt."[26]

---

23. Authorities have not been able to agree as to whether this refers to outright cannibalism or whether it means they "eateth up the inhabitants" of the land through constant strife.
24. Numbers 13:31-33
25. Numbers 14:2-3
26. Numbers 14:4

According to the prophet Nehemiah the rebels actually went through with the traitorous act of appointing a new leader.[27]

When Moses and Aaron both saw how far things had gone they simply bowed to the ground in grief before the Lord.[28] However, Caleb of Judah and Joshua of Ephraim refused to take this disgraceful collapse of Israel's morale without at least making one final attempt to rally their senses. Standing before the whole multitude they rent their clothes and cried out:

"The land, which we passed through to search it, is an exceeding good land. If the Lord delight in us, then he will bring us into this land, and give it us; a land which floweth with milk and honey. Only rebel not ye against the Lord, neither fear ye the people of the land: for they are bread for us; their defense is departed from them, and the Lord is with us; fear them not."[29]

But the rebellious Israelites were not to be diverted from their subversive plans. In reply to Caleb and Joshua they did not use words but stones![30] Had not the Lord intervened they would have undoubtedly both been killed. The thing which saved them was the sudden appearance of the cloud of God's glory over the Tabernacle. The multitude immediately knew that the Lord had come to converse with Moses and this temporarily sobered their murderous rage.

And indeed the Lord had come to converse with Moses. He passed a death sentence on the whole rebellious camp. Said He:

"How long will this people provoke me? and how long will it be ere they believe me, for all the signs which I have shewed among them? I will smite them with the pestilence, and disinherit them, and will make of thee [Moses] a greater nation and mightier than they."[31]

These were familiar words to Moses. This was exactly what the Lord had said when the Israelites had worshipped the golden calf. Because Moses knew how literally the Lord

27. Nehemiah 9:17
28. Numbers 14:5
29. Numbers 14:7-9

30. Numbers 14:10
31. Numbers 14:11-12

intended to fulfill this sentence he reacted just as he had on Mount Sinai. Almost in the same words, Moses took the defensive and pleaded for this traitorous and rebellious people. It was obvious that the love of Moses for these wayward Israelites was practically without bounds. Said he:

"Then the Egyptians shall hear it . . . and they will tell it to the inhabitants of this land; for they have heard that thou Lord art among this people, that thou Lord art seen face to face, and that thy cloud standeth over them, and that thou goest before them, by day-time in a pillar of a cloud, and in a pillar of fire by night. Now if thou shalt kill all this people as one man, then the nations which have heard the fame of thee will speak, saying, Because the Lord was not able to bring this people into the land which he sware unto them, therefore he hath slain them in the wilderness . . . Pardon, I beseech thee, the iniquity of this people according unto the greatness of thy mercy, and as thou hast forgiven this people, from Egypt even until now."[32]

This was a humble yet eloquent petition. The Lord could have answered the arguments of Moses very easily, but He did not. He consented to postpone the death of the rebellious Israelites until He had raised up a nation "mightier than they." How could He do that? The Lord said He would do it by condemning these rebellious men and women who were twenty years or older at the time they left Egypt, to wander in the wilderness until they had died and their places had been filled by their children. The Lord made only two exceptions to this decree of death for all adult Israelites. One exception was Caleb, the faithful son of Judah and the other was Joshua, the valiant son of Ephraim. Of all the adult Israelites only these two would enter the promised land. In making this solemn decree, this is the way the Lord said it:

"Your carcasses shall fall in this wilderness; and all that were numbered of you, according to your whole number, from twenty years old and upward, which have murmured against me . . . ye shall not come into the land concerning which I sware to make you dwell therein, save Caleb the son of Jephunneh, and Joshua the son of Nun. But your little ones, which ye said should be a prey, them will I bring in,

---

32. Numbers 14:13-19

"Wherefore now do ye transgress the commandment of the Lord? but it shall not prosper. Go not up, for the Lord is not among you; that ye be not smitten before your enemies."[36]

"But," the scripture says, "They presumed to go up."[37] They marched out to battle and ran head on into the strongly entrenched heathen Amorites who came pouring down out of the mountains and slaughtered the Israelite armies all the way from Hormah to Kadesh.[38] It was a mammoth defeat and no doubt Moses saw a broken and humiliated band of Israelites as the survivors came straggling back into camp carrying their dead and wounded. They had presumed to go up without the Lord.

So this was the end of Israel's attempt to conquer Canaan. Not at any time in that generation would it be attempted again. For over thirty-eight years they would wander up and down the region of the Arabah — the valley connecting the Dead Sea with the Akaba gulf of the Red Sea. Kadesh would remain the general headquarters but the camps would be moved from place to place as their flocks and other circumstances required it.

It is difficult to appreciate how slowly these 38 years dragged along for Moses. He makes no attempt to burden the record with painful details concerning it. Only occasionally does he refer to some incidents of critical importance. It is impossible to fix the dates of such incidents because Moses did not include them. We just know they occurred during the "wandering in the wilderness."

KORAH AND 250 LEADERS OF ISRAEL ASPIRE TO THE HIGHER PRIESTHOOD

Sometime during those weary years in the wilderness a rebellion occurred against Moses and Aaron because the Levites could not participate in the functions of the higher Priesthood.[39]

The leader of this priestly rebellion was Korah, great-grandson of Levi and first cousin of Moses and Aaron.[40]

---

36. Numbers 14:41-42
37. Numbers 14:44
38. Numbers 14:45; Deut. 1:42-45

39. Numbers 16:10
40. Exodus 6:18-21

He rallied about him 250 of the "princes of the assembly. famous in the congregation, men of renown."[41] Korah's complaint against Moses and Aaron was because they did not share the privilege of performing ordinances before the Lord's sanctuary in the Holy of Holies. They shouted out against Moses and Aaron in these defiant words:

"Ye take too much upon you, seeing all the congregation are holy, every one of them, and the Lord is among them: wherefore then lift ye up yourselves above the congregation of the Lord?

"And when Moses heard it, he fell upon his face: And he spake unto Korah and unto all his company, saying, Even tomorrow the Lord will show who are his, and who is holy; . . . This do: Take you censers, Korah, and all his company; and put fire therein, and put incense in them before the Lord tomorrow; and it shall be that the man whom the Lord doth choose, he shall be holy; ye take too much upon you, ye sons of Levi."[42]

At this point Moses decided to make the issue sufficiently clear-cut so that Korah and his co-conspirators would have no doubt as to the seriousness of their offense: Said he:

"Hear, I pray you, ye sons of Levi [leaders of the rebellion]: Seemeth it but a small thing unto you, that the God of Israel hath separated you from the congregation of Israel, to bring you near to himself, to do the service of the tabernacle of the Lord, and to stand before the congregation to minister unto them? And he hath brought thee near to him, and all thy brethren the sons of Levi with thee: and SEEK YE THE [higher] PRIESTHOOD ALSO?"[43]

Apparently two of Korah's conspirators of the tribe of Reuben named Dathan and Abiram were not present when all of this was going on, so Moses sent for them. They refused to come. They were so bitter in their denunciation of Moses that they even blamed him because Israel had not yet obtained the promised land.[44]

---

41. Numbers 16:2
42. Numbers 16:3-7
43. Numbers 16:8-10. It should be kept in mind that the Levites already had the Levitical Priesthood, but it would not permit them to perform the ordinances in the Tabernacle.
44. Numbers 16:12-14

As soon as Moses received this message the scripture says he "was very wroth."[45] He demanded that all these rebellious Levites and the princes of the congregation meet him the following day before the Tabernacle. He told them to each bring a censer, lighted with fire, and they would see whose offering would be accepted by the Lord.

When this meeting took place the following day, a vast congregation gathered to see what would happen. The first thing that occurred was the illumination of the cloud over the Tabernacle signifying the immediate presence of God. In fact, the Lord spoke to Moses and Aaron, saying, "Separate yourselves from among this congregation, that I may consume them in a moment."[46]

But Moses pleaded with the Lord and said, "O God, the God of the spirits of all flesh, shall one man sin, and wilt thou be wrath with all the congregation?"[47]

In response to the plea of Moses, the Lord once more spared the congregation but insisted that those who had led the rebellion should be punished.

The Fate of Korah and His Fellow Conspirators

The Lord told Moses to warn the Israelites to flee from the part of the camp where Korah, Dathan and Abiram had pitched their tents.[48] Moses therefore left the Tabernacle and went to the place where the warning needed to be given "and the elders of Israel followed him."[49] Raising his voice so all could hear him, Moses cried out:

"Depart, I pray you, from the tents of these wicked men, and touch nothing of theirs, lest ye be consumed in all their sins."[50]

The people immediately began to gather their belongings and flee from the place where God's wrath was about to strike. But Dathan and Abiram stood contemptuously with their families at the door of their tents. Since Korah was punished with Dathan and Abiram, he must have come down from the Tabernacle with Moses and joined his family.

---

45. Numbers 16:15
46. Numbers 16:21
47. Numbers 16:22

48. Numbers 16:23-24
49. Numbers 16:25
50. Numbers 16:26

When Moses had assembled the multitude at a safe distance, he gave the people a warning and a prophecy. He warned them that what was about to happen would be proof that he, Moses, was a true prophet. Then he prophesied exactly how Korah, Dathan and Abiram would die. Said he:

"Hereby ye shall know that the Lord hath sent me to do all these works; for I have not done them of mine own mind. If these men die the common death of all men . . . then the Lord hath not sent me. But if the Lord make a new thing, and the earth open her mouth, and swallow them up, with all that appertain unto them, and they go down quick into the pit, then ye shall understand that these men have provoked the Lord"[51]

And instantly, even as Moses "made an end of speaking,"[52] a terrible earthquake shook the camp so that "the earth opened her mouth, and swallowed them up, and their houses, and all the men that appertained unto Korah, and all their goods."[53]

The watching multitude were terrified by the scene and as they heard the "cry of them" who slid into the yawning abyss, they fled in wild disorder for fear they also would go crashing down into the bowels of the earth.[54]

Meanwhile, the 250 princes of Israel who were waiting with their censers at the Tabernacle to prove their acceptance by the Lord, found themselves caught in the same vortex of God's vengeance as Korah, Dathan and Abiram. However, the princes of Israel did not die by being swallowed up in the earth. Their death came through a consuming fire.[55]

The Lord then commanded Moses to tell Eleazar, the son of Aaron, to go out among these 250 dead princes and gather up all their brass censers. The Lord said the brass from these incense burners should be made into flat plates and these plates should then be used to cover the altar of sacrifice which stood before the Tabernacle.[56] Moses was

51. Numbers 16:28-30
52. Numbers 16:31
53. Numbers 16:32-33
54. Numbers 16:34
55. Numbers 16:35
56. Numbers 16:38. As a result, the altar of sacrifice became known as the "brazen" altar to distinguish it from the altar of incense inside the Tabernacle.

told that henceforth these brass plates on the altar were designed to memorialize the fate of those who rebelled against God.

The Congregation Rebels and 14,700 are Killed by a Plague

One would have expected that such manifestations of God's indignation would have left the hosts of Israel humble and repentant. In fact, if Moses had not interceded for them, they all would have been dead by now.[57] The record is clear, however, that instead of being repentant, those obstinate Israelites began pointing the finger of accusation at Moses and Aaron, demanding that *they* repent. The rebels saw no justice in the cataclysmic destruction of Korah and his fellow conspirators. They accused Moses and Aaron of murder, saying, "Ye have killed the people of the Lord."[58]

Before Moses could rebuke this latest outburst, the glory of God's presence appeared in a cloud above the Tabernacle and the Lord told Moses He was commencing immediately to consume these wretched mutineers. Moses once more decided to throw his own good offices on the scales of God's judgment in an effort to save these ungrateful sychophants. He said to Aaron: "Take a censer, and put fire therein from off the altar, and put on incense, and go quickly unto the congregation, and make an atonement for them, for there is wrath gone out from the Lord; the plague is begun."[59]

Aaron did as Moses commanded. He took the censer and quickly went through the prescribed ordinance of atonement, then he rushed into Israel's city of tents to discover how far the plague had spread. When Aaron had found its boundaries, "he stood between the dead and the living; and the plague was stayed."[60]

Then the incident closes with this sobering passage: "Now they that died in the plague were fourteen thousand and seven hundred, beside them that died about the matter of Korah. And Aaron returned unto Moses unto the door

---

57. Numbers 16:21-22
58. Numbers 16:41

59. Numbers 16:46
60. Numbers 16:48

of the tabernacle of the congregation: and the plague was stayed."[61]

THE MIRACULOUS ROD OF AARON

In fulfilling the prophecy of destruction which Moses had pronounced on Korah, Dathan and Abiram, the Lord had verified once more that Moses was His chosen prophet. In destroying the 250 princes the Lord had verified that no one is to serve in His sanctuary unless he is chosen through the divinely appointed channels of the Priesthood. Now the Lord had one final project in mind and that was to verify that Aaron was the priest over the people and that only he or his sons were to minister at the altar of incense and within the veil. To impress this upon all Israel forever, the Lord said to Moses, "Speak unto the children of Israel, and take of every one of them a rod according to the house of their fathers . . . twelve rods: write thou every man's name [who represents a tribe] upon his rod. And thou shalt write Aaron's name upon the rod of Levi: for one rod shall be for the head of the house of their fathers. And thou shalt lay them up in the tabernacle of the congregation before the testimony, where I will meet with you. And it shall come to pass, that the man's rod, whom I shall choose, shall blossom: and I will make to cease from me the murmurings of the children of Israel, whereby they murmur against you."[62]

So Moses had each tribe write its leader's name upon a rod or staff, and all of them were placed in the Holy of Holies before the Ark of the Covenant. There they remained until the next day.

The following morning, Moses brought forth the twelve rods. To the astonishment of everyone, the rod of Aaron which had been inscribed with his insignia for the tribe of Levi, had burst into live growth so that overnight it had produced buds, blossoms and matured almonds. And the Lord said, "Bring Aaron's rod again before the testimony [Ark of the Covenant] to be kept for a token against the rebels; and thou shalt quite take away their murmurings from me, that they die not."[63]

---

61. Numbers 16:49-50   62. Numbers 17:2-4   63. Numbers 17:10

As a result of this incident one more token of physical evidence or "testimony" was included in the Ark of the Covenant. Already, the Lord had consigned the golden bowl of manna and the Tablets of the Law to the Ark as a perpetual witness, but now the rod of Aaron was to be included.[64] Paul says the rod was "in" the Ark rather than "before" it, so this rod may have been the length of a cane rather than a staff since the Ark was only about 45 inches long.[65]

THE THREE LEVELS OF PRIESTHOOD DISTINGUISHED

It was at this point that the Lord reconfirmed the exact status of Aaron and his sons as well as the tribe of Levi.[66] In order to understand the Biblical account, it is helpful to consider all of the information which has now been revealed concerning the three levels of Priesthood — Melchizedek, Aaronic and Levitical.

We should point out, of course, that in reality there is only one Priesthood—the Melchizedek—which is after the Order of the Son of God.[67] This is the overspreading,

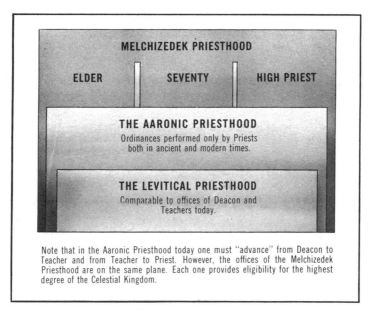

MELCHIZEDEK PRIESTHOOD

ELDER   SEVENTY   HIGH PRIEST

THE AARONIC PRIESTHOOD
Ordinances performed only by Priests
both in ancient and modern times.

THE LEVITICAL PRIESTHOOD
Comparable to offices of Deacon and
Teachers today.

Note that in the Aaronic Priesthood today one must "advance" from Deacon to Teacher and from Teacher to Priest. However, the offices of the Melchizedek Priesthood are on the same plane. Each one provides eligibility for the highest degree of the Celestial Kingdom.

64. Hebrews 9:4
65. Exodus 25:10
66. Numbers, Ch. 18
67. Doctrine and Covenants 107:2-4

all-encompassing authority of God which is delegated to righteous men in order to perform the work of God's kingdom here upon the earth. When men (or youth) are not prepared for the whole Priesthood, the Lord gives them a portion of it which, since the days of Moses, has been called the lesser or Aaronic Priesthood. And when individuals are not prepared for all of the Aaronic, they receive a somewhat lesser portion which, in the days of Israel, was called the Levitical Priesthood. Often the Aaronic and Levitical Priesthoods are considered as one, but this is not entirely accurate because the Levitical order represented only as much as the offices of Deacon and Teacher do today and did not include the right to perform any ordinances.[68] It is believed the student will get a clearer picture of these two Priesthoods if they are treated separately.

THE AARONIC PRIESTHOOD

The Aaronic Priesthood is a functional appendage to the higher or Melchizedek Priesthood.[69] In fact, the man who presides over the Aaronic Priesthood must be a High Priest and therefore a member of the Melchizedek Priesthood.[70] In the days of Moses, this privilege of presiding over the Aaronic Priesthood was made hereditary. Aaron was designated the "High Priest"[71] and when he died this privilege descended to his oldest living son, Eleazar.[72] As we shall see in a moment, worthiness was also required so that if the eldest living son was not worthy the privilege would descend to the next one in line who was worthy.

When Aaron presided over the Aaronic Priesthood in his day he set the pattern for his successors. He was allowed to wear and use the Urim and Thummim.[73] Except for Moses, he was the only one allowed to perform the sacred rites in the Holy of Holies.[74] He was the only one allowed to wear the mitre and the vestments of the High Priest.[75] For all of these reasons we see that the head of the Aaronic Priesthood is an office quite separate and distinct from the regular Aaronic Priesthood members.

---

68. Numbers 18:2
69. Doctrine and Covenants 107:14
70. Doctrine and Covenants 68:19
71. Leviticus 21:10; Numbers 35:25; Joshua 20:6

72. Numbers 20:28
73. Exodus 28:30
74. Hebrews 9:7
75. Leviticus 8:7-9

When the Gospel was restored in modern times, the Lord made it clear that if and when a literal descendant of Aaron came into the Church he would have the privilege of functioning in this hereditary position again: "And if they [future presidents of the Aaronic Priesthood which we call Presiding Bishops] be literal descendants of Aaron they have a legal right to the bishopric, if they are the firstborn among the sons of Aaron. For the firstborn holds the right of the presidency over this priesthood, and the keys or authority of the same. No man has a legal right to this office, to hold the keys of this priesthood, except he be a literal descendant and the firstborn [oldest living heir in the Church] of Aaron."[76]

In the next verse the Lord stresses the importance of worthiness. He states that even the firstborn among the literal descendants of Aaron cannot receive this calling automatically: "And a literal descendant of Aaron, also, must be DESIGNATED by this Presidency [President of the Church] and FOUND WORTHY, and ANOINTED, and ORDAINED under the hands of this Presidency, otherwise they are not legally authorized to officiate in their priesthood."[77]

So far no person has stepped forward to legitimately claim this privilege, nor has the Lord revealed one. The Lord stated that until this happens the First Presidency has the responsibility of selecting someone to fill this office from among the High Priests of the Church.[78]

Now that we have considered the office of the President or High Priest in charge of the Aaronic Priesthood, let us examine the office of the regular members of this Priesthood.

In the days of Israel, membership in the Aaronic Priesthood was hereditary just like the office of High Priest. It could only be given to those who were Aaron's descendants. So Aaron's eldest living heir became the High Priest and the rest of his descendants became holders of the Aaronic Priesthood. They were called "priests" to distinguish them from the members of the Levitical Priesthood who were simply called "Levites".

---

76. Doctrine and Covenants 68:16-18   78. Doctrine and Covenants 68:15, 19
77. Doctrine and Covenants 68:20

The "priests" in Aaron's day had a degree of authority comparable to the Priests in the Aaronic Priesthood today. The Lord says they ministered the preparatory gospel, "Which gospel is the gospel of repentance and of baptism, and the remission of sins, and the law of carnal commandments, which the Lord in his wrath caused to continue with the house of Aaron among the children of Israel until John. . . ."[79] Of course, the carnal commandments have been suspended since the coming of Jesus Christ, but all of the other functions of the priests of Aaron are performed by the priests of the Aaronic Priesthood today.

Here is a summary of the work which Aaronic Priesthood holders had to perform in the days of ancient Israel:

1. Watch over the fire on the altar of burnt offering. This refers to the altar of sacrifice out in front of the Tabernacle where the fire had to be kept burning day and night.[80]

2. Make the morning and evening sacrifice of a lamb accompanied by a Meat (meal) Offering and a Drink Offering.[81]

3. Perform the ordinance of burning incense on the golden altar of the Tabernacle every night and morning.[82]

4. Keep the lamps on the golden candlestick trimmed and burning.[83]

5. Maintain the table of shew-bread in the Tabernacle.[84]

6. Slaughter and offer up sacrifices brought in by the people.[85]

7. Receive and distribute offerings brought in by the people.[86]

8. Perform rites of circumcision.[87]

---

79. Doctrine and Covenants 84:27
80. Leviticus 6:12; 2 Chronicles 13:11
81. Exodus 29:38-44
82. Exodus 30:7-8. The performance of many of these rites is described as being done by Aaron, but he did so in his office of "priest" rather than High Priest. And the office of "priest'" belonged to Aaron's sons as well as to him. (See Exodus 30:30.)
83. Exodus 30:7-8
84. Leviticus 24:5-9
85. Leviticus 9:15
86. Leviticus 9:16-22
87. Joshua 5:8. While Joshua had the assignment notice that "they" (which would necessarily refer to the priests) helped him get it done.

9. Perform baptisms.[88]

10. Teach the children of Israel the statutes of the Lord.[89]

11. Sound the silver trumpets to give the alarm or troop signals in time of war and to announce the festivals of the Lord in times of peace.[90]

Whenever the sons of Aaron were ministering at the Tabernacle they were required to wear certain "holy garments" designed "for glory and for beauty."[91] The priests wore much simpler clothing than the High Priest. Their vestments consisted of linen breeches and a "coat" or cassock of linen that came nearly to the feet. The cassock was held close to the body with a girdle.[92] Their linen bonnets were in the shape of a round, cup-shaped flower.[93]

This clothing was not to be worn outside the precincts of the Tabernacle or Temple: "And it shall come to pass, that when they enter in at the gates of the inner court, they shall be clothed with linen garments; and no wool [apparently because of the heat] shall come upon them, while they minister in the gates of the inner court and within. They shall have linen bonnets upon their heads, and shall have linen breeches upon their loins; they shall not gird themselves with any thing that causeth sweat. And when they go forth into the utter [outer] court, even into the utter court of the people, they shall put off their garments wherein they ministered, and lay them in the holy chambers, and they shall put on other garments. . . ."[94]

The priests were forbidden to shave their heads or let their hair grow long so as to distinguish them as a separate class.[95]

In the days of King David when the sons of Aaron had become so numerous that there were more priests than were

88. Doctrine and Covenants 84:26-27. In this reference the Lord states that the ordinance of baptizing specifically belonged to the Aaronic Priesthood during the days of Israel.
89. Leviticus 10:11; Deuteronomy 33:10; 2 Chronicles 15:3; Ezekiel 44:23-24
90. Numbers 10:1-8
91. Exodus 28:40
92. Ibid.
93. Ibid, plus Peloubet's *Bible Dictionary*, under "Priest," p. 530.
94. Ezekiel 44:17-19
95. Ezekiel 44:20

needed in the Temple service at any one time, he divided them into 24 courses which represented the number of family chiefs at that time who had descended from Aaron's two sons, Eleazar and Ithamar.[96] (Nadab and Abihu, the two older sons, died without offspring—1 Chronicles 24:2.) Each of these courses or groups would serve at the Temple in rotation for one week.[97] Individual assignments to members of a group were determined by lot.[98]

While not occupied at the Temple, the priests were busy serving the people in their local communities. They had multiple duties of both a religious and temporal nature. They were teachers, preachers, baptists, judges, law enforcement officials and supervisors of the Levitical Priesthood which assisted them.

THE LEVITICAL PRIESTHOOD

To gather some idea of the gargantuan task which fell upon the priests while serving in the Temple, it only need be remembered that on occasions such as feast days there might be several thousand sacrifices and offerings. To assist the priests in these and similar duties, the Lord set up the Levitical Priesthood. The name is taken from the fact that membership in it was restricted to members of the tribe of Levi. In other words, it was a hereditary Priesthood just like the Aaronic Priesthood and also the position of High Priest.

The functional level of the Levitical Priesthood was comparable to the position of Deacon and Teacher in the lesser Priesthood today.[99] The Levites assisted the priests in the sacrifices just as Deacons and Teachers assist in preparing the sacrament. They collected, handled and delivered the various offerings just as the Deacons do today. They had charge of keeping order and seeing that everything was clean and comfortable, just as the Deacons are expected to do today.[100] The Levites were assigned to preach, teach, ex-

---

96. 1 Chronicles 24:1-19
97. 2 Chronicles 23:8
98. Luke 1:9
99. "And again, the offices of teacher and deacon are necessary appendages belonging to the lesser priesthood, which priesthood was confirmed upon Aaron and his sons." (Doc. and Cov. 84:30)
100. Doctrine and Covenants 84:111

hort, visit the people, detect evil, eliminate quarreling, encourage attendance at Sabbath services, and otherwise "watch over the church always" just as Teachers are required to do today.[101]

So much for the duties of the Levitical Priesthood. The Levites also had definite restrictions. For example, they could not perform any of the ordinances. The same restriction is put on Deacons and Teachers in modern times.[102] Concerning the Levites, the Lord said to Aaron, "And thy brethren also of the tribe of Levi, the tribe of thy father, bring thou with thee, that they may be joined unto thee, and minister [give assistance] unto thee: BUT THOU AND THY SONS WITH THEE SHALL MINISTER BEFORE THE TABERNACLE OF WITNESS."[103]

Since ordinances were performed only by the priests, therefore only the sons of Aaron were entitled to be called, "priests". All of the Levitical Priesthood were called, "Levites". Whenever the scripture mentions "the priests of Levi" it is always referring to those Levites who were sons of Aaron and who held the Aaronic Priesthood.

Members of the Levitical Priesthood did not have to actively serve longer than age fifty.[104] Their assignments were often extremely strenuous, particularly those involving the handling of sacrificial animals. After age fifty they merely moved among the congregation serving as watchmen and counsellors.[105]

We have already observed that during the wandering in the wilderness the Levites were divided into three courses and given separate assignments in connection with dismantling and transporting of the Tabernacle. In the days of David, the Levitical Priesthood had become so numerous that he divided them into 24 courses just as he did the sons of Aaron.[106] Each course of Levites was assigned to one of the courses of priests.[107] They would then go to the Temple together to serve on a rotating basis for one week. When not occupied at the Temple the Levites would assist the

---

101. Doctrine and Covenants 20:53-59
102. Doctrine and Covenants 20:58
103. Numbers 18:2
104. Numbers 8:25
105. Numbers 8:26
106. 1 Chronicles 24:20-30
107. 1 Chronicles 24:31

priests in teaching and administering to the temporal welfare of the various tribes in the area where they were assigned.

It will be readily appreciated why the Levites were not given an inheritance but were required to live in certain cities which were judiciously scattered among all the tribes.

It is important to note that the Levitical Priesthood was never considered a separate or independent order. It was always looked upon as simply an "appendage" to the Aaronic Priesthood. In modern times the Lord speaks of the Aaronic Priesthood as "including the Levitical Priesthood."[108] In fact, in modern times the distinction between the Levitical and Aaronic Priesthoods was dissolved so that we now speak of Deacons and Teachers as members of the Aaronic Priesthood right along with the Priests. Eventually, the Lord has indicated that the distinction between the Aaronic and Melchizedek Priesthood will be dissolved the same way. This will occur when "the sons of Levi do offer again an offering unto the Lord in righteousness."[109]

The offices and functions will not necessarily be dissolved, but they will be considered a part of the Melchizedek Priesthood just as they were in ancient times before apostasy and rebellion forced the Lord to divide the Priesthood into the three functional levels which we have described above.

THE LEGAL STATUS OF THE LEVITES

As we have previously pointed out, the Lord originally wanted Israel to be a "kingdom of priests"[110] instead of designating a specialized group from a single tribe to serve. We have also observed that the adoption of the tribe of Levi by the Lord was an emergency measure designed to maintain a fixed responsibility in one group for the spiritual welfare of the weaker and more rebellious groups. To make this procedure practical, the Lord resorted to a number of devices to protect and reward the Levites after they reached the promised land:[111]

---

108. Doctrine and Covenants 107:1
109. Doctrine and Covenants Section 13
110. Exodus 19:6
111. Numbers, Ch. 18. See also Clarke, *Bible Commentary*, Vol 1, pp. 674-675

First, they were deprived of any specific territorial inheritance in the promised land.

Second, in place of an inheritance they were awarded the tithes of all the production of the whole territory. The Levites, in turn, paid a tithe to the house of Aaron.

Third, they were excused from military service but at the same time were deprived of any political status.

Fourth, since they had no territorial inheritance they were scattered throughout Israel and occupied 48 cities each forming a square of 4,000 cubits.

Fifth, they also had 2,000 cubits of ground on the outskirts of each city. (The total amount of land in the possession of the Levites was 53,000 acres or approximately 1/212th of Israel's territory.)

Sixth, in addition to receiving the tithes of the whole land, the Levites received meat, bread, flour, grain and fruit from the offerings made at the Tabernacle. These were to be the "best of the land." Some of them had to be eaten within the Tabernacle courtyard, while others could be shared with their families.

This, in essence, was the legal status of the tribe of Levi provided by the Lord. Dr. Adam Clarke states that "while it was a slender remuneration for their services, yet their portion was such as rendered them independent, and kept them comfortable; so that they could wait on the Lord's work without distraction."[112]

The Ordinance of the Red Heifer

Before closing this chapter we need to mention one final incident. Sometime during the wandering in the wilderness the Lord added the ordinance of the Red Heifer to the ritual of the carnal commandments.[113] It will be recalled that persons who were "unclean" were required to stay outside of the camp for a period of time, particularly those who had been involved in disposing of the dead. Before they could return to the city they had to be inspected and pronounced ceremonially clean. To give emphasis to this procedure the ordinance of the Red Heifer was introduced.

This consisted of sacrificing a red heifer outside of the camp. Its blood was sprinkled in the direction of the sanctu-

---

112. Clarke, *Bible Commentary*, Vol 1, p. 675
113. Numbers, Ch. 19

ary seven times and then the entire carcass was burned in the place where the heifer was killed along with cedar wood, hyssop, and scarlet wool. The ashes were then carefully gathered together and put in a "clean place." A portion of these would be mixed with water to sprinkle on "unclean" persons preparatory to pronouncing them "clean." The water was also sprinkled around a tent or room where a person had died, thereby proclaiming it "clean" and habitable again.

The water (mixed with the red heifer ashes) was called the "water of separation" or water for the removal of ceremonial impurity. Obviously, this was just one more ceremonial appendage designed to teach the rebellious Israelites the rhythm of obedience.

CONCLUSION

Thus we come to the conclusion of a long series of monumental events in the history of Israel. During all this period the whole populace of Israel pursued a course which was continuously bordering on the brink of extinction. It was a strenuous, disappointing and frustrating period for Moses. As with the patriarchs before him, Moses found his family and his friends as much of a trial as his enemies. The Lord and His prophets have always had great ambitions for the human family, but the problem of the people has been to keep up with the Lord and His prophets. In the case of Israel, they often stopped trying. They replaced refinement with defilement, and cooperation with mutiny. During the ministry of Moses this became the story of his life. It finally brought him to the climax of his earthly career. We call it the fateful fortieth year in the ministry of Moses and this we will consider next.

Scripture Reading and Questions on Chapter Eighteen

Scripture Reading Assignment: Numbers, chapters 13 to 19.

1—Who first suggested that spies be sent into the land of Canaan? Did Moses agree? Did the Lord?

2—When the spies were selected, who represented Judah? Who represented Ephraim? Why wasn't Levi represented?

3—How many spies felt Canaan was too strong to be conquered? Who opposed them? Which side did the people choose to support?

4—When the people rebelled, how far did they actually go? What suddenly brought the rebellion to a halt?

5—What did the Lord say he was going to do to all the adult Israelites? What dissuaded the Lord from taking this action?

6—Nevertheless, the Lord did issue a decree against Israel—what was it? What special promise did the Lord make to Caleb and Joshua? What happened to the ten spies whose report had started the rebellion?

7—What drastic action did the Israelites decide to take in an effort to remove God's judgment? Why didn't Moses support this action?

8—What accusation did Korah and the princes of Israel make against Moses and Aaron? How did Moses say the question could be resolved?

9—What happened to Korah, Dathan and Abiram? What happened to the 250 princes of Israel?

10—Did the people accept this judgment from God? What did the Lord do? How many died as a result?

11—Relate the incident involving the blossoming of Aaron's rod. What was this intended to show? What happened to Aaron's rod afterwards?

12—Must a man be a High Priest to preside over the Aaronic Priesthood? Is this also true of a literal descendant of Aaron?

13—If a literal descendant of Aaron came forward would he automatically start functioning as the presiding bishop of the Church or would something else have to happen first?

14—What office in the Aaronic Priesthood today compares with the "Priests" in the days of Moses and Aaron?

15—What offices in the Aaronic Priesthood today compare with the basic responsibilities of the Levitical Priesthood of ancient Israel?

16—After Aaron's death what were the two requirements for the selection of a new High Priest to take his place?

17—What were the five distinctive vestments of the High Priest?

18—How many things can you recall concerning the inheritance promised to the Levites in the Promised Land?

19—Was the ordinance of the Red Heifer part of the substantive Gospel or was it added to emphasize obedience along with the other carnal commandments?

20—Why do you think the Saints of almost every dispensation have failed to keep up with the Lord and his prophets? Is this true today?

Chapter Nineteen

The Fateful Fortieth Year in the Ministry of Moses

When Moses sat down to record the highlights of his life he restricted himself almost exclusively to the events of five separate years.

There was the first year when he escaped being drowned in the Nile and through the providence of God became the adopted son of Pharaoh's daughter.

There was the fortieth year when he became a fugitive from Pharaoh's wrath and fled to Midian where he took up the role of a humble shepherd.

There was his eightieth year when he received his prophetic calling, returned to Egypt, rescued Israel, and marched them to the precincts of Mount Sinai.

Then came the eighty-first year when he built the Tabernacle, taught Israel the Mosaic Law and tried to prepare them to take over the promised land. When that failed, the rebellious Israelites were condemned to wander in the wilderness until that entire generation (except Caleb and Joshua) had died off. For Moses it was a period of 38 sterile, nomadic years about which he tells us practically nothing.

Finally he comes to the last year of his life when the significant events took place which we are about to relate. By this time Moses was nearing 120. Since he had received his calling at eighty, his prophetic mission had lasted thirty-nine years and he was now about to start the fateful fortieth year which would bring him to the end of his life.

MOSES LOSES HIS SISTER MIRIAM

The camps of Israel had moved many times during the long years since they had left Egypt. In his record Moses provides a chronological list of each encampment.[1] It appears, however, that he had maintained his headquarters fairly close to Kadesh on the borders of Canaan. This was the invasion base which he had set up thirty-eight years[2] before but was never used because the people mutinied and lost the support of the Lord. Now, however, it was time to bring the Israelites to Kadesh once more. According to Moses this was their thirty-second move since leaving Egypt.[3] Great changes had taken place in Israel between their first and second visit to Kadesh. During those thirty-eight years the rebels had died at the average rate of 16,000 per year. Only a few of them were left, and before the year was out even that remnant would be gone except for Caleb and Joshua.

However, not only the wicked died, the righteous had also. The scripture says it was at this time that Moses lost his sister Miriam. Just one year before the Israelites took possession of the Promised Land, Miriam died at Kadesh and there she was buried.[4]

It is known that Miriam was somewhat older that Moses, probably as much as ten years.[5] This would mean that she died around the age of 129. Moses could not have helped but feel an extremely deep sense of loss as this remarkable woman was finally laid to rest. As a young girl, Miriam had risked her life to guard the tiny ark which contained the infant Moses as he lay hidden among the bulrushes. After the Exodus from Egypt she had become known as "Miriam the prophetess"[6] which indicates that she had been endowed with great spiritual power and assumed a position of prominence in the affairs of Israel. It was she who led all the women of Israel in a song of rejoicing following their passage through the Red Sea and the destruction of Pharaoh and his armies.[7]

---

1. Numbers, Ch. 33. No one pretends to know where all of these camp sites were located. It is believed, however, that most of them were located between the Akaba Gulf of the Red Sea and Kadesh.
2. We usually speak of the "wandering in the wilderness" as lasting 40 years without realizing that "40 years" refers to the entire period from the time they left Egypt. Actually, the "wandering" did not begin until the second year away from Egypt when they were rejected at Kadesh for their rebellion. Hence we use "38 years" in describing the period of "wandering."
3. Numbers 33:36
4. Numbers 20:1   6. Exodus 15:20-21
5. See Clarke, *Bible Commentary*, Vol. 1, p. 678   7. Exodus 14:20-21

Except for the one tragic incident of jealousy and sedition when she and Aaron had rebelled against Moses, Miriam apparently enjoyed a long life of faithful service. As Aaron and Moses laid her to rest in a tomb at Kadesh they probably never suspected that within three months Aaron would follow his sister, and before the year was out Moses would be gone as well.

MOSES AND AARON OFFEND THE LORD

It was soon after the camps of Israel were established at Kadesh that Moses found the water supply completely exhausted. Whether this was due to the time of season or an unexpected failure of the usual supply we are not told. It is plain, however, that this place which had provided the Israelites with adequate resources thirty-eight years earlier was no longer habitable.

As was their custom in a time of tribulation, the people in the camps set up a cry of protest. They said to Moses, "Would God that we had died when our brethren died before the Lord! And why have ye brought up the congregation of the Lord into this wilderness, that we and our cattle should die there? And wherefore have ye made us to come up out of Egypt, to bring us in unto this evil place? It is no place of seed, or of figs, or of vines, or of pomegranates; neither is there any water to drink."[8]

Moses and Aaron appealed to the Lord and Moses was ordered to repeat a miracle which he had performed during the first year of the Exodus.[9] The Lord said to Moses, "Take the rod, and gather thou the assembly together, thou, and Aaron thy brother, and speak ye unto the rock before their eyes; and it shall give forth his water, and thou shalt bring forth to them water out of the rock: so thou shalt give the congregation and their beasts drink."[10]

The rod referred to by the Lord was apparently the sacred "rod of Aaron" which had blossomed and brought forth almonds in a single night.[11] This rod was kept in the Holy of Holies along with the golden bowl of manna and

---

8. Numbers 20:3-5   10. Numbers 20:8
9. Exodus 17:5   11. Numbers 17:8

the Tablets of the Law written by the finger of God.[12] So Moses "Took the rod from before the Lord," and went forth to perform the miracle of producing a spring of gushing water from a solid rock.

But knowing from experience how literally the Lord would perform this miracle and how impressive it would be, Moses could not resist the temptation of taunting the people for their miserable faithlessness. Somehow a spirit of boastfulness seemed to possess him for a moment. He referred to the power of bringing forth water from a rock as though it were something inherent in himself and Aaron. Here is the way Moses said it: "Hear now, ye rebels; must we fetch you water out of this rock?" [13]

Moses then stepped forward, struck the rock twice with the sacred rod, and immediately "the water came out abundantly, and the congregation drank, and their beasts also."[14]

But for the moment, Moses had forgotten himself. It was one of those rare occasions when a wave of pride engulfed him and he boasted in his own strength. Apparently Aaron likewise gave consent to it because the sharp rebuke of the Lord applied to both of them.

"And the Lord spake unto Moses and Aaron, Because ye believed me not, to sanctify me in the eyes of the children of Israel, therefore ye shall not bring this congregation into the land which I have given them."[15]

This pronouncement was a bitter blow to Moses and he later tried to get the Lord to rescind it. In fact, it made the Lord angry when he brought it up again.[16] In reporting this incident to Israel later, Moses said, "The Lord was angry with me for your sakes, saying, Thou shalt not go in thither."[17] For reasons best known to Himself, the Lord did not want Moses or Aaron to be with Israel when they invaded the Promised Land and He seems to have used this incident as the excuse to put the desired restriction upon them.

When one considers the problems involved in the conquest of Canaan perhaps the Lord was doing both of them

---

12. Hebrews 9:4
13. Numbers 20:10
14. Numbers 20:11
15. Numbers 20:12
16. Deuteronomy 3:25-26
17. Deuteronomy 1:37

a kindness. Nevertheless, the announcement to Moses at this time that neither he nor Aaron would enter the Promised Land came as a desolating disappointment, especially after all their privations and long-suffering to get there. Is seemed that the prize was being snatched away just as they were about to enjoy their long awaited triumph. Weaker men might have given up in disgust. They might have said, "Why help these multitudes to go over into the land of milk and honey, when we shall never set foot on it?" But Moses and Aaron were made of stronger stuff. They pressed forward as though they *would* inherit the Land.

However, it soon became apparent to Moses that the Lord no longer wanted them to enter Canaan from Kadesh but to pass around the east side of the Dead Sea and enter Canaan from Trans-Jordan. To do this, Israel had to pass through several well populated areas where they would be in direct contact with other tribes, many of whom were distant relatives but even more distant in their feelings toward Israel.

Moses Receives Specific Instructions Concerning the Inhabitants of the Land Through Which Israel Must Pass

Prior to this time Moses had been given very strict instructions concerning the relations to be maintained between Israel and the surrounding tribes and peoples. For several hundred years certain degenerate tribes in Canaan had been sacrificing their children and participating in the most inhuman, cruel and degenerate debaucheries. These the Lord now intended to cleanse from the face of the earth. He intended to destroy them in their entirety and sweep them back into the spirit world before they further contaminated the Second Estate of mortality. However, among these tribes whose barbaric behavior had marked them for extinction were other peoples who were also wicked and rebellious but who still had some possibility of regeneration. The Lord therefore instructed Moses tribe by tribe as to the policy which Moses should follow in dealing with them. Note the careful discrimination which the Lord made in judging each tribe. He said to Moses:

THE CHILDREN
OF ESAU:

"Ye are to pass through the coast of your brethren the children of Esau, which dwell in Seir; and they shall be afraid of you: take ye good heed unto yourselves therefore: meddle not with them; for I will not give you of their land, no, not so much as a foot breadth; because I have given mount Seir unto Esau for a possession."[18]

THE MOABITES:

"Distress not the Moabites, neither contend with them in battle: for I will not give thee of their land for a possession: because I have given Ar unto the children of Lot for a possession."[19]

THE AMMONITES:

"And when thou comest nigh over against the children of Ammon, distress them not, nor meddle with them: for I will not give thee of the land of the children of Ammon any possession; because I have given it unto the children of Lot for a possession."[20]

As it turned out, this advice was very timely, because Moses found some of these people resisting even the most reasonable requests to pass through their lands. Had not the Lord given this word of caution there easily could have erupted a violent conflict between Israel and these tribes who were their distant relatives.

MOSES SEEKS TO NEGOTIATE A PASSAGE THROUGH EDOM

The descendants of Esau (or Edom—brother of Jacob) occupied the area south of the Dead Sea and down the Arabah to Mount Seir. The great king's highway from Arabia to Babylon passed through Edom and was the only logical route for Israel to take as they travelled from Kadesh to the Trans-Jordan area where the Lord had instructed them to go. Since the people of Esau were related to Israel, Moses thought the king might let them pass through his territory as a matter of accommodation. He therefore sent messengers to the king of Edom, saying:

"Thus saith thy brother Israel, Thou knowest all the travail that hath befallen us: how our fathers went down into Egypt, and we have dwelt in Egypt a long time; and

---

18. Deuteronomy 2:4-7
19. Deuteronomy 2:9

20. Deuteronomy 2:19

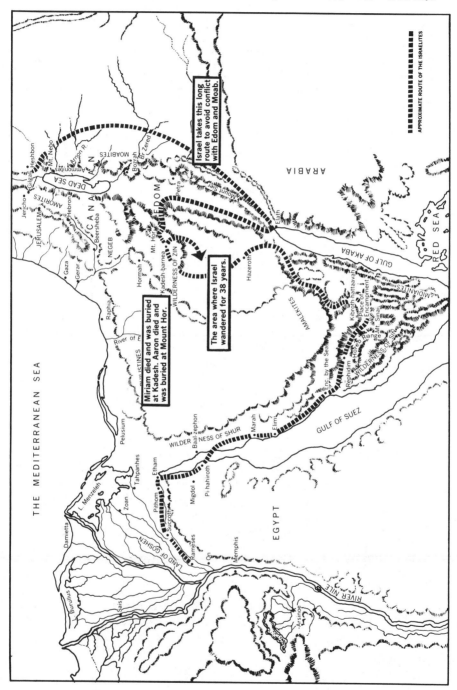

APPROXIMATE ROUTE OF THE ISRAELITES

Israel takes this long route to avoid conflict with Edom and Moab.

The area where Israel wandered for 38 years.

Miriam died and was buried at Kadesh. Aaron died and was buried at Mount Hor.

ARABIA

RED SEA

GULF OF AKABA

MIDIANITES

MOABITES

DEAD SEA

Ammonites

Mt. Nebo

Heshbon

Gilgal

Arnon R.

Bozrah

Br. Zered

CANAAN

EDOM

Petra

Mount Seir

Elath

Jericho

Jerusalem

AMORITES

Hebron

Beersheba

Gaza

Gerar

NEGEB

Mt. Hor

Hormah

Kadesh-barnea

WILDERNESS OF ZIN

Raphia

River of E

PHILISTINES

Hazeroth

AMALEKITES

Kibroth-hattaavah

Place of Encampment

Mt. Sinai

WILDERNESS OF SIN

Rephidim

Horeb Range

nc. by the Sea

Pelusium

WILDER

Baal-zephon

NESS OF SHUR

Marah

Elim

GULF OF SUEZ

Tahpanhes

Migdol

Pi-hahiroth

Etham

Pithom

Succoth

LAND OF GOSHEN

Rameses

Zoan

Sais

On

Memphis

EGYPT

THE MEDITERRANEAN SEA

Damietta

L. Menzeleh

Burullus

L.

Arsinoe

RIVER NILE

the Egyptians vexed us, and our fathers: and when we cried unto the Lord, he heard our voice, and sent an angel, and hath brought us forth out of Egypt: and, behold, we are in Kadesh, a city in the uttermost of the border: Let us pass, I pray thee, through thy country: we will not pass through the fields, or through the vineyards, neither will we drink of the water of the wells: we will go by the king's highway, we will not turn to the right hand nor to the left, until we have passed thy borders."[21]

One highly significant point emphasized by Moses in this message was the fact that the experiences of Israel were no secret but were widely known among all the people of this area. As we see later, even the heathen nations were aware of the miracle of the Red Sea crossing and practically every detail of the Exodus march was known to them.

Certainly the ambassadors from Moses could not have carried a more conciliatory plea than this one, but the king of Edom was many generations removed from his ancestor, Esau, who had loved Jacob or Israel. This king was in an ugly and suspicious mood. Therefore, his reply to Moses was brief and to the point: "Thou shalt not pass. . . ."[22]

The ambassadors reported this bad news to Moses and then returned with another message in which Moses declared: "We will go by the high way: and if I and my cattle drink of thy water, then I will pay for it: I will only, without doing any thing else, go through on my feet."[23] Moses was offering to cross through Edom on a forced march without even stopping to camp.

But the hostile king was adamant. He bluntly replied, "Thou shalt not go through."[24] And the next thing the Israelites knew the Edomite nation had taken up arms and had swept down toward the border to annihilate the Israelites in case they attempted a crossing.[25]

So the people of Israel removed from Kadesh and "turned away from him [the king of Edom]."[26] So far as we can tell they moved south to go around this kingdom

21. Numbers 20:14-17
22. Numbers 20:18
23. Numbers 20:19
24. Numbers 20:20
25. Ibid.
26. Numbers 20:21

and come up on the far side to the east. At some point along this journey around Edom they came to Mount Hor. Geographers are not at all certain where Mount Hor was located but if Israel moved south as we are almost compelled to conclude, it probably would have been somewhere along the Seir range and in the edge of the land of Edom (Num. 33:37).

MOSES LOSES HIS BROTHER AARON

It was at Mount Hor that the Lord said he was going to call Aaron across the veil and unite him with "his people" in the spirit world. To the Lord, death is that simple, and Aaron was put on notice that this great adventure was about to happen to him. The Lord said to Moses, "Take Aaron and Eleazar his son, and bring them up unto Mount Hor; and strip Aaron of his garments, and put them upon Eleazar his son and Aaron shall be gathered unto his people, and shall die there."[28]

Aaron had served as the High Priest of Israel for a full generation and had lived on the earth nearly a century and a quarter. Now it was all to suddenly end. The psychological impact of this revelation on the aged Aaron must have shaken the fibers of his innermost being. And the farewell scene between Aaron and his family, his friends and the vast multitude he had served, must have contained some sweeping tides of sorrow and mourning which no historian recorded. All the Bible tells us is the fact that Aaron, Moses and Eleazar began their ascent "in the sight of all the congregation."[29] It was a solemn moment to watch Aaron climb the rugged crags of Mount Hor knowing that in this life they would never see him again.

Somewhere up there among its forbidding volcanic peaks, a sacred ceremony took place. Carefully and reverently, the priestly robes were removed from Aaron and transferred to the new High Priest of Israel, Eleazar. No doubt all the keys and authority necessary to fill this new calling were consecrated upon Eleazar at the same time although there is no specific reference to it. Then the shadow of death

27. Numbers 20:22; 33:37   29. Numbers 20:27
28. Numbers 20:25-26

fell across the countenance of the aged Aaron as he slipped into the twilight of semi-consciousness, then of sleep, and finally the ultimate trauma of death came as his spirit was released to join his people on that higher plateau of reality which we call the spirit world.

Moses and Eleazar were alone. The body of the dead man before them was the brother of one and the father of the other. Together, they consigned the remains of Aaron to the encompassing embrace of a grave located near the summit of the mount. Then Moses and Eleazar descended the mountain to the plain below and told the people that the aged Aaron had passed to his reward. A dark shroud of sorrow enveloped all Israel. For thirty days they mourned the passing of their dead High Priest.[30]

THE CANAANITES ATTACK

During the time the camps of Israel were located at Mount Hor, a raiding party swept down out of the southern monarchy of King Arad, the Canaanite, and captured an important segment of the people of Israel.[31] They were not rescued at this time inasmuch as it would have brought Israel into a direct engagement with the powerful Canaanites at the wrong time and place. Eventually these Canaanites were utterly destroyed[32] but this did not happen until sometime later when Joshua entered the promised land to conquer it.[33]

Since it was the Lord's will that the Israelites approach Canaan from Trans-Jordan, Moses left Mount Hor and proceeded around the Edomites in order to travel north through the eastern wilderness.

THE BRAZEN SERPENT

As the people slowly dragged their cumbersome paraphernalia across the burning wilderness they began their customary complaint, saying, "Wherefore have ye brought us up out of Egypt to die in the wilderness? for there is no bread, neither is there any water; and our soul loatheth this light bread [manna]."[34]

---

30. Numbers 20:29
31. Numbers 21:1
32. Numbers 21:2-3

33. Joshua 11:14
34. Numbers 21:5

Almost immediately the great caravan of Israel found itself in a wild sector of desert which was teeming with serpents. The breed of snake which thrived in this particular area had a lethal bite which brought almost immediate death. Authorities believe this might have been the *prester* or *dipsas* species because the bite of these particular snakes is notorious for the fever, violent inflammation and thirst which are created in their victims.[35] It is also thought that this may have been the reason why they were called "fiery serpents."

An ancient poet describes the effect of the bite from a snake of the *prester* specie:[36]

> A fate of different kind Nasidius found,
> A burning prester gave the deadly wound,
> And straight, a sudden flame began to spread,
> And paint his visage with a glowing red.
> With swift expansion swells the bloated skin,
> Naught but an undistinguished mass is seen;
> While the fair human form lies lost within.
> The puffy poison spread, and heaves around,
> Till all the man is in the monster drowned.

This devastating plague of serpents spread death through the camps of Israel and stopped their progress completely. Moses asked the Lord to guide him in what he should do and was told to fashion a serpent of brass and place it on a high pole. The Lord promised that all who looked upon it would be saved from the deadly attack of these "fiery serpents."[37] In his writings, Moses confirms that this was literally fulfilled.[38] This great miracle was later quoted by Jesus as symbolic of the Messiah being "lifted up" and bringing salvation to all who would look upon him and believe.[39]

THE ISRAELITES ENTER THE LAND OF THE GIANTS

In the Book of Deuteronomy Moses emphasizes that much of the territory through which Israel now passed was inhabited in ancient times by "a people great, and many, and tall," who were known as giants. These were similar to

---

35. Clarke's *Bible Commentary*, Vol. 1, p. 682
36. Ibid.   38. Numbers 21:9
37. Numbers 21:8   39. John 3:14-15

"the Anakims" of Hebron who had frightened the spies of Israel out of their senses.[40]

Moses says that in the Arabah Valley at Mount Seir (just south of Edom) there had once been a tall and fearsome people called the Horims, and the people of Esau had been compelled to destroy them in order to live unmolested in this area.[41]

He states that the territory just north of Edom on the east side of the Dead Sea had been occupied by a tribe of giant-sized people know as Emims. This tribe had controlled everything up to the river Arnon. However, the Moabites, who were descendants of Lot, had conquered this tribe and now occupied this territory themselves.[42]

From the Arnon River up to the River Jabbock there once lived a giant tribe called the Zamzummims, but these had been conquered by another group of Lot's descendants called the people of Ammon or the Ammonites.[43]

Still further north, including the territory on the eastern side of the Sea of Galilee, was the kingdom of Bashan. This kingdom was presided over by the famous King Og, whom Moses describes as the only king who "remained of the remnant of giants."[44]

These details furnished by Moses help us to better understand the history of this area and the kind of people Israel would now encounter.

THE ARMIES OF ISRAEL MAKE THEIR
FIRST PERMANENT CONQUEST

As Moses led his people around Edom he had to come up along their eastern border and this forced him to seek passage through the territory occupied by the Moabites. In this negotiation he was turned down flatly. The Moabites were as stubborn as the Edomites in refusing to let the Israelites pass.[45] However, they did consent to sell them food and water so Moses continued to lead the Israelites up through the wilderness on the eastern border of the Moabites.[46]

---

40. Deuteronomy 2:21; Numbers 13:33
41. Deuteronomy 2:12, 22
42. Deuteronomy 2:9-11
43. Deuteronomy 2:19-21
44. Deuteronomy 3:11
45. Judges 11:17
46. Deuteronomy 2:28-29

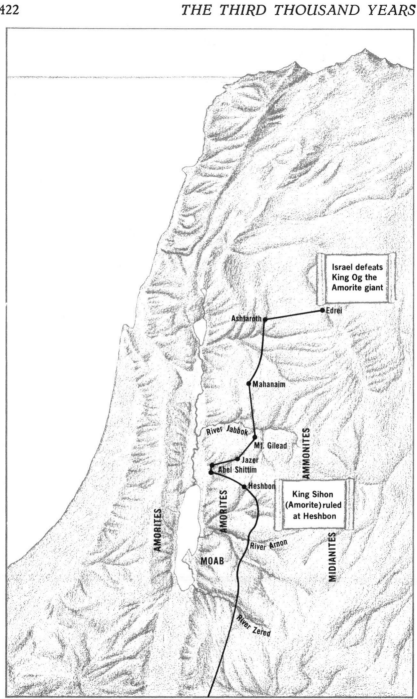

Israel defeats
King Og the
Amorite giant

● Edrei

Ashtaroth ●

● Mahanaim

River Jabbok
                ● Mt. Gilead

            ● Jazer
Abel Shittim ●
        ● Heshbon

AMMONITES

King Sihon
(Amorite) ruled
at Heshbon

AMORITES

River Arnon

MOAB

MIDIANITES

River Zered

Finally, Israel came to the banks of the Arnon River. This river flows into the Dead Sea at about half way between its two extremities. Since this river marked the end of the Moabite country, Moses was anxious to arrange for passage through the land of the Ammonites so that he could set up his base of operations along the Jordan river preparatory to launching the campaign into Canaan. He soon learned, however, that the Ammonites were no longer in charge of their own country. They had been recently conquered by a powerful heathen king from across Jordan named Sihon.

Sihon was an Amorite,[47] the tribe which occupied practically all of the mountain country of Canaan from Mount Hermon clear down to Hebron and a tribe which God had marked as an abomination unto him.[48] Sihon had conquered the Trans-Jordan area of the Ammonites (no relation to the Amorites) and had set up his capitol at Heshbon.

It will be recalled that the Lord had specifically commanded Moses to make no attack on the Ammonites,[49] but as for this Sihon who had conquered them, that was something else again. Concerning this Amorite king, the Lord said: "Rise ye up, take your journey, and pass over the river Arnon: behold, I have given into thine hand Sihon, the Amorite, king of Heshbon, and his land: begin to possess it, and contend with him in battle."[50] But Moses first extended a gesture of peace to Sihon. He wanted only one thing from the Amorite king and that was permission to pass through his kingdom to the river Jordan. If this could be worked out peacefully or even by some reasonable financial arrangement so much the better. Therefore Moses wrote to Sihon as follows:

"Let me pass through thy land: I will go along by the high way, I will neither turn unto the right hand nor to the left. Thou shalt sell me meat for money, that I may eat; and give me water for money, that I may drink; only I will pass through on my feet: (as the Children of Esau which dwell in Seir, and the Moabites which dwell in Ar, did unto me;)

47. Deuteronomy 2:24
48. Peloubet's *Bible Dictionary* under "Amorite."
49. Deuteronomy 2:19
50. Deuteronomy 2:24

until I shall pass over Jordan into the land which the Lord our God giveth us."[51]

But Sihon was defiant. He would neither accommodate nor negotiate. He mobilized his armies and came upon the children of Israel with enough hatred to annihilate them. He belonged to that polluted, corrupt civilization which had mocked God for generations and which had been condemned by the Lord to extinction. Therefore the Lord said, "Behold I have begun to give Sihon and his land before thee; begin to possess, that thou mayest inherit his land."[52]

The first battle was fought at Jahaz,[53] and then the war spread from the River Arnon to every section where Sihon had built his strongholds.[54] Even the Israelites must have been surprised as Sihon's fortified cities fell one after another in quick succession. These Amorites had declared war on Israel, now Israel brought the war to them. As the Israelites overran their walls and pulled down their gates they brought about their complete destruction. Nothing came out alive except the cattle which were taken as spoil.[55] They also stripped each city of the wealth which Sihon's people had stolen from those who had previously inhabited these towns and cities.

Moses made it clear that this war of extinction was aimed exclusively at Sihon's violent and perverted people and against none else. As he said to Israel afterwards, ". . . unto the land of the children of Ammon thou camest not, nor unto any place of the river Jabbok, nor unto the cities in the mountains, nor unto whatsoever the Lord our God forbad us."[56]

ISRAEL IS ATTACKED BY KING OG, ONE OF THE LAST OF THE GIANTS

Now another Amorite king came charging down on the armies of Israel. This time it was the great King Og who ruled everything west of Jordan from the River Jabbock to Mount Hermon. This territory was called "the land of giants"[57] and King Og is referred to by Moses as the only

---

51. Deuteronomy 2:27-29
52. Deuteronomy 2:31
53. Deuteronomy 2:32
54. Deuteronomy 2:36

55. Deuteronomy 2:35
56. Deuteronomy 2:37
57. Deuteronomy 3:13

king left of the "remnant of giants."[58] Moses says that an iron bedstead which the people of Ammon had apparently captured during a war with King Og had been taken to Rabbath and it was nine cubits long and four cubits wide. [59] This means it was approximately 13½ feet long and 6 feet wide! This is undoubtedly the earliest historical reference to a king-size bed.

As King Og came rushing down on Israel, the Lord said to Moses, "Fear him not: for I will deliver him, and all his people, and his land, into thy hand; and thou shalt do unto him as thou didst unto Sihon, king of the Amorites, which dwelt at Heshbon."[60]

The hosts of King Og met Israel at Edrei where the scripture says Og was killed and the whole city devastated. Then the armies of Israel swept through the land of Bashan cleansing it as they went. Moses says, "And we took all his cities at that time, there was not a city which we took not from them, threescore cities, all the region of Argob, the kingdom of Og in Bashan. . . ."[61] And just to keep the record straight, Moses wanted it understood that this monumental victory was no small achievement. He says, "all these cities were fenced with high walls, gates, and bars; beside unwalled towns a great many."[62]

When this broad arena of conflict was finally cleared of all opposition, the children of Israel occupied the cities, towns and villages and possessed the wealth of their first permanent conquest. Moses wrote, "And we took at that time out of the hand of the two kings of the Amorites the land that was on this [the east] side of Jordan, from the river of Arnon unto Mount Hermon."[63]

By attacking Israel, the war-mongering Amorites had reaped a whirlwind of devastation and defeat when all Moses had asked was the privilege of passing through their lands peacefully and paying for food and water as they went!

---

58. Deuteronomy 3:11
59. Ibid.
60. Deuteronomy 3:2

61. Deuteronomy 3:4
62. Deuteronomy 3:5
63. Deuteronomy 3:8

Moses Pleads With the Lord to Let Him Cross Over Jordan

The sudden reversal of Israel's affairs from nomadic wandering in the wilderness to the occupation of great cities and the enjoyment of the riches of the valleys in eastern Jordan, had its effect on the mind and heart of Moses. He knew that the hour of Israel's hopes was about to have its fulfillment. If these Israelites could stay half-way faithful and not rebel against the leadership of the Lord's chosen servants, they had a great triumph within their grasp. But Moses remembered the cowardly spirit of the people thirty-eight years before when a similar opportunity had confronted them. They had turned and run like craven, desert jackals.[64]

Moses knew that this second opportunity to take Canaan was their last, and much depended upon the valiant Joshua, commander in chief. Moses therefore said to him, "Thine eyes have seen all that the Lord your God hath done unto these two kings: so shall the Lord do unto all the kingdoms whither thou passest. Ye shall not fear them: for the Lord your God he shall fight for you."[65]

But the contemplation of this great day of imminent success for Israel was too much for Moses. He could not reconcile himself to leaving them just when they were to enter the promised land. Based on what he later said, it is easy to visualize what must have passed through his mind. Why could he not have the privilege of leading Israel to its goal of total victory now? Why leave it to another? Had not Moses been a highly successful general over Egypt's armies? Had he not led Israel to victory over Sihon and Og? Hopefully, Moses sought out the Lord, and pleaded:

"O Lord God, thou hast begun to shew thy servant thy greatness, and thy mighty hand: for what God is there in heaven or in earth that can do according to thy works, and according to thy might? I pray thee, let me go over, and see the good land that is beyond Jordan, that goodly mountain, and Lebanon."[66]

---

64. Numbers Chapters 13 and 14
65. Deuteronomy 3:21-22
66. Deuteronomy 3:24-25

But Moses knew immediately he had imposed upon the Lord. He had been told earlier that this was not his calling and now he was tempting the Lord. Moses later told the people what had happened. He said, "The Lord was wroth with me for your sakes, and would not hear me: and the Lord said unto me, Let it suffice thee; speak no more unto me of this matter."[67]

Then the Lord comforted Moses and said, "Get thee up into the top of Pisgah, and lift up thine eyes westward, and northward, and southward, and eastward, and behold it with thine eyes: for thou shalt not go over this Jordan."[68]

Then the Lord added a significant statement which must have stopped Moses short. Said he: "And when thou hast seen it, thou also shalt be gathered unto thy people, as Aaron thy brother was gathered."[69]

So that was it! No wonder he would not pass over Jordan. Only a few months before he had seen Aaron get this kind of message. Now it had come to the great Moses. The end of his days was near.

The Appointment and Anointing of Joshua

Moses immediately turned from his personal problems and began thinking about his people. When he was gone, what would they do? Moses addressed a new plea to the Lord:

"Let the Lord, the God of the spirits of all flesh, set a man over the congregation, which may go out before them, and which may go in before them, and which may lead them out, and which may bring them in; that the congregation of the Lord be not as sheep which have no shepherd."[70]

In reply the Lord said, "Moses, Take thee Joshua the son of Nun, a man in whom is the spirit, and lay thine hand upon him; and set him before Eleazar the priest, and before all the congregation; and give him a charge in their sight. And thou shalt put some of thine honour upon him, that all the congregation of the children of Israel may be obedient.

---

67. Deuteronomy 3:26
68. Deuteronomy 3:27
69. Numbers 27:13
70. Numbers 27:16-17

And he shall stand before Eleazar the priest, who shall ask counsel for him after the judgment of Urim before the Lord: at his [Eleazar's] word shall they go out, and at his word they shall come in, both he, and all the children of Israel with him, even all the congregation."[71]

So Moses called a great conference of all the people. He presented Joshua to them as the man who would be their leader when Moses was gone. And he presented Joshua to Eleazar, Aaron's son, who now held the office of High Priest. Then Moses laid his hands upon the head of Joshua and conferred upon him the keys of his new calling.[72]

Every Israelite present could see what was happening. They were about to lose Moses. A whole epic in Israel's history was about to come to an end. They knew it would never be the same without the prophet and lawgiver whom they had come to take for granted as though he were an immortal fixture among them. Suddenly things were going to change.

Moses knew this change would come when he went into Mount Pisgah to look at the land beyond Jordan. Once he went up to the Mount he would never come down again. He would be gathered to his fathers.[73] Moses therefore knew he must postpone that fatal journey until he had made all the necessary preparations.

As Moses set about to complete his writings and give his last instructions to the people, a strange drama began to be enacted in the surrounding hills. The children of Lot — the Moabites — were getting ready to massacre Israel!

THE AMAZING STORY OF BALAAM

This conspiracy to destroy Israel centered around the possibility of getting a famous prophet named Balaam to come down and curse Israel so that they could be more easily defeated.

It had begun shortly after Israel had conquered Sihon and Og and taken over all the cities of these two Amorite

---

71. Numbers 27:18-21   73. Deuteronomy 32:49-50
72. Numbers 27:22-23

kings which extended from the River Arnon to Mount Hermon. As the Moabites looked out upon the success of Israel they were "sore afraid of the people, because they were many."[74]

Moses, of course, had no intention of disturbing the Moabites since the Lord had specifically forbidden it.[75] In fact, the people of Israel had completely circumnavigated the borders of Moab on their way to Jordan in order to avoid any clash with them.

But the Moabites had become a wicked and licentious people and were closely associated with the Midianites (descendants of Abraham through Keturah).[76] Both the Moabites and Midianites had become worshipers of Baal-Peor, the obscene heathen deity whose rituals involved the most depraved sensual orgies. In their state of abysmal apostasy these peoples conspired together to destroy Israel.

Balak was king of the Moabites and he said "to the elders of Midian, Now shall this company [of Israelites] lick up all that are round about us, as the ox licketh up the grass of the field."[77] It was agreed to set up a mutual protection pact and launch a preventive war against Israel. The risk, however, was greater than either of them was willing to take. They therefore decided to send messengers to Balaam. He was a prophet who worshipped the same God as the Israelites and these messengers were instructed to induce Balaam to try and persuade his God to turn against Israel. They believed that if Balaam would curse the Israelites then they could be defeated and their wealth seized by the Moabite-Midianite armies. Obviously, this whole conspiracy was concocted by men who were the victims of their own superstitions and greed.

---

74. Numbers 22:3
75. Deuteronomy 2:9
76. Genesis 25:2. The Midianites were apparently scattered up and down the wilderness regions. It would seem that most of them had apostatized and turned to idolatry. Nevertheless, it will be recalled that Jethro's branch of the Midianites who lived near the Akaba Gulf of the Red Sea, had received the Priesthood. Jethro could trace his Priesthood back to Abraham and it was he who ordained Moses. (Doctrine and Covenants 84:6-14)
77. Numbers 22:4

The messengers found Balaam in the land of Haran[78] on the Euphrates River and delivered the following message from the Moabite king: "Behold there is a people come out from Egypt; behold, they cover the face of the earth, and they abide over against me: Come now, therefore, I pray thee, curse me this people; for they are too mighty for me: peradventure I shall prevail, that we may smite them, and that I may drive them out of the land."[79]

Balaam was puzzled by the request but told the messengers he would inquire of the Lord. The Lord's reply was prompt and emphatic. He said to Balaam: "Thou shalt not go with them; thou shalt not curse the people [of Israel] for they are blessed."[80]

Balaam returned to the messengers and said, "Get you into your land: for the Lord refuseth to give me leave to go with you."[81]

From this incident it is obvious that at this stage of his career Balaam was in direct communication with the Lord and apparently fulfilling his role as a spiritual leader among his people. Joshua 13:22 refers to Balaam as a "soothsayer" with the marginal note by the translators indicating that perhaps "diviner" is the more appropriate word. It seems clear from the record, however, that neither of these are satisfactory for God does not communicate with sorcerers, professional diviners and those who lay phoney claim to magical enchantments. As we shall see shortly, Balaam was very much like Cain of old who enjoyed direct revelations from the Lord but fell because of a desire to illegally "get gain." This is specifically spelled out in Jude, verse 11, where he says, "Woe unto them! for they have gone in the way of Cain, and ran greedily after the error of Balaam for reward. . . ." By keeping Balaam in the role of a true prophet who fell the student will understand his life better than if he tries to

---

78. Numbers 22:5 plus Deuteronomy 23:4. Note that in Numbers 22:5 Balaam is said to live "by the river of the children of his people," and Moses says this was Mesopotamia (Deuteronomy 23:4). Although the exact location of his residence is not known, it may have been part of the Shemite nation in Padanaram or Haran where the relatives of Abraham had built several communities. (See Genesis 28:2; 33:18)
79. Numbers 22:5-6
80. Numbers 22:12
81. Numbers 22:13

twist Balaam into the character of a wizard. God does not reveal Himself to wizards.

When King Balak learned that Balaam would not come he was deeply disappointed but was far from giving up. He immediately sent some of his most important officials to Balaam and this time he was prepared to offer tempting bribes. The king's message was as follows: "Let nothing, I pray thee, hinder thee from coming unto me: for I will promote thee unto very great honour, and I will do whatsoever thou sayest unto me: come therefore, I pray thee, curse me this people."[82]

At first, Balaam stood firm. He declared with boldness: "If Balak would give me his house full of silver and gold, I cannot go beyond the word of the Lord my God, to do less or more."[83] Had Balaam stood solidly on this righteous resolution he would never have fallen but would have gone down in history as a prophet hero. His mistake was in setting about to undermine the very policy he had announced. He told the king's messengers to linger overnight while he conversed further with the Lord. It was obvious Balaam intended to tempt the Lord.

Modern Revelation Solves a Scriptural Problem

The Biblical account states that when Balaam inquired the second time the Lord told him to "go with them," but only to do and say the things commanded of the Lord.[84] Balaam promptly launched forth on a journey to Moab and the Bible then says "God's anger was kindled because he went."[85]

At this point the story is contradictory. Why would the Lord tell Balaam to go and then be angry because he did so? Bible scholars have pondered this question through the centuries[86] but not until modern revelation clarified this passage was it possible to determine exactly what happened. The Inspired Version gives the text as Moses originally wrote it and in it we learn that the Lord did not order Balaam to go with the messengers. He left it up to him to decide. The Lord had already told Balaam not to go, but when Balaam

---

82. Numbers 22:16
83. Numbers 22:18
84. Numbers 22:20

85. Numbers 22:22
86. See *The Interpreters Bible*, Vol. 2, p. 250

asked the second time the Lord said "go if thou wilt."[87] Balaam jumped at this opportunity to override the previous instruction of the Lord and therefore hastened toward Moab with the messengers. This is why it says "God's anger was kindled because he went."[88]

THE ANGEL OF THE LORD STOPS BALAAM

Although it says Balaam started on his journey "with the princes of Moab,"[89] it is obvious that he soon fell behind because of the strange behavior of the donkey mare he was riding. At one point the donkey veered off the road and ran into a field so that Balaam could not control her. The scripture says this was because the donkey was given the power to see that the road was blocked by the angel of the Lord "standing in the way."[90]

Balaam then beat the donkey to make it go back to the road, but, failing in this, he started the donkey through the "path of the vineyard" which paralleled the road. The vineyards were often planted on terraces along the hillsides which were only about four feet wide. Since the donkey had a wall on one side against which the grapevines grew and a precipice or wall on the other side which led down to the next terrace, she was obliged to stay on the terrace ledge. When the angel stood before her the second time, the frightened donkey lunged sideways into the wall and bruised Balaam's foot. Balaam was so enraged that he beat the donkey again. Shortly afterwards the pathway narrowed sharply so that there was "no way to turn either to the right hand or to the left."[91] Here the angel appeared once more, and this time the terrified and bewildered donkey just collapsed to the ground in a heap beneath Balaam.

The infuriated Balaam was outraged beyond reason. He took his heavy staff and began belaboring the donkey with heavy blows. Suddenly a miraculous thing occurred. The donkey mare spoke to Balaam! Not since the serpent spoke to Eve in the Garden of Eden had such a phenomenon been reliably recorded.

---

87. Inspired Version, Numbers 22:20
88. Numbers 22:22
89. Numbers 22:21

90. Numbers 22:23
91. Numbers 22:26

In anguish the donkey pleaded with Balaam, "What have I done unto thee, that thou hast smitten me these three times?"[92]

Balaam must have been shocked and astonished at the unexpected capacity of the donkey to communicate orally with him, but if this amazing creature could speak, perhaps she could also understand. Therefore he cried out to her, "Because thou hast mocked me: I would there were a sword in mine hand, for now would I kill thee."[93] But the donkey reasoned with Balaam and asked if she had not always been obedient in the past. Balaam admitted she had. A moment later the eyes of Balaam were opened and the scripture says, "he saw the angel of the Lord standing in the way, and his sword drawn in his hand. . . ."[94] Immediately Balaam bowed himself to the ground. The angel rebuked Balaam for beating the donkey and said, "Behold, I went out to withstand thee, because thy way is perverse before me."[95] He then told Balaam that unless the donkey had turned aside, Balaam would already be dead.[96]

The prophet from Haran was shaken. He said, "I have sinned; for I knew not that thou stoodest in the way against me: now therefore, if it displease thee, I will get me back again."[97]

This appeared to be true humility but apparently the Lord was willing to let Balaam run the full course of the snare he had set for himself. Since this is what Balaam had been so anxious to do, the angel said, "Go with the men; but only the word that I shall speak unto thee, that thou shalt speak." So Balaam hurried forward to catch up with the messengers of King Balak and proceed toward Moab.

Balaam Totters Between God and Mammon

Having arrived in Moab, Balaam was welcomed by King Balak who said, "Wherefore camest thou not unto me? Am I not able indeed to promote thee to honour?"[98]

---

92. Numbers 22:28
93. Numbers 22:29
94. Numbers 22:31
95. Numbers 22:32
96. Numbers 22:33
97. Numbers 22:34
98. Numbers 22:37

Balaam said he had come indeed but only to speak what God would put in his mouth.[99] To King Balak this was no problem. The king intended to offer expensive sacrifices to Balaam's God so that He would tell Balaam to say that which the king wanted him to say. In other words, the wicked king would not only bribe Balaam, he intended to bribe the Lord as well. This was often done through the priests of local gods, why not Balaam and his God?

The fantastic part of the whole situation was the fact that Balaam went along with the king's scheme. The next thing we read, Balaam is in company with the king at one of the heathen sanctuaries.[100] There Balaam actually undertook to tempt the Lord. He said to the king, "Build me here seven altars, and prepare me here seven oxen and seven rams."[101] After these sacrifices were completed, Balaam said: "Stand by thy burnt-offering, and I will go: peradventure the Lord will come to meet me: and whatsoever he showeth me I will tell thee."[102]

When Balaam returned, the king waited anxiously for the terrible curse to be pronounced upon Israel, but Balaam said the Lord would give nothing but a blessing to Israel.

Very well, then Balaam's God must be further pacified. The heathen priests cunningly bargained this way for their gods all the time. This was to be expected. Said the king, "Come, I pray thee, with me unto another place, from whence thou mayest see them [the hosts of Israel]: thou shalt see but the utmost part of them, and shalt not see them all: and curse me them from thence."[103]

Then the king took Balaam high up on the Pisgah range where new altars were built and additional sacrifices made. Once more Balaam went before the Lord and once more he returned with only a blessing for Israel. Said Balaam, "Behold, I have received commandment to bless: and he hath blessed; and I cannot reverse it. He hath not beheld iniquity in Jacob, neither hath he seen perverseness in Israel: the Lord his God is with him, and the shout of a king is among them."[104]

99. Numbers 22:38
100. Numbers 22:41
101. Numbers 23:1

102. Numbers 23:3
103. Numbers 23:13
104. Numbers 23:20-21

In this statement Balaam leaves the hint that he had actually hoped to get the Lord to reverse his position but had been unable to do so.[105]   Therefore he continued, "God brought them out of Egypt: he hath as it were the strength of an unicorn.   Surely there is no enchantment against Jacob, neither is there any divination against Israel: according to this time it shall be said of Jacob and of Israel, what hath God wrought!"[106]

Balaam's reference to "enchantments" and "divination" were obviously used for the benefit of the heathen king who believed in such things.   These were not the kind of words a faithful member of the Priesthood should have been using.   It was as though he wanted the king to believe that Balaam had these powers of enchantment and occult divination but at the same time be able to blame the Lord for not allowing him to use his powers against Israel.   In this way perhaps he could carry out the Lord's instructions but still get an endow-ment or reward from the king.

But King Balak interpreted all this as a further demand for a better price — additional sacrifices — to pacify the appetite of Balaam's great God.   So he said, "Come I pray thee, I will bring thee unto another place; peradventure it will please God that thou mayest curse me them from thence."[107]   So once again Balaam tempted the Lord.   Once again he had the king build altars and once again there were sacrifices of seven bullocks and seven rams.   This series of sacrifices occurred on the most profligate heathen sanctuary of all, the abominable Mount Baal-Peor.[108]

From this mount, "Balaam lifted up his eyes, and he saw Israel, abiding in his tents according to their tribes; and the spirit of God came upon him."[109]   Immediately Balaam spoke the words of inspiration which came to him and the king heard it.   Balaam said: "How goodly are thy tents, O Jacob, and thy tabernacles, O Israel! . . . he shall eat up the

---

105. Moses himself seems to verify that this was Balaam's secret design when he says, "the Lord thy God would not hearken unto Balaam." (Deut. 23:5) The Lord also implies that Balaam made a direct plea but says, "I would not heark-en." (Joshua 24:10)

106. Numbers 23:22-23   108. Numbers 23:28

107. Numbers 23:27   109. Numbers 24:2

nations his enemies, and shall break their bones, and pierce them through with his arrows. He couched, he lay down as a lion, and as a great lion: who shall stir him up? Blessed is he that blesseth thee, and cursed is he that curseth thee."[110]

This is all King Balak could stand. In great anger he "smote his hands together" and said to Balaam: "I called thee to curse mine enemies, and, behold, thou hast altogether blessed them these three times."[111] Then he taunted Balaam saying, "I thought to promote thee unto great honour; but, lo, the Lord hath kept thee back from honour."[112]

In reply, Balaam was inspired by the Spirit to unload on the king a whole series of prophecies concerning the things which Israel would yet do to the Moabites.[113] Balaam said these prophecies were shown to him while "falling into a trance, but having his eyes open."[114] He predicted the glorious days of King David when the Moabites and all of the surrounding heathen tribes would be conquered or annihilated.[115] This was enough for King Balak and he departed in a state of highly frustrated vexation.

Then the spirit of the Lord departed from Balaam. The Lord had used him to warn King Balak, but the seeds of greed were already beginning to sprout in the heart of Balaam and once he was left to himself all kinds of dark shadows of intrigue clouded his intellect and polluted his calling. We know he started off for Mesopotamia but before long he was back among the heathens again. What happened to him we shall discover in a moment.

THE MIDIANITES CORRUPT ISRAEL BY SEDUCTION

Since King Balak had failed to get the Israelites cursed and conquered, the Midianites decided to try a different technique. They determined to divide and conquer Israel through internal subversion. The scheme was to send out their most beautiful Midianite girls to induce the handsome Israelites to come over to their heathen sanctuaries and participate in their obscene and licentious ceremonies.

---

110. Numbers 24:5, 8-9
111. Numbers 24:10
112. Numbers 24:11
113. Numbers 24:14
114. Numbers 24:16
115. Numbers 24:17-24

Whether the Israelites went first out of curiosity and then out of desire or whether they collapsed overnight in profligate apostasy we are not told. The record simply says that the Midianite plot met with great success and many of the men from the victorious Israelite armies joined in the heathen ceremonies which always ended in the wildest kind of sensual debauchery.[116]

The indignation of the Lord was promptly manifest as a devastating plague broke out among the Israelites. The people began dying off by the thousands.[117] The Lord commanded that the leaders who had been guilty of participating in these transgressions should be killed. Moses therefore called the congregation and the tribal leaders to assemble before the Tabernacle. While the meeting was in session, one of the Israelites named Zimri who was "a prince of a chief house among the Simeonites,"[118] came strutting along with a Midianite woman whose father was a chieftain in Midian. In the sight of Moses and all the congregation, Zimri took the woman into his tent.[119]

Since immorality was the very crime which had brought the plague of death upon Israel and since the Lord had commanded all such offenders to be slain, a young priest named Phinehas, the grandson of Aaron, took a javelin in his hand and raced toward the tent of Zimri. There he found the man and woman. The scripture says he "thrust both of them through, the man of Israel and the woman, through the belly."[120]

"And the Lord spake unto Moses, saying, Phinehas the son of Eleazar, the son of Aaron the priest, hath turned my wrath away from the children of Israel."[121]

So the plague was stayed, but not until it had taken the lives of more than 24,000 Israelites![122]

THE WAR AGAINST THE MIDIANITES

Now the Lord commanded Moses to destroy the Midianites.[123] A thousand soldiers from each tribe were called to

---

116. Numbers 25:1-3
117. Numbers 25:9
118. Numbers 25:14
119. Numbers 25:6
120. Numbers 25:8
121. Numbers 25:11
122. Numbers 25:9
123. Numbers 31:2

fulfill this assignment.[124] When they had been marshalled for war they launched an attack against the whole Midianite nation and the campaign immediately met with success. The scripture says, "They burnt all their cities wherein they dwelt, and all their goodly castles, with fire."[125] They slew all of the five kings of Midian and were ordered to wipe out the entire population except for female children.

During the conquest of the Midianite cities, the soldiers of Israel came upon a famous and most unexpected Shemite among these licentious heathens. It was Balaam!

Apparently, after going back to his home in Meso- potamia,[126] he had returned to Trans-Jordan and actually initiated the scheme to destroy the Israelites by seduction. In spite of all the Lord had shown him, this apparently brilliant and complex man had apostatized and become an advisor to the Midianite kings. The honors of men and the lure of mammon had overcome him. Jude states that he took this profligate course of action for "reward."[127] Moses said his great sin was deliberately advising the Midianites to use their beautiful women to ensnare the Israelites and get them to commit the licentious acts which had brought down the plague of death upon them.[128] John the Revelator was later told that Balaam had also given this same advice to King Balak, telling him to "cast a stumblingblock before the chil- dren of Israel, to eat things sacrificed unto idols, and to com- mit fornication."[129]

So Balaam, the fallen prophet from Mesopotamia, was caught by the Israelites. For a man whose prophetic calling had made him famous even among the heathens this was a tragic finale. He had partaken of the spirit of Cain and Judas,[130] turned apostate and betrayed his God. So the scrip- ture concludes, "Balaam . . . the son of Beor they slew with the sword."[131]

---

124. Numbers 31:4-5   128. Numbers 31:16
125. Numbers 31:10   129. Revelations 2:14
126. Numbers 24:25   130. Moses 5:31
127. Jude, verse 11   131. Numbers 31:8

Failure of the Israelite Soldiers to Carry Out Orders

In connection with the conquest of the Midianites, the 12,000 soldiers were under orders from the Lord to cleanse the land of this society. Only female children and young virgins were spared because it was felt they could be integrated into the culture of Israel without corrupting it. The soldiers, however, violated this commandment and brought back large numbers of captives who should have been destroyed. Moses was under the revolting necessity of requiring them to fulfill their orders before they could return to the camps of Israel.[132]

This was not the last time the troops of Israel would fail to execute their orders. In later years Joshua would find himself confronted with this same kind of problem. It was difficult to get the armies of the various tribes to cleanse the land of those totally corrupted tribes whom the Lord had warned would subvert Israel if they were allowed to live. With the Lord it was a question of dealing summarily with societies which had become as degenerate as those in the days of Noah. Failure of the Israelites to cleanse the land was paid for in the blood, sweat and tears of their descendants who fell victim to the snares and cruelty of these very nations which the Lord had ordered destroyed.[133]

Spoils of the Midianite War

When the Midianite war was over, the captains of Israel's hosts made an accounting of their losses. To their astonishment they discovered that this terrible conflict had been fought without the loss of a single man![134] As an expression of appreciation for the protection of his life, each soldier made a special offering to Eleazar, the High Priest. The offering was made in gold and amounted to 16,750 shekels.[135] It was brought as a sacred offering and laid before the Tabernacle by the soldiers.[136]

Moses also had the captains tally the flocks, cattle, donkeys and prisoners taken in the Midianite war. These

---

132. Numbers 31:14-24
133. Numbers 33:55-56
134. Numbers 31:49

135. Numbers 31:52
136. Numbers 31:54

figures illustrate that this war was certainly no minor skirmish. The 12,000 Israelite soldiers brought back:

675,000 sheep
72,000 head of beef
61,000 donkeys
32,000 prisoners

The prisoners, of course, as we have already mentioned
were restricted to female children and young virgins who had
not participated in the abominations of Baal.[137] Such a quantity of prisoners would necessarily imply a very extensive
population on the part of the Midianites.

The end of the Midianite war marked the last major
project required of the prophet Moses. The Lord had said
that when the affairs of this war were completed Moses
could get ready to be "gathered to his people."

With only a few days of life left to him, Moses still
had a number of monumental tasks to perform.

---

137. Numbers 31:18

Scripture Reading and Questions on Chapter Nineteen

Scripture Reading Assignment: Numbers, chapters 20 to 31; Deuteronomy, chapters 2 and 3.

1—In the writings of Moses which years of his life does he treat in detail?

2—Where were the Israelites when Miriam died? About how old was she?

3—What was the basis for Israel's complaint at Kadesh? What did the Lord tell Moses and Aaron to do?

4—In what way did Moses and Aaron offend the Lord at Kadesh? What penalty was imposed upon them? Might not this have been a blessing in disguise rather than a penalty?

5—How were the Edomites related to the Israelites? Were the Moabites and the Ammonites related to the Israelites? Through whom?

6—Why did the Israelites have to pass through Edom? What did the king of Edom say? What did he do to enforce his edict?

7—What happened to Aaron at Mount Hor? Who accompanied him into the mount? Where was Aaron buried? Who succeeded him?

8—As the Israelites detoured around Edom toward the east what new tribulation confronted them? What did the Lord tell Moses to do? What did Jesus say this symbolized?

9—What kind of people are described in the Bible as "giants?" Were they isolated individuals or had there been whole tribes of them?

10—Did Moses get permission from the Moabites to cross through their territory? What did they do with regard to food and water?

11—Moses was expecting the next territory to be occupied by the Ammonites. What nation had recently occupied this area? Were they related to the Ammonites? What was the king's name?

12—What overtures did Moses make to this king? Did he respond favorably? What did he do? What was the outcome?

13—Who was King Og? Why was he famous? What did he try to do to Israel? What were the consequences?

14—What happened when Moses asked the Lord to let him lead Israel across Jordan? What shocking news did Moses receive at this time? Whom did Moses ordain to take his place?

15—Was Balaam a soothsayer or a true prophet who fell? What scriptural support to you have for your answer?

16—What did King Balak want Balaam to do? Briefly recite the incident in which Balaam's donkey saw the angel of the Lord.

17—Did Balaam tempt the Lord? Did the Lord favor Balaam or Israel? What was the reaction of the Moabite king?

18—How did the Midianites subvert the Israelites? What affliction came upon the Israelites? What incident stopped the plague?

19—What was the outcome of the battle between the Midianites and Israel? What famous person was found among the Midianites? What had he been doing? What happened to him?

20—How many Israelites were killed in the war with the Midianites? Is there evidence that the Midianites were numerous or small in number?

Chapter Twenty

The Closing Chapter in the Life of Moses

During the closing days of his life, events came thick and fast for Moses. There were so many final details to complete before that fatal day when he would ascend into the mount "to be gathered to his people." There was a census to be taken, records to be written, others to be completed, inheritances to be defined, final exhortations to be delivered, blessings to be invoked and prophecies to be pronounced.

The exact order in which these events occurred is not entirely clear, but they all took place in the tightly compressed period which marked the very end of the fortieth year in the ministry of Moses.

THE SECOND GREAT CENSUS

When Israel was camped at the base of Mount Sinai some thirty-eight years earlier, Moses had conducted the first census of Israel's adult males who were "twenty years old and upward . . . that are able to go forth to war. . . ."[1] They had amounted to 603,550.[2] Now all of those men were dead except three — Moses, Joshua and Caleb.[3] During the thirty-eight years in the wilderness they had died off at the average rate of approximately 16,000 per year. Their places had been filled by their sons whom Moses now tabulated in the second great census.

When the tallies were all in it was found that the new generation of Israelites who were twenty years of age or older totalled 601,730. This meant that they came within 1,820 of being equal to the numbers of their fathers at the time they were enumerated at Mount Sinai. During the trek

---

1. Numbers 1:3, 26
2. Numbers 1:46
3. Numbers 26:64-65

through the wilderness some tribes had increased, others decreased. It is interesting to see what had happened to each tribe during this period.

Tribe	First Census	Second Census	Difference
Reuben	46,500	43,730	2,770 decrease
Simeon	59,300	22,200	37,100 decrease
Gad	45,650	40,500	5,150 decrease
Judah	74,600	76,500	1,900 increase
Issachar	54,400	64,300	9,900 increase
Zebulun	57,400	60,500	3,100 increase
Manasseh	32,200	52,700	20,500 increase
Ephraim	40,500	32,500	8,000 decrease
Benjamin	35,400	45,600	10,200 increase
Dan	62,700	64,400	1,700 increase
Asher	41,500	53,400	11,900 increase
Naphtali	53,400	45,500	8,000 decrease
TOTAL[4]	603,550	601,730	1,820 decrease

REUBEN AND GAD REQUEST AN INHERITANCE EAST OF JORDAN

Once the Israelites had seized the cities, fields and flocks of King Sihon, King Og and the five kings of Midian, it was a great temptation to settle down and forget the Lord's assignment to capture the territory west of Jordan.

Moses was fully conscious of the danger and therefore he was deeply disturbed when the two tribes of Reuben and Gad sent their princes before the congregation to suggest that they be given their inheritance immediately and not wait until West Jordan had been conquered. It seems that the tribes of Reuben and Gad had accumulated "a very great multitude of cattle"[5] and they gave this as their reason for settling in Trans-Jordan since it was found to be an excellent territory for pasturage.[6]

---

4. Note that this tally does not include the tribe of Levi since they were excused from going to war because of their special calling. However, at the time of the first census the Levites are known to have numbered 22,000 (Numbers 3:39). Thirty-eight years later they numbered 23,000 (Numbers 26:62).
5. Numbers 32:1
6. Numbers 32:4-5

But Moses was outraged. This was exactly the kind of talk that had made cowards out of Israel 38 years earlier. He rebuked the princes of Reuben and Gad saying, "Shall your brethren go to war, and shall ye sit here?"[7]

Then he challenged them: "Wherefore discourage ye the heart of the children of Israel from going over into the land which the Lord hath given them? Thus did your fathers. . . ."[8]

Moses recited the history of the tragic incident thirty-eight years earlier when the spies returned from the promised land with the report that Israel should not invade Canaan. He declared: "And the Lord's anger was kindled against Israel, and he made them wander in the wilderness forty years until all the generation, that had done evil in the sight of the Lord was consumed."[9] Then Moses told the princes of Reuben and Gad: "And, behold, ye are risen up in your fathers' stead, an increase of sinful men, to augment yet the fierce anger of the Lord toward Israel."[10]

Moses predicted that if they now refused to go forward and invade Canaan the wrath of the Lord would leave them once more in the wilderness and this time the whole nation of Israel would be ultimately wiped out.[11]

The princes of Reuben and Gad realized they had deeply provoked their aged prophet and so they immediately came forward in the most conciliatory spirit, saying, "We will build sheepfolds here for our cattle, and cities for our little ones; but we ourselves will go ready armed before the children of Israel, until we have brought them unto their place. . . . We will not return unto our houses, until the children of Israel have inherited every man his inheritance."[12]

When Moses saw that the people of Reuben and Gad appeared to be completely sincere in this pledge, he relented. However, he warned them that unless they fulfilled this promise they would get no inheritance east of Jordan but would have to take their chances in Canaan along with the other tribes.[13]

7. Numbers 32:6
8. Numbers 32:7-8
9. Numbers 32:13
10. Numbers 32:14

11. Numbers 32:15
12. Numbers 32:16-18
13. Numbers 32:30

The princes of Reuben and Gad agreed, so Moses assigned the land which Israel had captured east of Jordan to these two tribes and told them to divide it between them. Then, almost as an afterthought it would seem, Moses included half of the tribe of Manasseh in this agreement.[14] Perhaps they also had "much cattle" and even though they had not been among the original petitioners, Moses specifically named them as being heir to part of Trans-Jordan.

THE PROBLEM OF FIXED INHERITANCES

Moses told Joshua that when he had conquered Canaan the various tribes should receive their inheritances "by lot," and "To many thou shalt give the more inheritance, and to few thou shalt give the less inheritance: to every one shall his inheritance be given according to those that were numbered of him."[15]

This procedure involved two problems, however. First of all, since inheritances were always passed down from father to son through the male line, what about those who had no sons? Moses presented this to the Lord and received the famous "law of inheritance:"

"If a man die, and have no son, then ye shall cause his inheritance to pass unto his daughter. And if he have no daughter, then ye shall give his inheritance unto his brethren [brothers]. And if he have no brethren, then ye shall give his inheritance unto his kinsman that is next to him of his family, and he shall possess it."[16]

The second problem arose in connection with those inheritances which descended to a daughter. If she married outside of her tribe, the land would eventually pass on to her sons and thus be lost to the tribe which originally received this land as a permanent inheritance for its people. This problem was solved by providing that daughters who were in line to be their father's heirs were required to marry within their own tribe in order to qualify as heirs. If they elected to marry outside their tribe they forfeited their inheritance.[17]

---

14. Numbers 32:33
15. Numbers 26:54-55
16. Numbers 27:8-11
17. Numbers 36:5-9

The Last Great Sermons of Moses

Just thirty days before he completed his mission on earth, Moses called all of the hosts of Israel together and gave them the first of a series of sermons.[18] This sermon plus those which followed were his last words of instruction, encouragement, blessings and prophecies. They constitute almost the entire contents of the Book of Deuteronomy which means "The Second Presentation of the Law."

In later centuries the Book of Deuteronomy became one of the most popular books of the entire Old Testament and it is the book most frequently quoted by writers in the New Testament. It is a distillation of the history of Israel and a summary of the Gospel principles as Moses delivered them to the people of Israel in his day.

Moses had seen enough of Israel to know their future history would be a series of fatal disasters interspersed with an occasional moment of fleeting glory; nevertheless, he also knew that in the Lord's due time these stumbling, suffering, stiff-necked Israelites would pass through the mill-stones of adversity and rise to meet their day of judgment as refined, righteous, valiant servants. As with Jacob, Peter, Paul, and others, they would pass through the refiners fire to be glorified. However, Moses knew that with these Israelites the process would take longer, not only this lifetime but there would necessarily follow a long period of post-graduate work in the spirit world. In this life they had rejected a magnificent opportunity to duplicate the golden age of Enoch and having made that choice they were bound to pay the consequences.

Even though they were going to be blessed in conquering the heathen nations in Canaan the Lord made it very clear that they must not think they had been forgiven for their continuous rebellion since coming out of Egypt. Moses made a major issue out of this in one of his sermons: "Not for thy righteousness, or for the uprightness of thine heart, dost thou go to possess their land; but for the wickedness of these nations the Lord thy God doth drive them out from before thee, and that he may perform the word which the Lord

---

18. Deuteronomy 1:3

sware unto thy fathers, Abraham, Isaac, and Jacob. Understand, therefore, that the Lord thy God giveth thee not this good land to possess it for thy righteousnesss; for thou art a stiff-necked people. Remember, and forget not, how thou provokedst the Lord thy God to wrath in the wilderness: from the day that thou didst depart out of the land of Egypt, until ye came unto this place, ye have been rebellious against the Lord."[19]

These strong words were designed to help the Israelites reconcile themselves to the bitter days ahead. Moses wanted to inoculate their minds with humility so that they would not rise up and curse God in that fearful hour when they reaped the consequences of their earlier rebellion. As the Lord had said at Sinai, ". . . it is a terrible thing that I will do with thee."[20] The Lord was about to make them the military executioners of several nations who for generations had sacrificed their children,[21] who had created a culture in the land that "eateth up the inhabitants thereof,"[22] and who had corrupted their way upon the earth as completely as the perfidious and perverted population in the days of Noah.

If the earth were to be cleansed of this corruption, it would be necessary to root it out and replace it with a higher order of society. The Lord now offered this opportunity to Israel. The manner in which the old culture was to be rooted out depended upon the degree of corruption and the attitude of those who practiced it. The Lord had made it clear to Moses that His object was regeneration and repentance wherever possible. Only in those extreme cases of total degradation were the Israelites to completely destroy the heathens or force them to flee from this territory. Moses gave the Israelites a set of clearly defined principles to govern their actions during the conquest of Canaan.

PRINCIPLES GOVERNING THE LIBERATION AND OCCUPATION OF THE PROMISED LAND

Moses knew that Israel would be confronted with three types of situations in Canaan and he therefore gave them a set of guiding principles for each:

---

19. Deuteronomy 9:5-7
20. Exodus 34:10
21. Deuteronomy 12:31
22. Numbers 13:32

1 — *The rule for conquering city-states or nations in general.* "When thou comest nigh unto a city to fight against it, then PROCLAIM PEACE UNTO IT. And it shall be, if it make thee answer of peace, and open unto thee, then it shall be that all the people that is found therein shall be tributaries unto thee, and they shall serve thee."[23] In other words, any cities or tribes which occupied territory within the boundaries designated by the Lord as the Land of Israel's inheritance were to be peacefully integrated into the new central kingdom if at all possible. God was about to set up a higher type of government and a higher order of justice and law than existed anywhere in the world at that time. To do this, cities and nations were invited to participate by peacefully submitting to the new central authority and the new system of law under which it would function. However, they would be required to support the central government with their taxes or tribute and would have to submit to the new order which prohibited the idolatry, dishonesty and immorality that characterized practically all societies in that day.

2 — *The rule for city-states or nations which resisted.* "And if it make no peace with thee, but will make war against thee, then thou shalt besiege it; and when the Lord thy God hath delivered it into thine hands, thou shalt smite every male thereof with the edge of the sword. But the women, and the little ones, and the cattle, and all that is in the city, even all the spoil thereof, shalt thou take unto thyself. . . ."[24] In other words, rebellious peoples were to have their fighting forces liquidated (which in those days would include all adult males) and the remaining population with all its possession was to be absorbed into the various tribes of Israel as bond servants. If the Israelites took these survivors into their home there was a likelihood that with the passing of time many of them would adopt the ideals of Israel and be converted. As fast as they did so they could be treated as "the seed of Abraham"[25] and could then be liberated as "brethren" or fellow-Israelites at the next Sabbath Year.[26]

Had Israel strictly adhered to the commandments of God in this regard, the occupation of the Promised Land by

---

23. Deuteronomy 20:10-11   25. Galatians 3:7-8, 29
24. Deuteronomy 20:13-14   26. Leviticus 25:39-41

Israel could have been a great blessing to all the nations of Canaan. The subjugation of the heathen tribes could have turned out to be their pathway to liberty. Not only was it designed to prepare them for political freedom (through conversion and adoption into Israel) but it also would have liberated them from the bondage of licentious idolatry which had caught them in its cycle of self-perpetuating degradation.

As we shall see later, Israel's tragic mistake was failing to carry out this program with firmness. Instead, she fell for the very debauchery which this chosen people was supposed to cleanse from the face of the land. Rather than becoming the great people of liberty like the famous City of Enoch, the Israelites eventually found themselves tributaries — both politically and morally — to the heathens which they were supposed to subjugate. The Lord anticipated this by laying down a particularly strict rule with reference to the worst of the heathen nations.

3 — Rule for the six anathematized nations. The Lord specifically warned against six nations which had reached such a level of total human debauchery that he knew they would (with one notable exception) resist all efforts to regenerate them or incorporate them into the new order. Therefore, this rule was to apply: "But of the cities of these people [whom he is about to designate] which the Lord thy God doth give thee for an inheritance, thou shalt save alive nothing that breatheth: but thou shalt utterly destroy them; namely, the Hittites, and the Amorites, the Canaanites, and the Perizzites, the Hivites, and the Jebusites: as the Lord thy God hath commanded thee: that they teach you not to do after all their abominations, which they have done unto their gods; so should ye sin against the Lord your God."[27]

This is the rule of *anathema.* It meant that all of these six nations were to be wiped out or forced to flee from the land. Actually, as we have already seen, some of Abraham's own descendants such as the Midianites and the Moabites had been indulging in some of these same practices but were not "ripe" in their iniquity and therefore the Lord had held Israel back from totally destroying them.[28] Apparently the Lord will not order the anathematizing of a nation until it is

---

27. Deuteronomy 20:16-18   28. Deuteronomy 2:4-19

altogether corrupted. He had made this very clear in the days of Abraham when he had spoken about one of these very nations which was now about to be destroyed, and said: ". . . for the iniquity of the Amorites is not yet full."[29] But over four centuries had passed since the days of Abraham, and the iniquity of the Amorites and their fellow heathens was now full indeed. With them human sacrifices and debasing immoral debauchery were not occasional spasms of evil but a continuous frenzy of sub-human depravity. They had institutionalized these abominations and made them a mandatory way of life. The Lord knew that without any significant exception, these people would fight desperately and bitterly rather than abandon these practices. They reveled in them. Therefore the land was to be completely cleansed of them. They were *anathema*.

Of course, there were two things these nations could do to save themselves. They could flee from Canaan and settle in a new land,[30] or they could voluntarily repent and submit themselves to the new order by dissolving their own cultural and political existence and becoming subservient to the leadership of Israel.[31] As we shall see later, only one city — the Gibeonites of the Hivite nation — chose this latter course.[32] Once that city had capitulated, Israel not only considered it a part of the new order but went to war against the whole Amorite federation to keep the Gibeonites from being destroyed.[33] An equally favorable relationship could have been developed by all of the heathen nations if they had chosen to do so.

The decision of the heathens to make war against Israel was particularly contemptuous of the Lord because these nations were fully aware of the great things God had done for Israel. In fact, it was the knowledge of these very things which led the Gibeonites to seek asylum with the Israelites. Said they: "Because it was certainly told [to us] thy servants, how that the Lord thy God commanded his servant Moses to give you all the land, and to destroy all the inhabi-

---

29. Genesis 15:16
30. This is clear from Joshua 13:12-13 where the words "cast them out" and "expelled" are used in connection with anathematized nations.
31. Deuteronomy 20:11
32. Joshua, Chapter 9
33. Joshua, Chapter 10

tants of the land from before you, therefore we were sore afraid of our lives because of you. . . . And now, behold, we are in thine hand: as it seemeth good and right unto thee to do unto us, do."[34] Elsewhere, we learn that the heathen tribes knew "the Lord had dried up the waters of Jordan from before the children of Israel. . . ."[35] They also knew about the miraculous events in Egypt and Trans-Jordan. A resident in one of the heathen cities declared: "I know that the Lord hath given you the land, and that your terror is fallen upon us, and that all the inhabitants of the land faint because of you. For we have heard how the Lord dried up the water of the Red Sea for you, when ye came out of Egypt; and what ye did unto the two kings of the Amorites, that were on the other side of Jordan, Sihon and Og, whom ye utterly destroyed. And as soon as we had heard these things, our hearts did melt, neither did there remain any more courage in any man, because of you: for the Lord your God, he is God in heaven above, and in earth beneath. . . . save alive my father, and my mother, and my brethren, and my sisters, and all that they have, and deliver our lives from death."[36]

These were the words of Rahab, a woman of Jericho, who was spared with all her kindred because of her humble petition. It clearly demonstrates that this could have been the lot of every heathen nation in Canaan. The fact that the heathen nations elected to make war with Israel becomes increasingly significant when it is realized that they launched their "fight to the death" fully aware that they were defying God and attacking his people.

ISRAEL GETS A SECOND CHANCE TO DUPLICATE THE GOLDEN AGE OF ENOCH

When the Lord had first rescued the Israelites from Egypt He had offered them the ultimate in temporal blessings. He had said: "Now therefore, if ye will obey my voice indeed, and keep my covenant, then ye shall be a peculiar treasure unto me ABOVE ALL PEOPLE; for all the earth is mine: and ye shall be unto me a KINGDOM OF

---

34. Joshua 9:24-25
35. Joshua 5:1

36. Joshua 2:9-13

PRIESTS AND AN HOLY NATION."[37] Now, let us remind ourselves what happened.

When this proposition was presented to the people they gladly entered into this covenant saying, "All that the Lord hath spoken we will do."[38] The Lord therefore undertook to give Moses all the higher ordinances and prepare the people for the day when they could "behold the face of God."[39] Had this program been successful the Lord would have been able to build them into a great political power of righteous dominion which would have been similar to the City of Enoch. They would have been "above all people" and "a holy nation" unto God as indicated above.

Unfortunately, however, even while Moses was being instructed in the procedures for building a temple, setting up the ordinances, and governing the people under laws of perfect equity, the Israelites went braying off into the wilderness of apostasy, built a golden calf and flung themselves into the drunken, naked orgies of ancient Egypt. For this profligate act of covenant breaking the Israelites lost all of Enoch's blessings including the Melchizedek Priesthood, the temple ordinances, the promise of political dominion and the privilege of seeing the Lord face to face.[40] Just a year-and-a-half later, as they stood at the very gates of Canaan under mandate to conquer it, they turned away like abject cowards and tried to run back to Egypt.[41] For this second offense against Heaven they were condemned to wander in the wilderness for another thirty-eight years until they had all died off except Joshua and Caleb. Now a whole new generation had risen to take their places.

All of these facts need to be kept in mind in order to appreciate the exciting new proposal which the Lord now authorized Moses to make to this new generation of Israelites. During the last thirty days of his life, Moses was allowed to offer these fresh, younger Israelites a renewal of the original covenant. Said Moses:

"This day the Lord thy God hath commanded thee to do these statutes and judgments: thou shalt therefore keep

37. Exodus 19:5-6
38. Exodus 19:8
39. Doctrine and Covenants 84:23

40. Doctrine and Covenants 84:23-27
41. Exodus Chapter 4

and do them with all thine heart, and with all thy soul. Thou hast avouched [publicly proclaimed] the Lord this day to be thy God, and to walk in his ways, and to keep his statutes, and his commandments, and his judgments, and to hearken unto his voice: and the Lord hath avouched thee this day to be his PECULIAR PEOPLE, as he hath promised thee, and that thou shouldest keep all his commandments; and to MAKE THEE HIGH ABOVE ALL NATIONS WHICH HE HATH MADE, in praise, and in name, and in honour; and that thou mayest be an HOLY PEOPLE unto the Lord thy God, as he hath spoken."[42]

Even earlier in this series of sermons Moses had hinted that this great opportunity was coming. He had said to them, "Only if thou carefully hearken unto the voice of the Lord thy God, to observe to do all these commandments which I command thee this day. For the Lord thy God blesseth thee, as he promised thee: and thou shalt LEND UNTO MANY NATIONS, but thou shalt not borrow; and thou shalt REIGN OVER MANY NATIONS, but they shall not reign over thee."[43]

All of this was a prophetic commitment from the Lord that he was once more willing to make Israel an unexcelled political power of righteous dominion and great wealth.

Moses was so anxious that the new generation of Israelites appreciate exactly what the Lord was trying to do for them that he took one more occasion just before he left them to spell out in the most minute detail the magnificent blessings which awaited them if they would just obey the Lord. Israel had it within her power to change the whole course of world history and if she had risen to this occasion the human race might have been spared the subsequent series of blood-baths which drenched mankind with a scarlet flood from the swords of the Medes, Persians, Assyrians, Egyptians, Greeks and Romans. It is obvious that if Israel had prevailed in righteousness and become "high above all nations" there never would have been the political vacuum which later tempted these heathen kings to launch their campaigns of violent conquest in order to set up world empires.

---

42. Deuteronomy 26:16-19   43. Deuteronomy 15:5-6

THE TEN COMMANDMENTS — A Paramount Picture

"And Moses called all Israel and said unto them, Hear, O Israel, the statutes and judgements which I speak in your ears this day, that ye may learn them, and keep, and do them."

The Lord knew this and so did Moses. Consider, therefore, the solemnity of the occasion as the Lord's prophet pronounced these significant words:

"And it shall come to pass, if thou shalt hearken diligently unto the voice of the Lord thy God, to observe and to do all his commandments which I command thee this day, that the Lord thy God will set thee ON HIGH ABOVE ALL NATIONS OF THE EARTH:

"And all these blessings shall come on thee, and overtake thee, if thou shalt hearken unto the voice of the Lord thy God.

"Blessed shalt thou be in the city, and blessed shalt thou be in the field.

"Blessed shall be the fruit of thy body, and the fruit of thy ground, and the fruit of thy cattle, the increase of thy kine, and the flocks of thy sheep.

"Blessed shall be thy basket and thy store.

"Blessed shalt thou be when thou comest in, and blessed shalt thou be when thou goest out.

"The Lord shall cause thine enemies that rise up against thee to be smitten before thy face; they shall come out against thee one way, and flee before thee seven ways. . . .

"The Lord shall establish thee AN HOLY PEOPLE UNTO HIMSELF, as he hath sworn unto thee, if thou shalt keep the commandments of the Lord thy God, and walk in his ways.

"And ALL THE PEOPLE of the earth shall see that thou art called by the name of the Lord; AND THEY SHALL BE AFRAID OF THEE. . . .

"The Lord shall open unto thee his good treasure, the heaven to give the rain unto thy land in his season, and to bless all the work of thine hand: and THOU SHALT LEND UNTO MANY NATIONS, and thou shalt not borrow.

"And the Lord shall MAKE THEE THE HEAD and not the tail; and THOU SHALT BE ABOVE ONLY, and thou shalt not be beneath; if that thou hearken unto the commandments of the Lord thy God, which I command thee this day, to observe and to do them.''[44]

These superlative promises make it perfectly obvious that the Lord was offering Israel a second chance to duplicate the golden age of Enoch among mankind.

THE CURSE OF DISOBEDIENCE

The penalty for rejecting these blessings was ominous with ugly predictions for the future. Moses itemized with meticulous care the gruesome experience which awaited israel if they deliberately and contemptuously rejected this magnificent blessing which God now offered them. The consequences would be one prolonged series of persecution, bloodshed, slavery and total desolation.

Instead of prosperity there would be poverty.[45]

Instead of health there would be pestilence.[46]

Instead of fertility the land would become a desert.[47]

Instead of military victory there would be humiliating defeat.[48]

Instead of happy marriages wives would be kidnapped and ravished.[49]

Instead of happy families children would be sold into slavery.[50]

Instead of flocks and herds they would be left destitute.[51]

Instead of being the greatest Israel would be the lowest.[52]

Instead of enjoying religious freedom they would be compelled to worship manmade idols.[53]

Instead of comfort and abundance there would be hunger, thirst and nakedness.[54]

In anticipation of Israel's conquest Moses declared:

'The Lord shall bring a nation against thee from far, from the end of the earth, as swift as the eagle flieth; a na-

44. Deuteronomy 28:1-13
45. Deuteronomy 28:17-18
46. Deuteronomy 28:21-22
47. Deuteronomy 28:24
48. Deuteronomy 28:25
49. Deuteronomy 28:30
50. Deuteronomy 28:32, 41
51. Deuteronomy 28:31
52. Deuteronomy 28:44
53. Deuteronomy 28:36
54. Deuteronomy 28:48

tion whose tongue thou shalt not understand; a nation of fierce countenance, which shall not regard the person of the old, nor shew favour to the young. . . . And he shall besiege thee in all thy gates, until thy high and fenced walls come down, wherein thou trustedst, throughout all thy land. . . ."[55] Three different times this prophecy was fulfilled: by the Assyrians, the Babylonians, and finally by the Romans.

The worst prophecy of all was concerning the siege against Israel which would cause the mothers of Israel to resort to cannibalism and devour the bodies of their own starved children: "And thou shalt eat the fruit of thine own body, the flesh of thy sons and of thy daughters, which the Lord thy God hath given thee, in the siege, and in the straitness, wherewith thine enemies shall distress thee."[56]

This prophecy was also fulfilled on three different occaions: during the Assyrian siege,[57] during the siege of Jerusalem by Nebuchadnezzar,[58] and later during the final overthrow of Jerusalem by Titus.

Josephus was a personal witness to the terrible scenes of famine and death during the Roman siege by Titus in 70 A.D. In fact, he was an intermediary between the Romans and the Jews. He describes one instance where the guards inside the city found a woman who seemed to have food and Josephus says they "threatened her they would cut her throat immediately if she did not show them what food she had gotten ready. She replied that she had saved a very fine portion of it for them, and withal uncovered what was left of her son."[59]

Such were the horrors which Moses foresaw for his people if they rejected the covenant of God and apostatized.

Like a voice of thundering doom, Moses declared to Israel: "And the Lord shall scatter thee among all people, from the one end of the earth even unto the other; and there thou shalt serve other gods, which neither thou nor thy fathers have known, even wood and stone.

---

55. Deuteronomy 28:49-52
56. Deuteronomy 28:53
57. 2 Kings 6:28-29
58. Lamentations 4:10
59. Josephus, *Wars of the Jews*, Vol. VI, Chapter 3:4

"And among these nations shalt thou find no ease, neither shall the sole of thy foot have rest: but the Lord shall give thee there a trembling heart, and failing of eyes, and sorrow of mind.

"And thy life shall hang in doubt before thee; and thou shalt fear day and night, and shalt have none assurance of thy life:

"In the morning thou shalt say, Would God it were even! and at even thou shalt say, Would God it were morning! for the fear of thine heart wherewith thou shalt fear, and for the sight of thine eyes which thou shalt see."[60]

PROMISE OF THE GATHERING IN THE LAST DAYS

But after this doomsday prophecy Moses followed it with the famous message of hope contained in the thirtieth chapter of Deuteronomy. Looking down the long corridor of time to the great winding up scene of the latter days, Moses saw that in that far distant vista of the future the scattered Israelites would finally seek once more for the blessings of freedom and prosperity which they had lost:

"And it shall come to pass, when all these things are come upon thee, the blessing and the curse, which I have set before thee, and thou shalt call them to mind among all the nations, whither the Lord thy God hath driven thee,

"And shalt return unto the Lord thy God, and shalt obey his voice, according to all that I command thee this day, thou and thy children, with all thine heart, and with all thy soul;

"That then the Lord thy God will turn thy captivity, and have compassion upon thee, and will return and gather thee from all the nations, whither the Lord thy God hath scattered thee."[61]

Then Moses let fly a prophetic bolt which some students believe had reference to the lost Ten Tribes. Said he:

"If any of thine [people] be driven out unto the outmost parts of heaven, from thence will the Lord thy God gather thee, and from thence will he fetch thee."[62]

---

60. Deuteronomy 28:64-68   62. Deuteronomy 30:4-5
61. Deuteronomy 30:1-3

MOSES DELIVERS HIS FINAL CHARGE TO JOSHUA AND THE LEVITES

As one of his final acts Moses called a great conference of all the Israelites and said unto them: "I am an hundred and twenty years old this day; I can no more go out [to lead Israel] and come in [to bring them back victorious]: also the Lord hath said unto me, Thou shalt not go over this Jordan."[63]

Then Moses called Joshua forward and in the presence of this vast throng he gave him this charge: "Be strong and of a good courage: for thou must go with this people unto the land which the Lord hath sworn unto their fathers to give them; and thou shalt cause them to inherit it. And the Lord, he it is that doth go before thee: fear not, neither be dismayed."[64]

To the Levite priests Moses gave instructions that the law should be kept in the Ark of the Covenant[65] and brought out every seven years and read before all the people.[66] This was to take place "in the solemnity of the year of release, in the feast of the tabernacles, when all Israel is come to appear before the Lord thy God. . . ."[67]

At the end of this conference the Lord said to Moses: "Behold, thy days approach that thou must die; call Joshua, and present yourselves in the tabernacle of the congregation, that I may give him a charge."[68]

When they entered the Tabernacle the pillar of cloud became luminous as it always was when God's presence was there. By this means the people knew the Lord was conversing with Moses. And the Lord said to him: "Behold, thou shalt sleep with thy fathers; and this people will rise up, and go a whoring after the gods of the strangers of the land, whither they go to be among them; and will forsake me, and break my covenant which I have made with them."[69]

This was the one revelation Moses probably hoped he would never receive. It told him which way the Israelites

---

63. Deuteronomy 31:1
64. Deuteronomy 31:7-8
65. Deuteronomy 31:26
66. Deuteronomy 31:10-11
67. Ibid.
68. Deuteronomy 31:14
69. Deuteronomy 31:16

would choose to go. It was almost as though his whole life's work had come tumbling down around him in a shambles. But Moses was no more heartbroken than the Lord. He told Moses to write down a song which would be given by revelation that all Israel could memorize it and sing it in the day of her sorrow. This song was God's lamentation over fallen Israel.[70] In it He reminded them of their importance. He referred to their pre-existence when they were singled out to be leaders and the leaven of hope for humanity. Through the words of this song the Lord cried out:

"Remember the days of old, consider the years of many generations: ask thy father, and he will shew thee; thy elders, and they will tell thee. When the Most High divided to the nations their inheritance, when he separated the sons of Adam, he set the bounds of the people according to the number of the children of Israel."[71]

In this passage the Lord discloses the fact that the continuous ushering in of millions of human beings upon the earth, the rise and fall of nations, the ebb and flow of civilizations, all must be carefully supervised in terms of available leadership. In this song God is simply telling Israel that when they who have been chosen leaders let the Lord down, it slows the progress of the whole human race. There is nothing magic about the way God accomplishes his purposes. He performs his work through intelligent beings.[72] His plan is dependent upon the cooperation of these intelligent beings.[73] When they elect to disobey and fail in their role as Priesthood leaders, it affects the rate of progress for the entire human family.

So here was the purpose of this new song. It was to tell Israel that she could have become greater than any nation on the face of the earth, but that the Lord already knew she would flounder and lose her opportunity. They were going to get the promised land but because of unrighteousness they were eventually going to lose it.

After all Moses had gone through to save this people he could not help but remark sadly, "I know thy rebellion,

70. Deuteronomy Chapter 32
71. Deuteronomy 32:7-8
72. Abraham 3:22-23
73. Doctrine and Covenants 93:29-31

and thy stiff neck: behold, while I am yet alive with you this day, ye have been rebellious against the Lord; and how much more after my death? . . . I know that after my death ye will utterly corrupt yourselves. . . .''[74]

MOSES BLESSES EACH OF THE TWELVE TRIBES

Nevertheless, the hope of Moses was in the Lord. Several thousand years hence he knew that God would reap the victory and so would Israel. Therefore, Moses closed his ministry with a blessing on each of the tribes. The most singular of all these blessings was the one he pronounced on Joseph. For the other tribes Moses followed rather closely the blessings previously pronounced upon them by Jacob, but for Joseph there was to be a special calling, in a special land, in the latter days.

It should be kept in mind that Moses already knew a great deal about the last days. When he had been working on the Book of Genesis he had learned about the "Joseph" who would rise up to do God's great work in the last dispensation.[75] He knew this prophet would be like unto himself and that it would be the great day of gathering and the preparation of the earth for the coming of the Messiah. Therefore, with a note of triumph in his blessing, Moses declared concerning Joseph:

"Blessed of the Lord be HIS LAND, for the precious things of heaven, for the dew, and for THE DEEP that coucheth beneath; And for the precious fruits brought forth by the sun, and for the precious things put forth by the moon, and for the chief things of the ANCIENT MOUNTAINS, and for the precious THINGS OF THE LASTING HILLS. And for the precious things of the earth and the fulness thereof; and for the good will of HIM THAT DWELT IN THE BUSH: let the blessing come upon the head of Joseph and upon the top of the head of him that was separated from his brethren. His glory is like the firstling of his bullock, and his horns are like the horns of unicorns: with them he shall PUSH THE PEOPLE TOGETHER to the ends of

---

74. Deuteronomy 31:27, 29
75. Inspired Version, Genesis, Chap. 50

the earth: and they are the ten thousands of Ephraim, and they are the thousands of Manasseh."⁷⁶

The student of today has a great advantage in studying this passage because this prophecy is presently in process of being fulfilled and the more obscure phrases become vividly apparent. Moses knew that Joseph was to receive a land which would be a vast continental inheritance of his own and that it would be separate from the land of his brethren by the great deep even as Joseph had been separated from his brethren when he was taken into Egypt. Moses knew it would be a land of ancient mountains and its hills would be filled with the wealth of precious resources. He knew that the tens of thousands of Ephraim and the thousands of Manasseh would launch the great gathering of Israel in the last days and "push the people together" from the ends of the earth. What Moses was seeing was the rise of America and the setting up of Zion in the latter days.

As we have previously pointed out, the Jewish scholars have known from the most ancient times that there would be a "Joseph" raised up in the last days. Out of respect for his great mission they came to know him prophetically as "Messiah ben Joseph" and said he would prepare the way for the coming of "Messiah ben David." Today, the word is going forth to the Jews and all the scattered remnants of Israel: "Messiah ben Joseph has come!"

MOSES ASCENDS MOUNT NEBO TO MEET GOD

Having blessed the tribes of Israel, Moses prepared to ascend into the range of Mount Nebo and climb the heights of a certain peak called Mount Pisgah.⁷⁷ All Israel knew the earthly mission of Moses was through. What had happened to Aaron would now happen to Moses. He would ascend into the mount and they would never see him again.

In the person of Moses there was nothing to portend death. The people noted that "his eye was not dim, nor his natural force abated."⁷⁸ Having been notable for his beauty as a child, it seems he remained ruggedly handsome even

---

76. Deuteronomy 33:13-17   78. Deuteronomy 34:7
77. Deuteronomy 34:1

extends to the Sea of Galilee where Jesus would one day teach and fifteen miles from which he would be reared as a carpenter's son at Nazareth. Farther north lay Lebanon with its snow-capped Mount Hermon brooding over the valley of Damascus. Far beyond and toward the east lay the great Euphrates River. All of this was to be Israel's — from the "river of Egypt" to the great Euphrates.[84] What Moses could see was glorious. What lay beyond excited the imagination.

But this was all the Lord had promised Moses. He had seen the promised land and now the time for his departure had come. Josephus describes the final scene as it appeared to those who were there. He says Moses "dismissed the elders, and then, as he was embracing Eleazar and Joshua, and still speaking to them, a cloud suddenly stood over him and he vanished in a deep valley."[85]

For Moses it was a sudden, exciting, breathtaking metamorphosis. For Joshua and Eleazar, a heartbreak. Suddenly the two new leaders of Israel stood alone. Finally they descended into the valley to tell the people it was all over. Moses was gone.

This marked the end of a great historic epic in the annals of the race and, as the scripture declares, ". . . there arose not a prophet since in Israel like unto Moses, whom the Lord knew face to face."[86]

THE LORD REVEALS A GREAT SECRET CONCERNING MOSES

But this is not the end of the story. One of the most interesting things about the life of Moses is the way it ended. Unless they had been told, Joshua and Eleazar would never have guessed what actually happened. They saw Moses disappear in the cloud and for them this was the end of the matter. Therefore, when Joshua[87] later wrote his comments on the death of Moses he assumed that the Lord had buried

---

84. "In the same day the Lord made a covenant with Abram, saying, Unto thy seed have I given this land, from the river of Egypt unto the great river, the river Euphrates." (Genesis 15:18)
85. Josephus, *Antiquities of the Jews, Book IV*, Chapter 8:48
86. Deuteronomy 34:10
87. Authorities seem in general agreement that Joshua must have written the last chapter of Deuteronomy. In fact, they point out that it was originally part of the Book of Joshua. See Clarke, *Bible Commentary*, Vol. 1, p. 838.

his great prophet in the valley beyond, so he said: "And he [the Lord] buried him in a valley in the land of Moab, over against Beth-peor. . . ." Nevertheless, in the very next sentence he frankly admits that this is purely a presumption on his part because "no man knoweth of his sepulchre unto this day."[88]

The truth of the matter is that Moses did not die at all. He was *translated!*[89] Instead of laying his body down in the grave, it was quickened just as had happened to the entire city of Enoch, to the people of Melchizedek, and just as it would later happen to Elijah, John the Beloved, Alma and the Three Nephites.

In the New Testament Jude indicates that it was Adam (known in Heaven as Michael) who came to Mount Nebo to welcome Moses across the veil and introduce him into the higher dimension of eternity where translated beings have their home.[90] Jude says that Satan protested bitterly "about the body of Moses"[91] due, no doubt, to the fact that his body was not going to be consigned to the grave as is the common lot of mankind generally. However, Michael prevailed over Satan and said, "The Lord rebuke thee."[92]

We learn that there are certain functions of angelic administration which require possession of the physical body. For example, a person must be "in the flesh" (either as a translated or resurrected being) in order to pass on keys of authority and ordinations in the Priesthood. We are told that this was why both Moses and Elijah were translated. They both held special keys and powers of authority which would have to be conferred upon later servants of God *prior to the resurrection.* Speaking of this, Joseph Fielding Smith says, ". . . we understand why Elijah and Moses were pre-

---

88. Deuteronomy 34:6
89. For a discussion of this matter, see Joseph Fielding Smith, *Doctrines of Salvation,* Vol. 2, pp. 110-111.
90. Concerning translated beings, Joseph Smith wrote: "Many have supposed that the doctrine of translation was a doctrine whereby men were taken immediately into the presence of God, and into an eternal fulness, but this is a mistaken idea. Their place of habitation is that of the terrestrial order, and a place prepared for such characters He held in reserve to be ministering angels unto many planets, and who as yet have not entered into so great a fulness as those who are resurrected from the dead." (*Teachings of Joseph Smith,* p. 170)
91. Jude, verse 9
92. Ibid.

served from death: because *they had a mission to perform,* and it had to be performed *before* the crucifixion of the Son of God, and it *could not be done in the spirit. They had to have tangible bodies.* Christ is the first fruits of the resurrection; therefore if any former prophets had a work to perform preparatory to the mission of the Son of God, or to the dispensation of the meridian of times, it was essential that they be preserved to fulfill that mission *in the flesh.* For that reason Moses disappeared from among the people and was taken up into the mountain, and the people *thought* he was buried by the Lord. The Lord preserved him, so that he could come at the proper time and *restore his keys,* on the heads of Peter, James and John, who stood at the head of the dispensation of the meridian of time. He reserved Elijah from death that he might also come and bestow his keys upon the heads of Peter, James and John and prepare them for their ministry."[93]

THE POST-MORTAL APPEARANCES OF MOSES

In the above quotation Joseph Fielding Smith refers to the appearance of Moses on the Mount of Transfiguration. The New Testament account does not give the precise reason for this important meeting in which the Savior, Peter, James, John, Moses and Elijah all took part. Joseph Smith says one reason for the meeting was this: "The Savior, Moses and Elias (or Elijah), gave the keys to Peter, James and John, on the mount, when they were transfigured before him."[94] Obviously, this event was a much more important and significant meeting than the simple account in the New Testament implies.

In a modern revelation, the Lord states that Moses was one of those who was "with Christ in his resurrection."[95] This would seem to indicate that at the time of Christ's resurrection Moses was permitted to pass from that of a translated being to a state of glorified perfection in the resurrection. We are told this process can be accomplished "in the twinkling of an eye."[96]

---

93. Joseph Fielding Smith, *Doctrines of Salvation,* Vol. 2, pp. 110-111 (Italics in the original).
94. Teachings of Joseph Smith, p. 158   96. 3 Nephi 28:8
95. Doctrine and Covenants 133:55

From this it would therefore appear that when Moses was allowed to minister to the Lord's modern leaders in the Kirtland Temple, he came as a resurrected being. This modern appearance of the mighty Moses occurred in connection with the dedication and acceptance of the first temple built in modern times. Joseph Smith describes the moving events of that day:

"In the afternoon, I assisted the other presidents in distributing the Lord's Supper to the Church, receiving it from the Twelve, whose privilege it was to officiate at the sacred desk this day. After having performed this service to my brethren, I retired to the pulpit, the veils being dropped, and bowed myself, with Oliver Cowdery, in solemn and silent prayer. After rising from prayer, the following vision was opened to both of us. . . .

"We saw the Lord standing upon the breastwork of the pulpit, before us; and under his feet was a paved work of pure gold, in color like amber. His eyes were as a flame of fire; the hair of his head was white like the pure snow; his countenance shone above the brightness of the sun; and his voice was as the sound of the rushing of great waters, even the voice of Jehovah, saying:

"I am the first and the last; I am he who liveth, I am he who was slain; I am your advocate with the Father. . . . Let the hearts of your brethren rejoice, and let the hearts of all my people rejoice, who have, with their might, built this house in my name.

"For behold, I have accepted this house, and my name shall be here; and I will manifest myself to my people in mercy in this house.

"Yea, I will appear unto my servants, and speak unto them with mine own voice, if my people will keep my commandments, and do not pollute this holy house. . . .

"After this vision closed, the heavens were again opened unto us; and Moses appeared before us, and committed unto us the keys of the gathering of Israel from the four parts of the earth, and the leading of the ten tribes from the land of the north."[97]

---

97. See Doctrine and Covenants, Section 110 including the preface.

How appropriate that Moses, who had predicted the great gathering of Israel in the last day, should have been an active participant on this sacred occasion. And what a memorable experience it must have been for Joseph Smith and Oliver Cowdery as they felt the touch of the hands of Moses upon their heads and heard him bestow the keys for the gathering of Israel from the four corners of the earth in modern times!

Scripture Reading and Questions on Chapter Twenty

Scripture Reading Assignment: Numbers, chapters 31 to 35; Deuteronomy, chapters 4 to 34.

1—In round figures, how much had Israel decreased in population
during the 38 years in the wilderness?

2—Why was Moses alarmed when Reuben and Gad wanted to settle
down in Trans-Jordan? What finally convinced Moses to let
them do it?

3—Which other tribe received a partial inheritance in Trans-Jordan?

4—When Israel lay seige to a city what did the Lord say they had
to do before launching an attack? Why did the Lord want these
heathen nations to be subject to Israel?

5—Why did the Lord declare some of the heathen nations *anathema*?
What was to happen to them if they did not repent and resisted
Israel?

6—Just before the passing of Moses, what great blessing did the Lord
offer the new, uprising generation of Israel? If this second generation of the Israelites had remained valiant how could it have
changed world history?

7—List three blessings promised the Israelites if they were faithful.
List three afflictions which would follow if they were unfaithful.

8—What hope was Moses inspired to give the Israelites of the latter
days?

9—Did Moses have advance knowledge that Israel would fail in her
mission? Does it affect world history when Priesthood leaders fall
short of God's goals?

10—When Moses blessed the twelve tribes, which tribe received the
most attention?

11—Name three distinctive things about the blessing Moses gave this
tribe.

12—When Moses reached 120 years of age, was he sickly?

13—Where did Moses say the Levites should put his writings of the
law?

14—When Moses went up into the mountains of the Nebo range, what
did the Lord tell him he would see? Who was with Moses on
this occasion?

15—Why does the Bible say that no one knows where Moses was
buried? What actually happened to him? Why does it appear
this was necessary?

16—What did Moses, Elijah and the Savior do for Peter, James and
John on the Mount of Transfiguration?

17—Does Moses appear to have been resurrected at the time of the
resurrection of Christ?

18—Who had the great honor of seeing Moses in modern times?

19—What did Moses do when he appeared in the Kirtland Temple?

20—As you contemplate the long life of Moses, how would you rate
him among the prophets?

CHAPTER TWENTY-ONE

Joshua, the Great Ephraimite General, Takes Command

Now the children of Israel were in the hands of Joshua, the foremost military leader to be raised up by the Lord during the third thousand years of Biblical history.

Joshua was an Ephraimite, the son of Nun.[1] In fact, he was the patriarchal heir of Ephraim,[2] and on occasion was chosen to represent his entire tribe.[3]

Nothing is given concerning the birth or early life of Joshua except to state that his name was originally Hoshea (sometimes spelled Oshea),[4] and that during the second year of the Exodus, Moses changed his name to Joshua (sometimes spelled Jehoshua) which means "Jehovah is Salvation."[5] This is the identical name which was given to the Son of Mary some fifteen centuries later and which we have transliterated into English through the Greek as "Jesus."[6]

We know that Joshua was 110 years old when he died at the conclusion of Canaan's conquest,[7] and there is a variety of circumstantial data available in the scripture which has led Bible chronologists to estimate that Joshua was close to 57 years of age when the great Exodus began.[8]

Nevertheless, Joshua first appears in the scripture as "the servant of Moses, one of his young men," who is made the first captain-general over the hosts of Israel.[9] Age 57

---

1. Numbers 13:8, 16
2. 1 Chronicles 7:22-27
3. Numbers 13:8
4. Numbers 13:16
5. Ibid. plus Peloubet's *Bible Dictionary* under "Joshua."
6. See Clarke's *Bible Commentary*, Vol. 1, p. 387. Note that New Testament references to Joshua are translated "Jesus" (Acts 7:45; Hebrews 4:8).
7. Joshua 24:29
8. Clarke, *Bible Commentary*, Vol. 1, p. 883.
9. Exodus 17:9 plus Numbers 11:28 where Joshua is described as "the servant of Moses, one of his young men."

would be the prime of life for a man who was going to live 110 years, therefore Joshua is called a "young" man. His appointment came as a result of a cowardly attack by the Amalekites when Israel was just a few weeks out of Egypt and on the way to Mount Sinai.[10] The Amalekites did not dare assault the main body of Israel but struck at the stragglers who were too weak or weary to keep up.[11] Moses assigned Joshua the task of organizing the first army of Israel and driving off the Amalekites. This was a critical military contest which went badly for Israel part of the time,[12] but Joshua and his troops finally prevailed and the Amalekites were routed.[13]

Early in their association together Moses knew that Joshua would be his successor.[14] Perhaps he had sensed it even earlier. At least we know that he kept the Ephraimite captain-general close to him throughout his ministry. Moses saw to it that Joshua was among the seventy elders who were allowed to see the personage of the Lord in the lower regions of Mount Sinai.[15] Later that day when Moses went up higher into the mount, Joshua was the only one he took with him.[16] For six days Moses and Joshua waited for the Lord to give further instructions, and it was not until the seventh day that the Lord finally told Moses to proceed up to the summit alone.[17] During the thirty-four days and nights while Moses was being instructed by the Lord, Joshua waited patiently. How Joshua survived we are not told,[18] but the scripture is very specific that when Moses started down with the tablets of the law, Joshua was still waiting for him and the two came down from the mount together.[19]

---

10. Exodus 17:8-16
11. Deuteronomy 25:17-18
12. Exodus 17:11
13. Exodus 17:13
14. Deuteronomy 1:37-38
15. Exodus 24:9-13
16. Exodus 24:13
17. Exodus 24:16-18
18. If the traditional site which we now call Mount Sinai is indeed the correct location, there is a saddle between the highest peak and the one nearby which contains a cloistered vale with water, shade, shrubs and some animal life. The visitor comes upon it unexpectedly and is always amazed to find such an oasis on this otherwise barren pile of solid rock.
19. Joshua 2:15

The following year Moses sent 12 spies into Canaan to search out the land.[20] Joshua was one of them, being designated to represent the entire tribe of Ephraim.[21] When the tribes returned, only Joshua and Caleb of Judah had the faith to believe that with God's help Israel could conquer Canaan.[22] In fact, Joshua and Caleb almost lost their lives trying to get the people to support Moses and the Lord.[23] It will be recalled that as a result of this mutiny the Lord condemned Israel to wander in the wilderness for an additional 38 years. The Lord said that out of that entire generation of adults only Joshua and Caleb would live to enter the promised land.[24]

It will be further recalled that when Israel had finally raised up a new generation and Moses led them toward Trans-Jordan, the armies of Israel were amazingly successful in overcoming any tribes who tried to destroy or subvert them. All of these victories were under the military direction of Joshua which added tremendous stature to his image as Israel's commander in chief.

Finally, when Moses was told that it was time that he be "gathered to his people," he ordained Joshua to be his successor by the laying on of hands,[25] and gave Joshua the Lord's charge to him, "Be strong and of a good courage; for thou shalt bring the children of Israel into the land which I sware unto them: and I will be with thee."[26]

The passing of Moses came shortly afterwards and left the people of Israel in deepest mourning. After thirty days of lamentation they turned to their new leader: "And Joshua the son of Nun was full of the spirit of wisdom; for Moses had laid his hands upon him: and the children of Israel hearkened unto him, and did as the Lord commanded Moses."[27] Joshua knew that from this moment through to the end of his days, Israel would be his personal responsibility.

---

20. Numbers 13:1-2
21. Numbers 13:8
22. Numbers 13:31 plus 14:6-9
23. Numbers 14:10
24. Numbers 14:27-38. The Lord uses the term "40 years" but He is including the two years of wilderness travel which had already passed.
25. Numbers 27:18-23
26. Deuteronomy 31:23
27. Deuteronomy 34:9

JOSHUA FACES UP TO HIS NEW CALLING

Joshua knew that crossing into Canaan was far more hazardous than merely fording the waters of the Jordan River. He knew that once they crossed Jordan, Israel stood on enemy territory. They would be in Canaan as invaders and their very presence across the river would be an open invitation to attack. Joshua also knew that the conquest of Canaan would require that his troops "fight to the death" and that thousands of them would die in any event. Therefore this massive migration across Jordan was no casual nomadic excursion.

At this point Joshua received a personal revelation from the Lord containing both a promise and a plea. Here was the Lord's promise:

". . . arise, go over this Jordan, thou, and all this people, unto the land which I do give to them, even to the children of Israel. . . . There shall not any man be able to stand before thee all the days of thy life: as I was with Moses, so I will be with thee: I will not fail thee, nor forsake thee."[28]

Then came the Lord's plea. The Lord had a great blessing of military success in store for Joshua. Although the children of Israel were not collectively worthy of the blessing, nevertheless the Lord felt justified in granting them a great victory if Joshua, their leader, remained valiant. Knowing human nature, the Lord was well aware that Joshua could collapse just as easily as Saul several hundred years later. Therefore He pleaded with Joshua as a father pleads with a son:

"Be strong and of a good courage: for unto this people shalt thou divide for an inheritance the land, which I sware unto their fathers to give them. Only be thou strong and very courageous, that thou mayest observe to do according to all the law, which Moses my servant commanded thee: turn not from it to the right hand or to the left, that thou mayest prosper withersoever thou goest."[29]

---

28. Joshua 1:2, 5   29. Joshua 1:6-7

Joshua Sends Spies to Jericho

Joshua gave Israel just three days to pack up, "prepare . . . victuals" and get ready to cross into Canaan.[30] Meanwhile he ordered two spies to cross the Jordan and search out the military strength of Jericho which lay only six or seven miles beyond Jordan and was the most prosperous, powerful and well-fortified city in the entire south Jordan valley.

Following these instructions, the two spies somehow navigated the Jordan River and made their way to the gates of Jericho. Inside the city they made contact with an innkeeper named Rahab and there they made their lodging. Little did they realize that they had providentially come to the one woman in this teeming, licentious city who not only would save their lives but who already believed in Israel's God and was destined to become a maternal ancestor of Jesus Christ!

Because of her historical importance, it is necessary to pause for a moment and clarify an ugly error which has occurred in the English version of the Bible concerning this woman. The modern Bible says that the spies stayed at "an harlot's house, named Rahab."[31] Dr. Adam Clarke counts this a translator's error and says, "I am fully satisfied that the term *zonah* in the text, which we translate harlot, should be rendered tavern or inn-keeper or hostess."[32] There is nothing in the text to impute a tainted character in Rahab and Dr. Clarke feels there was no excuse for the translators to presume as much just simply because she kept a public house of lodging.

It would also seem apparent that Rahab was not a Canaanite even though she was living in a Canaanite city. This seems clear from the fact that she subsequently married a prince of Judah[33] which marriage would have been unlawful had she been of Hamitic lineage.[34] This conclusion is further supported by the fact that she was the direct lineage through which the Savior was born. It would not be unusual for a

---

30. Joshua 1:11
31. Joshua 2:1
32. Clarke's *Bible Commentary*, Vol. 2, p. 11
33. Matthew 1:5. The New Testament spelling is "Rachab."
34. Genesis 24:3. See discussion in note 65, Chapter two.

non-Hamitic woman to be living in this Canaanite city. The cross-currents of war and commerce had long since mixed the various nationalities so that people of many racial patterns and cultures were represented in every major city along the fertile crescent.

RAHAB SAVES THE LIVES OF THE SPIES

When the spies had first entered Jericho they were not aware that they had raised the suspicions of certain men of the city who had followed them to Rahab's house. These men immediately sent word to the king of Jericho who quickly sent his soldiers to have the two Hebrews arrested. Had Rahab been a woman of disrepute they would have no doubt raided her inn and dragged the Hebrew spies to the king's prison. But this is not what happened. The king sent his messengers to her respectfully asking that she deliver the two Hebrews to the authorities.[35]

However, instead of surrendering the men, Rahab immediately took them up onto the roof of her house where she was drying quantities of flax. There she hid them.[36] Then she gave the king's messengers a story which would divert them away from searching any longer in Jericho. She told them to hasten after the Hebrews and catch them before they had a chance to get back across Jordan. This they did.[37]

Rahab then quickly ascended to the roof of her house to talk to the spies. No doubt they were amazed that a woman of Jericho would befriend them in this manner, but when she returned from talking to the king's messengers she explained why she had done it. Rahab had a greater testimony of God's destiny for Israel than most of the Israelites! Said she, "I know that the Lord hath given you the land, and that your terror is fallen upon us, and that all the inhabitants of the land faint because of you. For we have heard how the Lord dried up the water of the Red sea for you, when ye came out of Egypt; and what ye did unto the two kings of the Amorites, that were on the other side Jordan, Sihon and Og, whom ye utterly destroyed. And as soon as we had heard these things, our hearts did melt, neither

35. Joshua 2:3   37. Joshua 2:5, 7
36. Joshua 2:6

did there remain any more courage in any man, because of you: for the Lord your God, he is God in heaven above, and in earth beneath."[38]

Having borne this testimony Rahab indicated that she wished to become their ally and friend and that in return she would expect protection when Israel occupied Jericho. She said: "Now therefore, I pray you, swear unto me by the Lord, since I have shewed you kindness, that ye will also shew kindness unto my father's house, and give me a true token: and that ye will save alive my father, and my mother, and my brethren, and my sisters, and all that they have, and deliver our lives from death."[39]

The grateful Hebrews agreed. They swore that if she would protect them and keep their whereabouts a secret they would guarantee her life with their own lives and also protect her kinsmen when Israel took Jericho.[40] They told her to bind a red or scarlet cloth to the window so the army of Israel would know which was her house and spare it. Rahab's house was built on the wall that protected the city,[41] so she helped them escape by lowering the scarlet cloth down the side of the wall from one of her windows. She told the spies to let themselves down by this device and flee into the mountains west of Jericho for three days. By that time she felt the king's soldiers would have become discouraged and discontinued their search. The spies did exactly as she suggested.

Three days later the two Hebrews crept down from their mountain hideout and crossed the River Jordan. They hurried to Joshua with the vital news he was awaiting. Said they, "Truly the Lord hath delivered into our hands all the land; for even all the inhabitants of the country do faint because of us."[42] That was all Joshua needed to know.

THE HOSTS OF ISRAEL CROSS OVER JORDAN

Early the following morning Joshua roused the camps of Israel. Apparently they had already broken camp and were ready to march whenever the signal was given. It was the intention of Joshua to get them down to the banks of the Jordan river by nightfall. The marching multitude was led by

38. Joshua 2:9-11
39. Joshua 2:12-13
40. Joshua 2:14
41. Joshua 2:15
42. Joshua 2:24

the Levite priests who were assigned to carry the Ark of the Covenant on their shoulders. No one was allowed to follow the Ark closer than 2,000 cubits.[44] Since the distance from their former camp site at Shittim to the banks of the Jordan was not a long journey, they were able to cover it in one day. Toward evening Joshua said to the people, "Sanctify yourselves: for tomorrow the Lord will do wonders among you."[44]

Joshua knew that a great historic event was about to take place. Both he and the people approached the dawn of the next day with mixed feelings of excitement and solemnity. To Joshua the Lord said, "This day will I begin to magnify thee in the sight of all Israel, that they may know that, as I was with Moses, so I will be with thee."[45]

Joshua then called all of the people together and told them they were about to see a miracle similar to one of those the Lord had performed for their fathers as they came up out of Egypt. For the most part, this younger generation of Israel had been born since that time. Only a few were old enough to remember the avalanche of divine power which God had exhibited during those early days of the Exodus. Now, he said, they too would be scientific witnesses to a display of that power.[46]

Joshua immediately ordered the priests who were carrying the Ark to march out ahead of the camp and approach the river. In fact, he ordered them to march into the river. The scripture says that as the feet of the priests touched the swirling tide along the banks of the river the great miracle happened. Before the eyes of all Israel a clean break appeared in the midst of this torrent of water. It was as though a huge invisible dam had been thrown across the river in an instant. The amazed Israelites watched as "the waters which came down from above stood and rose up upon an heap. . . ."[47] The waters below drained off and disappeared into the Dead Sea.[48] Furthermore, the muddy bottom of the river and the marshland along its banks became dry land so that the priests bearing the Ark were able to march down onto the riverbed

---

43. Joshua 3:3-4
44. Joshua 3:5
45. Joshua 3:7

46. Joshua 3:9-13
47. Joshua 3:16
48. Ibid.

and stand on "dry ground" while the great wall of water piled up miraculously just above them.[49]

Ordinarily the Jordan River is a moderate but steady flow of water which is difficult but not impossible to cross. However, the scripture says the season when Israel crossed was the time of harvest and "the Jordan overfloweth all his banks all the time of harvest."[50] Therefore Israel crossed Jordan at floodtide which made it all the more miraculous.

It must have made an impressive scene as 600,000 men of military age and the wives and children of 9½ tribes swarmed across the dry streambed of the lower Jordan. Since the water was dried up clear to the Dead Sea the crossing was not confined to a narrow passageway but they were able to cross en masse all along the dry river bottom which extended for several miles.

While the water was being held back, Joshua had the representatives from each tribe lift up a boulder from the bottom of the riverbed and carry it up the enbankment. These were later built into a memorial at the place of encampment.[51]

Finally, when Joshua was certain that all of his vast host with their herds and possessions had made a safe crossing he said to the Levite priests who carried the Ark, "Come ye up out of Jordan."[52] The priests promptly came up out of the riverbed and just as soon as they had reached high ground "the waters of Jordan returned unto their place, and flowed over all his banks, as they did before."[53]

The exact date of this momentous event is fixed in scripture as the tenth day of the first month.[54] Since the children of Israel had left Egypt on the fifteenth day of the first month,[55] this meant that they crossed into Canaan just five days short of a full forty years from the time they left Egypt.

---

49. Joshua 3:17
50. Joshua 3:15
51. Joshua 4:2-3, 8. Authorities point out that verse 9 of this passage contains an error when it states that the stones were "set up" in the midst of Jordan. Obviously this would be an impossible place to build a memorial with twelve boulders so small that each could be carried by a single man. Verses 3 and 8 make it clear that the stones were picked up in the midst of Jordan and carried to the place "where they lodged." Verse 20 then says, "and those twelve stones which they took out of Jordan, did Joshua pitch in Gilgal."
52. Joshua 4:17
53. Joshua 4:18
54. Joshua 4:19
55. Exodus 13:4 plus Numbers 33:3 which fixes the day of the month.

Joshua Establishes his Headquarters At Gilgal

The flat, fertile land immediately west of the Jordan river was called Gilgal and there Joshua set up a permanent camp.[56] This camp was very close to Jericho, the Canaanite capital for this whole region.[57] One of the first things Joshua did was to erect a memorial with the twelve stones which had been carried up from the Jordan river bottom.[58]

The massive migration of so large a company as the Israelites represented with a population of two to three million people is very difficult for some modern students to comprehend. However, those who have had the opportunity of watching the manner of life in the Middle East know that the moving, feeding and settling of this number of people is not nearly as difficult as western minds might envision it. Nomadic people learn to live simply. They can provide delicious meals with the most meager resources. They tend to crowd together in close quarters; in fact, setting up dense populations in modest space allotments is characteristic of them.

Of course, Joshua was well aware that his multitude of migrating Israelites were extremely vulnerable to attack as they came tumbling across the Jordan and faced Jericho. Had the Canaanite kings decided to attack just then they could have caught the Israelites in a strategically disastrous position, particularly since most of the men of war were involved in moving their families.

However, there was one large body of men who had brought no families. These were the men of Reuben, Gad, and half the tribe of Manasseh. They had already received their inheritance on the east side of the Jordan but were under covenant to help the rest of Israel become established.[59] Joshua used these men to provide a force of storm troops in case of attack. They were a sufficiently massive array of might to discourage any reckless assault. The scripture says, "And the children of Reuben, and the children of Gad, and

---

56. Joshua 4:19
57. Geikie, *Hours With the Bible*, Vol. 2, p. 445
58. Joshua 4:20-24
59. Joshua 1:12-16

half the tribe of Manasseh, passed over armed before the children of Israel . . . about forty thousand prepared for war passed over before the Lord unto battle, to the plains of Jericho."[60] The sight of 40,000 troops ready for war would be a frightening display of military might to the people of Jericho as they watched from the battlements of their fortified city and saw Israel's great city-camp being built within sight of their gates.

However, whether Joshua realized it or not, there was at that moment a far greater deterrent from attack than the sight of these 40,000 warriors. It was the psychological impact of the cry of alarm which was being spread all over Canaan by the inhabitants of Jordan Valley who had actually seen with their own eyes the miracle of the dividing of the waters of Jordan. This manifestation of God's power in behalf of Israel left the Canaanites panic-stricken. The scripture says, "And it came to pass, when all the kings of the Amorites,[61] which were on the side of Jordan westward, and all the kings of the Canaanites, which were by the sea, heard that the Lord had dried up the waters of Jordan from before the children of Israel . . . their heart melted, neither was there spirit in them any more, because of the children of Israel."[62]

From a military standpoint it would have seemed an ideal time to invade this new territory, but instead of giving the order to attack, the Lord instructed Joshua to put the people under covenant and circumcise all the male population. The scripture says the men of war who had been circumcised at the beginning of the Exodus had all died off (save Joshua and Caleb) and since no circumcision was performed in the wilderness, a whole new generation had arisen without this ordinance.[63] So Joshua did as he was commanded and the people rested until the male population had recovered from these operations.[64]

---

60. Joshua 4:12-13
61. The Amorites were a branch of the Canaanites. They lived mostly in the mountainous area of Canaan, some of whom had spilled over into the Jordan Valley and beyond.
62. Joshua 5:1
63. Joshua 5:4-6
64. Joshua 5:7-8

The Miracle of the Manna Disappears

The fourteenth of the month in which all of this happened was the time of the Passover. While they were resting, Joshua had them celebrate the Feast of the Passover and then immediately afterwards he had them commemorate the Feast of Unleavened Bread.[65]

However, in order to make unleavened bread, the people had to buy grain and make flour. In order to obtain these supplies it was apparently necessary to set up purchasing agreements with Canaanite farmers in the vicinity. They purchased "old corn" which was obtained from "the fruit of the land of Canaan that year."[66]

But as soon as these arrangements were made a strange thing happened. For the first time in nearly forty years there was no supply of manna provided for Israel.[67] This remarkable miracle food from heaven ceased as of this time and so far as we know was never again provided for these people.

Joshua Meets the Captain of God's Hosts

For Joshua and Israel this entire period of respite at Gilgal was a pleasant interlude, but not for the people of Jericho. The king of that city considered himself and his city in a state of siege. He did not allow his people to go in or come out.[68] And of course he could not figure out exactly what Joshua was up to with all of this circumcising and sermonizing and celebrating of religious feasts. It was terribly confusing, but not for long.

One day as Joshua looked over toward the city of Jericho he saw a man standing with his sword drawn. Joshua went out alone to challenge him. "Art thou for us, or for our adversaries?"[69] he said. To Joshua's astonishment the man replied, "Nay: but as captain of the host of the Lord am I now come."[70]

Suddenly realizing he was talking to a heavenly messenger, Joshua fell to the ground and asked, "What saith

---

65. Joshua 5:10-11   68. Joshua 6:1
66. Joshua 5:12   69. Joshua 5:13
67. Ibid.   70. Joshua 5:14

my Lord unto his servant?"[71] He was told to take off his shoes, for the ground on which he stood was holy. Joshua did so.

Following this "the Lord said unto Joshua, See, I have given into thine hand Jericho, and the king thereof, and the mighty men of valour."[72]

This was encouraging but not entirely reassuring. How could this be accomplished? How could the armies of Israel navigate a breach in the high, massive walls of Jericho? The Lord said this would be accomplished by a device which would involve the direct intervention of God's power. Joshua was given a procedure for the conquest of Jericho which no military leader is known to have attempted either before or since.[73]

THE FALL OF JERICHO

Having received his instructions, Joshua set about to carry them out. He organized the military might of Israel in a very special way and then ordered them to march directly toward Jericho. First came the army of Israel, then seven priests followed them blowing their trumpets of rams' horns. Behind the trumpeters came the Ark of the Covenant carried on the shoulders of several priests. Last of all came the special guard bringing up the rear.[74]

The sight of this great throng must have caused the people of Jericho to rush to their battle stations in expectation of an immediate attack, but they were in for a surprise. Instead of attacking, the Israelites made one complete circle around Jericho and then marched directly back to their camp site. They did not so much as unlimber their weapons. Another peculiar thing about this meaningless maneuver was its solemnity. Not a sound was uttered by the multitude as they marched around Jericho.[75] Only the mournful sound of the rams' horn trumpets and the muffled plodding of the thousands of marching feet ascended to the ears of Jericho's defenders mounted on her high walls. As they watched the hosts of Israel march back to their camp they were left with a feeling of puzzled anxiety. What were the Israelites up to?

---

71. Ibid.
72. Joshua 6:2
73. Joshua 6:3-5
74. Joshua 6:7-9
75. Joshua 6:10

The same thing happened the next day and the next. For six consecutive days this strange military exercise was repeated. Since the Israelites made no gesture of hostility it should have occurred to the king of Jericho that an overture of peace could be made to these people. He knew about the miracle of the Jordan drying up at floodtide. As we have already seen, the news of it had spread throughout the land. It is also likely that he knew about the dividing of the Red Sea and the many miracles which God had done for Israel in Egypt, because this also was widely known.[76] For Rahab the innkeeper, this had been sufficient, but not for the king of Jericho. What if these were God's armies? What if they did have God performing miracles for them? Perhaps the gigantic walls of Jericho would be a Nemesis to Israel's miracle-making God. In any event, he would lock his people behind them, and defy Israel.

This was the state of things when Israel came out to march around Jericho on the seventh day. By this time the people of the city had no doubt become bored with this idle parade-ground maneuver and may have assumed that it would continue indefinitely. But on this seventh day something unusual happened. After completing their encirclement of Jericho the hosts of Israel did not march back to camp. They began circling again. Even after the second encirclement they did not return to camp. Nor after the third, fourth, fifth or sixth. These Hebrews were maddening. Nothing could have drawn the manpower of Jericho's forces to the top of her high walls faster than this continuous circling of the city. Had the king known the mind of the Lord he would have realized that the worst place in the city for his soldiers was on top of this wall. It was a death trap.

As the armies of Israel started their seventh encirclement of Jericho every man in the ranks knew the hour for battle had come. As the Ark completed the final procession around the city the priests who carried it suddenly stopped and the long military line shuffled to a halt. Every man then turned toward that portion of the wall directly in front of him and drew his sword. A moment later the seven priests who stood before the Ark raised their trumpets of rams' horns and

---

76. Joshua 2:10-11

sounded a long clarion signal. Immediately a great shout went up from the hosts of Israel.

The roar which came from the dust-parched throats of the Hebrew soldiers seemed to reverberate back from the walls before them. Suddenly the great stacks of stone, mortar and dried mud which had been the pride of Jericho's defense, began to tremble and quake like teetering piles of collapsing building blocks. In one great thunderous debacle they came tumbling down upon themselves with soldiers, stones, mortar and bricks all grinding and crashing together in one mammoth avalanche of devastating destruction.[77] It was the miracle the Lord had promised.

For a moment the choking dust and falling debris must have held back the hosts of Israel, but as soon as they could see sufficiently well to press forward they climbed over the rubble and ruins to storm the city.

Joshua quickly sent in his two spies to locate Rahab and her family. Her house was located on the wall[78] so this section of the rampart must have remained intact for the scripture says Joshua told the spies to go to Rahab's "house" and bring her out together with all of her kindred and their various possessions.[79] "And the young men that were spies went in, and brought out Rahab, and her father, and her mother, and her brethren, and all that she had; and they brought out all her kindred and left them without the camp of Israel."[80]

Then the hosts of Israel performed their terrible task of destruction required of them: "And they utterly destroyed all that was in the city. . . ."[81] Nothing was left alive, neither of man nor beast. It was total extinction for Jericho. "And they burnt the city with fire, and all that was therein: only the silver, and the gold, and the vessels of brass and of iron, they put into the treasury of the house of the Lord."[82]

Even the ruins of Jericho were execrated. Joshua said, "Cursed be the man before the Lord that riseth up and buildeth this city Jericho. . . ."[83]

---

77. Joshua 6:20
78. Joshua 2:15
79. Joshua 6:22
80. Joshua 6:23
81. Joshua 6:21
82. Joshua 6:24
83. Joshua 6:26

"So the Lord was with Joshua; and his fame was noised throughout all the country."[84] A permanent beachhead had been established in Gilgal and the conquest of Canaan lay open before him.

THE FIRST DEFEAT

As soon as his armies were rested Joshua sent men up into the mountains overlooking the Jordan valley. They were specifically told to make a military estimate of the city called "Ai," which was located east of Bethel a short distance.[85] When the men came back they were bursting with abundant self-confidence. They said, "Let not all the people go up; but let about two or three thousand men go up and smite Ai; and make not all the people to labour thither; for they are but few."[86]

So a small task force of 3,000 men was sent up to conquer Ai. The next thing Joshua knew his soldiers were streaming back to camp weeping, wailing and gnashing their teeth. They had been completely routed! When the camps of Israel learned about it they felt routed, too. The whole morale of the camp collapsed. When Joshua saw what was happening, he went before the Lord lonely and discouraged. He threw himself prone upon the ground before the Ark and cried out, "O Lord, what shall I say, when Israel turneth their backs before their enemies!" The Lord was impatient with Joshua and all this weeping and whining in Israel. The Lord said to Joshua, "Get thee up; wherefore liest thou thus upon thy face?"[87] Then the Lord unloaded a complaint against Israel which no doubt came as a shock to Joshua. The Lord said, "Israel hath sinned, and they have also transgressed my covenant which I commanded them; for they have even taken of the accursed thing. . . ."[88]

THE SIN AND PUNISHMENT OF ACHAN

What was this? Joshua had put the whole army of Israel under oath that during the conquest of Jericho they would destroy every scintilla of heathen paraphernalia and save nothing except the things which the Lord had authorized to

---

84. Joshua 6:27
85. Joshua 7:2
86. Joshua 7:3

87. Joshua 7:8-10
88. Joshua 7:11

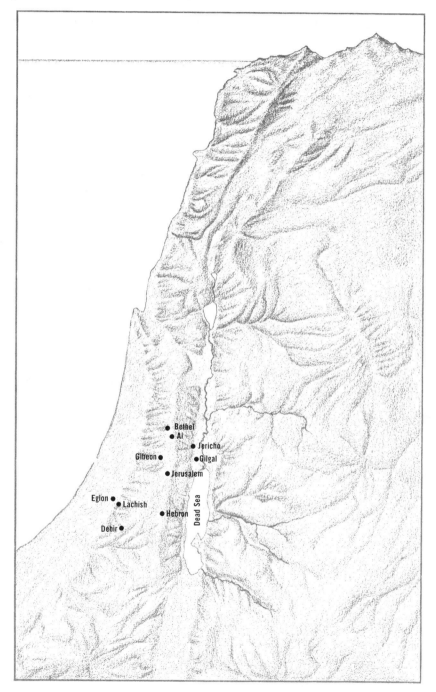

be placed in the Tabernacle treasury. The Lord said that not only had an "accursed thing" been brought out of Jericho but someone had also "stolen" part of the bounty that was supposed to go into the Lord's treasury.[89] The Lord therefore warned Joshua, "O Israel: thou canst not stand before thine enemies, until ye take away the accursed thing from among you."[90]

The Lord instructed Joshua to call a solemn assembly the following day. The Ephraimite Captain-General was to sit in judgment and the Lord promised to reveal who was responsible for this offense which could become the means of ensnaring Israel before she had barely begun to cleanse the land.

The following day the leaders of the various tribes came before Joshua one by one. The Lord revealed that the offense was in the tribe of Judah. Then Joshua had the heads of the various clans from the tribe of Judah pass before him. The Lord revealed that the offender belonged to the clan of the Zarhites. Joshua called before him the patriarch or oldest living progenitor of each family group from among the Zarhites. The Lord revealed to Joshua that the offender was within the family group of Zabdi. Now the search was closing in. Each man from Zabdi's family solemnly came before Joshua. Finally, when one of Zabdi's grandsons came forward the Spirit of revelation rested upon Joshua and proclaimed that this was the man. His name was Achan.[91]

All this time Achan had watched these proceedings knowing he was guilty but determined not to reveal himself. Only when the Lord had finally exposed his identity did Achan feel an overwhelming flood of remorse for what he had done.

Joshua said to Achan, "My son, give I pray thee, glory to the Lord God of Israel, and make confession unto him; and tell me now what thou hast done; hide it not from me."[92] Achan replied, "Indeed I have sinned against the Lord God of Israel. . . . When I saw among the spoils a goodly Babylonish garment, and two hundred shekels of silver, and a

---

89. Ibid.
90. Joshua 7:13

91. Joshua 7:18
92. Joshua 7:19

wedge of gold of fifty shekels weight, then I coveted them, and took them; and, behold, they are hid in the earth in the midst of my tent, and the silver under it."[93]

Joshua promptly sent messengers to the tent of Achan to retrieve the Babylonish garment and also the silver and gold. It would appear that the Babylonish garment was "the accursed thing" while the silver and gold were the things which the Lord said had been "stolen" from the bounty which was supposed to go into the Tabernacle treasury. Just how the Babylonish garment was connected with the accursed heathen cult we are not told. Most likely it was one of the costly embroidered robes of the idolatrous priests of Babylon. In any event the Lord declared it anathema (accursed) and required the maximum penalty for this act which could have been the means of once more corrupting all Israel.

As an object lesson Achan was taken some distance away from the camp together with his immediate possessions and there he was executed by stoning. Then he and all of his personal property were burned. Joshua had a large pile of stones erected over the place and called it Achor (trouble) to memorialize the displeasure of God which this man had brought down upon all Israel.[94]

CONQUEST OF THE CITY OF AI

Now the Lord told Joshua to march on the city of Ai and it would be delivered into his hands. However, He said Israel was not to send up a mere gesture of strength as before but go with power. In this revelation Joshua was told the exact strategy to follow. He was to use two armies. One army was to hide in the region just beyond Ai, and when the second army had feigned weakness and had fled from before the gates of Ai so as to draw out the men of Ai from their stronghold, then the hidden army could enter the city and destroy it.[95]

This stratagem worked out just as the Lord predicted it would. Joshua used 30,000 troops, 5,000 of whom were sent around Ai to hide on the western side of the city. The remainder went with Joshua to a position north of Ai.[96]

---

93. Joshua 7:20-21
94. Joshua 7:26

95. Joshua 8:2
96. Joshua 8:13

The next morning the king of Ai saw Joshua and his legions assembling in the valley. The King not only had his own soldiers ready and waiting but also the army of Bethel, the neighboring community, lying about three miles away· With confidence he therefore marched out against the Is-raelites.

"And Joshua and all Israel made as if they were beaten before them, and fled by the way of the wilderness. And all the people that were in Ai were called together to pursue after them: and they pursued after Joshua, and were drawn away from the city. And there was not a man left in Ai or Bethel, that went not out after Israel: and they left the city open, and pursued after Israel."[97]

At this point Joshua was instructed by the Lord to raise his spear on high and when he lifted it up, the lookouts for the army on the west signalled their companions who charged out in a body from the hiding places to seize the city and burn it.

"And when the men of Ai looked behind them, they saw, and, behold, the smoke of the city ascended up to heaven, and they had no power to flee this way or that way: and the people that fled to the wilderness turned back upon the pur-suers.

"And when Joshua and all Israel saw that the ambush had taken the city, and that the smoke of the city ascended, then they turned again, and slew the men of Ai."[98]

The soldiers of Ai found themselves completely trapped between the Israelites in front of them and the Israelites behind them. In this battle the entire population of Ai was destroyed, including an adult population of 12,000.[99] The king of Ai was hanged and buried at the gateway of his demolished city.[100] The city itself was reduced to a heap.[101]

THE GREAT CONFERENCE AT MOUNT EBAL

Now Joshua proceeded to assemble all the hosts of Israel in a nearby valley which separates Mount Ebal and Mount

---

97. Joshua 8:15-17
98. Joshua 8:20-21
99. Joshua 8:25

100. Joshua 8:29
101. Joshua 8:28

Gerizim. It must be remembered that Moses had been gone from Israel only a few weeks and just prior to his passing he had told Joshua to hold this conference in this valley after they had begun liberating Canaan.[102] Joshua proceeded to do exactly what Moses had commanded.

First, he built an altar of unhewn stones on Mount Ebal to use for sacrifices. These stones were bound together with mortar.[103] Joshua carved upon these uncut stones the blessings and cursings which Moses had prophesied and written down just prior to his departure.[104] When this had been done, Joshua divided the tribes of Israel on either side of the Ark, half of them toward Mount Ebal and half of them toward Mount Gerizim. The priests would then read the law of blessings and cursings and after each one the people would cry out, "Amen!"[105] The scripture says, "There was not a word of all that Moses commanded, which Joshua read not before all the congregation of Israel, with the women, and the little ones, and the strangers that were conversant among them."[106]

THE TRIBES OF CANAAN CONSOLIDATE TO DEFY ISRAEL

In ancient times when Cain had abandoned his righteous calling in the Priesthood and began to lust after the property of his brother, the Lord came to him and pleaded with him to turn back from the brink of disaster.[107] But the spirit of ugly defiance was in him. He is quoted as saying "Who is God that I should know him!"[108] In time, he went on to become the first murderer and the first son of perdition.

This mysterious phenomenon of men deliberately revolting against light and knowledge is one of the irrational aspects of human nature which is not easily explained. Nevertheless, it has always been characteristic of a certain percentage of the Father's children. They seem to revel in rebellion; not blind, ignorant, stupid rebellion, but open, flagrant, deliberate and premeditated defiance of light and truth.

---

102. Deuteronomy, chapter 27
103. Deuteronomy 27:2
104. Deuteronomy, chapters 27 and 28
105. Deuteronomy 27:15-26
106. Joshua 8:35
107. Moses 5:22-23
108. Moses 5:16

Joshua was now confronted by a rich and bounteous land filled to overflowing with this kind of people. Joshua had it in his power to spare these people, but only if they totally and irrevocably abandoned their heathen ways — their profligate immorality, their human sacrifices, their resistance to the cleansing of the land.

The scripture is clear that all of these tribes or nations in Canaan were fully aware that they were dealing with the chosen people of God. They knew what the Lord had done for Israel in Egypt, they knew about the dividing of the Red Sea,[109] they knew about the miraculous crossing of the Jordan,[110] and they even knew that God had told Moses that Israel was to take over Canaan and cleanse it of those vicious and dissolute practices which had corrupted the land.[111] With these tribes of Canaan it was not a question of knowing God's will. The stratagem they were seeking was to defy God's will and get away with it. From their point of view the problem was not to discover some way to save their homes and families since repentance and reform would do that automatically. What they really wanted to save — even at the risk of losing their homes and families — was their satanic, idolatrous culture of sensuous perversion and sadistic human sacrifice. It was for this that their Heavenly Father could not forgive them, and that is why the Lord had commanded Israel to purge them from the face of the earth.

As we previously mentioned, there were two things these tribes could do to save themselves. One was to flee to some new territory thereby cleansing Canaan so that the higher culture under the Lord's law could replace them. The other was to voluntarily repent and submit themselves to the new order by dissolving their cultural and political existence and becoming subservient to the leadership and laws of Israel. But apparently the heathen kings did not even consider this alternative. The scripture says, "And it came to pass, when all the kings which were on this side of Jordan, in the hills, and in the valleys, and in all the coasts of the great sea over against Lebanon, the Hittite, and the Amorite, the Canaanite, the Perizzite, the Hivite, and the Jebusite, heard thereof; that

---

109. Joshua 2:10   111. Joshua 10:24
110. Joshua 5:1

they gathered themselves together, to fight with Joshua and with Israel, with one accord."[112]

THE HEATHEN GIBEONITES SEEK A TREATY BY DECEPTION

There was one city of Canaanites which refused to join this alliance. It was the people of Gibeon, a large city which belonged to some of the Hivites.[113] The Gibeonites decided that what had happened to Jericho and Ai could soon befall every city in Canaan. They therefore determined to neutralize the hostility of the Israelites towards them by negotiating a treaty. However, instead of throwing themselves on the mercy of the Israelites and offering to submit to the new order, they undertook to obtain a guarantee of sanctuary by deception.

The scriptures says the leaders of Gibeon "did work wilily, and went and made as if they had been ambassadors. . . ."[114] They put on wornout clothing, used old wine bottles, moldy bread and stale provisions. "And they went to Joshua unto the camp of Gilgal, and said unto him, and to the men of Israel, We be come from a far country: now therefore make ye a league with us."[115]

But the leaders of Israel suspected something was wrong. They even hit upon the idea that these men might be from a local tribe and were putting on an act to escape destruction. They therefore said, "Peradventure ye dwell among us; and how shall we make a league with you?"[116]

Joshua even challenged them outright, "Who are ye? and from whence come ye?" To be more persuasive they mixed their lie with some truth. They said, "From a very far country thy servants are come because of the name of the Lord thy God: for we have heard the fame of him, and all that he did in Egypt, and all that he did to the two kings of the Amorites, that were beyond Jordan, to Sihon king of Heshbon, and to Og king of Bashan, which was at Ashtaroth. Wherefore our elders and all the inhabitants of our country spake to us, saying, Take victuals with you for the journey, and go to meet them, and say unto them, We are your serv-

112. Joshua 9:1-2
113. Joshua 9:3-7
114. Joshua 9:4

115. Joshua 9:6
116. Joshua 9:7

ants: therefore now make ye a league with us. This our bread we took hot for our provision out of our houses on the day we came forth to go unto you; but now, behold, it is dry, and it is mouldy: and these bottles of wine, which we filled, were new; and, behold, they be rent: and these our garments and our shoes are become old by reason of the very long journey."[117]

This was quite a tale. Furthermore it was persuasive. The scripture says the leaders of Israel "took of their victuals" and apparently their stale, moldy quality convinced them that these men had indeed come from a great distance. Therefore, without asking Eleazar, the High Priest, to get "counsel at the mouth of the Lord,"[118] Joshua went ahead and made "a league with them, to let them live: and the princes of the congregation sware unto them."[119]

It was not until three days later that they discovered the deception. This happened when the army of Israel marched into the land of the Gibeonites and found that "they [the Gibeonites] were their neighbours, and that they dwelt among them."[120] Joshua immediately called the leaders of Gibeon to him and demanded, "Wherefore have ye beguiled us, saying, We are very far from you: when ye dwell among us?"[121]

The Gibeonites replied, "Because it was certainly told thy servants, how that the Lord thy God commanded his servant Moses to give you all the land, and to destroy all the inhabitants of the land from before you, therefore we were sore afraid of our lives because of you, and have done this thing. And now, behold, we are in thine hand: as it seemeth good and right unto thee to do unto us, do."[122]

Note how much the heathens knew about the Lord's dealings with Israel and how thoroughly they understood God's commandment to Moses concerning the cleansing of the land. The Gibeonites would have fared better with the Israelites if they had honestly confessed their desire to collaborate with Israel instead of using deception. Nevertheless, they did not come off too badly. The princes of Israel decided to dissolve their political existence, put them under

---

117. Joshua 9:9-13
118. Joshua 9:14
119. Joshua 9:15

120. Joshua 9:16
121. Joshua 9:22
122. Joshua 9:24-25

Israel's law, and make them tributaries as the Lord had previously instructed in such situations.[123] So the Gibeonites were assigned the task of being "hewers of wood and drawers of water for the congregation and for the altar of the Lord. . . ."[124]

Then the army of Israel marched back to Gilgal.[125]

THE CANAANITE FEDERATION SEEKS TO ANNIHILATE THE GIBEONITES

As soon as the other tribes in central and southern Canaan learned that the Gibeonites had made peace with Israel, they wrathfully determined to make an example of them. They would show what happened to any Canaanites who defected from the national alliance! The next thing the Gibeonites knew they were besieged.

The scripture says this action was taken under the leadership of Adoni-zedec, king of Jerusalem. Some Bible scholars see an interesting implication in this man's name. It means "lord of righteousness" and is very similar to Melchizedek which means "king of righteousness."[126] Melchizedek's ancient capitol city had been called Salem and now the Jebusites (Canaanites of the Amorite branch) occupied the site of that city and called it Jeru-salem. Furthermore, their king had assumed a name remarkably similar to Melchizedek which seems to reflect a desire to imitate the famous king of Salem of earlier times. However that may have been, it is certain that the similarity between these two men ended with their names. Adoni-zedek was the very antithesis of the High Priest, Melchizedek. He not only intended to destroy Israel, but he first intended to destroy the Gibeonites because they had defected from the pan-Canaanite federation and joined Israel. Adoni-zedek mobilized the armies of five Amorite kings to besiege Gibeon.

The terrified Gibeonites immediately sent messengers to Gilgal saying, "Slack not thy hand from thy servants; come up to us quickly, and save us, and help us: for all the kings of the Amorites that dwell in the mountains are gathered together against us."[127]

---

123. Deuteronomy 20:11
124. Joshua 9:27
125. This becomes apparent in Joshua 10:6.
126. Clarke's *Bible Commentary*, Vol 2, p. 42
127. Joshua 10:6

Joshua now had a decision to make. His treaty with the Gibeonites was not a military alliance but an agreement that the Gibeonites would serve Israel. Was Israel duty-bound to defend those who had become their tributaries? Joshua decided in the affirmative. If the Gibeonites were to be under Israel's law, and if they were to support the government of Israel with taxes in the form of supplying water and wood, then the central government had the obligation to protect them. Joshua took immediate action.

The scripture says, "So Joshua ascended from Gilgal, he, and all the people of war with him, and all the mighty men of valour. And the Lord said unto Joshua, Fear them not: for I have delivered them into thine hand; there shall not a man of them stand before thee. Joshua therefore came unto them suddenly, and went up from Gilgal all night."[128]

Joshua caught the Amorites in a strategically weak position because they were in the process of launching an assault against Gibeon. By using a forced march during the night the Israelites were able to catch the Amorites by surprise. The initial assault was devastating. A great multitude of the Amorites were killed on the spot and the rest fled in the wildest confusion. The five kings of the Amorites were among those who fled. At first Joshua could not pursue these fleeing hosts because his troops were completely occupied at the center of the conflict at Gibeon. However, before the Amorites could reach the protection of their cities the Lord caught them with a deadly hail-storm somewhere between Beth-horon and Azekah. This was no ordinary storm for the hail stones were of such mammoth size that they killed more Canaanites than the whole army of Israel had slaughtered at Gibeon.[129]

The Miracle of the Sun and the Moon Standing Still

But the weary Israelites were hard pressed to do the mopping up which the Lord required of them. Having marched all night and fought all day they found the afternoon drawing to a close without their task being completed. Therefore Joshua did something which no prophet is known

---

128. Joshua 10:7-9   129. Joshua 10:11

to have done either before or since. He apparently climbed to some high place so as to be "in the sight of Israel" and then declared, "Sun, stand thou still upon Gibeon; and thou Moon, in the valley of Ajalon."[130]

Those who were close enough to hear what Joshua said must have turned in amazement to look up toward the sun and see if such a thing were possible. At first, it would have been impossible to perceive, but as the hours wore on it definitely became apparent that neither the sun nor the moon was moving. Concerning this unprecedented phenomenon the scripture simply says, "So the sun stood still in the midst of heaven, and hasted not to go down about a whole day. And there was no day like that before it or after it, that the Lord hearkened unto the voice of a man. . . ."[131]

These extra hours permitted Joshua to completely consume the Amorites at Gibeon and he then marched his troops back to Gilgal to recuperate.[132] Joshua did not know it but within a few days he would be launched into the great campaign which would bring to an end the stifling grip which the Canaanite kings held on this part of Israel's inheritance.

---

130. Joshua 10:12
131. Joshua 10:13-14

Scripture Reading and Questions on Chapter Twenty-One

Scripture Reading Assignment: Joshua, chapters 1 to 10 inclusive.

1—To which tribe did Joshua belong? How prominent was he in the tribe?

2—What other famous person had the same name as Joshua? Did Joshua receive any revelations or was he just a military man?

3—What can you recall in the early life of Joshua which reflects the quality of his character?

4—When the two spies were sent to Jericho, who saved their lives? What knowledge did she have which caused her to do it? Was this good news for the Israelites?

5—What was unusual about the Jordan River when the Israelites crossed? Once the river was miraculously dammed off did it leave a muddy riverbed? Did the Israelites cross through a narrow passage? Why?

6—Who protected the Israelites while they were crossing? Would this have been impressive to the Canaanites? What was more impressive?

7—Instead of ordering the Israelites to immediately attack Jericho, what did the Lord tell them to do?

8—What happened to the miracle of the manna? What were the circumstances?

9—Recite the incident when Joshua met the captain of the Lord's hosts.

10—How many details can you recall concerning the fall of Jericho? What happened to the woman who befriended the spies? What happened to her family?

11—What were the circumstances of Israel's first defeat in Canaan?

12—What was the sin of Achan? Why do you think that the Lord—who is filled with mercy and love—felt He had to be so strict with Israel?

13—Recite the incident of the fall of Ai. What other nearby Canaanite community was involved?

14—Describe what took place at the great conference which was held in the valley between Mount Ebal and Mount Gerizim.

15—What new force did Joshua now face? Tell how the Gibeonites became an ally of the Israelites.

16—What incident precipitated a war between Israel and the Canaanite federation? What did this reflect in Joshua's attitude toward heathen peoples who became subservient to Israel?

17—Why did Joshua catch the Canaanite armies at a disadvantage? How did the Israelites get to Gibeon so fast?

18—During this battle what great miracle occurred?

19—What was the name of the king who set up the Canaanites federation? What did his name mean? How was this significant?

20—How successful was the battle at Gibeon? What did Joshua do with the army of Israel after the battle was over?

CHAPTER TWENTY-TWO

Joshua Liberates Canaan, Divides the Promised Land, and Dies

One of the most fortunate political and military advantages which the Israelites enjoyed when they entered Canaan was the fact that they were united and the Canaanites were not.

It will be recalled that even though Joshua was camped within sight of Jericho for several weeks, no other Canaanites came to Jericho's rescue. When Israel attacked Ai the only help came from the small community of Bethel nearby. Even during the major conflict at Gibeon when five Amorite kings formed a federation to punish that city for defecting, the arrival of Joshua on the scene to protect the Gibeonites brought no additional Canaanites to reinforce Adoni-zedec. Therefore, the divided strength of the Canaanites was no match for the united strength of the Israelites. The five kings of Adoni-zedec's federation were beaten by Joshua and after having their armies smashed to fragments were forced to flee.

JOSHUA CAPTURES THE FIVE AMORITE KINGS

It was not until after Joshua had returned to the main headquarters at Gilgal (near the ruins of Jericho), that excited messengers came to tell him where the five Amorite kings were hiding. Instead of fleeing to their respective capitals, which were fortified cities, they had rallied the remnants of their scattered armies and set up their secret headquarters in a cave near Makkedah.[1]

---

1. Joshua 10:17

Joshua reacted to this information immediately. He sent out an advance contingent of assault troops and instructed them as follows:

"Roll great stones upon the mouth of the cave, and set men by it for to keep them: and stay ye not, but pursue after your enemies, and smite the hindmost of them; suffer them not to enter into their cities: for the Lord your God hath delivered them into your hand."[2]

The advance assault troops were successful in trapping the five kings in their cave and great stones were rolled over the entrance. The followers of these kings were apparently hiding in the vicinity but when they saw the Israelites returning in force they fled in every direction. By this time Joshua had arrived with the main body of Israel's army and it says "Joshua and the children of Israel" made havoc of the Amorites so that there was "a very great slaughter" and they were consumed except for the remnant which escaped into "fenced cities."[3]

After combing the hills and plains for any remaining vestiges of the enemy, the Israelites finally returned to the outskirts of Makkedah where Joshua had set up camp. Joshua then said to his military commanders, "Open the mouth of the cave, and bring out those five kings unto me out of the cave."[4] When the leaders of the Amorite federation who had intended to massacre Gibeon were brought before Joshua, he had them kneel to the ground before him. Joshua ordered each of the captains from the armies of Israel to come forward and place his foot on the neck of these kings. It was a token of their abject defeat. Joshua said to his troops: "Fear not, nor be dismayed, be strong and of good courage: for thus shall the Lord do to all your enemies against whom ye fight."[5]

Now the five kings who had expected in the near future to destroy Israel were destroyed themselves. They were first slain and then "hanged" upon five different trees until sunset. Before dark, Joshua had their bodies cut down and entombed in the cave where they had formerly hidden. Huge

2. Josshua 10:18-19
3. Joshua 10:20
4. Joshua 10:22
5. Joshua 10:25

boulders were placed over the entrance to seal it up. Thus came to a conclusion the federation of Adoni-zedec.

The next day Joshua ordered the extermination of the nearby city of Makkedah. This was the Amorite stronghold in this particular area and its leaders were obviously in collaboration with the five Amorite kings who headed up the anti-Israelite entente. Joshua therefore leveled Makkedah and hanged its slain king upon a tree until sunset just as he had done with the five Amorite kings the day before. Henceforth this was to be the pattern.

It was at this point that Joshua decided that now was as good a time as any to expand his military campaign into the south and establish a foothold which the hosts of Israel could occupy. He knew that the defending armies for a number of these cities had been practically wiped out during the battle at Gibeon and he therefore resolved to press forward and quickly strike their fenced cities or fortified pockets of resistance wherever he found them. Makkedah was the beginning.

The Conquest of Canaan in Historical Perspective

However, to gain a proper perspective of this campaign and those which followed it, two things should be kept in mind.

First, it should be realized that the hosts of Israel were not of the same caliber as their leader. Joshua was a man of consecrated devotion and integrity who was acceptable to God and received direct revelations from Him. The hosts of Israel, on the other hand, were of a different stripe. They continued to enjoy God's blessings only by the narrowest margin of worthiness. Their faith was continually on the brink of collapse and their integrity was never much more than a glimmer of borrowed light from the lamp of their leader.

The military efforts of Israel during this period of their history must be interpreted in this frame of reference. Not at any time did they come even close to cleansing the land of its abominations and setting up a bastion of liberty as Enoch had done. The lack of individual righteousness among the people of Israel was such that a just God could not do for them what He had done for Enoch.

The Lord had promised Israel a sweeping victory over Canaan if they were obedient and faithful, "And five of you shall chase an hundred, and an hundred of you shall put ten thousand to flight. . . ."[6] But a half-hearted righteousness produced a half-baked loaf of limited victory. As time went on Joshua seemed to sense the constricted capacity of his semi-righteous Israelites. The Lord was willing to give Joshua whatever victories were necessary to get a foothold in Canaan but little more. Joshua therefore limited his conquests to the establishment of beachheads where Israel could put down her roots. He avoided throwing the forces of Israel into a do-or-die contest of strength with the well-entrenched Canaanite cities on the coast. Only when Israel was confronted with confederations of force which threatened to annihilate them did they rally behind Joshua and exhibit the valiant heroism which the Lord had described. In the absence of such a threat they were willing to leave well-enough alone. Therefore, they never did cleanse the land as the Lord had commanded them. This is why the Book of Joshua is not like the Book of Enoch.[7] Instead of a momumental saga of well-deserved victory, the reader beholds an abortive conquest — a half-deserved and therefore half-achieved war of liberation. No wonder God cried out in lamentation over them.[8]

A Description of the Land of Canaan

The second factor to keep in mind while studying the conquest of Canaan is the restricted area of geography involved. Nothing was more astonishing to this author when he visited Palestine for the first time than to see how much had happened in so small a space. For a detailed physical description of every corner of Canaan, no writer has ever equalled the six-volume work of Dr. Cunningham Geikie. In discussing the period of the conquest he tries to share with the student some of the physical dimensions of this history-saturated section of the earth's surface:

6. Leviticus 26:8
7. See quotations from the Book of Enoch in Moses, 6:32 to 7:20.
8. Deuteronomy, Chapter 32

"The country which now invited conquest lay before the camp of Israel as a great mass of hills, rising from the back of Jericho in height above height, till its central elevation reached nearly 4,000 feet above the spot on which they stood. Western Palestine is, indeed, little more than a wide tangle of mountains, seamed by valleys, of all depths and breadths, which on both sides run east and west, and form the only roads through the labyrinth. The Dead Sea, close by Gilgal, lies 1,292 feet below the Mediterranean, the city of Jericho standing about 600 feet above it; but many of the heights before them tower, at 12 or 14 miles' distance, to a height of 2,500 feet above its level. Some of the cliffs on the Dead Sea rise 2,000 feet above the waters below, but some hills beyond them, north of Hebron, are 2,000 feet higher, and others, in various parts of the land are still loftier. Bethlehem is 2,500 feet above the Mediterranean; Jebus, the future Jerusalem, 43 feet more; the hill behind it on the east, our Mount of Olives, 2,683; Neby Samuel, a little to the north, 2,935; Mounts Gerizim and Ebal, in the centre of the land at Shechem, rise to the height of 2,849 and 3,076 feet respectively; and Shechem itself lies in a valley 1,800 feet high, while the tops of Mount Carmel and Mount Tabor have almost the same elevation. Mount Jurmuk, a few miles northwest of the Sea of Galilee, was 4,000 feet high; and the town of Safed, close by, looked over the country from a height of 2,800 feet. Nor were these the only heights worthy to be called mountains. Across the Jordan, 'the hill of Bashan' cast its shadow from an elevation of 5,900 feet, and, on the northern limit of the land, the vast peaks of Lebanon, 'the white,' shine down from the upper skies over a great part of the land. The long-drawn roof of Hermon, especially, over 9,000 feet high, flashes from its snowy rocks like a cloud of light to almost every point of the central northern landscapes, for I have looked up to it from the plain along the coast, from the hills of Samaria, and from the wide level of Hauran, its dazzling, unstained splendour filling the mind with awe and rapture from all, alike.

"The whole country, however, 'from Dan to Beersheba,' it a very small one, for it measures only one hundred and thirty-nine miles, north and south, from the one to the other, and the paltry breadth of twenty miles from the coast to the

Jordan, in the north of the land, increases slowly to only forty between the Dead Sea and the Mediterranean, at Gaza, in the south. Palestine is, in fact, only about the size of the small principality of Wales."[9]

JOSHUA'S CAMPAIGN IN THE SOUTH

This geographical description will help the student appreciate some of the problems which confronted Joshua as he attempted to fulfill the Lord's instructions concerning the conquest of Canaan. A few days before when his armies had been resting at their main headquarters in Gilgal and Joshua had been told about the five Amorite kings hiding in in the cave, Joshua had been under the necessity of bringing his army and supplies up nearly 3,000 feet to the summit and then down a considerable distance on the other side to Makkedah. Often major battles were only ten to fifteen miles apart, but the high peaks and deep valleys in between made it seem ten times that far.

As Joshua began moving forward, that branch of the Canaanites called the Amorites who had conspired together against Israel, knew they were in an extremely precarious position. Especially the five fortified cities belonging to the five kings who had been killed. They were now without kings and without armies. A few fragments from the ranks of their citizen-soldier fighting forces had escaped and gotten within their cities before the great gates had to be closed, but most of them were depleted of their military strength and were forced to rely upon their massive walls for protection. It did not seem to occur to any of them to seek sanctuary from the Israelites. They simply appointed new kings to replace the dead ones and resolved to hold out to the bitter end. But their walls were no match for the Israelites.

The first city of the Amorites confederation to go down was Libnah. Joshua "smote it with the edge of the sword, and all the souls that were therein; he let none remain in it; but did unto the king thereof as he did unto the king of Jericho."[10]

---

9. Cunningham Geikie, *Hours with the Bible*, Volume 2, pp. 452-453
10. Joshua 10:30

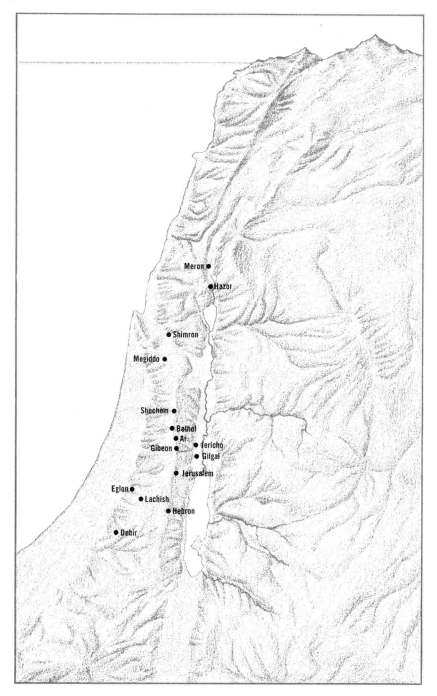

The next city was Lachish. It was the same story there except that Horam, king of Gezer, tried to help Lachish so Joshua extended the war to include Gezer. Once again all opposition was destroyed.[11]

The city of Eglon was the next to fall,[12] then Hebron,[13] and then Debir.[14]

In addition to these five cities which comprised the mainstays of the Amorite confederation, Joshua conquered much of the territory in between. Except for the powerful Canaanite city-states on the coast, it is plain from the scripture that Joshua rather thoroughly subdued the region in south Canaan. It says, "so Joshua smote all the country of the hills, and of the south, and of the vale, and of the springs, and all their kings: he left none remaining, but utterly destroyed all that breathed, as the Lord God of Israel commanded."[15]

Then the scripture says, "And Joshua returned, and all Israel with him, unto the camp to Gilgal."[16]

THE CAMPAIGN IN THE NORTH

Once again, however, the rest at Gilgal was of short duration. Word came to Joshua that a new confederation of Canaanite city-states was forming in the north. The leader of the new anti-Israel league was Jabin, king of Hazor.[17] This city was a Canaanite stronghold north of Galilee and very near Lake Merom. Jabin rallied around him a much stronger league than the one which had been formed in the south. Joshua therefore had an important decision to make. Should he allow these hosts to come down to fight Israel at Gilgal or should he keep the war away from the women and children of Israel's vast city camp by going up to meet the northern confederation in their own territory. He resolved to take this latter course.

However, as the Israelites moved up from their Jordan Valley home at Gilgal and ascended the 3,000 foot climb to

---

11. Joshua 10:31-33
12. Joshua 10:34-35
13. Joshua 10:36-37
14. Joshua 10:38-39

15. Joshua 10:40
16. Joshua 10:43
17. Joshua 11:1

the back of Canaan's mountain spine, they received some disquieting news. The military forces which were converging together at the frantic insistence of the king of Hazor was something Israel had never before faced. The scripture says Jabin, king of Hazor, had "sent to Jacob, king of Madon, and to the king of Shimron, and to the king of Achshaph, and to the kings that were on the north of the mountains, and of the plains south of Chinneroth, and in the valley, and in the borders of Dor on the west. And to the Canaanite on the east and on the west, and to the Amorite, and the Hittite, and the Perizzite, and the Jebusite in the mountains, and to the Hivite under Hermon in the land of Mizpeh. And they went out, they and all their hosts with them, much people, even as the sand that is upon the sea shore in multitude, with horses and chariots very many."[18]

Authorities point out that the manner in which the people along the western coasts of Canaan used their chariots had a particularly fearsome aspect inasmuch as they fastened iron scythes to the hubs of their chariots and chopped to pieces the infantry of an enemy by driving furiously through their ranks with several chariots abreast so that very few could escape.[19]

Nevertheless, the Lord said to Joshua, "Be not afraid because of them: for tomorrow about this time will I deliver them up all slain before Israel: thou shalt hough [wound or cut off] their horses, and burn their chariots with fire."[20]

The Canaanite kings had assembled their hosts of war at "the waters of Merom,"[21] which was a lake about halfway between Mount Hermon and the Sea of Galilee. Joshua concluded that this was as good a place as any to engage them in battle.

The strategy which he used was apparently designed to catch the Canaanites by surprise before they had time to harness their horses or mount their war chariots. The scripture says Joshua organized his army of Israel and then came sweeping down upon his enemy "suddenly."[22] By taking this initial offensive the Israelites gained an advantage which

---

18. Joshua 11:1-4
19. Clarke, *Bible Commentary*, Vol. 2, p. 53
20. Joshua 11:6
21. Joshua 11:5
22. Joshua 11:7

they never relinquished. Before long the hosts of Jabin's federation were completely demoralized and melted away under the pressure of Israel's smashing attack. As the Canaanite lines began to collapse those who were able fled in every direction. The Israelites took no prisoners but fought to the death as Joshua had commanded. The scripture says they pursued the heathen hosts as far north and west as Great Zidon (Sidon) the famous Phoenician seaport on the Mediterranean. Others were pursued clear to Misrephath-maim (hot waters) and into the valley of Mizpeh, eastward of Sidon, while others tried to escape south or west. Everywhere the Canaanites fled the Israelites followed in close pursuit until they were consumed. Because the horses they left behind with their chariots were looked upon as instruments of war during these early days, they were destroyed, and the chariots burned with fire.[23]

Following this great victory, Joshua did as he had done in the south. Having literally annihilated the offensive military forces which had been mobilized against him, he used selective tactics in besieging one city at a time until each of the kings and the cities they represented had been destroyed. It was a long, desperate campaign and appears to have taken six times as long as the campaign in the south. Authorities believe that of the seven years required for the conquest of Canaan, one year was utilized in the south and six years in the north.[24] Concerning the northern campaign the scripture says, "Joshua made war a long time with all those kings."[25]

Apparently, Joshua had hoped that some of these cities would respond to the proclamation of peace which the Lord had said to make,[26] but the scripture says, "There was not a city that made peace with the children of Israel, save the Hivites, the inhabitants of Gibeon: all other they took in battle."[27]

Concerning the cities which resisted Israel and determined to fight to the death, the record is clear that they received the Jericho treatment, "And all the cities of those kings, and all the kings of them, did Joshua take, and smote

23. Joshua 11:9
24. Clarke, *Bible Commentary*, Vol. 2, p. 54
25. Joshua 11:18

26. Deuteronomy 20:10-11
27. Joshua 11:19

with the edge of the sword, and he utterly destroyed them, as Moses the servant of the Lord commanded."[28]

However, the fortified cities which the Israelites expected to occupy as places of refuge after they took over the land, were preserved intact even though their populations were destroyed. The scripture says, "But as for the cities that stood still in their strength, Israel burned none of them save Hazor only: that did Joshua burn."[29]

The twelfth chapter of the Book of Joshua chronicles the total number of cities (with their kings) which Israel had conquered since coming out of the wilderness. Altogether there were thirty-one. Among all of these conflicts, both small and great, the prophet-historian was especially proud of Israel's troops for one thing: their refusal to be paralyzed with fear when they ran into the fearsome super-men of that day, the huge-bodied Anakims.[30] Everywhere these so-called giants appeared, the Israelites drove into them, out-fought them and conquered them. As we shall see in a moment, however, as soon as the Israelites had departed from an area, the Anakims would come in from Gaza, Gath, Ashdod and other refugee centers and immediately commence rebuilding their ruined cities. This was especially true in the south since the Israelites were gone somewhere around six years during their campaign in the north.

THE END OF JOSHUA'S CAMPAIGN

Following approximately seven years of continuous fighting, the aging Joshua decided it was time to give the land a rest from war. Certainly Joshua needed a rest. Israel may not have realized it, but they were about to lose their valiant commander-in-chief. The Lord said to Joshua, "Thou art old and stricken in years, and there remaineth yet very much land to be possessed."[31] The Lord then itemized every section of Canaan not yet cleansed and conquered. It was obvious that the Lord was holding Israel to its original commitment. Nevertheless, he was not expecting the job to be done by the battle-scarred Joshua. The Lord told Joshua to go ahead and divide the land which had been conquered

---

28. Joshua 11:12
29. Joshua 11:13

30. Joshua 11:21-22
31. Joshua 13:1

thus far and then it was apparently presumed that the various tribes could collaborate in expanding their respective inheritances until they had cleansed the land completely. Joshua therefore moved the Tabernacle and the entire camp of Israel from Gilgal to a more centrally located headquarters at Shiloh.[32]

THE TRANS-JORDAN TRIBES RETURN HOME

At this point it was apparent that the two-and-a-half tribes from Trans-Jordan had fulfilled their obligation to help Israel obtain an inheritance in Canaan and since the assignment of territory was now about to be made to each tribe, Joshua felt justified in releasing these troops. Joshua spoke to the troops from the tribes of Reuben, Gad and half the tribe of Manasseh, and said to them, "Ye have kept all that Moses the servant of the Lord commanded you, and have obeyed my voice in all that I commanded you: ye have not left your brethren these many days unto this day, but have kept the charge of the commandment of the Lord your God. And now the Lord your God hath given rest unto your brethren, as he promised them: therefore now return ye, and get you unto your tents, and unto the land of your possession, which Moses the servant of the Lord gave you on the other side of Jordan. But take diligent heed to do the commandment and the law, which Moses the servant of the Lord charged you, to love the Lord your God, and to walk in all his ways, and to keep his commandments, and to cleave unto him, and to serve him with all your heart and with all your soul."[33]

So Joshua blessed them and sent them away to their families across Jordan. His final words to them were: "Return with much riches unto your tents, and very much cattle, with silver, and with gold, and with brass, and with iron, and with very much raiment: divide the spoil of your enemies with your brethren."[34]

Having bade farewell to these faithful troops, Joshua prepared to take care of other pressing business, but they had been gone scarcely a few days when messengers brought

---

32. Joshua 18:1   34. Joshua 22:8
33. Joshua 22:2-5

word to the Israelites at Shiloh that an appalling thing had happened. The troops returning to Trans-Jordan had built a huge altar near the Jordan River and apparently had turned to idolatry!

The scripture says, "And when the children of Israel heard of it, the whole congregation of the children of Israel gathered themselves together at Shiloh, to go up to war against them."[35]

However, before sending across a whole expedition it was decided to make an investigation, so Phinehas, the son of the High Priest, and ten princes from each of the tribes made the journey. As they approached the Jordan they saw the large altar or monument which had been erected by the river.

When this solemn delegation arrived in Trans-Jordan the leaders of Reuben, Gad and Manasseh discovered this was no social call. These brethren from whom they had so recently separated were in an ugly mood. Said they: "What trespass is this that ye have committed against the God of Israel, to turn away this day from following the Lord, in that ye have builded you an altar, that ye might rebel this day against the Lord?"[36] They then went on to say that it was just such iniquity as this at Peor which brought down their last plague upon them wherein thousands of the Israelites died.[37] They said that if the children of Reuben, Gad and Manasseh were being tainted by the heathen influence in Trans-Jordan then they should join the rest of the tribes at Shiloh. Better to leave their homes than risk the wrath of God by indulging in the immoral rites of heathen idolatry.

To all of this the princes of Reuben, Gad and Manasseh were astounded. What were their brethren talking about? This whole thing was a misunderstanding. They called upon God as a witness that they had committed no such abomination as their accusers were charging. They admitted building the stone structure which their brethren had seen but they assured them it was no altar of sacrifice and no sacrifices had been made upon it, nor had any heathen debaucheries been involved in its consecration.

---

35. Joshua 22:12   37. Joshua 22:17
36. Joshua 22:16

Then they explained why they had built it. They said that as they prepared to cross over Jordan after seven years of service as comrades-in-arms with the other tribes, it occurred to them that in future generations the nine-and-a-half tribes in Canaan might disown the two-and-a-half tribes in Trans-Jordan. "Therefore we said, Let us now prepare to build us an altar, not for burnt-offering, nor for sacrifice; but that it may be a witness between us and you, and our generations after us, that we might do the service of the Lord . . . that your children may not say to our children in time to come, Ye have no part in the Lord."[38]

Phinehas and the princes from Canaan were greatly relieved. They were also probably chagrined. Their brethren who had served the other tribes for so many years had tried to memorialize the unity of the tribes and it had been mistaken for a token of disunity. Phinehas and the princes from Canaan assured their Trans-Jordan brethren they were "pleased" with the explanation and departed. The Israelites who waited anxiously at Shiloh for a report were also "pleased" to get the report. It had all turned out to be a tempest in a teacup.

THE FIRST DIVISION OF CANAAN

As Joshua prepared to divide the conquered portion of Canaan he did it in several logical steps. Some of the tribes were far from ready to assume their responsibilities while Judah and Joseph seemed prepared to go forward. As a result, Joshua first divided the land in two. Judah received a large portion of south Canaan while Joseph received the central portion. It appears to have been Caleb who was responsible for getting the southern portion of Canaan for Judah. As soon as he saw that the distribution of inheritances was in order he went before Joshua and made a most interesting speech. From it we learn a great deal about this man Caleb which might have otherwise been lost. Here is what he said:

"Thou [Joshua] knowest the thing that the Lord said unto Moses the man of God concerning me and thee in

---

38. Joshua 22:26-27

Kadesh-barnea. [The Lord had said that only Caleb and Joshua of that generation would live to gain an inheritance in Canaan — Num. 14:30].

"Forty years old was I when Moses the servant of the Lord sent me from Kadesh-barnea to espy out the land: and I brought him word again as it was in mine heart.

"Nevertheless my brethren that went up with me made the heart of the people melt: but I wholly followed the Lord my God.

"And Moses sware on that day, saying, Surely the land whereon thy feet have trodden shall be thine inheritance, and thy children's forever, because thou hast wholly followed the Lord my God.

"And now, behold, the Lord hath kept me alive, as he said, these forty and five years, even since the Lord spake this word unto Moses, while the children of Israel wandered in the wilderness: and now, lo, I am this day fourscore and five years old [85].

"As yet I am as strong this day as I was in the day that Moses sent me; as my strength was then, even so is my strength now, for war, both to go out, and to come in.

"Now therefore give me this mountain, whereof the Lord spake in that day; for thou heardest in that day how the Anakims were there, and that the cities were great and fenced: if so be the Lord will be with me, then I shall be able to drive them out, as the Lord said."[39]

There was no doubt that this eloquent plea touched Joshua deeply. Here was the only man alive, other than himself, who had been an adult and a mature witness to the exodus from Egypt and all of the amazing and miraculous things that had happened to Israel since. And here was this 85-year-old veteran who had fought and suffered right along with all the others but who still had the faith to go up to the vicinity of Hebron and drive out the dangerous and powerful Anakims who had reoccupied that city after its destruction some seven years earlier. This valiant Caleb

---

39. Joshua 14:6-12

felt that with the help of God he and his immediate relatives in the tribe of Judah could reconquer this territory and set up an inheritance just as the Lord had promised Caleb so many years before.

To all of this Joshua gave his enthusiastic consent. The scripture says, "And Joshua blessed him, and gave unto Caleb the son of Jephunneh Hebron for an inheritance. . . . because that he wholly followed the Lord God of Israel."[40]

The record is clear that Caleb was as good as his word. He found Hebron dominated by the three giant-sized sons of Anak. Their names were Sheshai, Ahiman and Talmai, and the scripture says Caleb and his warriors drove them out.[41] As we shall see later, Caleb was supported in this campaign by his nephew, Othniel, who became his son-in-law.[42] The name of Othniel should be remembered since he later became one of Israel's great heroes.[43]

THE INHERITANCE OF JOSEPH

Having consigned southern Canaan to the large tribe of Judah, Joshua assigned the central part of Canaan to the next largest tribe, that of Joseph. It will be recalled that Joseph consisted of two groups, Ephraim and Manasseh, so when both of these populous tribes were assigned to the mountain region of Samaria they bitterly complained. After all, Joshua himself was an Ephraimite. Surely they should expect something better than that from a relative.

The spokesmen for the tribes of Ephraim and Manasseh brought their complaint to Joshua. Their leader said, "Why hast thou given me but one lot and one portion to inherit, seeing I am a great people, forasmuch as the Lord hath blessed me hitherto?"[44]

Joshua shot back, "If thou be a great people, then get thee up to the wood country, and cut down for thyself there in the land of the Perizzites and of the giants, if mount Ephraim be too narrow for thee."[45]

---

40. Joshua 14:13-14
41. Joshua 15:14
42. Joshua 15:15-17

43. Judges 3:9-11
44. Joshua 17:14
45. Joshua 17:15

It was obvious that Joshua was assigning territory where the armies of Israel had created a foothold, but he was depending upon each tribe to enlarge its inheritance by mopping up the resistance forces in the areas still to be occupied. Joshua's announcement of this policy jolted the Josephites. They said, "The hill is not enough for us: and all the Canaanites that dwell in the land of the valley have chariots of iron, both they who are of Beth-shean and her towns, and they who are of the valley of Jezreel."[46]

But Joshua would not accept all this whimpering. He spoke very firmly to the Josephites, "Thou art a great people, and hast great power: thou shalt not have one lot only; but the mountain shalt be thine; for it is a wood, and thou shalt cut it down: and the outgoings of it shall be thine: for thou shalt drive out the Canaanites, though they have iron chariots, and though they be strong."[47]

So the Ephraimites moved out into their inheritance and so did the tribe of Manasseh. They never did obtain everything to which they were entitled but they did acquire enough living space to satisfy their needs for the time being.

The Seven Remaining Tribes Receive
their Inheritances

With Judah pushing out the frontier on the south and the two tribes of Joseph pressing for more territory in the north, the remaining seven tribes seemed satisfied to sit on their haunches at Shiloh as though the struggle were over. Joshua became very disturbed with them and cried out, "How long are ye slack to go to possess the land, which the Lord God of your fathers hath given you?"[48]

He commanded these tribes to nominate three men each to serve on a survey commission. When these twenty-one men had been appointed Joshua said to them: "Go and walk through the land, and describe it, and come again to me that I may here cast lots for you before the Lord in Shiloh."[49]

Apparently these tribes were to look over the entire territory allocated to Israel and divide it into reasonable re-

---

46. Joshua 17:16
47. Joshua 17:17-18
48. Joshua 18:3
49. Joshua 18:8

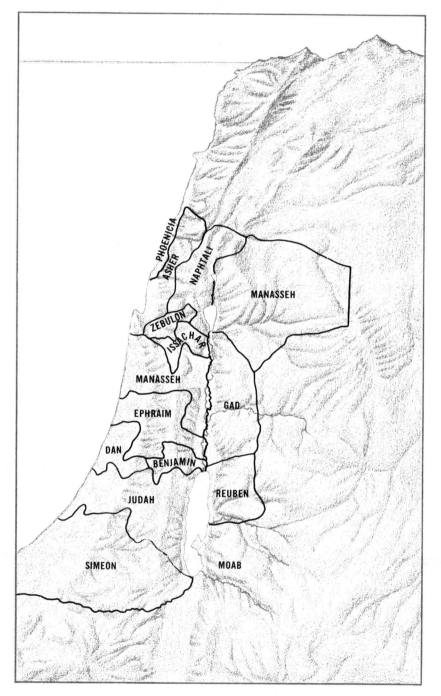

gions which could be assigned by choosing lots. As might be expected these representatives of the seven tribes took huge chunks of territory out of the theoretical inheritances of both Judah and Joseph in order to make room for themselves. Inasmuch as an important part of this land was still in the hands of the Canaanites, neither Judah nor Joseph appear to have made any objections.

The actions of the survey commission is described as follows: "And the men went and passed through the land, and described it by cities into seven parts in a book, and came again to Joshua to the host at Shiloh. And Joshua cast lots for them in Shiloh before the Lord: and there Joshua divided the land unto the children of Israel according to their divisions."[50]

Perhaps the least difficult way to remember the approximate area assigned to each tribe is to start at the south end of Canaan and work up toward the north. Reference to the "Map of Tribal Inheritances" will be of further assistance.

Tribe	Location	Number of Cities
Simeon	Extreme south (Negeb)	17
Judah	Between Dead Sea & Med. Sea	Not given
Benjamin	Jordan R. half-way to the Mediterranean Sea	26
Dan	From Benjamin to the Mediterranean Sea	17
Ephraim	Samaria—from Jordan R. to Mediterranean Sea	Not given
Manasseh	Above Ephraim from Jordan R. to Mediterranean Sea	Not given
Issachar	From Jordan R. half-way to Mediterranean Sea	16
Zebulon	Landlocked area half-way between Galilee and Med. Sea	12
Asher	Mt. Carmel north to Mt. Lebanon	22
Naphtali	Galilee to Mount Hermon	19

---

50. Joshua 18:9-10

When all of this work was completed the children of Israel asked Joshua to pick out the location for his inheritance. He modestly selected Timnath-serah in Mount Ephraim which had been destroyed during the war and had to be rebuilt.[51]

SIX CITIES OF REFUGE DESIGNATED AND FORTY-EIGHT CITIES ASSIGNED TO THE LEVITES

The Lord had designated six cities of refuge to be assigned where capital fugitives could flee and receive sanctuary until such time as they were given a fair trial. Three cities were designated in Canaan: Hebron in Judah, Shechem in Mount Ephraim, and Kedesh in Galilee (not to be confused with Kadesh-barnea in the Negeb).[52] Three cities were also designated in Trans-Jordan: "Bezer in the wilderness upon the plain out of the tribe of Reuben, and Ramoth in Gilead out of the tribe of Gad, and Golan in Bashan out of the tribe of Manasseh."[53]

At this point the "heads of the fathers of the Levites" decided it was time for them to receive their inheritances and so they came to Eleazar the High Priest and unto Joshua to ask for their cities. It will be recalled that the Levites were not to have any territorial inheritances but were to be given specific cities with a limited amount of space around the city for their flocks and crops. By scattering these cities among the various tribes it would greatly facilitate the administration of religious rites for which the Levites were responsible.

Consequently these cities were selected from among the tribes on both sides of the Jordan. Altogether there were forty-eight cities which the Levites were authorized to occupy.[54] Actually, there were only 23,000 Levites at the last census so this meant that they would not be the only inhabitants in these cities but would govern them and have special privileges and rights in connection with their calling in the Priesthood.[55]

---

51. Joshua 19:49-50
52. Joshua 20:7
53. Joshua 20:8
54. Joshua 21:41
55. Numbers 26:62

Only one final thought need be added concerning these inheritances which were given to the various tribes and that is the fact that these tribal boundaries were not intended to be inflexible. In other words, the children of Israel could live almost anywhere they wished among the other tribes, but their voting rights and many other privileges had to be claimed within the territory of the tribe to which each person belonged. This is why Mary and Joseph had to go from Nazareth to Bethlehem in order to register for the tax census at the ancestral home of David because they were both his descendants.[56]

Joshua's Last Instructions

Following the division of the land into inheritances, Joshua's active public life diminished. In fact, it would appear that no public act is referred to during the last seven years of his life. Authorities estimate that he was around ninety-six when the conquest of Canaan began and that after seven years of war he divided the land and then lived seven years longer.[57] His only remaining public act came right at the end of this period when he was approaching the end of his life.

Joshua gathered the people together in a large conference and gave them his next to the last sermon. He left no doubt as to his greatest concern.

First, he commanded them to press forward and cleanse the whole land, "And the Lord your God, he shall expel them from before you, and drive them from out of your sight; and ye shall possess their land, as the Lord your God hath promised unto you."[58] Under no circumstances were they to become indifferent to this assignment nor be negligent in driving the Canaanites out. If they did, Joshua wanted them to know the consequences. Said he: take good heed therefore unto yourselves, that ye love the Lord your God. Else if ye do in any wise go back, and cleave unto the remnant of these nations, even these that remain among you, and shall make marriages with them, and go in unto them, and they to you: know for a certainty that the Lord your God will no more drive out any of these nations from before you; but they shall

---

56. Luke 2:1-4
57. Clarke, *Bible Commentary*, Vol. 2, p. 90
58. Joshua 23:5

be snares and traps unto you, and scourges in your sides, and thorns in your eyes, until ye perish from off this good land which the Lord your God hath given you."[59]

A short time after this Joshua called a conference of Israel's leaders at Shechem,[60] and there he gave his last sermon. In the name of the Lord he reminded them of the idolatry of their fathers and the devastating consequences of such profligate indulgences. Then he reminded them of the goodness of God to Israel in all her tribulations. He warned them against the abominations of the heathens and then concluded with a declaration which is one of the most frequently quoted passages in the entire Bible. To the leaders of Israel he cried out: ". . . choose you this day whom ye will serve . . . but as for me and my house, we will serve the Lord."

"And the people answered and said, God forbid that we should forsake the Lord, to serve other gods."[61]

Joshua called upon the people to commit themselves to God in a covenant, which they did. Joshua then raised up a large stone and placed it under an oak "that was by the sanctuary of the Lord."

"And Joshua said unto all the people, Behold, this stone shall be a witness unto us; for it hath heard all the words of the Lord which he spake unto us: it shall be therefore a witness unto you, lest ye deny your God."[62]

In modern times the Lord has revealed that there is intelligence in matter[63] which is perfectly capable of revealing what it has witnessed. In fact, the Lord has disclosed that when the earth is perfected and made into a celestial planet it "will be a Urim and Thummin to the inhabitants who dwell thereon, whereby all things pertaining to an inferior kingdom, or all kingdoms of a lower order, will be manifest to those who dwell on it; and this earth will be Christ's."[64] The stone which Joshua raised up was perhaps more of a witness than even the children of Israel may have realized.

---

59. Joshua 23:11-13
60. Joshua 24:1
61. Joshua 24.15-16
62. Joshua 24:26-27
63. See discussion with sources cited in *The First 2,000 Years*, pp. 356-357.
64. Doctrine and Covenants 130:9

Joshua and Eleazar Die

So Joshua had preached his last sermon, fought his last battle and made his last plea to Israel. It was now up to them.

"And it came to pass after these things, that Joshua the son of Nun, the servant of the Lord, died, being an hundred and ten years old.

"And they buried him in the border of his inheritance in Timnath-serah, which is in Mount Ephraim, on the north side of the hill of Gaash. . . .

"And Eleazar the son of Aaron died; and they buried him in a hill that pertained to Phinehas his son, which was given in mount Ephraim."[65]

So these two illustrious servants of the Lord passed to their reward. This probably left only Caleb of Judah alive of all the adults who came out of Egypt with the Exodus. We are not told of the death of Caleb but since he was somewhat younger than Joshua it is likely that he was still alive.

One more important burial is mentioned as the Book of Joshua closes. It says: "And the bones of Joseph, which the children of Israel brought up out of Egypt, buried they in Shechem, in a parcel of ground which Jacob bought of the sons of Hamor the father of Shechem for an hundred pieces of silver: and it became the inheritance of the children of Joseph."[66] How ironical that the body of Joseph should come to its final resting place about four miles from the place where he was first seized by his brothers and thrown into a pit near Dothan. And how interesting that he should be buried in Shechem, the site of Dinah's kidnapping and assault, and the community which Joseph's older brothers had wiped out in vengeance. Now he was being buried in a plot purchased for a hundred pieces of silver from Hamor, the ruling prince of Shechem, whom his brothers had killed, and for which their father had disinherited one of them. For all the days to come, this plot was to be the inheritance of the tribe of Joseph, and the body of their great ancestor was placed there to perpetuate the memory of Joseph, the most illustrious of Jacob's sons.

---

65. Joshua 24:29-30, 33   66. Joshua 24:32

Scripture Reading and Questions on Chapter Twenty-Two

Scripture Reading Assignment: Joshua, chapters 11 to 24 inclusive.

1—What did the messengers tell Joshua concerning the five Amorite kings who had escaped from Gibeon? What did Joshua tell his soldiers to do?

2—What happened to the five kings? What happened to all their cities?

3—Approximately how long is Palestine from "Dan to Beer-sheba?" How far is it from the Mediterranean Sea to the Dead Sea?

4—In spite of the victories Israel achieved, were these as great as the Lord would liked to have given them? Why was this?

5—After conquering the Canaanite federation (usually referred to by their local name of Amorite federation) what new force challenged the Israelites? Who was their leader?

6—What military aspect of this new enemy was frightening to Israel? What did the Lord say about it? What was the outcome?

7—How many years do authorities believe Israel's campaign in the north required? How many in the south?

8—What happened after the campaign to the soldiers from Reuben, Gad and half the tribe of Manasseh? What had kept them with the armies of Israel all these years?

9—What did the Trans-Jordan troops do which almost started a civil war?

10—What action did Israel take? What was the outcome?

11—When Caleb asked for an inheritance, what tribe was he representing? How old was he at this time?

12—What part of Canaan did Caleb's tribe want for an inheritance? What did Caleb offer to do in order to win this inheritance? What had happened there since the Israelites first conquered it?

13—What was the first capital of the Israelites in southern Canaan? What did Caleb have to do to get possession of it?

14—What was the second major division of Canaan? Why did the princes of Ephraim and Manasseh complain? What was Joshua's answer?

15—What was the attitude of the other seven tribes at this time? Why did Joshua rebuke them? What does this indicate?

16—What procedure did Joshua follow to determine where the other seven tribes should settle? Did any of the tribes actually possess everything the Lord had intended them to get? Why?

17—How many cities were assigned to the Levites? Were they located in one area? Why?

18—What was the famous statement Joshua made in his last sermon to Israel?

19—How old was Joshua when he died? Where was he buried?

20—Who else died about this time? What does it say happened to the embalmed body of Joseph which the Israelites brought up out of Egypt?

CHAPTER TWENTY-THREE

Israel Plunges into the Dark Ages

When Joshua died the national spirit of Israel died also. No longer was there a massive gravitating force of unity which had been so apparent during the crusade in Canaan. With the death of Joshua the great federation of military and political solidarity melted away. Every man departed to his own inheritance and each tribe began to look to its own resources without giving help or asking aid from their fellow Israelites. Occasionally, there was a sudden stirring of the old spirit, but never for long. In fact, the generation immediately following Joshua brought the curses of Mount Ebal down upon their heads, and thereafter Israel elected to follow a course of weakness and disobedience which left this people feeble and fragmented for a period of nearly 400 years.

In every tribal inheritance the Israelites went through the three-step process of tolerating, collaborating with, and finally embracing the Canaanites. Some four-and-a-half centuries later David finally united the strength of Israel and conquered this whole land, but during the interim the Israelites were corrupted and plundered by their enemies. The following verses summarize the basic pattern of Israel's terrible dark ages:

". . . and there arose another generation after them [meaning after Joshua and the elders], which knew not the Lord, nor yet the works which he had done for Israel.

"And the children of Israel did evil in the sight of the Lord and served Baalim:

"And they forsook the Lord God of their fathers, which brought them out of the land of Egypt, and followed other gods, of the gods of the people that were round about them, and bowed themselves unto them, and provoked the Lord to anger."[1]

THE BOOK OF JUDGES

Thus we are introduced to the story in the Book of Judges. It is a sad and cluttered story, highlighted only here and there with the feats of some noble spirit who arose momentarily from among the tribes to provide a spark of hope. But none of these sparks kindled into a permanent flame. Always the smothering darkness of apostasy swept in to extinguish the light.

Because the Book of Judges is a compilation of many more or less independent incidents, scholars have never been able to arrange it in exact chronological sequence. From Adam down to the conquest of Canaan there is sufficient data in the scriptures to fix important historical events with relative accuracy. Then working backwards from the birth of Christ, we are able to fix with reasonable exactness the chronology of events back to the reign of Saul. This therefore leaves a period in excess of 400 years between the conquest of Canaan and the crowning of Saul which is difficult to chronicle with any degree of exactness. For convenience it is called the days of the Judges, but this could be more accurately called the Book of Israel's heroes. This is the period we will now discuss.

The student will note that the personalities treated in the Book of Judges are not judicial officers but primarily military leaders or liberators who rescued one or more of the tribes at a particularly critical moment. That is why we say it is really the book of Israel's heroes during this grim and ugly era. The student will also note that specific periods of time are allocated to enemy conquests and the subsequent period of "peace" or "rest" in the land. However, these periods are not necessarily in consecutive sequence. Many of these incidents seem to have overlapped because they involved different tribes and different sections of the land. This is why it is impossible to fix the exact chronology of this period with any genuine confidence.

---

1. Judges 2:10-12

Conditions in Canaan During the Days of the Judges

To understand the predicament of the Israelites during this period it is necessary to realize that the sea-coast population with its Hamitic tribes of Philistines, Canaanites and Phoenicians were all powerful nations in their own right. They maintained professional armies, lived in walled cities and had vast material wealth to protect. The Phoenicians, for example, had purchased their security from Egypt by paying tribute during more than 400 years and, in return, had been given a monopoly in Egyptian trade. Phoenician ships dominated the seas of the then known world and brought back to Sidon the luxuries which their commercial trade provided. The Canaanites and Philistines were also in league with Egypt and had become her well established tributaries. The opulence of the sea-coast peoples was a genuine snare to the Israelites as the years went by.

The wealth of Canaan was also attracting the greedy eyes of the Syrians and Babylonians. Around 1400 B.C., the armies of these nations were beginning to make increasingly deep penerations into this part of the fertile crescent. Israel soon found herself caught in the cross-fire of this bitter contest between Egypt and the empires of Mesopotamia. Had Israel built the mighty commonwealth of liberty as originally envisioned by the Lord, these great empire builders would have been held back and thereby weakened while Israel would have become more powerful than all of them. This could have changed the whole course of human history.

The Heathen Fertility Cults in Canaan

The greatest single factor of corruption among the Canaanites was their wild, sensuous fertility cults. Dr. Geikie furnishes a glimpse into the heathen religions of this age:

"The chief god of the Canaanites was Baal—the sun—who was worshipped under different names. In one part he was Moloch, in another, Chemosh, but his worship was everywhere alike, fierce and cruel. His consort, Ashtaroth, the Babylonian goddess Istar, the goddess of love, worshipped as the morning star Venus, and, perhaps, also, as the moon—the Greeks translating her name Astarte—fostered abominations in her worship, almost inconceivable in our times. Erech was her chief city, and there she had, attached to her temple, choirs of festival-girls, and troops of consecrated maidens, all recognized as harlots, whose pay went to the temple treasury; and crowds of priests — 'the festival makers who had devoted their manhood' — that is, emasculated themselves—that men 'might adore the goddess,' and these, in their rites, 'carried swords, and razors, and flint knives,' who in the wild frenzy of the sacred rites desired to dedicate themselves to the goddess, by self-mutilation, or to hack themselves as done by the priests, in Elijah's time, at Carmel."[2]

Even worse than their sensuous debaucheries were their sacrificial rites which often used children as the sacrificial victims. For centuries these people had indulged themselves in these practices and were therefore considered ripe for extinction by the Lord. But Israel failed in her calling and allowed herself to be conquered by the very elements she was supposed to cleanse from the land. The tragedy of these days is caught in the blistering lines from the 106th Psalm: "They did not destroy the nations concerning whom the Lord commanded them: but were mingled among the heathen, and learned their works. And they served their idols: which were a snare unto them. Yea, they sacrificed their sons and their daughters unto devils, and shed innocent blood, even the blood of their sons and of their daughters, whom they sacrificed unto the idols of Canaan: and the land was polluted with blood."[3]

The best preserved of the ancient heathen temples may be found at Baalbek in Lebanon. There are located in the Valley of the Sun not many miles north of Mount Carmel. We think it was from this heathen center that priests of Baal came to Mount Carmel to be challenged by Elijah. The Greeks and Romans added their embellishments to the original Canaanite structures but the pattern for heathen worship remained virtually the same through the centuries.

When this author visited Baalbek recently it was noted that the three essential structures for the heathen rites are

---

2. Cunningham Geikie, *Hours wih the Bible*, Vol. 2, p. 514
3. Psalms 106:34-38

still visible. There is the large temple which housed the mammoth image of their god, and contained the altar where the sacrifice of both animals and human beings took place. Next to it is a structure presently referred to as the "temple of Bacchus" which was used in ancient times for drunken and riotous festivities. Then some distance away in a grove, is the small shrine of Venus where the drunken reveler went with one of the so-called vestal virgins to fulfil the final phase of this profligate pilgrimage. These groves were usually called *Asherah* which was the name of the goddess of sexual promiscuity. They were filled with phallic sculptures in wood and stone representing various forms of obscenity.

As the years went by all of these forces had their impact on Israel. Their tolerance for the Canaanite culture led to intermingling and this, in turn, to intermarriage. The corruption of heathen worship dissipated the whole concept of living under the covenant and as the religious tone of the Israelites diminished so did their political and cultural strength. The Israelites became a diversified conglomerate of disunited tribes which were individually vulnerable to attack from any nearby heathen chieftain bent on conquest. All of this gives significance to the early chapters in the Book of Judges which is epitomized in the following:

"And the children of Israel dwelt among the Canaanites, Hittites, and Amorites, and Perizzites, and Hivites, and Jebusites: and they took their daughters to be their wives, and gave their daughters to their sons, and served their gods. And the children of Israel did evil in the sight of the Lord, and forgat the Lord their God, and served Baalim and the groves."[4]

THE DAYS OF OTHNIEL

The first outright conquest of Israel did not come from the Canaanites, but from Mesopotamia. Joshua and the elders of his day had been dead less than a quarter of a century when the Syrian troops from up around the headwaters of the Euphrates came sweeping down on Canaan and placed this whole region under heavy tribute to King Chushan-rishathaim. This oppression lasted for eight years.

---

4. Judges 3:5-7

Finally, conditions became so intolerable that one of the princes of Judah determined to muster sufficient strength to purge the land of the Syrian soldiers and tax-collectors. This prince of Judah was none other than Othniel, the nephew of Caleb. He had gained a reputation for valor in the conquest of Debir and had thereby gained the privilege of marrying Caleb's daughter.[5] Now he called upon the people of Israel to repent, reform and resist the invader.

Othniel was actually able to muster sufficient unity among the tribes to lead an assault against the Syrians and completely root them out of the land. Their defeat was so complete that they never again returned while Othniel was alive.

The scripture indicates that Othniel was a power for good during the remainder of his life and under his influence the peace and independence of Israel was maintained for forty years.[6]

THE RISE OF EHUD

The next invasion of Israel was by a federation of Semitic tribes from Trans-Jordan. The Moabites and Ammonites were both descendants of Lot; and the Amalekites were descendants of Esau. These distant relatives of the Israelites formed a military alliance under King Eglon (king of the Moabites) and determined to conquer the rich valley on the west side of Jordan where Jericho once stood. A new city had been constructed in the area called the "City of Palms" and this was inhabited by the Benjamites to whom the whole area belonged. However, the Moabite assault on the City of Palms was successful and the Moabite federation promptly took over this part of the Jordan valley. For 18 years King Eglon made this his capital and kept the tribe of Benjamin under tribute. As time went by the scripture says this King Eglon became exceedingly fat.[7]

One day the tribe of Benjamin sent its "present" or tribute money to King Eglon by a man named Ehud, the son of Gera, a Benjamite. Since this errand gave Ehud the

---

5. Judges 1:11-13   7. Judges 3:17
6. Judges 3:10-11

excuse to come in direct contact with the king, he decided it might be a good time to strike this despot down. The scripture says Ehud was left-handed,[8] therefore he constructed a stiletto or short sword and fastened its sheath to his right hip so that he could easily draw it forth with his left hand. When he came unto King Eglon with his associates, he gave the king the tribute money, looked the situation over, and departed. But as soon as he had reached the "quarries that were by Gilgal" (the old camp ground of Israel) Ehud told his companions to go ahead while he himself returned to King Eglon.

Ehud found the king "sitting in a summer parlour, which he had for himself alone."[9] Ehud said to the king, "I have a message from God unto thee."[10] The king rose from his seat, apparently in the greatest expectation of some good news. "And Ehud put forth his left hand, and took the dagger from his right thigh, and thrust it into his belly: and the haft also went in after the blade; and the fat closed upon the blade, so that he could not draw the dagger out of his belly; and the dirt came out."[11]

The lethal blow was so powerful and destructive that King Eglon apparently sank down without even crying out. Ehud closed the parlour doors and immediately escaped. Later on, the servants of the king came to inquire after his well-being, but, finding the door closed, they thought the king wished privacy and so they did not knock or enter. This gave Ehud time to carry out his plan.

Ehud climbed the 3,000-foot heights west of the city and sounded his ram's horn on the mountains of Ephraim as a distress signal. When the people rallied to him in contemplation of some kind of attack, he said, "Follow after me: for the Lord hath delivered your enemies the Moabites into your hand."[12] Ehud led these minutemen down the steep sandstone cliffs to the valley of Gilgal below. This sudden attack apparently struck the City of Palms just about the same time the alarm was spreading through the city that the king had been assassinated in his own house. The panic of the Moab-

---

8. Judges 3:15
9. Judges 3:20
10. Ibid.
11. Judges 3:21-22
12. Judges 3:28

ites led them to flee from the city and try to get over to their traditional territory on the east side of the Dead Sea, but Ehud and his men were too quick for them. They cut the Moabites off at the fords where they tried to cross the Jordan, "And they slew of Moab at that time about ten thousand men, all lusty, and all men of valour; and there escaped not a man."[13]

This is all we are told about Ehud. Once the Moabites and their allies had been routed from the west side of Jordan they left the Israelites alone. For eighty years there was peace.[14]

THE RISE OF SHAMGAR

It may have been sometime during this eighty year period or immediately thereafter that Judah and Simeon were having their own troubles when the Philistines attacked Israel down along the southwest corner of the land.

This invasion apparently began and ended very abruptly as a result of the bold and heroic behavior of a one-man army named "Shamgar, son of Anath."[15]

Shamgar took one of the long spiked poles which was used ordinarily as an ox-goad and charged into the Philistines like a ram-jet. For some reason or other the Philistines could not stop him with either spear or sword, and after they had lost a total of 600 men to this churning Hercules of Israel they turned tail and took off for their own territory. So peace was restored in this area also.[16]

THE RISE OF DEBORAH AND BARAK

The scripture says that after "Ehud was dead" the people once more forgot how vulnerable they were to their enemies and their need for the constant blessings of God. It says they "again did evil in the sight of the Lord," and as a result the whole northern section of Israel was conquered by King Jabin, a Canaanite, who reigned in his capital city of Hazor several miles above the Sea of Galilee.[17] The

13. Judges 3:29
14. Judges 3:30
15. Judges 3:31

16. Ibid.
17. Judges 4:1-2

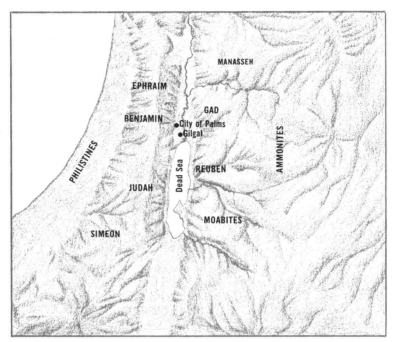

captain of Jabin's host was Sisera who lived in Harosheth. Sisera put down all resistance with military might and used 900 "chariots of iron" to enforce the king's dominion. For twenty years this oppression continued.[18]

Finally, when it was painfully apparent that the men of Israel were too slack and sluggish to take action, an inspired "mother in Israel," the wife of Lapidoth, who had received revelations from the Lord and was called a "prophetess," decided to strike for liberty against Jabin.[19] This woman had become widely known in Israel due to her wisdom. In fact, her fame in settling disputes had extended so far that she held court under a palm tree near her home located between Ramah and Bethel in Mount Ephraim.[20] Not being a holder of the Priesthood, and not being an ordained judge, she functioned in a private capacity, but her sagacity had become so famous that disputing parties would mutually agree to abide by her decision whatever it might be. Therefore, "the children of Israel came up to her for judgment."[21]

18. Judges 4:3   20. Judges 4:5
19. Judges 4:4; 5:7   21. Ibid.

Deborah (whose name meant "a bee")[22] was not satis-fied to sit in the pleasant security of her own tribe of Ephraim and see all of the northern tribes bullied about by King Jabin. She therefore sought the Lord and received an assurance that Jabin could be conquered. All Deborah needed was a leader. She finally decided to raise up Barak who lived at Kedesh-naphtali, very near to Hazor, and who was there-fore fully aware of the brutality and violence of this tribal enemy. Deborah said to him:

"Hath not the Lord God of Israel commanded, saying, Go and draw toward Mount Tabor, and take with thee ten thousand men of the children of Naphtali and of the children of Zebulun? And I will draw unto thee, to the river Kishon, Sisera, the captain of Jabin's army, with his chariots and his multitude; and I will deliver him into thine hand."[23]

But Barak hesitated. It turned out that he had plenty of confidence in Deborah but not so much in himself. Said he, "If thou wilt go with me, then I will go: but if thou wilt not go with me, then I will not go."[24] With feminine deftness she urged Barak to go forward and gain the glory of this great victory. She pointed out that if she went along, people would give her the credit whereas if Barak went alone he would be the nation's hero. However, Barak was not seeking personal glory but only the liberty of his people. He felt that Deborah's presence at the battle front was indispensable, so "Deborah arose, and went with Barak to Kedesh."[25]

This Deborah proved to be a veritable Joan of Arc. She did no actual fighting, but her presence in the campaign inspired not only the men of Zebulun and Naphtali but con-tingents of volunteers began pouring in from Ephraim, Ben-jamin and Issachar.[26] Other tribes, such as Reuben, Dan and Asher were condemned by Deborah for making no effort to come,[27] and a curse was placed on the city of Meroz be-cause it refused to help.[28]

Those who did come constituted an armed force of 10,000 men as the Lord had required and all of these were

---

22. Peloubet's *Bible Dictionary*, under "'Deborah."
23. Judges 4:6-7
24. Judges 4:8   26. Judges 5:14-15
25. Judges 4:9   27. Judges 5:15-17
                                   28. Judges 5:23

assembled together on top of Mount Tabor. Below them lay the great valley of Esdraelon, one of the most famous battlefields in the world.

DEBORAH AND BARAK AT MOUNT TABOR

Mount Tabor rises 1,500 feet above the valley floor in the northeast corner of the plain of Esdraelon. It stands out by itself and is connected only on the west by a narrow ridge which joins it to the hills of Nazareth. The top is relatively level and commands a wide view of the valley from one end to the other.

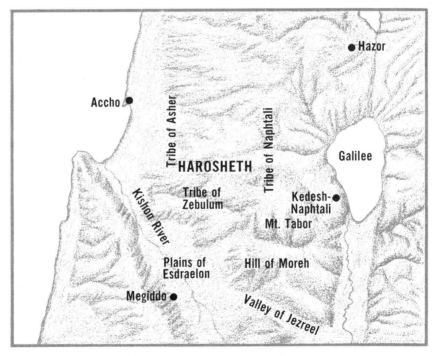

The plain of Esdraelon is one of the largest open spaces in Palestine, extending some sixteen miles from Engannim on the south to the foot of the hills of Nazareth on the north. The valley is about twenty-five miles from east to west and is seamed with shallow brooks which drain into the Kishon ("winding") river. In case of a flash flood this river becomes extremely dangerous. Its channel of fifteen feet in depth and twenty yards in width overflows and becomes a raging torrent as it sweeps down this valley and rushes into the Mediterranean Sea at the gulf of Acre.

This stream is also treacherous at its headwaters near the base of Mount Tabor where the springs which feed it form a chain of pools and brooks, fringed with reeds and rushes. In case of a storm this whole area of loose volcanic soil can be changed into a quagmire. Understanding these physical features helps to explain the amazing outcome of the battle which the Israelites fought here and which made Deborah and Barak famous.

The Battle at Mount Tabor

Scarcely had the Israelites established themselves when the hosts of King Jabin rumbled into view. The question immediately arises as to how Jabin and Sisera (Jabin's commanding general) knew the Israelites were going to assemble at this place. The scripture says a man named Heber who was of the people of Jethro and who lived near Kedesh-naphtali, had cut himself off from his own people and was friendly with the Canaanites. As soon as this Heber learned that the Israelites were meeting at Mount Tabor he communicated this information to Sisera.[29] Sisera immediately mobilized his 900 chariots and his "multitude" and set out for the plain of Esdraelon.[30]

"And Deborah said unto Barak, Up; for this is the day in which the Lord hath delivered Sisera into thine hand. . . ."[31] So the ten thousand Israelites went pouring down the sides of Mount Tabor to engage Sisera in battle. Although the details are not provided, it is evident that Sisera's band of chariots became mired down and many of them were lost because "The river of Kishon swept them away."[32] From this it has been assumed that a flash flood came to help the

29. Judges 4:11-12
30. "The plain of Esdraelon has in all ages been the battlefield of Palestine.. Here fought Thothmes III, Rameses II, Rameses III; here Pharaoh Necho won that sad battle of Megiddo, in which King Josiah was slain, amidst a slaughter so terrible that the great conflict of the Apocalypse is called, from it, the battle of Armageddon—'the hill of Megiddo.' Here have fought in turns the armies of Assyria, of the Crusaders, and of Bonaparte, and it was on the mountains of Gilboa, at east end, that Saul and Jonathan perished." Geikie, *Hours with the Bible*, Vol. 2, pp. 544-545.
31. Judges 4:14
32. Judges 5:21

Israelites and that Sisera's army was no match for the Israelites once they were forced to abandon their chariots. What few charioteers escaped headed for the hills of Nazareth where the roads led back into the wooded country, "But Barak pursued after the chariots, and after the host, unto Harosheth of the Gentiles: and all the host of Sisera fell upon the edge of the sword, and there was not a man left."[33]

However, Sisera, himself, did not go in that direction. The scripture says that when he was forced to abandon his war chariot he frantically fled toward the Sea of Galilee where Heber the Kenite lived, whom Sisera knew to be a friend. However, Heber was not at home. Nevertheless, Jael, his wife, went out to meet Sisera and beckoned the exhausted general to come in. He did so and pleaded with her to hide him. She had him lie down to rest in the cloistered part of the tent and "she covered him with a mantle."[34] Then Sisera asked for a drink, and after she had given him some milk, he promptly fell into a sound sleep.

Apparently Jael did not harbor the same sentiments toward Sisera as her husband, but was on the side of the Israelites. Therefore, as soon as Sisera was asleep, she took a "nail of the tent" or metal stake and using a carpenter's hammer she placed the spike on Sisera's temple and drove it clear through his head. The scripture says the blow was struck with such force that the nail of the tent not only passed completely through the frontal skull but "fastened it into the ground."[35]

"And, behold, as Barak pursued Sisera, Jael came out to meet him, and said unto him, Come and I will shew thee the man whom thou seekest. And when he came into her tent, behold Sisera lay dead and the nail was in his temples."[36]

So with Sisera disposed of, Barak was free to march his victorious army right up to the gates of Hazor. The scripture says, "And the hand of the children of Israel prospered, and prevailed against Jabin the king of Canaan, until they had destroyed Jabin. . . ."[37]

---

33. Judges 4:16
34. Judges 4:18
35. Judges 4:21

36. Judges 4:22
37. Judges 4:24

Deborah was so jubilant over this success that she composed a triumphant song of victory and this comprises the entire fifth chapter of the Book of Judges. It is one of the famous poetic passages in the Old Testament and furnishes the student with many of the details which we have set forth above. At the conclusion of the song, the scripture simply says, "And the land had rest forty years."[38]

By this time, at least two centuries had passed since the days of Joshua and the original conquest of Canaan. These last mentioned forty years of peace which had been gained through the leadership of Deborah could have been a season of revitalization and reform, but they were not. Once more the scripture says, "And the children of Israel did evil in the sight of the Lord."[39]

THE RISE OF GIDEON

The next invasion of Israel was like a plague of locusts. Once more the distant and apostate relatives of the Israelites came up the Arabah from the wilderness in the south and after gathering their allied tribes on the eastern highlands they crossed over Jordan into Canaan. This time the main core was a great wave of marauding Midianites, descendants of Abraham through Keturah.[40] With them came the Amalekites (descendants of Esau) and a host of other Semitic peoples who are referred to as "the children of the east."[41] These Gypsy-like nomads would wait until the Israelites had sown and cultivated their crops and after all the work was done they would swarm across the Jordan "with their cattle and their tents, and they came as grasshoppers for multitude; for both they and their camels were without number: and they entered into the land to destroy it."[42]

This plague of immigrants did not stop in the plain of Gilgal as the Moabites had done but climbed the spine of Canaan's range of central mountains and then swept westward as far as Gaza on the Mediterranean coastal plain.[43] They consumed and destroyed all before them "and left no sustenance for Israel" so that the people were greatly im-

---

38. Judges 5:31
39. Judges 6:1
40. Genesis 25:2; I Chronicles 1:32

41. Judges 6:3
42. Judges 6:5
43. Judges 6:4

poverished.[44] During these inroads each year, the Israelites would have to flee for their lives and make themselves "dens which are in the mountains, and caves, and strong holds."[45] For seven straight years,[46] Israel suffered from these annual raids and so they finally pleaded with the Lord for relief.

The Lord did not send help immediately. Instead, he sent a prophet whose name is not given but who reminded the Israelites that all of this was the direct result of disobedience.[47] Perhaps this brought them temporarily to their senses for the next thing we read is that "a mighty man of valour" had been raised up. His name was Gideon.

GIDEON RECEIVES HIS FIRST REVELATION

Gideon belonged to the tribe of Manasseh and lived at Ophrah which is no longer possible to identify with any specific location. His father was Joash, a man of prominence in the area, but he, like all the rest, had been reduced to poverty because of the ravages of the Midianites.

When the Lord's messenger came to Gideon, he was in the midst of trying to thresh out a little wheat for his family. Instead of doing it in the open field he had set up a small threshing floor behind a winepress, "to hide it from the Midianites."[48] The next thing Gideon knew, there was a personage who came "and sat under an oak. . . ."[49] This angel or messenger of the Lord was apparently like the "man" who appeared to Jacob at Peniel,[50] or the "men" who appeared to Abraham on the plains of Mamre.[51] As we have previously pointed out, these holy messengers were probably from the translated City of Enoch since the task of serving as ministering angels was the specific assignment given to Enoch's people until the Second Coming.[52] Whenever these messengers have appeared on the earth there is usually nothing to distinguish them from ordinary mortal men. Such was the case with the mesenger who came to Gideon.

"And the angel of the Lord appeared unto him, and said unto him, The Lord is with thee, thou mighty man of

44. Judges 6:4, 6
45. Judges 6:2
46. Judges 6:1
47. Judges 6:8-10
48. Judges 6:11

49. Ibid.
50. Genesis 32:24-29
51. Genesis 18:2
52. *Teachings of Joseph Smith*, p. 170

valour. And Gideon said unto him, Oh my Lord, if the Lord be with us, why then is all this befallen us? and where be all his miracles which our fathers told us of, saying, Did not the Lord bring us up from Egypt? but now the Lord hath forsaken us, and delivered us into the hands of the Midianites.''[53]

The messenger disregarded Gideon's complaint. Instead, he said, "Go in this thy might, and thou shalt save Israel from the hand of the Midianites. . . .''[54]

But Gideon could not imagine himself in such a role. He said, "Oh, my Lord, wherewith shall I save Israel? behold, my family is poor in Manasseh, and I am the least in my father's house.''[55]

The messenger, speaking in the first person, delivered the promise of the Lord to Gideon, "Surely I will be with thee, and thou shalt smite the Midianites as one man.''[56]

At this point Gideon had to determine for certain that he was dealing with an authorized servant of the Lord. Said he, "If now I have found grace in thy sight, then shew me a sign that thou talkest with me.''[57] In other words, "produce some evidence that this is not just a trick but is in very deed the message of the Lord unto me. But before any sign could be given, Gideon suddenly realized that he had not offered any refreshment to this important visitor. He therefore interrupted the conversation and said, "Depart not hence, I pray thee, until I come unto thee, and bring forth my present, and set it before thee.''[58] The messenger agreed to wait while these refreshments were prepared.

When Gideon returned, he had some meat in a basket together with unleavened cakes and a container of broth.[59] It will be recalled that when Abraham had offered food to his angelic messengers they had partaken,[60] but this messenger told Gideon to pour out the broth upon the ground as a libation (or drink offering) and place the meat and cakes on a nearby rock. After Gideon had done this, the Lord's messenger reached forth the shepherd's staff which he was carrying and touched the rock. Immediately a flame of fire shot

---

53. Judges 6:12-13   56. Judges 6:16   59. Judges 6:19
54. Judges 6:14   57. Judges 6:17   60. Genesis 18:2-8
55. Judges 6:15   58. Judges 6:18

out from the stone and consumed the food which Gideon had prepared. This was the sign. "And when Gideon perceived that he was an angel of the Lord, Gideon said, Alas, O Lord God! for because I have seen an angel of the Lord face to face."[61] But the reply came back to Gideon, "Peace be unto thee; fear not: thou shalt not die."[62]

It is important to note that up to this time there was nothing singular about this messenger to persuade Gideon that he was a true ambassador from God. The text is somewhat confusing due to the fact that Gideon is said to have addressed the messenger as "Lord," but it is perfectly clear that this was simply a form of respectful salutation and not an attempt to identify the messenger as *the* Lord. Once he had seen the power of the messenger manifest in the devouring flame from the rock, Gideon knew the man standing before him was an authorized servant of God.

GIDEON SMASHES HIS FATHER'S HEATHEN ALTAR

That very same night Gideon was told to "throw down the altar of Baal that thy father hath, and cut down the grove that is by it: and build an altar unto the Lord thy God upon the top of this rock, in the ordered place, and take the second bullock [the younger of the two bullock owned by Gideon's father][63] and offer a burnt-sacrifice with the wood of the grove which thou shalt cut down."[64]

This passage clearly demonstrates the depth of apostasy to which many of the Israelites had descended. Gideon's father, Joash, appears to have been the custodian for the heathen altar of Ophrah and the presence of a "grove" nearby implies the practice of the impure rites associated with Baal-worship. The Lord's command to destroy this heathen sanctuary involved the possibility of the most severe kind of retaliation by the people of Ophrah, and Gideon knew it.

For this reason, Gideon took ten men from among his servants and crept out at night to fulfill this command "because he feared his father's household, and the men of the city. . . .

---

61. Judges 6:22
62. Judges 6:23
63. Judges 6:25
64. Judges 6:25-26

"And when the men of the city arose early in the morn-ing, behold, the altar of Baal was cast down, and the grove was cut down that was by it, and the second bullock was offered upon the altar that was built."[65] Obviously, Gideon and his men had been engaged in a strenuous night's work!

The men of Ophrah were not only outraged but they were determined to find out who had desecrated their shrine. Apparently they had little difficulty discovering that it was Gideon and they immediately made demands upon Joash to bring his wretched son before them so that he could be killed. But a strange thing happened. The father of Gideon boldly defended his son. He said to the townspeople, ". . . if he [Baal] be a god, let him plead [contend] for himself, because one hath cast down his altar."[66] Joash seems to have taken pride in Gideon's display of courage. In fact, he gave him a new name—"Jerrubbaal"—which means "let the shameful thing contend [for itself]."[67] For the moment, the men of Ophrah were silenced.

It appears that immediately after this incident an alarm-ing report came through that a mighty host of more than 120,000 warriors of the Midianite federation had assembled in the valley of Jezreel. This was in the same vicinity where Deborah and Barak had fought the hosts of Jabin, so it appeared that the Midianites intended to press northward and devastate the more distant tribes the same way they had consumed those further south. Immediately "the Spirit of the Lord came upon Gideon"[68] and he found himself full of courage and determined to challenge this predatory power which was devouring the whole land.

He blew his trumpet near Ophrah and gathered all of the Manassites of the Abi-ezer clan around him,[69] then he sent messengers throughout Manasseh, Asher, Zebulun and Naphtali, because this seemed to be the territory which this enemy now threatened. He asked these tribes to rally a host of men to defend the liberties of Israel. Upwards of 32,000 men from among these specific tribes responded.

---

65. Judges 6:27-28   68. Judges 6:34
66. Judges 6:31   69. Ibid.
67. Clarke, *Bible Commentary*, Vol. 2, p. 131

While they were gathering, however, Gideon began to feel the weight of responsibility connected with this venture. Was he leading his brethren into a conflict which might turn out to be a death trap and a massacre? Militarily speaking, Gideon was outnumbered four to one. He therefore asked the Lord to bolster his confidence with an additional confirmation of a God-guaranteed victory. So Gideon prayed to the Lord and said, "If thou wilt save Israel by mine hand, as thou hast said, Behold, I will put a fleece of wool in the floor; and if the dew be on the fleece only, and it be dry upon all the earth beside, then shall I know that thou wilt save Israel by mine hand, as thou hast said."[70]

It is obvious that the valiant courage which had surged in Gideon while the Spirit of the Lord rested upon him was not nearly so strong when he was left unto himself. Somehow there was a lonely, empty feeling of incompetence and inadequacy. Instinctively, he was reaching for the iron rod of God's word to support him, or a manifestation of God's power to bolster him.

The next morning Gideon rose early to examine the fleece. Sure enough, the fleece was sodden wet while all around the ground was dry. Gideon wrung a whole bowl full of water from the fleece. But dealing with God was such a new experience for Gideon that he felt the need for just one more proof that this was not a mere coincidence. Therefore he took it upon himself to approach the Lord once more. Said he, "Let not thine anger be hot against me, and I will speak but this once: let me prove, I pray thee, but this once with the fleece; let it now be dry only upon the fleece, and upon all the ground let there be dew."[71]

Apparently the Lord was not offended by this additional request, for the next morning Gideon found everything exactly as he had requested. The fleece was dry while the ground all around was soaked with heavy dew. This was enough. At last Gideon was ready to gird up and go.

GIDEON'S BATTLE WITH THE MIDIANITES

The valley of Jezreel rises upward from the Jordan River toward the west where it passes over a summit and opens

---

70. Judges 6:36-37   71. Judges 6:39

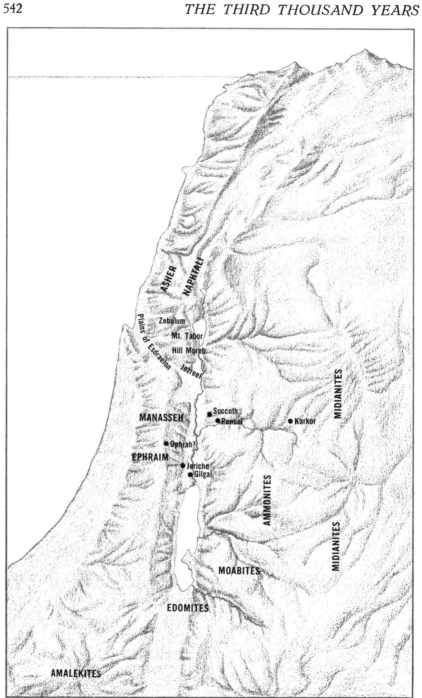

onto the plain of Esdraelon. Where the two come together stands Mount Moreh. It rises 900 feet from the valley floor and looks down like a giant sentinel upon the fertile fields of Jezreel and the receding vista of Esdraelon. The scripture makes it plain that the Midianites had not camped in the valley of Jezreel but had passed around Mount Moreh and camped on its northern side in that bay of Esdraelon which sweeps in between Mount Moreh and Mount Tabor.[72] This therefore left the valley of Jezreel unoccupied and was the logical place for Gideon to set up his camp. He chose a spot part way up the valley called the well of Harod.

However, at this juncture, the Lord said to Gideon, "The people that are with thee are too many for me to give the Midianites into their hands, lest Israel vaunt themselves against me, saying, Mine own hand hath saved me. Now therefore go to, proclaim in the ears of the people, saying, Whosoever is fearful and afraid, let him return and depart early from Mount Gilead."[73]

Being outnumbered four to one, it was not difficult to find the majority of these Israelites honestly admitting that they were approaching this battle with fear and trembling. Consequently, 22,000 departed, leaving Gideon with 10,000.[74]

"And the Lord said unto Gideon, The people are yet too many; bring them down unto the water, and I will try them for thee there. . . ."[75]

When the soldiers came down to the spring to drink, Gideon was told to pick out any who scooped up the water and drank by "putting their hand to their mouth."[76] Since nearly all men lie prone upon the ground or get down on their knees to drink from a stream, the number who drank from their cupped hands was small indeed—only 300. And that is precisely what the Lord wanted, just a few hundred. So another 9,700 Israelites were released to go home, and Gideon retained the remnant that was now left.

---

72. Judges 7:1
73. Judges 7:2-3 Authorities point out that Mount Gilboa near the well of Harod is meant here instead of Mount Gilead. Mount Gilead is clear over on the other side of Jordan.
74. Ibid.
75. Judges 7:4
76. Judges 7:6

Gideon then appears to have taken his 300 companions and ascended the heights of Mount Moreh. This would permit them to look into the next valley (the plain of Esdraelon) where the Midianites were camped. The scripture says "the host of Midian was beneath him in the valley."[77] On the far side of this valley or plain was Mount Tabor, so this would mean that Gideon was going to engage the Midianites in exactly the same locale where the famous battle was waged against Sisera by Deborah and Barak.

The scripture states that when Gideon gazed down upon the camp of the enemy it was anything but a comforting view. It says, "And the Midianites and the Amalekites and all the children of the east lay along in the valley like grasshoppers for multitude; and their camels were without number, as the sand by the sea-side for multitude."[78]

When it was dark the Lord commanded Gideon to prepare to attack. In view of the fact that he only had 300 men, this command seemed to border on the ridiculous. The Lord told Gideon that if he were afraid, he should take his servant, Phurah, and go down to the edge of the Midianite camp where he could hear what they were saying among themselves. Apparently Gideon was well aware of his own apprehensions and knew the Lord must be aware of them also, therefore he unashamedly took his servant and crept down to the valley floor where the tents of the enemy were pitched. Outside one of these tents Gideon was able to hear two men talking. One said he had a dream in which he saw a cake of common barley bread fall in among their army and it had knocked a tent flat upon the ground. His companion viewed the dream with alarm, saying, "This is nothing else save the sword of Gideon the son of Joash, a man of Israel: for into his hand hath God delivered Midian, and all the host."[79] When Gideon heard this he bowed his head and worshipped. He and his servant promptly climbed back up the mount and said to the men of Israel, "Arise, for the Lord hath delivered into your hand the host of Midian."[80]

Apparently, the Lord had told Gideon exactly what procedure to follow, so he divided his men into three groups of

77. Judges 7:8   79. Judges 7:14
78. Judges 7:12   80. Judges 7:15

100 each. Then each man was given a pitcher or jar containing a lighted lamp. He was also given a trumpet. The three groups of 100 each were directed to proceed to certain strategic positions around the area where the fighting men of the Midianites had pitched their tents. All of this was done under cover of darkness and when Gideon was certain that all were in their assigned places he blew a shrill blast on his war trumpet. Immediately all the Israelites did as they had been instructed. They broke their pitchers so the light of their lamps could be seen. Holding them aloft, each man blew his trumpet and then shouted, "The sword of the Lord, and of Gideon."[81]

The sleeping Midianites and all their allies awakened amidst the wild cries of alarm from their own watch. In the darkness there was pandemonium. It was impossible to tell who was friend and who was foe. The panic of a mob engulfed the army of the Midianites and all their federated allies. They charged into the darkness, scrambling and groping their way around Mount Moreh, and finally as daylight approached they hurried on down the valley of Jezreel and then pushed along the west bank of the Jordan toward the fords near old Jericho. This was the nearest escape route back to their own country.

Gideon made no attempt to become involved in combat. Instead, he sent messengers in every direction to arouse the Israelies to pursue the fleeing enemy. The men of Naphtali, Asher and Manasseh had been released by Gideon the day before because of their fear, but when they learned that the powerful Midianite federation had abandoned their camp and were at that moment racing madly toward home, these Israelites took courage and raced right after them.

However, Gideon hit upon another stratagem which really saved the day. While the Midianites were going the long way round to reach the fords of Gilgal, Gideon sent messengers directly into Mount Ephraim which overlooked Gilgal. Everywhere they cried out to the Ephraimites, "Come down against the Midianites, and take before them the waters unto Beth-barah and Jordan."[82] The Ephraimites responded

---

81. Judges 7:20   82. Judges 7:24

en masse. They reached the fords of Jordan in time to cut off the hosts of Midian and once the battle was joined a furious slaughter ensued. The scripture says that when it was over the dead among the Midianite hosts totaled 120,000.[83] The two princes of Midian were captured and slain. One was named Oreb who was slain upon a rock which afterwards bore his name. The other prince was named Zeeb who was caught and killed near a winepress which thereafter bore his name.[84]

The princes of Ephraim cut off the heads of Oreb and Zeeb and prepared to proceed to Ophrah and present Gideon with these ghoulish trophies along with their report on the outcome of the battle.

GIDEON CAPTURES KING ZEBAH AND KING ZALMUNNA

Meanwhile Gideon had troubles of his own. With what appears to have been a much smaller fighting force, Gideon traced the flight of the two kings of Midian, named Zebah and Zalmunna, who had engineered the conquest of Israel. These two kings had rallied a force of 15,000 men and separated themselves from the rest of their fleeing army. Instead of proceeding down the west side of Jordan to the river crossing in Gilgal, they had used the upper fords at the mouth of the valley of Jezreel and crossed over into the eastern mountains of Trans-Jordan.

As soon as Gideon had led his own men across the Jordan he stopped off at nearby Succoth to get supplies. He said to the leaders of the city, "Give, I pray you, loaves of bread unto the people that follow me; for they be faint, and I am pursuing after Zebah and Zalmunna, kings of Midian."[85] But the leaders of Succoth were contemptuous of Gideon and treated him as though he were unworthy of any help until he had actually won the victory. Gideon was filled with wrath. Here were some of the very people for whom his armies were fighting treating him as an enemy and refusing to give aid. Gideon swore in the presence of these men that he would not forget their treasonable conduct and he would deal with them on his return. He then pushed on further

---

83. Judges 8:10   85. Judges 8:5
84. Judges 7:25

to Penuel and made the same appeal. However, they, too, refused to help. Gideon said, "When I come again in peace, I will break down this tower," meaning the defenses of their city. He left notice that he intended to avenge their impudence.[86]

Gideon carried his campaign to the gates of Karkor where the Midianite kings had fled, and was eventually successful in destroying this remnant of the Midianite army. King Zebah and King Zalmunna were both captured alive and Gideon carried them back to Ophrah. On the way, however, he stopped off at Succoth and Penuel. At Succoth Gideon encountered a young man outside the city walls just before daybreak, and he obtained from the youth the identity of the seventy princes of Succoth. Gideon then marched into the city, seized these seventy treacherous leaders and had them flogged with thorn bushes.[87] He then went up to Penuel where he apparently met with some resistance, so he smashed down their watchtower and other defenses and destroyed the "men of the city" who had refused to aid their brethren in their hour of desperate need.[88]

Gideon then proceeded to Ophrah with his two royal captives. Not only had these two kings been responsible for the woes of the Israelites during many long years of suffering but Gideon had a personal score to settle with them. He had the two kings brought before him and said, "What manner of men were they whom ye slew at Tabor? And they answered, As thou art, so were they; each one resembled the children of a king."[89]

The scripture does not give us the slightest hint as to when this crime took place. It would appear that it must have been incidental to the setting up of the Midianite camp between Mount Moreh and Mount Tabor. In any event it is clear that the Midianites had killed a group of Israelites near Mount Tabor. Gideon promptly identified the victims of this ruthless act by saying, "They were my brethren, even the sons of my mother: as the Lord liveth, if ye had saved them alive, I would not slay you."[90]

---

86. Judges 8:9
87. Judges 8:15-16
88. Judges 8:17

89. Judges 8:18
90. Judges 8:19

Then Gideon turned to his oldest son, Jether, and said, "Up, and slay them." But Jether hesitated and the scripture says he drew not his sword "for he feared, because he was yet a youth."[91]

The two Midianite kings recognized that Gideon was trying to inure his son to the hardships and terrors of war, and so they said to the youth, "Rise thou, and fall upon us: for as the man is, so is his strength." But Jether could not bring himself to do it. So the scripture says, "Gideon arose, and slew Zebah and Zalmunna. . . ."[92]

GIDEON REFUSES TO BE THE KING OF ISRAEL

It would appear that it was about this time that the princes of Ephraim arrived from the great battle at the fords of Jordan. Not only had they destroyed 120,000 of the enemy but they had in hand the heads of Oreb and Zeeb. In the hour of their great victory, the Ephraimites could not resist chiding Gideon for taking on so great a venture without their help. Said they, "Why hast thou served us thus, that thou calledst us not, when thou wentest to fight with the Midianites?"[93] By this they meant that Gideon should have called in the Ephraimites at the very beginning instead of waiting until he had accidentally — so they thought — and by some undeserved good fortune put the enemy to rout.

However, Gideon knew that a soft answer turneth away wrath, and so, in the most conciliatory manner, he said to them, "God hath delivered into your hands the princes of Midian, Oreb and Zeeb: and what was I able to do in comparison of you?" Gideon could have vaunted before them the heads of two kings instead of two princes but he chose a course which is characteristic of great leaders. He deprecated his own achievements and lauded those who had faithfully followed his orders. The Ephraimites immediately caught the humble spirit of this man and the scripture says "their anger was abated toward him."[94]

In fact, the more the princes of Ephraim and the leaders of the other tribes thought about it, the more they felt the

---

91. Judges 8:20   93. Judges 8:1
92. Judges 8:21   94. Judges 8:3

need to have a king for Israel. And who could better serve them in such a capacity than this noble fellow from Ophrah? So the leaders of Israel said to Gideon, "Rule thou over us, both thou, and thy son, and thy son's son also: for thou hast delivered us from the hand of Midian."[95]

Gideon was being offered an hereditary monarchy which is the highest earthy honor men can confer upon one another. But Gideon was quick to give his reply. Said he, "I will not rule over you, neither shall my son rule over you: the Lord shall rule over you."[96]

However, Gideon did have one request to make of these princes. He asked that he be allowed to have the ear-rings which they had taken from the people of Midian. "And they answered, We will willingly give them. And they spread a garment, and did cast therein every man the ear-rings of his prey. And the weight of the golden ear-rings that he requested was a thousand and seven hundred shekels of gold. . . ."[97]

The record is clear that it was not the purpose of Gideon to make himself rich with this gold, but rather to make a gift to the Lord. However, many generations of apostasy had confused their understanding of God and the way in which men might best serve him. Gideon reflected this in attempting to honor the Lord by making a very rich priestly garment or ephod of gold. It was the procedure followed by the heathens in honoring their gods. It apparently did not occur to Gideon that this might not be the way to honor the God of Israel. As it turned out, this priestly garment was so magnificent that the people came to worship it instead of the Lord in whose honor and glory it had been made. Thus, the scripture says, it became a "snare unto Gideon, and to his house."[98]

Except for this one somber note, however, the life of Gideon appears to have proceeded along a pleasant and peaceful path. In fact the whole land now had peace for forty years.[99]

---

95. Judges 8:22
96. Judges 8:23
97. Judges 8:25-26

98. Judges 8:27
99. Judges 8:28

During all of this time Gideon raised up a numerous posterity. He had several wives and to these were born a total of seventy sons.[100] The number of daughters is not given. Fortunately, Gideon died before one of these sons went politically beserk and murdered sixty-eight of his brothers. But that is another story—the story of Abimelech—which must wait for another chapter.

---

100. Judges 8:30

Scripture Reading and Questions on Chapter Twenty-Three

Scripture Reading Assignment: Judges, chapters 1 to 8.

1—Why is the title to the Book of Judges misleading? What would be a more appropriate title?

2—What was there about the worship of idols which became such a source of corruption to ancient peoples, including the people of Israel?

3—Othniel had a famous relative, who was he? What tribe did Othniel belong to? Which invaders did he overthrow?

4—From which direction did the next invasion come? Recount briefly how Ehud killed King Eglon and overthrew the Moabites.

5—Why is Shamgar called a "one-man army?" Who did he attack?

6—What part of Israel did King Jabin conquer? Where was his headquarters?

7—What is indicated to you by the fact that Deborah—"a mother in Israel"—had to be the leader in overthrowing King Jabin?

8—Where did the battle against Sisera and the forces of King Jabin take place? What happened to Sisera's chariots?

9—How did King Jabin know the Israelites were assembling at Mount Tabor? What was the nationality of Heber?

10—What woman met Sisera when he fled to the tent of Heber? Whose side was she on? What happened to Sisera?

11—After the great victory of Deborah and Barak did the people of Israel reform and thereafter seek to become a righteous people?

12—How were the Midianites related to Israel? How were the Amalekites related to Israel? Why did both of these people attack Israel?

13—To which tribe did Gideon belong? Why did he have to thresh his grain secretly?

14—Did the Lord's messenger who appeared to Gideon come in glory? Would this be confusing? What did Gideon do about it?

15—Relate what happened when Gideon smashed his father's heathen altar.

16—How large an enemy did Gideon face at Mount Moreh? How many Israelites did he have? Did the Lord say he needed more?

17—Recount the device which Gideon used to put the Midianites to flight.

18—Who cut off the Midianites at the fords of the Jordan? How many did they slay? Why were they afterwards angry with Gideon? Did he appease them?

19—What military role did Gideon play in the overthrow of the Midianites?

20—What happened when the people asked Gideon to be their king?

CHAPTER TWENTY-FOUR

From Abimelech to Samson

Public acclaim is a fickle mistress. No one learns this more painfully than military heroes. When the very existence of a nation is at stake those who rise to put down the enemy usually receive the accolades and adulation of the populace, but let the crisis pass and the hero's glory fades like a gossamer phantom into the receding past. It was so with Israel's Gideon.

The scriptures say "as soon as Gideon was dead, that the children of Israel turned again" and once more became an unrighteous and ungrateful people.[1] "Neither shewed they kindness to the house of Jerubbaal, namely, Gideon, according to all the goodness which he had shewed unto Israel."[2] Nevertheless, Gideon had left behind him seventy sons, and from these there might have been built a sanctuary of righteousness which could have leavened all of Israel.

But it was not to be. Among those seventy sons was a man with avaricious political ambitions and a murderous heart.

THE SEIZURE OF POWER BY ABIMELECH

During his lifetime, Gideon had married several wives and concubines. One of the concubines was a "maid-servant" from Shechem. We are told nothing about this woman except that when she gave birth to a son she endowed him with a most pretentious name. She called him Abimelech which means "my father is king," or "my father hath reigned."[3] Any mother who would give such a name to a son could be expected to nurture in him a consuming ambition for power. As Abimelech reached maturity he reflected such an upbringing. Instead of possessing the normal aspirations of life, Abimelech exhibited a burning passion for power which bordered on insanity.

---

1. Judges 8:33
2. Judges 8:35

3. Clarke, *Bible Commentary*, Vol. 2, p. 139

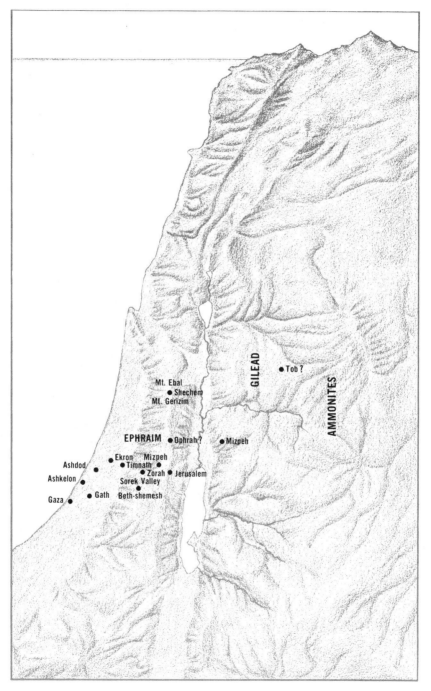

GILEAD

● Tob ?

AMMONITES

Mt. Ebal
● Shechem
Mt. Gerizim

EPHRAIM ● Ophrah ?   ● Mizpeh

Ashdod   ● Ekron   Mizpeh
Ashkelon ● Timnath ●
         ● Zorah ● Jerusalem
         Sorek Valley
Gaza ●   ● Gath   Beth-shemesh

He began his political career by arousing all of his mother's family — apparently called the "house of Millo"[4] — to support him in becoming the king of all Israel. Abimelech pretended that if he did not ascend to this high office then the other sixty-nine sons of Gideon would divide Israel among them and chaos would surely result. "And his mother's brethren spake of him in the ears of all the men of Shechem all these words: and their hearts inclined to follow Abimelech; for they said, He is our brother."[5]

Therefore, just as it was with Cain and his brethren who murdered to get gain and seize political power, so it was now with Abimelech and his secret combination of maternal relatives. They had planned their work and now they intended to work their plan.

First, they looted the sanctuary of their own heathen temple[6] and obtained the money to hire a band of "vain and light persons" to serve as an army of mercenary cutthroats. With these they intended to implement in practical terms their violent venture to make Abimelech the new king.

The first conquest of this band was at Ophrah, headquarters of Gideon's family. Abimelech's raiding party swept down on the hapless community and rounded up all of Gideon's sons. In the confusion Gideon's youngest son, Jotham, managed to hide himself and thereby escape; however, all of the other sixty-eight sons were dragged to a certain place and there Abimelech "slew his brethren . . . upon one stone."[7] By this brutal, fratricidal slaughter Abimelech hoped to make himself the uncontested king of Israel, and the people of Shechem so interpreted it. The scripture says, "And all the men of Shechem gathered together, and all the house of Millo, and went, and made Abimelech king, by the plain of the pillar that was in Shechem."[8]

---

4. Judges 9:6
5. Judges 9:3
6. Judges 9:4
7. Judges 9:5—Since Judges 8:30 says Gideon had a total of seventy sons, it would appear that only sixty-eight were actually killed (Abimelech and Jotham being excluded). Nevertheless this account always uses the round number of seventy when referring to the number who were slain.
8. Judges 9:6

The Parable of Jotham

The city of Shechem lies in a valley between Mount Ebal on the north and Mount Gerizim on the south. When Jotham, Gideon's youngest son, heard that Abimelech had been crowned king by the people of Shechem, he climbed upon Mount Gerizim and after gaining the attention of all the people, told them a parable.

Some students may wonder if it were possible to talk to a whole community from the top of this high hill or mountain. Gerizim rises 800 feet above the valley floor and from such a height a strange acoustical phenomenon often occurs. People standing below can clearly distinguish the words of normal conversation. Only recently this author stood on top of the Pyramid of the Sun near Mexico City and was surprised to find that words spoken clearly but without strain could be heard by friends standing on the ground several blocks away from the foot of the pyramid. A like phenomenon may have occurred as Jotham stood 800 feet above the city and told his parable.

He said that once upon a time the trees decided to have a king appointed over them. However, none of the fruitful trees would accept the crown because they felt there should be equality among the trees and not have one ruling over the rest. Even the vine was invited to rule, but it also refused. Finally the kingmakers asked the miserable bramble bush to reign over the trees and the bramble consented providing they would put their complete trust in him and obey his every command. If they did not obey he said he would send out a fire which would consume all the trees, including the magnificent cedars of Lebanon.[9]

To appreciate this parable it must be recalled that Gideon had been invited to be king but had declined. He had also said that none of his sons would be king. So Jotham applied his parable to Shechem. Said he, "For my father fought for you, and adventured his life far, and delivered you out of the hand of Midian. And ye are risen up against my father's house this day, and have slain his sons . . . upon one stone, and have made Abimelech, the son of his maid servant, king

---

9. Judges 9:8-15

over the men of Shechem, because he is your brother."[10]
Jotham predicted that because of their wicked aspirations
they had appointed an unworthy bramble bush son to be
their king. He told them that before they were through they
would want to destroy Abimelech and he would try to
consume them.[11]

Having finished his parable, Jotham ran quickly and
hid himself lest the men of Shechem find him and slay him.[12]

The scripture says Abimelech reigned for three years
but it is obvious that his influence never extended much
further than the environs of Shechem. When the three years
had passed the prophecy of Jotham began to be fulfilled.

By this time Abimelech was living at Arumah[13] while his
servant Zebul ruled over Shechem.[14] In Shechem there were
beginning to be signs of an insurrection against Abimelech.
This was being sparked by Gaal the son of Ebed who is
believed to have been a Canaanite since he speaks of wanting
to restore the ancient Canaanite government of Hamor.[15]

News of the plot leaked out as a result of Gaal getting
drunk with his companions at the heathen temple in Shechem.
Gaal fell to boasting what the men of Shechem would do to
Abimelech and his servant Zebul as soon as they seized
power. When Abimelech heard about the plot he came rushing down with his army and completely destroyed the followers of Gaal. He then "took the city and slew the people
that was therein, and beat down the city, and sowed it with
salt."

During the last stages of the siege he found that a
thousand men and women had hidden in the "hold" of the
heathen temple.[16] This was both a shrine and a fortress.
Archaeologists have now uncovered what is believed to be
the remnants of this massive structure. It had walls fifteen
feet thick and the building was cloistered in a heavily pro-

---

10. Judges 9:17-18
11. Judges 9:20
12. Judges 9:21
13. Judges 9:41
14. Judges 9:30
15. Judges 9:28—For a discussion of this point see Clarke, *Bible Commentary*, Vol.
    2, p. 144.
16. Judges 9:46

tected courtyard.[17] It could have easily accommodated 1,000 persons. The scripture says that when Abimelech was unable to get inside of the "hold" of the temple-fortress, he built a huge fire all around it and with flames and fumes killed all who were within it, thereby literally fulfilling Jotham's prophecy.

Not content with this scorched-earth policy against Shechem, he stormed the city of Thebez which apparently had joined the insurrection. During the siege the people climbed into a tower or fortress connected with the city and when Abimelech charged up to it with the intent of using fire to destroy the inmates, a woman took her household millstone (usually weighing around 25 pounds) and cast it down from the tower on Abimelech's head.

It appears to have struck him a glancing blow which fractured his skull but left him conscious. Abimelech may have actually seen the woman throw the millstone at him; at least he knew he had been struck by a woman. Therefore the scripture says, "Then he called hastily unto the young man his armour bearer, and said unto him, Draw thy sword and slay me, that men say not of me, A woman slew him. And his young man thrust him through, and he died. And when the men of Israel saw that Abimelech was dead, they departed every man unto his place."[18]

So the prophecies of Jotham were literally fulfilled. Abimelech had consumed Shechem and the insurrectionists, and they, in turn, had destroyed Abimelech. The scripture says, "Thus God rendered the wickedness of Abimelech, which he did unto his father, in slaying his seventy brethren."[19] All of which illustrates the age-old lesson of history: crime pays — but not for long.

THE DAYS OF TOLA AND JAIR

The next important defender of Israel was Tola, the son of Puah, the son of Dodo, a man of Issachar. This is the only man of Issachar who rose to prominence during the dark ages of Israel. We know nothing of this man except that

---

17. See McGraw-Hill, *World of the Bible*, Vol. 2, p. 94
18. Judges 9:54-55
19. Judges 9:56. As previously pointed out, this number should be sixty-eight.

Israel looked to him for protection for twenty-three years. He was followed by Jair, a Gileadite, which means he was a native of Trans-Jordan. He provided leadership against the enemies of Israel twenty-two years. All we know of this man is that he had thirty sons and gave each one of them a village in the land of Gilead.

After these two protectors were gone, the Israelites "did evil again in the sight of the Lord, and served Baalim, and Ashtaroth, and the gods of Syria, and the gods of Zidon, and the gods of Moab, and the gods of the children of Ammon, and the gods of the Philistines. . . ."[20]

But, as always, they paid the bitter penalty. This time it was eighteen years of conquest and oppression under the harsh cruelty of a two-pronged attack consisting of the Ammonites moving in from the east and the Philistines attacking from the west.[21]

It will be recalled that the Ammonites were descendants of Lot and they made their home in the highlands east of the Dead Sea. These people had grown into a great multitude and were probably among the "children of the east" who had fought against Gideon.[22] But Gideon's success in dealing with the Ammonites was a formula the Israelites were no longer able to duplicate. The scripture says, "Moreover the children of Ammon passed over Jordan to fight also against Judah, and against Benjamin, and against the house of Ephraim; so that Israel was sore distressed."[23]

However, when the children of Israel cried out in anguish the word of the Lord came (probably through a prophet or one of the priests) saying, "Did not I deliver you from the Egyptians, and from the Amorites, from the children of Ammon, and from the Philistines? [meaning, of course, on earlier occasions]. . . . Yet ye have forsaken me, and served other gods: wherefore I will deliver you no more. Go and cry unto the gods which ye have chosen; let them deliver you in the time of your tribulation."[24]

---

20. Judges 10:6
21. Judges 10:7
22. Judges 6:3

23. Judges 10:9
24. Judges 10:11-14

The afflicted Israelites pleaded with the Lord to give them one more chance. They "put away the strange gods from among them, and served the Lord. . . ." However, barely had they launched their project of reform when word came that a mighty host of Ammonites was marching into Israel's Trans-Jordan territory of Gilead. The leaders of Israel gathered at Mizpeh in Trans-Jordan (there was another Mizpeh west of the Jordan) and said one to another, "What man is he that will begin to fight against the children of Ammon? he shall be head over all the inhabitants of Gilead."[25] When no prince of Gilead arose to the occasion, the leaders finally agreed that they would have to turn to a certain Jephthah who was a "man of valour" but who had been ignored up to this time primarily because they rated him a social outcast. However, faced with imminent disaster they felt the need to stop quibbling over petty protocol.

THE RISE OF JEPHTHAH

Jephthah had the misfortune of being born to a mother who was a tavern keeper. The English Bible says she was a "harlot." The original Hebrew does not say she was a harlot, but this is the word the King James translators elected to use in describing her.[26] As we have mentioned earlier, the word *zonah* means "hostess" or "keeper of an inn" and in the absence of a specific reference to immoral conduct it is not believed the translators were justified in presuming it. Nevertheless, the mother of Jephthah was a woman of a lower element and perhaps of some separate Semitic people. Therefore, his brothers had ejected Jephthah from the family residence many years before, saying to him "Thou shalt not inherit in our father's house; for thou art the son of a strange woman. Then Jephthah fled from his brethren and dwelt in the land of Tob. . . ."[27]

While there he had gathered a band of soldiers of fortune around him and his exploits soon gave him the reputation of being a "man of valour."[28] It was this very reputation which now drew the leaders of Israel toward Jephthah. Both his brothers who had mistreated him and

25. Judges 10:18
26. Clarke, *Bible Commentary*, Vol. 2, p. 149
27. Judges 11:2-3
28. Judges 11:1

the princes of Israel who previously hated him, joined forces to beg that he return home and take over as commander-in-chief. Said they, "Come, and be our captain, that we may fight with the children of Ammon."[29] Jephthah was so astonished at this sudden turn of events that he challenged them, saying, "Did not ye hate me, and expel me out of my father's house? and why are ye come unto me now when ye are in distress?"[30]

However, his former antagonists were completely penitent; they had not come to quarrel but to plead for needed leadership. They replied, ". . . we turn again to thee now, that thou mayest go with us, and fight against the children of Ammon, and be our head over all the inhabitants of Gilead."[31] This last phrase was extremely significant. They were offering him the government of Gilead if he would only rescue them from the further oppression of Ammon.

Jephthah finally consented. He accompanied them back to Mizpeh and was there acclaimed the new leader — first by the elders of Trans-Jordan and then by the people.[32]

JEPHTHAH COMMUNICATES WITH THE KING OF THE AMMONITES

Like Moses of old, Jephthah was primarily a peace maker; therefore the first thing he did was to send messengers to the king of the Ammonites asking why they were continually oppressing the children of Israel.

In order to find an excuse for the Ammonite depredations during the past eighteen years, the king of the Ammonites had to go back three hundred years to the time when Moses was bringing the hosts of Israel out of the wilderness. The king said the reason for the present war was "because Israel took away my land, when they came up out of Egypt. . . . now therefore restore those lands again peaceably."[33]

Jephthah immediately sent back an answer. He told the king that never at any time had the Israelites taken land away from the Ammonites. He gave the king a brief history lesson,

29. Judges 11:6
30. Judges 11:7
31. Judges 11:8
32. Judges 11:10-11
33. Judges 11:13

reminding him that by the time Israel came up out of the wilderness the Ammonites had already been driven from their land by the Amorites. What Israel did was to conquer the Amorites and seize the land from them. Jephthah pointed out that what God had given the Israelites through a victory over the Amorites belonged to Israel. Jephthah then challenged the king by saying that if Chemosh, the god of the Ammonites, wanted the Ammonites to have this land, why hadn't he done something about it during the past 300 years? Obviously, Jephthah argued, even Chemosh knew that Israel held this territory legally!

To this the king of the Ammonites had no rational reply, so he answered by force of arms.

"Then the Spirit of the Lord came upon Jephthah and . . . he passed over unto the children of Ammon.

"And Jephthah vowed a vow unto the Lord, and said, If thou shalt without fail deliver the children of Ammon into mine hands, Then it shall be that whatsoever cometh forth of the doors of my house to meet me, when I return in peace from the children of Ammon, shall surely be the Lord's, and I will offer it up for a burnt-offering."[34]

Great difficulty has grown out of this passage. In its present form Jephthah is vowing to sacrifice "whatsoever" comes forth to greet him when he returns. Such a vow is completely illogical. Jephthah would realize that whoever or whatever came out to meet him would in all likelihood be a person rather than a domestic animal and therefore not lawful for a sacrificial offering. The vow, as stated, does violence to the known circumstances.

Some leading authorities believe that a single letter was inaccurately copied in the original Hebrew text and, if so, it would change the entire meaning of this passage. It is their belief that the original meaning was as follows: "Whatsoever cometh forth of the door of my house to meet me — shall be the Lords; and I will offer HIM [not "it"] a burnt offering." In other words Jephthah is saying that whoever comes to greet him when he returns home will be dedicated to the service of the Tabernacle (as later happened to Samuel),

---

34. Judges 11:29-31

and in addition, Jephthah vowed he would make a burnt offering of thanksgiving to the Lord.[35] As we shall see in a moment, this version fits in perfectly with subsequent developments whereas the King James version does not.

JEPHTHAH IS VICTORIOUS OVER THE AMMONITES

"So Jephthah passed over unto the children of Ammon to fight against them; and the Lord delivered them into his hands. And he smote them from Aroer, even till thou come to Minnith, even twenty cities, and unto the plain of the vineyards, with a very great slaughter. Thus the children of Ammon were subdued before the children of Israel."[36]

After this great victory was consummated, Jephthah returned home in triumph. Naturally no one would be more proud of him than his own family and so when Jephthah neared his residence, his only child—a daughter—came forth to meet him "with timbrels and with dances."[37]

"And it came to pass, when he saw her, that he rent his clothes, and said, Alas, my daughter! thou hast brought me very low, and thou art one of them that trouble me: for I have opened my mouth unto the Lord, and I cannot go back."[38]

This suddent complication did not disturb the daughter nearly so much as it did her father. She said, "My father, if thou hast opened thy mouth unto the Lord, do to me according to that which hath proceeded out of thy mouth; forasmuch as the Lord hath taken vengeance for thee of thine enemies, even of the children of Ammon."[39]

At this point Jephthah apparently explained to her that he had committed her to the service of the Lord and he assumed that this would necessarily involve the giving up of any prospective marriage. That this was precisely the way the daughter understood this vow is reflected in her next statement. Said she, "Let this thing be done for me; let me alone two months, that I may go up and down upon the mountains and bewail my virginity, I and my fellows.

---

35. Clarke, *Bible Commentary*, Vol. 2, p. 151
36. Judges 11:32-33
37. Judges 11:34
38. Judges 11:35
39. Judges 11:36

"And he said, Go. And he sent her away for two months: and she went with her companions, and bewailed her virginity upon the mountains."[40]

Note that she did not bewail the fact that she was going to die but simply that she would be required to forfeit marriage and the raising of a family.

"And it came to pass at the end of two months, that she returned unto her father, who did with her according to his vow which he had vowed: and she knew no man."[41]

This passage seems to make it perfectly clear that Jephthah's vow did not require his daughter to give up her life as some have suggested. The main issue in all of these passages is simply the daughter's virginity. It should be recognized that the only reason this passage has been interpreted to mean that the daughter was offered as a human sacrifice is to accommodate verse 31. But since that verse is believed to have had an entirely different meaning in its original form, this straining of the scripture is not really necessary. Certainly, from Jephthah, who is expressly described as having been blessed with the Spirit of the Lord we could expect more common sense than some have attributed to him. No true servant of the Lord would commit an abomination against God expecting that this would satisfy a vow to God. This alone should signal the fact that something is seriously wrong with verse 31 in our modern version.

A Civil War Breaks Out in Israel

Barely had Jephthah returned home from his victory over the Ammonites when he found himself confronted by a new kind of war.

By conquering the Ammonites Jephthah had been made the leader of all of the Israelites east of the Jordan. Suddenly, however, he found the Ephraimites from west of the Jordan coming up against him with a great force. Their complaint was that Jephthah had taken military action against their common enemy without giving the Ephraimites the privilege of participating. Said they:

40. Judges 11:37-38
41. Judges 11:39

"Wherefore passedst thou over to fight against the children of Ammon and didst not call us to go with thee? we will burn thine house upon thee with fire."[42]

At this point one cannot help wondering why it would make the Ephraimites so angry to be left out of the conflict. The Bible does not give the specific reason but more than likely it was because of the spoils involved. For eighteen years the Ammonites had been stealing from all of the tribes in southern Israel and now that they had been beaten the matter of dividing the spoils would loom large in the minds of the Ephraimites. They appeared to feel that Jephthah had cheated them by not giving them a chance to participate in the campaign and thereby get their fair share.

But Jephthah had a complaint of his own. Said he:

"I and my people were at great strife with the children of Ammon; and when I called you, ye delivered me not out of their hands. And when I saw that ye delivered me not, I put my life in my hands, and passed over against the children of Ammon, and the Lord delivered them into my hand: wherefore then are ye come up unto me this day, to fight against me?"[43]

This charge put the Ephraimites in a very defensive position. It looked as though they had neglected their duty when Jephthah had called for help, but after he had fought the Ammonites against great odds and God had delivered the enemy into his hands, then these greedy Ephraimites wanted to come forward and claim a share of the spoils. It was obvious that Jephthah considered them the offenders, not he.

The Ephraimites had no logical answer for Jephthah and so they did what people with criminal intentions usually do. They answered with force and violence. The Ephraimites made a proclamation that hereafter all Israelites on the east side of Jordan would be considered "fugitives of Ephraim,"[44] which meant they could be destroyed on sight.

Jephthah therefore mobilized the Israelites of Trans-Jordan (called the people of Gilead) and met the Ephraim-

---

42. Judges 12:1   44. Judges 12:4
43. Judges 12:2-3

ites head on. Not only did he match them in battle but he overwhelmed them so completely that few escaped and those who survived were scattered to the four winds. All the fleeing Ephraimites could do was to race toward the fords of the river in a frantic effort to cross over into their own territory. However, they found all of the Jordan crossings guarded and blocked by the soldiers of Jephthah.

The Ephraimites finally resorted to the stratagem of disguising themselves and pretending they were men of Gilead who merely wanted to cross the Jordan on business or to pursue the enemy. Concerning this development, the scripture says:

". . . when those Ephraimites which were escaped said, Let me go over; that the men of Gilead said unto them, Art thou an Ephraimite? If he said, Nay, then said they unto him, Say now Shibboleth [burden], and he said Sibboleth [without the 'Sh']: for he could not frame to pronounce it right. Then they took him, and slew him at the passage of Jordan."[45]

Thus the men of Gilead made fugitives of the Ephraimites instead of the Ephraimites making good their boast to run down and destroy the Gileadites. In this great civil war for which the scripture puts the blame squarely on Ephraim "there fell at that time of the Ephraimites forty and two thousand."[46]

The scripture concludes the story by saying that Jephthah only lived six years after his great victories, then he died.

THIRTY-SEVEN YEARS OF PEACE

In addition to the six years of peace which prevailed while Jephthah was alive, there were thirty-one additional years without serious oppression.

Following the death of Jephthah, it was Ibzan of Bethlehem who was looked to for protection. His period of leadership lasted seven years, but all we know about Ibzan is the fact that he had sixty children — thirty sons and thirty daughters — and that when he died he was buried in Bethlehem.[47]

---

45. Judges 12:6
46. Ibid.

47. Judges 12:9-10

Ibzan was followed by Elon, a Zebulonite, who functioned ten years as a leader.[48]

Then came Abdon, son of Hillel, who lived in Pirathon
of Ephraim. Here was another man with a large posterity.
The scripture specifically mentions his forty sons and thirty
nephews.[49]

However, it seems the Israelites were never able to maintain a semblance of stability for more than one generation.
When the thirty-seven years of peace had passed they once
more indulged themselves and "did evil again in the sight of
the Lord."[50] This time their corruption exposed them to the
military forays of the Philistines. These people were coming into their own as a nation and already they had driven
wedges into the Phoenician territory on the north and taken
outposts from the Egyptians on the south. It was inevitable
that someday their policies of expansion would bring them
into sharp collision with the Israelites on the east.

It appears that the Philistines finally made tributaries
out of all the tribes of Israel bordering their territory. This
included Judah, Simeon, Dan, Benjamin and Ephraim. But
it was the little tribe of Dan which took the brunt of the
Philistine assaults since the people of Dan lived on Israel's
western borders within sight of several cities belonging to
the Philistines. Furthermore, the tribe of Dan had settled
in the Sorek valley which was the main route of the highway
coming down from Jerusalem to the Mediterranean Sea. It
was therefore the logical route whenever the Philistines
marched inland. How often the people of Dan must have
lamented the fact that their forefathers had not cleansed the
land of the Philistines some 300 years earlier when the Lord
said he would help them do it!

But even though the tribe of Dan was exposed to the
most frequent assaults by the Philistines, nevertheless its
geographical location made it a logical place for the Lord to
commence a liberation movement. After forty years of Philistine oppression the Lord was ready to act.[51]

This then brings us to the story of Samson.

---

48. Judges 12:11-12
49. Judges 12:13-15

50. Judges 13:1
51. Ibid.

A FEW NOTES ON THE STORY OF SAMSON

Before presenting the biography of Samson it is important to understand the circumstances under which it was written. The student will find some statements in the scriptural account of Samson which are completely inconsistent with the rest of the scriptures. This is because Israel had just passed through three centuries of apostasy and we have learned from experience that periods of apostasy do not usually produce good historians. There is not the same sense of sacred responsibility associated with the keeping of records as that which prevails during a period when men are in close communication with God.

This point is especially evident when we compare the biography of Samson with that of Saul. Actually, the lives of these two men were very similar, but they are not written up the same. Both of them started out as favored servants of God. Both were extremely well-endowed physically. Both apostatized and betrayed their calling. Both committed suicide.

Nevertheless, the unknown writer who left us the history of Samson seemed anxious to present him as a great hero of Israel whom God favored in spite of his apostasy. The author may have thought that by taking this approach he was doing a favor to Samson. But it was certainly no favor to God. It made the Lord a partner to all the stupid antics of a wilful, defiant spirit who had abandoned his calling and betrayed his God.

In contrast to this, the biography of Saul was written at a time when inspired prophets of the Lord were back in the earth, and this account is far more discerning. It points out that the moment Saul apostatized and betrayed his calling, the spirit of God was offended and departed from him. His subsequent career, like that of Samson, led down the steep dark road toward failure and oblivion.

Keeping this point in mind will be helpful to the student who is reading the scriptural account of Samson for the first time. Had it been written up by a prophet of the Lord it undoubtedly would have been interpreted with deeper insight and therefore written in a framework similar to the biography of Saul. It would have emphasized that the Lord was never a partner in any man's sins even though that man may have started out as a servant of the Lord.

THE RISE OF SAMSON

Directly west of Jerusalem and about half-way to the Mediterranean Sea the mountains jut out from the central range in long, finger-like ridges. These overlook the lower levels of fertile, rolling hills as they gently fall away toward the maritime plain. On one of these ridges rising 2,000 feet above the sea, there used to be a city of Dan called Zorah. Nearby, and across the intervening valley of Sorek, was the more famous city of Beth-shemesh, and below, within clear sight, lay several of the properous and lecherous cities of the heathen Philistines. Each one of these Philistines cities paid homage to the monster-god, Dagon, and honored him with depraved, sensual rituals which had become notorious.

However, it was in Zorah that the Lord undertook to give Israel her new hope for freedom. The scripture says that during this particular time there lived in this highland community, a man named Manoah. He was married but his wife was barren. One day a messenger of the Lord came to Manoah's wife while she was alone and said:

"Behold now, thou art barren, and bearest not: but thou shalt conceive, and bear a son. Now therefore beware, I pray thee, and drink not wine nor strong drink, and eat not any unclean thing: for lo, thou shalt conceive, and bear a son; and no rasor shall come on his head: for the child shall be a Narazite unto God from the womb: and he shall begin to deliver Israel out of the hand of the Philistines."[52]

The messenger, we later learn, was like any ordinary man except that "his countenance was like the countenance of an angel of God, very terrible [or fearsome]."[53] The woman immediately ran and told her husband what had happened. She admitted being too excited to ask any questions: "I asked him not whence he was, neither told he me

52. Judges 13:3-5   53. Judges 13:6

his name."[54] The fact that he had promised her a son was the important thing. Manoah agreed. Nevertheless, he believed his wife should have gotten more details. Therefore he prayed fervently to the Lord, saying, "O my Lord, let the man of God which thou didst send come again unto us, and teach us what we shall do unto the child that shall be born."[55]

The Lord answered this prayer. Surprisingly, however, the messenger came back again when Manoah was absent. The scripture says "the man of God" appeared to the woman while she was alone in the field.[56] But this woman was determined that this time her husband should not miss the visitation so she left the messenger and ran quickly to find Manoah. After locating her husband she announcd excitedly, "Behold, the man hath appeared unto me, that came unto me the other day."[57] Manoah rose up and followed her quickly back into the field. He was relieved, no doubt, to find that the messenger was still there.

It was immediately apparent to Manoah that there was nothing particularly miraculous or angelic about this being. He seemed like any other man.[58] Manoah therefore said to him, "Art thou the man that spakest unto the woman?" The messenger replied, "I am." Manoah therefore asked to have the message repeated to him so he would know how to raise up this wonderful child which the man had promised. The messenger promptly repeated everything he had previously told Manoah's wife.

At this point Manoah felt he should detain the messenger long enough to run and prepare some refreshments for him. The scripture specifically says, "For Manoah knew not that he was an angel of the Lord."[59] But the messenger answered Manoah in a peculiar way, saying, "Though thou detain me, I will not eat of thy bread: and if thou wilt offer a burnt offering, thou must offer it unto the Lord."[60] Manoah was puzzled by the answer and therefore said, "What is thy name, that when thy sayings come to pass we may do thee honour?"

---

54. Ibid.
55. Judges 13:8
56. Judges 13:9
57. Judges 13:10

58. Judges 13:16
59. Ibid.
60. Ibid.

The angel answered abruptly, "Why askest thou thus after my name, seeing it is secret?"[61]

Somewhat abashed, Manoah said nothing more but went and obtained a young goat and some meal in order to make an offering as the man had suggested. The offering was made on one of the large flat rocks which so abundantly thrust themselves up from the ground in this area. Then something amazing happened. As the flames from this improvised altar ascended skyward the messenger suddenly arose and walked directly into the fire. Right before the eyes of the astonished man and woman the "angel of the Lord ascended in the flame of the altar."[62] It is likely that this messenger was a translated being and what he actually did was to manifest himself in glory at the last moment so that the brilliant light in which he ascended was not literally the flame of the sacrifice, for that would not be extensive, but rather the shaft of brilliant light which appeared above the altar and which received the messenger just as has happened to messengers of God on other occasions.[63]

The whole thing was so startling to Manoah that he not only concluded that this was an angel, but he decided that it must have been the Lord, Himself! He therefore fell flat on the ground and cried out, "We shall surely die, because we have seen God."[64] But now it was the wife who retained her good senses and calmly replied, "If the Lord were pleased to kill us, he would not have received a burnt offering and a meat [meal]-offering at our hands; neither would he have shewed us all these things, nor would as at this time have told us such things as these."[65]

Then the scripture continues, "And the woman bare a son, and called his name Samson: and the child grew, and the Lord blessed him. And the Spirit of the Lord began to move him at times in the camp of Dan between Zorah and Eshtaol."[66]

---

61. Judges 13:18
62. Judges 13:20
63. See, for example, *The Pearl of Great Price*, p. 52, verse 43; also verses 45 and 47.
64. Judges 13:22
65. Judges 13:23
66. Judges 13:24-25

Samson Makes a Fatal Mistake

There must have been great satisfaction for Manoah and his wife as they raised up this unusual son, seeing him grow in strength, and watching him race down the steep mountain terraces below Zonah with his long, uncut hair streaming in the wind. They knew they were raising another Joshua — a veritable soldier of God — in fact, a mighty man of valor who could lead the liberation forces of Israel against the smothering oppression of the Philistines.

But then Samson made his first fatal mistake. Even his parents may have had difficulty explaining just how it came about. It is the same thing that has happened to thousands of other young men whose parents have seen them rise to the threshold of phenomenal achievement, only to have it snatched away and smashed on the rocks of a passionate and all-consuming love affair with the wrong woman. With Samson, it involved a Philistine woman from Timnath.

Timnath was a Philistine town just below Zonah and a little further down the valley of Sorek toward Ekron. Even though he was an Israelite, Samson ventured into Timnath and it was there that he saw this Philistine woman with whom he fell madly in love. He rushed back up to his hilltop village and proclaimed the news to his parents. Said he, "I have seen a woman in Timnath of the daughters of the Philistines: now therefore get her for me to wife."[67]

His parents were shocked. Apparently it was his father who pleaded with him, "Is there never a woman among the daughters of thy brethren, or among all my people, that thou goest to take a wife of the uncircumcised Philistines?"

This speech strongly implies that this was not the first time Samson had been tempted to violate Israel's rule against intermarriage with the heathens. But the headstrong Samson was almost contemptuous of his father's counsel and said to him, "Get her for me: for she pleaseth me well."[68]

Any young man can make a mistake, especially when he is insanely in love, but to scornfully ignore the advice of his father on a matter involving an actual violation of a com-

---

67. Judges 14:2   68. Judges 14:3

mandment of God was a mistake Samson definitely could not afford. In fact, it was a mistake from which he never recovered.

It is at this point in the story that the unknown scriptural biographer of Samson starts making excuses for Samson and takes the side of the disobedient son rather than the parents. He interrupts the story to say that Samson's "father and his mother knew not that it [the marriage to the Philistine woman] was of the Lord, that he sought an occasion against the Philistines."[69]

The story itself repudiates the whole implication of this gratuitous editorial comment. Forty years of brutal oppression against Israel had given the Lord plenty of "occasion against the Philistines." And even before that, the centuries of human sacrifice and immoral debaucheries had given Him further occasion against them. What the Lord needed at this point was a liberator, not a collaborator. Samson's marriage to the woman from Timnath turned out to be the downfall of Samson. There is no evidence whatever that "it was of the Lord."

As the story unfolds we discover that once Samson had undertaken to defy his parents and lavish his passions on the heathen women with whom he hereafter continually fell in love, the calling of Samson disappeared into the bottomless limbo of an unfulfilled and illusionary dream. In twenty years Samson did not at any time attempt to organize the forces of Israel for their liberation. Nor was he even successful in matching the achievement of Shamgar, the man who had single handedly driven out the Philistines a century or so earlier. As we shall see in a moment, Samson's stories of slaughter, arson, gate-crashing and skull smashing were motivated by one single, feverish aspiration — his own personal revenge. It was not for Israel that Samson fought, it was for himself.

THE MARRIAGE OF SAMSON

When Samson found that his parents would not arrange his marriage, he apparently undertook to do it himself. His

---

69. Judges 14:4

SAMSON AND DELILAH — A Paramount Picture

". . . behold, a young lion roared against him. And the Spirit of the Lord came mightily upon him, and he rent him as he would have rent a kid, and he had nothing in his hand."

mother and father went along[70] but no doubt this was out of a sense of duty to see if they might not yet divert their son from his rash intentions. But Samson went right ahead with his plans. The scripture says, "he went down, and talked with the woman; and she pleased Samson well."[71]

It was while Samson was on this trip that he went out among the vineyards near Timnath and while alone was attacked by a young lion. The scripture says Samson "had nothing in his hand," neither knife, spear, sword, nor stone, so he met the attacking beast with his own brute strength. The magnificent physical power with which God had blessed Samson, saved his life. He seized the lion and "rent him as he would have rent a kid. . . ." The scripture says, "but he told not his father or his mother what he had done."[72]

The formalities of the betrothal having been completed, Samson and his parents returned home. "And after a time he returned to take her, and he turned aside to see the carcase of the lion: and, behold, there was a swarm of bees and honey in the carcase of the lion."[73]

At his seven-day wedding feast Samson entertained thirty young Philistines after the custom of the time. During the festivities he proposed a riddle to his newly acquired heathen friends. He wagered thirty "sheets" and thirty "changes of garments" that they could not solve it. If they failed in seven days to find the answer they were to reward him with the same amount of rich booty as he had offered them. His riddle was as follows, "Out of the eater came forth meat, and out of the strong came forth sweetness."[74] This, of course, referred to the lion he had killed.

When they could not solve the riddle even after three days of perplexity, the thirty young Philistines induced Samson's bride to inveigle it out of him. By teasing and using her feminine wiles on him she finally obtained the answer and promptly passed it on to the young Philistines. They waited until just before sunset on the seventh day and then came gloating into Samson with their answer, saying, "What is sweeter than honey? and what is stronger than a lion?"

---

70. Judges 14:5
71. Judges 14:7
72. Judges 14:5-6
73. Judges 14:8
74. Judges 14:14

Samson immediately knew his wife had betrayed the secret which he had shared with her. In a rage he shot out at them, "If ye had not ploughed with my heifer, ye had not found out my riddle."[75] Authorities point out that this strange figure of speech is a Hebrew aphorism which was intended to imply that Samson's wife had not only violated his confidence but also her marriage vows.[76] This may help to account for Samson's reaction. He stormed out of Timnath and headed for the main Philistine seaport at Ashkelon on the Mediterranean. No reason is suggested for this illogical behavior unless it would be the fact that he wanted to get far away from the scene of his sorrows. In any event, he fled to Ashkelon. Samson had not been there long when his mounting passion for vengeance boiled over on thirty unfortunate men of Ashkelon whom he slew and stripped. He took their "changes of garments" and trudged back to Timnath where he flung the clothes at the thirty young men who had solved his riddle by cheating. Then, in the deepest disgust, he climbed up the mountain to Zorah and went "to his father's house."[77]

Time, however, diminished his anger and resentment against his wife and her friends, so he decided to take a young kid and make peace with his wife. But when he came down to Timnath he found that she had already remarried. Her father said, "I verily thought that thou hadst utterly hated her; therefore I gave her to thy companion."[78] Apparently this "companion" was one of the young Philistines whom Samson had counted a friend. The father tried to interest Samson in one of his other daughters but Samson would have none of it. In a new outburst of rage he fled to the hills.

Samson immediately busied himself snaring a total of 300 foxes. Then he fashioned torches of combustible material which he fastened tightly to the tail of each fox. When everything was ready he lighted the torches and released the terrified foxes which ran wildly throughout all of the surrounding valleys. The results were devastating. The foxes set fire to all the crops which were then yellow-ripe. The conflagration destroyed both the standing grain and that

75. Judges 14:18
76. Clarke, *Bible Commentary*, Vol. 2, p. 163
77. Judges 14:19
78. Judges 15:2

which had been cut and shocked. It also spread to the vine-yards and then devoured the olive orchards.[79]

It did not take the Philistines long to discover who was responsible for this calamitous destruction. They could not find Samson at the moment but they did decide to avenge themselves upon the household of Samson's erstwhile wife and family because they had provoked Samson to commit this terrible outrage. They therefore moved in mob force to Timnath where they seized Samson's former wife and also her father. Both were burned alive.[80] But even this action by the Philistines did not pacify Samson. Before any of them realized what was happening, Samson came rumbling down out of the hills seeking further revenge. "And he smote them hip and thigh with a great slaughter. . . ." Then he fled and hid "in the top of the rock Etam."[81]

This latest flight took Samson into the mountains of Judea and apparently some of the Philistines followed him from a safe distance for they knew where Samson had hidden himself.

THE PHILISTINES SEND A WHOLE ARMY TO CAPTURE SAMSON

The Philistines now armed themselves and sent a great host into the mountainous terrain of Judah to capture Samson. As this great military host came in upon Judah the elders of the people cried out, "Why are ye come up against us? And they answered, To bind Samson are we come up, to do to him as he hath done to us.

"Then three thousand men of Judah went to the top of the rock Etam and said to Samson, Knowest thou not that the Philistines are rulers over us? what is this that thou hast done unto us? And he said unto them, As they did unto me, so have I done unto them."[82]

The sons of Judah were in no mood to allow the personal feelings of one man to jeopardize the safety of their whole tribe, therefore they shouted out to Samson, "We are come down to bind thee, that we may deliver thee into the

---

79. Judges 15:5   81. Judges 15:8
80. Judges 15:6   82. Judges 15:10-11

SAMSON AND DELILAH — A Paramount Picture

"And he found a new jawbone of an ass, and put forth his hand, and took it, and slew a thousand men therewith."

hand of the Philistines. And Samson said unto them, Swear unto me, that ye will not fall upon me yourselves.

"And they spake unto him, saying, No; but we will bind thee fast, and deliver thee into their hand: but surely we will not kill thee. And they bound him with two new cords, and brought him up from the rock."[83]

However, when Samson was finally given into the custody of the Philistines he waited for the appropriate moment and then exerted all his strength. The scripture says that "the cords that were upon his arms became as flax that was burnt with fire, and his bands loosed from off his hands."[84] As the Philistines scrambled about trying to recapture him, Samson reached for the nearest available device to defend himself. His hands fell upon "a new jaw bone of an ass" which was lying upon the ground. This hammer-like device in the hands of Samson turned out to be a lethal weapon. The scripture says Samson "took it, and slew a thousand men therewith. And Samson said . . . heaps upon heaps, with the jaw of an ass have I slain a thousand men."[85] Then he called the place Ramath-lehi which means "the lifting up of the jaw-bone."[86] Even with a modern machine-gun the slaying of a thousand men would be a formidable task. To do it with a piece of animal bone is almost inconceivable. Nevertheless, it was extremely impressive to the Philistines and terribly real besides. They were so panic-stricken by the onslaught that they completely lost control of the situation and allowed Samson to escape once more.

This time Samson did not go into any part of Israel but headed toward the southwest region of the Philistine domain. Perhaps he deliberately avoided the mountains of Israel lest it result in further retaliatory action by the Philistines. However, fear and frustration were taking their toll in Samson and he began exhibiting the senseless bravado of a defiant outlaw.

The scripture says, "Then went Samson to Gaza and saw there an harlot, and went in unto her. And it was told the Gazites, saying, Samson is come hither. And they com-

83. Judges 15:12-13
84. Judges 15:14
85. Judges 15:15-16
86. Clarke, *Bible Commentary*, Vol. 2, p. 166

passed him in, and laid wait for him all night in the gate of the city, and were quiet all the night, saying, In the morning, when it is day, we shall kill him."[87]

But during the night Samson arose and took "the doors of the gate of the city, and the two posts, and went away with them, bar and all," and carried them to the top of a nearby hill which is on the road to Hebron.[88] So once more he made the Philistines look foolish as he escaped out of their hands.

It is easy to imagine what a man of this ability could have done for Israel had he remained righteous and become the mighty leader of Israel's liberating hosts as God had originally intended!

Samson and Delilah

As one proceeds westward from Jerusalem the traveler soon encounters the valley of Sorek which we have previously mentioned. It is one of the principal valleys which sweeps down from the mountains of Judah toward the maritime plain and the sea. This was the valley which Samson had known all his life and it was the fertile channel of meadows and fields into which the encroaching Philistines were making continuous progress by building their communities and taking over broad tracts of land every decade. Samson's hometown of Zorah looked down on this valley so it was to be expected that eventually his hideout would be moved to this general area, which it was.

But once again Samson wandered into the snare of another Philistine woman. This one carried the name of Delilah, and she lived in the valley of Sorek.

Almost from the moment he met her, Samson knew she was trying to betray him, yet he recklessly and deliberately gambled with his life by continuing to consort with her. Delilah had become known as Samson's latest paramour and therefore "the lords of the Philistines came up unto her, and said unto her, Entice him, and see wherein his great strength lieth, and by what means we may prevail against him, that we

---

87. Judges 16:1-2   88. Judges 16:3

may bind him to afflict him: and we will give thee every one of us eleven hundred pieces of silver."[89]

To offer Delilah such a treasure was a striking indication of the desperate state of mind the five lords of the Philistines were in. Each of them represented a major city of the Philistines — Gaza, Gath, Ashkelon, Ekron and Ashdod. Each was willing to give eleven hundred pieces of silver to Delilah if she could somehow betray Samson into their hands.

Delilah immediately set out to earn her money and even though Samson knew precisely what she was doing, he childishly egged her on as though he enjoyed this flirtation with death at the hands of his enemies.

When she first asked him about the secret of his strength and the means by which he could be rendered helpless, he told her it could be done by using seven green withs to bind him. Delilah arranged to have a cadre of Philistines hiding in her apartment[90] and when Samson was asleep she bound him as he had instructed and then shouted, "The Philistines be upon thee, Samson." He instantly awakened and snapped the withs as though they were made of tissue, then he stood ready to defend himself. Apparently, the Philistines could see what had happened so they did not come out.

In the light of his past experiences, Samson should have fled from this valley and never returned. Instead, however, he continued flirting with the fates almost as though he were suffering from a death-wish.

Twice more Delilah tempted Samson, and twice more he told her various fictitious ways to bind him. Once it was with new cords, another time he said to tie the seven strands of his long hair to a beam with a web. When Delilah tried this second procedure, Samson awakened more frightened than even he would have wished to admit. He knew he was playing a game with his own life as the pawn and when Delilah fastened his hair securely to a beam and then shouted at him as before, "he awakened out of his sleep and went away with the pin of the beam, and with the web."[91]

89. Judges 16:5   91. Judges 16:14
90. Judges 16:9

SAMSON AND DELILAH — A Paramount Picture

"But the Philistines took him, and put out his eyes, and brought him down to Gaza, and bound him with fetters of brass; and he did grind in the prison house."

Finally, Delilah began a campaign of pestering and teasing combined with all of the feminine tricks she could contrive. She cried out, "How canst thou say, I love thee, when thine heart is not with me? thou hast mocked me these three times, and hast not told me wherein thy great strength lieth.

"And it came to pass, when she pressed him daily with her words, and urged him, so that his soul was vexed unto death;

"That he told her all his heart, and said unto her, There hath not come a rasor upon mine head; for I have been a Nazarite unto God from my mother's womb; if I be shaven, then my strength will go from me, and I shall become weak, and be like any other man.

"And when Delilah saw that he had told her all his heart, she sent and called for the lords of the Philistines, saying, Come up this once, for he hath shewed me all his heart. Then the lords of the Philistines came up unto her, and brought money in their hand.

"And she made him sleep upon her knees; and she called for a man, and she caused him to shave off the seven locks of his head; and she began to afflict him, and his strength went from him."[92]

Once more she cried out saying, "The Philistines be upon thee, Samson," but this time the mighty son of Dan awakened to find that he was just as other men. His super-strength was gone.

Originally the fate of Samson had been in the hands of God. Through obstinate defiance he had removed himself from the protection of God and taken his fate into his own hands. Now, at last, he had run his full course. His fate was in the hands of the Philistines.

With fiendish glee they dragged him from Delilah's house. They could have killed him on the spot but they decided to keep him for a trophy and abuse him for their pleasure. However, they were taking no chances on his becoming a threat in the future. They therefore put out both

---

92. Judges 16:16-19

of his eyes to make him helpless. Then they hauled him down to the great city of Gaza where he had pulled the doors of the gates from their sockets and carried them off. This time he entered the city with blind and vacant sockets and with his once powerful arms securely bound. Once they had him in the security of Gaza they called the smiths and had him permanently manacled with "fetters of brass." Then they put him in their prison house and forced him to grind grain.[93]

The tragic life of this fallen servant of God had finally reached the lowest stratum in the bedrock of mortal existence. In the depths of absolute degradation and misery he sweat out the suffering of each lonely day.

THE DEATH OF SAMSON

So grateful were the Philistines to be rid of the threat of Samson's perpetual attacks against them that they felt they owed it to their heathen god to offer him a great sacrifice of thanksgiving. The preparations for this festive celebration must have taken several weeks or months, for we are told that there was sufficient time for Samson's hair to grow out once more.[94] As it did so, Samson apparently found his strength gradually returning.

Of course, there was no direct relation between the two. It was not Samson's growing hair that brought back his strength but Samson's growing capacity to pray. His uncut hair had only been a token of his vow as a Nazarite. His miraculous strength had been a gift from God. If he were to receive it back again it would have to come through the beneficence of the same source from which it had come originally.

When the great celebration was ready, the joyous Philistines dragged Samson from his prison house and placed him where all could see his helpless plight. The scriptures say they "made them sport" with him, tantalizing their blinded prisoner, and rejoicing that Dagon, their heathen god, had finally delivered Samson into their hands.[95]

---

93. Judges 16:21
94. Judges 16:22
95. Judges 16:23-25

The temple of Dagon appears to have been built like the temple of Diana which the Greeks later erected at Ephesus. Diana's temple was an open pavilion suspended on many pillars, but the two center pillars were the key to the building. If these came down, the whole building collapsed under its own weight.

There is no doubt but what the temple of Dagon was also a massive affair. We are told that three thousand men and women were assembled on its roof.[96] Beneath them the woe-begotten Samson sat between the pillars where they had placed him after tormenting him.[97]

"And Samson said unto the lad that held him by the hand, Suffer me that I may feel the pillars whereupon the house standeth, that I may lean upon them. . . .

"And Samson called unto the Lord, and said, O Lord God, remember me, I pray thee, and strengthen me, I pray thee, only this once, O God, that I may be at once avenged of the Philistines for my two eyes.

"And Samson took hold of the two middle pillars upon which the house stood, and on which it was borne up, of the one with his right hand, and of the other with his left.

"And Samson said, Let me die with the Philistines. And he bowed himself with all his might."[98]

The dislodging of these two delicately but firmly balanced pillars by a single human being was something the Philistines would never have believed possible. For the moment they had completely forgotten about the tormented Samson and were getting under way to honor their great god Dagon. Then suddenly it happened. There was the grinding sound of heavy stones splitting away from their moorings and then the resounding crash accompanied by the horrified scream of the falling multitude. Their wild cries mingled with the roar of the thundering sandstone blocks as they came tumbling down from the heights of the temple. In virtually seconds the whole massive structure was reduced to a shambles as it collapsed into a shapeless heap of crumbled

---

96. Judges 16:27
97. Judges 16:25

98. Judges 16:26-30

SAMSON AND DELILAH — A Paramount Picture

"And Samson took hold of the two middle pillars upon which the house stood . . . And Samson said, Let me die with the Philistines. And he bowed himself with all his might; and the house fell upon the lords, and upon all the people that were therein."

stonework and mangled bodies. When the dust settled it revealed a demolished mass of total destruction.

Underneath it all was Samson, the son of Dan, the servant of God, who first lost his way, then lost his eyes, and finally lost his life. It was the pitiful and sorrowful conclusion to a violently hazardous life that could have been the most brilliant and successful career between Joshua and David. It lacked only one thing—a willingness to obey God.

With the rise and fall of Samson, the hopes of Israel stagnated. The liberation movement was postponed a century, and hundreds of thousands of lives continued in oppression and misery.

As for Samson, "his brethren and all the house of his father came down, and took him, and brought him up, and buried him between Zorah and Eshtaol in the burying place of Manoah his father."[99]

The adult career of the strong man from Zorah had lasted only twenty years.[100]

---

99. Judges 16:31
100. Ibid.

Scripture Reading and Questions on Chapter Twenty-Four

Scripture Reading Assignment: Judges 8:33 through chapter 16.

1—What was the significance of Abimelech's name? How many brothers did he have? How many did he kill? How did Abimelech die?

2—What did the Lord say to Israel when the people pleaded for relief after 18 years of oppression by the Ammonites?

3—Why did the Israelites wait so long to call Jephthah to leadership?

4—What was the excuse of the Ammonites for attacking Israel? What was Jephthah's reply? Did the Ammonites accept it? What did they do?

5—Why do we believe Jephthah's vow concerning his daughter has been misunderstood?

6—Why did the Ephraimites attack the people of Gilead? What was Jephthah's reply to their charges?

7—What happened when the Ephraimites tried to cross the Jordan in an effort to escape into their own territory?

8—What are the similarities between the lives of Samson and Saul?

9—What difference may be noted in the way their lives are recorded?

10—How did the Lord's messenger appear to the mother of Samson? Did she find out his name?

11—How did Manoah discover that the messenger was an angel of God? What did Manoah say? What did his wife say?

12—In what approximate area of Palestine did Samson live? How close was this to the cities of the Philistines?

13—What was Samson's first fatal mistake? What did his parents say to him? What was the deep significance of his reply?

14—Who apparently arranged Samson's marriage in Timnah? Where was Samson when he encountered the young lion?

15—When Samson lost his wager over the riddle, how did he get the thirty changes of garments to pay off his debt? What significance do you see in this behavior?

16—After being separated from his wife for a time, what did he discover upon his return? In his anger, what did Samson do?

17—How extensive was the damage from the 300 foxes with firebrands on their tails? What did the Philistines do to Samson's former wife and her father? Was Samson satisfied? What did he do?

18—Who captured Samson on the "rock Etam?" How did he happen to escape again?

19—What deterioration in Samson's personality does his journey to Gaza reflect?

20—Where did Delilah live? How did she get Samson to betray his secret? What were the results? How did he die?

CHAPTER TWENTY-FIVE

The Days of Ruth, Eli and Samuel

After Samson's death the tribe of Dan decided that there was no possibility of defeating the scourge of the Philistines and therefore they decided to make an exploration to discover some new territory which they might be strong enough to conquer and occupy. Five men were sent out to make a preliminary survey and they returned with the report that a city in the northernmost part of Israel's original inheritance, called Laish, could be taken because the people "dwelt careless, after the manner of Zidonians, quiet and secure. . . ."[1]

Therefore a body of men, 600 in strength and fully armed, left the vicinity of Zorah with their families and headed up into the mountains of Judah and then northward toward Ephraim. While in Mount Ephraim, the company stopped at the residence of an apostate Ephraimite, named Micah,[2] who boasted of the fact that he had his own personal Levite priest, a sacred ephod and some heathen images besides. The Danites decided they needed this private religious collection to provide an oracle and a sanctuary in their new home. They thereupon seized the "carved image, the ephod, and the teraphim, and the molten image."[3] They were also prepared to kidnap the Levite priest but when the priest found out that they intended to make him the spiritual leader of their tribe he went along cheerfully.[4] Micah tried to rally as much of a military force as possible to repossess his stolen property but these sons of Dan were as apostate and therefore as ruthless as Micah. Said they, "Let not thy voice be heard among us, lest angry fellows run upon thee, and thou

---

1. Judges 18:7
2. See Judges chapter 17 for the story of this dissolute character.
3. Judges 18:18
4. Judges 18:19-20

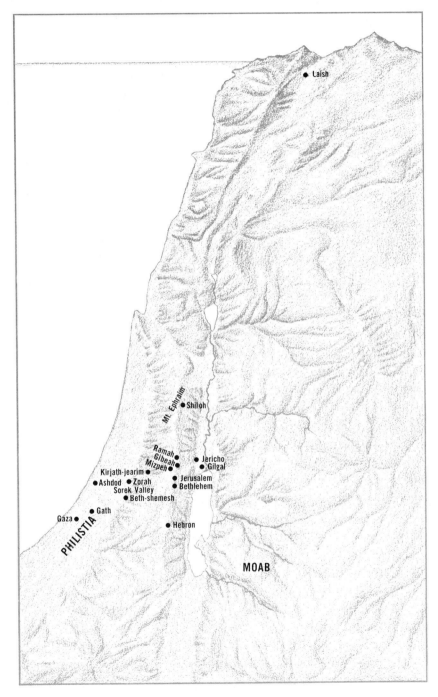

lose thy life, with the lives of thy household. And the children of Dan went their way: and when Micah saw that they were too strong for him, he turned and went back unto his house."[5]

Had the people of Laish realized that they were a target of immediate conquest and had they known what kind of men these Danites were they would have fled for their lives or mobilized their defenses. But their long years of careless living caught them completely unawares. There is no indication that the tribesmen of Dan made any attempt to give the initial proclamation of peace required by the Lord. It appears that they just went charging in against these heathens the same way these heathens had taken the city much earlier: "and they smote them with the edge of the sword, and burnt the city with fire. And there was no deliverer, because it was far from Zidon, and they had no business with any man; and it was in the valley that lieth by Beth-rehob. And they built a city, and dwelt therein. And they called the name of the city Dan. . . ."[6]

From this date on, the city of Dan marked the northernmost boundaries of Israel. Beer-sheba marked the southern extremity. It became a common saying to speak of the domain of Israel as being "from Dan to Beer-sheba."

Israel's Second Great Civil War

In order to catch the point of view of heaven concerning the sorrows and depravity of Israel's dark ages, the compiler of the Book of Judges has shared with us a number of incidents which might very well have been left untold. The compiler of the Book of Mormon, for example, refused to include in the record the sordid and monstrous acts of savage ferocity committed by the troops who participated in the great last war of the Nephite-Lamanite conflict.[7]

However, in order to include everything of significance which is covered by the Book of Judges we will refer briefly to the events which led up to Israel's Second Civil War.[8]

---

5. Judges 18:25-26
6. Judges 18:27-29
7. Mormon 5:8
8. There is some indication that this civil war may have occurred much earlier. However, we have elected to treat this material in the same order in which it appears in the Bible.

It seems that a certain Levite from Mount Ephraim had taken a maid-servant as a wife. The scripture says her status was that of a concubine. This woman lived with the Levite for a time and then became unfaithful. After violating her marriage vows she returned to her father's house in Bethlehem. The Levite eventually went down to see her in order to discuss the possibility of a reconciliation and the scripture says he was finally successful in getting her to agree to return with him.

On the way home the Levite and his concubine were urged by a servant to stop off with the Jebusites (which had reoccupied Jerusalem) but the Levite said he would not feel safe unless they stayed overnight with fellow Israelites. The party therefore pressed on to Gibeah, a town which was located in the territory of Benjamin. This turned out to be a mistake.

First of all, the people of Gibeah proved to be apostate Israelites who were grossly inhospitable. The Levite finally had to seek shelter with an old man who took pity on him. Furthermore, in the city of Gibeah there were "the sons of Belial" who not only had become apostates but had disgraced the tribe of Benjamin by adopting the abominations of Sodom. When these men heard that a stranger was in their midst they surrounded the house where the Levite was staying and demanded that his host release the Levite to them. This was a repetition of the precise problem which confronted Lot when he was living in Sodom before the destruction of that corrupt metropolis.[9] In the case of Lot the men of Sodom were frustrated by the servants of the Lord who were in the house, but in the case of the Levite at Gibeah there was no such good fortune. It was the custom in those apostate times to appease the vicious demands of such mobs by turning over to them the women of their households. In this case the concubine of the Levite was taken by the "sons of Belial" and by the next morning she was dead.[10] The Levite was so aghast at the atrocities of these depraved degenerates that he took the remains of the woman to his residence in Ephraim and there divided her body asunder so that there were twelve parts.[11] He sent one part to each tribe as a

---

9. Genesis 19:1-23
10. Judges 19:25-28

11. Judges 19:29

testimonial and to verify the story of what had happened to her at the hands of the tribe of Benjamin at Gibeah.

When the other tribes heard of this inhuman barbarity they assembled together in a vast conference and determined to send up a military force to avenge the woman.[12] Before doing so, however, they gave the tribe of Benjamin a chance to cleanse its own house.

"And the tribes of Israel sent men through all the tribe of Benjamin, saying, What wickedness is this that is done among you? Now therefore deliver us the men, the children of Belial, which are in Gibeah, that we may put them to death, and put away evil from Israel."[13]

One would have thought that the Benjamites, no matter how apostate or dissolute, would have been quick to take action on this problem, but the cancer of corruption had tainted this tribe to the core. They tried to justify the sons of Belial and swore to defend them.[14] This, then, was the setting for Israel's Second Civil War.

THE TRIBE OF BENJAMIN IS PRACTICALLY WIPED OUT

The Benjamites not only turned out to be completely devoid of any sense of decency or morality in this crisis, but they also turned out to be ferocious fighters. Altogether they had only 26,700 men.[15] Nevertheless, in the first encounter with the tribes of Israel they slew 22,000.[16] In the next encounter they slew 18,000.[17] In both of these battles the Benjamites seem to have lost no more than 1,000 men. This drove the tribes of Israel to give some belated attention to strategy. In the third encounter the other tribes succeeded in drawing the hosts of Benjamin away from their defenses at Gibeah with the result that the city was taken and burned and the whole army of the Benjamites was practically wiped out. Altogether a total of 25,100 Benjamites were slain[18] leaving only 600 alive. These escaped by fleeing into the wilderness.[19]

---

12. Judges 20:8-11
13. Judges 20:12-13
14. Judges 20:13-14
15. Judges 20:15

16. Judges 20:21
17. Judges 20:25
18. Judges 20:35
19. Judges 20:47

When the turmoil had settled down, the eleven tribes felt a sense of remorse because one whole tribe was now practically extinct. The problem was further complicated by the fact that each of the eleven tribes had sworn that none of their daughters would be allowed to marry a Benjamite.[20] It was finally decided that the solution might be found in Gilead. It seems that a certain Israelite city in Gilead had been marked for extinction due to its failure to respond to the call to arms. Therefore, they concluded to save the maidens from this condemned city and give them to the surviving Benjamites as wives. This action was taken and it resulted in the capture of 400 maidens,[21] but this still left 200 Benjamites without wives.

The calloused princes of Israel could only suggest that these remaining Benjamites kidnap additional girls during the dance festival which was held at Shiloh each year.[22] This procedure was actually followed[23] which demonstrates that the other tribes were about as depraved as the Benjamites themselves. This action saved the tribe of Benjamin from becoming extinct but one cannot read the account without contemplating the suffering and reckless indignities to which the daughters of Shiloh were subjected by these barbaric tactics.

However, knowing a few of these instances which were so common during these ugly days of apostasy helps the student appreciate the wisdom of God's original plan to cleanse this land and raise up a righteous people who could provide the following generations with the refining environment of the gospel. Instead, the Israelites had so corrupted themselves that they offered little more to their children than the harsh existence which typified the surrounding heathens.

The Book of Ruth

At this point in the Bible, it is wonderfully refreshing to come to the Book of Ruth. This book marks the beginning of the end for that long series of sterile and desolate years which had prevailed during Israel's dark ages. From this time onward, the course of Israel's progress begins lifting toward the light.

20. Judges 21:1   22. Judges 21:19-22
21. Judges 21:12-14   23. Judges 21:23

The Book of Ruth is not about one great woman, but two—Naomi and Ruth. As for the time of its occurrence, this is not fixed with certainty in the scriptures but we do know it was in the latter days of the judges and just three generations before the birth of David.

The scripture says that about this time a severe famine struck the mountains of Judah and preyed upon the land for a period of several years. It eventually became so severe that Naomi and her husband, Elimelech, decided to leave their land near Bethlehem and move to the Moabite country among the highlands east of the Dead Sea. The Moabites, it will be recalled, were descendants of Lot and therefore distant relatives of the Israelites. Naomi and Elimelech took with them their two sons, Mahlon and Chilion, who were now nearing maturity.[24]

Soon after arriving in Moab, however, Elimelech died and Naomi was left a widow. Nevertheless she continued making Moab her home and eventually her two sons married Moabite girls. One married Orpah and the other married Ruth.[25] Misfortune struck again within a short time and both of Naomi's sons died also, leaving their young widows childless.[26] By this time Naomi had received word that the famine had abated in Judea and so she determined to return to Bethlehem which was her original home. However, enroute it occurred to her that it was unfair to require Orpah and Ruth to return with her. Because they were Moabites Naomi realized that this move into a strange territory would separate them from both their families and friends. She therefore urged them to remain in Moab where they could re-marry, worship in their own religion, and live more happily among their own people.

But the older Naomi was such an inspiration to both of these younger Moabite women that they would have followed her anywhere. Nevertheless, she said to them, "Go, return each to her mother's house: the Lord deal kindly with you, as ye have dealt with the dead, and with me. The Lord grant you that ye may find rest, each of you in the house of her husband. Then she kissed them; and they lifted

---

24. Ruth 1:1-2   26. Ruth 1:5
25. Ruth 1:3-4

up their voice, and wept. And they said unto her, Surely we will return with thee unto thy people."[27]

However, Naomi continued to urge them to return and Orpah finally consented. Orpah embraced Naomi and kissed her and then sadly departed. Ruth, nevertheless, would not go with her. She pleaded with Naomi, saying:

"Intreat me not to leave thee, or to return from following after thee: for whither thou goest, I will go; and where thou lodgest, I will lodge; thy people shall be my people, and thy God my God: where thou diest, will I die, and there will I be buried: the Lord do so to me, and more also, if aught but death part thee and me."[28]

The heart of the older woman melted. She could not resist Ruth's overwhelming manifestation of love and confidence, so the two of them proceeded toward Bethlehem together. Naomi did not know it, but she was bringing back to Judeah one of the most noble spirits among Old Testament women. In Ruth was the mainstream of life which would produce in three generations the famous King David and centuries later, Jesus the Christ.

RUTH MEETS BOAZ

Because both Naomi and Ruth were widows and without a livelihood they were eligible to glean in the fields for whatever sustenance they could secure there. However, age or infirmity may have made it difficult for Naomi to participate because we find Ruth volunteering to go out alone. The scripture is clear that it was not by design but by providential good fortune that Ruth happened to gain permission to glean in one of the fields belonging to Boaz.

When Boaz came out from Bethlehem that day to inspect the fields and see how his reapers were progressing, he was immediately impressed with this young woman who was obviously a stranger in these parts. However, when he inquired of his foreman he found that she was well known among the workers as a virtuous young woman who had recently come to Judah out of love for Naomi, her mother-

---

27. Ruth 1:8-10   28. Ruth 1:16-17

in-law. This further impressed Boaz. He instructed his reapers not to molest her in any way and to treat her with kindness. Then he spoke to Ruth and invited her to continue gleaning in all of his fields as long as the harvest lasted. He also invited her to use the drinking supply of his own maidens who were working in the fields shocking the sheaves.[29]

Ruth was so impressed with this gesture of courtesy from a man who was known for his wealth and his prominence that she bowed before him, saying, "Why have I found grace in thine eyes, that thou shouldest take knowledge of me, seeing I am a stranger?

"And Boaz answered and said unto her, It hath fully been shewed me, all that thou hast done unto thy mother in law since the death of thine husband: and how thou hast left thy father and thy mother, and the land of thy nativity, and art come unto a people which thou knowest not heretofore. The Lord recompense thy work, and a full reward be given thee of the Lord God of Israel, under whose wings thou art come to trust."[30]

Her reply was humble but gracious. There was a certain nobility about this woman and the more Boaz observed her the more he became impressed. Therefore at noon he invited her to eat with the rest of his people who belonged to the crew of reapers.[31] He personally saw to it that she had food for apparently she had brought none with her. In the afternoon Boaz told the workers to "let fall also some of the handfuls of purpose for her, and leave them, that she may glean them, and rebuke her not."[32]

As a result, Ruth gleaned enough during the day to thresh out a whole ephah of grain which would be about 9½ gallons. In those days this was so much more than gleaners ordinarily gathered that Ruth felt more like a reaper than a gleaner as she proudly took this precious store of food home to Naomi. And Ruth was not disappointed in Naomi's enthusiastic reception. Not only was she surprised and delighted with Ruth's good fortune in securing so much grain but she was elated to learn that it was Boaz who had befriended her.

---

29. Ruth 2:8-9
30. Ruth 2:10-12
31. Ruth 2:14
32. Ruth 2:16

Naomi exclaimed, "The man is near of kin unto us, one of our next kinsmen."[33]

No further incident occurred during the harvest season. Boaz was further along in life than Ruth and having helped her he thereafter kept himself aloof without presuming to impose his attentions on her simply because he had assisted her in securing a better living.

NAOMI'S PLAN

But the mind of Naomi was filled with concern for the future of Ruth. Therefore, when the harvest was over she had formulated a plan. As a childless widow, Ruth had certain rights in Israel and Naomi felt the circumstances were propitious for those rights to be exercised. She was entitled to ask her husband's nearest kinsman to take her into his household as a wife. Naomi apparently assumed that since Boaz was the nearest kinsman and since he had befriended Ruth, it would be well to go forward with this arrangement if both Ruth and Boaz were willing. Ruth had implicit faith in Naomi and therefore she said to her, "All that thou sayest unto me I will do."[34]

It so happened that even though the harvest was over, Boaz was still staying out near the fields because the threshing was still in process. In fact, he was sleeping at the threshing floor as was required in those days to guard the store of grain from thieves. Naomi was no meddlesome matchmaker, but she was a wise and experienced woman who loved Ruth and wanted to see her enjoy the kind of home and security she deserved. Therefore she said to Ruth,

"Wash thyself, therefore, and anoint thee, and put thy raiment upon thee, and get thee down to the [threshing] floor: but make not thyself known unto the man [Boaz] until he shall have done eating and drinking. And it shall be, when he lieth down, that thou shalt mark the place where he shall lie, and thou shalt go in, and uncover his feet, and lay thee down; and he will tell thee what thou shalt do."[35]

For a modest person such as Ruth, this was a very bold and audacious plan, but Ruth had enough confidence in

---

33. Ruth 2:20
34. Ruth 3:5

35. Ruth 3:3-4

Naomi to try it. She did exactly as she had been told. After Boaz had completed his evening meal "and his heart was merry, he went to lie down at the end of the heap of corn; and she came softly, and uncovered his feet, and laid her down."[36]

Later, about midnight, Boaz "turned himself" and was startled to discover her there. "And he said, Who art thou? And she answered, I am Ruth thine handmaid: spread therefore thy skirt over thine handmaid; for thou art a near kinsmen."[37] This is a Hebrew phrase with technical implications which the Jewish *Targum* translates as follows: "Let thy name be called on thy handmaid to take me for wife, because thou art the kinsman to whom the right of redemption belongs."[38]

To Boaz this meant that this attractive young woman who could have gone husband-hunting among the rich and handsome young men of the region had elected to merely raise up children to her deceased husband in the home of her near kinsmen as provided under the law of Moses. Boaz was a spiritual man as well as a very successful farmer and merchant and he recognized in Ruth a supreme quality of spiritual integrity. He therefore blessed her for it and then counselled with her as follows:

". . . my daughter, fear not; I will do to thee all thou requirest: for all the city of my people doth know that thou art a virtuous woman. And now it is true that I am thy near kinsman: howbeit there is a kinsman nearer than I. Tarry this night and it shall be in the morning, that if he will perform unto thee the part of kinsman, well; let him do the kinsman's part: but if he will not do the part of a kinsman to thee, then will I do the part of a kinsman to thee, as the Lord liveth: lie down until morning."[39]

NAOMI'S PLAN IS THREATENED

Apparently neither Naomi nor Ruth knew about this other man who was a nearer kinsman than Boaz. This complicated things and was enough to keep Ruth awake the

---

36. Ruth 3:7
37. Ruth 3:9

38. Clarke, *Bible Commentary*, Vol. 2, p. 198.
39. Ruth 3:11-13

rest of the night. The scripture says, "And she lay at his feet until morning: and she rose up before one could know another."[40] However, Boaz stopped her before she could get away and had her take "six measures of barley" to Naomi which would be about as much as Ruth could comfortably carry.

When Ruth came into Naomi it was still dark, but Naomi awakened and said, "Who art thou my daughter?"[41] Ruth reassured her mother-in-law that it was she and then the two women sat together and discussed everything that had happened. Apparently Ruth was quite worried over this new and unexpected turn of events, but Naomi said, "Sit still, my daughter, until thou know how the matter will fall: for the man [Boaz] will not be in rest, until he have finished the thing this day."[42]

Naomi was right. That very day Boaz called the man who was Naomi's nearer relative and had him appear before ten elders of the city. Boaz started out by saying that since Naomi's husband was dead and both of his sons had died without issue this left certain lands in the hands of Naomi which should now be purchased by the next of kin to keep it on the male side of the family after the custom of the Law of Moses. The kinsman immediately said he would be willing to purchase it. But then Boaz pointed out that one of the dead sons had left a widow, a Moabite girl, who had never borne children and therefore the law provided that she would have to be taken as a wife by the person redeeming or purchasing the land. Immediately the next of kin was flustered and fuming. This changed everything. Not under any circumstances would he be interested in exercising his rights and duties as next of kin. He had no desire whatever to raise another family. He said to Boaz, "Buy it for thee."

In his quiet way, this was exactly what Boaz had expected and wanted, so he told the next-of-kin it was agreed. Boaz then turned to the elders of the city and said,

"Ye are witnesses this day, that I have bought all that was Elimelech's [Naomi's husband], and all that was Chili-

40. Ruth 3:14   42. Ruth 3:8
41. Ruth 3:16

on's and Mahlon's, of the hand of Naomi. Moreover Ruth the Moabitess, the wife of Mahlon, have I purchased [redeemed] to be my wife, to raise up the name of the dead upon his inheritance, that the name of the dead be not cut off from among his brethren, and from the gate of his place: ye are witnesses this day."[43] And all the people who heard the words including the elders of the city said, "We are witnesses."

How Ruth Became the Great Grandmother of David

Having made all the necessary legal arrangements, Boaz was now free to fulfill Ruth's request concerning him. The scripture says, "So Boaz took Ruth, and she was his wife. . . ."[44] In due process of time this union was blessed with a son and he was given the name of Obed. This little boy was not only a joy to his mother, but especially to Naomi, his grandmother. It gave her a complete new lease on life and her friends congratulated her, saying, "Blessed be the Lord, which hath not left thee without a kinsman [descendant], that his name may be famous in Israel. And he shall be unto thee a restorer of thy life, and a nourisher of thine old age; for thy daughter in law, which loveth thee, which is better to thee than seven sons, hath born him."[45]

The scripture leaves no doubt about the way Naomi felt toward this new little gift from heaven. It says, "And Naomi took the child, and laid it in her bosom, and became nurse to it."[46]

The scripture also says it was the neighbors who suggested the name of "Obed" which comes from a Hebrew word meaning "he served."[47] This is believed to have had reference to the great blessing he would be to his grandmother, Naomi, in her old age.

We should also note that in Obed two famous blood lines were joined. Since his mother, Ruth, was a descendant of Moab, this meant her line came through Lot. And since Boaz, the father of Obed, was an Israelite, this meant his

---

43. Ruth 4:9-10
44. Ruth 4:13
45. Ruth 4:14-15
46. Ruth 4:16
47. Clarke, *Bible Commentary*, Vol. 2, p. 202

line came down through Abraham. In Obed, therefore, these two great family branches were brought together.

Thus we come to the end of the Story of Ruth and Naomi. From it we are able to appreciate that in spite of all of the wretched and unrighteous degeneration of Israel during the dark ages, there were still certain choice spirits scattered here and there throughout the various tribes who longed for the happy and more abundant life which comes through obedience to God. Naomi, Ruth and Boaz were of this select nobility.

In due process of time Ruth saw her son, Obed, grow to the full stature of a man, and when he finally married, Obed had a son who was named Jesse. Jesse, in turn, begat David.[48] But once again we are getting ahead of our story. Our immediate concern must remain with the important events lying in between.

THE LIFE AND TIMES OF ELI

We now come to what was anciently called the first of the four Books of Kings. Today we call it the First Book of Samuel. In it we learn for the first time in nearly 400 years how things had been progressing at Shiloh where the High Priest presided over the sanctuary of the Tabernacle.

The high Priest at this juncture of Israel's history was a descendant of Aaron through Ithamar. His name was Eli.

The very fact that the Priesthood leadership had shifted from Eleazar and was now following the line of the younger Ithamar indicates some important ecclesiastical upheaval during the intervening centuries which is no longer in the record. However, the scripture is perfectly clear that for generations Israel had been wallowing in a sumphole of corruption. Not only had the forces of idolatry, immorality and general decay infested the people, but it had also corrupted the Priesthood. We saw strong evidence of what was happening in the case of the Levite who was employed by the Danites. He had received his ordination from the unauthorized hands of the apostate Micah, and had then undertaken to mix idol-worship with Jehovah-worship.[49]

---

48. Ruth 4:21-22   49. Judges 17:12; 18:20

We learn that even at Shiloh the dark spirit of apostasy had taken its toll. Eli presided over the formalities of the annual feasts and went through the rituals of the law of carnal commandments but the scripture says, "There was no open vision."[50] Apparently the Urim and Thummim no longer functioned and the heavens had become as brass. The Spirit of God had been offended. As the history of this era further unfolds, it is not difficult to understand why.

Eli, himself, appears to have plodded through life neither hot nor cold. He just carried out the dead letter of the law like the professional cleric that he was. He let the tide of Israel's cultural cesspool eddy about his feet without giving it much more than an occasional glance. Neither his nose nor his intellect would acknowledge the stench of the putrifying filth which had been spewed across the land during the four centuries of Israel's dark ages. Eli was not a man to engage the devil in controversy.

His policy of co-existence with the devil was particularly evident in dealing with his own two sons. These profligate offspring served in the Tabernacle like a couple of leeches. They corrupted the young girls and women who came to worship at the Tabernacle.[51] They used compulsion and extortion to extract excessive contributions in meat and offerings from the people.[52] They had made themselves so detestable that men "abhorred" coming to the Tabernacle to make an offering.[53] When things became so notorious that even Eli could no longer ignore them, the most he could muster was a mild rebuke as he said to them, "Why do ye such things? for I hear of your evil dealings by all this people. Nay, my sons; for it is no good report that I hear: ye make the Lord's people to transgress."[54] There the matter ended and the sons went blissfully along just as before. Eli may have felt that he had done his duty but the Lord did not. The High Priest was not aware of it, but the Lord was preparing to strip from him and his sons the entire management of Israel's spiritual and temporal government.

---

50. 1 Samuel 3:1
51. 1 Samuel 2:22
52. 1 Samuel 2:12-16
53. 1 Samuel 2:17
54. 1 Samuel 2:23-24

THE BIRTH OF SAMUEL

Among the ragged remnants of Israel there were still a few solid souls who yearned with all their hearts for the kingdom of God. Among these was a man named Elkanah who lived in Mount Ephraim.[55] Elkanah had two wives, Hannah and Peninnah, but only the latter had borne Elkanah any children. Each year when the family went up to Shiloh for the celebration of the various feasts, Hannah would go before the Tabernacle and pray for a son.

On one of these occasions, Hannah felt so desperate in her anxiety that she made a promise to the Lord that if he would bless her with a son she would make him a Nazarite and dedicate him to the service of the Lord all the days of his life.[56]

Eli was standing near and noting the great emotional distress of this woman as well as the fact that she was moving her lips but speaking no words, he concluded she must be drunk. Therefore he said to Hannah, "How long wilt thou be drunken? put away thy wine from thee."[57] But Hannah answered and said, "No, my Lord, I am a woman of a sorrowful spirit: I have drunk neither wine nor strong drink, but have poured out my soul before the Lord."[58]

Eli was pacified so he dutifully intoned upon her a benediction appropriate to the occasion. Said he, "Go in peace: and the God of Israel grant thee thy petition that thou hast asked of him."[59] Without realizing it, Eli had just endorsed a prayer which, when answered, would change the course of Israel's history and the direction of Eli's life.

With the passing of time Hannah did conceive and bear a son. The arrival of this long-awaited child was so thrilling to Hannah that she composed a song of rejoicing to the Lord and presented it to Him as a prayer of thanksgiving.[60]

Hannah called her son Samuel, which means "one asked of God,"[61] and then she undertook to raise him through a course of training that would make him a profitable servant of

55. 1 Samuel 1:1
56. 1 Samuel 1:11
57. 1 Samuel 1:14
58. 1 Samuel 1:15
59. 1 Samuel 1:17
60. 1 Samuel 2:1-10
61. 1 Samuel 1:20

the Lord. Josephus states that Samuel was twelve years old when his mother felt he was sufficiently mature to be turned over to the High Priest and consecrated to the service of God for the rest of his life.[62]

From the beginning young Samuel seems to have taken to this new calling. It appears that he had an earnest anxiety to fulfill his mother's highest aspirations. As for Hannah, the scripture says the Lord was so pleased with her devotion that he blessed her with five more children — three sons and two daughters.[63]

Each year Hannah would look forward to the annual sacrifice or feast of the Passover at Shiloh. It was her chance to visit with her son. The scripture says that each year she also brought along a "little coat" which she had made for him.[64] Of course, when Samuel ministered in the Tabernacle as a helper to the High Priest he wore a linen frock or ephod.[65]

ELI RECEIVES A WARNING

But while the son of Hannah was growing in the service of the Tabernacle, Eli's sons were continuing to corrupt it. One day "a man of God" came to Eli with a doomsday message. We do not know whether this was an angelic messenger similar to those who appeared to Abraham, Gideon and the parents of Samson or whether this was some righteous man in Israel who was especially endowed with the prophetic gift. In any event, the scripture is clear that the message came from the Lord.

The "man of God" declared to the aging Eli, "Thus saith the Lord, Did I plainly appear unto the house of thy father, when they were in Egypt in Pharaoh's house? And did I choose him out of all the tribes of Israel to be my priest, to offer upon mine altar, to burn incense, to wear an ephod before me? . . . Behold, the days come, that I will cut off thine arm, and the arm of thy father's house, and there shall not be an old man in thine house. . . . And this shall be a sign unto thee, that shall come upon thy two sons, on Hophni and Phinehas; in one day they shall die both of them."[66]

---

62. Josephus, *Antiquities of the Jews,* Book V, ch. 20:4
63. 1 Samuel 2:21
64. 1 Samuel 2:19
65. 1 Samuel 2:18
66. 1 Samuel 2:27-34

This ominous warning must have shaken Eli although it did not seem to change him. Knowing he would soon die, Eli must have wondered what the Lord would do for a leader if his sons were to be suddenly destroyed. The messenger from the Lord provided the answer. "And I will raise me up a faithful priest, that shall do according to that which is in mine heart and in my mind: And I will build him a sure house; and he shall walk before mine anointed for ever."[67]

SAMUEL RECEIVES A REVELATION

The next thing we read is that young Samuel received a revelation. He was awakened during the night by someone calling his name. By this time Samuel was in all probability nearing mid-adolescence, an age when the Lord has begun the tutoring of a number of his chosen servants.[68]

Samuel apparently slept in quarters adjacent to those of the High Priest so that he would be immediately available to serve him. When he heard his name spoken it was natural for him to assume that the elderly Eli had called him. But when Samuel went to ask the old man what he wished, Eli said he had not called him and instructed Samuel to go back to bed. The puzzled boy did so, but when the voice called to him again he knew something was wrong because he heard it distinctly. Once more Samuel reported to Eli but with the same results. A third time it happened. Finally Eli realized that Samuel may be receiving a call from a source which Eli himself had undoubtedly wished to have heard from. He therefore said to the youth, "Go, lie down: and it shall be, if he call thee, that thou shalt say, Speak, Lord; for thy servant heareth."[69]

So Samuel went and lay down as he had been told. Before long he heard the voice again, saying, "Samuel, Samuel." He immediately replied, "Speak; for thy servant heareth."

The message which Samuel received was undoubtedly a shock to him. The Lord said, "Behold, I will do a thing in

---

67. 1 Samuel 2:35
68. Enoch was called in his youth and so was Jeremiah . In fact, Jeremiah pleaded to be excused from his calling because he was so young (Jer. 1:6-7). Mormon was only ten when he received his call. Joseph Smith was fourteen.
69. 1 Samuel 3:9

Israel, at which both the ears of every one that heareth it shall tingle. In that day I will perform against Eli all things which I have spoken concerning his house: when I begin, I will also make an end. For I have told him that I will judge his house for ever for the iniquity which he knoweth; because his sons made themselves vile, and he restrained them not. And therefore I have sworn unto the house of Eli, that the iniquity of Eli's house shall not be purged with sacrifice nor offering for ever." (1 Samuel 3:11-14)

That was all. Young Samuel lay until morning wondering about the strange message he had received. When he arose he dared not tell Eli what had happened, but went directly to attend to his morning duties at the Tabernacle. Ulitimately, however, Eli came to Samuel. The aged High Priest was in a dark mood. He was prepared to extract from Samuel what the Lord had told him even if he had to do it by threats. Said he, "Samuel , my son. . . . What is the thing that the LORD hath said unto thee? I pray thee hide it not from me: God do so to thee, and more also, if thou hide any thing from me of all the things that he said unto thee."[70]

The scripture says that young Samuel then related "every whit" of the message from the Lord so that nothing remained hidden from Eli.[71]

This bold declaration of the Lord left Eli completely broken. He who had feared to have a controversy with the devil found he now had a controversy with the Lord. Eli solemnly listened to everything Samuel had to say and then, instead of being angry, he said to the youth, "It is the Lord: let him do what seemeth him good."[72]

The scripture says the word spread "from Dan even to Beer-sheba" that there was a youth attending the Tabernacle who had received a direct revelation from the Lord. They even went further. In spite of his youth, the scripture says "all Israel . . . knew that Samuel was established to be a prophet of the Lord."[73]

---

70. 1 Samuel 3:16-17   72. *Ibid.*
71. 1 Samuel 3:18   73. 1 Samuel 3:20

The Israelites Lose the Ark of the Covenant

It was sometime after this that the southern tribes of Israel suddenly found themselves involved in a new war with the Philistines. The enemy came swarming up from the maritime plains and pitched camp at Aphek. The Israelites rallied their available strength and pitched camp at what was later called Eben-ezer. When the battle began the Israelites found themselves in difficulty almost immediately. They were not only decimated and routed but 4,000 of their dead were left on the field of battle.[74]

A conference of the elders was hurriedly called and it was decided that things might go better in the next encounter with the Philistines if they sent to Shiloh and had the Ark of the Covenant brought onto the battle field. This strategy was enthusiastically approved so they sent messengers to Shiloh and petitioned for the Ark. It would have been well nigh impossible for these arrangements to have been made without the approval of Eli, although the details are not given. All we are told is the fact that when the Ark arrived in the camp of the Israelites it was accompanied by none other than Eli's two sons, Hophni and Phinehas.[75]

"And when the ark of the covenant of the Lord came into the camp, all Israel shouted with a great shout, so that the earth rang again.

"And when the Philistines heard the noise of the shout, they said, What meaneth the noise of this great shout in the camp of the Hebrews? And they understood that the ark of the Lord was come into the camp.

"And the Philistines were afraid, for they said, God is come into the camp. And they said, Woe unto us! for there hath not been such a thing heretofore.

"Woe unto us! who shall deliver us out of the hand of these mighty Gods? these are the Gods that smote the Egyptians with all the plagues in the wilderness.

"Be strong, and quit yourselves like men, O ye Philistines, that ye be not servants unto the Hebrews, as they have been to you; quit yourselves like men, and fight."[76]

---

74. 1 Samuel 4:2
75. 1 Samuel 4:4

76. 1 Samuel 4:5-9

With such a frenzied sense of fanatical desperation the Philistines went into battle with the fury of mad men. They lashed out at the Israelites in a gigantic avalanche of overwhelming destruction so that the guardians of the Ark and all the forces of Israel recoiled and then collapsed. The Philistines stormed through the broken lines to slaughter the Israelites by the thousands. Eventually they reached the spot where men were fighting to the death to protect the sacred Ark of the Covenant. To the Philistines this was the greatest prize of all because it would signify the victory of their heathen god Dagon over the God of the Israelites.

The scripture says, "And the ark of God was taken; and the two sons of Eli, Hophni and Phinehas were slain."[77] Not only that, but thirty thousand Israelites were slain with them.[78] In all her history there had not been so great a defeat of the armies of Israel as this one. And never before had the sacred Ark of God been in the idolatrous hands of the heathens. It was a cursed and evil day for Israel.

When one of the soldiers belonging to the tribe of Benjamin saw what a tremendous disaster had overtaken Israel, he extricated himself from the struggle and raced toward Shiloh. He arrived there the same day "with his clothes rent, and with earth upon his head."[79] As he went through the city shouting the news of the tragedy a great cry went up from the people. Eli heard the cry and feared that it harbingered bad news. The scripture says "his heart trembled for the ark of God."[80] And when he sent to find out the cause of the tumult, the messenger came to him personally. The scripture says that at this time Eli was ninety-eight years old and feeble with age.[81] As the messenger came up to where he was seated, Eli pleaded, "What is there done, my son? And the messenger answered and said, Israel is fled before the Philistines, and there hath been also a great slaughter among the people, and thy two sons also, Hophni and Phinehas, are dead, and the ark of God is taken."[82]

It was more than the old man could stand. He fainted and fell from the place on which he was sitting and was

---

77. 1 Samuel 4:11
78. 1 Samuel 4:10
79. 1 Samuel 4:12
80. 1 Samuel 4:13
81. 1 Samuel 4:15
82. 1 Samuel 4:16-17

instantly killed when his head struck the ground and broke his neck.[83] For forty years Eli had been the High Priest at Shiloh.[84] In one day he and his sons had been swept away.

But that was not the end·of the series of tragedies for Eli's house. We are told that the wife of Phinehas was expecting the birth of her baby and when she heard the news of Israel's catastrophe she went into a state of shock and her travail began. As the labor wore on it became apparent to her attendants that the unfortunate woman was not going to survive the ordeal. She did succeed in giving birth to the child but only lived long enough to give him the foreboding name of Ichabod, which means "no glory." She said as she died, "The glory is departed from Israel: for the ark of God is taken."[85]

GOD INTERVENES TO RECOVER THE ARK TO ISRAEL

However, the Philistines soon learned that the Ark of Jehovah was a catastrophic liability in the hands of the wrong people. First they carried it triumphantly into the heathen temple and placed it before the great idol of their god, Dagon. But the next morning their idol had fallen over and was lying face down before the Ark.[86] The Philistines set it upright again, but the next day it was found fallen over and smashed before the Ark.[87] Immediately afterwards the people of Ashdod, the city where this temple was located, suddenly began to suffer from a terrible plague which was character- ized by dysentery, a bloody flux and ulcerations.[88]

The leaders of the people in Ashdod decided it would be in the interest of their city to get the Ark of the Covenant transferred immediately to somebody else's city. They there- fore took it to the city of Gath.[89] But almost immediately the same plague broke out in Gath. The Ark was then sent to Ekron, but the people anticipated that they, too, would be stricken and therefore they urged the lords of the Philistines to get the Ark of the Israelites out of Philistia altogether and take it back to the people of Jehovah.

83. 1 Samuel 4:18
84. *Ibid.*
85. 1 Samuel 4:22
86. 1 Samuel 5:3

87. 1 Samuel 5:4
88. Clarke, *Bible Commentary*, Vol. 2, p. 223
89. 1 Samuel 5:8

"And the Philistines called for the priests and the diviners, saying, What shall we do to the ark of the Lord? tell us wherewith we shall send it to his place.

"And they said, If ye send away the ark of the God of Israel, send it not empty; but in any wise return him a trespass-offering: then ye shall be healed, and it shall be known to you why his hand is not removed from you."[90]

It was therefore decided to send "five golden emerods, and five golden mice, according to the number of the lords of the Philistines."[91]

The priests of the Philistines also instructed that a new cart should be constructed to carry the Ark and they said it should be drawn by two milk cows which had never before been under the yoke.[92] They said the ark should be placed on the cart and then the cows should be allowed to go withersoever they would. The priests said, if they took the highway up the valley of Sorek toward Israel it would mean that the God of Israel was guiding them homeward and they would also know that the plagues that had struck each city were indeed a direct manifestation of the wrath of Jehovah. However, they also said, that if the cows did not go back to Israel they would know that the hand of God was not in it and the plagues were therefore merely "a chance that happened to us."[93]

So the five lords of the Philistines watched anxiously to see what the cows would do. Sure enough, they "took the straight way to the way of Beth-shemesh, and went along the highway, lowing as they went, and turned not aside to the right hand or to the left; and the lords of the Philistines went after them unto the border of Beth-shemesh.

"And they [the Israelites] of Beth-shemesh were reaping their wheat harvest in the valley; and they lifted up their eyes, and saw the ark, and rejoiced to see it."[94]

It is interesting that once the two cows reached this area, they left the highway and went into the field of a man named Joshua of Beth-shemesh. They stopped near a large

90. 1 Samuel 6:3
91. 1 Samuel 6:4
92. 1 Samuel 6:7

93. 1 Samuel 6:9
94. 1 Samuel 6:12-13

stone and there they stood until the Israelites took possession of them.

The rustic wheat reapers were so overjoyed to get the Ark back that they decided to make a burnt offering on the spot. They slaughtered the two cows for that purpose and broke up the wooden cart or wagon to use for kindling.[95] The lords of the Philistines seemed satisfied that the hand of Israel's God had indeed been at work in bringing the Ark to his people, and so they returned home.

The scripture says there were several Levites with the wheat reapers and so they were apparently assigned the task of rummaging through the sacred Ark to see what they might discover. Inside they promptly came upon the coffer containing the golden mice and golden emrods which the Philistines had sent as a trespass-offering.

At this point the student cannot help wondering what had happened to the stone tablets containing the law as written by the finger of the Lord. And what had happened to the vessel of manna and the rod of Aaron? Did the Philistines steal them? This is unlikely in view of the fact that they were trying to return the Ark to pacify Israel's God. Perhaps Eli removed them before he allowed the Ark to go onto the battle field at Eben-ezer.

Surely these objects would have been mentioned if they had been found inside the Ark at the time the Levites searched it and discovered the coffer of golden mice and golden emrods. The fact that they were not mentioned leads us to assume that they were not there. (In the days of Solomon we are told that the tablets of stone were still in existence but the Ark contained nothing else. See 1 Kings 8:9)

But even if the tablets of the law and the other sacred testimonials were missing from the Ark, the Lord did not excuse the Levites and the wheat reapers for having ransacked the Ark and desecrating it. The Bible says that fifty thousand and seventy men were destroyed in consequence of this trespass. However, this figure is obviously an error

---

95. 1 Samuel 6:14

since the entire community of Beth-shemesh was not large, and certainly there would not be very many men involved in the reaping of the wheat. Bible scholars have recognized this passage as a problem down through the centuries and the different versions give different figures. Dr. Adam Clarke believed that the correct figure is probably the one given by Josephus. In his writings, Josephus makes no mention of any fifty thousand but says the number of men destroyed for this trespass against the Ark was "seventy."[96] For a community the size of Beth-shemesh this number of men would seem entirely plausible, especially since this number represents those who were in the field reaping the grain.

As soon as the people of Beth-shemesh saw how angry the Lord was with them for desecrating the Ark, it was decided that it should be moved at once to another location. The leaders of the city therefore sent messengers to nearby Kirjath-jearim on the borders of Benjamin and asked them to come and get the Ark. They apparently made no mention of the calamity they had suffered as a result of ransacking the Ark, but simply said, "The Philistines have brought again the ark of the Lord: come ye down, and fetch it up to you."[97] So the men of Kirjath-jearim came down and carried the Ark back with them. It was placed in the house of a man named Abinadab, and his son, Eleazar, was assigned the task of safeguarding it. For twenty years the Ark remained in this place.[98] Why didn't they take it back to Shiloh where the Tabernacle was located? The record doesn't say.

SAMUEL LAUNCHES A REFORM AND CONQUERS THE PHILISTINES

Sometime after Samuel had grown to maturity, and apparently a number of years following the events we have just described, a great program of reform took place in Israel.

The scripture says, "And Samuel spake unto all the house of Israel, saying, If ye do return unto the Lord with all your hearts, then put away the strange gods and Ash-

96. Josephus, *Antiquities of the Jews*, Book VI, Chapter 1:4
97. 1 Samuel 6:21
98. 1 Samuel 7:1-2

taroth from among you, and prepare your hearts unto the Lord, and serve him only; and he will deliver you out of the hand of the Philistines."[99]

In order to commit the people to a new era of righteousness, Samuel gathered the people of Israel in a huge general conference at Mizpeh (this Mizpeh was west of Jordan). As might be expected this great gathering was widely acclaimed and as soon as the Philistines heard about it they mistook it to be a council of war. Therefore they mobilized their armies and marched into the mountains of Israel to put down what appeared to be another act of insurgency against the Philistine masters.

"And the children of Israel said to Samuel, Cease not to cry unto the Lord our God for us, that he will save us out of the hand of the Philistines.

"And Samuel took a sucking lamb, and offered it for a burnt offering wholly unto the Lord: and Samuel cried unto the Lord for Israel: and the Lord heard him."[100]

The next thing the Philistines knew, a violent storm was beating down in their faces. It apparently became so severe that they decided to turn back, and as soon as they did so the men of Israel swept down upon them. The battle was fought at Eben-ezer, the same place where the Philistines had slaughtered so many Israelites when they captured the Ark. Now the Lord had returned to Israel and the outcome was reversed. The Philistines were so completely beaten that they not only evacuated their forces but turned back to Israel all of the territory they previously had held under their vassalage. What Samson and Eli tried to do without the Lord, Samuel was now able to accomplish because of the Lord. It was a great day in the history of Israel and marked the beginning of the return of the twelve tribes to light and liberty. The dark ages of Israel were almost past.

---

99. 1 Samuel 7:3
100. 1 Samuel 7:8-9

Scripture Reading and Questions on Chapter Twenty-Five

Scripture Reading Assignment: Judges, chapter 18 to 21 inclusive; The Book of Ruth; 1 Samuel, chapters 1 to 7 inclusive.

1—What characteristics would you ascribe to the people of Dan who conquered Laish?

2—What did it indicate when the Benjamites defended the "sons of Belial?" Were the Benjamites timid or ferocious? What happened to them?

3—What steps did the other tribes take to provide wives for the 600 surviving Benjamites? What kind of thinking does this reflect?

4—Why did Naomi and her husband leave Judah? Where did they go? Who went with them?

5—What nationality was Ruth? Would this make her a Shemite?

6—Why did Naomi leave Moab? Who started with her? Who turned back? Why did Naomi want Ruth to turn back? What did Ruth say?

7—For what is Ruth most famous? What is implied from the fact that she was a "gleaner" in the fields? Did Naomi glean also?

8—What did Boaz hear about Ruth that greatly impressed him? Was Boaz older or younger than Ruth? What did Boaz do to help Ruth?

9—After helping Ruth did Boaz make any romantic overture toward her? Who proposed marriage? On whose suggestion?

10—What did Boaz tell Ruth which she did not know before? Why did this complicate things? How was it solved?

11—What relation was Ruth to King David? What did Ruth name her son? Who suggested the name? Who became the baby's nurse?

12—In those days was Eli, the High Priest, accustomed to receiving revelations? Why didn't he use the Urim and Thummim?

13—What does it mean to refuse to engage the devil in controversy? Do you know any people who take this attitude? Does it have any advantages? Any disadvantages?

14—Why was the Lord angry with Eli's sons? Was Eli a good father? Give the reason for your answer.

15—When Eli saw Hannah praying what did he assume? After discovering he was wrong, what did he say to her?

16—What does "Samuel" mean? According to Josephus, how old was Samuel when he was taken to serve the High Priest?

17—About how old was Samuel when he received his first revelation? Name two other prophets who were called at about this age.

18—How did the Israelites lose the Ark? Did the Philistines intend to keep it? Why did they send it back?

19—Who drove the cart bearing the Ark back to Israel? What happened to the two cows? What happened to the cart?

20—When Samuel called upon Israel to reform and held a huge conference what did the Philistines think? What did they do? What happened?

CHAPTER TWENTY-SIX

The Rise of Saul

The setting for this present chapter occurs in the last century of the third thousand years.

Apparently Samuel was a relatively young man when he began the great reform movement which resulted in the expulsion of the Philistines and the revival of national unity among the twelve tribes. The scriptures imply that the years immediately following were pleasant ones as Samuel refurbished the spiritual armor of Israel and once more lifted before their eyes the vision of "liberty under law," and "freedom under God."

Time, however, once more wore away the high goals which Samuel had set and by the time he was an old man we find that the Philistines had once more established their garrisons among the southern tribes. Because the middle years of Samuel are completely missing from the scriptures we have no idea how or when the latest wave of Philistine oppression began. Perhaps, if we had those chapters we also would know who Samuel married and how he happened to move his headquarters from Shiloh to Ramah where he built an altar and thereafter maintained his headquarters.[1] In fact, from this time on, Shiloh fades out of history. The Ark of the Covenant had been removed under Eli's administration as we have already seen, and the Tabernacle seems to have been treated like an orphan as it began to be moved about from place to place.

When the scriptural history picks up the continuation of Samuel's story, his personal circumstances are none too pleasant. As an older man Samuel found himself in much the same position as Eli whom he had replaced. Israel was once more under the Philistines and worst of all, Samuel's sons were commencing to behave much like Eli's.

---

1. 1 Samuel 7:17

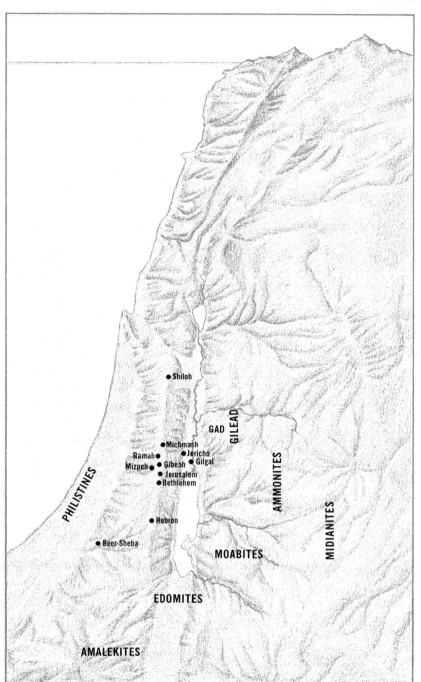

Samuel Discovers Apostasy In His Sons

Like all great men, Samuel had the highest aspirations for his two sons. He apparently trained them to be his successors and as soon as possible he made them judges. Samuel's firstborn son was named Joel and his second son was named Abiah. Both of these were assigned to positions of leadership in the district of Beer-sheba.[2]

However, it is the universal experience of the human family that the sons of famous fathers are often easily corrupted when thrust into positions of trust and responsibility. In the beginning it is not always their fault, but society makes them pay the penalty just the same.

In the first place the public gives to the sons of illustrious men the unearned accolades and certain undeserved favors as a vicarious tribute to their fathers. Often this is done in the utmost sincerity and yet it isn't long before these sons may come to take these gratuitous pleasantries for granted and accept them as though they had been earned. Some of these favors come in the form of "innocent" gifts which are given in the name of friendship. Later they turn out to be the material consideration for demanded favors. The problem is further complicated by the fact that when the sons of prominent fathers find they have compromised themselves, they seldom have the courage to forego the advantages they have been enjoying and therefore never get around to making a clean break so as to start afresh on their own.

So we learn from observing life that it is not any easy thing to be the son of an outstanding man. The biggest problem is having the patience to grow to greatness through personal initiative instead of exploiting the greatness which has been earned by a father. This was a lesson the sons of Samuel never learned.

It must have been a great disappointment to Samuel when he heard that his sons had acquired a reputation almost as abominable as the notorious sons of Eli. The scripture says, "And his sons walked not in his ways, but turned aside after lucre, and took bribes, and perverted judgment."[3] Worst of all, the corruption of Samuel's sons had led the people to

2. 1 Samuel 8:2
3. 1 Samuel 8:3

lose confidence in the system of government originally delivered to Moses by the Lord. Apparently Samuel had been
attempting to restore confidence in that system, but the bribes
and perverted judgment of Joel and Abiah had created a
spirit of revolutionary reaction. The people came marching up
to Ramah demanding that Samuel give them a whole new
system of government, headed by a king.

What Is the Nature of God's Government?

Since Israel was on the verge of discarding the last
vestigial remnants of what had originally been a God-given
government, it is important to analyze the principles of political science which would have prevailed if Israel had remained
a righteous people. As we go into this subject the student
will immediately realize that this is a matter which has
received very little attention and one which has suffered from
widespread misunderstanding.

In the first place, when the Lord is talking about
"judges" he is referring to community leaders, men of wisdom, men of discernment, men of initiative. Here is the way
Moses described this office, "Take you wise men, and understanding, and known among your tribes, and I will make
them rulers over you."[4] Note that these men were to be
selected by the people and had to be well known so that they
had the confidence of the people. If nominated by central
leadership they had to be approved by the people.[5]

These "wise men" under God's government were to
function at all levels. There were captains of tens, captains
of fifties, captains of hundreds, and captains of thousands.[6]
Each man held a sort of bishopric over those he served as
leader.[7] He was expected to know God's law and administer
it impartially.[8] He was to anticipate social problems, health
problems, and human relations problems.[9] In cases of dis-

---

4. Deuteronomy 1:13
5. This was demonstrated in the case of Jephthah—Judges 11:9-11.
6. Deuteronomy 1:15
7. A bishop is described by the Lord as an officer in charge of the temporal affairs
   of those over whom he presides. (Doctrine and Covenants 107:68)
8. Leviticus 19:15
9. Moses, himself, was the model community leader. He concerned himself with all
   of these fields.

putes he was to "inquire diligently" concerning the facts in each case.[10] He was to "hear the small as well as the great."[11] He was not to "be afraid of the face of man"[12] but judge justly. He was not to accept gifts of any kind, for "a gift doth blind the eyes of the wise, and pervert the words of the righteous."[13]

Under God's government there was strong emphasis on orderly processes. Problems were studied and solved to the greatest possible extent down on the level where they originated. Only the most profound and difficult problems were allowed to occupy the time and energies of the leaders in the central government. Early in his career, when Moses failed to recognize this principle and allowed the whole burden of the people to fall upon him personally, his father-in-law, Jethro, reprimanded him and taught him the principles of Priesthood government as follows:

"The thing that thou doest is not good. Thou wilt surely wear away, both thou, and this people that is with thee: for this thing is too heavy for thee; thou art not able to perform it thyself alone. Hearken now unto my voice, I will give thee counsel, and God shall be with thee . . . and thou shalt teach them ordinances and laws, and shalt shew them the way wherein they must walk, and the work that they must do. Moreover thou shalt provide out of all the people able men, such as fear God, men of truth, hating covetousness; and place such over them, to be rulers of thousands, and rulers of hundreds, rulers of fifties, and rulers of tens: and let them judge [govern] the people at all seasons: and it shall be, that every great matter they shall bring unto thee, but every small matter they shall judge: so shall it be easier for thyself, and they shall bear the burden with thee. If thou shalt do this thing, and God command thee so, then thou shalt be able to endure, and all this people shall also go to their place in peace."[14]

God's way is to provide men with correct principles and then teach them to govern themselves. Note that Moses was to use God's law to show them "the way wherein they must

---

10. Deuteronomy 17:4; 19:18
11. Deuteronomy 1:17
12. *Ibid.*

13. Deuteronomy 16:19
14. Exodus 18:17-23

walk and the work they must do." Then he was to select, with the approval of the people, those who would administer these principles. By decentralizing authority to rulers of tens, fifties, hundreds and thousands, it provided an orderly pattern of problem solving. It provided a systematic filtering system with channels of appeal which lifted only the most weighty problems to the top of the Priesthood pyramid. Most important of all, it provided the means to get things done in the most efficient, economical and direct manner. People did not have to stand in line waiting for some ranking official with choke-hold authority to approve some trivial matter which even a child could discern to be necessary.

Bad government is the kind which does not meet people's needs. People need to have a remedy if they are wronged, which we call *Justice*. They need to be secure in their lives, their property and their privacy which we call *Civil Rights*. They need to be free to choose their vocation and avocation, their religion, their residence, their travel, their education, what they shall write and what they shall speak. This we call *Liberty*. Finally, they need to know that whatever rights or duties exist shall be universal in their application — that there shall be no privileged class — that there shall be one law for all the people. This we call *Equality*.

Self government is always a dynamic and volatile affair. It takes initiative and patience, forcefulness and restraint. But the Lord knows it is the only system under which men can "go to their place in peace." As Thomas Jefferson said, "Liberty is a boisterous sea. Timid men prefer the calm of despotism."

What makes men too timid to govern themselves? What makes them reach for a monarchy, despotism or tyranny which will cost them their freedom? Usually it is because they were using a bad system of government or had corrupted a good one. In Samuel's day it was the latter.

The Children of Israel Demand a Monarchy

When the people of Israel came clamoring to Samuel demanding a new system of government they embarrassed him by blaming Samuel's sons for their loss of confidence in the Lord's way. Said they, "Behold, thou art old, and thy sons walk not in thy ways: now make us a king to judge us like all the nations."[15]

Samuel knew they were making a tragic mistake. He also knew that even though their complaints against his sons were true, their use of this as an excuse to demand a king was false. There had been corrupt judges in Israel during the entire dark ages. Corruption in office had been the watchword of Israel for some 400 years. No, this was only a handy excuse for their demand. Even their own speech betrayed them. They had openly admitted that they wanted a king so they could be "like all the nations." It was pride that moved them. Samuel knew that if a king were appointed his own lifetime of work to restore the framework of God's pattern of government would be practically wasted. Nevertheless, he had to admit that his own sons had not supported that pattern. It was aggravating, frustrating, discouraging. In a spirit of desperation he went to the Lord in prayer.

"And the Lord said unto Samuel, Hearken unto the voice of the people in all that they say unto thee for they have not rejected thee, but they have rejected me, that I should not reign over them."[16]

Nowhere in scripture is there a better example of God's respect for human free agency than here. He had given them a system of theocratic government which, if practiced, could build another City of Enoch. However, they had rejected it and demanded a king "like all the nations." Very well, they would have one. The Lord said to Samuel, ". . . hearken unto their voice: howbeit yet protest solemnly unto them, and shew them the manner of the king that shall reign over them."[17]

What the Lord now had Samuel say to the Israelites was a bill of particulars against monarchies as a system of government. In essence He was telling them that liberty once lost is regained only by the shedding of blood.

Here is what He told them to expect from a king no matter how carefully he was chosen:

15. 1 Samuel 8:5
16. 1 Samuel 8:7

17. 1 Samuel 8:9

"This will be the manner of the king that shall reign over you: He will take your sons, and appoint them for himself, for his chariots and to be his horsemen; and some shall run before his chariots. And he will appoint him captains over thousands, and captains over fifties; and will set them to ear his ground, and to reap his harvest, and to make his instruments of war, and instruments of his chariots. And he will take your daughters to be confectionaries, and to be cooks, and to be bakers. And he will take your fields and your vineyards, and your oliveyards, even the best of them, and give them to his servants. And he will take the tenth of your seed, and of your vineyards, and give to his officers, and to his servants. And he will take your menservants, and your maidservants, and your goodliest young men, and your asses, and put them to his work. He will take the tenth of your sheep; and ye shall be his servants. And ye shall cry out in that day because of your king which ye shall have chosen you; AND THE LORD WILL NOT HEAR YOU IN THAT DAY."[18]

This speech was an unveiled, naked prophecy. It should have sent the Israelites fast-footed back to their homes filled with a resolve to enjoy their liberties and make the political science of God's theocracy work. But it fell on their ears like thistledown instead of thunder. They spurned these words of warning and cried out, "Nay, but we will have a king over us; That we also may be like all the nations; and that our king may judge us, and go out before us and fight our battles."[19]

Samuel reported back to the Lord and received this instruction: "Hearken unto their voice, and make them a king."[20]

So the stage was set. A whole new era was about to begin for Israel. It might be called the era of the grand illusion. Israel was about to try man's age-old fantasy of pomp and pageantry and thereby create for herself a mirage of illusionary greatness as a substitute for God's reality of greatness.

18. 1 Samuel 8:11-18
19. 1 Samuel 8:19-20
20. 1 Samuel 8:22

The Calling of Saul

Nevertheless, the Lord intended to start them out with every possible advantage. From all of Israel he would indicate by direct revelation the man best fitted to be a king. This man turned out to be Saul. The scriptures says he was "a choice young man, and a goodly: and there was not among the children of Israel a goodlier person than he: from his shoulders and upward he was higher than any of the people."[21] By calling him a "young" man, the implication seems to be that he was in the prime of his life. Actually, he had a grown son, Jonathan, so we know his age was around forty at the time of his call.

Saul belonged to the tribe of Benjamin, the tribe which had nearly become extinct as a result of the slaughter at Gibeah.[22] However, Saul was the son of Kish who had the reputation of being "a mighty man of power."[23] Therefore Saul came by his physical attributes naturally.

Saul's destiny caught up with him while he was on a rather humble mission. He was out hunting some lost asses which belonged to his father. These animals were larger and faster than the common donkey and were counted the most valuable domestic animals a person might possess. To have a whole herd of them escape was a serious blow to the household of Kish. Saul went north and searched throughout the hills and valleys of Ephraim. Failing to find them he turned toward Shalisha, then Shalim (perhaps Salem) and then through the territory of Benjamin. In three days Saul and his servant covered the rough terrain of approximately twenty-five square miles but the animals were nowhere to be seen. Finally, as they came down into a region called Zuph (believed to be below Bethlehem), they passed near a city where Samuel often stayed while traveling about the country. The servant urged Saul to stop off long enough to ask Samuel where they should go next. Saul was reluctant because he had no gift of food or money to present to Samuel. The servant had a fourth of a shekel so he loaned it to his master.

When Saul and his servant came near to the city they asked the maidens who were drawing water out of the well if

---

21. 1 Samuel 9:2
22. Judges, Chapters 20 and 21
23. 1 Samuel 9:1

Samuel were in the city. "And they answered them, and said, He is; behold, he is before you: make haste now, for he came to day to the city; for there is a sacrifice of the people to day in the high place: As soon as ye be come into the city, ye shall straightway find him, before he go up to the high place to eat: for the people will not eat until he come, because he doth bless the sacrifice: and afterwards they eat that be bidden. Now therefore get you up; for about this time ye shall find him."[24]

Little did these maidens realize that one of the men they were addressing would be anointed king of Israel within twenty-four hours.

Already the Lord had spoken to Samuel the previous day and said: "To morrow about this time I will send thee a man out of the land of Benjamin, and thou shalt anoint him to be captain over my people Israel, that he may save my people out of the hand of the Philistines: for I have looked upon my people, because their cry is come unto me."[25]

So on this day of sacrifice Samuel knew he was about to meet the Lord's selection for Israel's king. In fact, as Samuel was walking toward the altar or "high place" to officiate at the sacrifice he saw a man of magnificent stature coming toward him with a servant. The Spirit of the Lord whispered to Samuel: "Behold the man whom I spake to thee of! this same shall reign over my people."[26]

Saul and his servant were just coming through the city gate, so when he saw the elderly man standing in the way, he said, "Tell me, I pray thee, where the seer's house is."[27] To Saul's surprise the old man replied, "I am the seer: go up before me unto the high place; for ye shall eat with me today, and tomorrow I will let thee go, and will tell thee all that is in thine heart."[28]

Of course, about the only thing in Saul's heart at the moment was the worry over his father's lost animals, so Samuel undertook to add a word of comfort. Said he, "And as for thine asses that were lost three days ago, set not thy

---

24. 1 Samuel 9:12
25. 1 Samuel 9:16
26. 1 Samuel 9:17
27. 1 Samuel 9:18
28. 1 Samuel 9:19

mind on them; for they are found."[29] To Saul this was the best news he could have heard, but Samuel decided to lay upon the heart of this tall and kingly man a new worry. He said to him in all solemnity, "And on whom is all the desire of Israel? Is it not on thee, and on all thy father's house?"[30]

What kind of talk was this? The puzzled Saul looked at the aged Samuel and said, "Am not I a Benjamite, of the smallest of the tribes of Israel? and my family the least of all the families of the tribe of Benjamin? wherefore then speakest thou so to me?"[31]

But Samuel had said enough. He went on up to the altar where the people were awaiting him and after offering the sacrifice he invited Saul and his servant to join Samuel and his thirty guests for dinner. During the meal Samuel had his cook give Saul a special portion of meat which had been set aside the day before when Samuel first learned that the identity of Israel's new king was about to be disclosed.

This meal appears to have taken place in some residence or structure near the place of sacrifice, for Samuel afterwards took Saul back into the city with him to the house where he was staying. The two of them visited at length the remainder of the day.[32]

Early the next morning "about the spring of the day," Samuel awakened Saul and his servant to get them started on their journey homeward. Samuel walked down the empty streets with them toward the city gates. "And as they were going down to the end of the city, Samuel said to Saul, Bid the servant pass on before us . . . but stand thou still a while, that I may show thee the word of God."[33]

When the servant had gone ahead, Samuel took a vial of oil and poured it on the head of Saul and kissed him. Apparently Saul did not understand what Samuel was doing, and so the elderly prophet answered Saul's quizzical look with a question. Said he, "Is it not because the Lord hath anointed thee to be captain over his inheritance?"[34]

So that was it. Saul had just been anointed king!

---

29. 1 Samuel 9:20
30. Ibid.
31. 1 Samuel 9:21

32. 1 Samuel 9:25
33. 1 Samuel 9:27
34. 1 Samuel 10:1

Samuel then told the new ruler of Israel what would happen to him all the way home, how he would be met by two men at Rachel's sepulchre near Bethlehem. They would tell him that his father had found the lost animals but was greatly worried over what had happened to Saul.[35] Next he would meet three men who would give him some bread to eat.[36] Then he would meet "a company of prophets" who would have in them the spirit of prophecy which Saul would also receive and he would be able to prophesy right along with them. Samuel said that from this moment on Saul would have the spirit of revelation in him.[37]

Saul, of course, was well aware by this time that part of his calling as the new king would be to mobilize the forces of Israel and liberate them once again from the Philistines.[38] Concerning this aspect of his calling Samuel said, ". . . go down before me to Gilgal; and behold, I will come down unto thee, to offer burnt-offerings, and to sacrifice sacrifices of peace-offerings: seven days shalt thou tarry, till I come to thee, and show thee what thou shalt do."[39]

With this, Samuel bade the new king farewell and sent him home. Everything happened to Saul just as Samuel had said it would. Saul and his servant met the men near Rachel's tomb who told them the animals had been found, then they met the three men who gave them bread. When the company of prophets came along Saul felt the Spirit of God come upon him so that he could prophesy as well as the others. People standing around were astonished and said, "What is this that is come unto the son of Kish? Is Saul also among the prophets?"[40] All of this was a new and wonderful sensation for Saul.

SAUL IS PRESENTED TO THE PEOPLE

As soon as Samuel could arrange it, he called a general conference of all the tribes at Mizpeh which was located about ten miles north of modern Jerusalem. Said he, ". . . ye have this day rejected your God, who himself saved you out of all your adversities and your tribulations; and ye have said

---

35. 1 Samuel 10:2   38. 1 Samuel 10:7
36. 1 Samuel 10:3-4   39. 1 Samuel 10:8
37. 1 Samuel 10:5-6   40. 1 Samuel 10:11

unto him, Nay, but set a king over us. Now therefore present yourselves before the Lord by your tribes, and by your thousands."[41]

When the huge throng had assembled they waited with the greatest expectation for Samuel to tell them who the new king would be. Every tribe present hoped it would be one of their sons. But Samuel surprised them by announcing that the new king would come from the most feeble tribe of them all, Benjamin. Then he announced that it would be from the family of Matri among the Benjamites. Finally he told them that the new king was named Saul, son of Kish.

Undoubtedly there was a great straining of necks to get a glimpse of the great new leader. However, Saul did not come forward. The people began looking about in every direction for the new king and Samuel especially must have felt perturbed. Surely the man would have enough sense to come to his own coronation! Nevertheless, Saul could not be found. Finally Samuel went to the Lord. After all, it was He who had selected Saul. Samuel wanted to know where he was. The Lord said he was in the camp but hiding amongst the baggage. A frantic search was undertaken and finally they found him. In all the history of kings there was nothing quite like this. We are not told whether it was through modesty or fear that Saul had hidden himself. In any event Samuel was relieved to see him eventually brought forward. There is no doubt but that Saul made a magnificent impression as he strode through the throng. The scripture says "he was higher than any of the people from his shoulders and upward."[42] Samuel pointed to him and declared, "See ye him whom the Lord hath chosen, that there is none like him among all the people?"[43]

A great shout went up from the vast assembly as they said, "God save the king."[44]

Samuel then gave a dissertation on the manner in which the kingdom should be governed under the new system. Later he wrote it in a book and laid it up before the Lord for safe-

---

41. 1 Samuel 10:19
42. 1 Samuel 10:23
43. 1 Samuel 10:24
44. *Ibid.* The literal meaning of the original Hebrew is: "May the king live."

keeping.[45] It is unfortunate that we do not have this book today for undoubtedly it would make an interesting study. In another book we do have the words of a righteous king which would perhaps fit the kind of policies that Samuel most likely recommended. How different the history of Israel might have been if Saul, her first king, had captured the spirit of the great King Benjamin. This latter king lived in America a little over a thousand years after Saul. At the end of his life this is what he was able to say to his people:

"My brethren . . . I have not commanded you to come up hither that ye should fear me, or that ye should think that I of myself am more than a mortal man.

"But I am like as yourselves, subject to all manner of infirmities in body and mind; yet I have been chosen by this people, and consecrated by my father, and was suffered by the hand of the Lord that I should be a ruler and a king over this people. . . .

"I say unto you that as I have been suffered to spend my days in your service, even up to this time, and have not sought gold nor silver nor any manner of riches of you;

"Neither have I suffered that ye should be confined in dungeons, nor that ye should make slaves one of another, nor that ye should murder, or plunder, or steal, or commit adultery; nor even have I suffered that ye should commit any manner of wickedness, and have taught you that ye should keep the commandments of the Lord, in all things which he hath commanded you —

"And even I, myself, have labored with mine own hands that I might serve you, and that ye should not be laden with taxes, and that there should nothing come upon you which was grievous to be borne. . . .

"Behold, I say unto you that because I said unto you that I had spent my days in your service, I do not desire to boast, for I have only been in the service of God·

". . . I tell you these things that ye may learn wisdom; that ye may learn that when ye are in the service of your fellow beings ye are only in the service of your God.

---

45. 1 Samuel 10:25

"Behold, ye have called me your king; and if I, whom ye call your king, do labor to serve you, then ought not ye to labor to serve one another?"[46]

Here indeed was a king after the Lord's design. With this man the key to kingship was service, not pomp and pageantry. With God's true servants it has always been so, and could have been so with Saul. Note that Samuel did not put him in a fine house, nor surround him with servants and luxury. Samuel sent Saul home to Gibeah to work in the field and perform his daily tasks until the government could be reorganized under the new system.[47] It was a humble beginning. In fact so humble that the "sons of Belial" and similar apostate spirits scoffed at Saul saying, "How shall this man save us?" The scripture says, "And they despised him, and brought him no presents. But he held his peace."[48]

SAUL'S FIRST TEST — THE AMMONITE WAR

Saul's calling was to rid the land of the Philistines, but his first call to duty came from the other direction. A generation earlier, Jephthah had driven the Ammonites (descendants of Lot) out of Trans-Jordan and pushed them back into the Moabite mountains east of the Dead Sea. Now, however, they had regrouped, re-mobilized and were back in Gilead with a vengeance. Their new leader was named Nahash.

The attack against Gilead in Trans-Jordan was so quick and overwhelming that the Israelites surrendered and told Nahash that if he would not destroy them they would serve him as tributaries. But Nahash was a ruthless ruler and said he would only spare their lives if they would allow him to blind the right eye of every male. Apparently this was intended to make them less effective in rising up to regain their freedom. This cruel proposal made the Israelites of Gilead reconsider. They asked Nahash for seven days during which time they hoped to rally some help from the Israelites on the other side of the Jordan. When Nahash agreed to the seven day truce, the frantic Gileadites sent word to Saul pleading with him to rescue them.

---

46. Mosiah 2:9-18
47. 1 Samuel 10:26
48. 1 Samuel 10:27

As Saul listened to their story a spirit of righteous wrath rose in him. He took two oxen and dismembered them and sent pieces of the butchered animals to all parts of Israel with this message: "Whosoever cometh not forth after Saul and after Samuel, so shall it be done unto his oxen."[49] This was a call to arms and Saul wanted any slackers among the Israelites to know that failure to respond carried a definite penalty.

In response to this call, thirty thousand came up out of Judah while the other tribes rallied three hundred thousand. As this massive tide of humanity came pouring out of Bezek where they had been mobilized there was no doubt that Israel was once more a united body like it was in the days of Joshua. These forces moved down the mountains of Judah and Benjamin, crossed the plains of Gilgal, pushed through the Jordan at the southern crossing and then charged into the Ammonites before they were even out of their beds. The scripture says they "slew the Ammonites until the heat of the day: and it came to pass, that they which remained were scattered, so that two of them were not left together."[50] There had been nothing like it in Israel in four hundred years!

The people were so proud of this revived national spirit and the success of this venture that it made Saul a hero overnight. The people said to Samuel, "Who is he that said, Shall Saul reign over us? bring the men, that we may put them to death."[51] They were referring to the "sons of Belial."

But Saul interrupted this enthusiastic display of misdirected loyalty and said, "There shall not a man be put to death this day: for today the Lord hath wrought salvation in Israel."[52] Saul was no Abimelech. He felt no need to assassinate everyone who might resist him or criticize him. This statement was worthy of a king. If only Saul could have retained the same spirit later on when David came into his life how different things might have been. In righteousness, Saul and David could have made a tremendous team.

---

49. 1 Samuel 11:7
50. 1 Samuel 11:11
51. 1 Samuel 11:12
52. 1 Samuel 11:13

THE CONFERENCE AT GILGAL

After this great victory Samuel felt it would be an appropriate time to gather all of the people into conference for a sacrifice of thanksgiving and further instructions. Therefore the word was sent out and the people gathered in a great multitude on the very plain where the mighty host of Joshua had camped after their miraculous crossing of the Jordan.

On this occasion Saul was confirmed once more as their king and it was a time of great rejoicing together. After the various sacrifices and rites had been completed, Samuel addressed the multitude as follows:

"Behold, I have hearkened unto your voice in all that ye said unto me, and have made a king over you. And now, behold, the king walketh before you: and I am old and gray-headed; and, behold, my sons are with you: and I have walked before you from my childhood unto this day. Behold, here I am: witness against me before the Lord, and before his anointed: whose ox have I taken? or whose ass have I taken? or whom have I defrauded? whom have I oppressed? or of whose hand have I received any bribe to blind mine eyes therewith? and I will restore it you."[53]

To appreciate this speech it must be kept in mind that this is the man the people had rejected in favor of a king. Samuel was just setting the record straight. The people assured him, "Thou hast not defrauded us, nor oppressed us, neither hast thou taken ought of any man's hand."[54]

Samuel then told the people that even though the Lord had given them a king they must still look to the Lord for liberation from the Philistines or any future oppressors. In other words, their king without God could be nothing. After teaching them this principle Samuel pointed out to them that it was the harvest season (May and June in that country) and that it was a season when it never rained. Then he said, ". . . stand and see this great thing, which the Lord will do before your eyes."[55] Immediately a great storm arose which poured down a flood upon the people and thundered mightily in their ears. They pleaded with Samuel, saying, "Pray for

53. 1 Samuel 12:1-3
54. 1 Samuel 12:4

55. 1 Samuel 12:16

thy servants unto the Lord thy God, that we die not: for we
have added unto all our sins this evil, to ask us a king.''[56]

Apparently after the storm had ceased he told them in
essence that to have a king or not to have a king was of little
importance providing they remained faithful to the Lord. No
doubt he was repeating some of the things he had written in
his book about government by kings. There could be great
kings like King Benjamin if only the people would remain
righteous and serve one another, "But if ye shall still do
wickedly, ye shall be consumed, both ye and your king.''[57]

This was a true doctrine as both Saul and the people
would shortly learn.

THE BEGINNING OF THE WAR WITH THE PHILISTINES

Although the Israelites were able to attack the Ammonites and overwhelm them with sheer weight of numbers, they
did not have the same confidence in dealing with the Philistines. The Ammonites were nomads. They could be fought
with clubs, rocks, knives and staves. Not so with the Philistines. They had chariots, infantry, and all the paraphernalia
of professional warriors· Furthermore, the Philistines were
coming up in the world. They were becoming a powerful
maritime power in their own right and were respected by
both Egypt and Mesopotamia as a force to be reckoned with.

At the same time the Philistines knew the Israelites were
no shabby crew of fighters either. After seeing what they
did to the Ammonites the Philistines made it a rule that the
Isarelites could not have any forges for the manufacture of
weapons. The scripture says, "Now there was no smith found
throughout all the land of Israel: for the Philistines said,
Lest the Hebrews make them swords or spears.''[58] As a result
of this ". . . all the Israelites went down to the Philistines, to
sharpen every man his share, and his coulter, and his axe,
and his mattock.''[59]

Only when these circumstances are kept in mind is it
possible to understand what Saul was trying to accomplish
when he made his first attack on the Philistines. He took

---

56. 1 Samuel 12:19   58. 1 Samuel 13:19
57. 1 Samuel 12:25   59. 1 Samuel 13:20

three thousand men and divided them with two thousand in Michmash under his own command and one thousand at Gibeah under his son, Jonathan. These were both major Philistines garrisons and it appears to have been the intention of Saul to attack these points first for the purpose of seizing their arsenals of weapons.

Jonathan made the first assault and successfully took over the garrison in his area. However, the Philistines did not look upon this as a mere skirmish as Saul might have hoped but considered it the signal for an all-out war. Saul sent an emergency message throughout Israel ordering every man over twenty to rally to the standard, but the courage of the people wilted within them. The scripture says, ". . . the people did hide themselves in caves, and in thickets, and in rocks, and in high places, and in pits. And some of the Hebrews went over Jordan to the land of Gad and Gilead."[60]

SAUL MAKES HIS FIRST SERIOUS MISTAKE

This whole development occurred so quickly that Saul could only rally what forces were available and wait for Samuel to tell him what to do. Samuel had said that in any situation such as this he should go to Gilgal "and behold, I will come down unto thee, to offer burnt offerings, and to sacrifice sacrifices of peace offerings: seven days shalt thou tarry, till I come to thee, and shew thee what thou shalt do."[61]

Apparently Samuel thought that in case of an emergency he would always be able to reach Saul within seven days, no matter where his travels may have taken him. In this case, however, he failed to make it in the prescribed time and Saul began to panic. The hosts of the Philistines had camped at Michmash in numbers that were terrifying to the Israelites. There were three thousand chariots and six thousand horsemen, not to mention a great body of infantry.[62]

As Saul saw his own troops begin to flee from him he decided to take matters into his own hands. He apparently felt the need to join the enemy in battle as soon as possible in order to rally his forces before they lost all willingness to

---

60. 1 Samuel 13:6-7
61. 1 Samuel 10:8
62. 1 Samuel 13:5. The text says 30,000 chariots but this is believed to be an error in transcription. Dr. Clarke discusses the problem and gives the opinion that the correct figure is 3,000 chariots (Clarke, *Bible Commentary*, Vol. 2, p. 247).

fight. However, he dared not do this without first asking for the benediction of heaven on his efforts and since Samuel had not arrived he decided to take on the Priesthood function himself. He therefore went forward as though he were the priest and made the offerings.[63]

But barely was the act completed when Samuel did arrive. "And Samuel said, What hast thou done? And Saul said, Because I saw that the people were scattered from me, and that thou camest not within the days appointed, and that the Philistines gathered themselves together at Michmash: therefore said I, the Philistines will come down now upon me to Gilgal, and I have not made supplication unto the Lord: I forced myself therefore, and offered a burnt-offering."[64]

Samuel immediately detected a fundamental weakness in Saul which would ultimately destroy him. Under pressure he could not maintain personal discipline. Therefore Samuel said, "Thou hast done foolishly: thou hast not kept the commandment of the Lord thy God, which he commanded thee: for now would the Lord have established thy kingdom upon Israel for ever."[65]

Apparently the Lord had already told Samuel that he was about to manifest a great display of power for Israel and wipe out their enemies in a smashing victory for the Israelites. Now Samuel knew that Saul's impetuous act had destroyed this possibility. He said to Saul, "But now thy kingdom shall not continue: the Lord hath sought him a man after his own heart, and the Lord hath commanded him to be captain over his people, because thou hast not kept that which the Lord commanded thee."[66]

All of this was in anticipation of the calling up of David which was still in the future. However, in the prophetic mind of Samuel it was a present, accomplished fact.

Samuel immediately left for Gibeah which was Saul's home. Bewildered and deflated, Saul followed him. His total military strength had now dwindled to six hundred men.[67]

---

63. 1 Samuel 13:9
64. 1 Samuel 13:11-12
65. 1 Samuel 13:13
66. 1 Samuel 13:14
67. 1 Samuel 13:15

JONATHAN TRIGGERS A SURPRISING VICTORY

When the Philistines found that the Israelites were avoiding open combat they divided their forces and sent three groups of spoilers or marauders to roam the land. This was a dangerous military maneuver and opened up the Philistines to possible ambush. Jonathan thought he saw an opportunity to put the Philistines on the defensive. It involved the risk of his own life but little more. Jonathan plainly had more faith than his father and son, without telling anyone else of his plan, he said to his armor-bearer, "Come, and let us go over unto the garrison of these uncircumcised: it may be that the Lord will work for us: for there is no restraint to the Lord to save by many or by few."[68] Jonathan told his companion that he would attract the attention of the garrison and if the soldiers invited them to approach then he would consider it an omen that God was delivering them into his hands. He thought that once he was close enough to attack he could dispatch the lot. Jonathan told the armor-bearer to come behind him so that as Jonathan knocked each man down the armor-bearer could slay him.

This plan worked out even better than Jonathan had expected. Altogether, he and his companion succeeded in disposing of about twenty soldiers at the garrison but when the alarm was sounded and a wild cry went forth that the Israelites were attacking it caught the Philistines in their own psychological trap. From a military standpoint they knew they were in an extremely vulnerable position with their forces so completely scattered. Their own fears had built up to such a point that when the alarm sounded they went into a stampede trying to escape. They were so frantic that they "went on beating down one another."[69]

Saul was just as surprised as the Philistines and lost a lot of valuable time trying to figure out what to do. He assumed that some of his troops must have attacked so he ordered a roll call and found that only Jonathan and his armor-bearer were missing. Then he held a consultation with the Levite Priest who was with him to determine if they should send for the Ark of the Covenant before attacking. Finally, after

---

68. 1 Samuel 14:6   69. 1 Samuel 14:16

a great deal of wasted motion he ordered his troops to tread down the fleeing Philistines. The scripture says that two factors contributed to this great victory near Gibeah. One was the fact that the Israelites finally generated enough courage to come out of hiding and join the fray and the other was the fact that the Philistines had brought many Hebrew servants along with them and these mutinied against their masters when they saw them in a state of panic.

SAUL ATTEMPTS TO KILL JONATHAN

Once King Saul had felt the fever of victory he could not restrain himself. After the great victory at Gibeah he ordered them into battle at Beth-aven the next day without allowing any of them to eat. He rated it a waste of time. Said Saul, "Cursed be the man that eateth any food until evening, that I may be avenged on mine enemies." As a result, "none of the people tasted any food."[70]

However, Jonathan had not heard this command and when he went through a wood he saw a quantity of wild honey. He was famished and fatigued so he used a rod he was carrying to dip into the honey and eat as he went along the way. Immediately afterwards he felt refreshed and renewed in strength. When some of the others noticed what Jonathan was doing they told him about his father's command. Jonathan was angry with his father's stupidity and said, "My father hath troubled the land: see, I pray you, how mine eyes have been enlightened, because I tasted a little of this honey. How much more, if haply the people had eaten freely to-day of the spoil of their enemies which they found? for had there not been now a much greater slaughter among the Philistines?"[71] It was apparent that the son was a man of sounder judgment that the father.

That night the people took the cattle of the Philistines and used them for meat. However, they did not kill the animals in the manner required by the Mosaic law so Saul once more presumed to function in a Priesthood capacity by building an altar. Then he said to the priest who was Ahiah (great-grandson of Eli)[72] "Shall I go down after the Philistines?"

---

70. 1 Samuel 14:24
71. 1 Samuel 14:29-30

72. 1 Samuel 14:3

But when this Priest attempted to make contact with the Lord there was no answer. A whole day was spent waiting for an answer. Finally Saul decided that someone had committed a sin and he swore, saying that whoever had committed this sin should die "though it be in Jonathan my son." At that time he did not know that Jonathan had broken his command of the previous day but he spoke his oath in this form so the people would know he truly meant it.

In those days the Urim and Thummim was used by the High Priest to discern judgment. When Saul asked who had been involved in violating an order the answer pointed to Jonathan. Saul was greatly surprised and said to his son, "Tell me what thou hast done." Jonathan knew he had done nothing to offend the Lord. He frankly told his father, "I did but taste a little honey with the end of the rod that was in mine hand, and, lo, I must die."[73] Now, if Saul had gone back to the Urim and Thummim to discover the will of the Lord concerning Jonathan he would have no doubt learned than Jonathan's actions had nothing to do with the Priest's inability to communicate with the Lord concerning the Philistines. But Saul relied upon his own judgment and determined to fulfill his oath by slaying Jonathan.

But by this time the word had apparently circulated among the fighting men of Israel that it had been Jonathan's strategy which had precipitated their great victory. They therefore said to their king, "Shall Jonathan die, who hath wrought this great salvation in Israel? God forbid: as the Lord liveth, there shall not one hair of his head fall to the ground; for he hath wrought with God this day." Then the scripture concludes, "So the people rescued Jonathan that he died not."[74]

THE CAMPAIGN AGAINST THE AMALEKITES

From this time on, King Saul became almost completely preoccupied with war. But he fought as a man, not as a servant of God. Every time he received an instruction from the prophet of the Lord he always seemed to fall short of the mark. The campaign against the Amalekites was typical of his problem.

---

73. 1 Samuel 14:43   74. 1 Samuel 14:45

Samuel told Saul it was the will of the Lord that the Amalekites should be cleansed from the face of the land and that they should be destroyed as completely as ancient Jericho. So Saul went forth, but instead of fulfilling the commandment he listened to his troops who thought they should bring home the best of the flocks from the Amalekites. Saul also decided to save the king of the Amalekites whose name was Agag. Israel's four hundred years of dark ages had been the direct result of disobeying God's commandments in this same manner. Nevertheless, Saul thought he had done a tremendous job. When Samuel came down to him, the king welcomed the aged prophet and said,

"Blessed be thou of the Lord: I have performed the commandment of the Lord."[75]

Samuel looked solemnly at the king and said, "What meaneth then this bleating of the sheep in mine ears, and the lowing of the oxen which I hear?"[76]

King Saul tried to pass it off lightly. He said, "They have brought them from the Amalekites: for the people spared the best of the sheep and of the oxen, to sacrifice unto the Lord thy God; and the rest we have utterly destroyed."[77]

Even if this were completely true, it once more reflected the stubborn habit which Saul possessed of rationalizing his own disobedience and continuously presuming to impose his own judgment over that of the Lord.

"Then Samuel said unto Saul, Stay, and I will tell thee what the Lord hath said to me this night. And he said unto him, Say on.

"And Samuel said, When you wast little in thine own sight, wast thou not made the head of the tribes of Israel, and the Lord anointed thee king over Israel? . . . Wherefore then didst thou not obey the voice of the Lord?"[78]

King Saul tried to argue with Samuel, saying, "Yea, I have obeyed the voice of the Lord, and have gone the way which the Lord sent me, and have brought Agag the King of Amalek, and have utterly destroyed the Amalekites. But

---

75. 1 Samuel 15:13   77. 1 Samuel 15:15
76. 1 Samuel 15:14   78. 1 Samuel 15:16-19

the people took of the spoil, sheep and oxen, the chief of the things which should have been utterly destroyed, to sacrifice unto the Lord thy God in Gilgal·

"And Samuel said, Hath the Lord as great delight in burnt offerings and sacrifices, as in obeying the voice of the Lord? Behold, to obey is better than sacrifice, and to hearken than the fat of rams.

"For rebellion is as the sin of witchcraft, and stubbornness is as iniquity and idolatry. Because thou hast rejected the word of the Lord, he hath also rejected thee from being king."[79]

These final words penetrated the calloused conscience of Saul where all else had failed. He suddenly threw himself on the mercy of Samuel and pleaded for forgiveness. As Samuel turned away, Saul seized his mantle so that it ripped. Samuel said, "The Lord hath rent the kingdom of Israel from thee this day, and hath given it to a neighbour of thine, that is better than thou."[80]

As Saul contemplated his fate his pride once more asserted itself· He just could not face his troops as a king rejected of God. He therefore pleaded with Samuel to at least stand by him in the presence of the people while he worshipped the Lord. To this request, Samuel consented as a parting gesture. Afterwards he said to King Saul, "Bring ye hither to me Agag the king of the Amalekites."[81]

Apparently this Agag was a vicious and cruel ruler who above all his people deserved to die. We do not have a catalogue of his crimes but simply the judgment of God that he and his people had become so depraved and violent that the Supreme Judge had ordered them summarily returned to God. When Agag was brought before Samuel the Vulgate version says he came in "very fat and trembling."[82] The scripture says he exclaimed to Samuel, "Surely the bitterness of death is past."[83] But he knew better the moment Samuel spoke. The aged prophet declared with words which give us a suggestion of Agag's crimes, "And thy sword hath made women

79. 1 Samuel 15:20-23
80. 1 Samuel 15:28
81. 1 Samuel 15:32

82. Clarke, *Bible Commentary* ,Vol. 2, p. 257
83. I Samuel 15:32

childless, so shall thy mother be childless among women."[84] With that the prophet Samuel took a weapon and dispatched the trembling Agag himself.

The death of Agag marked the end of the Amalekites. Their crimes had been accumulating during the years. They were the first to attack the children of Israel as they came up out of Egypt,[85] and they had been among the most depraved of all the nomadic tribes of the desert. Now they were no more.

This was also the last time Samuel ever conversed with Saul.[86] Already the Lord had told Samuel that a new star was rising over Israel. It was the star of David.

84. 1 Samuel 15:33
85. Exodus 17:8-16
86. 1 Samuel 15:35

Scripture Reading and Questions on Chapter Twenty-Six

Scripture Reading Assignment: 1 Samuel, Chapters 8 to 15 inclusive.

1—How much does the scripture tell us about the middle years of Samuel's life? What important changes obviously took place during those years?

2—In what respects did Samuel's later years compare with those of Eli's?

3—What was the excuse given by the Israelites for wanting a king? What was the real reason?

4—Were "judges" in the Bible judicial officers or something much broader? Why does the Lord sometimes call them "rulers"?

5—What kind of men were to be selected as judges or captains?

6—What is Justice? What are Civil Rights? What is Liberty? What is Equality?

7—What were some of the things Samuel said a king would do to them? Is this typical of most kings?

8—Why did the Lord let the people of Israel have a king when he knew it was not the best form of government?

9—How did Samuel happen to pick out Saul to be the king? Was Saul humble or proud about his new calling?

10—To which pride did Saul belong?

11—What happened when Saul was presented to the people at Mizpeh? Did this show good judgment?

12—What were the qualities of King Benjamin which made him such an excepional ruler? What was the key word in his administration? Would this apply to all public offices?

13—Why did the Gileadites decide to fight Nahash after they had previously offered to surrender and be tributaries?

14—Why do you think Samuel asked the people if they had anything against him? Do you think he was hurt when the people had rejected him in favor of a king? What did he do to show the power of the Lord was still with him?

15—Why didn't the Israelites fight the Philistines as readily as they had the Ammonites?

16—What was the reaction of the people when war finally broke out with the Philistines? What was Saul's first serious mistake?

17—How did Jonathan trigger a great victory? Was Saul surprised?

18—What were the circumstances when Saul attempted to kill Jonathan? Who saved him?

19—What was Saul's mistake in the war with the Amalekites? What was Saul's recurring weakness?

20—Who killed King Agag? Who was going to be raised up to replace Saul? When was the last time Samuel conversed with Saul?

APPENDIX

Herodotus Describes the Egyptian Embalming Process

"When they (the relatives) have agreed upon the price they depart; and those with whom the dead corpse is left proceed to embalm it after the following manner: First of all, they with a crooked iron draw the brain out of the head through the nostrils; next, with a sharp Ethiopic stone they cut up that part of the abdomen called the *ilia,* and that way draw out all the bowels, which, having cleansed [the cavity] and washed with palm wine, they again rinse and wash with wine perfumed with pounded odours: then filling up the belly with pure myrrh and cassia grossly powdered, and all other odours except frankincense, they sew it up again. Having so done, they salt it up close with nitre seventy days [with Jacob it was 40 days — Gen. 50:3] for longer they may not salt it. After this number of days are over they wash the corpse again, and then roll it up with fine linen, all besmeared with a sort of gum, commonly used by the Egyptians instead of glue. Then is the body restored to its relations, who prepare a wooden coffin for it in the shape and likeness of a man, and then put the embalmed body into it, and thus enclosed, place it in a repository in the house, setting it upright against the wall. After this manner they, with great expense preserve their dead." (Taken from *Euterpe,* by Herodutus, p. 120, and quoted with additional related material in Clarke's *Bible Commentary,* Vol. 1, p. 273-274.)

APPENDIX

The History and Significance of the Urim and Thummim

"Urim" and "Thummim" appear to be individual names assigned to each of two transparent stones which were used by the servants of God from Adam on down, to 1—facilitate revelation,[1] 2—to give righteous judgments,[2] and 3—to translate ancient records written in an unknown tongue.[3]

Students of Hebrew tell us that the literal meaning of "Urim" is "lights," and the literal meaning of "Thummim" is "perfection." However, Dr. Sidney B. Sperry of the Brigham Young University points out that more ancient languages have similar words with a fuller meaning. The Assyrian word, *uru*, means "to give an oracle" or prophecies and revelations. The Babylonian word, *tamu*, may be related to the Hebrew word, *Thummim*, and means "to speak."

Abraham is the first prophet mentioned in scripture as having these instruments, although Orson Pratt is the authority for saying that Noah also had them.[4] We have the following statement from Abraham concerning his possession of these instruments:

"And I, Abraham, had the Urim and Thummim, which the Lord my God had given unto me, in Ur of the Chaldees. . . . And the Lord said unto me, by the Urim and Thummim, that Kolob was after the manner of the Lord."[5]

Abraham also had the sacred history of God's chosen servants going back to Adam and he may have received these at the same time he received the Urim and Thummim. Said he: "But the records of the fathers, even the patriarchs, concerning the right of the Priesthood, the Lord my God

---

1. Numbers 27:21
2. Exodus 28:30
3. Doctrine and Covenants 10:1; Ether 3:23-24
4. *Journal of Discourses*, Vol. 16, p. 50
5. Abraham 3:1-4

preserved in mine own hands; therefore a knowledge of the beginning of the creation, and also of the planets, and of the stars, as they were made known unto the fathers, have I kept even unto this day. . . ."[6]

The fact that Abraham had a record from "the beginning" and at the same time had the Urim and Thummim implies that those instruments might have been in the possession of Noah (as Orson Pratt has stated) and also in the possession of all the patriarchs back to Adam. This seems rather strongly supported by the Book of Mormon which says: "And now he [Mosiah] translated them [certain ancient records] by means of those two stones which were fastened into the two rims of a bow. Now these things were prepared FROM THE BEGINNING, and were handed down from generation to generation, for the purpose of interpreting languages . . . and whosoever has these things is called seer, after the manner of old times."[7]

If these sacred instruments were prepared "in the beginning" and handed down "from generation to generation," then they must have originated with Adam and must have been passed down through the Patriarchs until they finally came into the possession of Abraham.

What happened to these two transparent stones between Abraham and Moses we do not know. They may have been handed down through Isaac, Jacob, and Joseph but it is more likely that they were taken back into divine custody and were then returned to Moses either on the Mount or shortly thereafter. After Abraham no further mention is made of them until Moses is told to put them in the jewelled linen container (called a "breastplate") which Aaron wore on the front of his Priesthood vestment, called the ephod. The ephod was a multi-colored waistcoat with two large onyx stones on the shoulders. The names of six tribes were carved on each stone. From these stones hung woven golden chains which were attached to the linen container called the "breastplate of judgment." Concerning it the Lord said: "Thou [Moses] shalt put in the breastplate of Judgment the Urim and the Thummim; and they shall be upon Aaron's heart,

6. Abraham 1:31
7. Mosiah 28:13-16

when he goeth in before the Lord: and Aaron shall bear the judgment of the children of Israel upon his heart before the Lord continually."[8]

Later, these instruments were turned over to Aaron's son, Eleazar, and Joshua was told to get the word of the Lord through this means. The Lord said: "And he [Joshua] shall stand before Eleazar the priest, who shall ask counsel for him after the judgment of Urim before the Lord: at his word shall they go out, and at his word they shall come in, both he, and all the children of Israel with him, even all the congregation."[9]

There is another lapse of around 400 years and then we are told, "When Saul inquired of the Lord, the Lord answered him not, neither by dreams, nor by Urim, nor by prophets."[10] This implies that these sacred instruments were available but would not function during a period of apostasy.

Following the return of the Jews from Babylon (538 B.C.) the sacred instruments appear to have been lost from among them. "And the Tirshatha [Governor] said unto them, that they should not eat of the most holy things, till there stood up a priest with Urim and Thummim."[11] However, they appear to have been very familiar with these instruments so their disappearance may have been just before the captivity. This would imply that Jeremiah was probably the last of the Israelites of Old Testament times to have access to them.

REFERENCES TO A URIM AND THUMMIM IN THE BOOK OF MORMON

It is highly probable that there were two or more sets of these so-called "Urim and Thummim." At least we know that around 2,000 B.C. the Lord said to the brother of Jared who was about to leave for the western hemisphere: ". . . wherefore, ye shall treasure up the things which ye have seen and heard, and show it to no man. . . . ye shall write them and shall seal them up, that no one can interpret them; for ye shall write them in a language that they cannot be read. And behold, THESE TWO STONES will I give unto thee, and

---

8. Exodus 28:30
9. Numbers 27:21
10. I Samuel 28:6
11. Nehemiah 7:65; Ezra 2:63

ye shall seal them up also with the things which ye shall write. For behold, the language which ye shall write I have confounded; wherefore I will cause in my own due time that these stones shall magnify to the eyes of men these things which ye shall write. And when the Lord had said these words, he showed unto the brother of Jared all the inhabitants of the earth which had been, and also all that would be; and he withheld them not from his sight, even unto the ends of the earth."[12]

The Jaredites were wiped out around 600 B.C. and their records fell into the hands of their successors. Somehow the Lord also transferred "the interpreters" for we read that around 121 B.C. the prophet Mosiah "has wherewith that he can look, and translate all records that are of ancient date; and it is a gift from God. And the things are called INTERPRETERS, and no man can look in them except he be commanded, lest he should look for that he ought not and he should perish. And whosoever is commanded to look in them, the same is called seer. . . . a seer is a Revelator and a prophet also; and a gift which is greater can no man have. . . . But a seer can know of things which are past, and also of things which are to come, and by them [the interpreters] shall all things be revealed, or, rather, shall secret things be made manifest, and hidden things shall come to light, and things which are not known shall be made known by them . . . Thus God has provided a means that man, through faith, might work mighty miracles; therefore he [the seer] becometh a great benefit to his fellow beings. . . . These interpreters were doubtless prepared for the purpose of unfolding all such mysteries to the children of men."[13]

It is obvious that the so-called "interpreters" were used for revelation of all kinds[14] and were identical in purpose with the Urim and Thummim used by Abraham and Aaron. In fact, these stones are those which were delivered to Joseph Smith with the gold plates and are specifically referred to by the Lord as the Urim and Thummim.[15] They are also identified as the "Urim and Thummim which were given to the brother of Jared upon the mount. . . ."[16]

---

12. Ether 3:21-25
13. Mosiah 8:13-19
14. Alma 37:21-25

15. Doctrine and Covenants 10:1
16. Doctrine and Covenants 17:1

How did these "interpreters" get from the Brother of Jared to Mosiah and then to Joseph Smith? As already indicated, we do not know how Mosiah received the interpreters. However, we are told that by about 121 B.C., which was long after the Jaredites had been wiped out, he did have them. It is interesting that the interpreters were not listed among the sacred items such as the sword of Laban, the records, and the Liahona, which Mosiah received from his father.[17] It is therefore likely that Mosiah received the interpreters during his ministry and was the first custodian of these sacred instruments insofar as the Nephites were concerned. They were handed down to each succeeding generation. The next Nephite prophet to receive the interpreters from Mosiah was Alma the younger. The record says Mosiah gave him "the interpreters, and conferred them upon him, and commanded him that he should keep and preserve them, and also keep a record of the people, handing them down from one generation to another. . . ."[18] That this was actually done seems evident from the fact that by 400 A.D. Moroni had custody of the Urim and Thummim and was commanded to seal them up with the gold plates (and other sacred objects) to come forth in the last days.[19]

Joseph Smith Receives the Urim and Thummim

It is impossible to tell from the record whether the Lord had prepared one set of Urim and Thummim for the prophets of the Bible and another for the people of the Book of Mormon, or whether He may have used the same Urim and Thummim and transferred them back and forth.

All we know is that the interpreters which Joseph Smith received were the same "Urim and Thummim which were given to the brother of Jared upon the mount. . . ."[20]

Concerning the circumstances under which Joseph Smith first saw these instruments, he says, "Convenient to the village of Manchester, Ontario County, New York, stands a hill of considerable size, and the most elevated of any in the neighborhood. On the west side of this hill, not far from the top, under a stone of considerable size, lay the plates,

---

17. Mosiah 1:16
18. Mosiah 28:20
19. Ether 4:5
20. Doctrine and Covenants 17:1

deposited in a stone box· [This box and its location had been previously shown to Joseph Smith in a vision, and identified to him as the sanctuary of the sacred scriptural record of the Nephites.] This stone was thick and rounding in the middle on the upper side, and thinner towards the edges, so that the middle part of it was visible above the ground, but the edge all around was covered with earth. Having removed the earth, I obtained a lever, which I got fixed under the edge of the stone, and with a little exertion raised it up. I looked in, and there indeed did I behold the plates, the Urim and Thummim, and the breastplate, as stated by the messenger."[21]

Two objects in this stone box are of particular interest in our present discussion — the set of Urim and Thummim and the breastplate to which they were attached.

DESCRIPTION OF THE BREASTPLATE

The mother of Joseph Smith has given us the most detailed account of the breastplate. She personally examined the breastplate and says: "It was wrapped in a thin muslin handkerchief [which in those days was large and much like a scarf], so thin that I could feel its proportions without any difficulty. It was concave on one side, and convex on the other, and extended from the neck downwards, as far as the center of the stomach of a man of extraordinary size. It had four straps of the same material, for the purpose of fastening it to the breast, two of which ran back to go over the shoulders, and the other two were designed to fasten to the hips. They were just the width of two of my fingers, (for I measured them) and they had holes in the end of them, to be convenient in fastening· After I had examined it, Joseph placed it in the chest with the Urim and Thummim."[22]

DESCRIPTION OF THE URIM AND THUMMIM

The Book of Mormon simply describes the Urim and Thummim as "two stones which were fastened into the two rims of a bow."[23]

---

21. *Documentary History of the Church*, Vol. 1, p. 16
22. Quoted by B. H. Roberts in *Comprehensive History of the Church*, Vol. 1, pp. 92-93
23. Mosiah 28:13

Joseph Smith described them as follows: "With the records was a curious instrument, the Urim and Thummim, which consisted of two transparent stones, set in the rim of a bow fastened to a breast plate. Through the medium of the Urim and Thummim I translated the record by the gift and power of God."[24]

A more detailed account of the Urim and Thummim and how they were fastened to the breast plate is given by William Smith.

"The Urim and Thummim was set in a double silver bow which was twisted into the shape of a figure eight, and the two stones were placed literally between the two rims of a bow. At one end was attached a rod which was connected with the outer edge of the right shoulder of the breastplate. By pressing the head a little forward, the rod held the Urim and Thummim before the eyes much like a pair of spectacles. A pocket was prepared in the breastplate on the left side, immediately over the heart. When not in use the Urim and Thummim was placed in the pocket, the rod being of just the right length to allow it to be deposited. This instrument could, however, be detached from the breastplate when away from home, but Joseph always used it in connection with the breastplate when translating, as it permitted him to have both hands free to touch the plates. The instrument was too large for Joseph's eyes; they must have been used by larger men."[25]

Just as ancient prophets very seldom refer to the Urim and Thummim because of their sacred character, so also the modern custodians neither discuss them nor display them. Concerning this, Joseph Smith said: "Again he [Moroni] told me, that when I got those plates . . . I should not show them to any person; neither the breastplate with the Urim and Thummim; only to those to whom I should be commanded to show them; if I did I should be destroyed."[26]

---

24. *Documentary History of the Church*, Vol. 4, p. 537
25. Quoted in *Saints Herald* Mar. 9, 1932, p. 258
26. *Documentary History of the Church*, Vol. 1, p. 13

APPENDIX

The Law of Moses—What Was It? How Did It Work?

One of the most baffling aspects of the Old Testament is the famous "Law of Moses." However, gaining an understanding of this law can be one of the most gratifying rewards available in the Bible.

Two things make the Law of Moses difficult to grasp. First of all, it is not in one book, but is spread throughout Exodus, Leviticus, Numbers and Deuteronomy. Secondly, the original statement of the law which was clear-cut and relatively simple had to be amended by the Lord following Israel's apostasy. In its amended form the Law became burdened with an elaborate system of ceremonial rituals which fulfilled God's intention to teach Israel the rhythm of obedience, but which, for the modern student, obscured the underlying beauty of righteous living, equity and justice that the original Law contained.

In the following digest of the Law of Moses we will clearly distinguish between the laws which constituted a permanent part of the Gospel (the Law of the Covenant) and those laws which were called, "the Law of Carnal Commandments" that were added as a "schoolmaster" to guide the Israelites to Christ.

The Law of Carnal Commandments consisted of 1—dietary laws, 2—sanitation laws, and 3—an elaborate system of special sacrifices, special offerings, special sabbaths and special ordinances prescribed for ceremonial cleanliness. All of these were temporary in nature and were geared exclusively to the circumstances of the period in which they were given. This is why they were all eliminated as soon as the Savior had fulfilled his mission. They had no permanent value.

It is for this very reason that none of the Carnal Commandments are included in this present digest. Our interest is entirely with those principles which have always been a permanent part of the government of God's kingdom whenever it has been upon the earth. They worked for Enoch and they worked for Melchizedek. Unfortunately, the Israelites would not allow them to work and that is why the Carnal Commandments had to be added. Nevertheless, Moses wrote them down for us to study and a deeper appreciation of the Society of Zion or the City of Zion can be gained from a study of these principles.

As we shall see in a moment, the Law of the Covenant as given to Moses, covered practically every aspect of life's daily problems. However, the solution to these physical, practical problems always grew out of certain spiritual or eternal principles. Therefore, in order to appreciate the reason for the code of laws given to Moses it was important for the people to understand the spiritual laws on which they were based. This was the reason for the Ten Commandments.

The Significance of the Ten Commandments

The Ten Commandments describe various aspects of two sacred and eternal principles — the relationship between God and man, and the relationship between each man and all other men. The whole purpose of the Law of the Covenant as given to Moses was rooted in these two sacred relationships. The Lord undertook to digest His code of conduct or Law of the Covenant into a simple decalogue which anyone could memorize with a little effort. This is what we call, "The Ten Commandments."

For the purpose of memorizing the Ten Commandments, the following simplified form is suggested:

1 — THOU SHALT HAVE NO OTHER GODS BEFORE ME.
2 — THOU SHALT NOT MAKE UNTO THEE ANY GRAVEN IMAGE.
3 — THOU SHALT NOT TAKE THE NAME OF THE LORD THY GOD IN VAIN.
4 — REMEMBER THE SABBATH DAY TO KEEP IT HOLY.
5 — HONOR THY FATHER AND THY MOTHER.
6 — THOU SHALT NOT KILL.

7 — THOU SHALT NOT COMMIT ADULTERY.

8 — THOU SHALT NOT STEAL.

9 — THOU SHALT NOT BEAR FALSE WITNESS.

10 — THOU SHALT NOT COVET.

In the Bible these commandments are not numbered. The above breakdown is the one customarily given; however, the Catholic and Lutheran faiths combine the first two and then divide the last one into two different kinds of coveting. The principles are the same, the numbering is merely a matter of convenience.

It is interesting that when Jesus ministered among men he was challenged to name the one law which might be considered fundamental to all the rest. In other words, if the Law could be reduced to ten commandments, was it perhaps possible to reduce it to one?

In reply, Jesus put the whole law in proper perspective. He emphasized the two sacred relationships upon which all law must rest. The first and most important relationship is between God and man and the second is between one man and all other men. Here is the way the Savior said it:

"THOU SHALT LOVE THE LORD THY GOD WITH ALL THY HEART, AND WITH ALL THY SOUL, AND WITH ALL THY MIND. THIS IS THE FIRST AND GREAT COMMANDMENT. AND THE SECOND IS LIKE UNTO IT, THOU SHALT LOVE THY NEIGHBOR AS THYSELF. ON THESE TWO COMMANDMENTS HANG ALL THE LAW AND THE PROPHETS." (Matthew 22:37-40)

As we now go through a digest of the Law of the Covenant or God's revealed "code of conduct," note how completely these principles permeate every aspect of it. For convenience the Law has been broken down into the following classifications and arranged aphabetically for quick reference:

ADULTERY

See also Fornication, Idolatry, Incest, and Rape.

Definition: Unlawful sexual intercourse between a married person and one of the opposite sex, whether married or single.

"Thou shalt not commit adultery." (Exodus 20:14)

" . . . he that committeth adultery with his neighbour's wife, the adulterer and the adulteress shall surely be put to death." (Lev. 20:10)

ANIMALS — RESPONSIBLITY OF OWNER

"If an ox gore a man or a woman, that they die: then the ox shall be surely stoned, and his flesh shall not be eaten; but the owner of the ox shall be quit.

"But if the ox were wont to push with his horn in time past, and it hath been testified to his owner, and he hath not kept him in, but that he hath killed a man or a woman; the ox shall be stoned, and his owner also shall be put to death.

"If there be laid on him a sum of money, then he shall give for the ransom of his life whatsoever is laid upon him." (Ex. 21:28-30) This would be in the form of damages to the family of the victim.

The same rules apply to the goring of a child by an ox. (Ex. 21:31)

"If the ox shall push a manservant or a maidservant: he shall give unto their master thirty shekels of silver, and the ox shall be stoned." (Ex. 21:32) The damages were paid to the master since it was his responsibility to care for the injured servant until he had recovered.

"And if one man's ox hurt another's, that he die: then they shall sell the live ox, and divide the money of it; and the dead ox also they shall divide.

"Or if it be known that the ox hath used to push in time past, and his owner hath not kept him in; he shall surely pay ox for ox: and the dead shall be his own." (Ex. 21:35-36)

"If a man shall cause a field or vineyard to be eaten, and shall put in his beast, and shall feed in another man's field; of the best of his own field, and of the best of his own vineyard, shall he make restitution." (Ex. 22:5)

ANIMALS — PUREBRED STRAINS TO BE MAINTAINED

Purebred cattle are those with distinctive characteristics which have been maintained through generations of unmixed descent. The Israelites were to perpetuate the strains of purebred cattle in their possession:

"Thou shalt not let thy cattle gender with a diverse kind." (Lev. 19:19)

ARSON OR FIRE-SETTING

"If fire break out, and catch in thorns, so that the stacks of corn, or the standing corn, or the field, be consumed therewith; he that kindled the fire shall surely make restitution." (Ex. 22:6)

BATTERY

Definition: "The unlawfull beating of another."

"And if men strive together, and one smite another with a stone, or with his fist, and he die not, but keepeth his bed: if he rise again, and walk abroad upon his staff, then shall he that smote him be quit: only he shall pay for the loss of his time, and shall cause him to be thoroughly healed." (Ex. 21:18-19)

BESTIALITY

Definition: Sexual relations between mankind and an animal.

"Whosoever lieth with a beast shall surely be put to death." (Ex. 22:19)

"Neither shalt thou lie with any beast to defile thyself therewith: neither shall any woman stand before a beast to lie down thereto: it is confusion." (Lev. 18:23)

"And if a man lie with a beast, he shall surely be put to death: and ye shall slay the beast. And if a woman approach unto any beast, and lie down thereto, thou shalt kill the woman, and the beast: they shall surely be put to death; their blood shall be upon them." (Lev. 20:15-16) The animal was killed because it had often been trained for this purpose. Dr. Clarke cites authorities on the heathen practices of women committing immoral acts with animals. (*Bible Commentary*, Vol. 1, pp. 565 and 569)

BLASPHEMY

"And he that blasphemeth the name of the Lord, he shall surely be put to death, and all the congregation shall certainly stone him. . . ." (Lev. 24:16)

BOND SERVANT

See: Servitude.

BORROWING

See also: Lending.

"And if a man borrow ought of his neighbour, and it be hurt, or die, the owner thereof being not with it, he shall surely make it good." (Ex. 22:14)

However, if a man were hired to plow a field or perform some other service, and his animals were hurt or killed, the employer would not be held responsible since the risk of such injuries was included in the amount of the hire. (Ex. 22:15)

"The wicked borroweth, and payeth not again. . . ." (Psalms 37:21)

"If thou borrowest of thy neighbor, thou shalt restore that which thou hast borrowed; and if thou canst not repay, then go straightway and tell thy neighbor, lest he condemn thee." (Doc. & Cov. 136:25)

"And I would that ye should remember, that whosoever among you borroweth of his neighbor should return the thing that he borroweth, according as he doth agree, or else thou shalt commit sin; and perhaps thou shalt cause thy neighbor to commit sin." (Mosiah 4:28)

These last two quotations are included to demonstrate that the Law of the Covenant is the same in different ages and in different places.

BREACH OF TRUST

See: Embezzlement

BRIBERY

"And thou shalt take no gift; for the gift blindeth the wise, and perverteth the words of the righteous." (Ex. 23:8)

The violation of this commandment lies as the root of all corrupted governments and institutions.

BUSINESS ETHICS

"Thou shalt not defraud thy neighbor. . . ." (Lev. 19:13)

"Ye shall do no unrighteousness in judgment, in meteyard, in weight, or in measure. Just balances, just weights, a just ephah, and a just hin, shall ye have." (Lev. 19:35-36)

"Thou shalt not have in thy bag divers weights, a great and a small. Thou shalt not have in thine house divers measures, a great and a small. But thou shalt have a perfect and just weight, a perfect and just measure shalt thou have. . . . For all that do such things [as using dishonest weights and measures], and all that do unrighteously, are an abomination unto the Lord thy God." (Deut. 25:13-16)

BURGLARY

Legal Definition: "The act of breaking into any building at any time to commit a theft or other felony."

"Thou shalt not steal." (Exodus 20:15)

"If a thief be found breaking up [or breaking into a building], and be smitten [at nighttime] that he die, there shall no blood be shed for him." (Ex. 22:2) In other words, it is considered an excusable homicide.

The next verse makes it clear that this is referring only to the killing of a burglar at night because it says:

"If the sun be risen upon him, there SHALL be blood shed for him; for he should make full restitution. . . ." (Ex. 22:3) In other words, if the burglary occurs in the daytime the thief can be identified and a restitution made by him. At nighttime the burglar cannot be identified and the property owner has no remedy. Therefore, slaying the burglar at night was excusable homicide whereas deliberately slaying a burglar in the daytime was an unlawful killing.

CHILDREN — THEIR RIGHTS AND RESPONSIBILITIES

"Thou shalt not avenge, nor bear any grudge against the children of thy people, but thou shalt love thy neighbour as thyself. . . ." (Lev. 19:18)

"The fathers shall not be put to death for the children, neither shall the children be put to death for the fathers: every man shall be put to death for his own sin." (Deut. 24:16)

However, as children grew to maturity, the Mosaic law required that they begin to assume responsibility and conduct themselves according to the laws which their parents taught them. Special provision was made for the criminal delinquent who became "stubborn and rebellious," and was a "glutton and a drunkard." (Deut. 21:20) The penalty for such defiant profligacy was death, (Deut. 21:21) providing, of course, the parents who were witnesses against him, would cast the first stone (Deut. 17:7; 13:9). As might be expected, there is no single instance recorded where this extremity was ever used, nevertheless, every son of Israel knew that it was a most serious offense to rebel against parents because it was a capital crime.

The Lord requires parents to teach their children eternal truths: "And ye shall teach them your children, speaking of them when thou sittest in thine house, and when thou walkest by the way, when thou liest down, and when thou risest up." (Deut. 11:19)

Parents were to teach their children religious history so they would understand the purposes of God in giving certain commandments and requiring certain rituals or procedures. (Deut. 6:20-24)

CONTRACTS

When an Israelite made a vow or contract he was under religious as well as a legal obligation to fulfill it: "If a man vow a vow unto the Lord, or swear an oath to bind his soul with a bond; he shall not break his word, he shall do according to all that proceedeth out of his mouth." (Numbers 30:2)

A vow by a minor could be disavowed by a father and therefore made of no effect. (Numbers 30:3-5)

If a wife made a vow or contract it could be disavowed by her husband for the very practical reason that in all liklihood he would have to provide the money or otherwise help fulfill the vow. (Num. 30:6-8)

However, if the husband learns of the vow and keeps silent it is assumed that he has confirmed it and will therefore be held to support it. (Num. 30:14)

CULTS — RELIGIOUS AND FRATERNAL

It was customary among some of the heathens to identify themselves with fellow-believers of a particular cult by cutting their hair and beards in a round style. Herodotus makes special mention of those who worshipped Bacchus as shaving or cutting their hair "round." (Clarke, *Bible Commentary*, Vol. 1, p. 573) Concerning this the Lord said:

"Ye shall not round the corners of your heads, neither shalt thou mar the corners of thy beard." (Lev. 19:27)

Another heathen custom which still prevails among many primitive peoples was cutting the flesh to show remorse for the death of a relative or friend. In Barneo the natives still cut off joints of fingers as funeral offerings. Often children are badly maimed before reaching adolescence because of this practice. Another widespread practice condemned by the Lord was tatooing or marking the body with elaborate religious symbols:

"Ye shall not make any cuttings in your flesh for the dead, nor print any marks upon you: I am the Lord." (Lev. 19:28)

DIVORCE

It is obvious that the Mosiac law was designed to preserve the family and implement the marriage relationship. To maintain its integrity, adultery was equated almost as serious as murder (Deut. 22:22-23). To get a marriage off to a good start not even war was allowed to disrupt it: "When a man hath taken a new wife, he shall not go out to war, neither shall he be charged with any business: but he shall be free at home one year, and shall cheer up his wife which he hath taken." (Deut. 24:5)

Jesus made it plain that God had intended the marriage vow to be so sacred that it could not be broken except for extremely serious reasons. However, the Pharisees tempted him, by pointing out that Moses had authorized husbands in ancient Israel to put away their wives whenever they desired by simply giving them a bill or declaration of divorcement (see Deut. 24:1-4):

"And Jesus answered and said unto them, For the hardness of your heart he wrote you this precept. But from the beginning of the creation God made them male and female. For this cause shall a man leave his father and mother, and cleave to his wife; And they twain shall be one flesh: so then they are no more twain, but one flesh. What therefore God hath joined together, let not man put asunder." (Mark 10:5-9)

Later, the disciples of Jesus asked him further concerning this subject: "And he saith unto them, Whosoever shall put away his wife, and marry another, committeth adultery against her. And if a woman shall put away her husband, and be married to another, she committeth adultery." (Mark 10:11-12) In other words, in the sight of God, it is adultery for the offending partner to leave his or her spouse and then remarry.

In his Sermon on the Mount, Jesus had enunciated the restrictive basis on which a marriage could be dissolved when he said: ". . . whosoever shall put away his wife, saving for the cause of fornication, causeth her to commit adultery: and whosoever shall marry her that is divorced [when she had no excuse for abandoning her husband] committeth adultery." (Matthew 5:32)

EMBEZZLEMENT BY A TRUSTEE

Legal Definition: The fraudulent appropriation to one's own use or benefit, of property or money entrusted to him by another.

"If a man shall deliver unto his neighbour money or stuff to keep, and it be stolen out of the man's house; if the thief be found, let him [the thief] pay double. If the thief be not found, then the master of the house [the custodian of the goods or money] shall be brought unto the judges, to see whether he have put his hand unto his neighbour's goods." (Ex. 22:7-8)

If the investigation by the judges failed to implicate the custodian or trustee then he was asked to take a sacred oath "in the name of God" that he was innocent and if he did so he was absolved. Dr. Adam Clarke's comment on the principle is as follows: "Whatever goods were thus left in the hands of another person, that person, according to the Mosiac law, became responsible for them: if they were stolen, and the thief was found, he was to pay double; if he could not be found, the oath of the person who had them in keeping, made before the magistrates, that he knew nothing of them, was considered a full acquittance." (*Bible Commentary*, Vol. 1, p. 412)

If a trustee is careless and allows bailments to be stolen from him, "he shall make restitution unto the owner thereof." (Ex. 22:12)

If an animal given into his custody and care is "torn in pieces," then let him bring it for witness, and he shall NOT make good that which was torn." (Ex. 22:13)

ELDERLY PEOPLE — ENTITLED TO RESPECT

"Thou shalt rise up before the hoary head, and honour the face of the old man, and fear thy God. . . ." (Lev. 19:32)

EMPLOYER-EMPLOYEE RELATIONS

If a man hires another to work for him and the employee uses his own animals to plow, haul, etc., the injury or death of any such animals is considered to be the responsibility of the hired employee since his wage included the risk of such injuries. (Ex. 22:15)

"Ye shall not therefore oppress one another; but thou shalt fear thy God. . . ." (Lev. 25:17)

"Thou shalt not rule over him with rigour; but shalt fear thy God." (Lev. 25:43)

"Thou shalt not oppress an hired servant that is poor and needy, whether he be of thy brethren, or of thy strangers that are in thy land within thy gates: at his day thou shalt give him his hire, neither shall the sun go down upon it: for he is poor, and setteth his heart upon it: lest he cry against thee unto the Lord, and it be a sin unto thee." (Deut. 24:14-15)

FATHER

See: Parents

FIRE HAZARD

See: Arson

FORNICATION

See: Adultery, Bestiality, Idolatry, Incest, Sodomy

Definition: Any unlawful sexual intercourse.

In all ages and dispensations, sexual purity has been required. As Paul wrote, "For ye know what commandments we gave you by the Lord Jesus. For this is the will of God, even your sanctification, THAT YE SHOULD ABSTAIN FROM FORNICATION: that every one of you should know how to possess his vessel in sanctification and honour; not in the lust of concupiscence, even as the Gentiles which know not God." (1 Thessalonians, 4:2-5)

"Nevertheless, to avoid fornication, let every man have his own wife, and let every woman have her own husband." (1 Cor. 7:2)

"And if a man entice a maid that is not betrothed, and lie with her, he shall surely endow her to be his wife. If her father utterly refuses to give her unto him, he shall pay money, according to the dowry of virgins." (Ex. 22:16-17) According to Dr. Adam Clarke, this meant a "person who might feel inclined to take the advantage of a young woman knew that he must marry her, and give her dowry, if her parents consented; and if they did not consent that their daughter should wed her seducer, in this case he was obliged to give her the full dowry which could have been demanded had she been still a virgin." (Bible Commentary, Vol. 1, p. 413)

FRAUD

See: Business Ethics

GOSSIPING

"Thou shalt not go up and down as a tale-bearer among thy people; neither shalt thou stand against the blood of thy neighbour; I am the Lord." (Lev. 19:16)

"Thou shalt not raise a false report; put not thine hand with the wicked to be an unrighteous witness." (Ex. 23:1)

HATE

"Thou shalt not hate they brother in thine heart: [but] thou shalt in any wise rebuke thy neighbour, and not suffer sin upon him." (Lev. 19:17)

Note that it is not "hate" to point out to someone that they are following a path which leads to a snare and a blunder. Some people cannot stand criticism no matter how kindly or constructive it may be. Like small children they resist criticism by equating it with "hate" and throw a frenzied tantrum of protest claiming "that man hates me!" The Lord makes it clear in the above passage that each person has a duty to call attention to an error which another is observed to be making. This is not to be equated as hate.

HANDICAPPED SHOULD BE TREATED KINDLY

"Thou shalt not curse the deaf, nor put a stumblingblock before the blind, but shalt fear thy God: I am the Lord." (Lev. 19:14)

In other words, those who offend the weak and helpless shall be answerable to God.

HOMO-SEXUALITY

Definition: Unnatural sexual relations, particularly with a person of the same sex.

"Thou shalt not lie with mankind, as with womankind: it is abomination." (Lev. 18:22, 24, 29)

"If a man also lie with mankind, as he lieth with a woman, both of them have committed an abomination: they shall surely be put to death; their blood shall be upon them." (Lev. 20:13)

"And likewise also the men, leaving the natural use of the woman, burned in their lust one toward another; men with men working that which is unseemly, and receiving in themselves that recompence of their error which was meet." (Romans 1:27)

"Know ye not that the unrighteous shall not inherit the kingdom of God? Be not deceived: neither fornicators, nor idolaters, nor adulterers, nor effeminate, nor abusers of themselves with mankind." (1 Cor. 6:9)

"Defile not ye yourselves in any of these things: for in all these the nations are defiled which I cast out before you. . . . For whosoever shall commit any of these abominations, even the souls that commit them shall be cut off from among their people." (Lev. 18:24, 29)

"If a man also lie with mankind, as he lieth with a woman, both of them have committed an abomination: they shall surely be put to death; their blood shall be upon them." (Lev. 20:13)

One of the characteristics of the habitual homo-sexual is the inclination to wear the clothing of the opposite sex. Therefore, this was strictly forbidden by the Lord: "The woman shall not wear that which pertaineth unto a man, neither shall a man put on a woman's garment: for all that do so are abomination unto the Lord thy God." (Deut. 22:5)

HUMAN SACRIFICE

See: Idolatry

In the days of ancient Israel, human sacrifice, particularly of children, was a common practice among the heathen religions. Although the penalty for human sacrifice was death under the Law of Moses, nevertheless, the Israelites indulged in it during the days of their apostasy:

"Yea, they sacrificed their sons and their daughters unto devils, and shed innocent blood, even the blood of their sons and of their daughters, whom they sacrificed unto the idols of Canaan: and the land was polluted with blood." (Psalms 106:37-38)

The Lord made capital punishment mandatory for this crime because it involved premeditated murder: "Whosoever he be of the children of Israel, or of the strangers that sojourn in Israel, that giveth any of his seed unto Molech; he shall surely be put to death: the people of the land shall stone him with stones." (Lev. 20:2) The Lord went on to say that any of his people who refused to destroy those who were guilty of human sacrifices would be cut off themselves. (Lev. 20:4-5)

IDOLATRY

"He that sacrificeth unto any god, save unto the Lord only, he shall be utterly destroyed." (Ex. 22:20)

"If there be found among you, within any of thy gates which the Lord thy God giveth thee, man or woman, that hath wrought wickedness in the sight of thy Lord thy God, in transgressing his covenant, and hath gone and served other gods, and worshipped them, either the sun, or moon, or any of the host of heaven, which I have not commanded; and it be told thee, and thou hast heard of it, and inquired diligently, and behold, it be true, and the thing certain, that such abomination is wrought in Israel: then shalt thou bring forth that man or that woman, which have committed that wicked thing, unto thy gates, even that man or that woman, and shalt stone them with stones, till they die." (Deut. 17:2-5)

"And they shall no more offer their sacrifices unto devils, after whom they have gone a whoring." (Lev. 17:7) Devil-worship is as old as written history and apparently began with Cain (Moses 5:29-31).

Heathen idolatry almost invariably involved some form of fertility worship, implicating the worshippers in acts of degeneracy, bestiality, perversion and promiscuous sexual indulgence. 24,000 Israelites were destroyed as a result of involvement in the corrupting idol worship and immorality of Baal-peor in Moab. (Numbers 25:1-9)

Dr. Adam Clarke says: "It is well known that Baal Peor and Ashtaroth were worshipped with unclean rites; and that public prostitution formed a grand part of the worship of many deities among the Egyptians, Moabites, Canaanites, Greeks, and Romans." (*Bible Commentary*, Vol. 1, p. 565, see also 569)

Speaking of heathen worship and the related rites, the Lord said: "And thou shalt not let any of thy seed pass through the fire to Molech, neither shalt thou profane the name of thy God: I am the Lord. Thou shalt not lie with mankind, as with womankind: it is abomination. Neither shalt thou lie with any beast to defile thyself therewith: neither shall any woman stand before a beast to lie down thereto: it is confusion. Defile not ye yourselves in any of these things: for in all these the nations are defiled which I cast out before you. . . . Ye shall therefore keep my statutes and my judgments, and shall not commit any of these abominations: neither any of your own nation, nor any stranger that sojourneth among you: (For all these abominations have the men of the land done, which were before you, and the land is defiled:) that the land spue not you out also, when ye defile it, as it spued out the nations that were before you. For whosoever shall commit any of these abominations, even the souls that commit them shall be cut off from among their people." (Lev. 18:21-29)

"Whosoever he be of the children of Israel, or of the strangers that sojourn in Israel, that giveth any of his seed unto Molech; he shall surely be put to death: the people of the land shall stone him with stones. And I will set my face against that man, and will cut him off from among his people; because he hath given of his seed unto Molech, to defile my sanctuary, and to profane my holy name. And if the people of the land do any ways hide their eyes from the man, when he giveth of his seed unto Molech, and kill him not; then I will set my face against that man, and against his family, and will cut him off, and all that go a whoring after him, to commit whoredom with Molech, from among their people." (Lev. 20:2-5)

In connection with the immorality rites of the heathen nations, the Lord condemned them for engaging in human sacrifice of their children to Molech (see above), also for adultery, homosexuality, sodomy, bestiality and degenerate immorality between parents and their children and between others who were near relatives. (Lev. 20:10-21) After describing these "abominations" the Lord said:

"And ye shall not walk in the manners of the nation, which I cast out before you: for they committed all these things, and therefore I abhorred them." (Lev. 20:23)

"When thou art come into the land which the Lord thy God giveth thee, thou shalt not learn to do after the abominations of those nations. There shall not be found among you any one that maketh his son or his daughter to pass through the fire, or that useth divination, or an observer of times, or an enchanter, or a witch, or a' charmer, or a consulter with familiar spirits, or a wizard, or a necromancer. For all that do these things are an abomination unto the Lord: and because of these abominations the Lord thy God doth drive them out from before thee." (Deut. 18:9-12)

What did it mean to have "his son or his daughter to pass through the fire?" Perhaps we have a clear indication of it in this passage: "Take heed to thyself that thou be not snared by following them, after that they be destroyed from before thee; and that thou inquire not after their gods, saying, How did these nations serve their gods? even so will I do likewise. Thou shalt not do so unto the Lord thy God: for every abomination to the Lord, which he hateth, have they done unto their gods; for even their sons and their daughters they have burnt in the fire to their gods." (Deut. 12:30-31)

INCEST

Definition: Sexual cohabitation between near relatives.

Among primitive or degenerate heathen cultures it was customary to have the most promiscuous sexual relations within family groups or among close relatives. These often included elements of incest such as immoral relations between mothers and sons, fathers and daughters, brothers and sisters, etc. Sometimes, however, such unions were solemnized by actual marriage. This was particularly true of brothers and sisters, and became a regular practice in Egypt among the ruling Pharaohs. Concerning the problem of incest and consanguinity (marriage with close relatives) the Lord said:

"After the doings of the land of Egypt, wherein ye dwelt, shall ye not do: and after the doings of the land of Canaan, whither I bring you, shall ye not do: neither shall ye walk in their ordinances. . . . None of you shall approach to any that is near of kin to him, to uncover their nakedness: I am the Lord." (Lev. 18:3-6; the laws of consanguinity are verses 7-19)

Immorality between near relatives carried the death penalty. (See Lev. 20:11-12, 17, 19-21)

Parents have a responsibility to prevent a daughter from engaging in prostitution. (Lev. 19:29)

"And the man that committeth adultery with another man's wife, even he that committeth adultery with his neighbour's wife, the adulterer and the adulteress shall surely be put to death." (Lev. 20:10)

JUDGES

A "judge" in Israel was more than a judicial officer. He was a "ruler" (Deut. 1:13) who had responsibilities in a wide variety of administrative capacities. However, deciding disputes between contending parties was no small part of these responsibilities.

Judges and public officers were supposed to be of the highest caliber: "Moreover thou shalt provide out of all the people able men, such as fear God, men of truth, hating covetousness; and place such over them . . . and let them judge the people at all seasons: and it shall be, that every great matter they shall bring unto thee [Moses], but every small matter they shall judge: so it be easier for thyself, and they shall bear the burden with thee." (Exodus 18:21-22)

The Judges were to be "wise men, and understanding, and known among your tribes" (Deut. 1:13) so that they would have the confidence of the people.

They were to accept no gifts for "a gift doth blind the eyes of the wise, and pervert the words of the righteous." (Deut. 16:19)

Judges were to make decisions only after a thorough investigation. They were to "inquire diligently" concerning the facts in each case. (Deut. 19:18)

Judges were not to find a person guilty of a capital crime unless there were at least "two or three witnesses" who could prove his guilt. One witness was never sufficient. (Numbers 35:30; Deut. 17:6)

When a matter had been appealed to the chief judge or High Priest and the matter had been settled it was a capital offense to stir up insurrection against the decision. (Deut. 17:12) This applied to the judges of original jurisdiction as well as the parties to the case.

Moses said to the judges: "Hear the causes between your brethren, and judge righteously between every man and his brother, and the stranger that is with him. Ye shall not respect [discriminate against] persons in judgment; but ye shall hear the small as well as the great; ye shall not be afraid of the face of man; for the judgment is Gods." (Deut. 1:16-17)

"Ye shall do no unrighteousness in judgment: thou shalt not respect [discriminate against] the person of the poor, nor honour the person of the mighty; but in righteousness shalt thou judge thy neighbour." (Lev. 19:15)

KIDNAPING

"And he that stealeth a man, and selleth him, or if he be found in his hand, he shall surely be put to death." (Exodus 21:16)

"If a man be found stealing any of his brethren of the children of Israel, and maketh merchandise of him, or selleth him, then that thief shall die; and thou shalt put evil away from among you." (Deut. 24:7)

KINGS — THEIR CALLINGS AND RESPONSIBILITIES

The Lord anticipated that eventually the Israelites would want a king. He knew they would thereby abandon the open society of a theo-democracy and make themselves subject to the whims of a central authority. All such concentrations of power have eventually ended in tyranny because power corrupts and absolute power corrupts absolutely. Nevertheless, the Lord knew it was possible to have righteous kings even though they were a phenomenal rarity. He therefore outlined the requirements for a righteous king:

1—He must be a citizen of Israel and not a stranger. (Deut. 17:15)

2—It should be a person whom "the Lord thy God shall choose." (*Ibid.*)

3—He should not "multiply horses" which was a common characteristic of heathen kings, especially the extravagant and war-making kings of Egypt. (Deut. 17:16)

4—The king was not to multiply wives. (Deut. 17:17)

5—The king was not to "multiply to himself silver and gold," which would have to be at the expense of his people. (Deut. 17:17)

6—The task of the king was to be a great scholar, judge, general, and righteous policy maker. To do this, he was to have his own personal copy of the law and he was to "read therein all the days of his life: that he may learn to fear the Lord his God, to keep all the words of this law and these statutes, to do them." (Deut. 17:19)

One of the most notable examples of a king who fulfilled all of these high requirements was King Benjamin who ruled over the Nephites around 124 B.C. At the end of his long and illustrious reign he was able to say:

"My brethren . . . I have not commanded you to come up hither that ye should fear me, or that ye should think that I of myself am more than a mortal man. But I am like as yourselves, subject to all manner of infirmities in body and mind; yet I have been chosen by this people, and consecrated by my father, and was suffered by the hand of the Lord that I should be a ruler and a king over this people; and have been kept and preserved by his matchless power, to serve you with all the might, mind and strength which the Lord hath granted unto me.

"I say unto you that as I have been suffered to spend my days in your service, even up to this time, and have not sought gold nor silver nor any manner of riches of you; neither have I suffered that ye should be confined in dungeons, nor that ye should make slaves one of another, nor that ye should murder, or plunder, or steal, or commit adultery; nor even have I suffered that ye should commit any manner of wickedness, and have taught you that ye should keep the commandments of the Lord, in all things which he hath commanded you—

"And even I, myself, have labored with mine own hands that I might serve you, and that ye should not be laden with taxes, and that there should nothing come upon you which was grievous to be borne — and of all these things which I have spoken, ye yourselves are witnesses this day. Yet, my brethren, I have not done these things that I might boast, neither do I tell these things that thereby I might accuse you; but I tell you these things that ye may know that I can answer a clear conscience before God this day. Behold, I say unto you that because I said unto you that I had spent my days in your service, I do not desire to boast, for I have only been in the service of God." (Mosiah 2:9-16)

LAND

No person was to look upon land as "his" but rather as a steward-ship from the Lord: "The land shall not be sold for ever: for the land is mine: for ye are strangers and sojourners with me." (Lev. 25:23)

In other words, once a man and his family had received a steward-ship inheritance in the promised land they could not quit-claim the land lest it disinherit their children after them. The most they could do was to lease the land for 49 years. Every fiftieth year (at the time of Jubilee) the land went back to the family who originally received it as a stewardship. (Lev. 25:13) As a result, the cost of leasing land depended upon the length of time remaining until the next Jubilee. (Lev. 25:17)

If a poor Israelite had been forced to lease his land through economic necessity he was able to redeem it and get it back at any time by paying the pro-rated amount for the remainder of the lease. (Lev. 25:24-28)

In all of these transactions the Lord required the utmost honesty on the part of both the buyer and the seller: "Ye shall not therefore oppress one another; but thou shalt fear thy God." (Lev. 25:17)

The above rules applied not only to land but also to any house or real estate located in the villages and unwalled cities. (Lev. 25:31) However, a different rule applied to a house located in a fortress city— a walled city. There the owner of a house could sell it and have just one year to buy it back. If he did not do so within the prescribed time, the property went to the new owner in fee simple or as a perman-ent stewardship and was not affected by the Jubilee. (Lev. 25:29-30)

A special rule also applied to the Levites. These people had no inheritance except certain cities which were given them. It was there-fore impossible for a Levite to dispose of his land in the suburbs of his city even under lease. (Lev. 25:34) Nevertheless, a Levite could lease his house but at the time of Jubilee it had to be returned to him. Even in a walled city, a Levite could not permanently dispose of a house. (Lev. 25:33)

Each Israelite was to try to increase the ownership of land among those who lived under God's laws. Therefore if a poor Israelite came into the community who had no inheritance, the other Israelites were to try to get him on his feet financially and help him buy an inheritance:

"And if thy brother be waxen poor, and fallen in decay with thee; then thou shalt relieve him: yea, though he be a stranger, or a sojourner; that he may live with thee." (Lev. 25:35) If money were loaned to a fellow Israelite on this basis it was to be without interest or usury: "Take thou no usury of him, or increase: but fear thy God; that thy brother may live with thee [i.e. in harmony, not necessarily in the same domicile]. Thou shalt not give him thy money upon usury, nor lend him thy victuals for increase." (Lev. 25:36-37)

This program of expanding the ownership or inheritances of the Israelites until they occupied all of the territory may have been considered unfair by non-Israelites. However, it was done on the open market like any other business transaction and did not involve any extortion or compulsion against the seller. The object was to fill up the land with people who were willing to live under God's law. If a gentile or heathen became converted and covenanted to live according to revealed principles of righteousness he automatically became an Israelite and was counted the "seed of Abraham" as much as any other Israelite. (See Paul's comment on this in Gal. 3:7-9, 29; also Abraham 2:9-10.) He was therefore entitled to all of the same privileges.

This is undoubtedly one of the reasons the Lord urged Israelites to buy bond servants from among the non-Israelites (Lev. 25:45) so that by living with the Israelites they could see the advantages of such a life and become converted. If they did so, they could be looked upon as a "brother" and would then be released at the next Jubilee along with their families. (See Lev. 25:39-41 for the treatment of any "brother" serving as a bond servant.) Thereafter they could obtain an inheritance like any other Israelite.

The scripture is clear, however, that if a gentile bond servant did not respond to the message he would be considered a chattel possession just as all other nations considered them at that time. (Lev. 25:45-46) Nevertheless, an Israelite was under obligation to treat all bond servants with consideration. (See "Servants — Treatment of")

The land, like the people, had its sabbath: "Six years thou shalt sow thy field, and six years thou shalt prune thy vineyard, and gather in the fruit thereof; But in the seventh year shall be a sabbath of rest unto the land, a sabbath for the Lord: thou shalt neither sow thy field, nor prune thy vineyard. That which groweth of its own accord of thy harvest thou shalt not reap, neither gather the grapes of thy vine undressed: for it is a year of rest unto the land." (Lev. 25:3-5)

"And six years thou shalt sow thy land, and shalt gather in the fruits thereof: but the seventh year thou shalt let it rest and lie still; that the poor of thy people may eat: and what they leave, the beasts of the field shall eat. In like manner thou shalt deal with thy vineyard, and with thy oliveyard." (Ex. 23:10-11)

The question automatically arises, what did the people eat during the seventh year and on up to the beginning of the ninth year when the new harvest was available? Concerning this the Lord said: "And if ye shall say, What shall we eat the seventh year? behold, we shall not sow, nor gather in our increase: then I will command my blessing upon you in the sixth year, and it shall bring fruit for three years. And ye shall sow the eighth year, and eat yet of old fruit until the ninth year; until her fruits come in ye shall eat of the old store." (Lev. 25:20-22) As noted in Lev. 25:3-5 only the poor and the stranger could go into the field or the vineyard to gather that which "groweth of its own accord." Technically, even the owner could do this if he were "poor," and did not have enough to carry him over until the beginning of the ninth year.

"When thou comest into thy neighbour's vineyard, then thou mayest eat grapes thy fill at thine own pleasure; but thou shalt not put any in thy vessel. When thou comest into the standing corn of thy neighbour, then thou mayest pluck the ears with thine hand; but thou shalt not move a sickle unto thy neighbour's standing corn." (Deut. 23:24-25)

LENDING

The Lord makes a distinction between lending for commercial purposes, (that is for interest or usury), and lending to a person in desperate need:

"If thou lend money to any of my people that is poor by thee, thou shalt not be to him as an usurer, neither shalt thou lay upon him usury.

"If thou at all take thy neighbour's raiment to pledge, thou shalt deliver it unto him by that the sun goeth down: for that is his covering only, it is his raiment for his skin: wherein shall he sleep? and it shall come to pass when he crieth unto me, that I will hear: for I am gracious." (Ex. 22:25-27)

"And if thy brother be waxen poor, and fallen in decay with thee; then thou shalt relieve him: yea, though he be a stranger, or a sojourner: that he may live with thee. Take thou no usury of him, or increase: but fear thy God; that thy brother may live with thee. Thou shalt not give him thy money upon usury, nor lend him thy victuals for increase." (Lev. 25:35-37)

"At the end of every seven years thou shalt make a release. And this is the manner of the release: Every creditor that lendeth ought unto his neighbor shall release it; he shall not exact it of his neighbour, or of his brother; because it is called the Lord's release. Of a foreigner thou mayest exact it again: but that which is thine with thy brother thine hand shall release: save when there shall be no poor among you. . . ." (Deut. 15:1-4) Note that this rule is to help Israelites who are poor. There need not be a release of debtors "when there shall be no poor among you."

Throughout this discussion the Lord continues to distinguish between commercial lending and lending to the poor:

"If there be among you a poor man of one of thy brethren within any of thy gates in thy land which the Lord thy God giveth thee, thou shalt not harden thine heart, nor shut thine hand from thy poor brother: but thou shalt open thine hand wide unto him, and shalt surely lend him sufficient for his need, in that which he wanteth. Beware that there be not a thought in thy wicked heart, saying, The seventh year, the year of release, is at hand; and thine eye be evil against thy poor brother, and thou givest him nought; and he cry unto the Lord against thee, and it be sin unto thee. Thou shalt surely give him, and thine heart shall not be grieved when thou givest unto him: because that for this thing the Lord thy God shall bless thee in all thy works, and in all that thou puttest thine hands unto. For the poor shall never cease out of the land: therefore I command thee, saying, Thou shalt open thine hand wide unto thy brother, to thy poor, and to thy needy, in thy land." (Deut. 15:7-11)

LYING
"Thou shalt not bear false witness against thy neighbour." (Ex. 20:16)

"Ye shall not steal, neither deal falsely, neither lie one to another." (Lev. 19:11)

MILITARY SERVICE
Moses was asked to set up the military service of Israel in such a way that it would be counted a great honor to serve in its ranks. Battalions were formed from each tribe (Num. 31:3-5). This would tend to make each contingent anxious to uphold the standard of its tribe.

Then Moses was told to eliminate from the ranks of the armies of Israel any who would tend to be distracted by affairs at home: "And the officers shall speak unto the people, saying, What man is there that hath built a new house, and hath not dedicated it? let him go and return to his house, lest he die in the battle, and another man dedicate it. And what man is he that hath planted a vineyard, and hath not yet eaten of it? let him also go and return unto his house, lest he die in the battle, and another man eat of it. And what man is there that hath betrothed a wife, and hath not taken her? let him go and return unto his house, lest he die in the battle, and another man take her." (Deut. 20:5-7)

Moses was also told to eliminate any who were fearful or faint hearted: "And the officers shall speak further unto the people, and they shall say, What man is there that is fearful and faint-hearted? let him go and return to his house, lest his brethren's heart faint as well as his heart." (Deut. 20:8)

A dramatic illustration of how these principles worked in actual practice is found in Gideon's campaign against the Midianites. When

Gideon had assembled 32,000 troops who were all duty-bound to fight, the Lord told Gideon to subject the army to the self-purging process as previously outlined by Moses. When this was done Gideon had only 10,000 men left. (Judges 7:3) The others fought after the initial assault. In Gideon's case this was carried out by only 300. (See Judges 7:7 plus 7:22-24)

Modern armies tend to build elite corps out of their best fighting components and these make the first contact with the enemy. The mopping up, building of installations, and general occupation is then assigned to the followup units. It is considered a great honor to belong to one of these elite corps or crack assault units. It was intended to be likewise in the armies of Israel.

When the tribal battalions were assembled they were to select "captains of the armies to lead the people." (Deut. 20:9) Apparently this selection was by a democratic process.

All military campaigns were to be preceded by a proclamation of peace to the enemy (Deut. 20:10-11). If the enemy resisted, then it was to be besieged and conquered, and its fighting forces (adult males) destroyed. The women and children were to be saved except in those totally profligate nations which were corrupting the whole region. Among the latter nothing that breathed was to be spared. (See Deut. 20:12-18)

MOBOCRACY

"Thou shalt not follow a multitude to do evil; neither shalt thou speak in a cause to decline after many to rest judgment." (Ex. 23:2) This last phrase has reference to those who decline to accept a judgment of the court and who gather in a mob to "rest judgment" or take the law into their own hands.

MOTHER

See: Parents

MURDER AND ACCIDENTAL HOMICIDE

The law clearly distinguished between premeditated killing and accidental homicide. There were four types of homicide problems which the Law of Moses covered:

1 — MURDER:

This is the premeditated, deliberate killing of another. The penalty was death. (Lev. 21:12, 14; Num. 35:16-18, 20-21, 30; Deut. 19:11)

No amount of "satisfaction" could ameliorate the crime of murder: "He shall surely be put to death." (Numbers 35:31)

A murder conviction had to be on the testimony of two or more witnesses, otherwise the matter must wait on God's judgment. (Numbers 35:30; Deut. 19:15)

The victim's nearest kinsman had the responsibility of bringing the murderer to trial and avenging his death. (Numbers 35:19)

2 — ACCIDENTAL HOMICIDE:

The accidental killing of another was not punishable. (Lev. 21:13; Num. 35:22-23, 32; Deut. 19:4-5)

If the victim's kinsman accused the accidental killer of murder, then the latter was to flee to the altar of the temple (Ex. 21:14) or to a city of refuge where he was to remain until he could have a fair trial. He had to be returned to the city where the killing occurred for his trial. If he were found innocent of deliberate homicide (murder) but the kinsman would not believe the findings of the judge, then the accused was to be sent back to the city of refuge and remain there until the High Priest died. (Numbers 35:24-25) Once assigned to a city of refuge he was not allowed to give "satisfaction" to the avenger of blood in order to return home before the High Priest died. It was felt that he might be tricked. (Numbers 35:32) However, if he wandered from the city of refuge before the appointed time and was slain, the kinsman would not be punished because the accused had violated the limits of his sanctuary. (Numbers 35:26-28) After the High Priest died the accused could return to his own city and the avenger of blood or kinsman had to leave him unmolested. (Numbers 35:28) The application of this law was the same for "strangers" as it was for Israelites. (Numbers 35:15; also 15:16)

3 — EXCUSABLE HOMICIDE:

"If a thief be found breaking up (into a building), and be smitten (at nighttime) that he die, there shall no blood be shed for him." (Ex. 22:2) In other words, it is considered excusable.

"If the sun be risen upon him, there shall be blood shed for him." (Ex. 22:3) To kill a person in broad day light was not excusable because the thief could be identified and apprehended with much greater facility than at night.

4 — UNSOLVED MURDERS:

In order to preserve the sanctity of human life, the Lord required that every murder be treated as a major issue whether the perpetrator were found or not. In those cases where "it be not known who hath slain him," the elders of the city nearest to the place where the body was found were required to take a heifer into "a rough valley, which is neither eared nor sown, and shall strike off the heifer's neck. . . ." (Deut. 21:4) They would then wash their hands over the heifer and say, "Our hands have not shed this blood, neither have our eyes seen it. Be merciful, O Lord, unto thy people Israel, whom thou hast redeemed, and lay not innocent blood unto thy people of Israel's charge." (Deut. 21:7-8) The Lord said that in this manner "shalt thou put away the guilt of innocent blood from among you. . . ." (Deut. 21:9)

NEIGHBOR — DUTIES TOWARD

"Thou shalt not avenge, nor bear any grudge against the children of thy people, BUT THOU SHALT LOVE THY NEIGHBOR AS THYSELF. . . ." (Lev. 19:17)

If a person saw any of the domestic animals of a neighbor going astray, "thou shalt surely bring it back to him again." (Ex. 23:4)

"Thou shalt not see thy brother's ox or his sheep go astray, and hide thyself from them: thou shalt in any case bring them again unto thy brother. And if thy brother be not nigh unto thee, or if thou know him not, then thou shalt bring it unto thine own house, and it shall be with thee until thy brother seek after it, and thou shalt restore it to him again.

"In like manner shalt thou do with his ass; and so shalt thou do with his raiment; and with all lost thing of thy brother's, which he hath lost, and thou hast found, shalt thou do likewise: thou mayest not hide thyself.

"Thou shalt not see thy brother's ass or his ox, fall down by the way, and hide thyself from them: thou shalt surely help him to lift them up again." (Deut. 22:1-4)

"Thou shalt not defraud thy neighbour, neither rob him. . . ." (Lev. 19:13)

"Thou shalt not hate thy brother in thine heart: thou shalt in any wise rebuke [give timely reproof to] thy neighbour, and not suffer sin upon him." (Lev. 19:17)

The Lord imposed heavy duties on an Israelite concerning any of his neighbors who were poor. The poor were to be given assistance without usuary. (Exodus 22:25-27; Lev. 25:35-37)

If a poor neighbor could not pay his debts by the end of the Sabbath Year, the debt was to be written off and forgotten. (Deut. 15:1-2)

An Israelite was not to be hindered in lending to a poor neighbor just because the Sabbath Year was near when the debt could be automatically cancelled. (Deut. 15:7-11)

It is obvious that the Law of the Covenant called for the generosity of mature Christianity which is exactly what the Law of the Covenant was.

OATHS

The oath was originally designed as the most solemn procedure for covenant-making that men could invoke. It was designed as a covenant with God to perform a certain thing, therefor the oath was to be taken in the name of God and nothing else: "Thou shalt fear the Lord thy God, and serve him, and SHALT SWEAR BY HIS NAME." (Deut. 6:13)

Once the oath was taken, it was to be given the highest priority in the life of the covenant-maker so that it was carefully fulfilled. This is the meaning of the commandment: "Thou shalt not take the name of the Lord thy God in vain; for the Lord will not hold him guiltless that taketh his name in vain." (Exodus 20:7)

Oaths have been primarily reserved for the temple, for judicial proceedings, for the acceptance of an important office or calling and for comparable *official* acts. The oath was never intended to be a daily vehicle for confirming a questioned statement or superfluous triviality. Nevertheless, the Israelites followed the heathen practice of "swearing" by the heavens, the earth, the head, etc., that such and such was true or that such and such would be done. This type of "swearing" was actually a form of profanity, therefore Jesus forbade it altogether saying, ". . . Swear not at all; neither by heaven; for it is God's throne: nor by the earth; for it is his footstool: neither by Jerusalem; for it is the city of the great King. Neither shalt thou swear by thy head, because thou canst not make one hair white or black. But let communications be, Yea, yea; Nay nay: for whatsoever is more than these cometh of evil." (Matt. 5:34-37)

Some interpreted this to mean that Jesus had outlawed sacred oaths. However, they missed the point. Jesus was talking about daily "communications" or conversation. It was the continuous "swearing" by the head, by the heavens, by the City Jerusalem, etc., to which he was objecting. The sacred oath was an entirely different subject. In modern revelation the Lord has referred to the use of oaths in covenant-making which clearly indicates that this procedure was never outlawed. (See Doc. & Cov. 132:7; 84:39)

The use of the oath in judicial matters was an important part of the Law of the Covenant. For example, "If a man deliver unto his neighbour an ass, or an ox, or a sheep, or any beast, to keep; and it die, or be hurt, or driven away, no man seeing it: then shall an oath of the Lord be between them both, that he hath not put his hand unto his neighbour's goods; and the owner of it shall accept thereof, and he shall not [be required] to make it good." (Exodus 22:10-11) Another example is found in Deut. 21:4-9.

PENALTIES

Some have thought that the punishment or penalties under the Law of the Covenant was a form of *Lex Talionis* (Law of Retaliation or Revenge). However, it turns out to be a law of *reparation* designed to repair the wrong which was done. Note the following:

If a man stole cattle and they were found in his hand still alive, he had to restore two for each one stolen. (Exodus 22:4)

If the stolen cattle had been killed and the meat sold it was considered proof that the offender was a professional criminal engaged in commercial crime. He therefore had to restore five oxen for each one stolen and four sheep for each sheep stolen. (Exodus 22:1)

If a person committed a trespass against his neighbor he was required to pay the damages plus one fifth. (Numbers 5:7)

If the offended person or his relatives could not be found the recompense for the offense was to be given as a contribution to the sanctuary of the Lord. (Numbers 5:8)

This same principle applied in cases of injury to a person. The offender had to make "satisfaction" to the injured person or have the same affliction imposed on him. This is the meaning of passages such as the following: "And he that killeth a beast shall make it good; beast for beast. And if a man cause a blemish in his neighbour: as he hath done, so shall it be done to him; breach for breach, eye for eye, tooth for tooth: as he hath caused a blemish in a man ,so shall it be done to him again." (Lev. 24:18-20)

Taken by itself this passage would indicate that the law required the offender to be punished exactly in the same way that he had injured his neighbor, but later we learn that this is what would happen to him IF he did not make proper satisfaction. This is particularly emphasized in connection with the death penalty. "Satisfaction" could be made by the offender in most cases but not one involving the shedding of innocent blood. As Moses said: "Moreover ye shall take no satisfaction for the life of a murderer, which is guilty of death: but he shall be surely put to death." (Numbers 35:31) Satisfaction was usually in the form of money payment: "If there be laid on him a sum of money, then he shall give for the ransom of his life whatsoever is laid upon him." (Exodus 21:30) If a person did not have enough money he could sell his personal services for a period not to exceed six years. (Exodus 22:3 plus 21:2)

The death penalty was invoked for practically all offenses which would destroy the culture of this society, but, as we have noted, it was not compulsory unless the offender was involved in the deliberate taking of human life such as a murderer or one who had offered up his children as human sacrifices. In all other cases it appears that the death penalty was designed as a punishment only where the offender failed to make satisfaction or refused to leave the society under self-exile. It is interesting that an offender could be "cut off from among his people" and thereby escape the death penalty. In other words, if he would not repent and make satisfaction he remained in Israel at the peril of his life. This was to motivate him in accepting self-exile so he would not further corrupt the society which Israel was supposed to build. There are numerous references to the use of exile as a punishment for those who would not repent or make satisfaction. (See Exodus 30:33; 30:38; Leviticus 7:20-21, 25; 17:4; 19:8; 20:6; 23:29; Numbers 9:13)

It is important to observe the strong element of equity in the Law of the Covenant. Penalties were designed first of all to restore the victim to a *status quo* insofar as possible. Secondly, if a person were a renegade who would not repent and make satisfaction then he was threatened with an extremely severe penalty if he did not leave the country. This was to protect the society from the depredations of the habitual criminal.

In those cases where the offender had no opportunity to make satisfaction but nevertheless wanted to remain in the community, his punishment could be whipping. However, this was not to be a brutal flogging and in no case could the number of "stripes" exceed a total of 40: "If there be a controversy between men, and they come unto judgment, that the judges may judge them; then they shall justify the righteous, and condemn the wicked. And it shall be, if the wicked man be worthy to be beaten, that the judge shall cause him to lie down, and to be beaten before his (the judge's) face, according to his fault, by a certain number. Forty stripes he may give him, and not exceed: lest, if he should exceed, and beat him above these with many stripes THEN THY BROTHER SHOULD SEEM VILE UNTO THEE." (Deut. 25:1-3)

THE POOR

The Law of the Covenant required more than mere compassion for the poor. It required constructive generosity. Although men are created equal before the law, they are never equal in their circumstances. Some are rich, some are poor, and some who are rich today will be poor tomorrow. This is the nature of a constantly changing existence.

Societies do best by encouraging and rewarding those with productive capacity while at the same time protecting the less fortunate from undue hardship or suffering.

It has always been a principle of the Lord to help people help themselves. This is achieved by having those with means lending a hand, and those in need working for what they get. A modern scripture states it as follows:

"Wo unto you rich men, that will not give your substance to the poor, for your riches will canker your souls; and this shall be your lamentation in the day of visitation, and of judgment, and of indignation; The harvest is past, the summer is ended, and my soul is not saved!

"Wo unto you poor men, whose hearts are not broken, whose spirits are not contrite, and whose bellies are not satisfied, and whose hands are not stayed from laying hold upon other men's goods, whose eyes are full of greediness, and who will not labor with your own hands!" (Doc. & Cov. 56:16-17)

Under the Law of the Covenant as given to Moses there were many requirements designed to favor the poor which were appropriate to the circumstances of those times:

"When thou doest lend thy brother any thing, thou shalt not go into his house to fetch his pledge. Thou shalt stand abroad, and the man to whom thou dost lend shall bring out the pledge abroad unto thee. And if the man be poor, thou shalt not sleep with his pledge: In any case thou shalt deliver him the pledge again when the sun goeth down, that he may sleep in his own raiment, and bless thee: and it shall be righteousness unto thee before the Lord thy God.

"Thou shalt not oppress an hired servant that is poor and needy, whether he be of thy brethren, or of thy strangers that are in thy land within thy gates: At his day thou shalt give him his hire, neither shall the sun do down upon it: for he is poor, and setteth his heart upon it: lest he cry against thee unto the Lord, and it be a sin unto thee. . . .

"When thou cuttest down thine harvest in thy field, and hast forgot a sheaf in the field, thou shalt not go again to fetch it: it shall be for the stranger, for the fatherless, and for the widow: that the Lord thy God may bless thee in all the work of thine hands.

"When thou beatest thine olive tree, thou shalt not go over the boughs again: it shall be for the stranger, for the fatherless, and for the widow. When thou gatherest the grapes of thy vineyard, thou shalt not glean it afterward: it shall be for the stranger, for the father-less, and for the widow." (Deut. 24:10-21)

"And when ye reap the harvest of your land, thou shalt not wholly reap the corners of thy field, neither shalt thou gather the gleanings of thy harvest. And thou shalt not glean thy vineyard, neither shalt thou gather every grape of thy vineyard; thou shalt leave them for the poor and stranger: I am the Lord your God." (Lev. 19:9-10)

At the end of every seven years creditors were expected to cancel outstanding debts from the poor. (Deut. 15:1-2)

This was a special dispensation to the poor since it did not apply to non-Israelites nor was it required "when there shall be no poor among you." (Deut. 15:3-4)

People of means were specifically instructed by the Lord to be generous even though the Sabbath Year was near when debts would be cancelled. (Deut. 15:7-11)

The Lord said generous and charitable people would be blessed with even more riches. (Deut. 15:10)

PROPHETS — TRUE OR FALSE?

The prophetic calling is based on a scientific principal rather than mystical imagination. A prophet speaks what he is told and describes what he has seen. Unless he has received instructions or has been shown a vision he has no more knowledge on the subject than other men and must not pretend otherwise.

Sometimes, however, those who aspire to the prophetic calling presume to speak in the name of the Lord when He has not spoken to them. There have been such people in all ages and it has therefore resulted in confusion among the Saints. Accordingly, the following test was given in the days of Moses by which a person pretending to speak in the name of the Lord could be judged:

"And if thou say in thine heart, How shall we know the word which the Lord hath NOT spoken? When a prophet speaketh in the name of the Lord, if the thing follow not, nor come to pass, that is the thing which the Lord hath not spoken, but the prophet hath spoken it presumptuously, thou shalt not be afraid of him." (Deut. 18:21-22)

Not only were the people free to ignore men who thus violated their calling, but the Lord reflected His indignation against those who presume to speak in his name without authority. Said He, "But the prophet which shall presume to speak a word in my name which I have not commanded him to speak, or that shall speak in the name of other gods, even that prophet shall die." (Deut. 18:20)

PUBLIC NUISANCES

"And if a man shall open a pit, or if a man shall dig a pit, and not cover it, and an ox or an ass fall therein; the owner of the pit shall make it good, and give money unto the owner of them; and the dead beast shall be his." (Exodus 21:33-34)

PARENTS

"Honour they father and thy mother: that thy days may be long upon the land which the Lord thy God giveth thee." (Exodus 20:12)

"And he that curseth his father or his mother, shall surely be put to death." (Exodus 21:17; Lev. 20:9)

"And he that smiteth his father, or his mother, shall be surely put to death." (Exodus 21:15)

RAPE

Special laws were set up to apply in cases of criminal assault. "But if a man find a betrothed damsel in the field, and the man force her, and lie with her: then the man only that lay with her shall die: But unto the damsel thou shalt do nothing." (Deut. 22:25-26) However, if the assault occurred in the city the damsel was expected to cry out, otherwise there was a presumption of guilt on her part. (Deut. 22:23-24) Of course, if she could prove she was intimidated and dared not cry out, the judges would treat her case accordingly.

If the problem was one of seduction of a maiden rather than forced rape, the rule was as follows:

"If a man find a damsel that is a virgin, which is not betrothed, and lay hold on her, and lie with her, and they be found; then the man that lay with her shall give unto the damsel's father fifty shekels of silver and she shall be his wife; because he hath humbled her, he may not put her away all his days." (Deut. 22:28-29)

SABBATH DAY

"Remember the Sabbath day, to keep it holy. Six days shalt thou labour, and do all thy work: But the seventh day is the Sabbath of the Lord thy God: in it thou shalt not do any work, thou, nor thy son, nor thy daughter, thy man-servant, nor thy maid-servant, nor thy cattle, nor thy stranger that is within thy gates." (Ex. 20:8-10)

"Speak thou also unto the children of Israel, saying, Verily my Sabbaths ye shall keep: for it is a sign between me and you throughout your generations; that ye may know that I am the Lord that doth sanctify you.

"Ye shall keep the Sabbath therefore; for it is holy unto you: every one that defileth it shall surely be put to death: for whosoever doeth any work therein, that soul shall be cut off from among his people." (Exodus 31:13-14)

SERVITUDE

No adult Israelite could be forced into servitude unless he were guilty of a theft and had been compelled to take up servitude in order to make retribution. (Ex. 22:3)

But whether an Israelite had become a servant voluntarily or under the above circumstances, he could not be compelled to serve longer than six years. (Ex. 21:2)

Occasionally, however, a person would become almost like a member of his master's household and would wish to remain. In this situation he would go with his master before the "judges" of the community and declare his desire. If the judges were confident that the man was making this decision voluntarily and without duress they would then consent, and the man's earlobe would be pierced as an insignia of permanent servitude (Ex. 21:5-6).

Israelites were required to treat fellow Hebrews as "hired servants" not as bond servants (Lev. 25:39-40). Furthermore, the Lord said, "Thou shalt not rule over him with rigour; but shall fear thy God." (Lev. 25:43) Cruel masters would be answerable to God.

"And if a man smite his servant, or his maid, with a rod, and he die under his hand; he shall be surely punished [avenged — marg. note]." (Ex. 21:20) He would be treated like any other deliberate murderer.

However, if the servant is injured but does not die, the master is not to be punished, and this seems to be true even if the person died a few days later. (Ex. 21:21) The need to leave punishment of servants to the judgment of the master seems to be the rule, and interference from the outside was only permitted where the servant was killed "under the hand" of his master.

If a master punished or mistreated a servant to the extent that an eye or a tooth were lost, the master was compelled to let the servant go free. (Ex. 21:26-27)

STEALING

"Thou shalt not steal." (Ex. 20:15; Lev. 19:11)

"If a man shall steal an ox, or a sheep, and kill it, or sell it; he shall restore five oxen for an ox, and four sheep for a sheep." (Ex. 22:1)

"If the theft be certainly found in his hand alive, whether it be ox, or ass, or sheep; he shall restore double." (Ex. 22:4)

"If he (the thief) have nothing (with which to make restitution), then he shall be sold for his theft." (Ex. 22:3) But not in excess of six years. (Ex. 21:1)

SPIRITUALISM

"Regard not them that have familiar spirits, neither seek after wizards, to be defiled by them: I am the Lord your God." (Lev. 19:31)

"And the soul that turneth after such as have familiar spirits, and after wizards, to go a whoring after them, I will even set my face against that soul, and will cut him off from among his people." (Lev. 20:6)

"When thou art come into the land which the Lord thy God giveth thee, thou shalt not learn to do after the abominations of those nations. There shall not be found among you any one that maketh his son or his daughter to pass through the fire, or that useth divination, or an observer of times, or an enchanter, or a witch, or a charmer, or a consulter with familiar spirits, or a wizard, or a necromancer. For all that do these things are an abomination unto the Lord: and because of these abominations the Lord thy God doth drive them out from before thee." (Deut. 18:9-12)

STRANGERS — TREATMENT OF

God has always required that his chosen servants extend the greatest courtesy and consideration to the stranger "within thy gates."

Moses emphasized this doctrine repeatedly as it was given him by the Lord:

"For the Lord your God . . . loveth the stranger, in giving him food and rainment. Love ye therefore the stranger: for ye were strangers in the land of Egypt." (Deut. 10:17-19)

"Thou shalt neither vex a stranger, nor oppress him. . . ." (Exodus 22:21)

"But the stranger that dwelleth with you shall be unto you as one born among you, and thou shalt love him as thyself. . . ." (Lev. 19:34)

"One law and one manner shall be for you, and for the stranger that sojourneth with you." (Numbers 15:16)

However there is one glaring contradiction to all of this in the Book of Deuteronomy. Here is what it says: "Ye shall not eat of any thing that dieth of itself; thou shalt give it unto the stranger that is in thy gates, that he may eat it; or thou mayest sell it unto an alien." (Deut. 14:21)

This would mean that an animal which had died of a disease could be butchered and given to strangers to eat or sold deceptively to aliens as good meat. This passage violated the whole spirit of the Law of the Covenant. It contradicts everything else the Lord has said concerning strangers.

Modern revelation has solved this problem and eliminated the contradiction. When the inspired version was being compiled by Joseph Smith, here is the way this passage was given: "Ye shall not eat of anything that dieth of itself; thou shalt NOT give it unto the stranger that is in thy gates, that he may eat it; or thou mayest NOT sell it unto an alien. . . ." (Inspired Version, Deut. 14:21)

Apparently some ancient scribe with an eye to business changed this passage. It is not probable that the elimination of two "nots" in a single sentence would happen by accident!

Strangers who were poor were to have all the privileges of Israelites who were poor. (Lev. 19:9-10; Deut. 24:10-21)

TITHES

"And all the tithe of the land, whether of the seed of the land, or of the fruit of the tree, is the Lord's: it is holy unto the Lord. And if a man will at all redeem ought of his tithes, he shall add thereto the fifth part thereof. And concerning the tithe of the herd, or of the flock, even of whatsoever passeth under the rod, the tenth shall be holy unto the Lord. He shall not search whether it be good or bad, neither shall he change it: and if he change it at all, then both it and the change thereof shall be holy; it shall not be redeemed." (Lev. 27:30-33)

"And, behold, I have given the children of Levi all the tenth in Israel for an inheritance, for their service which they serve, even the service of the tabernacle of the congregation. . . . But the tithes of the children of Israel which they offer as an heave-offering unto the Lord, I have given to the Levites to inherit: therefore I have said unto them, Among the children of Israel they shall have no inheritance. And the Lord spake unto Moses, saying, Thus speak unto the Levites, and say unto them, When ye take of the children of Israel the tithes which I have given you from them for your inheritance, then ye shall offer up an heave-offering of it for the Lord, even a tenth part of the tithe. . . . Thus ye also shall offer an heave-offering unto the Lord of all your tithes, which ye receive of the children of Israel: and ye shall give thereof the Lord's heave-offering to Aaron the priest." (Numbers 18:21-28)

The Israelites also had a SECOND tithe which was disposed of as follows: it was used as pervender for the tithe-payer when he went up to the temple city. He was supposed to go up for at least three feasts each year and this was to provide the means. (Deut. 24:24) If it were not practical to transport his grain and flocks he could convert them into money and use this for his journey and sustenance. (Ibid. vv. 24-25) This was to be the procedure for the first and second year's increase. Then on the third year all of this was to be turned over to the poor. The fourth and fifth years he used them to go to the temple city to rejoice before the Lord and the sixth year he once more gave it to the poor. In other words, each three years repeated itself. The procedure for each of the three years is described in Deut. 14:22-29. (See Clarke, *Bible Commentary*, Vol. 1, p. 776)

If a person gave the finest of his flock or his harvest to the Lord and then wished to redeem it or buy it back, he could do so by adding one fifth to its value and paying the total amount into the sanctuary. (Lev. 27:31)

WIDOWS AND ORPHANS

"Ye shall not afflict any widow, or fatherless child. If thou afflict them in any wise, and they cry at all unto me, I will surely hear their cry; and my wrath shall wax hot, and I will kill you with the sword; and your wives shall be widows, and your children fatherless." (Ex. 22:22-24)

"Thou shalt not pervert the judgment . . . of the fatherless: nor take a widow's raiment to pledge." (Deut. 24:17)

"When thou cuttest down thine harvest in thy field, and hast forgot a sheaf in the field, thou shalt not go again to fetch it: it shall be for the stranger, for the fatherless, and for the widow: that the Lord thy God may bless thee in all the work of thine hands. When thou beatest thine olive tree, thou shalt not go over the boughs again: it shall be for the stranger, for the fatherless, and for the widow. When thou gatherest the grapes of thy vineyards, thou shalt not glean it afterward: it shall be for the stranger, for the fatherless, and for the widow." (Deut. 24:19-21)

Widows and orphans also were allowed to glean the fields, including the corners which the owner refrained from harvesting. (Lev. 19:9-10)

WITNESSES

The Law of the Covenant had a very strict rule concerning witnesses. Here is what the scripture says concerning them:

"At the mouth of two witnesses, or three witnesses, shall he that is worthy of death be put to death: but at the mouth of one witness he shall not be put to death. The hands of the witnesses shall be first upon him to put him to death, and afterwards the hands of all the people." (Deut. 17:6-7)

Not only was this the rule for capital crimes but for all other criminal charges: "One witness shall not rise up against a man for any iniquity, or for any sin, in any sin that he sinneth: at the mouth of two witnesses, or at the mouth of three witnesses, shall the matter be established." (Deut. 19:15)

The law governing false witnesses was equally strict:

"Thou shalt not bear false witness against thy neighbor." (Ex. 20:16)

"Thou shalt not raise a false report: put not thine hand with the wicked to be an unrighteous witness." (Exodus 23:1)

"If a false witness rise up against any man to testify against him that which is wrong: then both the men, between whom the controversy is, shall stand before the Lord, before the priests and the judges, which shall be in those days; and the judges shall make diligent inquisition: and, behold, if the witness be a false witness, and hath testified falsely against his brother; then shall ye do unto him, as he had thought to have done unto his brother: so shalt thou put the evil away from among you." (Deut. 19:16-19)

WEIGHTS AND MEASURES

See also: Business Ethics

"Ye shall do no unrighteouness in judgment, in mete-yard, in weight, or in measure. Just balances, just weights, a just ephah, and a just hin, shall ye have. . . ." (Lev. 19:35-36)

Index

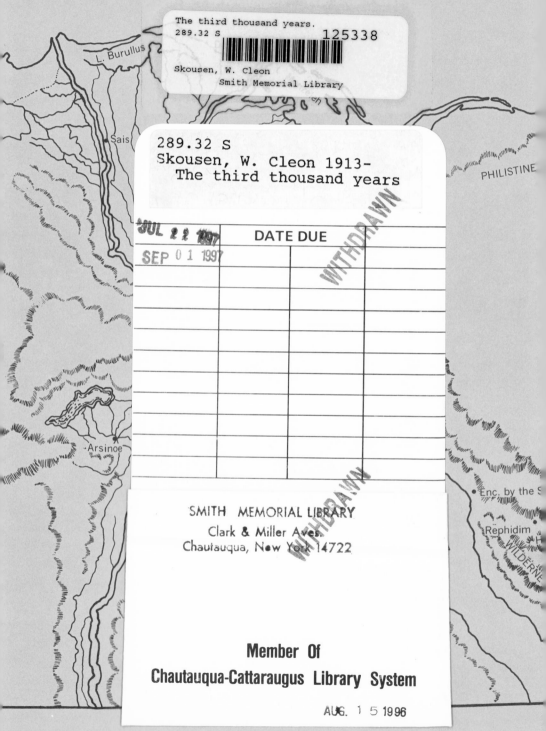